Beate Ego, Ulrike Mittmann (Eds.)
Evil and Death

Deuterocanonical and Cognate Literature Studies

Edited by
Friedrich V. Reiterer, Beate Ego and Tobias Nicklas

Volume 18

Beate Ego, Ulrike Mittmann (Eds.)
Evil and Death

Conceptions of the Human in Biblical, Early Jewish,
Greco-Roman and Egyptian Literature

DE GRUYTER

ISBN 978-3-11-055921-7
e-ISBN (PDF) 978-3-11-031571-4
e-ISBN (EPUB) 978-3-11-038203-7
ISSN 1865-1666

Library of Congress Cataloging-in-Publication Data
A CIP catalog record for this book has been applied for at the Library of Congress.

Bibliographic information published by the Deutsche Nationalbibliothek
The Deutsche Nationalbibliothek lists this publication in the Deutsche Nationalbibliografie; detailed bibliographic data are available on the Internet at http://dnb.dnb.de.

© 2017 Walter de Gruyter GmbH, Berlin/Boston
This volume is text- and page-identical with the hardback published in 2015.
Printing and binding: CPI books GmbH, Leck
♾ Printed on acid-free paper
Printed in Germany

www.degruyter.com

In Memoriam
Ellen Bradshaw Aitken (1961–2014)

Foreword

Der vorliegende Band enthält die Beiträge eines internationalen Forschungssymposiums zum Thema „Evil and Death in Light of Present and Future Existence. Conceptions of the Human in Biblical, Early Jewish, Greco-Roman and Egyptian Literature", das vom 21.–25. August 2011 an der Universität Osnabrück stattfand. Die Veranstaltung wurde durchgeführt im Verbund der beteiligten Universitäten Bochum (Beate Ego) und Osnabrück (Ulrike Mittmann) in Kooperation mit der Forschungsstelle für christlich-jüdische Studien der Universität Osnabrück.

Wir danken der Deutschen Forschungsgemeinschaft und der Universitätsgesellschaft Osnabrück für die Förderung der Tagung. Für ihre Mitarbeit in der Vorbereitung und Durchführung des Symposiums sowie der Drucklegung der Beiträge danken wir Frau Frauke Giesmann, Frau Ann-Christin Grüninger; Frau Jutta Kemper, Frau Carmen Jäger; Frau Sabine Liphardt, Herrn Antti Lück, Frau Lara Muchall, Frau Charlene Remane, Frau Rieke Schole und Frau Anne Danielle Turck.

Im Zentrum der Diskussionen stand der Mensch, im interdisziplinären Diskurs also die Frage einer kulturell divergierenden Anthropologie. Die Frage nach dem Menschenbild gehört zu den zentralen Fragen menschlicher Welt- und Selbstreflexion. Sie zielt auf die Stellung des Menschen im Ganzen der Wirklichkeit und gewinnt ihre stete Aktualität aus dem unauflöslichen Widerstreit von Selbstbezug und Fremdbezug im Akt der kognitiven Daseinsbewältigung. In einer nicht säkularisierten Welt stellt sich die Frage nach dem Selbstbild des Menschen unausweichlich als Frage des menschlichen Gottesbezuges: Wie der Mensch über sich selber denkt, steht in unmittelbarer Beziehung zu seinem Verhältnis zu Gott bzw. zur Gottheit im allumfassenden Sinn des Begriffs. Die Frage, ob ein monotheistischer oder polytheistischer Gottesbezug den Menschen in unterschiedlicher Weise über sich selbst nachdenken lässt, war daher das zentrale Thema der fächerübergreifenden Diskussion, die durch die Einbeziehung der Ägyptologie eine religionsgeschichtlich größtmögliche Breite gewann.

Ziel des Forschungssymposiums war es, den Grund zu legen für eine systematisch erstmals übergreifende Analyse der Anthropologie der frühjüdischen Literatur in der hellenistisch-jüdischen Zeit nach dem Vorbild anthropologischer Gesamtentwürfe in den biblisch-exegetischen Fächern und im Bemühen, interdisziplinär all jene Fächer in den Prozess zu integrieren, die gleichfalls mit der hellenistischen Zeit befasst sind: die Alte Geschichte, die vergleichende Religionswissenschaft und die Ägyptologie. Insbesondere auf dem Sektor des

Kulturvergleichs hat die interdisziplinäre Diskussion neue Horizonte eröffnet und wurde die Erkenntnis der fundamental verschiedenartigen Prägung des Menschenbildes durch die Religion für jedes der beteiligten Fächer in je eigener Weise zum Schlüssel der anthropologischen Rekonstruktion.

Die Verschiedenartigkeit der Menschenbilder war angesichts der Grundkonstanten individuellen Menschseins – der Endlichkeit des irdischen Lebens (Tod) und der Erfahrung lebensmindernder Kräfte und Einflüsse („das Böse") – für viele Tagungsteilnehmer durchaus überraschend. Dementsprechend war in den Diskussionen das Hauptinteresse auf den Bereich eines direkten oder indirekten wechselseitigen Einflusses im Bereich der zum Synkretismus tendierenden multireligiösen Gesellschaft und ihrer im Herrscherkult auch „politischen" Religion gerichtet. Gleichzeitig wurde wegen der Aktualität der Thematik in den das Symposium ausrichtenden biblischen Fächern die anthropologische Verankerung „des Bösen" zum Gegenstand fortdauernder Diskussion. Aus der Wahrnehmung und Differenzierung der religiösen Phänomene und anthropologischen Denkmuster haben sich für die einzelnen Fächer ganz unterschiedliche Impulse zur Weiterarbeit am Thema ergeben, die zum Teil bereits in den hier veröffentlichen Beiträgen ihren Niederschlag gefunden haben.

Im Einzelnen kamen folgende Themenbereiche zur Sprache: Viele der Beiträge aus dem Bereich der Bibelwissenschaften und der Judaistik stellten die Verbindung des Bösen bzw. der Sünde mit dem Tod heraus mit besonderem Akzent auf der Frage nach dem Strafcharakter des Todes. Da Sünde und Tod vielfach in einem kausalen Zusammenhang erscheinen, können diese Beiträge im weitesten Sinne der Vorstellung vom Tun-Ergehen-Zusammenhang zugeordnet werden. Die Frage nach der Verbindung von Gebotsübertretung und Tod wird grundlegend im einführenden Beitrag von Beate Ego gestellt und auf der Basis von Gen 2-3 beantwortet. Der Verknüpfung von Sünde und Tod sind mit unterschiedlichen literarischen Schwerpunkten die Beiträge von Gerbern S. Oegema (frühjüdische Literatur allgemein), Ulrike Mittmann (Sapientia Salomonis 1-2), Ekaterina Matusova (1 Henoch), Hermann Lichtenberger (Qumran) und Rouven Genz (Lk 16,19-31) gewidmet, theologisch vertieft durch die Frage nach dem Ursprung des Bösen und dem freien Willen des Menschen, die einmal im Kontext der Genesis (Ulrike Mittmann), ein andermal im apokalyptischen Kontext (Gerbern S. Oegema) beantwortet wird. Das Hoffnungs- und Gegenbild der Befreiung des Menschen von den ihn zerstörenden Mächten thematisiert der Beitrag von Georg Steins zu Psalm 107, der den an Gottes Weisheit partizipierenden Menschen der Rettermacht Gottes unterstellt weiß.

Ganz anders akzentuiert sind die Beiträge, die sich der Problematisierung des Kausalzusammenhangs von Sünde und Tod widmen. Hier zeigt die Auseinandersetzung mit der Hiobüberlieferung und dem Buch Kohelet in den Aufsätzen von Patricia G. Kirkpatrick und Christoph Berner, dass der genannte Zusammenhang der Phänomene in der Spätzeit des Alten Testaments aufgebrochen wird. Gleichzeitig wird, wie David A. deSilvas Analyse des 4. Makkabäerbuches belegt, die Hoffnungen auf ein Leben nach dem Tod immer deutlicher zu einem konstitutiven Element der anthropologischen Reflexion, und zwar im Sinne einer radikalen Transformation des Seins bei gleichzeitigem Erhalt individueller Identität.

Den Leidensaspekt der unter der Macht des Bösen und des Todes stehenden menschlichen Existenz thematisieren im Gesamtkontext des Christusgeschehens schließlich die Untersuchungen von Ian H. Henderson und Ellen Bradshaw Aitken zum Markusevangelium und zum Hebräerbrief, zwei Beiträge, welche mit der Frage nach der Überwindung des menschlichen Sündenverhängnisses programmatisch auch die Brücke zur Soteriologie schlagen.

Im Bereich der klassischen Antike kommen vor allem die unterschiedlichen Todesvorstellungen paganer Religiosität in den Blick – im Beitrag von Veit Rosenberger unter dem Aspekt der Privat-Deifikation, im Beitrag von Wolfgang Spickermann unter rituellem Aspekt (Trauer, Totenkult) und, im Rückbezug auf Lukian von Samosata, mit Schwerpunkt auf der Frage postmortaler Existenz. Das anthropologische Gegenkonzept zur Divinisierung, die *damnatio memoriae* als Phänomen postmortaler Existenzvernichtung, stellt Christiane Kunst vor. Den soziologischen Aspekt des Themas beleuchtet Darja Šterbenc Erker, die auf die bedeutsame Rolle der Priester und Magistrate als Vermittler zwischen den Göttern und den Menschen zum Wohle der Gemeinschaft verweist. Marlis Arnhold beantwortet die Frage nach der Bedingtheit menschlichen Lebens mythologisch vom Schicksalsgedanken her.

Im Beitrag der Ägyptologie zum Thema von Joachim Friedrich Quack schließlich erscheinen die von den anderen Fachrichtungen unter dem Vorzeichen monotheistischer bzw. polytheistischer Religiosität ganz unterschiedlich erhobenen anthropologischen Aspekte in neuer Zuordnung. Auch in den Texten der ägyptischen Spätzeit wird die kausale Verknüpfung des Bösen mit dem Tod als Frage individuellen Menschseins zum Thema gemacht, allerdings im polytheistischen Gottesbezug, was Jenseitserwartungen ganz eigener Art aus sich heraussetzt. Forschungsgeschichtlich noch nicht abschließend geklärt ist dabei die motivische Deckungsgleichheit der im Mittelpunkt der Reflexion stehenden ägyptischen Beispielerzählung mit dem von Rouven Genz behandelten neutestamentlichen Stoff.

Dass der Mensch im Leben vom Tod umfangen ist, gehört aber noch in ganz anderer Weise zu den tiefen Erfahrungen aller am Symposium Beteiligten. Ellen Bradshaw Aitken hat das Erscheinen des Sammelbandes nicht mehr erlebt. Ihrem Andenken ist dieser Band gewidmet.

Contents

Part I: Old Testament and Early Jewish Literature

Beate Ego
Das Böse und der Tod in der Paradieserzählung – Biblische und auslegungsgeschichtliche Aspekte —— 3

Georg Steins
An des Todes Pforten weise werden – Überlegungen im Anschluss an Psalm 107 —— 21

Patricia G. Kirkpatrick
Curse God and Die – Job's Wife and the Struggle for Job's Transformation —— 43

Christoph Berner
Evil and Death in the Book of Qohelet —— 57

Gerbern S. Oegema
Different Approaches to Evil and Death in the Ethics of the Non-Canonical Jewish Writings —— 75

Ulrike Mittmann
Das Bild des Menschen im Wandel – Die Rezeption von Genesis 1–3 in Sapientia Salomonis 1 und 2 —— 97

David A. deSilva
Human Experience and the Problem of Theodicy in 4 Maccabees —— 127

Ekaterina Matusova
The Post-mortem Divisions of the Dead in 1 Enoch 22:1–13 —— 149

Hermann Lichtenberger
„Dem Tode verfallen war ich wegen meiner Sünden" (11QPs^a XIX,1–18) —— 179

Part II: New Testament

Ian H. Henderson
The Child, Death and the Human in Mark's Gospel —— 199

Rouven Genz
Reversal of Fate after Death? —— 221

Ellen Bradshaw Aitken
Death and *Cultus* as Constitutive of the Human in the Epistle to the Hebrews —— 259

Part III: Greco-Roman and Egyptian Literature

Wolfgang Spickermann
Trauer und Tod in der 2. Sophistik am Beispiel des Lukian von Samosata —— 275

Veit Rosenberger
Privatdeifikationen in der römischen Kaiserzeit – Tod, Trauer und Memoria —— 295

Christiane Kunst
Tod auf der Latrine— Zum Ende von Caracalla und Elagabal —— 313

Darja Šterbenc Erker
Der Religionsstifter Numa im Gespräch mit Jupiter —— 333

Marlis Arnhold
Narrating Meleager's Deeds and Death in Words and Images —— 355

Joachim Friedrich Quack
„Sage nicht: ‚Der Frevler gegen Gott lebt heute'; auf das Ende sollst du achten!" —— 377

Index of Names and Subjects (German) —— 411

Index of Names and Subjects (English) —— 415

Bible Citation Index —— 417

Part I: **Old Testament and Early Jewish Literature**

Beate Ego
Das Böse und der Tod in der Paradieserzählung – Biblische und auslegungsgeschichtliche Aspekte

Auch wenn sich die Thematik des Bösen und des Todes einem roten Faden gleich durch weite Teile der Hebräischen Bibel bzw. des Alten Testaments zieht,[1] so ist es doch insbesondere die Geschichte vom Paradies und Sündenfall in Gen 2,4a–3,24, die im kollektiven Gedächtnis der christlich-abendländischen Tradition eine herausragende Rolle spielt. Fast jeder kennt das erste Menschenpaar Adam und Eva—oder meint dies zumindest: Schnell sind da die Assoziationen von Eva, die den Tod in die Welt bringt, vom Apfel und der bösen Schlange. Ein genauer Blick auf die biblische Überlieferung zeigt aber deutlich, dass diese uns so bekannten Vorstellungen keineswegs dem biblischen Text selbstverständlich zu entnehmen sind, sondern vielmehr ein Produkt einer langen Auslegungsgeschichte darstellen. Vor diesem Hintergrund soll es die Aufgabe dieses Beitrags sein, zunächst zu zeigen, dass die Erzählung vom sog. „Sündenfall" zahlreiche narrative Leerstellen enthält und somit eine semantische Polyvalenz aufweist (1). In einem weiteren Schritt soll dann deutlich gemacht werden, wie in der Auslegung des Textes in der frühjüdischen Tradition jenes Bild entstanden ist, das für das christlich-abendländische Verständnis der Paradieserzählung bestimmend geworden ist (2). Ein Blick auf die rabbinischen Auslegungen, die durchaus auch als eine Reaktion auf diese christlichen Entwicklungen verstanden werden können (3), und ein kurzes Fazit (4) sollen den Beitrag abrunden.[2]

1 Der biblische Text und sein Auslegungshorizont

Wenn wir uns zunächst der biblischen Erzählung von Gen 3 zuwenden, so lässt sich diese folgendermaßen zusammenfassen: Allerlei Bäume hatte Gott im Garten für den Menschen wachsen lassen, die—so die Lutherübersetzung—„verlo-

---

[1] S. hierzu die instruktiven Beiträge von SCHÜLE, Diskurs; WAGNER, Das Böse; GRUND, Bewältigung.
[2] Die hier vorgelegten Ausführungen bilden eine Zusammenfassung meiner Ausführungen in EGO, Adam und Eva, 11–78.

ckend anzusehen und gut zu essen" waren, sowie „den Baum des Lebens mitten im Garten und den Baum der Erkenntnis des Guten und Bösen" (Gen 2,9).³

Während das Motiv des Lebensbaumes auch außerhalb der Hebräischen Bibel in der altorientalischen Ikonographie zu finden ist und höchstwahrscheinlich ein Fruchtbarkeitssymbol darstellt,⁴ konnte die Vorstellung von einem „Baum der Erkenntnis von Gut und Böse" in diesen Quellen bislang nicht nachgewiesen werden. Gerade an diesem Baum aber soll sich die weitere Handlung entzünden, wenn Gott dem Menschen mitteilt, dass er von allen Bäumen des Gartens essen darf, diesen einen Baum aber von seiner Erlaubnis ausnimmt. An dem Tag nämlich, an dem der Mensch von ihm isst, soll er des Todes sterben (Gen 2,16–17). Ein Blick in die Konkordanz zeigt, was mit der Erkenntnis von Gut und Böse gemeint ist: Demnach besaß der König Salomo nach der Darstellung des Deuteronomistischen Geschichtswerks einen verständigen Geist und die Fähigkeit, zwischen Gut und Böse zu unterscheiden (1Kön 3,9); kleinen Kindern steht diese Fähigkeit aber noch nicht zur Verfügung (Dtn 1,39; Jes 7,15–16). Aus 1QSa 1,10–11 geht eindeutig hervor, dass es gerade diese Fähigkeit ist, die den Erwachsenen vom Kind unterscheidet, wenn nämlich hier die Fähigkeit der Erkenntnis von Gut und Böse mit dem Erreichen des 20. Lebensjahres verbunden wird. Es kann also angenommen werden, dass die Wendung von der Erkenntnis von Gut und Böse das Vermögen des Menschen meint, vernünftige und verantwortliche Entscheidungen zu treffen. Die Begrifflichkeit zielt—um die Worte Erhard Blums zu wählen—auf die „Unterscheidung zwischen Lebensförderlichem und Lebensabträglichem, die Befähigung zu einer eigenverantwortlichen Lebensorientierung, also die Urteilsfähigkeit des mündigen Menschen".⁵

---

3 Syntaktisch handelt es sich hier um eine „gespaltene Koordination", da sich die Ortsangabe „in der Mitte des Gartens" zwischen den koordinierten Objekten befindet; d.h. zwei Bäume stehen in der Mitte des Gartens nebeneinander. Unabhängig von der Frage, ob einer der Bäume tatsächlich sekundär in den Text eingefügt wurde, kann somit allgemein festgestellt werden, dass die Syntax des Textes nicht regelwidrig ist; zum Ganzen s. MICHEL, Gespaltene Koordination; BLUM, Gottesunmittelbarkeit, 19–20.
4 Die entsprechenden Darstellungen zeigen einen Baum, häufig eine Zedernart, neben dem rechts und links Tiere, meist Kapriden, stehen, die von seinen Blättern fressen. Daneben findet sich aber auch das Bildensemble eines Baumes, von dem Ströme ausgehen; zum Ganzen s. KEEL, Bildsymbolik, 164–169. Verwandt mit dieser Vorstellung ist das „Kraut des Lebens", das im Gilgamesch-Epos eine wichtige Rolle spielt.
5 Hierzu BLUM, Gottesebenbildlichkeit, 21 (mit Hinweisen auf die ältere Literatur). Vor diesem Hintergrund kann man durchaus von praktischer Weisheit sprechen. Andere Ausleger—so z.B. Hans-Peter Müller—nehmen an, dass unter der „Erkenntnis von Gut und Böse" ursprünglich die „Erfahrung mit Lust und Leid der Liebe" zu verstehen gewesen sei. Die Wendung sei dann später im Sinne eines magischen Wissens und schließlich im „epistemologischen Sinne als Erkenntnis

Erst nach der Erschaffung der Tiere und der Frau und ihrer Zusammenführung mit dem Mann (Gen 2,18–2,25) wird dieser Handlungsstrang weitergeführt. Nun soll sich die anfängliche Idylle in der Beziehung der beiden ersten Menschen schnell ändern, wenn von der Übertretung des göttlichen Gebotes und seinen Folgen erzählt wird. Recht unvermittelt setzt Gen 3,1 ein, wo die Schlange erscheint, die als ein Tier charakterisiert wird, das klüger oder listiger als alle anderen Tiere des Feldes ist. Es folgt ein Gespräch zwischen der Frau und der Schlange, das—so Odil Hannes Steck—ein meisterhaftes Stück hebräischer Erzählkunst darstellt. Die Schlange nämlich spricht eigentlich kein falsches Wort; es gelingt ihr aber, „mit winzigen Umakzentuierungen, mit Halbwahrheit und Doppelsinnigkeit den arglosen Partner soweit zu bringen, dass er von sich selbst in ihrem Sinne mitspielt und agiert, wie sie es haben will."⁶ Mit dem Hinweis, dass das Essen der Frucht keineswegs zum Tode führt, sondern vielmehr gottgleich macht, zeichnet die Schlange ein Bild von JHWH, das diesen so erscheinen lässt, als ob er dem Menschen etwas vorenthalten möchte. Als die Frau sieht, dass „es gut wäre, von dem Baum gut zu essen und ... und begehrenswert, um Einsicht zu gewinnen" (Gen 3,6), nimmt sie von seiner Frucht und isst davon. Anschließend gibt sie auch dem Mann von der Frucht des Baumes (Gen 3,6). Schnell werden die Konsequenzen dieser Tat deutlich: Die erste Erkenntnis, die Mann und Frau zuteil wird, ist die, dass sie beide nackt sind. Weil sie sich deshalb voreinander schämen, flechten sie sich eine Art Bekleidung aus Feigenblättern (Gen 3,7). Dann werden durch die verschiedenen Fluchworte eine ganze Reihe von Daseinsminderungen in Kraft gesetzt, die fortan das menschliche Leben durch Arbeit, Schwangerschaften, Geburtsmühen und der Feindschaft zur Schlange bestimmen (Gen 3,14–19). Mit der Benennung der

---

des Wirklichkeitsganzen" aufgefasst worden (MÜLLER, Drei Deutungen des Todes, 119). Damit kann die Erzählung—um einen Begriff von Hans-Peter Müller aufzunehmen—als „Adoleszenzmärchen" verstanden werden. Der Tod als Folge des Essens vom Baum der Erkenntnis wäre dann weniger als göttliche Strafe aufzufassen, sondern würde vielmehr den auch in anderen Mythen belegten Zusammenhang von Eros und Tod reflektieren. Deshalb sei es auch kein Zufall, dass unmittelbar nach dem Verzehr der verbotenen Frucht als einer Art Symbol für das Erwachen der Geschlechtlichkeit dann auch die Entdeckung der Nacktheit, die Scham und die Bekleidung folge. Geschlechtlichkeit und Tod könnten dabei ganz unterschiedlich aufeinander bezogen werden: So ist—nach Hans-Peter Müller—mit „einem primitiven Zusammenhang von Erkenntnis und Verfehlung" zu rechnen: „Da ‚das Wissen um das Geheimnis der Zeugung und des Gebärens ... etwas Göttliches ist', verletzt der Mensch durch das Erwachen zur bewußten Geschlechtlichkeit ein Tabu; aber die Verfehlung ist versehentlich, allenfalls tragisch, kann er doch gar nicht anders, als auf diese Weise die Unsterblichkeit verscherzen" (MÜLLER, Erkenntnis und Verfehlung, 197; s. auch MÜLLER, Drei Arten des Todes, 118).
6 STECK, Paradieserzählung, 91.

Frau als *Chawa* (חוה) im Sinne der „Mutter allen Lebens" und der Vertreibung aus dem Garten Eden, die damit begründet wird, dass der Mensch nun auch noch nach dem Baum des Lebens greifen könnte und damit ewig leben würde, schließt die Erzählung (Gen 3,20–24).

Wie bereits eingangs erwähnt, enthält unsere Erzählung zahlreiche Leerstellen. So ist zunächst darauf hinzuweisen, dass im vorliegenden Kontext von Gott keine Begründung für das Verbot, vom Baum der Erkenntnis zu essen, gegeben wird. Auch die Rolle, die Eva bei der Übertretung des Gebotes spielt, ist nicht eindeutig, denn hier erscheint unser Text wieder seltsam unbestimmt. Alles wirkt irgendwie beiläufig und recht unreflektiert, und man möchte daran zweifeln, ob es tatsächlich der Wunsch der Frau nach Gottgleichheit war, der sie zum Essen der Frucht bewegte. Weitaus wahrscheinlicher ist es, an dieser Stelle weniger das Autonomiebestreben des Menschen, der hybrisartig Gott gleich sein möchte, in den Vordergrund zu stellen; vielmehr spiegelt sich in dem Gespräch zwischen Frau und Schlange eine gewisse naive Unbekümmertheit. Die Frau hat ja noch gar nicht das Vermögen, zwischen Gut und Böse zu unterscheiden; zudem ist ihr die Kenntnis dessen, was der Tod eigentlich bedeutet, fremd. So wird man folgern können, dass sie einfach zugreift, ohne viel nachzudenken und zu reflektieren, vielleicht so ähnlich, wie man dies von einem unbekümmerten Kind erwarten würde, das sich über die Folgen seines Handelns noch gar keine Gedanken machen kann.

Wenn im Kontext dieser Erzählung traditionellerweise auch vom „Sündenfall" gesprochen wird, so ist doch darauf hinzuweisen, dass dieser Begriff hier in dieser Erzählung gar nicht erscheint. Explizit ist von der Sünde (חטאת) erst in Gen 4 in der Erzählung von Kain und Abel die Rede: Für Kain wird Abel zum „Anlass" für eine Sünde, die er freilich—so Gen 4,7—durch sein richtiges und gutes Handeln verhindern hätte können. Wie Bernd Janowski prägnant formuliert hat, steht nun zum ersten Mal im Anschluss an Gen 2,17 und Gen 3,5.22 die „Erkenntnis von Gut und Böse" auf dem Spiel. Trotz der durch das Essen der Frucht erworbenen Fähigkeit zum rechten Urteil, eben zur Unterscheidung von Gut und Böse, handelt Kain falsch, und somit lässt sich das Fazit ziehen: „Damit ist der Brudermord die grausige Konkretion der vom ersterschaffenen Menschen ergriffenen Möglichkeit, zwischen gut und böse wählen zu können."[7]

In diesem Kontext muss auch offen bleiben, was die Schlange zu ihrer Handlung, gegen Gottes Weisung zu opponieren, motiviert. Wieso kommt es zu einer Störung der anfänglichen Harmonie zwischen Gott, Mensch und Natur? Und warum ist es gerade die Schlange, die aus der Ordnung der göttlichen

---

[7] Zum Ganzen s. JANOWSKI, Jenseits von Eden, 156.

Schöpfungswelt ausbricht? Diese Frage wird weder hier noch an einer anderen Stelle in dieser Geschichte beantwortet. Die negative Rolle, die der Schlange im vorliegenden Kontext zukommt, ist sicherlich vor dem Hintergrund der bäuerlichen Lebenswelt zu erklären, in der dieses Tier bei der Feldarbeit als der natürliche Feind des Menschen erscheint. Man kann zudem auch erwägen, ob an dieser Stelle auch Einflüsse von anderen Mythen vorliegen, denn auch im Gilgamesch-Epos ist die Schlange pejorativ besetzt, wenn sie Gilgamesch das Kraut des Lebens stiehlt. Auch wenn es so möglich ist, das Auftreten der Schlange motivgeschichtlich näher zu umreißen, bleiben die Fragen, die mit dem Auftreten der Schlange verbunden sind, weitgehend offen. Es wird zwar erzählt, dass Falschheit und Ungehorsam in die Welt des Menschen einbrechen; worin diese negativen Größen aber ihren Grund haben und woher diese destruktiven Elemente letztlich kommen—diese Antwort bleibt uns die Erzählung, wie übrigens die gesamte Hebräische Bibel, schuldig.[8]

Schließlich enthält unser Text noch eine weitere Leerstelle, wenn es nämlich um die Frage nach der Bedeutung des Todes geht. Denn es bleibt letztlich in der Schwebe, ob es sich hier um die Androhung der Todesstrafe handelt und damit die Sterblichkeit des Menschen als schöpfungsbedingt bereits vorausgesetzt wird oder ob diese Geschichte eine Art Ätiologie für die Sterblichkeit der Menschen darstellt. Und wenn dem so sein sollte, worin liegt dann der tiefere Grund für diese Konsequenz aus der Übertretung? Ist der Tod die göttliche Strafe für den menschlichen Ungehorsam gegenüber Gott oder gleichsam die logische Folge für die Missachtung des Verbots, vom Baum der Erkenntnis von Gut und Böse zu essen?

Wie schwierig diese Frage zu beantworten ist, zeigt nicht zuletzt der kontroverse Diskurs in der alttestamentlichen Forschung. So gibt es hier prinzipiell mehrere Möglichkeiten: Wenn man sich einmal die Mühe macht, die verschiedenen Argumente zusammenzutragen, die hier angeführt werden, ist Folgendes festzustellen: Darauf, dass die Sterblichkeit des Menschen schöpfungsbedingt und der Tod somit von Anfang an Teil der menschlichen Natur ist, deutet das Motiv, wonach der Mensch aus dem Staub der Erde erschaffen wurde (Gen 2,7). Dieses Motiv wird dann im Strafwort gegen den Mann wieder aufgenommen (Gen 3,19). Außerdem wird in diesem Zusammenhang häufig dahingehend argumentiert, dass die Todesandrohung in Gen 2,17 an die sog. *mot-yumat*-Sätze der gesetzlichen Überlieferungen der Hebräischen Bibel erinnere, wie sie z.B. im sog. Bundesbuch in Ex 21–23 zahlreich belegt sind. Die in Gen 2,17 vorliegende Formulierung *mot tumat* in der 2. (und nicht wie üblich in der 3.) Pers. wird

---

8 Zur Rolle der Schlange s. u.a. WESTERMANN, Genesis, 322–327.

dabei durch die narrative Einbindung der Wendung erklärt (vgl. in diesem Kontext auch Gen 20,7; Num 26,65; Ri 13,22; Ez 3,18 oder 2Kön 1,16). Des Weiteren deuten die Ausleger, die sich für eine gleichsam naturhafte Sterblichkeit des Menschen aussprechen, die Tatsache, dass die ersten Menschen nach der Übertretung des Gebotes de facto gar nicht gleich sterben müssen, sondern zunächst nur verschiedene Daseinsminderungen auf sich zu nehmen haben, als Ausdruck der göttlichen Gnade. Wenn der Text eine Ätiologie der Sterblichkeit hätte bieten wollen, dann wäre zu erwarten gewesen, dass dies auch explizit ausgedrückt worden wäre. Die Vertreibung aus dem Paradies und damit die Trennung vom Baum des Lebens habe danach den Zweck, dem Menschen die im Paradies bestehende *Möglichkeit*, das ewige Leben zu erlangen, endgültig zu nehmen. Ganz ähnlich wird auch im Gilgamesch- und Adapa-Epos die Sterblichkeit des Menschen ebenfalls von Anfang an vorausgesetzt, und der Mensch verpasst auf unglückliche Art und Weise jeweils die ihm einmalig gegebene Chance, die Unsterblichkeit zu erringen.

Gegen diese Interpretationsmöglichkeit, Tod und Sterblichkeit von Anfang an als integralen Bestandteil der menschlichen Natur zu verstehen, lassen sich auf der anderen Seite zahlreiche wichtige Gegenargumente anführen. Das größte Gewicht liegt dabei sicherlich auf der Beobachtung, dass der Mensch nach dem Übertreten des göttlichen Gebots keineswegs unmittelbar vom Tode ereilt wird. Vielmehr erfolgen hier zunächst die Fluchsprüche, die nicht den sofortigen Tod, sondern die prinzipielle Möglichkeit des Todes ins Auge fassen. Dabei ist zu beachten, dass das einleitende *ki* (כי) keineswegs im Sinne einer Begründung gelesen werden muss, welche die Sterblichkeit gewissermaßen als „Hintergrundphänomen" für die menschliche Lebenszeit darstellt. Eine andere Interpretationsmöglichkeit von Gen 3,19 besteht vielmehr darin, diese Partikel in einem deiktischen Sinne aufzufassen und die Wendung mit den Worten „Wahrlich, du bist Erde und sollst wieder zur Erde werden" wiederzugeben. Gen 3,19b würde dann den letzten und abschließenden Teil für die drei Fluchworte darstellen, in dem diese noch einmal alle überboten werden.

Ein weiteres Argument besagt, dass das Hebräische die Aussage, dass der Mensch sterblich werde, ja nur in der hier vorliegende Form mit den Worten *mot tumat* formulieren könne, da es auch für den Modus der Notwendigkeit im Hebräischen keine andere Möglichkeit als die Verwendung des Imperfekts gebe. Die erforderlichen Vereindeutigungen erfolgten durch den Kontext.

Eine weitere Überlegung, die es nahelegt, die Paradieserzählung als eine Ätiologie für menschliche Sterblichkeit zu verstehen, wird in Gen 3,16.20 gegeben. Denn die Tatsache, dass die Erzählung das Motiv der menschlichen Reproduktion erst an dieser Stelle nennt und mit einem Ausblick auf Eva als die Mutter alles Lebendigen und somit auf die Generationenfolge endet, ist letztlich nur auf der Basis der menschlichen Sterblichkeit denkbar und passt daher an dieser Stelle besonders gut in den Kontext. Dementsprechend kann Erhard Blum an dieser Stelle ausführen:

> In dieser Perspektive (sc. einer tröstlichen Verheißung) liegt nun auch auf der Hand, weshalb der Mensch im Anschluß an die Fluchworte des Schöpfers zuerst seiner Frau einen Namen gibt: Der Mensch *kann* erst hier seine Frau als Mutter aller Lebendigen bezeichnen, weil er es seit den Gottesworten verstehen kann. Und er verleiht den Eva-Namen *gerade* hier, weil dieser Name gegenüber den vorausgehenden Todesworten die Zukunfts- und Lebensperspektive der neuen Existenz zum Ausdruck bringt.[9]

Der Tod, so Erhard Blum, ist keine Strafe für die Übertretung des göttlichen Gebotes, sondern vielmehr die logische Konsequenz daraus: Denn die beiden Bäume repräsentieren

> als Wirkgrößen zwei Aspekte des Göttlichen, die damit buchstäblich in Reichweite des Menschen liegen: An dem einen, der unerschöpflichen Lebenskraft können die Menschen von Anfang an partizipieren! Deshalb muß vom Baum des *Lebens* auch erst ganz am Ende wieder die Rede sein, als der Zugang zu ihm versperrt wird. [...] Würden die Menschen an der Fülle des Göttlichen partizipieren, wie sie durch die beiden Bäume repräsentiert wird, wäre die Differenz zwischen Schöpfer und Geschöpf nivelliert. Deshalb ‚muß' der eine Aspekt der Gottähnlichkeit mit der Aufhebung der anderen sanktioniert werden.[10]

So ließe sich als Fazit die Erzählung vom sog. „Sündenfall" folgendermaßen erklären: Der anfänglich potentiell unsterbliche Mensch erwirbt somit seine Sterblichkeit durch seine Übertretungen; diese Todesverfallenheit des Menschen realisiert sich zunächst in den von Gott verhängten Daseinsminderungen, die allesamt auf den Tod hinführen. Damit der Mensch sich dieses verwirkte ewige Leben nicht wieder zurückerobern kann und damit sowohl im Hinblick auf seine Erkenntnisfähigkeit als auch im Hinblick auf das ewige Leben gottgleich würde, muss er das Paradies verlassen. Seine Todesverfallenheit ermöglicht aber gleichzeitig den Grund für die Reproduktivität des Menschen.[11]

---

9 BLUM, Gottesunmittelbarkeit, 24.
10 BLUM, Gottesunmittelbarkeit, 24–25.
11 Die beschriebene exegetische Problematik erfährt dadurch eine noch größere Komplexität, dass manche Ausleger auch das diachrone Moment in ihre Überlegungen einbeziehen. Wenn man davon ausgeht, dass die Paradiesgeschichte ältere Überlieferungen in sich aufgenommen hat, so besteht zumindest theoretisch die Option, bei der Erklärung der Erzählung motivgeschichtlich bzw. literarkritisch zu argumentieren. Dabei wäre der Hinweis wichtig, dass das Motiv des Lebensbaums und des Staubs als Materie für die Menschenschöpfung nur relativ lose in der Erzählung verankert sind. Prinzipiell wäre also eine Erzählung denkbar, die zunächst nur das Motiv des Baumes der Erkenntnis von Gut und Böse enthielt, wie es in Gen 2,16 formu-

Es ist nicht die Aufgabe dieses Beitrags, eine definitive Entscheidung zwischen diesen verschiedenen Deutungen zu fällen. Aus meiner Sicht hat die zweite Deutung, die die Geschichte als eine Ätiologie des Todes deutet, mehr Plausibilität, da hier die Androhung des Todes durch die Daseinsminderungen eingelöst und zudem das Motiv der Reproduktivität des Lebens organisch mit der Gesamterzählung verbunden wird. Wichtiger als diese historisch-kritische Fragestellung erscheint mir im vorliegenden Kontext aber die Tatsache, dass diese Erzählung in ihrer Synchronizität eine ihr eigene „Polysemie" aufweist und mehrere Deutungen des Todes zulässt. Man kann die Erzählung sowohl in dem Sinne lesen, dass der Tod als eine schöpfungsbedingte Größe zu verstehen ist und dass hier primär Ätiologien für Daseinsminderungen im Vordergrund stehen; es gibt aber auch gute exegetische Gründe, von einer Ätiologie der menschlichen Sterblichkeit und des Todes auszugehen.[12] Somit handelt es sich um einen durchaus ambivalenten Text, und genau dies ist die Basis für die weitere Rezeption des Motivs, die ich im Folgenden wenigsten in Umrissen andeuten möchte.

2 Apokryphen und Pseudepigraphen

Es ist zunächst überraschend, dass in der gesamten Hebräischen Bibel keine weiteren Referenzen auf die Paradiesgeschichte erfolgen. Vielmehr bleibt es aus Gründen, über die wir nur spekulieren können, der apokryphen Literatur des zweiten bzw. ersten vorchristlichen Jahrhunderts vorbehalten, sich diesem Stoff wieder zuzuwenden. Aber auch hier spielen Rückgriffe auf die Paradiesgeschichte und die in ihr enthaltene Verbindung zwischen der menschlichen

---

liert ist: „Und JHWH Elohim gebot dem Menschen und sprach: Du darfst essen von allen Bäumen im Garten, aber vom Baum der Erkenntnis von Gut und Böse sollst du nicht essen, denn an dem Tage, an dem du von ihm isst, musst du des Todes sterben." Durch die Todesthematik und das Motiv vom Verlust des ewigen Lebens wäre dann sekundär das ältere, auch in der Umwelt belegte Motiv des Lebensbaumes in die Erzählung integriert worden, um so durch das Motiv der Vertreibung aus dem Paradies das Todesgeschick des Menschen plastischer werden zu lassen. Vor diesem Hintergrund könnte dann auch der etwas plump wirkende Nachsatz in Gen 2,9 als sekundäre Fortschreibung erklärt werden. Für die hier vorliegende Fragestellung sind solche Überlegungen eher sekundär. Denn selbst wenn der Text nicht einheitlich wäre, muss ja mit einer reflektierten Endredaktion gerechnet werden. Deshalb ist der Ausleger in keinem Fall seiner Aufgabe enthoben, den Sinnzusammenhang des Textes auf synchroner Ebene darzulegen; vgl. hierzu SCHMID, Unteilbarkeit der Weisheit, 26.
12 S. hierzu MÜLLER, Deutungen des Todes; DERS., Erkenntnis und Verfehlung.

Übertretung des göttlichen Gebots und dem Tod eine eher marginale Rolle. Eine wichtige Weichenstellung in der Auslegung erfolgt bei dem jüdischen Weisheitslehrer Jesus Sirach in Sir 25,24, wo dieser sagt, dass „die Sünde bei einer Frau ihren Anfang nahm und ihretwegen wir alle sterben müssen". Die Aussage steht im Kontext eines Abschnittes, der die Boshaftigkeit des weiblichen Geschlechts im Allgemeinen sowie das Unheil, das durch verschiedene Verhaltensweisen von Frauen in die Welt gebracht wird, thematisiert. In diesem Zusammenhang dient die implizite Anspielung auf Eva und ihre Sünde gleichsam als Begründung für die allgemeinen Ausführungen des Autors zur Natur der Frau, die wiederum in dem breiteren kultur- und geistesgeschichtlichen Umfeld des jüdisch-hellenistischen Kulturkontaktes zu kontextualisieren sind.[13] Für unsere Zusammenhänge ist dieser Beleg insofern wichtig, als nun die in der Paradiesgeschichte ambivalent gestaltete Aussage zum Ursprung des Todes eindeutig beantwortet wird: Der Tod kam erst durch das Übertreten des Gebotes in die Welt und war eben nicht von Anfang an Teil der göttlichen Schöpfungsordnung.[14] Wichtig ist auch, dass Evas Übertretung des Gebotes hier explizit als „Sünde" bezeichnet und dass sie nun für das Todesgeschick der gesamten Menschheit verantwortlich gemacht wird.[15]

In den Apokryphen wird die biblische Überlieferung insofern auf eindeutige Art und Weise ausgelegt, wenn nach der Sapientia Salomonis der Tod durch den Neid des Satans in die Welt gekommen ist (Sap 2,24). Damit benennt dieser Text nun nicht mehr die Schlange als ein natürliches Lebewesen als den Auslöser der Übertretung des Gebotes, sondern eine in gewisser Weise metaphysische Größe.[16]

So kann in jedem Fall festgestellt werden, dass das Motivensemble vom „Sündenfall", das neben der Sünde Evas die Schlange als das personifizierte Böse sowie eine Ätiologie der menschlichen Sterblichkeit enthält, bereits in den

---

13 S. hierzu weiterführend den Beitrag von CAMP, Understanding Patriarchy. Zu dem entsprechenden Abschnitt bei Jesus Sirach s. SAUER, Sirach, 190–192.
14 Das Motiv der Erschaffung des Menschen aus Erde und seine Rückkehr zu derselben wird in Sir 17,1 aufgenommen. Es erfolgt allerdings keine Verbindung mit der Thematik von Evas Verfehlung.
15 Zum Verständnis der Sünde in der Schrift Jesu Sirachs s. MURPHY, Sin, 261–270. Murphy weist darauf hin, dass für den Siraziden die Sünde in Verbindung mit Stolz und Hybris (10,13) sowie mit Reichtum (31,5) steht; insbesondere ist darauf hinzuweisen, dass in diesem Werk der freie Wille des Menschen betont wird (15,11–17). Eine ausführliche Beschreibung der Sünde findet sich in Sir 21,1–9. Danach führt der Weg des Sünders in die Scheol. Auf die Sünde Evas geht der Autor allerdings nicht ein.
16 Zur Überlieferung in der Sapientia Salomonis s. die grundlegenden Ausführungen in dem Beitrag von MITTMANN in diesem Band.

alttestamentlichen Apokryphen vorgegeben ist. Wie eng diese Elemente in der frühjüdischen Tradition miteinander verbunden sein können, zeigen die Überlieferungen in der Schrift „Griechisches Leben Adam und Evas" (auch „Apokalypse des Mose" genannt), einem Werk, das ins 1. oder 2. Jh. n. Chr. zu datieren und im palästinisch-jüdischen Milieu in griechischer Sprache entstanden ist.[17] In seiner richtungsweisenden Studie zu diesem Werk hat Jan Dochhorn gezeigt, dass dieser Text unterschiedliche Konzepte im Hinblick auf das Todesschicksal des Menschen enthält: Das sog. Testament Evas (ApkMos 15–30; 33,2–37,6) als der ältere Teil dieser Überlieferung basiert auf der Annahme, dass der Mensch sterblich geschaffen wurde, wohingegen in den jüngeren Teilen dieses Werkes Evas Übertretung des Gebotes als Grund für die Sterblichkeit des Menschen genannt wird: Nachdem Adam krank geworden ist, kann er nämlich seinen Kindern berichten, dass er um Evas willen den Tod erleiden muss (ApkMos 7). Des Weiteren wirft er seiner Frau auch ausdrücklich vor, dass sie es war, die den Tod über die gesamte Menschheit gebracht habe (ApkMos 14; s. auch ApkMos 28.41). Der Text bestätigt somit die der biblischen Paradieserzählung innewohnende Polysemie, da sich beide Verständnismöglichkeiten hier finden. Gleichzeitig belegt diese Überlieferung aber auch eine bestimmte Entwicklung im Verständnis des Todes, denn Adam und damit die gesamte Menschheit werden nun auch mit zahlreichen Krankheiten geschlagen (ApkMos 8).

Aus dem Munde Adams geht eindeutig hervor, dass Eva hier die Schuld an dem ganzen Geschehen trägt (ApkMos 7).[18] Die Erzählung enthält aber auch eine eindeutige Entlastung der Frau, da der Teufel als der eigentliche Initiator ihrer Handlungen portraitiert wird. Ausführlich wird nämlich geschildert, mit welcher List der Teufel ans Werk ging, um Eva durch die Schlange zur Übertretung des Gebotes zu verführen (ApkMos 16–19). Als sie Adam dazu überredete, ebenfalls von der verbotenen Frucht zu essen, redete sie gar nicht selbst, sondern war vielmehr vom Teufel besessen, da er es war, der aus ihrem Munde sprach (ApkMos 21). Geradezu rührend wirkt es, wenn Eva ihrem Mann anbietet, die Hälfte der Krankheit auf sich zu nehmen (ApkMos 9), und wenn sie mit ihrem Sohn Seth die nicht gerade ungefährliche Reise zum Paradies auf sich nimmt, um für Adam Fürbitte zu leisten und das Öl des Lebens zu holen (ApkMos 10–13). Evas Appell an ihre Nachkommen, sich künftig von der Sünde fernzuhalten, zeigt, dass sie ihre Schuld eingesehen hat, und impliziert, dass sie ihr

---

17 Zu den Einleitungsfragen s. DOCHHORN, Apokalypse, 149–172.
18 Aber auch weitere antik-jüdische Texte geben der Frau die Schuld für das Todesgeschick des Menschen. Insbesondere ist hier auf die sog. Adamsliteratur zu verweisen; andere Texte wie die Syrische Baruch-Apokalypse und 4. Esra sehen dagegen sowohl in Adam als auch in Eva die Verantwortlichen für das Todesgeschick der Menschheit; zum Ganzen s. KOCH, Adam.

Handeln bitter bereut (ApkMos 30). So kann abschließend festgestellt werden, dass Eva nicht durchweg negativ dargestellt wird, sondern vielmehr in einem ambivalenten Licht erscheint.[19]

Wie Thomas Knittel, der ebenfalls eine bedeutende Studie zu diesem Werk vorgelegt hat, zeigen konnte, hat die Erzählung damit auch eine paradigmatische Funktion. Eva spricht nämlich in ihrem Rückblick auf die Paradiesgeschichte auch die Warnung an ihre Kinder aus, künftig nicht vom rechten Wege abzuweichen. So bildet ihre eigene Geschichte ein negatives Exempel und impliziert damit eine konkrete Aufforderung zum rechten Handeln.[20] Schließlich enthält die Geschichte auch eine eschatologische Dimension, da Gott Adam bei seiner Bestattung verheißt, dass er ihn und alle anderen Menschen, die von ihm abstammen, am Ende der Zeiten auferwecken wird (ApkMos 41,2).

Die Existenz des Menschen stellt damit eine Existenz „zwischen Sündenfall und Erlösung" dar: „Gegenwärtig muss er (sc. der Mensch) aufgrund seiner Sünde mancherlei Bedrängnisse erfahren, und ein Ausweg aus seiner Not scheint innergeschichtlich nicht möglich zu sein. Am Ende der Zeit aber wird ihm das Paradies zurückgegeben und er somit wieder in seinen ursprünglichen Stand eingesetzt werden."[21]

Diese Überlieferungen bilden wohl auch den breiteren Vorstellungshintergrund für die christliche Überlieferung: Bereits Paulus kann in Röm 5,12–21 davon sprechen, dass durch einen Menschen die Sünde und der Tod in die Welt gekommen sind. Eine metaphysische Deutung der Schlange wiederum wird wohl schon in Apk 12,9 vorausgesetzt, wenn der in der Heilszeit vom Himmel herabgestürzte Satan als die „alte Schlange" und als der „Verführer" der ganzen Erde bezeichnet werden kann. Die explizite Verbindung von Evas Sündenfall, welcher der Menschheit generell den Tod bringt, und der Schlange als Inkorporation der bösen, widergöttlichen Macht ist in der christlichen Überlieferung dann sehr häufig anzutreffen.[22]

---

19 Zu dieser literarkritischen Analyse des Werkes s. DOCHHORN, Apokalypse, 124–138.
20 KNITTEL, Leben Adams und Evas, 302.
21 KNITTEL, Leben Adams und Evas, 303.
22 Zu den patristischen Auslegungen von Gen 3,1 s. LOUTH, Ancient Christian Commentary, 74–76, wo unter anderem Belege von Augustin, Ambrosius und Johannes von Damaskus genannt werden; zum Ganzen s. auch WESTERMANN, Genesis, 325.355.

3 Die rabbinische Literatur

Wenn wir uns abschließend der rabbinischen Überlieferung zuwenden, so ist an dieser Stelle eine Beschränkung auf einige ausgewählte Texte geboten. Während in den apokryphen und pseudepigraphischen Überlieferungen eine Auslegung der biblischen Paradieserzählung greifbar ist, die diese im Sinne einer Ätiologie der menschlichen Sterblichkeit sieht, wird in den rabbinischen Texten ein anderer Zugang zu dieser Erzählung offensichtlich. Bei aller Problematik, diese vielfältigen Traditionen zu systematisieren und einer kohärenten Lesart zu unterziehen, kann als generelle Linie des rabbinischen Verständnisses der Paradies- und Sündenfallgeschichte festgehalten werden, dass hier die Sterblichkeit des Menschen schöpfungsbedingt und von Anfang an gegeben ist: Bereshit Rabbah 9,5 kann sogar ganz prononciert in einem Al-Tiqre-Midrasch anstelle von טוב מאד (sehr gut) die Worte טוב מות (gut ist der Tod) lesen.

Manche der rabbinischen Überlieferungen erwecken sogar den Eindruck, als wollten sie gegen die Vorstellung einer Erbsünde Adams polemisieren. Nach einer Überlieferung im Babylonischen Talmud Sabbath 55b mussten lediglich vier Personen, nämlich Benjamin, der Sohn Jakobs, Amram, der Vater Moses, Isai, der Vater Davids und Kilab, der Sohn Davids, aufgrund der Verführung Adams und Evas durch die Schlange sterben. All den hier genannten Figuren ist gemeinsam, dass sie sich in ihrer geringen Bedeutung von ihren Vätern bzw. Söhnen unterschieden und wir nichts über ihre Sünden wissen. Alle anderen Menschen sind für ihren Tod aber selbst verantwortlich.[23]

Eine direkte Auseinandersetzung mit der Vorstellung von der Erbsünde scheint sich auch in Midrasch Tanchuma Buber Bereshit 29 (S. 11a) zu finden. Danach bittet Adam darum, dass Gott nicht über ihn schreiben möge, dass er den Tod in die Welt gebracht habe. Gott sichert ihm daraufhin zu, dass die Heilige Schrift einem jeden, der von der Welt scheidet, offenbaren wird, dass seine eigenen Werke, die während seines Lebens aufgeschrieben wurden, den tatsächlichen Grund seines Todes darstellen.[24] Das Ziel dieser Überlieferungen

---

[23] S. auch Babylonischer Talmud Baba Bathra 17a; zum Ganzen s. EGO, Adam und Eva, 65; OBERHÄNSLI-WIDMER, Biblische Figuren, 142–147.
[24] Eine andere rabbinische Überlieferung kann den Gedanken einer Erbsünde, die in Adam ihren Anfang nahm, sogar auf den Kopf stellen. Der Tod—so weiß es Bereshit Rabbah 9,5—war nur wegen Hiram und Nebukadnezar, die sich als Götter hatten anbeten lassen, über Adam verhängt worden. Damit wird die Ansicht, dass Adam für den Tod der folgenden Generationen verantwortlich sein könnte, geradezu umgedreht und er selbst wird entlastet. In der überwiegenden Zahl der Belege wird Adam trotz seiner Sündhaftigkeit als positive Figur beschrieben, die in einer engen Beziehung zu Israel steht. So kann er zum Ahnvater der Weisen und Schrift-

liegt wohl weniger in dem Anliegen, die Herkunft des Todes metaphysisch zu erklären, als vielmehr darin, die Wahl- und Willensfreiheit des Menschen zu betonen. Diese anthropologische Grundaussage wiederum steht in einem engen Bezug zur Vorstellung der Schöpfungsallmacht des einzigen Gottes, außer dem es keine andere, und schon gar keine widergöttliche Macht gibt. Gott schuf beide Triebe, den guten wie den bösen Trieb, und der Mensch hat die Freiheit (und die Aufgabe), sich auf die Seite des guten Triebes zu begeben.

Aber auch hier in der rabbinischen Überlieferung folgt aus der Übertretung des göttlichen Gebots eine Vielzahl von Daseinsminderungen: Adams Gestalt, ursprünglich von einem Ende der Welt zum anderen reichend, wurde nach der Verletzung der göttlichen Weisung, nicht vom Baum zu essen, vermindert (Bereshit Rabbah 12,6; 19,8; Babylonischer Talmud Baba Bathra 75a). Nach dem Midrasch Avot deRabbi Natan B 42, S. 116 hat Adam (und haben damit alle Menschen) als Folge der Verletzung des göttlichen Gebots zehn Strafen bekommen. So wurde ihm unter anderem seine schöne Kleidung genommen; seine Nahrung musste er fortan unter Mühen finden; seine Nachkommen müssen von Land zu Land wandern; der böse Trieb herrscht über ihn; nach seinem Tode verfällt er der Fäulnis und den Würmern; er ist den wilden Tieren ausgeliefert; sein Leben insgesamt ist nur kurz und voller Unruhe, und nach seinem Tod wird er vor das göttliche Gericht gestellt werden (vgl. Bereshit Rabbah 12,6 mit insgesamt sechs Verminderungen).

Der Midrasch Bereshit Rabbah 19,7 wiederum kann erzählen, dass sich die Schekhinah wegen der Verletzung des göttlichen Gebotes von der Erde in den ersten Himmel zurückzog. Durch jede weitere Sünde—so z.B. Kains Brudermord, den Götzendienst zur Zeit Enoschs, die Vergehen der Flutgeneration oder den Turmbau—findet diese Entfernung der göttlichen Gegenwart dann seine Fortsetzung. Das Gegengewicht zu dieser schrittweisen und stetigen Entfernung der Gottesgegenwart aus der Welt stellt die Wirksamkeit von sieben gerechten Männern dar. So bringen Abraham, Isaak, Jakob, Levi, Kehat, Amram und schließlich Mose mit der Gabe der Tora die göttliche Gegenwart wieder auf die Erde zurück.

---

kundigen Israels werden (Bereshit Rabbah 24,2); eine eindeutige Zuordnung zu Israel erfolgt auch in Bereshit Rabbah 58,4, wonach Adam (und natürlich Eva) zusammen mit Abraham, Isaak und Jakob sowie Sara, Rebekka und Lea in der Höhle Machpela begraben sind (vgl. Bereshit Rabbah 58,8). Zudem kann Adam zum Empfänger verschiedener Gebote und Gebräuche werden: So beobachtete er den Sabbat (Midrasch Tehillim zu 92,6), begründete den Habdala-Ritus (Bereshit Rabbah 12,6; 82,14) und brachte sogar als erster ein Opfer dar (Babylonischer Talmud Avodah Zarah 8a).

Insbesondere ist es Eva und die Frau überhaupt, die von solchen Daseinsminderungen betroffen ist. Denn die Frau muss die Beschwerde der Schwangerschaft, der Empfängnis, der Fehlgeburten, der Niederkunft und die der Kindererziehung auf sich nehmen (Bereshit Rabbah 20,6). Um ihre Scham über ihre Schuld zum Ausdruck zu bringen, muss eine jede Frau mit bedecktem Haupt gehen. Aber auch weitere Regelungen der Halakha und des Brauchtums werden auf Eva zurückgeführt: Weil Eva den Tod über Adam gebracht hat, müssen Frauen einem Trauerzug vorausgehen; weil sie das Blut Adams vergossen hat, müssen Frauen die Niddavorschriften beachten; weil Eva die Seele Adams ausgelöscht hat, müssen Frauen—gleichsam als Gegenpol—am Sabbat die Lichter entzünden (Bereshit Rabbah 17,8; siehe auch Avot deRabbi Natan Version B 9, S. 25; Avot deRabbi Natan Version B 42, S. 117). Die Halakha und das Brauchtum, die das Leben einer jeden jüdischen Frau bestimmen, haben ihren Grund bereits in der Urzeit am Anfang der Schöpfung. Auch wenn diese Texte nicht von einer Erbsünde sprechen, so liegt Evas Übertretung des göttlichen Gebots im Paradies doch wie ein Schatten über dem Leben einer jeden Frau.

Eine explizite Identifizierung der Schlange mit der Figur des Satans erfolgt dann in der jüngeren Midraschüberlieferung: Die Schlange, die vor der Übertretung des Gebotes ja noch Beine hatte und wie ein Kamel aussah, wird nun – so Pirqe de Rabbi Eliezer 13–14 – zum Reittier Sammaels, eines Engels, der die himmlische Welt verlassen hat. Dieser gibt sich allerdings nicht damit zufrieden, Eva zum Essen der verbotenen Frucht zu verführen, sondern begibt sich vielmehr nach der Vertreibung aus dem Garten nochmals zu Eva und geht zu ihr ein. Der Abkömmling dieser Verbindung ist kein anderer als der Brudermörder Kain, mit dem Mord und Totschlag auf die Erde kommen (Pirqe deRabbi Eliezer 22). Die Herkunft des Bösen und des Todes wird damit auch hier nun gleichsam metaphysisch interpretiert und in transpersonalen Zusammenhängen gesucht.

4 Fazit

Als Fazit lässt sich festhalten, dass die biblische Paradieserzählung vom sog. „Sündenfall" ein polysemantischer Text ist, der aufgrund zahlreicher Leerstellen ganz unterschiedliche Lesemöglichkeiten bietet. Vor diesem Hintergrund überrascht es nicht, dass wir es in den Auslegungen der frühjüdischen und frühchristlichen bzw. rabbinischen Literatur mit einer Vielzahl von narrativen Entwürfen zu tun haben, die den Sinngehalt der Überlieferung eindeutiger machen. Bemerkenswert ist dabei, dass die Erzählung von der Übertretung des Gebots in den Überlieferungen der hellenistischen Zeit eine eher marginale

Rolle spielt; eine breitere Rezeption findet sich—neben Philo—erst in den Pseudepigraphen bzw. der Midraschliteratur, also in Überlieferungen, die um die Zeitenwende und in den ersten nachchristlichen Jahrhunderten entstanden sind.

Generell kann festgestellt werden, dass bereits in hellenistischer Zeit eine eindeutige Fokussierung auf die Gestalt der Eva erfolgt, wenn es darum geht, nach der Verantwortung für den sog. „Sündenfall" zu suchen. Diese Linie wird dann auch in der rabbinischen Literatur, die mit der Tempelzerstörung und zudem noch mit dem gescheiterten Bar-Kochba-Aufstand ringen muss, vertreten. Die Überlieferungen machen aber auch deutlich, dass Evas Verfehlung, die ja wiederum Ergebnis der Überredungskunst der Schlange ist, in einem metaphysischen Zusammenhang zu betrachten ist. In diesem Kontext ist insbesondere auf die Dämonisierung der Schlange zu verweisen, die—so zum ersten Mal in der Weisheit Salomos—als Inkarnation des Satans verstanden werden kann. Damit berühren sich die hier vorgestellten Texte mit der Geschichte von den gefallenen Wächtern im Wächterbuch des Äthiopischen Henoch (1 Hen 6–14), die im Kontext einer Ätiologie von Gewalttat und Sünde in der frühjüdischen Überlieferung eine ganz zentrale Rolle spielt. Danach sind es Engelsmächte, die den ihnen angestammten himmlischen Bereich verlassen und Blutvergießen und Sünde über die Menschheit bringen.[25]

Während aber die Pseudepigraphen die Verbindung von Sünde und der Sterblichkeit der Menschheit generell in den Vordergrund stellen, macht die später entstandene rabbinische Literatur jeden Einzelnen für seinen Tod verantwortlich; hier führen die Ereignisse im Paradies und die erste Begegnung des Menschen mit dem Widergöttlichen und Bösen lediglich zu Daseinsminderungen ganz unterschiedlicher Art, die wiederum in der Existenz der Frau am deutlichsten zu greifen sind.

Trotz der zahlreichen Auslegungen, die den biblischen Basistext ausdeuten und so konkreter fassbar machen, ist festzustellen, dass die frühjüdischen Interpretationen bei Weitem nicht alle Leerstellen der biblischen Erzählung ausfüllen. Auch wenn die Schlange als das Wesen, durch welches das Böse und Daseinsminderungen bis hin zum Tod des Menschen in die Welt gebracht wurden, in metaphysischen Zusammenhängen gesehen wird, so bekommen die Leser und Leserinnen in diesen Überlieferungen doch keine Auskunft über dessen Ursprung. Die Erzählungen schweigen über das Woher dieser Figur und des

---

25 S. hierzu ausführlich BACHMANN, Ausnahmezustand; DIES., Engel (mit ausführlichen Literaturangaben zur älteren Forschung); zu dieser Überlieferung s. auch den Beitrag von OEGEMA in diesem Band.

Bösen, und es soll der Lurianischen Kabbala des 16. Jahrhunderts vorbehalten bleiben, hier mit dem Mythos vom „Bruch der Gefäße" eine Antwort zu finden, die Gottes Allmacht mit der Existenz der Sünde zu vereinbaren vermag.

Bibliographie

BLUM, Erhard, Von Gottesunmittelbarkeit zur Gottähnlichkeit. Überlegungen zur theologischen Anthropologie der Paradieserzählung, in: Eberhardt, Gönke/Liess, Kathrin (Hg.), Gottes Nähe im Alten Testament (SBS 2002), Stuttgart 2004, 9–29.

CAMP, Claudia, Understanding a Patriarchy. Women in Second Century Jerusalem Through the Eyes of Ben Sira, in: Levine, Amy-Jill (Hg.), "Women like this". New Perspectives on Jewish Women in the Greco-Roman World (Early Judaism and its Literature 1), Atlanta, Georgia 1991.

DOCHHORN, Jan, Die Apokalypse des Mose. Text, Übersetzung, Kommentar (TSAJ 106), Tübingen 2005.

GRUND, Alexandra, „Wer steht mir bei wider die Übeltäter?" (Ps 94,16). Zur Bewältigung des Bösen in den Psalmen, in: JBTh 26 (2011) 55–84.

JANOWSKI, Bernd, Jenseits von Eden. Gen 4,1–16 und die nichtpriesterliche Urgeschichte, in: Lange, Armin/Lichtenberger, Hermann/Römheld, K.F. Diethard (Hg.), Die Dämonen – Demons. Die Dämonologie der israelitisch-jüdischen und frühchristlichen Literatur im Kontext ihrer Umwelt, Tübingen 2003, 137–158 (wiederabgedruckt in: Janowski, Bernd, Der Gott des Lebens. Beiträge zur Theologie des Alten Testaments 3, Neukirchen-Vluyn 2003, 134–156).

KEEL, Othmar, Die Welt der altorientalischen Bildsymbolik und das Alte Testament. Am Beispiel der Psalmen, Göttingen 1996.

KNITTEL, Thomas, Das griechische „Leben Adams und Evas". Studien zu einer narrativen Anthropologie im frühen Judentum (TSAJ 88), Tübingen 2002.

KOCH, Klaus, »Adam, was hast du getan?« Erkenntnis und Fall in der zwischentestamentlichen Literatur, in: Rendtorff, Trutz (Hg.), Glaube und Toleranz. Das theologische Erbe der Aufklärung (Veröffentlichungen der Wissenschaftlichen Gesellschaft für Theologie 2), Gütersloh 1982, 211–242.

LOUTH, Andrew (Hg.), Genesis 1–11 (Ancient Christian Commentary on Scripture. Old Testament I), Downers Grove, Illinois 2001, 74–76.

MICHEL, Andreas, Theologie aus der Peripherie. Die gespaltene Koordination im biblischen Hebräisch (BZAW 257), Berlin 1997.

MÜLLER, Hans-Peter, Drei Deutungen des Todes. Gen 3, der Mythos von Adapa und die Sage von Gilgamesch, in: JBTh 6 (1991) 117–134.

MÜLLER, Hans-Peter, Erkenntnis und Verfehlung. Prototypen und Antitypen zu Gen 2–3 in der altorientalischen Literatur, in: Rendtorff, Trutz (Hg.), Glaube und Toleranz. Das theologische Erbe der Aufklärung, Gütersloh 1982, 191–210.

MURPHY, Roland E., Sin, Repentance, and Forgiveness in Sirach, in: Egger-Wenzel, Renate /Krammer, Ingrid (Hg.), Der Einzelne und seine Gemeinschaft bei Ben Sira (BZAW 270), Berlin 1998, 261–270.

OBERHÄNSLI-WIDMER, Gabrielle, Biblische Figuren in der rabbinischen Literatur. Gleichnisse und Bilder zu Adam, Noah und Abraham im Midrasch Bereschit Rabba (Judaica et Christiana 17), Bern 1998.

SAUER, Georg, Jesus Sirach/Ben Sira (ATD Apokryphen Bd. 1), Göttingen 2000.

SCHMID, Konrad, Die Unteilbarkeit der Weisheit. Überlegungen zur sogenannten Paradieserzählung Gen 2f und ihrer theologischen Tendenz, in: ZAW 114 (2002) 21–39.

SCHÜLE, Andreas, „Und siehe, es war sehr gut ... und siehe, die Erde war verdorben" (Gen 1,31; 6,12). Der urgeschichtliche Diskurs über das Böse, in: JBTh 26 (2011) 3–28.

STECK, Odil Hannes, Die Paradieserzählung. Eine Auslegung von Gen 2,4b–3,24, Neukirchen-Vluyn 1970.

WAGNER, Andreas, Das Böse im Gefüge prophetischer Anthropologie und Theologie, in: JBTh 26 (2011) 29–54.

WESTERMANN, Claus, Genesis 1–11 (BK.AT I/1), Neukirchen-Vluyn 1974.

Georg Steins
An des Todes Pforten weise werden –
Überlegungen im Anschluss an Psalm 107

1 Einleitung

Weisheit ist ein todernstes Thema, denn alle Weisheit hat sich zu bewähren vor der ebenso alltäglichen wie bedrängenden und niederdrückenden Tatsache des Bösen—und schließlich vor dem Tod. Diese Wirklichkeiten, die letztlich eine sind (vgl. Dtn 30,15–16), entscheiden über Stellung und Rolle, über Wert und Wirkung der Weisheit. Psalm 107 empfiehlt in seinem dicht formulierten Schlussvers 43, sowohl die Kraft der Erinnerung als auch die Fähigkeit zur sorgfältigen Unterscheidung aufzubieten, um weise zu werden, und er gibt zugleich den Grund und den Gegenstand aller Weisheit an: die zahlreichen gnadenvollen Zuwendungen JHWHs:

מי־חכם וישמר־אלה ויתבוננו חסדי יהוה

> Wer ist weise, so dass er diese (gemeint: Wunder)[1] bewahrt
> und sie acht geben/man acht gibt[2] auf die Zuwendungen JHWHs?

Die Bibel stellt bereits auf den ersten Seiten klar, dass dem Menschen eine Fähigkeit mitgegeben ist, die ihn zwar auf eine letztlich nicht zu durchschauende Weise aus dem Gottesgarten herausgeführt hat, die ihm aber auch das (Über-)Leben „jenseits von Eden" ermöglicht: die Fähigkeit der Erkenntnis, d.h. die Unterscheidung des Guten und des Bösen oder Schlechten. Im Deutschen fehlt

---

[1] Der Rückbezug des pluralischen Demonstrativpronomens in V. 43a auf „Wunder" ist angesichts der parallelen Nennung von „Zuwendung" und „Wunder" in V. 8.15.21 und 31 naheliegend, vgl. ZENGER, Psalm 107, 144. Der Wechsel vom Singular zum Plural der 3. Person in V. 43b ist syntaktisch schwierig, semantisch bereitet der Text dagegen weniger Probleme. Eventuell ist durch die Variation eine Generalisierung als Schlussakzent intendiert: Nach der stereotypen singularischen Frage schwingt der Psalm am Schluss wieder in den pluralischen Duktus der vier Beispielerzählungen (s. unter 2) ein.
[2] Vgl. jüngst RUWE, Psalmen, 165, der übersetzt: „Wer weise ist, bewahre diese Dinge,/und man gebe acht auf die Gunsterweise Adonais!" HIRSCH, Psalmen, 578, übersetzt: „Wer weise ist, der achte auf solches, so werden sich begreifen lassen die Liebeswirkungen Gottes", und er erwägt 579, ob nicht „die Liebeswirkungen Gottes" auch Subjekt sein können: „Sie lassen sich von andern begreifen, sie bringen andere dazu, Einsicht in sie zu gewinnen."

ein umfassender Begriff für Letzteres, man könnte auch von Unheil sprechen, das aber in gleicher Weise als Tat und als Resultat zu verstehen ist. Es geht um die Erkenntnis dessen, was einerseits das Leben fördert und was ihm andererseits abträglich ist und den Menschen in den Bereich des Todes führt.[3]

In ihrer stark von der Weisheit geprägten Endgestalt und unter dem Eindruck einer weisheitlichen Synthese der großen Traditionen (beides ist in der Septuaginta-Überlieferung noch stärker ausgeprägt als im hebräischen Überlieferungsstrang) lässt sich die Bibel auch lesen als ein Angebot unterschiedlicher Inszenierungen des Weges zur Weisheit. Anpassung an wie Absetzung von der zeitgenössischen griechisch-hellenistischen Welt, die auch die Welt der Bibel geworden ist, haben darin einen beträchtlichen Einfluss auf die Durchformung „biblischen" Denkens und der biblischen Literatur ausgeübt. Nicht nur das eher randständige Buch Kohelet, auch der Psalter sind tief weisheitlich geprägt, worauf schon die Eröffnung Psalm 1 hinweist.

Die sprachlichen Kunstwerke der Psalmen wollen die Rezipierenden mit ästhetischen Mitteln auf einen Weg bringen, der vom Tod zum Leben führt. Die Aneignung der Texte ist eine religiöse Praxis als ritualisierte Rettung, die das Leben formt, verändert und „erlöst". Entscheidende Aspekte des Lebens werden in der Kunst literalisiert, sind sowohl Ausdruck des Erlebten als auch Muster und Formular, das neue Erfahrungen generiert. Der Formularcharakter der Psalmen ist ein wesentliches Moment seiner Wirkung durch die Jahrhunderte, wie Martin Luther bereits gültig beschrieben hat.[4] Psalm 107, der hier genauer in den Blick genommen werden soll, geht noch einen Schritt darüber hinaus, da in diesem Text nicht nur die Literalisierung des Erlebens vollzogen, sondern auf einer weiteren Stufe reflektiert und schließlich explizit als Programm gefasst wird. Psalm 107 zeigt zwar zahlreiche Gemeinsamkeiten mit den vorausgehenden Hymnen auf Gottes Macht in Schöpfung (vgl. Ps 104) und Geschichte (vgl. Ps 105–106), er hebt sich aber auch deutlich von diesen ab, und zwar vor allem in seinem Aufbau und in seiner Pragmatik.

Die damit angedeutete Richtung der Interpretation von Psalm 107 gehört nicht zur Standardsicht auf Psalm 107, denn diese ist noch stark beeinflusst von der gattungskritischen Bestimmung als Danklied, denkt also nach meinem Eindruck noch zu sehr von einer postulierten ursprünglich kultischen Verwendung des Psalms insgesamt oder zumindest angenommener ursprünglicher Bestand-

---

3 Vgl. SPIEKERMANN, Ambivalenzen; DOHMEN, Zwischen Gott und Welt.
4 Vgl. BORNKAMM, Luthers Vorreden.

teile her.⁵ Zwar betont die Forschung, wie stark der Psalm konzeptionell und sprachlich vor allem von der Prophetie (besonders der zweiten Hälfte des Jesajabuches) und der Weisheit (hier besonders des Ijobbuches, und ganz speziell der Elihureden) geprägt ist,⁶ aber auch diese Einsicht in den hochgradig schriftgelehrt anthologischen (und intertextuellen) Charakter des Psalms hat nicht zur Postulierung einer Sonderstellung im Nahkontext geführt. Diese legt sich aber bei einer gründlichen Textanalyse und im Blick auf einige Probleme (oder auch nur Halbherzigkeiten) der neueren Forschungsgeschichte nahe.

2 Psalm 107—Beobachtungen zur Textstruktur

Die Arbeitsübersetzung von Psalm 107 ist so weit wie möglich um Konkordanz bemüht. Die nachfolgend begründete Textgliederung, die bis auf die Frage der Zuordnung von V. 33–42 nahezu unbestritten ist, wird bereits eingetragen. Eingezogene Textteile in Kursivdruck gehören einer von den Beschreibungen zu unterscheidenden Ebene an, auf der Äußerungen des Lobes zitiert werden. Auf diese Weise werden zwei Textebenen etabliert:

Ebene 1: das Gotteslob im Zitat; *Ebene 2*: die Aufforderungen an die „Erlösten", deren Status beschrieben und erzählend entfaltet wird; man könnte in den narrativen Passagen eine dritte Textebene sehen, aber sie ist an die beschreibenden Passagen angehängt.

THEMASETZUNG

1 „Dankt JHWH, fürwahr, er (ist) gut,
fürwahr, auf ewig (ist) seine Zuwendung" –

2 (sollen/können) sprechen die Erlösten JHWHs,
die: er hat sie erlöst aus der Hand der Bedrängnis,
3 und (die): aus Ländern hat er sie gesammelt,

---

5 Anders jedoch ZENGER, Psalm 107, 144–146, der aus den zahlreichen Übereinstimmungen mit Psalm 106 auf die nicht-kultische Herkunft des Psalm schließt; er sieht in Psalm 107 meines Erachtens zurecht ein redaktionelles Produkt im Zusammenhang der Formung des 5. Psalmenbuches (Ps 107–Ps 144 oder Ps 150); diesen Ansatz gilt es konsequent fortzusetzen.
6 So schon DELITZSCH, Psalmen, 707: „In allen dreien (= Ps 105.107: GSt) zeigt sich der D.(ichter: GSt) heimisch in Jes. C. 40–66 und daneben im B.(uch: GSt) Iob. Am vollsten von Reminiscenzen aus beiden BB. (= Büchern: GSt) in Ps 107, wo der D. sich freier bewegt, ohne schriftlich gewordene Geschichte zu recapituliren. Alles spricht dafür, dass Ps 105.106.107 ein Trifolium sind, zwei Hodu und in der Mitte ein Halleluja."

vom Sonnenaufgang und vom Sonnenuntergang,
vom Norden und vom Meer.

Sample (1)

4 Sie irrten in der Wüste, im Ödland,
den Weg (zu) einer bewohnten Stadt fanden sie nicht.
5 Hungernde, auch Dürstende (waren sie),
ihre Lebenskraft (/Kehle) in ihnen schwand dahin.
6 Und sie schrien zu JHWH in der Bedrängnis für sie;
aus ihren Engen riss er sie heraus.
7 Er führte sie auf einen geraden Weg,
zu gehen zu einer bewohnten Stadt.
8 Sie sollen JHWH danken für seine Zuwendung
und (für) seine Wunder an den Söhnen eines Menschen:

> 9 „Fürwahr, er hat gesättigt die lechzende Kehle,
> und die hungernde Kehle hat er gefüllt mit Gutem."

Sample (2)

10 Die Bewohnenden von Finsternis und Todschatten,
Gefangene von Elend und Eisen—
11 Fürwahr: sie lehnten sich auf gegen die Aussprüche Els,
und den Rat des Höchsten verachteten sie.
12 Und er beugte durch Mühsal ihr Herz,
sie strauchelten, und es gab keinen Helfer.
13 Und sie schrien zu JHWH in der Bedrängnis für sie;
aus ihren Engen rettete er sie.
14 Er führte sie heraus aus Finsternis und Todschatten,
und ihre Fesseln zerriss er.
15 Sie sollen JHWH danken für seine Zuwendung
und (für) seine Wunder an den Söhnen eines Menschen:

> 16 „Fürwahr, er hat zerbrochen die Türen aus Bronze,
> und die Riegel aus Eisen hat er zerschmettert."

Sample (3)

17 Die Törichten: vom Weg ihres Vergehens
und von ihren Sünden stöhnten sie.
18 Jede Speise verabscheute ihre Kehle,
und sie reichten heran an die Tore des Todes.
19 Und sie schrien zu JHWH in der Bedrängnis für sie,
aus ihren Engen rettete er sie.
20 Er sandte sein Wort, und er heilte sie,
er ließ (sie) entkommen aus ihren Gruben.

21 Sie sollen JHWH danken für seine Zuwendung
und (für) seine Wunder an den Söhnen eines Menschen.
22 Und sie sollen schlachtopfern Dank-Schlachtopfer,
und sie sollen erzählen seine Taten mit Jubel.

Sample (4)

23 Die Herabsteigenden auf das Meer in Schiffen,
die Arbeit Machenden auf großen Wassern:
24 Diese sahen die Taten JHWHs
und seine Wunder in der Tiefe.
25 Und er sprach, und er ließ stehen einen Sturmwind,
und der ließ hochgehen seine Wellen.
26 Sie stiegen hinauf zum Himmel, gingen hinab in die Urfluten;
ihre Lebenskraft (/Kehle) im Unheil zerfloss.
27 Sie torkeln, und sie schwanken wie der Betrunkene,
und all ihre Weisheit wurde verwirrt.
28 Und sie schrien zu JHWH in der Bedrängnis für sie;
aus ihren Engen führte er sie heraus.
29 Er ließ den Sturm zum Säuseln werden,
und er beruhigte „ihre" Wellen.
30 Und sie freuten sich, fürwahr, sie wurden ruhig,
und er leitete sie zum Hafen ihres Wunsches.
31 Sie sollen JHWH danken für seine Zuwendung
und (für) seine Wunder an den Söhnen eines Menschen.
32 Und sie sollen/werden ihn rühmen in einer Volksversammlung,
und am Wohnsitz der Ältesten sollen/werden sie ihn preisen:

> 33 *„Er bestallt(e) Ströme zu Wüste*
> *und Austritte von Wasser zu Trockenheit,*
> *34 Land der Frucht zu Salzigem*
> *wegen des Unheils der auf ihm Wohnenden.*
> *35 Er bestallt(e) Wüste zum Wasserteich*
> *Und dürres Land zu Austritten von Wasser.*
> *36 Und er ließ dort Hungernde wohnen,*
> *und sie gründeten eine bewohnte Stadt.*
> *37 Und sie besäten Felder und pflanzten Weinberge,*
> *und sie machten Frucht des Ertrages.*
> *38 Und er segnete sie, und sie wurden sehr zahlreich,*
> *und ihr Vieh wurde nicht weniger.*
> *39 Und sie wurden weniger und sie krümmten sich*
> *wegen des Druck des Unheils und des Kummers.*
> *40 Ausgießend Spott auf die Edlen,*
> *und er lässt sie irren in der Wildnis ohne Weg.*

41 Und er hob den Geringen aus dem Elend,
und er bestallte wie das Kleinvieh Sippen.
42 Sehen sollen/werden die Geraden, und sie sollen/werden sich freuen,
und jede Verkehrtheit soll/wird ihren Mund schließen. "

KOMMENTAR/„DIE MORAL"

43 Wer (ist) weise, so dass er diese (scil. Wunder) bewahrt
und sie Acht geben/man Acht gibt auf die Zuwendungen JHWHs?

Die Texteinteilung ist bis auf die Frage nach der Stellung eines Abschnitts im letzten Viertel nicht kontrovers:[7] Nach einem Auftakt in V. 1–3, der „die Erlösten JHWHs" zum Dank auffordert, folgen vier Beispiele von Gruppen, die für ihre Erlösung danken sollen: Menschen, die sich in der Wüste verirrt hatten, befreite Gefangene, geheilte Kranke und aus dem Sturm errettete Seefahrer (V. 4–32, bzw. 42[8]). In V. 33 schwenkt der Kegel des Scheinwerfers um; jetzt richtet er sich nicht mehr auf unterschiedliche Menschengruppen, sondern auf Gottes Handeln. Umstritten ist, wieweit dieser „Abschlusshymnus" reicht, ob V. 42 dazu gezählt wird oder ob dieser Vers mit V. 43 eine Art kommentierenden Abschluss bildet. Die Frage ist jedoch zu entscheiden, denn unter Berücksichtigung der engen sprachlichen Parallelen in Hi 5,16 und 22,19 muss man V. 42 eindeutig als eine Art „Chorschluss im Aufforderungsmodus" mit der vorangehenden Beschreibung der Gottestaten verbinden.[9] Mit dem Stilwechsel zur Frageform hat der Schlussvers (V. 43) ohnehin ein ganz eigenes Gewicht.

Der Psalm ist kunstvoll bis in die Details hinein durchgestaltet. Gerade an seinem Herzstück, den sogenannten vier „Rettungserzählungen" in V. 4–32, lässt sich das demonstrieren. Es fällt schon beim ersten Lesen/Hören auf, dass die vier „Strophen" alle nach demselben Schema strukturiert sind: Auf die Schilderung der Notsituation und den Hilfeschrei der Bedrängten folgt die Aussage über die Rettung durch Gott; die Strophen schließen mit einer Aufforderung zum Dank für die erfahrene Hilfe. Zwei Bikola wiederholen sich nahezu identisch in jeder Strophe; sie bilden eine Art Doppel-Refrain, durch den die vier Rettungserzählungen auf das engste miteinander verbunden werden:

---

[7] Für viele Detailfragen ist immer noch anregend BEYERLIN, Werden und Wesen, auch wenn die Frage der Einheitlichkeit diese Untersuchung dominiert; s. ferner AUFFRET, Qui est sage; BALLHORN, Telos z.St.; LEVINE, Vertical Poetics; WEBER, Werkbuch II, 203–211.
[8] Zur strittigen Abgrenzung des vierten Samples vgl. die nachfolgenden Überlegungen.
[9] Der Subjektwechsel vermag angesichts der genannten Parallelen aus Ijob die Zuordnung des Verses zum Schlussteil V. 43 nicht zu begründen, anders ZENGER, Psalm 107, 144. Aber auch nach ZENGER, Psalm 107, 157, ist V. 43 „viel entscheidender" als „Schlussappell", so dass sich die hier vorgeschlagene Trennung von V. 42 und V. 43 auch von daher nahe legt.

6 ויצעקו אל־יהוה בצר להם ממצוקותיהם יצילם

„Und sie schrien zu JHWH in der Bedrängnis für sie;
aus ihren Engen riss er sie heraus (o.ä.)." (V. 6.13.19.28)

8 יודו ליהוה חסדו ונפלאותיו לבני אדם

„Sie sollen JHWH danken für seine Zuwendung
und für (seine) Wunder an den Söhnen eines Menschen." (V. 8.15.21.31)

Im hebräischen Text ist die Komposition noch sehr viel stärker ausgestaltet; die Parallelisierungen und Entsprechungen gehen bis in die Ebene der Orthographie hinein. Der erste Refrain, also die Verse 6.13.19 und 28, lassen eine kunstvolle chiastische Fügung erkennen: In den äußeren Versen 6 und 28 wird das Verbum צעק verwendet, in den inneren Versen 13 und 19 dagegen die Variante זעק. Mag man das noch für ein singuläres Phänomen halten, so wird das Argument unterstützt durch zwei weitere Variationen in den genannten Versen: ממצקותיהם/ממצוקתיהם „aus ihren Engen" wird in den äußeren Versen plene geschrieben, in den Innenversen defektiv. Außerdem wechselt das Verb im jeweiligen zweiten Kolon; die äußeren Verse verwenden נצל hif. und יצא hif., die Innenverse ישע hif. Semantisch liegen die Ausdrücke, die alle die Rettung bezeichnen, sehr nahe beieinander, ja können als Synonyma gelten; um so bemerkenswerter ist die lexematische Variation in Verbindung mit der gezielten Positionierung, die man kaum als Zufall ansehen kann.

Inhaltlich decken die vier „Strophen" verschiedene Erfahrungsbereiche ab und sind chiastisch aufeinander bezogen: „Die beiden äußeren Abschnitte zeigen Menschen, die unterwegs sind, und zwar umherirrend bzw. umhergeworfen in den beiden nach biblischer Tradition typischen ‚Chaos-Regionen', das sind die Wüste (1. Abschnitt) und das Meer (4. Abschnitt); für diese Gruppen ereignet sich die Rettung aus dem Tod, weil JHWH sie in eine bewohnte Stadt bzw. in den sicheren Hafen führt. Den beiden inneren Abschnitten ist gemeinsam, dass die Not dieser Menschen eine Folge ihrer Sünde ist (davon ist in den Außenabschnitten nicht die Rede)." Deren Notlage wird nicht topographisch verbildlicht, sondern durch Metaphern des Gefangenseins (Fesseln, Eingesperrtsein, Grube=Grab; Totenstadt=Unterwelt) ausgedrückt; das Eingesperrtsein steht für verschiedene Erfahrungen der Lebensminderung und „die Zerstörung der Vitalität", „sodass ihre Rettung als Befreiung und als Heilung beschrieben wird". „Beide Abschnitte sind durch die Bilder von den ‚Türflügeln' (korr: GSt)/‚Toren' in V. 16 bzw. V. 18 miteinander verkettet."[10] Eine interessante Variante in der

---

10 ZENGER, Psalm 107, 143.

Zuordnung der vier Strophen skizziert Samson Raphael Hirsch: „Die beiden ersten jener vier Rettungen treffen den Menschen in seinen Beziehungen zur Gesellschaft: der verirrte Wanderer in der Wüste kommt um durch Entfernung von den Wohnstätten der Menschen, den Gefangenen im Kerker hat eine menschengesellschaftliche Gewalt seiner Freiheit beraubt. Die beiden letzten Rettungen, die Rettung aus Krankheit und Seesturm, treffen den Menschen im Kampf mit der Natur. Ferner, der ersten und vierten Gefahr, den Gefahren der Wanderung durch Wüsten und über Meere, setzt sich der Mensch freiwillig infolge seiner Berufsunternehmungen aus. Die zweite und dritte Not, Krankheit und Gefängnis, treffen Menschen unfreiwillig als Erziehungsleiden aus Verirrungen. Dies scheinen die natürlichen Motive ihrer Gruppierung zu sein."[11]

Auf diese Weise entsteht ein kompaktes Gefüge von vier Abschnitten über Personengruppen in Todessituationen. Es werden Gruppen vorgestellt, die beispielhafte Erfahrungen gemacht haben. Zur Bezeichnung wähle ich aus der empirischen Sozialforschung den Ausdruck „Samples". Es handelt sich nicht um Erzählungen über diese Gruppen, da in den Strophen lediglich einige narrative Anteile vorliegen, vielmehr wird auf diese Gruppen hingewiesen, um göttliches Handeln zu exemplifizieren: Das hatte bereits die traditionelle Psalmenforschung erkannt, die allerdings von diesen Strukturbeobachtungen rasch zu einer kultischen Kontextualisierung des Psalms gelangte.[12]

Der Textaufbau verdient noch weitere Aufmerksamkeit, da die Strukturanalyse des Psalms wichtige Impulse für die hier hauptsächlich interessierende besondere Sicht von Unheil und Tod bietet. Der in der Forschung unbefriedigend beantwortete Aspekt der Textstruktur betrifft die Stellung des hymnischen Abschnitts gegen Ende, also V. 33–42. Wenn dieser Abschnitt als zweiter Hauptteil neben dem ersten, aus den vier Samples gebildeten verstanden oder als Schlusshymnus von den vorangehenden Beispielschilderungen abgehoben wird, bleibt das Zuordnungsproblem merkwürdig in der Schwebe, genauer: Es wird über den Rückgriff auf eine postulierte kultische Verortung geklärt, nicht aber zunächst einmal literarisch. Gibt es eine weiterführende Idee? Um diese

---

[11] HIRSCH, Psalmen, 572.
[12] Vgl. dazu beispielhaft die „anschauliche" Verortung bei DEISSLER, Psalmen, 427: „Von Hause aus ist der erste Teil kein eigentliches Danklied des Volkes, sondern einzelner Gruppen von Festpilgern […] Sie bringen anscheinend bei einer großen Dankliturgie gruppenweise ihr Dankopfer dar, wobei unser Psalm wohl das von den Leviten vorgetragene Geleitgebet abgibt. Der hymnische Schlußteil (33–43) war wohl als gemeinsamer Dankgesang aller zum Gottesdienst Versammelten gedacht." Weiterführend fügt DEISSLER jedoch an, es handele sich „um einen nachexilischen Psalm, der bei aller kultischen Abzweckung zugleich die Erziehung zur Dankbarkeit und damit zu wahrer Weisheit im Auge hatte."

Frage beantworten zu können, empfiehlt es sich, nicht direkt auf das fragliche Textstück zu schauen, sondern Konstruktion und Struktur des Psalms insgesamt in den Blick zu nehmen und von seinem Anfang her zu betrachten.

Schon der Blick auf den Anfang des Psalms liefert einen wichtigen Hinweis: Aus V. 2, der nachgestellten Einleitung einer wörtlichen Rede, geht unmissverständlich hervor, dass der Einstiegsvers des Psalms nicht nur der Beginn eines Dankliedes ist, sondern dass es sich um ein Zitat handelt. V. 1 ist „das liturgische Lied, das die Erlösten singen sollen".[13] Die Formulierung ist stereotyp[14] und für sich genommen merkwürdig. Es handelt sich um eine Lobaufforderung (scil. Dritter), die selber Gegenstand einer Aufforderung an die „Erlösten JHWHs" ist. Die Lobaufforderung ist selbst bereits der vollgültige Lobvollzug: Das unmittelbar Ausgedrückte und das eigentlich Gemeinte treten also in diesem Fall auseinander. Andreas Wagner hat dieses Sprachphänomen, das typisch ist für das Gotteslob der Psalmen, als „indirekten Sprechakt" bezeichnet.[15] Das Phänomen ist vergleichbar mit dem Stilmittel der rhetorischen Frage, die ebenfalls eine sprachliche Erscheinung für eine vom unmittelbaren Wortlaut abweichende Pragmatik nutzt.

Im Zusammenhang dieses Psalms lässt sich jedoch noch ein tieferer Sinn dieser auf den ersten Blick eigenartigen Formulierung erkennen: Der Lobdank ist doppelt ausgerichtet. Er gilt natürlich zuerst und vor allem dem rettenden Gott und rühmt dessen Zuwendung und Wunderwirken. Aber zugleich geht es um das Gottesverhältnis „der Menschenkinder" (und nicht nur der „Kinder Israels"), das vor der „Versammlung des Volkes" und „im Kreis der Alten" (V. 32) bezeugt werden soll. In Bezug auf die „Erlösten" benennt V. 1 einen indirekten Sprechakt, aber im Kontext der Adressaten dieses Zeugnisses wird aus dem indirekten Sprechakt eine Aufforderung zur Einstimmung in den Lobdank. Wenn man diese Verhältnisse und wechselnden Perspektiven beschreibt, wirkt das alles ein wenig kompliziert; im konkreten Vollzug—der nicht nur liturgisch gedacht werden kann, sondern auch „literarisch" funktioniert—ist die Sache einfacher und klarer.

Halten wir fürs Erste nur fest, dass der Auftakt von Psalm 107 auf zwei Kommunikationsebenen „spielt": V. 1 ist Zitat wörtlicher Rede und als Kommunikationsebene II in die Kommunikationsebene I, zu der V. 2–3 gehören, eingebettet. Für die Strukturierung des weiteren Psalms ist nun die Erkenntnis entscheidend, dass das Muster der Arbeit mit zwei Kommunikationsebenen nicht

---

13 ZENGER, Psalm 107, 141.
14 Dazu unten mehr.
15 WAGNER, Lobaufruf, 143.

auf die Eröffnungspartie des Psalms beschränkt bleibt. Vielmehr ist dieser Wechsel in jedem Abschnitt anzutreffen, so dass das Muster als Gestaltungsprinzip des Psalms gelten kann. Eine feinsinnige Überlegung von Klaus Seybold weist bereits in diese Richtung; seiner Meinung nach wäre nach jeder Strophe, also in jedem der vier Samples, eigentlich der Vollzug des Dankes angezeigt. Man könnte, so Seybold, den Eröffnungsvers an jede der vier Strophen anfügen.[16] Das muss jedoch nicht hypothetisch erwogen werden, sondern ist in der Tat bereits im gegebenen Text der Fall, wie zunächst an den Rettungsbeispielen 1 und 2 erläutert werden soll: Die abschließenden, jeweils mit כי eingeleiteten Bikola in V. 9 und V. 16 können als Begründungen für die vorangehenden jussivischen Dankaufrufe verstanden werden; das spiegelt sich auch in der gängigen Übersetzungspraxis wider.[17] Es spricht jedoch mehr dafür, in den genannten Versen keine Begründung zu sehen, sondern in Fortführung, Variation und Konkretisierung von V. 1 ebenfalls Zitate des Lobdanks. Darauf hat auch Klaus Koenen hingewiesen: „Am Ende der 1. und 2. Strophe klingt der Dank schon in kurzen, mit כי eingeleiteten hymnischen Lobliedern an."[18]

Dafür gibt es außerhalb von Psalm 107 überzeugende Beispiele: In Ps 118,2–4 werden wie in Ps 107 verschiedene Gruppen zum Lob aufgerufen, und es wird jeweils das Motto des Lobs zitiert. In 1Chr 16,41; 2Chr 5,13; 7,3.6; 20,21 und Esra 3,11 ist die Zeile כי לעולם חסדו, die „Ewigkeitsprädikation der Liebe (Gottes)"[19], jeweils als Beispiel für das Gotteslob in den Erzählzusammenhang eingebettet (=Kommunikationsebene II). Von daher spricht viel dafür, auch Ps 107,9 und 16 als Zitate zu interpretieren. Bei diesen Kurzhymnen handelt es sich nicht um Eigenbildungen des Verfassers von Psalm 107, sondern um die Neuverwendung von überkommenen Formulierungen.[20] Deshalb muss es nicht stören, dass sich die Verse konzeptionell und sprachlich nicht völlig in die jeweiligen Kontexte einfügen, obwohl sie durchaus passen. Dieser Zug unterstreicht vielmehr die gerade vorgetragene Überlegung, dass die genannten Verse zur Kommunikati-

---

16 Vgl. SEYBOLD, Psalmen, 428: „Am Anfang der Komposition steht die liturgische ‚Dankformel', die für ein der Toda-Feier eigenes Responsorium steht, vgl. 118,1–4; 136; 1Chr 16,34.41 u.a. Sie wäre dementsprechend nach den Aufrufen 8–9.15–16.21–22.31–32 als Antiphon einzufügen."
17 Die „Bibel in gerechter Sprache" lässt die satzeröffnenden Konjunktionen in Ps 107,9 und 16 jedoch unübersetzt und bewahrt damit die syntaktische Mehrdeutigkeit.
18 KOENEN, Jahwe, 99.
19 FELDMEIER/SPIECKERMANN, Gott, 410.
20 Ein ähnliches Hantieren mit markanten „biblischen" Zitaten, die schon den Rang von dekontextualisierten und vielfältig einsetzbaren „geflügelten Worten" gewonnen haben, hat von Rad für die Ansprachen in den ebenfalls sehr spät zu datierenden Büchern der Chronik beschrieben, vgl. VON RAD, Levitische Predigt.

ons-ebene II gehören und als Zitate funktionieren, die den allgemeinen Lobausdruck von V. 1 situativ spezifizieren.

In Ps 107,17–22 (Sample 3) wird dieses Muster nicht fortgesetzt. Am Ende steht nicht das Zitat eines Kurzhymnus oder eine hymnische Äußerung, sondern ein Ritus, das Dank-Schlachtopfer. Auch diese parallele Stellung der Opfernotiz als Abschluss der Strophe unterstützt die These, die zuvor behandelten כי-Sätze als performative Äußerungen und nicht als Begründungen zu deuten.

Auf der Basis dieser Beobachtungen zur Zweisträngigkeit in Psalm 107 lässt sich die Frage nach der Stellung von Abschnitt 107,33–42 neu bearbeiten und beantworten.[21] Klaus Koenen hat dazu bereits einen wichtigen Hinweis gegeben, indem er feststellte: „Zu einer umfangreichen Entfaltung kommt das Gotteslob […] im zweiten Teil des Psalms, V. 33–42."[22] Seybold hatte konstatiert, der Abschnitt habe keine Anbindung an das Vorhergehende. Zugleich hält er jedoch fest, dass dieser unter dem Gattungsaspekt nicht deplatziert sei. Die Aussagen werden bei Seybold merkwürdigerweise nicht miteinander vermittelt. Auch Zenger bleibt auf dieser Argumentationslinie: „In formgeschichtlicher Hinsicht ist die hymnische Dichtung V. 33–41 das Lied, dass die Dankenden singen."[23] In solchen Äußerungen wirkt noch ein stark gattungsgeschichtlicher Zugang zum Psalter nach, der dazu neigt, der Fügung und Pragmatik des Einzelpsalms nicht genug Aufmerksamkeit zu schenken. Wenn schon viel dafür sprach, V. 1, V. 9 und V. 16 als Kurzhymnen zu verstehen, so liegt es nahe, die voranstehenden Überlegungen zusammenzuführen und die These von Klaus Koenen zu bestätigen und zugleich zu präzisieren: Ps 107,33–42 sind kein eigenständiger neuer Hauptteil, sondern die konsequente Fortsetzung des vierten Samples. Der größere Umfang dieses hymnischen Stücks passt auch zum Stil des vierten Beispiels, denn dieses ist deutlich ausladender und aspektreicher als die vorausgehenden ähnlich strukturierten Abschnitte.

Als gewichtiges Zusatzargument für den Zusammenhang des vierten Samples und des Schlusshymnus ist noch auf die inhaltliche Übereinstimmung zwischen beiden Teilen hinzuweisen, denn auch im vierten Beispiel geht es um eine ambivalente Gotteserfahrung: Gott wird nicht nur als Retter aus der Todesnot dargestellt; „seine Wunder" bezeichnet nicht nur die Rettungstaten, sondern nach V. 24 auch seine Schöpfungswerke, zu denen das Staunen erregende Meer mit seiner unergründlichen Tiefe gehört. An die vierte Rettungserzählung

---

21 Zu den lexematischen Verbindungen zwischen diesem Stück und den vier Samples vgl. VESCO, Le psautier II, 1028–1030.
22 KOENEN, Jahwe, 99; er rechnet jedoch noch V. 43 dazu.
23 ZENGER, Psalm 107, 155.

schließen sich zudem die V. 33–35 mit dem Thema „JHWH als Herr des Wassers" gut an.[24]

Zugleich markiert der Hymnus auf die „Umschaffungsmacht"[25] JHWHs in V. 33–42 den Abschluss des gesamten Psalms und verleiht ihm mit der differenzierten Theologie eine Hintergründigkeit, die in den vorangehenden Erzählungen über Not, Klage und Rettung nicht anzutreffen war, jedoch vielfach in hymnischen Kontexten thematisiert wird: Gottes schöpferisches Tun umfasst Gutes und Unheil, Leben und Tod, denn monotheistisch kann es nur eine Quelle der Wirklichkeit geben (vgl. Dtn 32,39; 1Sam 2,6; Jes 45,6–7; Am 3,6; Hi 1,21; 5,17–18; Sir 11,14, Tob 13,2 u.ö.).

Die Forschung hat sich immer schwer getan mit der Gattungsbestimmung von Psalm 107. Es führt nicht viel weiter, nach einem irgendwie passenden Terminus (etwa „Weisheitshymnus"[26]) zu suchen, erst recht nicht, wenn dieser gewissermaßen *ad hoc* gebildet oder eher uneigentlich gebraucht wird, was der Definition von „Gattung" per se widerspricht. Wichtiger ist es, einige formale Merkmale des Textes festzuhalten. Der Psalm drückt nicht einfachhin einen Lobdank aus, er erzählt auch nicht nur—gerahmt von hymnischen Elementen—von erfahrener Gottesnähe, sondern *reflektiert* auf eine literarisch kunstvolle und theologisch komplexe Weise, nämlich durch die Verbindung mehrerer Ebenen, das Geschehen der Überwindung des Unheils und der Rettung aus der Macht des Todes durch Gott.

a. Der Psalm benennt vier Gruppen, die je eigene Rettungserfahrungen gemacht haben. Er wendet sich nicht an sie, sondern spricht über sie und unterstreicht so den reflektierenden Ansatz.

b. Die Schilderung von Not und Rettung ist „zwar plastisch, aber wenig alltagsbezogen"; die Prägung ist—wie gleich noch näher zu zeigen ist—eher „,weltbildhaft' und metaphorisch", so dass die Ausführungen zu Sinn-Bildern, zu „Paradigmen"[27] werden.

c. Die Gruppen werden als Exempla vorgestellt, die Lobdank vortragen und Dank-Schlachtopfer vorbringen (sollen).

d. Der Schlussvers formuliert die didaktische Tendenz des Gesamttextes: Der Erkenntnisweg geht vom Eingedenken der Erfahrung zum Verstehen des

---

24 ZENGER, Psalm 107, 156; zum vierten Sample vgl. auch FORTI, Ships and Seas.
25 ZENGER, Psalm 107, 147.
26 BEYERLIN, Werden und Wesen, 11; der Gattungsterminus lässt eher an eine hymnische Feier der göttlichen Weisheit denken und holt das paradigmatisch-didaktische Programm des Psalms nicht ein.
27 ZENGER, Psalm 107, 149.

Wesens Gottes. Vorbereitet wird das didaktische Resümee bereits im letzten Vers des Schlusshymnus (V. 42), der die „Geraden" zur Erkenntnis auffordert und—typisch für die Zwei-Wege-Lehre der Psalmen—das Schicksal der „Toren" nicht direkt benennt, sondern abstrakt über die „Verkehrtheit" redet.[28]

e. Der Psalm weist über sich hinaus: Der Weise oder zur Weisheit Gelangte wird sich die den vier Gruppen von Geretteten geltende Aufforderung, Gott in Wort und Tat/Opfer zu danken, zu eigen machen.

f. Folglich reflektiert der Psalm die Bedingungen der Kommunikation, der Übernahme und der Verinnerlichung des öffentlichen Zeugnisses vom rettenden Gott und bietet so eine spezifische Ausformung von *Weisheit als religiöse Praxis*. Er wird zu einem Skript für den Weg zur Weisheit, der über die Reflexion der Erfahrungen des Unheils und der Rettung führt. Die in Psalm 107 gemeinte Weisheit ist weder allgemeines Weltwissen noch kundiges Verhalten oder kluges Gebaren in schwierigen Situationen. Weisheit ist religiöse Lebensdeutung und entsprechende „Glaubenspraxis".

Der besonderen Präsentation der Unheils- und Heilsthematik in Psalm 107 ist nun in einem weiteren Schritt nachzugehen.

3 Heil und Unheil in Psalm 107

Der Psalm inszeniert einen komplexen Diskurs über göttliche Rettung, der die Lesenden „weise" machen soll. Im Rahmen des Textes, in V. 1–3 und V. 43, wird nachdrücklich das Gut-Sein Gottes und seine nicht enden wollende Zuwendung hervorgehoben; ich übersetzte חסד bewusst mit „Zuwendung", um einerseits den antiquierten Ausdruck „Huld" oder den Klischeeausdruck „Gnade" und andererseits die seit einigen Jahren beliebte Wiedergabe mit „Liebe"[29] zu vermeiden, die in der Gefahr steht, die Konnotationen des Gefälles und den Machtaspekt der Gottesbeziehung zu minimieren, der am Ende des Psalms im Schlusshymnus so deutlich hervortritt. Die Wiedergabe von חסד mit „Zuwendung" hat zudem den Vorteil, dass sich auch der resümierende חסדי יהוה aus dem letzten Vers problemlos konkordant übersetzen lässt: „seine, d.h. JHWHs Zuwendung" ist das den ganzen Psalm durchziehende Leitwort. Die Bearbei-

---

28 Vgl. zu diesem häufig belegten Phänomen STICHER, Rettung.
29 Vgl. ZENGER, Psalm 107, 139 und 141, und VESCO, Le psautier II, 1026 und 1028.

tung der differenziert vorgetragenen Unheilsthematik geschieht unter diesem positiven Vorzeichen.

Um die Komplexität der Reflexion anschaulich zu machen, empfiehlt sich eine Sortierung der Beschreibungen nach den dominierenden Kategorien, das sind die topographischen und anthropologischen Aspekte, also Räume und menschliche Zustände oder Befindlichkeiten. Dazu kommt als dritte Ebene die des göttlichen und menschlichen Verhaltens oder der Praxen.

Der Auftakt des Psalms verbindet Raum- und Machtkonzepte und gibt damit schon einen Einblick in die dominierenden Vorstellungen. V. 2 redet mit einem familienrechtlichen Terminus von den „Losgekauften" (vgl. Lev 25,47– 54) und trägt verdeutlichend ein, dass die „Erlösten" aus der „Hand der Bedrängnis (oder des Bedrängers)" freigekauft sind. Damit ist das Thema der Macht gesetzt: JHWHs „Zuwendung" zeigt sich in seiner Überlegenheit über „Bedrängnis" (צר), das zweite Leitwort, dessen Erstreckung aber weniger weit reicht als die vom Ausdruck „Zuwendung" gebildete Leitwortkette. „Bedrängnis" tritt außer in V. 2 in festen Verbindungen auf: V. 6.13.19 und 28 steht es in Parallele zu מצוקות, V. 39 in Verbindung mit יגון („Kummer, Betrübnis"). Die Ausdrücke bezeichnen weit mehr als eine missliche Lebenslage; es sind Termini für die Macht des Todes. Ps 116,3 stehen „Tod", „Scheol" und צרה ויגון in Parallele. Sie veranlassen den Beter, um die Rettung seines Lebens (נפשי = „mein Leben") zu flehen (Ps 116,4), wofür er später dankt: „Fürwahr, du hast mein Leben aus dem Tod herausgerissen" (Ps 116,8; vgl. Ps 107,6).

In dieser Machtperspektive gelesen ist der folgende V. 3 mehr als eine Zusammenstellung von Himmelsrichtungen in einer Reminiszenz an die Rückführung israelitischer Bevölkerungsteile aus dem Exil und deren theologische Deutung als göttliche Sammlung der Deportierten. Die Angaben „vom Sonnenaufgang und vom Sonnenuntergang" „benennen die Ränder des horizontalen Weltbildes"[30] und zeigen die Erstreckung der Rettungsmacht JHWHs auf. Auch das zweite Paar der topographischen Angaben („vom Norden und vom Meer", nicht: „vom Süden", wie manchmal emendiert wird) ist weltbildlich imprägniert. Mit „Norden" und „Meer" sind mythische Orte benannt, die die Chaosmacht symbolisieren: Der Feind kommt stets „von Norden" (sogar wenn der Pharao aus dem *südlich* gelegenen Ägypten anrückt, so in Jer 47,2.4[31]), und das „Meer" ist die Bedrohungsmetapher schlechthin[32]. Der Fluchtpunkt dieser welt-

---

30 ZENGER, Psalm 107, 148.
31 Vgl. JARICK, Four Corners, 277; ferner FASS, The Symbolic.
32 Vgl. den kleinen Nachsatz in Offb 21,1–„auch das Meer ist nicht mehr"–, der die ganze Rettungsbotschaft zusammenfasst.

umspannenden Sammlungsbewegung der Erlösten bleibt ungenannt; die Leerstelle wird aber kontextuell eindeutig gefüllt: Es ist Jerusalem, genauer: der Zion mit dem Tempel, als Ort des Lobdanks (V. 1 u.ö.) und der Volksversammlung (V. 39).

Zwischen den vier Gegenden aus V. 3 und den vier Samples lassen sich gewisse Beziehungen erkennen, aber dennoch ist das eine Viererschema nicht auf das andere projizierbar, wie das gelegentlich in der Forschung vorgeschlagen wird.[33] Man könnte etwa die in Sample 1 genannte Wüste mit dem Sonnenaufgang verbinden, das Land der Finsternis aus Sample 2 mit dem Sonnenuntergang; und natürlich liegt eine Beziehung zwischen dem in V. 3b genannten Meer und dem Meer aus Sample 4 auf der Hand. Aber abgesehen davon, dass nur Sample 4 sich sprachlich eindeutig mit der mythischen Geographie von V. 3 berührt, ist schon die Verbindung von Wüste und Finsternis mit dem Sonnenaufgang/Osten und dem Sonnenuntergang/Westen nicht zwingend. Vollends nicht in dieses Schema einzuordnen ist das Sample 3 mit der Erfahrung von Krankheit, die als Todesnähe gedeutet wird; hier wirken alle Versuche, eine Verbindung zur Thematik des Nordens herzustellen, gewunden und lassen es angeraten erscheinen, diese zunächst nahe liegende Parallelisierung nicht zu forcieren. Bevor man nun bei einer spekulativen entstehungsgeschichtlichen Lösung Zuflucht sucht und etwa V. 3 als exilsbezogene Nachinterpretation für sekundär erklärt, gilt es zu beachten, dass der Psalm insgesamt mit Zitaten spielt (V. 2 und 3 sind lexematisch und konzeptionell von Jes 43 und 45 geprägt); man wird es in Kauf nehmen müssen, dass aufgrund des Patchworkcharakters nicht alle Elemente fugenlos zueinander passen. Die vier Samples halten typische Notsituationen fest, aus denen JWHH „erlöst" (hat).[34]

Mit V. 3 haben die vier Samples gemeinsam, dass sie die Not *vorrangig* topographisch fassen; die Rettung vom Tod wird räumlich konzipiert. Die Verbindung religiöser oder metaphysischer Konzepte mit Raumvorstellungen ist biblisch und religionsgeschichtlich ein breit belegtes Phänomen.[35] Psalm 107 zeigt *einen* Grund für diese Verbindung auf: Wenn der Tod räumlich konzipiert wird, kann der Machtaspekt, das dynamische Verständnis, besonders gut vermittelt werden. Macht ist wesentlich Verfügungsgewalt über den Raum. In der Bibel

---

33 So bes. JARICK, Four Corners, auch WEBER, Werkbuch II.
34 Die These, V. 2 und 3 seien sekundär (so etwa SEYBOLD, Psalmen, 428), nimmt einen harten Übergang von V. 1 nach V. 4 in Kauf und opfert die explizite Markierung von V. 1 als Zitat. Wer den Patchworkcharakter von Psalm 107 erkennt, kann auf diese rigide Kohärenzforderung verzichten.
35 Vgl. GEHLEN, Raum, 377; GAENZLE, Raum, 425.

bestimmt dieses Konzept schon den ersten Text, die Schöpfungsdarstellung in Gen 1. Machtausübung ist wesentlich „Raumordnungskompetenz".

Was leistet die topologische und dynamische Beschreibung des Todes? Zum Wesen des Todes gehört biblisch „ein ständiges ‚Über-die-Ufer-Treten'"[36]. „Die Domäne des Todes lag für Israel nicht draußen am äußersten Rand des Lebens, sondern war tief in den Bereich des Lebens vorgeschoben."[37] Dieses Konzept des Todes hat gegenüber unserem naturwissenschaftlich-medizinisch geprägten Verständnis vom Tod als Exitus—gerade weil es so viel weiter gespannt und so unpräzise ist—einige Vorteile. Der Tod wird aus der Sphäre des Unanschaulichen geholt. Weil er so weit in die Lebenszusammenhänge hinein ausgreift, ist er „erfahrbarer" und „greifbarer", ist er leichter kommunizierbar als ein Verständnis, das den Tod vor allem zeitlich fasst und eng als Erlöschen der Vitalfunktionen bestimmt. Es scheint, dass der Erfahrungsraum durch die Verschiebung der Grenzen größer ist, so dass sich sehr viel mehr darüber sagen lässt, lange vor dem Verstummen angesichts des Unvermögens, dieser Grenze ansichtig zu werden und darüber zu sprechen.

Eine zweite Leistung der topologisch-topographischen Konzeption vom Tod und seiner Überwindung lässt sich ebenfalls an Psalm 107 beobachten: Die Raummetaphern scheinen poetisch besonders produktiv zu sein.[38] Das lässt sich sehr gut am ersten Sample beobachten, dessen Metaphern zum Teil auch im Schlusshymnus wiederkehren. An dem topographischen Konzept „Wüste" hängen per Assoziation (1) weitere topographische Konzepte wie „Ödland" und das Oppositum „Stadt", (2) die Beschreibung der Stadt als „Wohnort" und (3) die Definition der Wüste als „Weglosigkeit".

Schon allein diese wenigen Begriffe lösen Kaskaden von Assoziationen und Konnotationen aus, in denen die Raumvorstellungen immer mehr in anthropologische Themen übergehen: Zur Wüste gehört die Erfahrung von Hunger und Durst, damit ist das Leben selbst bedroht. Wenn nun in V. 6 von „Bedrängnis" oder „Engen" die Rede ist, sind diese Raumkonzepte bereits „aufgeladen" mit existentiellen Grund- und Grenzerfahrungen. Entsprechend ist die „Rettung", wie sie in V. 7 konkretisiert wird, nicht nur eine Ortsveränderung, sondern eine Lebenswende.

Die Raummetaphern sind offenbar besonders anschlussfähig und durchlässig für anthropologische Aspekte. Dies hängt mit der dreidimensionalen „kör-

---

36 JANOWSKI, Raum, 324.
37 VON RAD, Theologie I, 400; s.a. JANOWSKI, Raum, 324; ferner BERLEJUNG, Tod, und PERI, Li ha riscattati.
38 Vgl. auch ROFFEY, Beyond Reality.

perlichen" Verfasstheit des Menschen und seiner Sinnestätigkeit zusammen, durch die der Raum „anthropozentrisch" strukturiert wird. Zugleich ist das Raumkonzept anschlussfähig für die Aufladung mit Wertaspekten. Die wichtigste dieser werthaltigen Metaphern ist der „Weg", „Weisheit" wird geradezu als Wege-Lehre dargeboten und als „richtige" Positionierung im Beziehungsraum entwickelt. Die topographische Metaphorik gelangt scheinbar mühelos vom Äußeren zum Inneren und vom Einzelnen zur Gemeinschaft.

So wie die Rettung räumlich gefasst wird, kann auch das Unheil mit topographischen Vorstellungen präsentiert werden: „Sich auflehnen" und durch Gottes Reaktion „gebeugt werden", nicht auf dem Weg zu gehen, sondern „zu straucheln" (V. 11–12)—wieder überlagern sich Raumkonzepte, anthropologische Zustände und Bewertungen in den verwendeten Bildern. Im Lichte von V. 3 und durch die Landmetaphorik des Schlusshymnus wird das Raumkonzept noch einmal geweitet oder spezifiziert, und zwar auf Israel und seine Geschichte hin. Aber diese Konkretisierung verbleibt in einer Schwebe, so dass die Übertragbarkeit auf und die Anschlussfähigkeit für andere Erfahrungen gewährleistet ist.

Gerade darin unterscheidet sich Psalm 107 signifikant von seinen beiden Vorgängern im Psalter, von Psalm 105 und Psalm 106, mit denen er sprachlich so viele Berührungen aufweist: Diese Psalmen rufen umfassend und sehr detailfreudig Israels Geschichte in Erinnerung, Psalm 107 dagegen fasst alles auf wenige Grunderfahrungen hin zusammen. Das Leitkonzept, der weisheitliche Ansatz, ist nicht originell, die Sprache ist ebenfalls entliehen (aus den Prophetenbüchern und der Weisheitsliteratur[39]), und dennoch gelingt eine kreative Gesamtsicht. Schaut man diese Leistung aus einer gewissen Entfernung an, so fällt eine interessante Parallele auf: Die Zusammenführung prophetischer und weisheitlicher Konzepte unter dem Aspekt der Rettung ist auch das Thema der sogenannten „Apokalyptik", die man vielleicht präziser als „apokalyptische Eschatologie" bezeichnen sollte. Natürlich spielen dort noch andere Themen hinein (im Danielbuch zum Beispiel die Auseinandersetzung mit einer konkreten Bedrohung jüdischer Existenz), aber die Parallelen in der Produktion von Literatur lassen es doch ratsam erscheinen, dem neueren Trend der Forschung zu folgen und diesen Zweig alttestamentlich-frühjüdischer Literatur nicht zu sehr vom Mainstream abzurücken, wie das in der Vergangenheit lange und zum Teil sehr massiv der Fall war. Literaturgeschichtlich stehen Psalm 107 und die Danieltexte ohnehin nahe beieinander.

---

39 Zu den Details vgl. die Kommentare.

Gottes Rettungshandeln wird in Psalm 107 auch mit dem Ausdruck נפלאות („Wunder") beschrieben; der Kontext des Psalms bietet die Möglichkeit, das biblische Wunderverständnis zur profilieren und als Schlüsselkategorie für die theologische Bearbeitung von Todeserfahrungen aufzuweisen.

4 Das Wunder – eine „Beziehungstat"

Die Rede vom „Wunder", wie sie sich in Psalm 107 leitwortartig findet (vgl. V. 8.15.21.31, dazu V. 24 in einem anderen Kontext), ist aus vielerlei Gründen wissenschaftlich und theologisch in der Moderne schwierig geworden; um so bemerkenswerter ist die neue Beachtung, die das Thema aktuell zum Beispiel in der Kulturwissenschaft erfährt.[40] Das neue „profane" Interesse am Wunder trägt vielleicht dazu bei, die theologische Peinlichkeitsschwelle einzureißen, die gerade auch in der Exegese zu einer Minimierung und Depotenzierung dieses Themas geführt hat, man denke nur an die Versuche einer formgeschichtlichen „Bändigung" dieser Irritation. Psalm 107 kann als Mustertext für ein biblisches Verständnis vom „Wunder" betrachtet werden; ich sage bewusst „biblisch", nicht nur „alttestamentlich", denn mit den Stichworten „Brot", „Finsternis" (subjektiv: „Blindheit"), „Krankheit" und „Seenot" wird unmittelbar die Bedeutung auch für den neutestamentlichen Wunderdiskurs deutlich. Psalm 107 könnte als eine Partitur auch des neutestamentlichen Wunderdiskurses verstanden werden, was jedoch nach meiner Beobachtung nicht geschieht.[41]

Ein Grund neuzeitlicher Probleme mit der Wunderthematik beruht auf der Isolierung des Phänomens und der Suche nach einer kausalen Erklärung. Psalm 107 könnte den Blick korrigieren im Sinne eines Zugangs, der der Bibel, ihrer Sprach- und Vorstellungswelt gemäßer ist. Auf den Machtaspekt habe ich bereits eingehend hingewiesen; er ist für das biblische Wunderverständnis zentral. Im Ausgang von Psalm 107 kann noch ein anderer Gesichtspunkt als für das biblische Wunderverständnis leitend erhoben werden: Biblisch ist ein Wunder niemals ein isoliertes Phänomen, das spezieller Erklärungsanstrengungen bedürfte. Die Bibel erklärt Wunder nicht; wenn sie ausbleiben, werden sie – bei Gott! – eingeklagt; wenn sie geschehen, sind Dank und Gotteslob die angemessene Reaktion.

---

40 Vgl. Geppert/Kössler (Hg.), Wunder; das Thema „Wunder" gehört zu den unerledigten Themen der Moderne (auch der Exegese), die als lange Zeit verdrängte um so heftiger wiederkehren.
41 Vgl. Steins, The Old in the New.

Ein Wunder ist somit Teil eines kommunikativen Zusammenhangs, genauer: einer Interaktion, die wesentlich von kommunikativen Akten getragen ist. Klagen und Loben „rahmen" das Wunder ein, bereiten es vor, indem sie den Menschen „einstellen" auf eine Erfahrung, die seine Möglichkeiten übersteigt. Im Klagen und Loben wird die Wirklichkeit unter dem Aspekt der Not und dem der Verwandlung wahrgenommen, in die Gottesbeziehung integriert und diese Sicht „öffentlich" an Dritte vermittelt. Kurz gesagt: Das Wunder ist biblisch eine „Beziehungstat"; es darf nicht aus der Gottesbeziehung herausgelöst werden, sonst wird es zum Mirakel, zu einem absonderlichen Phänomen der Medizin oder Physik. Die modernen Probleme mit dem Phänomen des Wunders beruhen zu einem großen Teil darauf, dass eine bestimmte Weltsicht die dem biblischen Wunder inhärente Mischung aus Schöpfungs- und Bundesaspekten—um es einmal in der Sprache biblischer Theologie zu formulieren—bereits im Ansatz nicht mitvollzogen hat.

Psalm 107 präsentiert eine komplexe Mischung von Vorstellungen, die sich eher auf natürliche Begebenheiten beziehen, und solchen, die an geschichtliche Erfahrungen Israels anklingen. Auf beiden Feldern, mit Bezug auf die Natur wie auf Geschichte (oder Gesellschaft), wird so offen formuliert, dass sich die Metaphern berühren und ergänzen und überlagern. Die Bilder sind nicht zu greifen und festzulegen. Der Moderne ist ein solches Denken fremd, weil für sie die Trennung von Natur und Gesellschaft/Geschichte einen prinzipiellen Status einnimmt. In der modernen Wissenssoziologie—ich denke hier an die so genannte „symmetrische Anthropologie" von Bruno Latour[42]—wird diese Grenzziehung wieder problematisiert. Es geht nicht um einen Rückfall in die Vormoderne oder eine postmoderne Spielerei. Die Verflüssigung der Grenze im aktuellen wissenschaftstheoretischen Diskurs ist aus bibelwissenschaftlicher Sicht anregend, geradezu aufregend, weil sich immer eine Grenze des Verstehens auftut, wo die Bibel scheinbar mühelos zwischen Natur und Gesellschaft hin und her springt. Das Phänomen des Todes ist ein Musterbeispiel, wie eine Aufweichung der Grenzziehung Möglichkeiten der Wahrnehmung und der Positionierung und der Lebensbewältigung im Angesicht dieser „Bedrängnis" eröffnet. Ich kann an dieser Stelle nur andeuten, nicht ausführen, weil die Auseinandersetzung der Bibelwissenschaft mit diesen modernekritischen Positionen der Wissenssoziologie noch nicht begonnen hat; nach meinem Eindruck liegen hier Möglichkeiten bereit, die die eigene Hermeneutik bereichern und aus mancher Enge herausführen könnten.

---

42 Vgl. LATOUR, Wir sind.

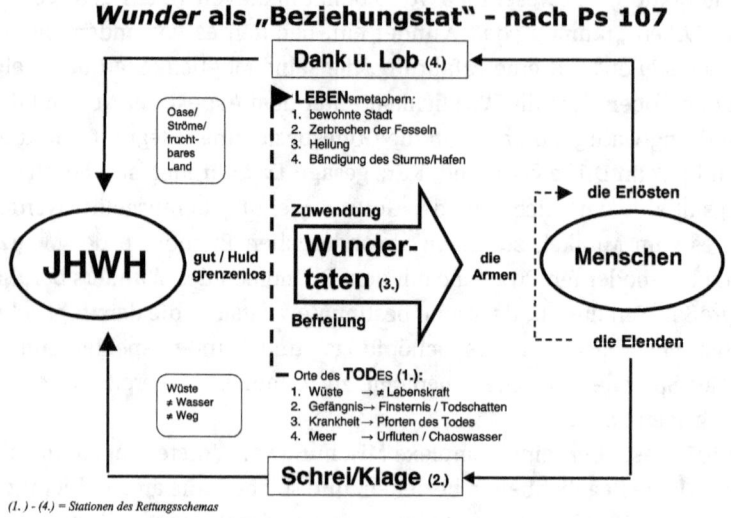

Abb. 1: Wunder als Beziehungstat

5 Schluss

Ich greife am Ende meiner Ausführungen noch einmal auf das Anfangsbild zurück. „Der weisheitliche Schluss (scil. von Ps 107: GSt) gewährt den Hörenden und Sehenden keinen ‚neutralen' Status, sondern weist in grundlegende Lebenskategorien ein und fordert mit der Abschlussfrage indirekt zum Bewahren dieser ‚Lehre' auf, was zur Erkenntnis und zur Hinwendung an die Gnadenerweisungen JHWHs führt. Damit weist der Schluss zum Anfang zurück, die Weisheit des Menschen führt zum Lobpreis Gottes."[43] Im Kontext des Psalters führt die „literarisch-fiktionale Dankliturgie"[44] immer wieder auf den Weg nach Jerusalem[45], „aus Unheil-Welten"[46] zum Ort der göttlichen Gegenwart. Anders formuliert: Weisheit „wohnt" dort, wo die Schwelle vom Tod zum Leben über-

---

43 WEBER, Werkbuch II, 211.
44 ZENGER, Psalm 107, 146.
45 Vgl. WEBER, Werkbuch II, 209.
46 WEBER, Werkbuch II, 206.

schritten und diese Erfahrung individuell wie kollektiv erinnert und erschlossen wird. Die Quelle der Weisheit ist das Wunder der Rettung. Noch einmal anders gesagt: Weisheit meint das Vernehmen-Können der Schöpfung—und der Neuschöpfung[47], die in „Gottes Wundern an den Söhnen eines Menschen" auf den Plan tritt.

Bibliographie

AUFFRET, Pierre, Qui est sage? Qu'il regarde cela! Nouvelle étude structurelle du psaume 107, in: BN 129 (2006) 25–52.
BALLHORN, Egbert, Zum Telos des Psalters. Der Textzusammenhang des Vierten und Fünften Psalmenbuches (Ps 90–150) (BBB 138), Berlin 2004.
BERLEJUNG, Angelika, Tod und Leben nach den Vorstellungen der Israeliten, in: Janowski, Bernd/Ego, Beate (Hg.), Das biblische Weltbild und seine altorientalischen Kontexte (FAT 32), Tübingen ²2004, 465–502.
BEYERLIN, Walter, Werden und Wesen des 107. Psalms (BZAW 153), Berlin 1979.
BORNKAMM, Heinrich (Hg.), Luthers Vorreden zur Bibel, Göttingen 1989.
CARBAJOSA, Ignacio, Salmo 107. Unidad, organización y teologia, in: EstBib 59 (2001) 451–485.
DEISSLER, Alfons, Die Psalmen, Düsseldorf 1964.
DELITZSCH, Franz, Biblischer Commentar über die Psalmen, Leipzig 1883.
DOHMEN, Christoph, Zwischen Gott und Welt. Biblische Grundlagen der Anthropologie, in: Dirscherl, Erwin et al. (Hg.), In Beziehung leben. Theologische Anthropologie, Freiburg 2008, 7–45.
FASS, David E., The Symbolic Uses of North, in: Judaism 37 (1988) 465–473.
FELDMEIER, Reinhard/SPIECKERMANN, Hermann, Der Gott der Lebendigen. Eine biblische Gotteslehre (Topoi Biblischer Theologie 1), Tübingen 2011.
FORTI, Tova, Of Ships and Seas, and Fish and Beasts. Viewing the Concept of Universal Providence in the Book of Jonah through the Prism of Psalms, in: JSOT 35 (2011) 359–374.
GAENZLE, Martin, Art. „Raum", in: Wörterbuch der Religionen, Darmstadt 2006, 424–425.
GEHLEN, Rolf, Art. „Raum", in: HRWG 4, Stuttgart 1998, 377–398.
GEPPERT, Alexander C.T./KÖSSLER, Till (Hg.), Wunder. Poetik und Politik des Staunens im 20. Jahrhundert (stw 1984), Frankfurt 2011.
HIRSCH, Samson Raphael, Psalmen, Frankfurt 1883 (Nachdruck Basel 1995).
JANOWSKI, Bernd, Der Gott des Lebens. Beiträge zur Theologie des Alten Testaments Bd. 3, Neukirchen-Vluyn 2003.
JANOWSKI, Bernd, „Du hast meine Füße auf weiten Raum gestellt" (Psalm 31,9). Gott, Mensch und Raum im Alten Testament, in: Hossfeld, Frank-Lothar/Schwienhorst-Schönberger,

---

[47] Das betont CARBAJOSA, Salmo 107, 484–485.

Ludger (Hg.), Das Manna fällt auch heute noch. Beiträge zur Geschichte und Theologie des Alten, Ersten Testaments (HBS 44), Freiburg 2004, 312–339.

JARICK, John, The Four Corners of Psalm 107, in: CBQ 59 (1997) 270–287.

KOENEN, Klaus, Jahwe wird kommen, zu herrschen über die Erde. Ps 90–110 als Komposition (BBB 101), Weinheim 1995.

LATOUR, Bruno, Wir sind nie modern gewesen. Versuch einer symmetrischen Anthropologie (stw 1861), Frankfurt 2008.

LEVINE, Nachman, Vertical Poetics. Interlinear Phonological Parallelism in Psalms, in: JNSL 29 (2003) 65–82.

PERI, Chiara, Li ha riscattatti dalle mani del nemico. Un'interpretazione mitologica del Salmo 107, in: Materia giudaica 9 (2004) 129–136.

ROFFEY, John W., Beyond Reality. Poetic Discourse and Psalm 107, in: Carpenter, Eugene E. (Hg.), A Biblical Itinerary. In Search of Method, Form and Content (JSOTS 240), Sheffield 1997, 60–76.

RUWE, Andreas, Die Psalmen zum Betrachten, Studieren und Vorlesen. Eine textanalytische Übersetzung, Zürich 2012.

SEYBOLD, Klaus, Die Psalmen (HAT I/5), Tübingen 1996.

SPIECKERMANN, Hermann, Ambivalenzen. Ermöglichte und verwirklichte Schöpfung in Genesis 2f., in: Grauper, Axel et al. (Hg.), Verbindungslinien. Festschrift für Werner H. Schmidt zum 65. Geburtstag, Neukirchen-Vluyn 2000, 363–376.

STEINS, Georg, "The Old in the New" – What Does that Mean? Considerations following Psalm 107, in: Steins, Georg/Sumpter, Philip/Taschner, Johannes (Hg.), Relationships Between the Two Parts of the Christian Bible (Osnabrücker Studien zur Jüdischen und Christlichen Bibel), Göttingen 2015 (im Druck).

STICHER, Claudia, Die Rettung der Guten durch Gott und die Selbstzerstörung der Bösen. Ein theologisches Denkmuster im Psalter (BBB 137), Berlin 2002.

VESCO, Jean-Luc, Le psautier de David traduit et commenté, Vol. II, Paris 2006.

VON RAD, Gerhard, Die levitische Predigt in den Büchern der Chronik, in: Ders., Gesammelte Studien zum Alten Testament (TB 8), München ⁴1971, 248–261.

WAGNER, Andreas, Der Lobaufruf im israelitischen Hymnus als indirekter Sprechakt, in: Ders., Studien zur hebräischen Grammatik (OBO 156), Göttingen 1997, 143–154.

WEBER, Beat, Werkbuch Psalmen II. Die Psalmen 73–150, Stuttgart 2003.

ZENGER, Erich (Hg.), Stuttgarter Altes Testament. Einheitsübersetzung mit Kommentar und Lexikon, Stuttgart 2004.

ZENGER, Erich, Psalm 107, in: Hossfeld, Frank-Lothar/Zenger, Erwin, Psalmen 101–150 (HThKAT), Freiburg 2008, 139–161.

Patricia G. Kirkpatrick
Curse God and Die — Job's Wife and the Struggle for Job's Transformation

The short phrase[1] that Job's wife throws out at her husband, "(do) you still hold on to your integrity (?) Curse god and die"[2] (Job 2:9) is one which has occupied a modicum of discussion by interpreters both Jewish and Christian. For the most part, however, Job's wife is dealt with in as many words as she speaks and given no more thought. The most recent example of this being Antonio Negri's reading of Job which includes the following reference to Mrs. Job: "Sores cover Job's body and he lies on a dunghill, listening to his wife's vulgarities."[3] Negri does, however, attempt to redeem Job from the tradition which sees him as a misogynist on the basis of a faulty translation given to his response in 2:10 to his wife.[4] Nevertheless, his description of Mrs. Job as spewing vulgarities is typical of a particular trajectory of interpretations which have sought either to ignore or erase her contributions to the story entirely.

In addition to theological debate over the meaning of her words, it is clear that the history of the transmission of this phrase has resulted in either a rewriting of the story or/and extending the story so as to give Mrs. Job more of a personality and character than is actually offered in the Hebrew text. By these extensions and/or rewritings Mrs. Job becomes arguably a much more sympathetic character with whom the reader can better empathise. She certainly becomes a woman who it can be seen has suffered, and is almost to be pitied.

---

1 The use of ברך for "curse" or "blaspheme" has been argued for by many for at least a century. See for example GEIGER, Urschrift, 62–66. It has also been taken as a *tiqqun sopherim*, so DHORME, Commentary, 4–5; HABEL, Book, 88. It has also been argued that ברך contains both the meanings "curse" and "blessing," so ANDERSEN, Job, 81; VAN WOLDE, Development, 201–221. There is also the argument to keep both meanings possible, see LINAFELT, Undecidability, 154–172.
2 The MT literally reads "Bless God and die." This is normally accepted in English translations as a euphemism for curse and in his recent commentary CLINES considers it so "without question," Job, 16. But as some have suggested the phrase may in fact be Mrs. Job's sincere attempt to have Job bid farewell to his belief in God and accept the inevitable metaphoric death which is practically upon him anyways. Cf. LEGASPI, Job's, 71.
3 NEGRI, Labor, 20.
4 NEGRI, Labor, 82.

The Septuagint translation[5] of the book of Job is approximately one sixth the length of the MT Job and has a different ending not found in the Hebrew. I find it intriguing that the words of Mrs. Job have been added to by what I will call "filler." These added words give a more robust image with which to contemplate the horrors that she has been made to suffer in an extended and arguably interpretative monologue. Whether or not the additions in Job are reflective of a very early Hebrew text tradition no longer extant has elicited a fair amount of discussion amongst scholars. The editors of the NETS argue that when assessing Greek Job the "usual categories of characterizing a translation fail us when we assess Job. [...] OG Job is one of a kind in the Septuagint corpus." With regards to the additions in Job's wife's speech the editors suggest that this may be a later addition. Regardless of whether or not these additions are early or late they are tantalizing bits with which to contemplate how and why corpuses of traditions are allowed to vanish from parts of the religious core. This, however, is not my main focus. It is sufficient for us to note that the Greek translation adds significantly to what we have in the MT.

In the Testament of Job, however, this "filler" becomes a complete expansion of Job's wife's trials and tribulations spoken of instead by Job himself. The dating of the original composition of the work is difficult as the earliest evidence is fragmentary and is a Coptic translation of what has been argued was an original Greek text. Indeed, some see the Testament of Job as clearly dependent on LXX Job.[6] To date there are no versions of this fragment in Hebrew, Aramaic or Syriac.[7] Arguing that the text was originally composed in Greek, Spittler suggests a fifth century B.C.E. or first century C.E. date,[8] while Charlesworth settles on a first century C.E. date composed amongst the therapeutae.[9]

As the story unfolds Job's second wife, who in the Testament is named Sitido, becomes a servant in the household of a certain nobleman to earn enough money to buy bread to bring to Job. Even this is eventually denied her and one day as she goes to market to beg for bread for Job she meets Satan who is disguised as a seller of bread. She is convinced to give Satan her hair as payment for the bread and in anguish she laments her situation in life. Throughout the lament Job is not moved to compassion but instead calls to Satan to stop hiding behind his wife. Here we have a glimpse of who the writer of the Testament

---

5 The dating of the various texts of the Greek translation of the Hebrew Bible is notoriously difficult.
6 SPITTLER, Testament, 831.
7 Scott, Testament of Job.
8 SPITTLER, Testament, 833.
9 CHARLESWORTH, Pseudepigrapha, 135.

would have us understand was responsible for her attitude and both hers and her husband's predicament. It is Satan who is identified as prolonging their terrors.

Susan Garrett arguing against van der Horst[10], who suggests that the presentation of Mrs. Job is of a positive 'good wife' such as is found in Proverbs 31, argues with John J. Collins that the image of Mrs. Job is negative in the Testament and akin to the presentation of women in Philo as symbolic of ignorance and associated with sense perception.[11] Indeed, she suggests that a negative attitude exists throughout the document which has Job's wife epitomize

> the feminine preoccupation with the cycle of birth, life, death, and burial. Her heart is weighed down, trapped in the realm of the corruptible and therefore easily led astray by Satan. She errs not "in spite of her virtues" as van der Horst contends but because of them.[12]

Interesting as these tradition trajectories are however, we need to look carefully at the biblical text from which these and other interpretations gain their perspectives.[13] What I would like to explore is the insight Mrs. Job demonstrates in trying to resolve her husband's problem and how the author/theologian of the dialogues resolves the problem and has Job "see" what it was that he only "heard of" before. I do not suggest that by doing this I am finally resolving the problem of theodicy to be found in Job. I do, however, wish to suggest that the term theodicy is a polite way of speaking about what Mrs. Job understands and wants Job to understand and is nothing less than the bankruptcy of the theology of the day in dealing with the notion of God's sovereignty. With Whybray,[14] I would argue that it is the proper concept of God which is the focus of the book. I would suggest that it is Mrs. Job, who Adele Reinhartz dubs a "bit player" who first signals that there is something very wrong with the way God is being conceived of by her husband. This "incidental" figure is so very important precisely because she expresses the "moral judgments and values of the narrator."[15]

---

10 VAN DER HORST, Images, 99–100; VAN WOLDE, Mr. and Mrs. Job, 23.
11 COLLINS, Structure, 41.
12 GARRETT, Weaker, 57.
13 Targum of Job although not offering much of a commentary on Job's wife does proceed to identify her as Dinah and so we read in the Targum its rendering of the above as "And Dinah his wife said to him, 'Are you steadfast in your integrity until now? Curse (lit. bless) the word of the Lord and die.'" It would appear that the Targum picks up the tradition of a second wife for Job and names her as Dinah. Contra LEGASPI, Job's Wives, 79.
14 WHYBRAY, Wisdom, 238.
15 REINHARTZ, Why, 30–31.

1 Mrs. Job

There is no introduction to Mrs. Job, no biographical details are given. Her existence is first surmised because of the reference to Job's children. Then suddenly, out of the blue she utters a fateful phrase which will determine the outcome of the book.

We have become so accustomed to not seeing female characters in the biblical text as instigators of important shifts of theological perspective that Job's wife has rarely been seen as the catalyst she is to her husband's salvation. If she is not altogether ignored she is often portrayed by commentators, agreeing with Augustin, that her function is that of the "diabolic adjutrix."[16] Even worse, although atypical, are what I consider as the expected remarks of Chrysostom, who when asked why the "devil" had not killed Job's wife answered: because he thought of her as the worst plague with which to burden Job.[17] These positions give only the negative interpretation of her presence, there are others which are far more positive, thus, her role and function in the text remains if nothing else a lively topic.

2 Mrs. Job's Statement

It is important to remember that what is now usually translated as a question is not self evident and in this case can produce quite different understandings if the question mark is removed. Assuming a question mark, "Are you still holding on to your integrity?" can imply a criticism of Job's faithfulness, a sarcastic denegration of his faith, and/or a shallow and coarse reproach to Job's suffering. But, if the question mark is removed leaving but the statement, a quite different result occurs which could have the following meaning, "Hold on to your integrity, Job, for you have done no wrong, what has happened is the consequence to a god who has lost all integrity."

Mrs. Job knowing her husband better than anyone deduces that whatever else has happened, this God that Job believes in, maybe even she too believed in, must himself be the origin and instigator of the evil which befalls her hus-

---

[16] HABEL, Book, 96.
[17] Chrysostom, On the First Letter to the Corinthians, Homily XXVIII[5] (NPNF Series 1 vol. XII), 166. "For if even out of paradise," saith he, "I cast mankind by her means, much more shall I be able to trip him up on the dunghill." See also BROC, La Femme, 396–403.

band and as such must be condemned. Like Job, she is not to know that the two of them are now caught up in the maelstrom of sadistic horrors from which neither can extricate themselves. They are sucked into a vortex of such malevolence that the silence that Job keeps betrays the level of his anger regardless of his half-witted attempts to console his wife. And if not to console her at least to answer her, as he replies saying, "You are talking like a foolish woman. Shall we accept good from God, and not trouble?" Tell the mother of your children now dead, the woman who directs the day to day workings of your household now obliterated, the beloved of your now spent passions that she speaks like a foolish woman and the chances are that you will not hear from her again. Mrs. Job is not reacting as an hysteric. Nor is she responding as someone which the wisdom tradition considers foolish. Like Job she has watched her life disappear, her identity both personal and public relinquished to an inconceivable evil and now the very object of her passion is being ravished physically by a slew of skin rotting diseases. Her only wish now is to save Job's integrity by unmasking the true horror of this god's actions.

What then of the second phrase in her statement "bless God and die?" The use in Hebrew of the term ברך has often been identified as a euphemism for curse,[18] even though it is by no means a scribal convention and, as Tod Linafelt has argued, must gain its meaning in each occurrence thus making the term at least multiply ambiguous.[19] Does Mrs. Job mean ברך literally or euphemistically? If literally is she being sarcastic and suggesting that Job's actions of blessing the creator in his suffering will eventually lead to his death? Or does she mean it euphemistically, that it is better to curse God and die to this tyrannical religion than continue to suffer. [20]

3 The Wisdom Tradition

The wisdom tradition more than any other is the least sympathetic to theologies of revelation. Nor is it generally persuaded by the somewhat pietistic notions found in other parts of Tenach which emphasize the calling upon God for help. The wisdom tradition although never denying God's ability to help is nevertheless adamant that the individual is capable of monitoring their own actions and

---

18 GEIGER, Urschrift, 268
19 LINAFELT, Undecidability, 169–170.
20 NEWSOM, Job, 55 argues that the idea of "to curse" does not fit into the narrative world as it would threaten the harmony of the very world it depicts.

is basically in control of their own destiny if only they would follow the path which leads to wisdom and therefore life as opposed to foolishness and therefore death. The covenant relationship which Israel has with God is maintained to be sure by a sacrificial system which is itself regulated by a legal system so often alluded to by Job.

The book of Job as a whole, if not in its various parts, not only questions covenant theology not in order simply to reject it but rather to embrace it by enlarging the very idea of covenant. In Israel's covenant theology as conceived by the prophets, God does not act capriciously. Israel trusts that God will act with steadfast loving kindness and will not seek to destroy life. The very basis of covenant theology depends on this trust. Here now it would seem is the crux of the matter. Mrs. Job recognizes that this covenant God cannot be trusted and is one which should now be repudiated by Job. Mrs. Job understands that her husband is suffering not despite his righteousness but actually because of it. Of course the reader knows that Job is suffering not because of some freak accident of nature but rather because of a deliberate action taken by a God whose ego it would seem has been ruffled by a secondary divine figure. As Green puts it:

> It is crude and religiously pointless, an extreme case of covenant violation. Nothing in the structure of the covenant prepares Job—or Israelite readers of the book for that matter—to deal with this kind of behaviour.[21]

The prologue is explicit about the cause of Job's suffering and there is nothing that he can do to atone as he is not the instigator of his suffering. Meticulous as he was to offer sacrifices on behalf of his children there is no offering which can be given to restore his situation, which may be why the issue is never pursued in the dialogues. You cannot seek redemption for an action you have not committed. No, the solution as to how a relationship between the God of Israel and Job can be retrieved is something which must be done outside accepted forms of covenantal maintenance and so outside the cult. The issue of Job's innocence will be pursued via a lawsuit launched by Job. Now, this is not what Mrs. Job suggests her husband should do. If we understand, as with Magdalene, that Mrs. Job does not ask a question and therefore we should read her words as a statement instead without a question mark "Hold on to your integrity. Curse God and die" she provides the catalyst sufficient for Job to launch his protest. To be sure Job continues for a while to trust god, hence his response, which need not be thought of as a reproof nor necessarily as a harsh put down, but one last gasp of a theological reflection on the covenant formulary of exact retribution.

---

21 GREEN, Stretching, 574

Following contemporary studies of the psychological effects of various techniques used on torture victims and the consequences of torture generally, Rachel Magdalene draws various analogies between victims of torture with what Job is depicted as having to experience. Magdalene speaks of "the torture that Job endures" as "theocratic violence of the greatest magnitude." She further speaks of Job's friends as "God's police force" albeit self-appointed police force. Their interest is in demonstrating the truth of a theological doctrine which "supports a specific divine legal system"[22] and certainly not in discovering a possible fault system in the doctrine.

It is quite possible to consider Mrs. Job's response to the situation as one which recognizes the odious nature of this God and the way in which Job has been made to become complicit with an unjust legal system governed by a deity without moral scruples.

Indeed, it has been suggested that Mrs. Job's phrase denotes her advice to her husband that he should literally take his own life. That given his circumstances, it would be better were he to die literally. "That is the meaning of the words: 'You must still hold onto your integrity! Curse God and die!' The first colon of this verse is not a question, but a statement—one to both Job and the court. Mrs. Job just might save Job from condemnation by this tactic."[23] She also offers Job a means by which to perform the ultimate act of resistance to the violence of oppressive legal systems, that is martyrdom. Ellen van Wolde contends that, because the root ברך means both "to bless" and "to curse," Job's wife sends a double message to Job[24] and forces him to choose whether he will bless God or blaspheme God. She forces him either to accept or reject passivity. She forces him to confront the possibility of death.[25] Keeping in line with the possibility of ambiguity Newsom argues that Mrs. Job asks Job to stop trying to uphold his integrity and blaspheme God, as traditional interpreters suggest, or the reader may understand that she may be saying to him that if he still wishes to maintain his integrity he must "say what is truly in [...] [his] heart." Newsom suggests that this possibility has been lost on later interpreters:

---

22 MAGDALENE, Job's Wife, 221–231.
23 MAGDALENE, Job's Wife, 233.
24 VAN WOLDE, Development, 203–204. Newsom also suggests that Mrs. Job's words are ambiguous, s. NEWSOM, Job, 139.
25 VAN WOLDE, Development, 204. Cf. VAN WOLDE, Mr. and Mrs. Job, 25.

> However Job has understood her words, his reply, criticizing her in the strongest terms [...] has generally set the tone for her evaluation by commentators from ancient times to the present.[26]

The most notable exception to this interpretation being Samuel Terrien who renders the term נבל as implying crazy with suffering, and not simply foolish.[27]

4 Job's Religious Transformation — the Narrator's Critique of Retributive Justice

We are told that Job is "innocent and straight, and one who feared God and turned away from evil," character traits that are repeated twice more in identical fashion. Although we are told that Job "fears" God he is not depicted as one who loves God. To be sure he is said to turn away from evil but he is not said to do good and we nowhere read that he is "wise," "righteous," and "good." Whatever else may be his piety it is one which can be said to be motivated by fear and blind deference. As Dor-Shav has suggested a term associated with Job, that of תם, is often translated as "perfect" when in fact it has more the meaning of "innocent" which can also have the connotation of naiveté, and therefore a bit of a simpleton.[28] Understood this way, the author goes out of his way to show Job as someone who accepts a mechanical understanding of sacrifice thinking somehow that he can offer efficacious sacrifices on behalf of his sons without needing his sons repentance. And to make matters worse we are told that Job does this continually and as a reader we are left thinking that he does so only out of fear when contemplating the efficacy of sacrifice.

To the calamities that befall him his responses are hollow and sound like rote memorizations of someone whose faith is quite shallow.

> In fact, a careful reading of the text reveals that the early Job is not a spiritual man in any sense of the term. Job's understanding of God is deeply flawed. His formulaic responses—"The Lord gave and the Lord has taken away," "shall we receive the good at the hand of the Lord and shall we not receive the bad?"—indicate a belief in a God who demands pure, unthinking obedience. Job's God [...] is defined by blind power and absolute authority and

---

26 Newsom, Job, 140, and Newsom, Book, 356.
27 Terrien, Job, 60–61.
28 Dor-Shav, Job's Path, 107.

has no relationship with man, no presumption of justice, and no inner resonance with the conscience of humankind.[29]

This is the faith that Mrs. Job would have her husband abandon and it is this faith which the narrator would have Israel recognize it must abandon, and from the ending of Job it is what God would have him abandon as well. Job will undergo a transformation of such magnitude that he will come to "see" what before he had only "heard of". Does Mrs. Job then "see" what Job only "hears?" I do not think it too much of a stretch to think that Mrs. Job has grasped the ramifications of Job's original faith. But on the other hand Mrs. Job reminds us all that the God Job believed in is not a God of integrity and honest relationship, he is not the God of covenantal חסד.

As Job's faith is in the process of transformation, he begins, ever so gingerly, to reflect on an unjust world (chs. 24–27) and I would argue with many others since Maimonides that Job's words about himself in ch. 29 are but boastfulness on his part. Nevertheless, they certainly indicate that he is aware of a certain moral responsibility towards others and in his depictions of grieving for the down trodden comes a glimmer that he feels for others and their plight. With the last speech he demonstrates a full blown understanding of what it is to do right by others and ends in ch. 31 with a series of oaths, thus signaling a complete transformation.

At the cosmic level, Job also comes to a fuller understanding of the nature of good and evil as he moves from darkness and death to light and life. It is darkness and death which are the abode of the shades of Sheol; light and life being the physical incarnation of Wisdom.

5 What then Does Job "See?"

What then does Job see that brings him understanding into God's nature and the right attitude to have towards God? Throughout Hebrew Scriptures mortals are not permitted to see God. Not even Moses is given this privilege as even he is required to hide in a cleft in the mountainside and can only experience the presence of God as God passes behind him. Mortals can experience the "mysterium tremendum" as Otto once put it but they may never see it. So complete is this prohibition that it would be odd for there to be this one instance in which this righteous man was permitted what had been denied all others.

---

29 Dor-Shav, Job's Path, 109.

William Green has suggested that what Job undergoes, and therefore what the narrator wants the reader to undergo is a "cognitive shift." What Job sees is an understanding of the Divine nature. As a consequence to understanding correctly Job is rewarded. At minimum what he sees is that God does not operate by means of "mechanistic retributive relationship built on a fixed calculus of reward and punishment."[30] God's complexity is such that a one-dimensional relationship is inadequate when trying to understand God's nature. It would also seem that blind fidelity to God and to the covenant is not what is called for but rather a commitment to understanding the relationship between God and Israel. As Job's unrelenting questioning of God's justice yields finally to God appearing before Job and revealing more of God's self the reader comes to understand that what Job "sees" is that his relationship with God entails unpredictability. The covenant however cannot work if it is "grounded in misconceptions and flawed knowledge of the relationship."[31] If the covenant mechanism is that which the book undermines and, then, to use the language of the satan, "fearing God for nothing" or depending solely on faith, would be to undermine certain fundamental aspects of Israelite religion and certainly negate certain fundamental tenets of wisdom theology.

What it is that Job sees is never articulated except that Job has been transformed in his faith and withstood God's response from the whirlwind. An onslaught that at no time explains the horrific actions of God but one which certainly does not deny God's active role in their relationship however unequal it may be. What is of a surety, however, is that God cannot and will not be manipulated. The relationship between God and the individual is based on the covenant but is not to be equated with exact retributive justice.

It does matter that Job refused to accept his condition. It does matter that he categorically denied any wrong doing. It does matter that God acted contrary to covenant stipulation. It does matter that Job was willing to confront God, whose actions were unacceptable. Anything else would have been tantamount to aiding and abetting a capricious and narcissistic god whose actions amounted to moral indifference.

Seen in this light, Mrs. Job's statement to her husband is neither stupid nor foolish. She it was who has understood that to remain silent in the face of Job's brutalizing experience and to stand by and allow him to accept such brutality would in effect be to undermine if not overturn the nature of the covenant.

---

30 GREEN, Stretching, 575.
31 GREEN, Stretching, 576.

Mrs. Job is not mentioned again after her one phrase except indirectly. There is no further utterance from her in the epilogue. No comment from the narrator accept that someone must have given birth to the children? If not the same Mrs. Job of the introduction than who? She has remained steadfast and remained by her husband's side refusing to allow evil to gain the upper hand. In the epilogue, although unmentioned, she is not reprimanded and indeed from the outcome she receives God's blessing, not least in the form of children and unlike Job's friends she is not chastised. Mrs. Job of the prologue did not ask Job to abandon God but rather to abandon his preconceived notions of how God should act. It may in fact mean that Job will have to die a metaphoric death or rather a death to his old religious beliefs. Mrs. Job does not supply him with anything else except to act as a spur to grate against his conscience. A spur which will prevent the sado masochism of unjust retribution, the spur that will redefine a covenant relationship which Israel will be able to acknowledge both at the individual and at the national level.

Have I overstated Mrs. Job's role? Have I taken the thunder away from Job? I do not think so. I have simply shown that the reader need not diminish nor in any way trivialize her role. This reading allows for the narrator's perspective to be even more nuanced and in a certain very real sense to take seriously wisdom's understanding of the wise wife. The portrayal of Job's wife is not a piece of ancient misogyny but rather an insightful presentation of wifely concern for justice and the maintenance of righteous covenantal relationship. The author has remained true to the understanding of what is expected of a wise wife whilst at the same time delivered to Israel an extended understanding of covenant, presented by a hero of perhaps long standing in Israelite tradition.

In a paper entitled "The concept of God after Auschwitz: A Jewish Voice," Hans Jonas developed the theme of immortality which he first wrote about in 1961. His primary focus or rather aim was to bring light to bear on our conception of God in the aftermath of the Shoah, to provide a further perspective to the question "what is the matter with God?" Having posited a God who suffers, is in the process of becoming and a god who runs a risk, Jonas offers one other postulate for this, his speculative theology, that is, that God is not omnipotent.[32] It is however a quotation from Etty Hillesum which Jonas refers to which struck me especially if the book of Job is to resonate with readers today who are not so interested in God's sovereignty. Hillesum was a Dutch Jew who in her mid twenties kept a diary of life in Amsterdam during the period of the Shoah. She was sent to Auschwitz where in 1943 she was murdered by Nazi thugs. She writes:

---

32 JONAS, Concept, 8.

[I shall] try to help you, God, to stop my strength ebbing away, though I cannot vouch for it in advance. But one thing is becoming increasingly clear to me: that You cannot help us, that we must help ourselves [...] Alas there does not seem to be much you yourself can do about our circumstances, about our lives. Neither do I hold you responsible. You cannot help us but we must help you and defend your dwelling place in us to the last.[33]

Is this what Job sees? This dwelling in us that must at all costs be preserved? Is this what Mrs. Job wanted her husband to acknowledge and thereby keep his integrity? Is this not what the narrator's Mrs. Job sought to gain for Israel's covenantal relationship with God and in so doing enlarge the parameters of her covenant theology?

Bibliography

ANDERSEN, Francis I., Job. An Introduction and Commentary (TOTC), Downers Grove, Illinois 1976.
BROC, Catherine, La Femme de Job dans la predication de Jean Chrysostome, in: StPatr 37 (2001) 396–403.
CHARLESWORTH, James H. (Hg.), Old Testament Pseudepigrapha, vol. I: Apocalyptic Literature and Testaments, Garden City, New York et al. 1983.
CHARLESWORTH, James H., The Pseudepigrapha and Modern Research with a Supplement (SBLSCS 75), Atlanta 1981.
CHRYSOSTOM, John, On the First Letter to the Corinthians, Homily XXVIII[5] (NPNF[1]), vol. XII, Grand Rapids, Michigan 1988.
CLINES, David J.A., Job 1–20 (WBC 17), Dallas, Texas 1989.
COLLINS, John J., Structure and Meaning in the Testament of Job, in: MacRae, George W. (Hg.), Society of Biblical Literature. Seminar Papers, vol. 1, Cambridge, Massachussetts 1974, 35–52.
DHORME, Edouard, A Commentary on the Book of Job (Original title: Le Livre de Job [1926]), Nashville, Tennessee 1984.
DOR-SHAV, Ethan, Job's Path to Enlightenment, in: Azure 32 (2008) 102–148.
GARRETT, Susan R., The 'Weaker Sex' in the Testament of Job, in: JBL 112 (1993) 55–70.
GEIGER, Abraham, Urschrift und Übersetzung der Bibel in ihrer Abhängigkeit von der inneren Entwicklung des Judentums, Frankfurt 1928.
GREEN, William Scott, Stretching the Covenant. Job and Judaism, in: RevExp 99 (2002) 569–577.
HABEL, Norman L., The Book of Job. A Commentary (OTL), Philadelphia, Pennsylvania 1985.
HILLESUM, Etty, An Interrupted Life. The Diaries and Letters of Etty Hillesum 1941–1943, New York 1984.

---

33 HILLESUM, Interrupted, 178, quoted in JONAS, Concept, 13.

JONAS, Hans, The Concept of God After Auschwitz. A Jewish Voice, in: JR 67 (1987) 1–13.
LEGASPI, Michael C., Job's Wives in the Testament of Job. A Note on the Synthesis of Two Traditions, in: JBL 127 (2008) 71–79.
LINAFELT, Todd, The Undecidability of *brk* in the Prologue to Job and Beyond, in: BibInt 4 (1996) 154–172.
MAGDALENE, F. Rachel, Job's Wife as Hero. A Feminist-Forensic Reading of the Book of Job, in: Biblical Interpretation 14 (2006) 209–258.
NEGRI, Antonio, The Labor of Job. The Biblical Text as a Parable of Human Labor (Original title: Il lavoro di Giobbe. Il famoso testo biblico come parabola del lavoro umano [2002]), London 2009.
NEWSOM, Carol, Job (New Interpreters Bible 4), Nashville, Tennessee 1996.
NEWSOM, Carol, The Book of Job. A Contest of Moral Imaginations, Oxford 2003.
REINHARTZ, Adele, 'Why Ask My Name?' Anonymity and Identity in Biblical Narrative, Oxford/New York 1998.
SCOTT, Ian W., Testament of Job, Edition 1.0. No pages; in: Penner, Ken M./Miller, David M. and Scott, Ian W. (Hg.), The Online Critical Pseudepigrapha, Atlanta, Georgia 2006; http://ocp.tyndale.ca/testament-of-job/introduction.
SPITLER, Rudolph, Testament of Job, in: Charlesworth, James H. (Hg.), The Old Testament Pseudepigrapha, vol. I: Apocalyptic Literature and Testaments, Garden City, New York 1983, 329–368.
TERRIEN, Samuel, Job. Commentaire de l'Ancien Testament, Neuchatel 1963.
VAN DER HORST, Pieter, Images of Women in the Testament of Job, in: Knibb, Michael A./van der Horst, Pieter (Hg.), Studies on the Testament of Job (SNTSMS 66), Cambridge 1989.
VAN WOLDE, Ellen, The Development of Job. Mrs. Job as Catalyst, in: Brenner, Athalya (ed.), Feminist Companion to Wisdom Literature (FCB 9), Sheffield 1995, 201–221.
VAN WOLDE, Ellen, Mr. and Mrs. Job, (Original title: Meneer en mevrouw Job. Job in gesprek met zijn vrouw, zijn vrienden en God [1991]), London 1997.
WHYBRAY, Norman, Wisdom, Suffering and the Freedom of God, in: Ball, Edward (ed.), In Search of True Wisdom. Essays in Old Testament Interpretation in Honour of Ronald E. Clements, (JSOTSup 300), Sheffield 1999, 231–245.

Christoph Berner
Evil and Death in the Book of Qohelet

Throughout the Hebrew Bible, there is a wide variety of writings and passages which deal with evil and death in light of present and future existence. Yet, there is hardly a place where these issues are treated more distinctly and more radically as in the Book of Qohelet, a collection of wisdom teachings dating to the third century B.C.E.[1] This treatment finds its most vivid expression in the following sentence from Qoh 9:3:

> The hearts of men are full of evil, and insanity is in their hearts throughout their lives, and after that they go to the dead.[2]

A fairly depressing sentence, to be sure. According to Qoh 9:3, human existence is characterized entirely by evil and insanity with death waiting as the final and inescapable reality. Anyone familiar with the basic ideas expressed in the Book of Qohelet will not be surprised when reading these reflections on human existence. They fit smoothly in the overall skepticism of the book, and with a certain right one may even designate Qoh 9:3 as a short summary of Qohelet's anthropology. Nevertheless, it is also clear that an isolated reading of the verse does hardly allow for the reconstruction of a precise anthropological concept. Many aspects are only alluded to, and the verse thus poses more questions than it actually answers. What are, for instance, the origins of human evil and what its effects? Is there a causal relationship between evil and death, with death possibly being the punishment for human wickedness? And finally, although not less important: what are the theological implications of this anthropology? Was man created with a heart receptive for evil, and does Qohelet make use of the concept of a divine judgment which restores righteousness?

In the following, I wish to assess these issues related to the anthropology of the Book of Qohelet by introducing and discussing a number of central passages. In my interpretation of these passages I will place special emphasis on Qohelet's reception of the biblical tradition.[3] I will begin with observations on

---

1 Detailed information to support a Hellenistic dating of Qohelet is provided by KRÜGER, Kohelet, 11–92; SCHWIENHORST-SCHÖNBERGER, Kohelet, 41–134. Differently e.g. CARR, Formation, 448–455, who argues that the core of the book might date back to the time of Solomon.
2 All Biblical references are quoted according to the NRS, partly revised by the author.
3 The crucial importance of the biblical tradition (especially Gen 1–11) for determining the profile of Qohelet's anthropology has variously been stressed in the past, most recently by SCHÜLE, Evil, 157–176.

human mortality (1) and continue with reflections regarding the moral status of mankind (2) and the relationship between human wickedness and suffering (3). Against this background, I will deal with the issue of divine judgment in the final section (4) of this article.

1 The Fate of Mortality and the Joy of Life

That all humans have to die one day is an observation which does not originate with Qohelet. Reflections on human mortality belong to the central topics of biblical anthropology and are attested throughout the writings of the Hebrew Bible.[4] The Book of Qohelet, however, introduces one new aspect in the treatment of the topic. Here, human mortality is interpreted in the light of the concept of fate or destiny. The Hebrew term used when referring to this concept is מקרה—literally "that which befalls". The term only occurs nine times in the writings of the Hebrew Bible, with five occurrences belonging to the Book of Qohelet.[5] All these five occurrences have in common that מקרה is used to express the idea that death is the common fate of all human beings, regardless of their social or moral status.

For the first time, the issue of the common fate is addressed in Qoh 2:(12)13–17. In this section, Qohelet ponders the advantages of wisdom against those of folly and comes to a clear conclusion:

> 2:13 Then I saw that wisdom excels folly as light excels darkness. 14a The wise have eyes in their head, but fools walk in darkness.

There is nothing spectacular about this conclusion which expresses a fundamental belief of wisdom literature. Very few wisdom teachers would object to the idea that the wise is superior to the fool like light is superior to darkness. However, Qohelet does not content himself with this commonplace statement but connects another observation which continues the argument in quite an unexpected way:

> 2:14b Yet I perceived that the same fate befalls all of them. 15 Then I said to myself, "What happens to the fool will happen to me also; why then have I been so very wise?" And I said to myself that this also is vanity. 16 For there is no enduring remembrance of the wise

---

4 See e.g. WOLFF, Anthropologie, 152–177.
5 Moreover, the term מקרה is attested in Deut 23:11; 1Sam 6:9; 20:26; Ruth 2:3 where it designates something (positive or negative) happening by chance.

or of fools, seeing that in the days to come all will have been long forgotten. How can the wise die just like fools? 17 So I hated life, because what is done under the sun was grievous to me; for all is vanity and a chasing after wind.

Qohelet would not disagree that compared to folly wisdom does provide a clear advantage inasmuch as it helps the wise to orient himself in his life. However, this advantage is entirely devaluated, because despite his wisdom the wise is subject to the same fate that befalls the fool.[6] Though this concept of fate may certainly include all kinds of life-experiences, it is nevertheless clear that the main issue is death.[7] The wise will die like the fool, it is their common fate. This idea of being subject to fate is nothing Qohelet has inherited from the tradition of the Hebrew Bible. Rather, the notion of fate (τύχη) is firmly rooted in the Hellenistic worldview which in this point seems to have strongly influenced the thinking of Qohelet.[8] This influence is also tangible in the motif of enduring remembrance which is broadly attested in Greek literature.[9] Yet, the same motif also occurs in biblical wisdom literature where it is stated several times that a person's deeds will be remembered beyond death.[10] Not so Qohelet. For him, the deeds of a person will surely be forgotten, so there is no hope that after death anyone will continue in the memory of future generations.

In Qoh 2:13–17, the observation of death as inescapable fate leads Qohelet to question the sense of a life devoted to wisdom. In a similar way, the argument recurs in Qoh 9:1–6. Here, however with the decisive difference that the categories under discussion are no longer wisdom and folly. Now Qohelet deals with righteousness and wickedness as well as related categories of religious observance:

> 9:2 The same fate comes to all, to the righteous and the wicked, to the good and the evil, to the clean and the unclean, to those who sacrifice and those who do not sacrifice. As are the good, so are the sinners; those who swear are like those who shun an oath. 3 This is an evil in all that happens under the sun, that the same fate comes to everyone.

The text continues in Qoh 9:3b with the observation on human wickedness and mortality which I have quoted at the beginning of this article. In its context, the sentence introduces a side-aspect whereas the main line of the argument contin-

---

6 Cf. Qoh 9:10; Ps 49:11–12.
7 See Schwienhorst-Schönberger, Kohelet, 225.
8 See e.g. Krüger, Kohelet, 144.
9 Cf. e.g. Platon, Symposion 208c-e; see Schwienhorst-Schönberger, Kohelet, 226.
10 Cf. Prov 10:7; Ps 112:6; Sir 15:6; 37:26; 39:11; 41:11–13.

ues in Qoh 9:4–6. After his reference to the one fate of all human beings (9:1–3), Qohelet now turns towards the advantages of life compared to death:

> 9:4 But whoever is joined with all the living has hope, for a living dog is better than a dead lion. 5 The living know that they will die, but the dead know nothing; they have no more reward, and even the memory of them is lost. 6 Their love and their hate and their envy have already perished; never again will they have any share in all that happens under the sun.

While the dead will inevitably fall into non-existence and oblivion, the living can lead their lives in awareness of this future fate. This may not be much, but it is at least more than nothing. "A living dog is better than a dead lion"—Qohelet quotes this traditional saying[11] in order to make his point: Life, even in its most miserable form, is always preferable over the nonexistence in death. The awareness of mortality leads one to appreciate life despite the fact that this life may be characterized by misery and hardship. Actually, Qohelet leaves little doubt that human life "under the sun" is a toil- and troublesome business. Nevertheless, he also points out frequently that there is one aspect through which human life gains a positive quality and meaning. It is the joy which human beings may experience in their toilsome lives. In Qoh 8:14–15, this central motif is expressed in the following way:

> 8:14 There is a vanity that takes place on earth, that there are righteous people who are treated according to the conduct of the wicked, and there are wicked people who are treated according to the conduct of the righteous. I said that this also is vanity. 15 So I commend enjoyment, for there is nothing better for people under the sun than to eat, and drink, and enjoy themselves, for this will go with them in their toil through the days of life that God gives them under the sun.

With his appreciation of joy, Qohelet stands in a long tradition. Similar thoughts are already expressed in ancient near eastern texts like the Mesopotamian Gilgamesh Epic or the Egyptian Harpers' Songs.[12] Moreover, there are also certain parallels to popular Hellenistic concepts inspired by the philosophy of Epikur.[13] Like Epikur, Qohelet should be accused by his opponents for propagating a primitive hedonism, a critique which in both cases completely misses its point. For both Epikur and Qohelet, joy is not mindless enjoyment, but rather a desirable state of mind or experience which even has a certain theological quality.

---

11 See e.g. SCHWIENHORST-SCHÖNBERGER, Kohelet, 449.
12 See SEOW, Ecclesiastes, 296–306; KRÜGER, Kohelet, 308–310.
13 See SCHWIENHORST-SCHÖNBERGER, Kohelet, 464–466.

For Epikur, it is the imitation of the gods' state of permanent bliss,[14] while to Qohelet it is nothing less than a divine gift. In a work like the Book of Qohelet which generally presumes a great distance between God and man, this theological qualification of joy can hardly be overestimated. Joy is nothing that man can create himself, but it can only be received as a gift from God (Qoh 3:13; 5:18). Therefore, it is hardly surprising that Qohelet concludes his book with a poetic exhortation to grasp joy in the days of youth, because old age and death leave little to no room for enjoyment (cf. Qoh 11:9–12:7).

It is time for a short summary of the observations made so far. For Qohelet, death is the common fate of humanity. Regardless of whether a person is wise or a fool, just or wicked he or she has to die, and there is no way, in which his or her personality and achievements may continue beyond death. Sooner or later everyone will be forgotten. In consequence, there can be no room for any conception assuming that the life of a person finds its earthly fulfillment after he or she has died. Moreover, in light of the passages discussed so far it also seems unlikely that Qohelet should assume any form of eschatological perfection of human existence. As I will try to show later, the Book of Qohelet in its original form did not contain any kind of eschatological expectation. The few passages which express this kind of expectation are due to an editorial reworking of the book.[15]

Contrary to any attempt to elude the finality of death, Qohelet finds the only positive meaning of human existence in the earthly moments of joy which man experiences as a divine gift. With the advice to grasp these moments, we are at the heart of Qohelet's practical teaching. Yet, the anthropological basis for this teaching has so far only been touched at its surface. What Qohelet has to say about the creational state of human beings in relation to other creatures, shall therefore be discussed in the following paragraph.

2 Homo Homini Lupus — the Relationship between Human Beings and Animals

The discussion of Qoh 2 and 9 has made clear that according to Qohelet all human beings are subject to the same fate of death. However, Qohelet goes much

---

14 For a recent treatment of Epikur's teachings regarding human joy, see HELD, Hēdonē.
15 See BERNER, Gott, 253–269.

further than this. In Qoh 3,19–22, he again employs the concept of fate, but it is no longer applied to human beings alone, but to animals as well:

> 3:19 For the fate of humans and the fate of animals is the same; as one dies, so dies the other. They all have the same spirit, and humans have no advantage over the animals; for all is vanity. 20 All go to one place; all are from the dust, and all turn to dust again. 21 Who knows whether the human spirit goes upward and the spirit of animals goes downward to the earth? 22 So I saw that there is nothing better than that all should enjoy during their work, for that is their lot; who can bring them to see what will be after them?

Qohelet starts with the observation that both human beings and animals are subject to the fate of death. This observation alone would hardly be remarkable. What is striking, however, are the reflections that follow, because now Qohelet presents an outline of his anthropology against the background of biblical creation theology. It has long been noted that Qoh 3:19–21 reflect a critical reading of both creation accounts from the Book of Genesis.[16] For instance, when Qohelet claims in 3:19 that all creatures have the same spirit (רוח) he obviously contradicts the non-Priestly creation account. According to this version, both human beings and animals are formed out of the ground, but it is only to the humans that God grants the breath of life (Gen 2:7):

> Then the LORD God formed man from the dust of the ground, and breathed into his nostrils the breath of life (נשמת חיים); and the man became a living being (נפש חיה).

For Qohelet, there is no such advantage of human beings over animals, because they all share the same spirit. Although this claim clearly contradicts the second creation account, it is—at least to a certain extent—supported by the Priestly version in Gen 1. According to Gen 1:30, animals are living beings (נפש חיה); the Priestly author thus employs the same terminology which is used in Gen 2:7 where it expresses the unique status of man.

An even closer parallel to the terminology employed by Qohelet is provided by the Priestly version of the flood story: According to Gen 6:17 (cf. 7:15.22) "all flesh in which is the spirit of life" (רוח חיים) shall be exterminated by the flood. Obviously, the Priestly writer assumes that humans and animals share the same vivifying spirit. When Qohelet claims in 3:19 that all creatures have the same spirit he may therefore contradict the non-Priestly creation account, but he goes quite conform with Priestly theology.

Yet, already the conclusion, which Qohelet draws from his claim that all creatures share the same spirit, no longer seems to be compatible with Priestly

---

16 See KRÜGER, Kohelet, 179–185; SCHWIENHORST-SCHÖNBERGER, Kohelet, 276–287.

thought. "Humans have no advantage over the animals," Qohelet concludes (Qoh 3:19). This sounds like an open contradiction to the Priestly concept according to which man has been created in the image of God to rule as God's representative over all other works of creation. Qohelet's denial of an advantage of humans over the animals reads like the attempt to revoke the Priestly writer's claim that humans enjoy a distinguished creational state.

However, it also seems worthwhile to consider an alternative interpretation of Qoh 3:19 which is in line with Priestly creation theology. It could be that Qohelet's denial of an advantage of humans over animals only applies to the specific issue of mortality. Thus, he would argue that *in death* human beings and animals are equal because they share the same fate. This interpretation would not contradict Priestly anthropology and at first glance it seems to be corroborated by the way the argument continues in Qoh 3:20–21. In 3:20, Qohelet describes that after death both human beings and animals return to dust. So, in the end the bodies of all living creatures will again resolve into the basic matter from which they were created.[17] Evidently, in this respect there is no advantage of human beings over animals.

This said, Qohelet turns towards discussing the consequences of death for the spirit. As both human beings and animals suffer the decomposition of their bodies, is it not reasonable to assume that their spirits also share an identical fate? After all, there is only one spirit to all creatures (Qoh 3:19). Who may therefore know, Qohelet asks rhetorically 3:21, "whether the human spirit goes upward and the spirit of animals goes downward to the earth?" At least to him, such a distinction does not seem very convincing. With this argument, Qohelet most likely turns against representatives of an early Jewish apocalypticism according to whom the righteous would receive their reward in death.[18] For Qohelet, this expectation is unfounded because to him there is no evidence that the human spirit continues beyond death. Despite nourishing hope for an eternal life, he therefore repeats his basic advice: man should enjoy life, because this is in fact all one can do (Qoh 3:22).

My short interpretation of Qoh 3:19–22 seems to confirm the above made suggestion that Qohelet's denial of an advantage of human beings does only apply to the specific issue of mortality: in death, there is no difference between human beings and animals as both share the identical fate. This interpretation

---

17 Cf. Gen 2:7.19; 3:19; Job 34:14–15; Ps 104:29–39.
18 Cf. 1 En. 9:3; 13:6; 22:3.5. On Qohelet's criticism of early Jewish apocalypticism see e.g. MICHEL, Untersuchungen, 126–137; FISCHER, Kohelet. Yet, one should not overlook that the discourse between Platonism and Epikureism on the issue of the immortality of the human soul may be reflected in Qoh 3:21 as well; see KRÜGER, Kohelet, 184–185.

of the verses is certainly true, but it reveals only one part of the truth. There is more to these verses than an isolated reading suggests, because Qohelet's reflections on the common fate of humans and animals are part of a larger argument, which begins with the following observation in Qoh 3:16:

> Moreover I saw under the sun that in the place of justice, wickedness was there, and in the place of righteousness, wickedness was there as well.

This observation is followed by two entirely different conclusions. While the second conclusion (Qoh 3:18) proves to be an integral part of the argument, the first one (Qoh 3:17) stands rather isolated. The verse which introduces the concept of divine judgment is not original but represents a later addition[19] we may ignore for the time being. Without this verse, Qohelet's argument runs as follows:

> 3:16 Moreover I saw under the sun that in the place of justice, wickedness was there, and in the place of righteousness, wickedness was there as well. 18 So I said in my heart with regard to human beings that God had singled them out, but had to see that they are but animals.[20]

In an equally remarkable and surprising way the argument develops a fundamental anthropological statement: Starting with the observation that earthly justice is corrupted and perverted by humans, Qohelet concludes that humans are in fact no better than animals. Their behavior towards each other shows that they do not substantially differ from animals. Evidently, this implies a harsh criticism of the Priestly concept according to which man enjoys a unique status among his fellow creatures. For Qohelet, there is no such status, because humans lack the appropriate moral quality. That they behave like animals makes him conclude that they are not fundamentally different from animals. He finds the confirmation for this conclusion in the fact that both human beings and animals share the fate of mortality. The respective verses Qoh 3:19–21 which deal with this issue now appear in an entirely different light. They are not the

---

19 See BARTON, Book, 111; VOLZ, Hiob, 254; MICHEL, Qohelet, 138; FISCHER, Kohelet, 340–345. Differently e.g. SEOW, Ecclesiastes, 175–176; KRÜGER, Kohelet, 179–185; SCHWIENHORST-SCHÖNBERGER, Kohelet, 280–287.
20 As the syntax of Qoh 3:18 is problematic, the correct translation of the verse is disputed. I follow the suggestion of KRÜGER, Kohelet, 164, who connects the inf. constr. ולראות Qal (MT) with God as subject (differently e.g. SEOW, Ecclesiastes, 167–168, who follows the reading of the LXX in assuming an original hif. ולראות "to show"). Krüger's interpretation seems to be corroborated by the intertextual link between Qoh 3:18 and Gen 6:5 which is discussed below.

main point of the argument, but provide additional evidence for Qohelet's refusal of the idea that man enjoys a unique status among his fellow creatures.

This refusal is certainly the main point of the argument developed in Qoh 3:16–22. Yet, there still remains much to say about the way it is presented. A close look reveals that the reflections in Qoh 3:18 do again deliberately allude to crucial events narrated in the Book of Genesis. In stating that human beings had been singled out by God, Qohelet obviously refers to the Priestly creation account which finds its climax with the creation of man and God commissioning him to rule in his stead over all other works of creation (Gen 1:26–29). According to Gen 1:26, God decides to create man in his own image, thus granting him a privilege which Ancient Near Eastern thought would attribute to the king exclusively. For the Priestly author of Gen 1, mankind as a whole enjoys a royal status, and it is therefore consequently entrusted with the dominion over all fellow creatures.

This concept is subject to a critical revision in Qoh 3:18: Qohelet does not deny that God has granted humans a special status among their fellow creatures. What he contests, however, is the notion that this status is justified. To him, human beings are but animals, because they do behave like animals. Yet, it must not be overlooked that this striking insight is presented from God's own perspective: "God had singled them out, but had to see that they are but animals." Thus, according to Qoh 3:18 God himself had to learn that humans did not live up to the role he had chosen for them. The wickedness of humans seems to have a quality that even surprises God. Despite its offensiveness, this notion does not lack a biblical background. This background is found in Gen 6:5, the prelude to the flood story, where it says:

> The LORD saw (ראה) that the wickedness of humankind was great in the earth, and that every inclination of the thoughts of their hearts was only evil continually.

This divine observation is obviously alluded to in Qoh 3:18: God "had to see" (ראה) that human beings are but animals. As I have already noted earlier, the following verses Qoh 3:19–21 adduce additional evidence for the accuracy of this judgment by referring to the common fate of mortality. Humans are but animals, because the one will die like the other. However, read against the background of the reference texts in the Book of Genesis, the argument in Qoh 3 still reveals another dimension. In Gen 6, God's recognition of human wickedness will eventually lead to the extinction of all living beings in the flood. This context in mind, it becomes possible to conclude that for Qohelet the common fate of mortality was not only proof for his equation of humans and animals. There may also exist the notion of divine punishment: death applies to humans and animals alike, because humans due to their animal-like behavior do not deserve any better.[21]

The argument in Qoh 3:16–22 underscores that there is a close connection between human wickedness and mortality, just like the quotation from Qoh 9:3 had indicated: "The hearts of men are full of evil, and insanity is in their hearts throughout their lives, and after that they go to the dead." It also shows that God is not made responsible for the origins of human wickedness;[22] quite to the contrary, he seems surprised when confronted with this anthropological reality. Precisely this issue also seems to be reflected in Qoh 7:29 where it says that "God made human beings upright (ישר), but they have devised many schemes."[23] Evidently, man has developed in a different way than God originally meant him to. Created as an upright being and thus theoretically capable of a corresponding behavior, man has nevertheless become a being with a heart full of evil.

It is not explicitly stated how this dramatic change could occur. There are, however, a number of passages which discuss the influence of human wickedness on everyday life and in doing so also shed further light on the theological and anthropological aspects of evil. I will briefly deal with these passages in the following paragraph.

3 Caught in a Vicious Circle – Human Wickedness and Suffering

Apparently, Qohelet took a special interest in the corruption of earthly justice. The discussion of Qoh 3:16 has already shown how he can draw conclusions on general anthropological issues from observations regarding the miserable state of the justice system. Quite a similar argument recurs in Qoh 8:11–12:

> 8:11 Because sentence against an evil deed is not executed speedily, the human heart is filled with evil. 12 Because sinners may do evil a hundred times and yet prolong their lives.

While Qoh 9:3 simply states that the human heart *is* full of evil, Qoh 8:11 gives a striking explanation for this condition. This explanation is not ontological, but rather combines sociological and psychological aspects: the inclination towards

---

21 Similarly e.g. KRÜGER, Kohelet, 180–181.
22 See MAUSSION, Le mal, 69–70.
23 Cf. Qoh 7:20.

evil deeds grows in the hearts of human beings because crimes are not punished fast enough. A criminal is thus not hindered from committing another crime, and he is even confirmed by the success of his wrongdoings as long as a quick judgment stays away. This observation is strongly reminiscent of the current debate about the necessity of accelerating legal proceedings in order to show the delinquent that there is a direct connection between deed and punishment. Despite its currentness, the subject of this debate is not a new one, as the evidence in Qoh 8:11 demonstrates.

What now are the consequences of this evidence for the issue of human wickedness? One may conclude that, for Qohelet, human wickedness constitutes a kind of a self-nourishing sphere, insofar as evil deeds remain unsanctioned and thus strengthen the inclination towards other evil deeds. In theory, the improvement of the justice system would constitute a way of breaking this vicious circle. Yet, Qohelet's reflections in other parts of the book suggest that he hardly deemed this a realistic option. For instance, in Qoh 5:7 he observes:

> If you see in a province the oppression of the poor and the violation of justice and right, do not be amazed at the matter; for the high official is watched by a higher, and there are yet higher ones over them.

Evidently, there is system to the corruption of the justice system. The elites cover and protect each other in order to prevent that the violation of justice from which they themselves draw profit comes to an end. For the ones suffering from this system, there seems to be no hope that their situation might improve. This hopeless situation of the oppressed is vividly reflected in Qoh 4:1–3:

> 4:1 Again I saw all the oppressions that are practiced under the sun. Look, the tears of the oppressed—with no one to comfort them! On the side of their oppressors there is power—with no one to comfort them! 2 And I thought the dead, who have already died, more fortunate than the living, who are still alive; 3 but better than both is the one who has not yet been, and has not seen the evil deeds that are done under the sun.

What Qohelet presents here is a sober and pitiless analysis of human oppression. The oppressed are completely and utterly at the mercy of their oppressors, without any hope of escaping that situation. In fact, their situation is so hopeless that to Qohelet even death and non-existence seem preferable. This is indeed a strong statement in a book that praises the living dog over the dead lion (Qoh 9:4) and leaves little doubt about its high appreciation of the enjoyments of life. Yet, for the oppressed enjoyment does not seem to be a reality anymore—at least not such reality that may outweigh their suffering. This explains why death suddenly seems to develop a certain appeal to Qohelet.

In sum, Qohelet offers a fairly depressing analysis of the structures that determine human life: With no one to step in, injustice and oppression thrive, and the poor and oppressed suffer without anyone to comfort them. It must, however, not be overlooked that this reference to the missing comforter has strong theological implications. The Hebrew Bible frequently refers to God himself as to the one who gives comfort in suffering and despair. For instance, this notion is attested in the following famous quotation from Ps 23:4:

> Even though I walk through the darkest valley, I fear no evil; for you are with me; your rod and your staff—they comfort me.

Qohelet obviously does no longer expect God to intervene on behalf of the oppressed. "On the side of their oppressors there is power—with no one to comfort them" (Qoh 4:1bβ). In a certain respect, this missing expectation of divine intervention is only consequent. After all, the evil of the human heart which causes all this suffering is not of God's doing but apparently self-inflicted: "God made human beings upright (ישר), but they have devised many schemes" (Qoh 7:29). One could certainly argue that this deviation from God's creational design makes man alone responsible for his own fate so he may no longer expect comfort or deliverance from God.

However, this plain pattern of cause and effect would be an oversimplification. Despite the fact that Qohelet gives a pitiless description of human wickedness, he does not seem to claim that the state of the human heart is something man alone is responsible for or even guilty of. Rather, it seems that man is in a dilemma, with God having a certain responsibility for the state of human affairs as well. After all, God has intentionally devised and ordered his creation in a way that makes it impossible for human beings to grasp the meaning of the whole.[24] This notion is expressed quite frequently throughout the Book of Qohelet, for instance in Qoh 7:13–14:

> 7:13 Consider the work of God; who can make straight what he has made crooked? 14 In the day of prosperity be joyful, and in the day of adversity consider; God has made the one as well as the other, so that mortals may not find out anything that will come after them.

Obviously, it can not be easy for an upright being to exist in a crooked world. Is it, therefore, not understandable that human beings have devised many schemes, as it says in Qoh 7:29? When dealing with the issue of human wickedness in the Book of Qohelet, it seems important to consider it in all its aspects. It

---

[24] See SPIECKERMANN, Suchen, 321–322. For a comprehensive discussion of Qohelet's reflections on the limits of human understanding, see the recent study of SCHELLENBERG, Erkenntnis.

is certainly true that the evil in the hearts of men has developed its own dynamics that completely account for all kinds of oppression and suffering, but the hearts of humans are not only full of evil. They are also full of misunderstanding and disorientation in a world which in its totality remains hidden from them.

This latter aspect finds its most vivid expression in Qoh 8:6b–7. "The misery (רעה) of man is great (רבה) upon him," Qohelet notes in 8:6b to conclude: "For they do not know what is to be, for who can tell them how it will be?" (Qoh 8:7). In Hebrew, great misery and great wickedness can be referred to in the identical manner as רעה רבה. It is hardly a coincidence that precisely this terminology is used in Gen 6:5 where God observes that "the wickedness (רעה) of humanity was great (רבה) in the earth." In Qoh 8:6 (cf. 6:1) this wording is taken up, but it is construed in a different way. Here, the text is no longer dealing with human wickedness (*malum morale*), but focuses entirely on human misery (*malum physicum*) which is found in the inability to tell what will be in the future.

Thus, the central anthropological statement from Gen 6:5 has been interpreted by Qohelet in two different ways: While on the one hand, he agrees in Qoh 3:18, 8:11 and 9:3 on the corruption of the human heart, he does on the other hand deliberately change the original meaning of Gen 6:5 by relating the verse to human misery (Qoh 8:6b–7). This twofold use of the quotation suggests that for Qohelet, human misery and wickedness are closely connected. The fatality of human existence lies in man's inability to comprehend the world in its totality, a defect which in turn generates wickedness. This, however, implies that God as the one who devised this creational design is also at least partially responsible for the results of this design in the form of human wickedness and suffering. Taking up a formulation coined by Hermann Spieckermann one may, therefore, say that evil is worked by God and man in "a crooked alliance."[25]

The notion that God created a world in which human wickedness could thrive is the only example in the Book of Qohelet for a causal relationship between God and evil. Apart from this, God plays no role in Qohelet's reflections on corruption and wickedness he had experienced in his own days: God is neither imagined to comfort the oppressed, nor is he expected to make an end with injustice and judge the evildoers. It is the absence of these aspects that are so closely connected to the God of Israel in most other writings of the Hebrew Bible which eventually gave rise to an editorial reworking of the book. In the process of this reworking, the editor introduced the concept of divine judgment which had originally played no role at all. I will close my paper with some brief notes

---

25 See SPIECKERMANN, Suchen, 325 ("in krummer Koalition").

regarding this editorial process which supplemented the Book of Qohelet with an entirely new perspective.

4 One Fate — One Judgment

In Qoh 12:9–14, the book closes with two epilogues. There has long been a consensus among biblical scholars that at least the second epilogue (Qoh 12:12–14) does not belong to the original version of the book.[26] Despite a certain tendency in recent scholarship to take even this second epilogue as original,[27] the evidence clearly points in the opposite direction. The second epilogue introduces categories which clearly contradict many of the central issues in Qohelet's teaching. Instead, it supplements a perspective which conforms to the basic creeds of what I would call "Biblical Judaism," a Judaism focused on the commandments of the Mosaic Torah:

> 12:13 The conclusion of the matter, when all has been heard, is: Fear God, and keep his commandments; for that is the whole duty of everyone. 14 For God will bring every deed into judgment, including every secret thing, whether good or evil.

It is sometimes asked, why someone who found the teachings of Qohelet problematic or even offensive should have supplemented the book with an epilogue that gives the entire composition an "orthodox" coloring. Thus, did the author not contribute to the spreading of a book that he should have rather wished to suppress?[28] Yet, this objection misses the point. Is it not easily conceivable that the author of the second epilogue was equally fascinated and disturbed by Qohelet's teachings? The study of these teachings was something he would not want to miss, but at the same time he found it necessary to state what to him was an indispensable creed: any Jew should obey the commandments of the Torah, because God himself will make him accountable in the final judgment.[29]

Qohelet himself had not conceived the possibility of a final judgment. Quite to the contrary, he sharply opposed any such position in Qoh 3:21:

---

26 See e.g. ZIMMERLI, Buch, 250–251; LOHFINK, Kohelet, 13–14; FISCHER, Skepsis, 35.
27 This tendency is most apparent in the commentaries of SEOW, Ecclesiastes; KRÜGER, Kohelet; FOX, Ecclesiastes; SCHWIENHORST-SCHÖNBERGER, Kohelet.
28 See the discussion in KRÜGER, Kohelet, 365–376.
29 An identical perspective has been supplemented in Qoh 11:9b; see e.g. BARTON, Book, 185; ZIMMERLI, Buch, 242–245; FISCHER, Skepsis, 35; BERNER, Gott, 254.

> Who knows whether the human spirit goes upward and the spirit of animals goes downward to the earth?

Apparently, for Qohelet there is no positive evidence to make him believe in any form of future existence after death. This, however, also excludes the possibility of an individual judgment of the dead as it is implied at the end of the second epilogue in Qoh 12:14. The editor who introduced this concept of judgment was well aware of the fact that he contradicted Qohelet's teaching about the finality of death. He tried to solve this contradiction by adding a short note in Qoh 12:7b. While in 12:7a Qohelet states that after death human beings return to dust (cf. Qoh 3:20) the editor adds that "the spirit returns to God who gave it." The rhetoric question from Qoh 3:21 ("who knows whether the human spirit goes upward [...]?") is thus taken literally and receives a belated answer. For the editor, there can be no doubt that the human spirit *does* return to God where the final judgment is pending.

The example of Qoh 12:7b shows that the concept of final judgment is not mechanically imposed on a book it does not easily fit with. On the contrary, the editor makes every effort to connect the respective concept with Qohelet's teaching as closely as possible. This editorial technique cannot only be observed in Qoh 12:7b, but also finds an even clearer expression in Qoh 3:17, a verse which was supplemented by the same author. As I have tried to demonstrate earlier, the original argument in Qoh 3:16–22 starts with the observation that the justice system is severely corrupted. From this observation, Qohelet then concludes that there is in fact no difference between human beings and animals. This original transition between the observation in 3:16 and the conclusion in 3:18 was disrupted by the addition of 3:17 which draws a completely different conclusion from the same observation:

> 16 Moreover I saw under the sun that in the place of justice, wickedness was there, and in the place of righteousness, wickedness was there as well. 17 I said in my heart, God will judge the righteous and the wicked, for he has appointed a time for every matter, and for every work (that is done) there.

The editor evidently shares Qohelet's conviction that the earthly justice system is corrupt without any hope this might ever change. Yet, he is not willing to accept that there is no divine deliverance. For him, there will be an eschatological judgment over all human beings, the righteous as well as the wicked. In this judgment, God himself will restore righteousness.[30] Although this expectation of a final judgment would have hardly been shared by Qohelet, the editor has again found a way to connect this notion with central issues of the book. "For everything there is an appointed time" (Qoh 3:1)—thus begins one of the most famous passages of the book which demonstrates that God has determined an appropriate moment for everything that happens under the sun. The editor who introduced the notion of divine judgment in Qoh 3:17 concluded that God had also appointed a time for the final judgment.[31]

Finally, even the notion that this judgment applies to the righteous and the wicked could be easily derived from Qohelet's teaching. For Qohelet, death is the one fate that all human beings are subject to. However, when one takes this one step further, it becomes possible to conclude that this fate continues beyond the moment of death. As all humans have to die, all of them will be finally made accountable for their deeds by the divine judge. It is their fate as well. At least, this is what the editor claims in Qoh 3:17.

Against the background of this editorial reworking of the Book of Qohelet, it seems worthwhile to take another look at the fundamental anthropological statement from Qoh 9:3:

> The hearts of men are full of evil, and insanity is in their hearts throughout their lives, and after that they got to the dead.

The editor who reworked the Book of Qohelet would most likely agree. However, he would add that one decisive point is missing. After death, God will restore justice. He had appointed the time when each individual—as fated—would be judged according to their deeds. The hopelessness that echoes throughout Qohelet's treatment of human wickedness and suffering is thus overcome through the addition of an eschatological perspective. Qohelet himself would hardly agree with this development. Yet, at the same time he would have to acknowledge that the seed which should eventually bring forth these redactional expansions had been laid with his very own teaching.

---

30 That Qoh 3:17 reflects an eschatological concept of judgment has been convincingly shown by FISCHER, Kohelet, 343. Differently e.g. SCHWIENHORST-SCHÖNBERGER, Kohelet, 552, according to whom the verse might as well refer to intramundane judgment through divine punishment.
31 Similarly FISCHER, Kohelet, 343–344.

Bibliography

BARTON, George Aaron, The Book of Ecclesiastes (ICC), Edinburgh 1947 (1908).
BERNER, Christoph, Der ferne Gott als Richter? Zur theologischen Deutung weltlicher Ungerechtigkeit im Koheletbuch, in: ZThK 108 (2011) 253–269.
CARR, David M., The Formation of the Hebrew Bible. A New Reconstruction, Oxford et al. 2011.
FISCHER, Alexander Achilles, Skepsis oder Furcht Gottes? Studien zur Komposition und Theologie des Buches Kohelet (BZAW 247), Berlin/New York 1997.
FISCHER, Alexander Achilles, Kohelet und die frühe jüdische Apokalyptik. Eine Auslegung von Koh 3,16–21, in: Schoors, Antoon (Hg.), Qohelet in the Context of Wisdom (BEThL 136), Leuven 1998, 339–356.
FOX, Michael V., Ecclesiastes קהלת (The JPS Bible Commentary), Philadelphia, Pennsylvania 2004.
HELD, Katharina, Hēdonē und Ataraxia bei Epikur, Paderborn 2007.
KRÜGER, Thomas, Kohelet (Prediger) (BK 19 Sonderband), Neukirchen-Vluyn 2000.
LOHFINK, Norbert, Kohelet (NEB), Würzburg ²1980.
MAUSSION, Marie, Le mal, le bien et le jugement de Dieu dans le livre de Qohéleth (OBO 190), Fribourg/Göttingen 2002.
MICHEL, Diethelm, Untersuchungen zur Eigenart des Buches Qohelet (BZAW 183), Berlin/New York 1989.
SCHELLENBERG, Annette, Erkenntnis als Problem. Qohelet und die alttestamentliche Diskussion um das menschliche Erkennen (OBO 188), Fribourg/Göttingen 2002.
SCHÜLE, Andreas, Evil from the Heart. Qoheleth's Negative Anthropology and its Canonical Context, in: Berlejung, Angelika et al. (Hg.), The Language of Qohelet in its Context (OLA 164), Leuven 2007, 157–176.
SCHWIENHORST-SCHÖNBERGER, Ludger, Kohelet (HThKAT), Freiburg et al. 2004.
SEOW, Leong, Ecclesiastes (AncB 18C), New York et al. 1997.
SPIECKERMANN, Hermann, Suchen und Finden. Kohelets kritische Reflexionen, in: Bib. 79 (1998) 305–332.
VOLZ, Paul, Hiob und Weisheit (Das Buch Hiob, Sprüche und Jesus Sirach, Prediger) (SAT 3/2), Göttingen ²1921 (1911).
WOLFF, Hans Walter, Anthropologie des Alten Testaments. Mit zwei Anhängen neu hg. v. Bernd Janowski, Gütersloh 2010.
ZIMMERLI, Walther, Das Buch des Predigers Salomo (ATD 16/1), Göttingen 1962.

Gerbern S. Oegema
Different Approaches to Evil and Death in the Ethics of the Non-Canonical Jewish Writings[1]

1 Introduction

Neither the more general question about "Ethics in Early Judaism" nor the more specific question about "Different Approaches to Evil and Death in the Ethics of the Pseudepigrapha" can be dealt with in the same way as the questions of ethics in the Hebrew Bible/Old Testament or in the New Testament.[2] The writings of Early Judaism—i.e. not only the Pseudepigrapha, but also the Apocrypha, the Qumran Scrolls, Philo and Josephus—neither represent a specific religious group or a sociological movement nor do they all originate from the same geographical area and period in history, nor do they present a uniform theology or set of religious views, let alone a tradition they would have in common.[3] Instead, they come to us from different life settings and represent many different, often unknown, groups and socio-religious traditions in Second Temple Judaism (538 B.C.E. to 70/135 C.E.).[4] Furthermore, equally unlike the Jewish or Christian Bible, the Pseudepigrapha and the other early Jewish writings of Early Judaism do not have a present-day faith community to represent them.

And still, the topic "Ethics in Early Judaism" and the question belonging to it, namely whether the "Ethics of the Pseudepigrapha" represent a specific response to evil and death, do presuppose a theological perspective on it and therefore, within the context of the more recent history of research a truly novel approach to Early Judaism, namely a theological one and not a mere literary,

---

[1] The article is partly based on a paper read as "Ethics in the Pseudepigrapha" for the section "Ethics and Biblical Interpretation," Society of Biblical Literature Annual Meeting, New Orleans, November 21–24, 2009.
[2] See further MARGUERAT, Eschatology; MASTON, Ethics. The Review of Biblical Literature website (accessed on April 17th 2010) lists 64 book reviews on aspects of ethics, of which the overwhelming majority deal with ethics in both the Old and New Testament, some in Rabbinic Judaism and the Greco-Roman world, but none with ethics in the non-canonical literature.
[3] See BLOCH, Book; SCHNABEL, Law; ZERBE, Retaliation.
[4] See further CRONBACH, Ideals, 119–156; KEE, Models, 17–54; SCHÜRER, History, Vol. III, 177–379.

historical and comparative one.⁵ Given the lack of research on the topic, this treatment of the material can only have an introductory character.

In this paper, we will first focus on the ethics in a number of individual writings, from the Pseudepigrapha and also from the Apocrypha, and then for comparative purposes briefly continue with the ethics in the Dead Sea Scrolls, Philo and Josephus. After that we can draw a more complete picture of ethics in Early Judaism, of which the non-canonical or early Jewish writings are indeed the main witness.⁶ The description of ethics in these non-canonical writings, which follows the organizing principle of the Jewish Writings of the Hellenistic-Roman Period (JSHRZ), is completed with a second part with a more systematic and theological overview of their ethics in its larger context.

Whereas the organizing principle of the *Jüdische Schriften aus hellenistisch-römischer Zeit* (JSHRZ) may be known to most of the readers, it will be important to mention the five theological themes or red threads with which I try to cover the different aspects of ethics within its larger context, namely 1) Torah and wisdom; 2) Divine revelation and intervention; 3) The origin of and ways to deal with evil; 4) Human responsibility and one's role in society; and 5) Practical ethics between the "love command" and the "Golden Rule." Only within this broader theological context it makes sense to speak about the question whether and how early Jewish ethics, and specifically that of the Pseudepigrapha, is a response to evil and death.

2 Ethics in the Non-Canonical Jewish Writings

2.1 Apocrypha

First and Second Maccabees, Wisdom of Solomon, and Sirach are substantial writings with clearly distinguishable ethics representing religious and philosophical views held in Judaism during the early Hellenistic periods (3rd to 1st century B.C.E.).

The books of First and Second Maccabees were commissioned by the Hasmonean rulers in the century after the Maccabean Revolt (164 B.C.E.) and represent an inner-Jewish ethic focused on national unity and a fight against

---
5 See OEGEMA, Writings, 491–512; IDEM, Ethics, 321–328, and IDEM, Judaism, 97–111.
6 Some of the older works to be mentioned here are: HERFORD, Talmud; MALDWYN HUGHES, Ethics; LEWIS, Ethics; CHATELION COUNET, Pseudepigraphy; MERGUET, Glaubenslehre.

Hellenistic-Syrian culture and religion. Their ethics highlight the values that are connected with Judaism as a way of life and are most visible in their identity markers, such as dietary laws, circumcision, and temple worship. The example of martyrdom for the Jewish cause is employed to stress the importance of keeping God's commandments, as preserved and handed down by ancestral traditions. Moral and, above all, military resistance against the Syrian occupancy is glorified using vivid descriptions of the God-given success of the Maccabean brothers in the war with Antiochus IV Epiphanes. The ethics of First and Second Maccabees are, therefore, national, social, and inner-Jewish at the same time, all subordinated to the concept of Jewish identity and the struggle for the survival of the Jewish nation. Even the Mosaic laws are subject to this, as the example of the temporary abolishment of the Sabbath laws during the war in order to save Jewish life shows (1Macc 2:41).[7]

Wisdom of Solomon from 1st-century C.E. Egypt represents a synthesis between biblical teaching and Greek philosophy in its treatment of the concept of wisdom. The first six of its 19 chapters are addressed to the ungodly rulers of the earth and urge them to love justice and avoid perverse words and deeds, as God sees everything and no one escapes final judgment. It describes two opposing ways of life: the just life and the ungodly life. Solomon is the perfect example of the wise person or sage, and personifies wisdom, which existed since the creation of the world and is its ruling principle (chapters 7-9). Although there are few examples of practical wisdom or ethics, it is obvious that all ethical principals are to be derived from the leading principle of God's wisdom and righteousness, which rules this world.[8]

In Sirach, the Greek translation of an originally Hebrew work ascribed to Ben Sira around 200 B.C.E. and written down by his grandson in the year 132 B.C.E., we find the commandment to love oneself connected with the command to love (and free) one's slave (7:21). It has also been linked to the Golden Rule with the anthropological argument that the neighbour, including the slave, is a human being too (31:15). As in Tobit, but more explicitly employing Greek philosophical concepts as in the Wisdom of Solomon, the author of Sirach equates the divine teaching found in the Books of Moses with the Greek concept of wisdom. In both cases, divine teaching and wisdom include the practical call to act righteously. Believing and acting are here seen as two sides of the same coin. If

---

[7] See on the "male" virtues of endurance in 1 and 2 Maccabees and other writings from the Greco-Roman period: ADAMOPOULO, Endurance; and see on the socio-political aspects of the Maccaean Revolt: STROUMSA/STANTON, Tolerance. See further XERAVITS/ZSENGELLÉR, Books.
[8] See more general on wisdom in the Bible: PERRY, God's Twilight Zone.

you believe that a human being is like you, that is to say, that others have been created in the image of God in just the same way as you, you will love them like yourself, whether they are slave or free.[9] This is simultaneously found in Torah and in the Hellenistic principle of the Golden Rule.[10]

2.2 Pseudepigrapha

Whereas the Pseudepigrapha are usually considered to belong to the conceptual world of the latter parts of the Hebrew Bible/Old Testament and of Early Judaism, at least in North America, many in Europe see them as presenting more of the Early Christian and Patristic traditions. Although Judaism has produced these writings to a large extent, Christianity, indeed, has preserved most of them. The emerging church had a clear and well founded interest in them, whereas rabbinic Judaism rejected most of the Pseudepigrapha or was even unfamiliar with them.[11] Despite their large number (over 70) and diverse character, for which reason they cannot be summarized under one title or one theology, the Pseudepigrapha can be arranged, though imperfectly, by genre, as is done here following the guiding principle of the JSHRZ, namely, in:

1. Historiography and Legend;
2. Ethical Writings in Narrative Form;
3. Ethical Writings in Pedagogical Form;
4. Poetic Writings; and
5. Apocalyptic Writings.

In the following we will select a few examples from each of these five categories.

2.2.1 Historiography and Legend

Two books should be mentioned here. The Fourth Book of Baruch (Paraleipomena of Jeremiah) and the Lives of the Prophets, in particular, give examples of the lives of the prophets, which because of their martyrdom are worthy to be

---

9 Compare KENWORTHY, Nature.
10 See BURKES, Wisdom, 253–276; COLLINS, Ben Sira's Ethics, 62–79.
11 For introductions to and translations of the Pseudepigrapha, see CHARLESWORTH, Pseudepigrapha. For a bibliography, see DITOMMASO, Bibliography.

held in memory, and because of their exemplary lives, are worthy to be followed. Although these two writings do not elaborate on ethical themes in a systematic or a practical way, they do call, for example, that the graves of the prophets are kept in honour, and, in The Fourth Book of Baruch, underline the importance of remembering the horror of the destruction of Jerusalem and the Temple.

2.2.2 Ethical Writings in Narrative Form

In total five books need to be mentioned here, the book of Tobit, the Letter of Aristeas, Jubilees, Pseudo-Philo and Joseph and Aseneth. In the legendary tale of Tobit from the 3rd century B.C.E. featuring Tobit, Sara, and their son Tobias, Tobit teaches his son to live a righteous life after his father's death. Of the examples from practical wisdom his father gives in order to teach him, the Golden Rule is one: "And what you hate, do not do to anyone" (4:15). Although the booklet gives no explanation, as it just quotes it, it is the oldest example of the use of the Golden Rule in Judaism (see also Letter of Aristeas § 207), a popular ethical maxim taken over from the Greek world. The context of the book of Tobit is that of Diaspora Judaism and the need to find a middle way between the adoption of foreign customs and philosophical/ethical principles on the one hand and the living according to the commandments of the Torah on the other hand, as the book concludes. It is easier to find this middle way in the realm of ethics than in the observance of the more specifically Jewish customs.

Jewish identity—or, more generally speaking, the question of what constitutes Jewish practices and beliefs—remains the ruling principle behind this cultural mediation. As the example of the Golden Rule shows, non-Jewish ethical principles do not have to oppose or question this identity, as they are of a more universal nature. They can also be found in the Books of Moses, which according to Hellenistic Judaism communicate universal values and, as they are of very old age, are even the origin of it. Understood in this way, Tobit reveals its deeper meaning, as it points to the Torah as the source of all moral guidelines. The book of Tobit, theologically and anthropologically speaking, then emphasizes three main concepts and employs them as keywords throughout the book: truth, righteousness, and mercy, the classical virtues of Judaism.

These concepts are first of all attributed to God, but are also expected from human beings as a response to God. Righteousness is understood in a very practical way as being merciful and doing good deeds (4:7), and it is in the end Tobit himself who gives the best example of how to act righteously in a foreign land (1:17–20; 2:1–8). Finally, the didactic parts of the book underline the importance of righteousness especially towards the needy, one's brothers, and one's parents (4:3.7–13.16–17 et al.).

In the Letter of Aristeas, written between 127 and 118 B.C.E. and narrating the Greek translation of the Hebrew Bible into Greek produced in commission for the Ptolemaic king Ptolemaeus II Philadelphus, the king asks: "What does wisdom teach?" The thirteenth of the 72 Jewish translators answers with the Golden Rule: "Insofar as you do not wish evils to come upon you, but to partake of every blessing, (it would be wisdom) if you put this into practice with your subjects, including the wrongdoers, and if you admonished the good and upright also mercifully. For God guides all men in mercy" (§ 207). This is one of the earliest examples of the Jewish use of the Golden Rule in its negative and positive form, here understood against the background of the command to love one's neighbor and argued for with the theological concept of *Imitatio Dei*: Loving one's neighbor is a way of following, obeying, and imitating God. At the same time, the author shows that, as far as ethics are concerned, he considers Greek philosophy and biblical teaching to basically say the same thing.

In the book of Jubilees, an example of the "Rewritten Bible" genre from between the Maccabean Revolt in 164 B.C.E. and 150 B.C.E. that divides Israel's history into periods of 50-year jubilees, we find the Golden Rule in its most popular context, namely, as practical wisdom teaching from parents to children: Love your brothers like someone loves his own soul and do good (36:4). The command to love one's neighbour is listed here among other commandments, equated with the Golden Rule, and defined as doing good. At the same time, it is presented as biblical teaching and as the wisdom taught by life itself; in other words, neighbour love is part of human and natural law.

In this context, Pseudo-Philo or Liber antiquitatum biblicarum, written after 70 C.E., is of interest, too, because it employs a style and expresses a point of view that is also found in other writings, though much less consistently used, i.e. that of ideal or exemplary biblical figures, who, because of their exemplary lives or righteous deeds or moral behaviour, are worthy of imitation.

Finally, the romance of Joseph and Aseneth gives an impressive and entertaining example of how Judaism seems to have attracted non-Jews, as it tells the story of chaste Joseph and the Egyptian princess Aseneth, who falls in love with him and, after a mysterious transformative experience, takes over all the practices and beliefs taught by Moses.

2.2.3 Ethical Writings in Pedagogical Form

In the Testaments of the Twelve Patriarchs, a collection of twelve single smaller works, of which some go back to a Jewish source from the 2nd and 1st centuries B.C.E., but which as a whole have been edited in final Christian form in the 1st and 2nd centuries C.E., we find the commandment to love one's neighbour combined with the commandment to love God (T. Iss. 7:6), a combination otherwise found only in the New Testament (Mark 12:28-34 and parallels), but as such going back to the Hebrew Bible, where the commandment to love one's neighbour (Lev 19:18) is argued for with the call of *Imitatio Dei* (Lev 19).[12]

In other passages, the Love Command is connected with the promise of blessing (T. Sim. 4:6), with a call to show mercy to those who are poor and ill (T. Iss. 5:2), with the call to include the animals in one's neighbour love (T. Zeb. 5:1), and with the call to do good (T. Benj. 4:3). Whereas there is no systematic treatment of ethics or a connection with philosophical reasoning or Greek philosophy in the Testaments of the Twelve Patriarchs, ethics is very much understood in its practical form as moral teaching with an emphasis on doing good and being merciful, much in line with the teachings of the Hebrew Bible.

All twelve testaments, but especially the Testament of Joseph, consider the patriarchs to be ethical models due to their exemplary behaviour and high moral standards. For this reason, the patriarchs are narrated here giving farewell speeches to their children while lying on their death beds. Within this narrative framework, a life according to the Torah is depicted as an *exemplum*, and lists of practical ethical directives are given that form the main content of these moral teachings from parents to children. Other testaments than the Testaments of the Twelve Patriarchs, such as the Testament of Job, employ more or less the same technique and share a similar theology and ethics.[13]

2.2.4 Poetic Writings

Among the Poetic Writings most relevant for a study of their ethics are the Psalms of Solomon and Pseudo-Phocylides.

The Psalms of Solomon are a compendium of (wisdom-)theological and anthropological beliefs of Pharisaic origin in the form of psalms dating from the second third of the first century B.C.E. The ethics in these 18 psalms are shaped

---

12 See HARRELSON, Significance; DE JONGE, Commandments, 371–392; SLINGERLAND, Nature, 39–48.
13 See GRAY, Points, 406–424.

by the eschatological expectations of the author, who expected that, at the end of days soon to come, the sinners would be punished and the righteous would be rewarded. Until then, education about righteousness plays an important role and at the end of days a Davidic messiah is expected to play a leading part.

In the description of the importance of righteousness, education, and the punishment of the sinners and rewards of the righteous at the end of days (in order to do justice to their present suffering), the author reflects what Pharisaic circles had considered to be important since the second century B.C.E., and much ethical teaching would be derived from this basic way of thinking: God's teachings are not only mediated through the Law of Moses, but also revealed directly. God is judge and king, He is merciful and loves His people, helps the needy, and is thus the perfect exemplar for human beings to follow and imitate. However, in all of this, humanity has a free will to choose to follow or not, and the righteous one has the ability to ask for forgiveness, to repent, to fast, etc. The fact that humankind is divided at all into righteous and sinners is partly due to God's *providentia*. In the background stands a concept of God as universal king, who allows the righteous to suffer only in order to try them, and an understanding of punishment as a means for God to express his love (see Pss. Sol. 3:3-10; 10:1–3; 13:8–10; 16:14 and 18:4).

Pseudo-Phocylides is a Jewish writing dating from the first century B.C.E. or very early first century C.E. wholly dedicated to ethical teaching, as it consists of *sententiae* or *gnomai* in the form of a moral poem in 219 hexameters later divided into 230 verses. It epitomizes the teaching of the Torah for Hellenized Jews by incorporating non-biblical material, both post-biblical wisdom literature and Greco-Roman popular ethical and philosophical concepts. However, it also has parallels with the rabbinic writing of Derekh Eretz Zuta, as it employs the 7 Noachidic laws. Its main ethical teachings can be divided into: 1) sexual ethics; 2) mercy towards the weak; and 3) sincerity towards the neighbour. The ethics of Pseudo-Phocylides is furthermore universalistic in outlook and consists of practical rules for every day life, both personal and social.

The teachings of this writing can be divided by verses as follows: Prologue (1–2); Summary of the Decalogue (3–8); Exhortations to Justice (9–21); Admonitions to Justice (22–41); Love of Money and its Consequences (42–47); Honesty, Modesty, and Self-Control (48–58); Moderation in All Things (59–69); The Danger of Envy and other Vices (70–96); Death and Afterlife (97–115); The Instability of Life (115–121); Speech and Wisdom, Man's Distinction, Avoidance of Wickedness, and Virtuous Life (122–152); The Usefulness of Labour (153–174); Marriage, Chastity, and Family Life (175–227); Epilogue (228–230).

Behind the book stands a concept of God as someone who is creator and king of the universe, who is mighty and wise, whose universe exists in harmony, who judges humankind after death, and who is the ruler of everyone's soul. As far as moral behaviour is concerned, one is expected to honour God in everything and above everything, share everything God has given with those in need, use the ability to reason with wisdom and to acquire wisdom, and to avoid evil, especially sexual sins (verses 177–194). Furthermore, one is expected to labour in honesty (153–174), limit oneself and be modest, execute justice and mercy, and have stable social relationships, i.e. between husband and wife (195–197), parents and children (207–209), masters and slaves (223–227), and even between friends and enemies (140–142.218).[14]

2.2.5 Apocalyptic Writings

The most important apocalyptic writings in Early Judaism also mark the beginning and end of apocalyptic thinking in Judaism: the books of 1 Enoch partly going back to the 4th/3rd centuries B.C.E., but mostly from the 1st centuries B.C.E. and C.E.; the canonical Book of Daniel dating from the 2nd century B.C.E.; and 4 Ezra as well as 2 Baruch, originating from the beginning of the 2nd century C.E.[15]

Most of the apocalypses have a detailed and explicit explanation of how evil came into the world, how evil has influenced the course of history, and how evil will do so until the end of this world. In that sense, of all the writings discussed so far, the apocalypses are the clearest examples of early Jewish writings having developed a response to evil and death. For the apocalypses, evil is mostly represented in the oppression of Israel by cosmic and/or foreign powers as well as in a variety of sins that come with this oppression. In this respect, the apocalyptic authors differ from the Prophets of Israel, who blame mankind and the evil heart for bringing sin and destruction upon the world and not the heavenly or other powers. The teaching of the apocalypses basically consists of the knowledge of mankind's origin, how to follow the path of righteousness, and how to develop patience in times of distress.

The ethics found in these writings is in principal interim ethics, i.e. ethics for the brief period between the presence of the authors and the expected end of days, and is meant for a minority group, not developed for the members of society at large, but for a group of persecuted martyrs and saints. This "holy remnant" sees itself still living according to the Laws of Moses in an otherwise basically vicious and violent environment with no hope for survival. The goal of this

---

14 See COLLINS, Jewish Ethics, 158–177.
15 See BAUCKHAM, Conflict, 181–196; GAMMIE, Dualism, 356–385.

kind of interim ethics is to help the group endure the final days of humanity, which will be a time of wars, famine, and global destruction, and in order to prepare for the days of the Messiah. He is about to come soon and bring a new law and a time of righteousness to the world.

Understood within the context of early Jewish society, the followers of these apocalyptic thinkers did not consider themselves obliged to uphold the moral standards and ethical rules of the society in which they lived, as they were basically opposed to this society and everything that it represented, including its ethics and morals. The apocalyptic authors considered society's *mores* and ethics to be expressions of wickedness, and offered many examples of this. The holy remnant they thought themselves to be would endure until the time of distress was over, when they could give up their "interim ethics" and begin to live according to the new or newly explained Torah of the Messiah.

1 Enoch has a long history and the origin of some of its oldest parts may date back to the 4th and 3rd centuries B.C.E. Like no other apocalypse before or after, the Ethiopic book of 1 Enoch sees only one reason for the origin of evil in the world in that it blames the fallen angels and the Great Adversary for having brought destruction in all of its forms to the world and humankind. Between God and His angels, and the Adversary and the fallen angels, there is an ongoing cosmic battle, in which the nations of the world are mere marionettes (see 1 En. 1-36).

Here, there is a great distance between God and humankind, with hardly any room left for human free will, as everything depends on the outcome of this cosmic battle. What awaits human beings, who possess an eternal soul, is the final judgment and, with it, either reward or punishment depending on which side of the battle they stood. As everything had been determined and evil existed before creation, it is predestination that defines one's fate and hardly anything can be done on the basis of moral reasoning.

Also for the author of 2 Baruch from the 2nd century C.E. one of the main reasons to employ a strict eschatological interpretation of Israel's origin, history, and future is to find an answer to the question of the origin of evil. He finds it in the first sin committed by Adam, which since then has inhabited human hearts, and has led to death and destruction. With this worldview, there is little space left for human action; only a holy remnant has remained to live according to the Law and it is only at the end of time that God will intervene by sending a Messiah, not only to save Israel, but also to punish the nations of the world. In this sense, the author considers it crucial to teach his audience about the origin of evil, to call for repentance like the biblical prophets, and to comfort the people in times of distress.

Even stronger and probably with more impact than 2 Baruch is the theology of 4 Ezra from the same period, which also uses the genre of apocalyptic visions to draw a picture of Israel's history as defined by the evil heart of humankind. This evil heart since Adam is the source of all destruction and because of it the course of history cannot be changed anymore until the very end of days. Then, God will intervene by sending a Messiah. Until then the ethical imperative is to return and repent from doing evil.

2.3 Dead Sea Scrolls

It is worth to look beyond the Apocrypha and Pseudepigrapha and to also include other writings from the Greco-Roman Period in order to get a more complete picture of ethics in this period. Among the Dead Sea Scrolls we find Essene and non-Essene writings, the latter being, for example, Biblical manuscripts and writings the Qumran community collected and copied but did not write itself. The former writings were the result of a longer tradition and redaction process during the existence of the community at the shore of the Dead Sea from the 150ties B.C.E. to 68 C.E., for which reason it is difficult to get a clear and complete picture of the ethics of the Essenes.[16]

Already Philo and Josephus praised and admired the high moral standards of the Essenes, and the Essene writings, such as the Rule of the Community, the Damascus Document and the Rule of the Congregation as well as the Hodayot, seem to confirm this. They describe an abstemious, moderate, and simple life of a community shunning pleasure and passions and nourishing themselves only to beat hunger. Their members did not amass any richness, but shared everything among themselves, and used their clothes until they were completely unusable.

Apart from their practical way of life, the Essenes also had an ethical theory, in which they taught their pupils and each other: no slavery, no swearing, no anointing, bathing in cold water before every meal as well as after contacts with non-members, wearing white clothes, being extra modest to their natural functions, no marriage, no animal offerings for the Temple, and sharing common meals. It is not clear whether they were also abstemious of wine and meat. In all, the members were called to live a righteous life, be meticulous in their daily

---

16 For a general introduction in some of the problems, see GARCÍA MARTÍNEZ/POPOVIĆ, Identities.

practice, separate themselves from the surrounding world and search the Scriptures.

Behind their ethics lies a theology, dualistic in nature and with a clear idea of predestination. God has created man and has appointed two spirits to rule over him: the good spirit of light, truth and righteousness, and the evil spirit of darkness, error and perversity, both limited in power until the end of this age (1QS 3–4). It is only through discipline and cooperation with the good spirit, that man can improve himself. More about this Essene theology, without which the Essene ethics is unthinkable, is found in the Hodayot, though not in a systematic but in a more poetic language. Furthermore, there are specific rules for becoming a member of the Community or entering the Covenant, both ritualistic and moral in nature (Damascus Document). And finally, many of the rules were stricter than generally accepted in the world of the Hebrew Bible, Early Judaism or the New Testament, such as those connected with keeping the Sabbath or those relating to wars. This set them apart in the eyes of everyone else.

2.4 Philo and Josephus

The ethics of Philo of Alexandria (ca. 10 B.C.E. to 45 C.E.) depend on his anthropology, which on its turn largely depends on Platonic views. In this sense, mankind lives in a dual world. On the one hand, his divine soul belongs to the spiritual world and the realm of angels and daemons, whereas his mortal and more animal-like body is part of the earth and the world of the senses. Individual human beings can live closer to the one or to the other world, the latter being the case with the majority of mankind, and the former more rarely taking place in the lives of the truly wise and righteous men, such as Abraham. From this it follows for Philo that man's spirit is close to reason and righteousness, whereas his body is the source of all evil and for the soul a mere prison.[17]

Consequently, the ethics derived from this is an emphasis of shunning every desire, passion and sensuality, an effort to achieve complete liberation from emotions and the world of the vices and at the same time being taught in how to live a life defined by the cardinal virtues, in all quite similar to the way the Stoics taught. For Philo, however, there was one important difference with Stoic ethics, namely that for him this liberation comes from God and not from man himself. The latter gives his ethics a distinctly mystical twist, as it is contemplation, openness towards the Word of God and the final surrender to Him, which

---

17 See the older work BELKIN, Philo.

enables man to see his true nature and to have faith in his own destiny, being that of a divine soul, whose realm belongs to God. The goal of Philo's ethics, therefore, seems to be the return of the soul to its original bodiless and transcendent condition.

It is not clear, where to situate the ethics of Flavius Josephus (ca. 37/38–100 C.E.). According to his own account, he had the background of a Sadducee, but by choice had become a member of the party of the Pharisees. In his youth he had stayed with the Essenes, whereas before and during the First Jewish War against Rome (66–70 C.E.) he was the leader of a resistance movement in Galilee and closely related to the Zealots and *Sicarii*, but at the end of that war he would turn to the Romans, where he would stay until his death. With such a *Vita* the right label for his ethics seems to be that of an opportunist. And still, his Jewish War contains many theological reflections and questions about responsibility and Jewish suffering, whereas the Antiquities contain elements of morality and Jewish rights.

From the perspective of the conclusions he reaches at the end of his life, Josephus argues that it is best to accept the fate bestowed by God, even if this means the victory of Rome, the loss of a Jewish state and the destruction of Jerusalem and the Temple. Those, who have not only resisted this fate, but have also actively fought against Rome, are the revolutionaries, the Zealots and the *Sicarii*, whom Josephus blames for almost everything, not the least for their violation of the Law of Moses and the desecration of the Temple.[18]

In this sense, the good resides with the Romans, as God is on their side, and evil and suffering is caused by the revolutionaries, who act against God's will and against fate and destiny, as Josephus often puts it. Behind Josephus' reflections lies the concept of Divine guidance, Divine providence as well as the language of Destiny, in which Hellenistic historiographers often expressed how God controls everything in history. At other times, he uses the language of prophecy applied by the historical authors and prophets of the Bible.

It is in his Antiquities that Josephus is more explicit about the practical side of the belief in Divine providence. In writing his history of the Jewish people, he emphasizes the importance of piety, courage, wisdom, humanity and other virtues, and shows this in great detail in the exemplary life of individual leaders and other central figures in Biblical history, such as that of Moses. At the same time, he can use selected Biblical stories to moralize against vices, such as

---

18 On the particular problem of suicide, which occupies an important role in Josephus' deliberations and speeches (cf. Masada), see the articles on Josephus in HANKOFF/EINSIEDLER, Suicide.

pride, greed, corruption, etc. By using these literary techniques Josephus follows a didactic purpose, for which he clearly had a Jewish audience in mind, whereas for the purpose of an apology of the Jewish rights in the context of the Roman Empire (see for his Against Apion) he may also have written for a non-Jewish audience.

3 Overarching Theological Themes

Let us now come to the five theological themes we have identified, in order to place the ethics in the Pseudepigrapha in particular and in Early Judaism in general in its broader context.

3.1 Torah and Wisdom

In a number of non-canonical Jewish writings, especially in the Wisdom literature from the Apocrypha and Pseudepigrapha, we find evidence that the Torah is philosophically equated with the Greek concept of Wisdom and that divine teaching is identified with the law of nature or of the cosmos. In both cases, Torah/Wisdom functions as the foundation of all of the laws of society and consists of many moral teachings for humanity. Furthermore, in connection with the philosophical concept of *sophia*, we find the frequent employment of practical wisdom, specifically in the form of practical wisdom sayings, *sententiae* or *gnomoi*, most notably narrated within the framework of the pedagogical teachings of parents to their children or in general of an older generation to a newer one. Moreover, it is also repeatedly stated that it is never enough to simply have knowledge of what is wise, but that one should also act wisely, that is to say, approach one's neighbour with mercy and righteousness. A popular example here is the employment of the Golden Rule, as it best exemplifies the philosophical equation of Torah and Wisdom and at the same time is the *epitome* of practical wisdom. Ethics is thus embedded in a philosophical and theological system.[19]

---

[19] See for an introduction to the world of Biblical wisdom literature PERDUE, Wisdom.

3.2 Divine Revelation and Intervention

For most Jews in antiquity it was unquestionably true that all knowledge comes from God and that revelation is therefore divine. However, that God would still actively intervene in history was a view held mostly by the Prophets and their followers; for the apocalyptic thinkers and in a way also for the Essene community there existed a second power in heaven, which was capable of influencing mankind in a negative way: God's Adversary together with his helpers, the fallen angels. Although few doubted that God would prevail in the end, it was indeed only at the end that God would intervene through a Messiah. Until then, humanity would be mostly the victim of a cosmic battle, a war between good and evil (either personified or seen as abstract powers): a clash between God and his angels and the fallen angels and their leaders.

Although there was some room for human action and responsibility within this battle, the course of history was in principal pre-determined, namely as a sequence of good and bad periods heading towards a catastrophic climax. Even in the end, God would not intervene directly, but send an Anointed or Messiah together with a host of angels to speak and execute the final judgment.

With this concept in mind, human responsibility is by nature limited and ethical teaching consists mainly of a call to follow the laws of the course of history and of the cosmos. Within the micro-cosmos of the individual's place in the family, clan, or smaller society, various wisdom sayings and collections of teaching that had been growing throughout history and that had come from the whole of the Ancient Near Eastern cultural environment to enter Judaism during its post-exilic period as Wisdom theology, would give someone meaning and direction in life. The authors of the apocalyptic writings would see man's ethics being limited in time and subject: they therefore developed an interim ethics for a minority.[20]

3.3 The Origin of Evil and How to Deal with It

Human responsibility, the need to act morally wise, and the necessity of developing moral teaching begins with accepting that there is at least some space for human action. This space depends on the answers given to the question on the

---

[20] As for one aspect of the much wider question of the "religion" or "theology" of Early Judaism and its various branches, that follows from the belief in divine revelation and intervention, see NICKELSBURG, Resurrection.

origin of evil and death and whether and how to deal with it.[21] The Prophets of Israel considered the wicked human heart to be the origin of evil, and without interruption called people to return to the moral teaching of the God of Abraham, Isaac, and Jacob. However, in the Persian and Hellenistic period, the apocalyptic authors, beginning with those of the early parts of 1 Enoch and then continuing with those of 4 Ezra and 2 Baruch, mostly blamed the fallen angels for having brought about evil and death on earth and divided mankind into two groups: those under influence of these fallen angels, who were acting accordingly in a wicked manner, and those under the influence of the angels of God acting righteously. Wise was the one who had the knowledge of where mankind came from and belonged to and acted accordingly righteous, wicked was the one, who had no knowledge of his or her origin and acted like a marionette in the hands of the evil powers. In all of this, the possibility of human action was seen as principally limited due to a lack of own responsibility.

During the Hellenistic period, under the influence of both Stoic philosophy and apocalyptic thinking, the various Jewish groups in society (especially after the Maccabean revolt of 164 B.C.E.) were divided on questions of the interaction of fate and human responsibility. As Flavius Josephus later reports, the Sadducees thought everything to be dependent on fate and left no room for human action. As they also did not believe in a life after death, a novel belief since the second century B.C.E., their maxim was to enjoy life as long as possible, as there was nothing one could do to change one's fate.

Contrary to the Sadducees, the Essenes and Pharisees believed in the possibility of different degrees of interaction between fate and one's own action and responsibility, with the Pharisees giving somewhat more room to free will and independent human action than the Essenes. For the latter, it was important that one could know one's fate by studying Scripture and reading it through the lens of their eschatological and apocalyptic worldview: there was a cosmic battle going on between the good and evil angels, who were able to influence humankind in both directions. For the Pharisees, more than for the Essenes, it was more important to develop a strategy for making the best of one's place in society and acting politically prudent.

For both the Essenes and the Pharisees it was clear that one can decide which direction to take by acting either foolishly or wisely, wickedly or righteously. Knowledge of one's fate and one's destiny and teaching the right kind of action were therefore of the utmost importance. Again, for the Pharisees there was more room for human acting than for the Essenes, who believed that,

---

[21] See as introduction to the problem the texts quoted in LARRIMORE, Problem.

through predestination, every man had a given portion of good and evil parts in him, and it was difficult, though not impossible, to change one's course in life.

Therefore, the Pharisees were best prepared to develop a more advanced ethics and moral teaching for society at large, which they were also able to adjust to the needs of an ever changing society and politics by constantly updating their interpretation and adaptation of the Mosaic Law. It was the Pharisees, then, who laid the foundations of the Oral Torah and later rabbinic Judaism, whereas the Essenes developed only a group ethic with an emphasis on inner-social values, and the Sadducees produced an ethic, if at all, that served only themselves and was meant to allow their own party to survive as best as possible.

3.4 Human Responsibility and Society

The idea of human responsibility, at least for the world of Ancient Israel, goes back to the authors of the books of Moses and the Prophets and especially their Deuteronomistic editors during and after the Babylonian exile. Ezra and Nehemiah would renew and implement this concept in post-exilic Jewish society and base every moral teaching on the Laws of Moses. The authors of 1 Enoch would question this idea of human responsibility and point to the fallen angels as the cause of all evil, until, much later, the Maccabees, supported by the authors of the Book of Daniel, would take a reverse turn, and again stress the need for human action in order to defend divine teachings and especially the freedom to live according to one's own religion.

Thus, between the fifth/fourth century B.C.E. and the Maccabean revolt in 164 B.C.E. as well as during the following period of the independent Jewish state ruled by the Hasmoneans until the coming of the Romans and the Herodian rule at the end of the first century B.C.E., the ethical values of Judaism in the Persian and Hellenistic period developed from a Prophetic acceptance through a post-Prophetic and apocalyptically inspired denial of human responsibility to a more balanced approach between the need for human action, a call for religious freedom, and the fight for what by then would be called "Judaismos," a set of Jewish values simply called the traditions of the ancestors and, as such, consisting of the essence of Mosaic teachings. From then on, man's principle obligation in society was to defend these traditions against anyone endangering them, whether from the outside or the inside. In other words, ethics often functioned to define and defend Jewish identity with or against the definitions of other groups within Jewish society.

3.5 The Love Command and the Golden Rule

The concept of love in the Old Testament (אהב ἀγαπάω; God's love, love for God, love for others, erotic love) is distinct from that of Greek thought (ἐρᾶν, φιλεῖν, ἀγαπᾶν; passionate love, love of people/friends, honor, etc.). However, in Hellenistic Judaism, efforts were made to combine the two, in that it stresses the love of or for God and the love for others both as the faithful fulfillment of the biblical commandments, even if this required suffering and unconditional martyrdom, as human love is the ultimate response to God's love.[22]

Furthermore, the importance of the commandment to love one's neighbour, often linked with philanthropy, is stressed again and again and often combined with or understood as an example of the originally Greek Golden Rule. Finally, authors like Philo underline the importance of both commandments for the well-being of humanity. Here, it should also be noted that wisdom as such or God's teaching can be the object of love. However, *eros* is typically downplayed as being important only to the "unchaste" Greeks.

Theologically, the ethical maxim of either the Love Command or the Golden Rule or both can be founded on three arguments: 1) equality (because everyone as God's creature is equal, everyone, even the slave, deserves the same treatment and respect); 2) the importance of doing good and being merciful (this is especially expected from those in a higher position); and 3) the call for *Imitatio Dei* (as God is good and does good, one should follow this).

In the later rabbinic literature, the first and third aspect are also found to be based on the biblical teaching that humanity is created in the image of God (and for that reason everyone is equal) and that one should be holy, because God is holy (Lev 17–26; t. Sanh. 9:11; Sifra, Kedoshim 4:12; Gen. Rab. 24:7), whereas the second aspect becomes a cornerstone of rabbinic ethics (see especially Talmud Sotah 14a). Both rabbinic Judaism and early Christianity would employ all three reasons to stress the importance of the commandments to love God and the neighbour at the same time.

---

[22] See KLAUCK, Love, 144–156; MALAMAT, Neighbor, 111–117; OEGEMA, Neighbour, 77–86.

4 Conclusion

In conclusion, the relation of ethics in the early Jewish writings is as diverse as the non-canonical Jewish writings are themselves. They all witness a many-sided Early Judaism, in which many groups with sometimes very differing opinions existed next to each other. The hermeneutical background and practical application of ethics in their writings not only expresses the vividness of their dialogue between themselves and with society at large but also the diversity of Torah interpretation in the Second Temple period. In most if not all cases ethics functions within the realm of the "religion" or "theology" of Early Judaism and its many branches and is interconnected with the various conceptions of Torah as teaching and/or derived from the theological concepts: Torah, wisdom, divine revelation, divine intervention, evil, human responsibility, and love.

Bibliography

ADAMOPOULO, Themistocles A., Endurance, Greek and Early Christian. The Moral Transformation of the Greek Idea of Endurance, from the Homeric Battlefield to the Apostle Paul, Dissertation Brown University, Providence, Rhode Island 1996.

BAUCKHAM, Richard J., The Conflict of Justice and Mercy. Attitudes to the Damned in Apocalyptic Literature, in: Apocrypha 1 (1990) 181–196.

BELKIN, Samuel, Philo and the Oral Law. The Philonic Interpretation of Biblical Law in Relation to the Palestinian Halakah, Cambridge, Massachusetts 1940 (reprint New York 1968).

BLOCH, Abraham P., A Book of Jewish Ethical Concepts. Biblical and Postbiblical, New York 1984.

BURKES, Shannon, Wisdom and Law. Choosing Life in Ben Sira and Baruch, in: JSJ 30 (1999) 253–276.

CHARLESWORTH, James H. (Hg.), The Old Testament Pseudepigrapha, 2 vols., Garden City, New York 1983-1985.

CHATELION COUNET, Patrick, Pseudepigraphy and the Petrine School. Spirit and Tradition in 1 and 2 Peter and Jude, University of Pretoria, 2007.

COLLINS, John J., Ben Sira's Ethics, in: Idem, Jewish Wisdom in the Hellenistic Age, Edinburgh 1997, 62–79.

COLLINS, John J., Jewish Ethics in Hellenistic Dress. The Sentences of Pseudo-Phocylides, in: Idem, Jewish Wisdom in the Hellenistic Age, Edinburgh 1997, 158–177.

CRONBACH, Abraham, The Social Ideals of the Apocrypha and Pseudepigrapha, in: HUCA 18 (1944) 119–156.

DE JONGE, Marinus, The Two Great Commandments in the Testaments of the Twelve Patriarchs, in: NovT 44/4 (2002) 371–392.

DITOMMASO, Lorenzo, A Bibliography of Pseudepigrapha Research, 1850–1999, Sheffield 2001.

GAMMIE, John G., Spatial and Ethical Dualism in Jewish Wisdom and Apocalyptic Literature, in: JBL 93 (1974) 356–385.
GARCÍA MARTÍNEZ, Florentino/POPOVIĆ, Mladen, Defining Identities. We, You, and the Other in the Dead Sea Scrolls. Proceedings of the Fifth Meeting of the IOQS in Groningen, Leiden/Boston, Massachusetts 2008.
GRAY, Patrick, Points and Lines. Thematic Parallelism in the Letter of James and the Testament of Job, in: NTS 50/3 (2004) 406–424.
HANKOFF, Leon D./EINSIEDLER, Bernice, Suicide. Theory and Clinical Aspects, Littleton, Massachusetts 1979.
HARRELSON, Walter, The Significance of 'Last Words' for Intertestamental Ethics, in: Crenshaw, James L./Willis, John T. (Hg.), Essays in Old Testament Ethics. J. Philip Hyatt in Memoriam, New York 1974, 203–214.
HERFORD, Robert Travers, Talmud and Apocrypha. A Comparative Study of the Jewish Ethical Teaching in the Rabbinical and Non-Rabbinical Sources in the Early Centuries, New York 1971.
KEE, Howard C., Models of Community in the Literature of Postexilic Judaism, in: Idem (Hg.), Who Are the People of God? Early Christian Models of Community, New Haven, Connecticut 1995, 17–54.
KENWORTHY, Alexander W., The Nature and Authority of Old Testament Wisdom Family Ethics. With Special Reference to Proverbs and Sirach, Dissertation University of Melbourne, Melbourne 1974.
KLAUCK, Hans-Josef, Brotherly Love In Plutarch and in 4 Maccabees, in: Balch, David L./Ferguson, Everett/Meeks, Wayne A. (Hg.), Greeks, Romans, and Christians. Essays in Honor of Abraham J. Malherbe, Minneapolis, Minnesota 1990, 144–156.
LARRIMORE, Mark J., The Problem of Evil. A Reader, Oxford/Malden, Massachusetts 2001.
LEWIS, John James, The Ethics of Judaism in the Hellenistic Period, from the Apocrypha and the Pseudepigrapha of the Old Testament, Dissertation University of London, London 1958.
MALAMAT, Abraham, You Shall Love Your Neighbor as Yourself. A Case of Misinterpretation?, in: Blum, Erhard/Macholz, Christian/Stegemann, Ekkehard W. (Hg.), Die Hebräische Bibel und ihre zweifache Nachgeschichte. Festschrift für Rolf Rendtorff, Neukirchen-Vluyn 1990, 111–117.
MALDWYN HUGHES, Henry, The Ethics of Jewish Apocryphal Literature, London 1909.
MARGUERAT, Daniel, La nouvelle eschatology dans les bas-judaïsme palestinien et dans l'evangile selon Matthieu. Une approche de la relation entre l'eschatologie et l'ethique, Dissertation Universität Lausanne, Lausanne 1975.
MASTON, Thomas B., Biblical Ethics. A Guide to the Ethical Message of the Scriptures from Genesis through Revelation, Cleveland, Ohio 1967.
MERGUET, Victor Karl Hermann, Die Glaubens- und Sittenlehre des Buches Jesus Sirach, Teil 1 (Programm des Königlichen Friedrichs-Collegiums zu Königsberg in Preussen), Königsberg 1874.
NICKELSBURG, George W. E., Resurrection, Immortality, and Eternal Life in Intertestamental Judaism and Early Christianity, Cambridge, Massachusetts 2006.
OEGEMA, Gerbern S., Love Your Neighbour as Yourself. Jesuanic or Mosaic?, in: BN 116 (2003) 77–86.
OEGEMA, Gerbern S., Non-Canonical Writings and Biblical Theology, in: Henderson, Ian H./Oegema, Gerbern S. (Hg.), The Changing Face of Judaism. Christianity and Other Religions

in Greco-Roman Antiquity (Studien zu den Jüdischen Schriften aus hellenistisch-römischer Zeit 2), Gütersloh 2006, 491–512.

OEGEMA, Gerbern S., Ethics in the Noncanonical Jewish Writings, in: New Interpreter's Dictionary of the Bible, Vol. 2, Nashville, Tennessee 2007, 321–328.

OEGEMA, Gerbern S., Early Judaism and Modern Culture. Essays on Early Jewish Literature and Theology, Grand Rapids, Michigan 2011.

PERDUE, Leo G., Wisdom Literature. A Theological History, Louisville, Kentucky 2007.

PERRY, Anthony, God's Twilight Zone. Wisdom in the Hebrew Bible, Peabody, Massachusetts 2008.

SCHNABEL, Eckhard J., Law and Wisdom from Ben Sira to Paul. A Tradition Historical Enquiry into the Relation of Law, Wisdom, and Ethics (WUNT II/16), Tübingen 1985.

SCHÜRER, Emil, The History of the Jewish People in the Age of Jesus Christ, 3 vols., Edinburgh 1973–1987.

SLINGERLAND, H. Dixon, The Nature of Nomos (Law) within the Testaments of the Twelve Patriarchs, in: JBL 105/1 (1986) 39–48.

STROUMSA, Guy G./STANTON, Graham N. (Hg.), Tolerance and Intolerance in Early Judaism and Christianity, Cambridge/New York 2008.

XERAVITS, Géza G./ZSENGELLÉR, József, The Books of the Maccabees. History, Theology, Ideology. Papers of the Second International Conference on the Deuteronomical Books, Pápa, Hungary, 9–11 June 2005, Leiden/Boston, Massachusetts 2007.

ZERBE, Gordon M., Non-Retaliation in Early Jewish and New Testament Texts. Ethical Themes in Social Contexts (JSPSup 13), Leiden 1993.

Ulrike Mittmann
Das Bild des Menschen im Wandel – Die Rezeption von Genesis 1–3 in Sapientia Salomonis 1 und 2

1 Einführung

Die Frage nach dem Wesen des Bösen gehört zu den großen Menschheitsfragen. Was hat es auf sich mit der Macht der Destruktion, mit der Macht, die den Menschen immer wieder zwingt, das zu zerstören, was sein Leben ausmacht, was ihn selbst ausmacht, was menschliches Miteinander ermöglicht? Die Frage nach dem Wesen des Bösen ist die zentrale Menschheitsfrage, weil sie den Menschen selbst fraglich macht, ihn in Frage stellt. Sie ist daher die Frage auch nach dem Wesen des Menschen, nach seiner inneren Verfasstheit im Ganzen des irdischen Lebens. Ja, sie ist die anthropologische Kernfrage, die auch dort nach Antwort drängt, wo das Denken keinen transzendenten Bezugspunkt sucht. Wo aber der Mensch, wenn er nach sich selber fragt, von Gott her denkt und den Gottesbezug seines Daseins als gegeben voraussetzt, unternimmt er den Versuch, das Wesen des Bösen zu ergründen, automatisch von der Erkenntnis her, dass durch das Böse die Gottesgemeinschaft gefährdet und zerstört wird.

Im alttestamentlich-jüdischen Schrifttum ist die Gefährdung der Beziehung des Menschen zu Gott im Bannkreis des Bösen das anthropologische Thema schlechthin. Es wird behandelt als ein sowohl individuelles als auch universelles Problem, dessen geschichtswirksame Dynamik im Kontext der Erwählung Israels, und das heißt: im Kontext nationaler Identität, zur Sprache kommt. Dass dabei das Böse Machtcharakter hat, also ein selbstwirksames Seinsphänomen ist, zeigt schon die Tatsache, dass es vor allem in den späteren Schichten des Alten Testaments personifiziert erscheint und in seinem gottfeindlichen Wirken als Schlangen- bzw. Drachenwesen (Hi 7,12; 26,12–13; Jes 27,1; 51,9; Ez 29,3; zu Leviathan vgl. Hi 3,8; 40,25; Ps 74,14; Jes 27,1) mit Sitz im Meer dargestellt wird[1] oder in der Figur Satans, griech. σατανᾶς oder διάβολος (2Sam 19,23; 1Chr 21,1; Hi 1,6–9.12; 2,1–7; Sach 3,1–2), irdischen Handlungsspielraum erhält. Die Personifizierung des Bösen bedeutet aber nicht *per se*, dass es eine Existenz im individuellen Sinne hätte. Individualisierung – die kategorial streng von der Personifizierung

---

1 Zu Rahab vgl. Hi 26,12; Jes 51,9; Ps 87,4; 89,11, zu Behemot Hi 40,15–24; äthHen 59,8.

zu unterscheiden ist – findet sich vornehmlich in dualistischen oder polytheistischen Denksystemen, in welchen Gott und Gegengott oder die Götter allgemein ein von anderen Mächten unabhängiges Sein und uneingeschränkte Wirkmächtigkeit besitzen. Dagegen ist im Rahmen des jüdisch-christlichen Monotheismus die Personifizierung der Wirkmacht des Bösen, aber auch die Personifizierung des irdischen Offenbarwerdens Gottes in Gestalt der Weisheit, ein Mittel reflexiver Abstraktion zur Konkretisierung theologischer Erkenntnisse, die dem Bereich der sinnlichen Anschauung entnommen sind.[2] Wenn aber das Böse nicht individuell existiert, wie dann? Dann bleibt nur die Möglichkeit, das Böse anthropologisch oder kosmologisch zu verankern, d.h. es als Phänomen des Menschseins zu begreifen und als Dimension der Schöpfung. Und in der Tat ist dies, wie gleich zu zeigen ist, das genuin biblische Denkmodell. Mit der Einordnung des Bösen in das Schöpfungsganze aber endet das Fragen nicht, sondern beginnt es eigentlich erst. Denn nun wird die Frage nach dem Menschen zur Frage nach Gott: Wie verträgt sich, wenn das Böse als ein der Schöpfung inhärentes Phänomen das Menschsein des Menschen qualifiziert, seine schiere Existenz mit dem Gedanken an einen alles durchwaltenden Gott? Wie verträgt es sich mit dem Gedanken an Gottes Souveränität? Und wie verträgt es sich mit dem Gedanken an den allein zum Guten wirkenden Gott?

Es sind diese Fragen, die aller jüdisch-christlichen anthropologischen Reflexion zugrunde liegen. Die Antwort auf die Frage nach dem Wesen des Bösen hängt ab vom Bild des Menschen in Korrelation zum monotheistischen Gottesbild, das in der Antike in diametralem Gegensatz zum griechisch-römischen und zum ägyptischen Gottes- bzw. Götterglauben steht. Gleichzeitig steht in hellenistischer Zeit das Judentum unter dem Einfluss der griechisch-römischen Kultur und zeigt sich gerade auch dort von den Geistesströmungen seiner Umwelt geprägt, wo es sie abzuwehren versucht. Es ist daher höchst aufschlussreich, zu beobachten, wie im antiken Judentum unter der unveränderten Prämisse der Einheit und Einzigkeit des Gottes Israels sich in dem Moment die Antwort auf das Wesen des Bösen verändert, in welchem das Menschenbild unter dem Einfluss fremder Kulturen erhebliche Modifikationen erfährt.

Die Sapientia Salomonis eignet sich ganz besonders als Anschauungsbeispiel für einen anthropologischen Paradigmenwechsel in bestimmten Kreisen

---

2 Ausführlich zur Personifizierung der Weisheit MITTMANN-RICHERT, Heil, 14–15 mit Anm. 41; zur Personifizierung des Bösen DIES., Dämonen, 499.

des hellenistischen Judentums, weil sie multikulturell verankert ist. Als eine jüdische Weisheitsschrift alexandrinischer Herkunft[3] gründet sie in der älteren Weisheit Israels, transformiert dieselbe aber im multikulturellen Kontext der ägyptischen Diaspora in spezifischer Weise. Dabei lässt schon der weisheitliche Charakter der Schrift vermuten, dass ihr Autor bzw. der Trägerkreis entsprechender Traditionen sich bewusst mit der „Weisheit" der sie umgebenden Völker auseinandersetzte, und zwar sowohl mit den griechisch-philosophischen Strömungen der Zeit als auch mit der Weisheit Ägyptens, die ebenfalls hoch in Blüte stand.[4]

Die Veränderungen lassen sich am besten an denjenigen Textstellen zeigen, an welchen explizit auf die alten Überlieferungen zurückgegriffen wird, darunter an erster Stelle auf den anthropologischen Schlüsseltext Gen 3, die Erzählung vom sogenannten Sündenfall. Sein auch für spätere Generationen programmatischer Charakter gründet in der Tatsache, dass er die Frage nach dem Bösen im Schöpfungskontext stellt (Gen 1–2) und die Beziehung des Menschen zu dem, der ihn schuf, aus der Perspektive der von Anfang an gegebenen Gebrochenheit analysiert.

2 Der Bezug auf Gen 3: Textbefund

Die Anspielung auf Gen 3 findet sich in Sap 2,21–24. Sie bildet innerhalb des Sap 1,1–6,21 umfassenden großen ersten Hauptteils der Schrift den Abschluss des Einleitungsteils, der als Ermahnung zu einem Leben in Gerechtigkeit beginnt (Sap 1,1–15) und das Gegenbild eines in Gottesfeindschaft geführten Lebens als dramatischen Bühnenakt[5] in zwei Aufzügen inszeniert (Sap 1,16–2,22). Im ersten stellen sich die Gottesleugner persönlich vor und erheben den rein immanent ori-

---

3 Aus der Fülle an Literatur zur Sapientia Salomonis seien hier nur einige ausgewählte Werke genannt: WINSTON, Wisdom, 3–69; ENGEL, Buch der Weisheit, 13–36; HÜBNER, Weisheit Salomos, 13–22; dort auch zur Diskussion der Einleitungsfragen. Zum geistesgeschichtlichen Hintergrund speziell s. KEPPER, Hellenistische Bildung; NEHER, Wesen. Text: ZIEGLER, Sapientia.
4 Die systematische Erschließung der ägyptischen Literatur aus hellenistischer Zeit, speziell der weisheitlich-apokalyptischen Literatur, gehört zu den jüngeren Forschungszweigen der Ägyptologie. Wegweisend sind die Studien und Texteditionen von Quack, von denen hier nur eine Auswahl genannt werden kann: QUACK, Einführung III; DERS., Ein neuer ägyptischer Weisheitstext; DERS., Chronologie der demotischen Weisheitsliteratur; DERS., Ein neuer prophetischer Text; QUACK/HOFFMANN, Anthologie.
5 Vgl. SCHMITT, Wende, 20–40, zu den dramatischen Elementen in Sap 1,16–6,21.

entierten, autonomen Daseinsvollzug zum Ideal, ja, proklamieren ihn als allgemein gültige Wahrheit (Sap 1,16–2,9); im zweiten wird der Unglaube zur Tat in der Verfolgung und Tötung des Gerechten und im Spott über seine vermeintliche Rettungslosigkeit und Unfähigkeit, die Existenz Gottes durch die Wendung seines Schicksals zu beweisen (Sap 2,10–20).[6] Die Irrigkeit dieser rein diesseitig argumentierenden Abwehr des Glaubens an den Gott Israels (Sap 2,21–22) erweist die Abschlusssentenz Sap 2,23–24, in welcher Leiden und Tod des Gerechten in einen protologisch-eschatologischen Gesamtkontext gestellt und die Unvergänglichkeit des geschöpflichen Lebens jenseits der irdischen Gegebenheiten festgehalten wird. Dabei nimmt der Verfasser in äußerster Verknappung Bezug auf die Schöpfungserzählung Gen 1–3, und zwar unter dem Doppelaspekt der Gottebenbildlichkeit des Menschen nach Gen 1,26–27 und seiner irdischen Todverfallenheit nach Gen 3,19:

[23] ὅτι ὁ θεὸς ἔκτισεν τὸν ἄνθρωπον ἐπ' ἀφθαρσίᾳ
καὶ εἰκόνα τῆς ἰδίας ἀϊδιότητος[7] ἐποίησεν αὐτόν·
[24] φθόνῳ δὲ διαβόλου θάνατος εἰσῆλθεν εἰς τὸν κόσμον,
πειράζουσιν δὲ αὐτὸν οἱ τῆς ἐκείνου μερίδος ὄντες.

[23] Gott hat den Menschen zur Unvergänglichkeit erschaffen
und hat ihn zum Ebenbild seiner eigenen Ewigkeit gemacht.
[24] Aber durch den Neid des Teufels kam der Tod in die Welt.
Es erleiden ihn aber diejenigen, die zu seinem Anteil gehören.

Auffällig ist im Blick auf den Menschen, der zunächst von seiner schöpfungsgemäßen Bestimmung her ganz allgemein betrachtet wird, die Unterscheidung zweier Seinsweisen mit eschatologisch weitreichenden Implikationen: der Existenz in Bindung an Gott und der Existenz in Bindung an den Teufel. Die unterschiedlichen Relationen implizieren im eschatologischen Horizont den Zerfall der Menschheit in zwei Gruppen, bedeuten also für den im Machtbereich des Teufels lebenden Teil den Verlust des ewigen Lebens. Damit bekommt der Tod, θάνατος (V. 24), als ein Phänomen, das unmittelbar an die Wirksamkeit des Bösen in der Welt gekoppelt wird, eine das Irdische transzendierende Bedeutung: Er ist nicht das Ende des irdischen Lebens, sondern der Ausschluss vom ewigen

---

6 S. auch die Strukturanalyse von SCHMITT, Komposition, 403–408.
7 Gegen HÜBNER, Weisheit Salomos, 47, ἀϊδιότητος als *lectio difficilior* gegenüber der Lesart ἰδιότητος; mit GEORGI, Weisheit Salomos, 409 Anm. 23 c). Hinzuweisen ist auch auf den Parallelismus der Begriffe „Unvergänglichkeit" und „Ewigkeit". Vgl. auch Sap 7,26, wo die Weisheit als εἰκὼν τῆς ἀγαθότητος αὐτοῦ betitelt wird.

Leben Gottes, das dem Mensch als Geschöpf Gottes eigentlich bestimmt ist.[8] Durch die Eschatologisierung des rezipierten Textes Gen 1–3 verschieben sich ganz offensichtlich die anthropologischen Nuancen der Ursprungserzählung. Die Akzentverschiebungen betreffen dabei nicht allein die Todesvorstellung, sondern auch und eigentlich zuerst das Bild des Bösen als einer vom Menschen bezwingbaren Macht, d.h. sie betreffen, auch wenn der Begriff selbst im vorliegenden Textausschnitt nicht genannt wird, das Sündenverständnis. Der Autor der Weisheitsschrift definiert also gegenüber seinem Referenztext die Bedingungen menschlich-irdischer Existenz im Ganzen neu und entwirft ein Bild vom Menschen, das in wesentlichen Aspekten im Gegensatz zu dem seiner Vorlage steht.

Die Frage, die sich angesichts dieser Modifikation des Menschenbildes von Gen 1–3 stellt, ist die nach den geistigen Einflüssen, die auf den in Ägypten beheimateten Verfasser oder Trägerkreis der Weisheitsschrift einwirkten. Sie lassen sich allerdings nur identifizieren, wenn das anthropologische Profil von Gen 3 klar vor Augen steht und wenn erkannt ist, welche Vorstellung die biblische Schöpfungserzählung von der Existenz und Wirkweise des Bösen hat. Wer allerdings bei einem Text aus hellenistischer Zeit den Blick zurück richtet und hinsichtlich der rezeptionsgeschichtlichen Prozesse nach der Entwicklung des Menschenbildes bzw. nach der Diversität von Menschenbildern fragt, kann dies nur im Bewusstsein der hermeneutischen Problematik tun, die dort aufbricht, wo die Auslegung von Texten in der Forschung strittig ist. Dies betrifft die sogenannte Sündenfallerzählung Gen 3 in besonderem Maße, da aufgrund ihrer Verankerung im altorientalischen Mythos das Verhältnis von Narration und Abstraktion und daher ihr Skopus ganz unterschiedlich bestimmt werden. Die im folgenden Exkurs gebotene Deutung stellt den Versuch dar, die anthropologische Dimension des Textes jenseits der bildlichen Motivik zu erfassen und die Frage nach dem Bösen und dem Tod in einer Systematisierung der Aspekte zu beantworten.[9]

---

8 Zu ἀφθαρσία vgl. auch Sap 12,1; 18,4.
9 Zum Text und seiner Auslegung s. auch im vorliegenden Sammelband den Beitrag von EGO.

Exkurs: Das Menschenbild der sogenannten Sündenfallgeschichte Gen 3

Der hier in aller Kürze gebotenen Deutung[10] liegt die Überzeugung zugrunde, dass der Text in anthropologischer Sicht kein Geschehen vor Augen stellt, sondern eine allgemeingültige Erkenntnis formuliert. Es geht nicht um einen „Unglücksfall", durch welchen den Menschen in kausaler Ereignisfolge ein Schicksal ereilt, das ihm von Gott nicht zugedacht war, sondern um menschliche Selbsterkenntnis in einem alle Aspekte des Seins umfassenden Sinne.[11] Es geht um den Grundkonflikt der menschlichen Existenz *coram Deo*, wie er aus der Spannung von Selbstbezug und Gottesbezug resultiert. Im Zentrum steht die Frage nach dem Bösen und dem Tod als Signum irdisch-geschöpflichen Lebens. Da allerdings die zur allgemeinen Wahrheit erhobene menschliche Selbsterkenntnis narrativ vermittelt und als Ereignisfolge präsentiert wird, muss zunächst dennoch nach dem Geschehensverlauf gefragt werden. Erst wenn die gegenläufige Dynamik des Geschehens erfasst ist, treten die spezifischen Aspekte des Menschenbildes zutage, das der szenischen Ausgestaltung zugrunde liegt.

Der allgemeingültige Charakter der Erzählung drückt sich in der Kennzeichnung der Handlung als Urgeschehen aus: Der Mensch – als Mann und Frau: Adam und Eva – lebt im Paradies, in welchem das Leben keinerlei Beschränkungen unterliegt als der einen (Gen 2,16–17): „Du darfst essen von allen Bäumen im Garten, aber von dem Baum der Erkenntnis des Guten und Bösen sollst du nicht essen, denn an dem Tag, da du von ihm isst, musst du des Todes sterben." Der Baum der Erkenntnis des Guten und Bösen ist der Dreh- und Angelpunkt der Erzählung. Das heißt anthropologisch gesprochen: Sie handelt von der Selbsterkenntnis des Menschen, die hier als Wissen um dasjenige definiert wird, was innerhalb der paradiesischen Gottunmittelbarkeit keinen Platz hat, nämlich das

---

10 Der Text wird im Folgenden strikt synchron ausgelegt in Anlehnung an die redaktionsgeschichtlichen Überlegungen von BLUM, Gottesunmittelbarkeit. Zu neueren redaktionsgeschichtlichen Analysen mit z. T. erheblich divergierenden Ergebnissen zu Wachstum und Komposition der Paradieserzählung s. den Überblick ebd., 27. Da die Auslegung auch als Beitrag zur alttestamentlichen Exegese gedacht ist, wird ihr der masoretische Text zugrundegelegt. Die anthropologischen Ergebnisse sind aber durchgehend auf den nur wenig abweichenden Text der LXX übertragbar, auf welchen sich die Sapientia Salomonis beziehen dürfte.
11 Dies bedeutet gegenüber vielen Deutungen, wie sie in den Kommentaren geboten werden, eine grundsätzlich andere Sicht auf den Stoff, entspricht aber dem vielfältig im biblischen und frühjüdischen Schrifttum geübten Brauch, abstrakte Sachverhalte narrativ zu fassen. Zur rein erzählerisch im Sinne des Mythos verfahrenden Interpretation vgl. etwa MCKEOWN, Genesis, 34–39 und zusammenfassend 270–272.

Böse. Es geht, da der Mensch am Anfang als ein *Nicht*wissender vorgestellt wird, um die drängende Frage, ob es dieser Selbst-Bewusstheit überhaupt bedarf. Die Antwort scheint „nein" zu lauten, da die Erkenntnis des Guten und des Bösen von Gott unter Strafe gestellt und mit dem Tod belegt wird. An dieser Stelle setzt in Gen 3 mit dem Auftreten der Schlange die eigentliche Handlung ein. Die Schlange ist die Verkörperung des Bösen,[12] dessen Erkenntnis Gott unter Strafe gestellt hatte. Die Schlange beschwichtigt den Menschen mit der Zusage, er werde keineswegs des Todes sterben, sondern zum Sehen gelangen und in der Erkenntnis des Guten und Bösen sein wie Gott (Gen 3,4–5). Diese Einflüsterung führt den Menschen in den Konflikt, der am Ende als der Grundkonflikt seines irdischen Lebens erkennbar wird. Der Konflikt verdichtet sich in dem Wunsch, Gott gleich zu sein, zu „sein wie Gott". Und in der Tat scheint sich sein Wunsch zu erfüllen und die Schlange Recht zu behalten. Denn als Adam und Eva der Versuchung erliegen und vom Baum der Erkenntnis essen, erleiden sie nicht den jähen Tod, sondern erfahren die Öffnung ihrer Augen. Sie sehen, was vorher nur Gott sah. Die Erkenntnis aber, die sich in diesem Akt Bahn bricht, ist die Erkenntnis der eigenen Nacktheit (Gen 3,7.10). In der Nacktheit manifestiert sich die Geschöpflichkeit des Menschen, und da der Mensch seiner Geschöpflichkeit ansichtig wird, erkennt er, dass er mit demjenigen, mit dem er in paradiesischer Gemeinschaft lebt, nichts gemein hat; er erkennt, dass ein diametraler Unterschied besteht zwischen dem ewigen Gott und dem geschöpflichen Menschen.[13]

---

12 Gegen BRUEGGEMANN, Genesis, 41. Vgl. aber LEVIN, Das verlorene Paradies, 94: „Die Schlange ist ... so etwas wie das *alter ego* der Frau." Dass die Schlange ihrem Wesen nach nicht Tierisches, sondern Menschliches verkörpert, zeigt sich auch an ihrem Sprachvermögen, das Charakteristikum des Menschen, das ihn zum personalen Gegenüber Gottes macht und ihn aus der Tierwelt heraushebt.

13 Vgl. BLUM, Gottesunmittelbarkeit, 17, der die Paradieserzählung von „eine[r] elementaren Grundfrage" bestimmt sieht: der „Frage der Unterscheidung von Schöpfer und Geschöpf, von Gott und Mensch". S. auch ebd., 24–25. Vgl. auch HARTENSTEIN, „Und sie erkannten, dass sie nackt waren ...", 283, der die Nacktheit „als die Wahrnehmung der eigenen Niedrigkeit angesichts des als ‚hoch' erfahrenen Gottes" definiert (im Original z.T. kursiviert). Dass die Erkenntnis der Nacktheit auf das Erwachen der Sexualität ziele, wie häufig behauptet wird (s. z.B. VON RAD, Genesis, 71), ist wenig wahrscheinlich oder nur im Sinne aller mit der Geschöpflichkeit des Menschen verbundenen Aspekte. Da das „Sein wie Gott" unmittelbar konkret wird in der Erkenntnis der Nacktheit, kann diese Erkenntnis nur bedeuten, dass der Mensch erst jetzt sieht, wie er vor Gott dasteht: nackt und bloß, als Geschöpf vor seinem Schöpfer, in seiner Körperlichkeit ein Staubwesen. Das „Sein wie Gott" zielt nicht auf die Gleichheit der Existenzweise, sondern auf die Gleichheit der Erkenntnis. Ihr Inhalt aber ist die *Un*gleichheit von Gott und Mensch. Dementsprechend zielt auch die Scham, die nach Gen 2,25 noch kein Empfinden des Menschen angesichts seiner Nacktheit ist, nicht auf die sexuelle Selbstwahrnehmung des Menschen, sondern

Dass diese Erkenntnis als Erkenntnis von Gut und Böse klassifiziert ist, wird verständlich von der Reaktion des Menschen her. Denn die Erkenntnis der eigenen Nacktheit als Erkenntnis des durch die Geschöpflichkeit konstituierten Abstands zwischen Gott und Mensch veranlasst den Menschen zur *willentlichen* Trennung von Gott. Der Mensch kehrt dem den Rücken, von dem er sich seinem Wesen nach ohnehin unüberbrückbar getrennt sieht, und verbirgt sich vor Gottes Angesicht (Gen 3,8). Diese willentliche Abkehr des Geschöpfs von seinem Schöpfer aber ist das, was der Text als das Böse qualifiziert, die Ursünde des Menschen. Sie wird als Tragik des Menschseins begriffen, weil die in der Erkenntnis der Nacktheit durchbrechende Selbsterkenntnis des Menschen das Erwachen des Ich-Bewusstseins markiert.[14] Sie ist die unvermeidliche Ich-Wahrnehmung, Ich-Erkenntnis des Menschen und damit Wahrnehmung des autonomen Selbst, wie sie aus dem Person-Sein des Menschen im Gegenüber zu Gott, gleichzeitig in Unterschiedenheit zu Gott erwächst. Indem der Mensch sich als Ich-Wesen erkennt, erkennt er sich als ein in *Abgrenzung von Gott* existierendes Wesen. Das aus dieser Erkenntnis autonomer Existenz resultierende selbstbestimmte Handeln des Menschen wird dabei schon deshalb als ein Handeln unter der Macht des Bösen klassifiziert, weil der Mensch sich zum Souverän seines Lebens macht und damit Gott die Herrschaft über sein Leben aberkennt – in Furcht zwar vor dem, der ihm plötzlich als der ganz andere vor Augen steht, aber gerade deshalb mit dem unbezwingbaren Impetus, Gott den Rücken zu kehren, vor ihm wegzulaufen und nach neuen Möglichkeiten des Lebensvollzugs zu suchen. In Trennung von Gott zu leben, bedeutet nach biblischem Verständnis immer, sich außerhalb des Bereichs wahren Lebens zu begeben, bedeutet, in die Sphäre des Todes überzutreten. Es ist daher konsequent, dass der zum Ich-Bewusstsein gelangte und als Souverän seines Lebens handelnde Mensch aus dem Paradies, dem Bereich ungebrochenen Lebens bei und mit Gott, vertrieben wird. Der Mensch lebt sein Leben unter den Bedingungen seiner Geschöpflichkeit, das heißt: als Wesen, das der Macht des Bösen und des Todes ausgeliefert ist.

Während allerdings dieser Gedankenzusammenhang sich narrativ als eine Ereignisfolge präsentiert, die auf ein bestimmtes Ziel zuläuft, muss in der anthropologischen Auswertung das Ende zum Ausgangspunkt des Verständnisses gemacht werden. Nicht das Ich-Bewusstsein, zu dem der Mensch nach der Übertretung des göttlichen Gebots erwacht ist, fordert das Todesschicksal, sondern

---

meint das aus dem unüberbrückbaren Abstand resultierende Zuschanden-Werden des Menschen vor Gott. S. dazu die philologisch erhellenden Bemerkungen von HARTENSTEIN, ebd., 286–288.
14 Zum tragischen Impetus der Erzählung s. auch BLOCHER, Original Sin, 32.

das Bewusstsein, dem irdischen Tod unterworfen zu sein, konstituiert das Ich-Bewusstsein als das Bewusstsein menschlich-geschöpflicher Identität.[15] Der Mensch – das ist der Skopus der Erzählung – vermag sich im Angesicht Gottes erst in dem Augenblick als Ich zu erkennen, wo er in der Erkenntnis seines Geschaffenseins der Auflösung dieses Ich ansichtig wird, damit aber der Verfallenheit an das Böse. Ich-Erkenntnis ist nach Gen 3 Erkenntnis des Bösen als einer Macht, welcher der Mensch als Mensch unentrinnbar ausgeliefert ist. Da der Mensch kraft seiner Geschöpflichkeit als autonomes Wesen lebt, tritt die Selbstbestimmung des Menschen in Konkurrenz zu der Gott allein vorbehaltenen Lebensbestimmung. Diesem Mechanismus kann der Mensch nicht ausweichen. Und der biblische Mensch erfährt diesen Mechanismus als eine unselige, sein Gottesverhältnis zerstörende Macht. Wenn er diese Macht personifiziert, dann ist auch dies ein Mittel der Abstraktion. Die Sünde, unter welcher nach Gen 3 der Menschen steht, wird als Schlange verkörpert. Sie ist der Sache nach aber nichts anderes als der dem Menschen inhärente Mechanismus zur Selbstdestruktion.

Die Tatsache, dass die Geschöpflichkeit des Menschen einen Unheilszusammenhang konstituiert, ist allerdings nur die eine Seite des Urverhältnisses von Gott und Mensch. Ihr steht auf der anderen Seite die Erkenntnis gegenüber, dass Gott der Schöpfer des Menschen ist und dass daher alles, was den Menschen in seinem geschöpflichen Gegenüber zu Gott betrifft, in Gottes Ratschluss liegt und vom Willen Gottes umschlossen ist, damit aber auch die Existenz des Bösen als einer das Gottesverhältnis des Menschen stetig gefährdenden Macht. Das Böse ist demnach kein Gott in eigener Mächtigkeit gegenüberstehendes Phänomen, kein Gegengott wie in dualistischen Denkhorizonten, sondern es ist der Schöpfung ein- und Gott somit untergeordnet. Die Erschaffung des Menschen als eines zur Autonomie und Selbstdetermination, damit auch zur Selbstverantwortung bestimmten Wesens wird damit als das *gute* Werk Gottes erkannt und die Selbstverantwortung des autonomen und ich-bewussten Menschen als die dem Menschen von Gott selbst zugeeignete Aufgabe.[16] Dass der Mensch an der Erfüllung dieser

---

15 Vgl. LEVIN, Das verlorene Paradies, 97, der gegen die beliebte Deutung, dass die Sterblichkeit des Menschen in der Erzählung nicht von vornherein vorausgesetzt, sondern Folge der Gebotsübertretung ist, festhält: „Das Sein zum Tode ist […] mit der Schöpfung gegeben." Der Text geht nicht „von einer verlorenen Unsterblichkeit" aus (ebd., 98).
16 Hierin liegt die eigentliche Bedeutung des verschiedentlichen Hinweises darauf, dass mit der Erkenntnis von Gut und Böse an anderen Stellen (Dtn 1,39; 2Sam 19,36; Jes 7,15-16) die Urteilskraft des Erwachsenen im Gegensatz zu der des Kindes bezeichnet ist; s. z.B. BLUM, Gottesunmittelbarkeit, 21-22; SCHMID, Loss of Immortality?, 61; KRÜGER, Sündenfall?, 101. Die Urteilskraft ist Zeichen der Individuation und Ausweis menschlicher Autonomie. Sie aber allein unter dem positiven Aspekt des göttlichen Schöpfungswillens zu betrachten und abzusehen von der gerade

Aufgabe scheitern wird und scheitern muss, wie auch der Fortgang der Ereignisse in Gen 4–11 zeigt, lässt seine Abhängigkeit von der Fürsorge Gottes desto schärfer hervortreten. Dieser lebensbegleitenden Fürsorge sieht die Erzählung Gen 3 am Ende den todgeweihten Menschen anheim gegeben. Die Frage nach der immerwährenden Herstellung eines vom Schuldverhängnis ungebrochenen Gottesverhältnisses des Menschen wird in diesem Zusammenhang nicht gestellt. Sie erscheint aber am Horizont als die Frage, die im Laufe der Geschichte immer dann auf Antwort drängt, wenn die aktuelle Situation unter dem Vorzeichen des Gerichts erscheint, wenn also der Mensch im Scheitern an seiner Verantwortung vor Gott seine Gottesbeziehung im Zeichen des Zornes Gottes und im Angesicht des Todes reflektieren muss. Die sogenannte Sündenfallerzählung hat also einen eschatologischen Impetus, ohne dass die Erzählung selbst die Existenz des Menschen mit und gegen Gott im eschatologischen Denkhorizont reflektiert.[17]

Angesichts der beklemmenden Dringlichkeit, mit der in Gen 3 anthropologisch grundlegend reflektiert und die universelle Verfallenheit *aller* Menschen an das Böse als die das Gottesverhältnis zerstörende Macht vor Augen gestellt wird, verwundert es zunächst, dass die Stoßrichtung der Sapientia Salomonis eine ganz andere ist. Die allgemeine Todverfallenheit des Menschen wird strikt negiert und der Tod als Schicksal nur derjenigen deklariert, die mit dem Teufel paktieren, was zu vermeiden als Möglichkeit des Menschen und damit von Gott her als Pflicht des Menschen erkannt wird. Wie ist diese völlig andere Sicht auf den Men-

---

aus der Individuation resultierenden Gebrochenheit menschlicher Existenz im Gegenüber zu Gott, bedeutet den Verlust der Tiefendimension des Textes, sofern nicht gleichzeitig auch das Böse, d.h. der aus dem Ich-Bewusstsein und dem Ich-Bezug des Menschen resultierende Impetus zur Selbstdestruktion, zur Frage des göttlichen Schöpfungswillens gemacht wird. Ganz anders KRÜGER, Sündenfall?, 102–104, der die Ansicht vertritt, dass der Ablösungsprozess des Menschen von Gott modellhaften Charakter habe im Sinne „der Ablösung der Kinder von ihren Eltern im Zuge des Erwachsenwerdens", weshalb die Erzählung nicht als Reflexion über den Mensch als Sünder zu verstehen sei. Allerdings ist diesem Deutungsversuch wohl doch vorzuwerfen, dass er „moderne kulturelle Gestaltungen der Adoleszenz in die antiken Texte [...] projizier[t]", ein Vorwurf, den in diesen Worten der Autor selbst als Gefahr seines Ansatzes in den Raum stellt (ebd., 103). Die Emanzipation aus der „Bevormundung" (ebd., 104) Gottes als von Gott selbst ins Werk gesetzt? Wohl kaum.

17 Auf diesen eschatologischen Impetus zielt auch BARR, Garden, 4.19, wenn er den Verlust der dem Menschen von Gott her eigentlichen zugedachten Unsterblichkeit als das eigentliche Thema des Textes bestimmt, wobei er „Unsterblichkeit" nicht als Leben nach dem Tod, sondern als Fortdauer eines Lebens ohne Tod definiert. Ähnlich im Anschluss an Barr SCHMID, Loss of Immortality?, 64, der in der Frage der Unsterblichkeit auch den Anknüpfungspunkt für die Rezeption von Gen 1–3 durch Ben Sira und die Sapientia Salomonis sieht (ebd., 65–69).

schen und seine Möglichkeiten zu erklären? Um hier einen Schritt weiterzukommen, bedarf es einer genauen Analyse der Sap 2,23–24 konstituierenden Begriffe und Motive.

3 Tod und Leben, Tod und Teufel in Sap 1 und 2

Die gegenüber Gen 3 vollzogene Neubewertung des Verhältnisses von Gott und Mensch gründet ganz offensichtlich in der ganz anderen Sicht auf den Tod. Auffällig ist, dass der Tod *nicht* gleichgesetzt wird mit dem Ende des irdischen Lebens. Es scheint, als sei hier vorweggenommen, was in der Johannesoffenbarung als zweiter Tod bezeichnet wird (Apk 20,14): der Verlust nicht der diesseitigen, sondern der jenseitigen Existenz. Diesem Todesverständnis entspricht in Sap 2,23 das Verständnis des Lebens. Leben, eigentliches Leben, ist für den Autor des Textes das ewige Leben, das Leben bei und mit Gott, das Leben im Transzendenzbereich Gottes. Diese ganz auf die jenseitige Existenz ausgerichtete Lebensvorstellung findet sich auch an zahlreichen anderen Stellen der Weisheitsschrift (Sap 3,4; 4,7; 5,15 u.ö.). Aber der Text geht noch einen Schritt weiter: Er redet, wenn er den Menschen als Ebenbild der göttlichen Ewigkeit charakterisiert, von einer Seinseinheit von Gott und Mensch, bei der die Grenze zur Wesenseinheit zu fallen scheint. Denn Ewigkeit und Unvergänglichkeit sind genuin göttliche Epitheta. Und wenn in Sap 2,23 die Ebenbildlichkeit des Menschen vom ewigen Sein Gottes her bestimmt und dem Menschen Unvergänglichkeit zuerkannt wird, dann ist die axiomatische Fixierung des existentialen Getrenntseins von Gott und Mensch in Gen 3 grundsätzlich infrage gestellt. Hier ist das „ihr werdet sein wie Gott" aus Gen 3,5 ganz neu und anders definiert als in der alten Schöpfungserzählung, nämlich nicht erkenntnistheoretisch im Sinne der Partizipation des Menschen am göttlichen Wissen um die schöpfungsbedingte Unterschiedenheit von Gott und Mensch, sondern existential im Sinne der Partizipation des Menschen an Gottes ewigem Sein. Damit ist das Paradoxon der Geneiserzählung aufgehoben, d.h. eben jene gerade benannte Tatsache, dass das „ihr werdet sein wie Gott" auf die göttliche Erkenntnis nicht der Gleichheit, sondern der *Ungleichheit* von Gott und Mensch zielt, die Gott vor dem Menschen im Uranfang gnädig verborgen hat. Er hat sie nach Gen 3 aber gerade deshalb verborgen, weil der Mensch nur solange am Leben *mit* Gott Anteil haben kann, solange er *nicht* autonom agiert. Damit ist in der Sapientia Salomonis auch der tragische Knoten aufgelöst, der den sehend gewordenen Menschen an sich selbst fesselt, da er nicht anders kann, denn als Souverän seines Lebens und also gegengöttlich zu handeln. Die Weisheitsschrift behaftet den Menschen bei seiner Willensfreiheit und macht von seiner Entscheidung für das Gute oder das Böse abhängig, ob der Weg zum Leben oder in den Tod führt, beides allerdings als Ziele jenseits der Schranken irdischen Lebens und irdischen Sterbens. Da aber der Tod in dieser Weise neu qualifiziert wird, muss konsequenterweise auch das Verständnis des Bösen, das in Sap 2,23–24 als Herrschermacht über den Tod erscheint, irdisch entgrenzt und als Dimension jenseitiger Existenz verstanden werden.

Die ganz andere und neue Sicht auf das Böse ergibt sich aus der Tatsache, dass mit der Negation eines in der Geschöpflichkeit des Menschen selbst liegenden Unheilzusammenhangs das Böse aus dem Schöpfungsplan Gottes ausgegrenzt wird und eine Eigenmächtigkeit erhält, wie sie der alte Schöpfungstext strikt negiert. Die Schlange aus Gen 3 wird jetzt als Teufel (διάβολος) identifiziert und damit auch titular dämonisiert. Dies geschieht ganz selbstverständlich und entspricht der Vermischung der Titel für das personifizierte Böse und der Austauschbarkeit der Konzepte in frühjüdischer Zeit. Der Teufel agiert als Souverän eigener Provenienz. Er ist Person im Sinne eigenständiger Individualität, weshalb er auch Gefühlsregungen haben kann: Er ist neidisch. Hier wird das Wirken der Schlange aus Gen 3 ganz auf den missgünstigen Impetus dieser gegengöttlichen „Person" reduziert, ohne dass die Einzelaspekte der alten Erzählung aufgenommen würden (Sap 2,24): „Durch den Neid des Teufels kam der Tod in die Welt." Worauf ist der Teufel neidisch? Das wird nicht gesagt. Vermutlich auf die im Urzustand intakte Gottesbeziehung des Menschen, der er als Gegenspieler Gottes nicht zustimmen kann. Nicht *das* Böse, sondern *der* Böse wird hier zum Verhängnis des Menschen. Dieses Verhängnis ist der Tod, nicht der irdische, sondern der ewige Tod. Er ist – als Geschehen irreversibler Existenzvernichtung – ganz der Wirksphäre Gottes entnommen. Der alte Text Gen 3 erfährt hier eine ausdrückliche Korrektur: Der Tod kam durch den Teufel in die Welt, *nicht* auf Geheiß und Veranlassung Gottes. Gott als ewiger Herr über das Leben kann nicht – das ist die Überzeugung des Autors – gleichzeitig Herr über das ewige Nichts sein, dem „Reich", dem diejenigen zugehören, die Gott und damit dem wahrhaften Leben den Rücken kehren. Hier wird im Blick auf den alten Schöpfungsbericht dem Missverständnis gewehrt, die Macht des Bösen und des Todes sei ein genuiner Teil der guten Schöpfung Gottes, die Ausfluss der Weisheit Gottes und bereits in ihrer irdischen Gestalt auf Ewigkeit hin angelegt ist. Mitzuhören ist an dieser Stelle all das, was bereits in Sap 1,13–15 zum Tode gesagt war:

¹³ ὁ θεὸς θάνατον οὐκ ἐποίησεν.

¹³ Gott hat den Tod *nicht* gemacht!

Daher hat der Tod – so führt der Verfasser die Argumentation im anschließenden Vers weiter – auf Erden kein Reich:

¹⁴ ἔκτισεν γὰρ εἰς τὸ εἶναι τὰ πάντα,
καὶ σωτήριοι αἱ γενέσεις τοῦ κόσμου,
καὶ οὐκ ἔστιν ἐν αὐταῖς φάρμακον ὀλέθρου
οὔτε ᾅδου βασίλειον ἐπὶ γῆς.
¹⁵ δικαιοσύνη γὰρ ἀθάνατός ἐστιν.

¹⁴ Er hat nämlich zum Sein das All geschaffen,
und zum Heil bestimmt sind die Erschaffungen des Kosmos,
und es ist in ihnen kein Gift des Untergangs,
wie auch Hades keinen Herrschaftsort auf der Erde besitzt.
¹⁵ Denn Gerechtigkeit ist unsterblich.

Der programmatische Abschluss des Einleitungsteils in Sap 2,23–24 knüpft thematisch unmittelbar an diese Schlussverse des ersten Unterabschnitts an. Der Tod ist dort als Hades bezeichnet, ein Titel, der in der LXX durchaus geläufig ist als Synonym für θάνατος.[18] Er stammt aus der griechischen Mythologie und erscheint dort in doppelter Verwendung, nämlich als Name für den Totengott und als Name für die von ihm regierte Totenwelt.[19] Diese Totenwelt ist in Sap 1,14 im Blick, wenn vom Herrschaftsort (βασίλειον) des Hades als einem dem Irdischen entnommenen Raum gesprochen wird.

An der Hades-Rezeption zeigt sich, dass die Anthropologie der Sapientia Salomonis nicht allein von alttestamentlich-jüdischen Vorstellungen geprägt, sondern auch von griechisch-mythologischen Konzepten beeinflusst ist. Diese werden allerdings nicht unmittelbar adaptiert, sondern mit althergebrachten Denkmustern korreliert. Das zeigt sich im Gesamtzusammenhang der Kapitel Sap 1–2 daran, dass Hades zwar als Herrscher über das Reich des Todes vorgestellt wird, er selbst aber seine Existenz einer übergeordneten Macht verdankt, nämlich dem Teufel, durch dessen Neid, wie es in Sap 2,24 heißt, der Tod überhaupt erst in die Welt kam. Bemerkenswert ist, dass diese Unterordnung des Totenherrschers Hades unter den Teufel kosmologisch eine grundsätzliche Korrektur griechischer Vorstellungen darstellt. Denn in der griechischen Mythologie ist Hades als Bruder des Zeus ein Gott mit eigener Herrschergewalt über einen Teil des

---

18 Nebeneinander begegnen die Begriffe θάνατος und ᾅδης in Jes 38,18 LXX und Ψ 114,3.
19 Vgl. BREMMER, Hades.

Weltganzen, zu dem die Totenwelt als dunkler, aber genuiner Teil gehört[20]; und da die Notwendigkeit eines solchen „Seins"bereichs für die Toten empfunden wird, ist die Vorstellung des Bösen nicht mit Hades verbunden, zumindest nicht in der Weise, dass Hades als ein Gegengott zu den anderen Göttern vorgestellt würde mit dem Impetus, den Menschen zur Selbstdestruktion zu verführen und ihm die Lebensgrundlagen zu entziehen. Im Gegenteil, Hades gehört zur Ordnung der Welt. Wenn daher in der Sapientia Salomonis der Teufel als der eigentliche Herrscher über den Tod erscheint und die Macht des Todes und die Macht des Bösen in ihrer Wirkweise miteinander identifiziert werden,[21] dann wird Hades seines göttlichen Wesens entkleidet bzw. wird sein göttlicher Status in der griechischen Mythologie pervertiert. Hades erscheint als gegengöttliche Macht mit einem Anspruch auf den Menschen, der ihm nicht zukommt. Diese Korrektur der griechischen Todesvorstellung ist als Konsequenz des jüdischen Monotheismus zu begreifen, der die Welt nicht mehreren Göttern, sondern nur einem Herrscher unterstellt weiß: dem Schöpfer und Erhalter des Kosmos.

Da allerdings die Sapientia Salomonis im Blick auf die Macht des Bösen auch die Ordnung von Gen 1–3 aufhebt und dem Tod als Wirkmacht Satans keine Funktion im Schöpfungsganzen einräumt, entsteht an dieser Stelle ein Problem. Denn durch die kosmologische Ausgrenzung des als Todesmacht agierenden Bösen verliert es seinen „Ort" in der Welt. Als „Ort" bleibt „das Nichts", das der Verfasser in der Tat als einen transkosmischen Machtbereich versteht, in den einzutreten er als Möglichkeit menschlichen Lebensvollzugs – eigentlich „Todesvollzugs" – vor Augen stellt. Hier zeigt sich auch, dass im Blick auf das Verständnis des Bösen die Rezeption der griechischen Hadesvorstellung nicht folgenlos bleibt. Denn der Teufel wird jetzt zum Regenten mit eigener Herrschermacht und nimmt in der Abgrenzung der Herrschaftssphären plötzlich doch eine Rolle ein, wie sie in der Vorstellung der griechischen Umwelt mit Hades verknüpft ist, wenn Hades auch nicht als Feind seines Bruders Zeus auftritt. In dieser neuen Rolle erhält das Böse eine Eigenmächtigkeit im feindlichen Gegenüber zu Gott, wie sie ihm in Gen 3 nicht zu eigen war und wie sie in anderen Kontexten Kennzeichen einer dualistischen Weltsicht ist.[22]

Muss man auch die Sapientia Salomonis als Vertreterin einer dualistischen Sicht auf die Welt und den Menschen ansehen? Das zu beurteilen kann nur geschehen, wenn nach Tod und Teufel auch der von Gott zum Leben bestimmte

---

20 Vgl. Hom. Il. 9,457 (Ed. MONRO/ALLEN): Hades als „Zeus der Unterwelt".
21 Identifikation in der Wirkweise bedeutet aber nicht, dass Satan und Hades als ein und dieselbe Gestalt vorgestellt werden. Gegen AMIR, Thanatos, 53–55.
22 Zur dualistischen Tendenz s. auch AMIR, Thanatos, 53–54.

Mensch ins Blickfeld rückt, der Mensch im Spannungsfeld von Gut und Böse und in steter Auseinandersetzung mit sich selbst.

4 Das Böse und die Bösen in Sap 1 und 2

Die Ausgrenzung des Teufels aus dem Bereich der Schöpfung hat notwendig anthropologische Konsequenzen. Sie zwingt zur Aufgabe der in Gen 3 anschaulich gemachten Erkenntnis, dass der Mensch kraft seiner Geschöpflichkeit im Gegenüber zu Gott einem tragischen Impetus zur Selbstdestruktion ausgeliefert ist, der ihn sein Leben als Existenz im Machtbereich des Bösen erfahren lässt. Und so wird in der Sapientia Salomonis zur Möglichkeit des Menschen, was vorher unmöglich schien: ein Leben *außerhalb* der Todessphäre des Bösen, ein Leben in ungebrochener Gottesnähe. Für sie steht in Gen 3 das Paradies, aus dem Gott den sich seiner selbst bewussten Menschen vertreibt. Auf die mit der Vertreibung verbundene Existenz im Machtbereich des Todes spielt auch Sap 2,24 an, ordnet diesem Seinsbereich aber nicht den Menschen als solchen zu, sondern nur einen Teil der Menschen, und zwar diejenigen, die Anteil am Teufel haben: οἱ τῆς ἐκείνου [sc. διαβόλου] μερίδος ὄντες.[23]

Mit der Zweiteilung der Menschheit in diejenigen, die dem Teufel zugehören und damit dem ewigen Tod verfallen, und diejenigen, die auf Seiten Gottes zu stehen kommen und ihrer Bestimmung gemäß das ewige Leben erlangen, eröffnen sich ganz neue Probleme. Sie kulminieren in der Frage der Prädestination: Hat der Mensch die Wahl, ob er Gott oder dem Teufel angehören will? Oder ist die Zugehörigkeit zu einer der beiden Menschengruppen unabänderliches Geschick? Letzteres würde die anthropologische Fixierung eines streng dualistischen Weltbildes bedeuten, wie es auch im weisheitlichen Qumranschrifttum begegnet.[24]

Die Antwort ergibt sich aus denjenigen Textpassagen, welche vom Sein und Wirken der gottabgewandten Menschheit handeln. In ihnen wird deutlich, dass die Gefahr der Verführung durch die Ränke des Teufels zunächst grundsätzlich besteht, also auch für diejenigen, die in den Eingangskapiteln der Weisheitsschrift der Seite Gottes zugeordnet und als Gerechte (Sap 2,10.12.16.18) tituliert

---

[23] Zum inneren Zusammenhang von Ethik und Todeskonzept s. auch den instruktiven Beitrag von ENGEL, Gerechtigkeit.
[24] Zum Text und theologischen Profil der Zwei-Geister-Lehre 1QSIII 13–IV 26 s. LANGE, Weisheit und Prädestination, 121–170.

werden.²⁵ Ja, man könnte sagen, dass diese Gefahr des Abfalls von Gott überhaupt den Anlass zur Abfassung der Schrift gab, da sie ermahnenden Charakter hat und in den hier zur Diskussion stehenden Kapiteln 1 und 2 den Preis der Weisheit und des Weisen mit der Aufforderung verbindet, nach Gerechtigkeit zu streben und auch im Leid an Gott festzuhalten. Nicht von ungefähr beginnt die Schrift mit einem dreifachen Imperativ (Sap 1,1):

> Ἀγαπήσατε δικαιοσύνην οἱ κρίνοντες τὴν γῆν,
> φρονήσατε περὶ τοῦ κυρίου ἐν ἀγαθότητι
> καὶ ἐν ἁπλότητι καρδίας ζητήσατε αὐτόν.

> Liebt die Gerechtigkeit, die ihr die Erde richtet,
> denkt nach über den Herrn in Güte²⁶,
> und sucht ihn in der Einfalt des Herzens!

Die Mahnung wird am Schluss des Eingangsteils in negativer Wendung warnend wiederholt (Sap 1,12):

> μὴ ζηλοῦτε θάνατον ἐν πλάνῃ ζωῆς ὑμῶν
> μηδὲ ἐπισπᾶσθε ὄλεθρον ἐν ἔργοις χειρῶν ὑμῶν.

> Eifert nicht nach dem Tod im Irrtum eures Lebens,
> und zieht nicht den Untergang herbei durch die Werke eurer Hände!

Der Mensch kann sich also selbst den Untergang bereiten.²⁷ Das ist die Gefahr, welcher der Mensch in seinem irdischen Leben beständig ausgesetzt ist. Und der Gottlose ist eben jener Mensch, der in seinem Handeln mit dem Bösen paktiert und sich damit unweigerlich und unabänderlich in die Hände des Todes begibt. Diese Erkenntnis, in Form einer Sentenz, leitet den dramatischen zweiten Teil der Eingangskapitel ein, in welcher die Gruppe der Gottlosen selbst das Wort ergreift und ihre Lebens- und Handlungsmaximen vorstellt, bevor sie zur Tötung des Gerechten schreitet (Sap 1,16):

---

25 Grundlegend zum Verständnis von δικαιοσύνη in der Sapientia Salomonis ENGEL, Gerechtigkeit, 180–184. S. auch HÜBNER, Ethik.
26 Zu ἀγαθότης s. auch Sap 7,26 und 12,22.
27 Ὄλεθρος wird hier im synonymen Parallelismus mit θάνατος identifiziert und meint ebenfalls den Tod in seiner individuellen Wirkmächtigkeit.

ἀσεβεῖς δὲ ταῖς χερσὶν καὶ τοῖς λόγοις προσεκαλέσαντο αὐτόν,
φίλον ἡγησάμενοι αὐτὸν ἐτάκησαν
καὶ συνθήκην ἔθεντο πρὸς αὐτόν,
ὅτι ἄξιοί εἰσιν τῆς ἐκείνου μερίδος εἶναι.

Die Gottlosen aber riefen ihn [den Tod] mit Händen und Worten herbei.
Da sie ihn für einen Freund hielten, schmolzen sie dahin
und schlossen einen Bund mit ihm,
weil sie es wert sind, zu seinem Teil zu gehören.

Dass jeder Mensch in Gefahr steht, mit dem Bösen zu paktieren, ist, wie in Gen 3, Ausdruck der Erkenntnis menschlicher Autonomie. Da aber diese Autonomie nicht als ein Wesensmerkmal klassifiziert wird, dem ein unentrinnbar selbstdestruktiver Impuls eignet, stellt sich die Frage, was den Menschen befähigt, selbstbestimmt und doch in ungebrochenem Einklang mit dem Gotteswillen zu leben.

Die Antwort ist klar: Es ist die Weisheit, griech. σοφία (Sap 1,4.6), die den Menschen, indem sie ihm wahre Gotteserkenntnis verleiht, befähigt, dem Willen Gottes zu entsprechen. Bevor allerdings die Textstellen, die von der Weisheit handeln, genauer analysiert werden können, ist auf das spezifische Verständnis des Begriffs „Weisheit" hinzuweisen und sind die Denkmuster zu fixieren, welche die Argumentation im Eingangsteil der Weisheitsschrift bestimmen. Denn die Aussagen zur Weisheit erscheinen hier nur in negativer Verkehrung, bezogen auf diejenigen, die *keinen* Anteil an der Weisheit haben. Gerade im Blick auf sie als Repräsentanten der gottabgewandten Welt ist festzuhalten, dass mit „Weisheit" keine dem Menschen eigene Fähigkeit zu intellektueller Reflexion bezeichnet ist wie etwa in der griechischen Philosophie und auch nicht ein in Anwendung des Intellekts erworbener Wissensschatz. „Weisheit" ist vielmehr eine dem Menschen von außen zukommende Gabe Gottes, deren Besitz unverfügbar ist, weil sich in ihr Gott selbst manifestiert. Sie ist Gottes Anteilgabe an sich selbst, göttlicher Geist, der im Menschen Wohnung nimmt. Sie ist eine personale Größe, die dem Menschen Gott in Person in der Anteilhabe an Gott selbst erschließt.

Die theologiegeschichtliche Entwicklung dieser weisheitlichen Zusammenhänge darzustellen, kann hier im Einzelnen nicht geschehen;[28] wie selbstverständlich sie die Gesamtsicht des Autors prägen, zeigt sich aber in seiner Auseinandersetzung mit demjenigen Teil der Menschen, die er als Anhänger des Teufels und als dem Tod verfallen klassifiziert (Sap 1,4–6aα):

---

28 S. dazu ausführlich MITTMANN-RICHERT, Thesen, 317–324.

⁴ [...] εἰς κακότεχνον ψυχὴν οὐκ εἰσελεύσεται σοφία
οὐδὲ κατοικήσει ἐν σώματι κατάχρεῳ ἁμαρτίας.
⁵ ἅγιον γὰρ πνεῦμα παιδείας φεύξεται δόλον
καὶ ἀπαναστήσεται ἀπὸ λογισμῶν ἀσυνέτων
καὶ ἐλεγχθήσεται ἐπελθούσης ἀδικίας.
⁶ φιλάνθρωπον γὰρ πνεῦμα σοφία.

⁴ [...] In eine vom Bösen regierte Seele wird die Weisheit nicht eingehen,
und sie wird nicht Wohnung nehmen in einem Leib, der von der Sünde beherrscht ist.
⁵ Denn der heilige Geist der Erziehung wird den Betrug fliehen
und Abstand nehmen von unverständigen Gedanken;
wird er doch geschmäht werden, wenn sich die Ungerechtigkeit naht.
⁶ Denn ein menschenfreundlicher Geist ist die Weisheit!

Die Identifikation der Weisheit mit dem göttlichen Geist, der als „der heilige Geist der Erziehung" betitelt ist, wird hier vermittelst der Parallelisierung der Aussagen in V. 4 und 5 ausdrücklich vollzogen und in V. 6 noch einmal bekräftigt. Die Weisheit erscheint als eine personale Größe, deren gott-menschliche Mittlerfunktion sich in der Erziehungsfunktion des Geistes ausdrückt: Es ist Gott selbst, der den Menschen, indem er ihm Anteil an der Weisheit gibt, zu einem Leben nach dem Willen Gottes zurüstet. Die Weisheit nimmt Wohnung im Menschen in einem seine ganze Existenz—Seele (ψυχή) und Leib (σῶμα)—umfassenden Sinn. Bemerkenswert ist, dass mit dem Motiv der Einwohnung (κατοικέω) der Weisheit im Menschen das Theologumenon von der Einwohnung Gottes im Irdischen aufgenommen wird, das in der Zionstradition verankert ist (vgl. Sir 24,8). Es wird aus seiner Zionsbindung herausgelöst und in den Bereich des Menschen verlagert, also individualisiert, damit aber auch universalisiert, was nur vermeintlich ein Paradox ist, da die Individualisierung mit einer geographischen Entgrenzung einhergeht.

Diese Individualisierung einer offenbarungsgeschichtlich auf Israel als Volk ausgerichteten Vorstellung erklärt zunächst die Diasporasituation, in welcher sich aufgrund der Ferne vom kultischen Zentrum Israels und damit vom „Wohn"-Ort Gottes das religiöse Bedürfnis nach real erfahrener Gottesnähe neue Wege des Denkens erschließt. Mit Hilfe der Vorstellung von der Selbstvermittlung Gottes an die Welt in Gestalt der Weisheit und der menschlichen Partizipation an Gott kraft der Anteilhabe an Gottes Weisheit wird das Problem der Unmöglichkeit, die heilvolle Gegenwart Gottes kultisch zu erfahren, einer Lösung zugeführt. Sie bestimmt das Verhältnis des Einzelnen in Israel zu seinem Volk perspektivisch, und das heißt soteriologisch, neu: Der Einzelne erscheint nicht mehr dadurch als Anteilseigner des Heils, dass er kraft der Erwählung Israels Teil dieses Volkes ist, sondern Israel in seiner wahren Gestalt muss sich geschichtlich erst konstituieren, und zwar als Gemeinschaft derer, die sich in ihrer persönlichen Beziehung zu Gott als „die Gerechten" erweisen. Gerecht aber wird der Mensch allein durch das Geschenk der Weisheit, das unverfügbar bleibt.

Die Individualisierung der ursprünglich auf den Zion ausgerichteten Vorstellung von der Einwohnung Gottes im Irdischen verdankt sich aber auch der vertieften geistigen Auseinandersetzung mit der—aus Sicht des Judentums—heidnischen Umwelt. Das hat schon die abwertende Adaption der griechischen göttlich-personalen Hadesvorstellung gezeigt, die zur Scheidelinie zwischen den Gerechten und den Gottlosen in Israel wird, da das Paktieren mit Tod und Teufel den ewigen Ausschluss des Individuums aus der Israelgemeinschaft bedeutet. Es zeigt sich aber auch an Stellen, wo die gleichzeitig skeptisch-pessimistische und in der Konsequenz hedonistische Daseinshaltung der Gottesleugner sich in Begriffen und Motiven popularphilosophischer Art ausdrückt, ohne dass dieselben einer bestimmten philosophischen Richtung zugeordnet werden können.[29] Ganz deutlich wird dies am Anfang des 2. Kapitels, wo nach der Ermahnung zu einem Streben nach Gerechtigkeit die Gottesfrevler selbst zu Wort kommen (Sap 2,1–2a):

> ¹ εἶπον γὰρ ἐν ἑαυτοῖς λογισάμενοι οὐκ ὀρθῶς
> Ὀλίγος ἐστὶν καὶ λυπηρὸς ὁ βίος ἡμῶν,
> καὶ οὐκ ἔστιν ἴασις ἐν τελευτῇ ἀνθρώπου,
> καὶ οὐκ ἐγνώσθη ὁ ἀναλύσας ἐξ ᾅδου.
> ² ὅτι αὐτοσχεδίως ἐγενήθημεν
> καὶ μετὰ τοῦτο ἐσόμεθα ὡς οὐχ ὑπάρξαντες·

> ¹ Sie sprachen nämlich untereinander unrichtigerweise:
> Kurz und traurig ist unser Leben.
> und es gibt keine Heilung beim Ende des Menschen,
> und es ist keiner bekannt, der vom Hades erlöst.
> ² Denn nur zufällig sind wir entstanden,
> und danach werden wir sein, als wären wir nie gewesen.

Die skeptische Weltsicht ist mit Händen zu greifen: Das Leben des Menschen endet unweigerlich mit dem Tod. Es gibt keine Jenseitshoffnung. Daher ist auch der Mensch, solange er lebt, ganz auf sich selbst geworfen. Der Skeptizismus offenbart sich hier als Atheismus; daher auch die Kennzeichnung derer, die so argumentieren, als ἀσεβεῖς (Sap 1,16). Der Gedanke radikaler Diesseitigkeit des Lebens in all seinen Vollzügen wird in Sap 2,2b–5 noch vertieft. Er kulminiert in Sap 2,6–9 im Blick auf den praktischen Lebensvollzug im hedonistischen Aufruf zum ungezügelten Lebensgenuss: Carpe Diem!

---

[29] Zum Problem generell HÜBNER, Weisheit Salomos, 13–14; NEHR, Wesen, 164–228.

⁶ δεῦτε οὖν καὶ ἀπολαύσωμεν τῶν ὄντων ἀγαθῶν
καὶ χρησώμεθα τῇ κτίσει ὡς ἐν νεότητι σπουδαίως·
⁷ οἴνου πολυτελοῦς καὶ μύρων πλησθῶμεν,
καὶ μὴ παροδευσάτω ἡμᾶς ἄνθος ἔαρος·
⁸ στεψώμεθα ῥόδων κάλυξιν πρὶν ἢ μαρανθῆναι·
⁹ μηδεὶς ἡμῶν ἄμοιρος ἔστω τῆς ἡμετέρας ἀγερωχίας,
πανταχῇ καταλίπωμεν σύμβολα τῆς εὐφροσύνης,
ὅτι αὕτη ἡ μερὶς ἡμῶν καὶ ὁ κλῆρος οὗτος.

⁶ Wohlan, lasst uns also die vorhandenen Güter genießen
und die Schöpfung wie in der Jugend eifrig in Gebrauch nehmen!
⁷ Lasst uns voll werden von kostbarem Wein und Salben,
und die Blüte des Frühlings soll nicht an uns vorüber gehen!
⁸ Bekränzen wir uns mit der Knospe von Rosen, bevor sie verwelken!
⁹ Keine Wiese soll ausgeschlossen sein von unserem ausgelassenen Treiben,
Überall lasst uns Zeichen der Freude hinterlassen!
Denn dies ist unser Anteil und unser Los!

Anthropologisch führt die pointierte Individualisierung der Gottesbeziehung als Grundlage der Bestimmung der Israelzugehörigkeit zu einer dualistischen Sicht auf die Menschheit und zu einer Scheidung Israels. Israel teilt sich in das wahre Israel der Gerechten, die auch den Titel „Söhne Gottes" tragen (Sap 2,18), und in die Gruppe der Gottesfrevler, die sich selbst als „Nicht-Israel" qualifiziert. Als Nicht-Israel erhält diese Gruppe Anteil (μερίς) am Los (κλῆρος) der gottfernen Welt, und d.h. Anteil am Geschick all der Völker, die ebenfalls Nicht-Israel sind, also der Heidenvölker, die kraft ihrer Nicht-Erwählung der Sphäre des Todes zugehören.[30]

Dass mit den Begriffen μερίς und κλῆρος indirekt, d.h. in negativer Verkehrung, auf die Erwählung Israels am Sinai angespielt wird, zeigt die bereits zitierte Stelle Sap 1,16, die Einleitung der Selbstvorstellung der Gottesleugner. Denn in ihr wird – in Anspielung auf Jes 28,15[31] – die Anteilhabe der Gottlosen am Tod auf den Bundesschluss mit dem Tod zurückgeführt (συνθήκην ἔθεντο πρὸς αὐτόν). Dieser Bund ist das negative Pendant zum Bund zwischen Gott und seinem Volk der Gerechten und Gottessöhne, ein Gegenbund gewissermaßen. Allerdings liegt er—das ist sein Geheimnis—nicht im Willen der Menschen, sondern im Willen

---

30 Im Hintergrund steht Jes 57,1–13, die große Rede über das Geschick der verfolgten Gerechten und der Gottlosen in Israel, die in V. 6 den Anteil und das Los der Gottesfrevler von Gottes Urteilsspruch bestimmt sieht. Er zielt auf die vollständige Vernichtung der Gottlosen und Götzendiener (V. 13).
31 [...] εἴπατε Ἐποιήσαμεν διαθήκην μετὰ τοῦ ᾅδου καὶ μετὰ τοῦ θανάτου συνθήκας – [...] Ihr habt gesagt: Wir haben mit Hades einen Bund geschlossen und mit dem Tod Verträge.

Gottes begründet, da Gott als Souverän des wahren Bundes verwirft, indem er erwählt.

Dass die Heidenvölker in ihrer geschichtlichen Gestalt kraft der Erwählung Israels von Gott selbst ausgeschlossen wurden von der Erkenntnis des einen und wahren Gottes und keinen Anteil haben am Leben der Gottesgemeinschaft, ist alttestamentlich-jüdische Grundgewissheit (Dtn 7,6–8). Das Gleiche gilt für die Überzeugung, dass diejenigen, die keine Gotteserkenntnis haben, im Irrtum vermeintlicher Autonomie befangen sind. Der Widerstand, den der ägyptische Pharao im Buch Exodus dem Gott Israels leistet im irrigen Bewusstsein, der Souverän über Land und Volk sein, und in Unkenntnis dessen, dass Gott selbst sein Herz verstockt (Ex 7,13), ist das Paradebeispiel für den in Gottes eigenem Willen verankerten Ungehorsam der Heidenvölker als Grund für ihren Verbleib in der Gottesferne. Dementsprechend eint auch in Sap 2 diejenigen, die der Verfasser zu den Gottlosen (ἀσεβεῖς) zählt, der Glaube, sie besäßen die Herrschaft über ihr Leben und würden den Kampf gegen den Gott Israels nach eigenem Willen führen. Der Bundesschluss mit dem Tod ist daher die unausweichliche Konsequenz der ihnen von Gott verordneten Gottesferne. Dass eine solche aber auch Israel treffen kann, dass ein Teil des Volkes seinem Wesen nach als Teil der Heidenvölker ausgewiesen wird und damit als Anteilseigner an der Sphäre des Todes auf ewig, ist eine Erkenntnis, die in letztgültiger eschatologischer Zuspitzung nicht von ungefähr in der Diaspora formuliert wird, in einer Situation also, in der die Frage nach Abgrenzung oder Assimilation zur jüdischen Identitätsfrage wird. Dabei scheint der Verfasser der Weisheitsschrift die eigentliche Gefahr für das Judentum nicht im heidnischen Polytheismus zu sehen, sondern in der intellektuellen Herausforderung durch alle Spielarten heidnischer „Weisheit", philosophischer Denksysteme verschiedenster Couleur, aber alle mit dem Anspruch, die Welt in ihren Bezügen samt dem Menschen als Teil eines ihn transzendierenden Ganzen geistig zu durchdringen.

Dass gerade in gebildeten jüdischen Kreisen die intellektuelle Auseinandersetzung auch Apostaten schuf, die den jüdischen Glauben im Chor der Gelehrten der Lächerlichkeit preisgaben, dokumentiert in Sap 2,10–20 eindrücklich das Spottlied auf den Gerechten und das gewaltsame Vorgehen gegen ihn zum Beweis des jüdischen Aberglaubens an ein dem Tod entnommenes Leben in Gemeinschaft mit Gott.[32] Das eigentliche Problem manifestiert sich in den Versen 17 und 18:

---

32 Zum alttestamentlichen Bezugsrahmen s. HÜBNER, Ethik, 169–174, und SCHMITT, Komposition, 408–411.

¹⁷ ἴδωμεν εἰ οἱ λόγοι αὐτοῦ ἀληθεῖς,
καὶ πειράσωμεν τὰ ἐν ἐκβάσει αὐτοῦ·
¹⁸ εἰ γάρ ἐστιν ὁ δίκαιος υἱὸς θεοῦ ἀντιλήμψεται αὐτοῦ
καὶ ῥύσεται αὐτὸν ἐκ χειρὸς ἀνθεστηκότων.

¹⁷ Lasst uns sehen, ob seine Worte wahr sind,
und lasst uns prüfen, was bei seinem Lebensaustritt passiert.
¹⁸ Wenn nämlich der Gerechte Gottes Sohn ist, wird er sich seiner annehmen
und ihn retten aus der Hand der Widersacher.

Es ist der irdische Tod, die Sterblichkeit des Menschen, die den Dreh- und Angelpunkt der Diskussion bildet. Hier wird offenbar, dass die Endlichkeit des Lebens das anthropologische Grundproblem ist, das dem Menschen über die Grenzen von Religion und Geisteshaltung hinweg eine individuelle Lösung abverlangt und integriert werden muss in eine Gesamtschau auf das Leben. Auch die Gegner des Gerechten erheben—wenn auch in ironischer Überheblichkeit—den irdischen Tod zum „Prüfstein" der Wahrheit des angefeindeten Glaubens, damit aber auch ihres eigenen Gedankengebäudes.

Die Sapientia Salomonis begegnet den von ihr als Atheisten und freidenkerischen Genussmenschen titulierten Gegnern mit vehementer Abwehr. Dennoch zeigt gerade die Heftigkeit der Diskussion, dass der Trägerkreis der Schrift sich zur Auseinandersetzung mit Anfragen gezwungen sieht, die an die jüdische Gemeinschaft „von außen" herangetragen werden— „von außen" durchaus auch im Sinne einer Kritik ehemaliger Mitglieder der Gemeinde. Die Kontroverse ist Zeichen der unlösbaren Zugehörigkeit des Verfassers zu einer multireligiösen und multikulturellen Gesellschaft hellenistischer Prägung. Sie äußert sich auch darin, dass er sich formal vielfältig der hellenistischen literarischen und rhetorischen Konventionen bedient. Ihre Kenntnis und ihr Gebrauch waren offenbar so selbstverständlich, dass sie in den jüdischen Lehrbetrieb Eingang gefunden haben. Um so drängender stellt sich die Frage nach den Grenzen kultureller Adaption.[33] Sie sind für den Verfasser deutlich dort verletzt, wo die Übernahme neuer

---

[33] Ob man tatsächlich von einer im Grundsatz ausschließlich positiven Haltung der griechischen Literatur und hellenistischen Popularphilosophie gegenüber ausgehen darf, wie ENGEL, Weisheit Salomos, 3.1., es tut, wenn er das Anliegen der Schrift in „moderner" Wertebildung verwirklicht sieht und im pointierten Versuch, den „alten Glauben neu zur Sprache" zu bringen (vgl. DERS., Buch der Weisheit, 58), erscheint fraglich angesichts der intensiven Auseinandersetzung mit Kritikern des jüdischen Glaubens, deren Judenfeindschaft nach Sap 2,10–20 bis zu massiver Verfolgung geht. Auch die dem Verfasser geltende Aussage (ebd., 4.): „Er zeigt einen angstfreien Umgang mit hellenistischen Errungenschaften und verteufelt sie nirgends", ist im Lichte der Tatsache zu revidieren, dass der Verfasser in Sap 1,16 die außerhalb des Judentums stehenden Gottesleugner als Bundesgenossen des Todes und damit nach Sap 2,24 des Teufels tituliert.

Gedanken und Formen zum Zweifel am Althergebrachten führt und in Religionskritik umschlägt.

Die eigentliche Antwort, die die Sapientia Salomonis auf jegliche Religionskritik gibt, ist der Verweis auf die Exklusivität der Gemeinschaft der Gerechten vor Gott, die sich in der Verleihung der Weisheit durch Gott manifestiert. Gott selbst ist es, der die Gemeinde abgrenzt von der Außenwelt als dem Zusammenschluss all derer, die dem Tod huldigen, d.h. ihm dadurch Selbstmächtigkeit verleihen, dass sie sich selbst aus der Lebensbeziehung zu Gott herausbegeben (Sap 1,16). Die Selbst- und Wirkmächtigkeit des Todes aber erweist sich darin als eine nur vermeintliche, dass er allein die gefangen hält, die Gott die Herrschaft über den Tod und damit die Existenz absprechen.

Von einer streng dualistischen Weltsicht ist hier insofern nicht zu sprechen, als die Souveränität Gottes dem Tod gegenüber strikt gewahrt bleibt. Allerdings ist eine Tendenz zum Dualismus dort zu erkennen, wo schöpfungstheologisch argumentiert und das Reich des Todes, anders als in der Genesis, aus dem Schöpfungsganzen ausgeklammert und der Herrschermacht des Teufels unterstellt wird, dessen Geschöpf und Vasall der Tod ist. Die Ausklammerung dieses Reiches aus der Schöpfung, die nach Sap 2,23 zur Unvergänglichkeit bestimmt ist, liegt aber in der Konsequenz eines den irdischen Tod transzendierenden Todesverständnisses. Sie zielt auf die Unterscheidung des ewig Seienden vom Nichts als einer „Existenzform" jenseits der Schranken des irdischen Todes, einer „Existenzform", die eigentlich keine ist und die sich allein darin realisiert, dass sie das Ende jeder Seinsmöglichkeit darstellt, die eigentlich das Charak-teristikum der Schöpfung ist. Zugehörigkeit zu diesem „Reich" bedeutet letztgültige, irreversible Existenzvernichtung als Folge des Paktes mit Satan, der als Herr des „Nichts" Sachwalter der von Gott selbst der Vernichtung anheimgegebenen Menschheit ist. Die jenseits der irdischen Todesschranken irreversible Zweiteilung der Menschheit in diejenigen, die im Glauben an den Gott Israels das Leben der Unvergänglichkeit gewinnen, und diejenigen, die als Bundesgenossen des Todes ihm auf ewig verfallen, entspricht der genannten dualistischen Tendenz.

Diese Art dualistischen Denkens wird aber – das zeigt die durchgehende Handlungssouveränität Gottes – nicht gespeist vom Glauben an Gott und Gegengott im Sinne zweier voneinander unabhängiger wirkmächtiger Entitäten, sondern wurzelt im Erwählungsglauben Israels, allerdings in der weisheitlich weiterentwickelten und individualisierten Form, wie sie oben als Reflex der

---

Anders als Engel klassifiziert HÜBNER, Weisheit Salomos, 25, daher die Schrift als Trostschrift, die „bedrängten Glaubensbrüdern und -schwestern" „in schwieriger Situation Trost und Halt" bieten wolle; vgl. ebd., 30.

Diasporaexistenz des Judentums in hellenistischer Zeit herausgestellt wurde. Die Individualisierung entspringt der Erfahrung, dass erwählungsgeschichtlich die Scheidung zwischen Israel und der Völkerwelt in der Gegenwart des Verfassers zu einer Israel selbst betreffenden Scheidung wird. Sie wird zur Scheidung in einer Zeit, in welcher der Großteil des Volkes in der Fremde lebt und die notwendige Auseinandersetzung insbesondere mit der hellenistischen Kultur zur Verlockung wird, die im Einzelfall bis hin zur Abwendung vom Gott Israels führt.

Dass dabei die Gemeinschaft der Gerechten, die den Glauben an den Gott Israels bewahrt, dies nach eigenem Zeugnis letztlich nur deshalb vermag, weil ihr von Gott her das Geschenk der Weisheit zuteil wurde, ist insofern noch nicht Ausdruck einer prädestinatianisch akzentuierten Anthropologie, als der mahnende Charakter der Kapitel die Entscheidungsfreiheit des Menschen impliziert, dem für die Wahl des rechten Weges entsprechender Lohn verheißen wird (μισθός, Sap 2,22). Hier sei noch einmal auf Sap 1,14 verwiesen, wo die Einwohnung der Weisheit im Menschen als Akt der göttlichen Selektion erscheint nach Maßgabe dessen, was zuvor auf Seiten des Menschen als gut oder schlecht zutage tritt. Andererseits ist gerade in diesem Zusammenhang nach dem Wirkmechanismus der Weisheit zu fragen und nach der Möglichkeit wahrer Gotteserkenntnis und wahrer Gottesfurcht.

In Sap 1–2 bleibt der Befund schillernd. Der Text gibt keine Antwort auf die Frage nach dem, was den Menschen zur Gotteserkenntnis und zu einem Leben in Gerechtigkeit befähigt. Programmatisch gestellt und beantwortet wird die Frage erst in Kapitel 9. Die Antwort umschließt die Erkenntnis, dass die Rettung des sterblichen und grundsätzlich unverständigen Menschen aus der *zuvor*kommenden Gabe der Weisheit erwächst (Sap 9,5–6.13–18).[34] Mit diesem Hinweis ist kein Urteil über die Einheitlichkeit der Gesamtschrift verbunden, die Gegenstand vielfältiger Diskussionen ist.[35] Er eröffnet nur den Blick auf die anthropologische Gesamtproblematik, mit welcher die Schrift in all ihren Teilen befasst ist. Man wird aber mit gebührender Vorsicht festhalten dürfen, dass die Individualisierung der Erwählungs- und der Bundesvorstellung und damit – ganz entscheidend – auch der Erlösungsvorstellung, wie sie in Sap 1 und 2 in der Auseinandersetzung mit Tod und Teufel zu greifen ist, die Grundlage für die christliche Ausformung einer

---

34 Vgl. ENGEL, Weisheit Salomos, 2.2.3.: „Die Suche nach ihr [sc. der Weisheit]" ist „bereits Teilhabe an ihr."
35 Die Einheitlichkeit der Gesamtkomposition vertreten u.a. HÜBNER, Weisheit Salomos, 22–24; ENGEL, Weisheit Salomos, 1. und 3.

prädestinatianischen Erlösungsvorstellung bildet. Sie prägt insbesondere das Johannesevangelium.[36]

Damit geht der Blick zurück zu Gen 3 als dem Hauptbezugstext für die Auseinandersetzung mit dem Menschen als sterbliches und der Macht des Bösen ausgeliefertes Wesen. Das Beispiel der Sapientia Salomonis zeigt, dass die Frage nach dem Sein des geschöpflichen Menschen in dem Moment zu einer über den alten Text hinausgehenden Antwort zwingt, in welchem das Ende der Schöpfung und damit das endzeitliche Werden des Menschen, sein Geschick bei Verlust seiner geschichtlichen Existenz, in den Blick kommt.

5 Die Eschatologisierung der Genesiserzählung

Die Rezeption von Gen 1–3 im Kontext der Kapitel Sap 1–2 ist ganz von der geschichtlichen Situation des alexandrinischen Diasporajudentums vor der Zeitenwende bestimmt. Was als die Grundgefährdung jüdischer Existenz und daher als Bedrohung durch das Böse bzw. den Bösen, Satan, erfahren wird, ist die fremde Gedankenwelt – nicht weil sie abstößt, sondern, ganz im Gegenteil, weil sie anzieht, weil sie den Menschen fesselt. Sie fesselt ihn als Möglichkeit, neu und anders zu denken, als Möglichkeit, den geistigen Standort zu wechseln und das eigene Leben in neuer Perspektive zu betrachten. Diese Möglichkeit erscheint aus der Sicht der in dieser Weise in Bann Geschlagenen als geistige Freiheit, sie erscheint aus der Sicht der Bewahrer des väterlichen Glaubens als Trugbild des Bösen, Verführung zur Apostasie und Verlust des wahren Lebens. Da aber der Umgang mit der fremden Kultur zur innerjüdischen Scheidelinie wird, bricht mit der Frage nach den Konsequenzen geistigen Freidenkertums die Frage nach der Macht auf, die den Menschen dazu bringt, seinem Gott den Rücken zu kehren. Es ist die Frage nach dem Bösen, die als Zukunftsfrage nur im eschatologischen Horizont beantwortet werden kann.[37] Und so wird, was in Gen 1–3 als heilvoller Urzustand vor Augen gestellt wird – die ungebrochene Paradiesesgemeinschaft des

---

36 Auch das Johannesevangelium ist, wenn auch aus anderer Perspektive, ganz deutlich mit dem Problem der *inner*jüdischen Scheidung befasst. Seine prädestinatianisch akzentuierte Soteriologie verdankt sich der weisheitlichen Prägung der johanneischen Theologie in all ihren Teilen, nicht nur der Christologie, sondern auch der Kosmologie und Eschatologie. Auf diesem Feld herrscht allerdings noch erheblicher Forschungsbedarf. Er betrifft im Bereich der Anthropologie und Soteriologie auch die vielfältigen Parallelen zur Sapientia Salomonis, die bislang nicht systematisch analysiert und ausgewertet wurden.
37 Vgl. auch HÜBNER, Weisheit Salomos, 23.46–47.

Menschen mit Gott – über Zeit und Geschichte hinweg zur endzeitlichen Bestimmung des Menschen: ein Leben bei und mit Gott unter den Bedingungen nicht des Irdischen, sondern in Anteilhabe an Gottes transzendentem, ewigen Sein.

Die eschatologische Rezeption des rein protologisch reflektierenden Textes Gen 1–3 führt dabei schon deshalb zu einer Umformung des Menschenbildes, weil der alte Text mit der Vertreibung des Menschen aus dem Paradies diesem ein ewiges Leben aberkennt und seine Existenz auf seine irdische Lebenszeit beschränkt. Die Anteilhabe an Gottes ewigem Sein steht allerdings mit dem Baum des Lebens als die von Gott her dem Menschen ursprünglich zugedachte Lebens*möglichkeit* im Raum. Sie bildet für die spätere Rezeption in der Sapientia Salomonis den Anknüpfungspunkt der Erkenntnis, dass der Mensch zur Unvergänglichkeit geschaffen sei, eine Erkenntnis, die auch durch das Wort von der Gottebenbildlichkeit des Menschen in Gen 1,27 gespeist wird. Die deutliche Bezugnahme auf die genannte Stelle in Sap 2,23, wo der Hinweis auf die dem Menschen von Gott zugedachte Unvergänglichkeit (ἀφθαρσία) expliziert wird durch die Parallelaussage, dass der Mensch Anteil an Gottes eigener Ewigkeit hat, schließt ein nur spirituelles Verständnis des Begriffs „Unvergänglichkeit" aus.[38] Die Umformung des Menschenbildes führt notwendig zu einer Umformung auch der Sicht auf den Tod und die Macht des Bösen. Da das Sterben-Müssen am Ende des irdischen Lebens zu den unumstößlichen Lebensrealitäten gehört, dem Menschen aber Unvergänglichkeit zuerkannt wird, bleibt nur die Möglichkeit, den Tod ohne die irdisch gesetzte Grenze zu denken: Tod nicht mehr als das Ende der diesseitigen Existenz, sondern als Ausschluss vom jenseitigen Leben, Abgeschnittensein vom Leben der ewigen Gottesgemeinschaft. Die Notwendigkeit schließlich, auch das Verhältnis von Gott und der Macht des Bösen neu und anders zu bestimmen, ergibt sich daraus von selbst. Die endzeitliche Zweiteilung der Menschheit, wie sie aus dem eschatologisierten Todesverständnis erwächst, zwingt zu einer Modifikation der Vorstellung vom Bösen als einer über alle Menschen herrschenden Macht. Denn da die Todverfallenheit des Menschen nicht mehr als ein gesamtmenschliches Phänomen verstanden wird, muss die Frage des menschlichen Ausgeliefertseins an diese Macht und muss die Frage nach den geschöpflichen Bedingungen ihrer Wirksamkeit anders beantwortet werden, als der alte Schöpfungsbericht es vorgibt. Auf die Tatsache, dass im Gegensatz zu

---

38 Gegen COLLINS, Fall, 297; DERS., Root of Immortality, 187.191, und SCHMID, Loss oft Immortality?, 67. Die Diskussion wird an dieser Stelle deshalb unpräzise, weil mit dem Streitbegriff „Unsterblichkeit", engl. immortality (s. den Titel des Beitrags von Schmid), eine falsche Alternative eröffnet wird, da die Unvergänglichkeit des Menschen ja gar nicht in Konkurrenz tritt zu seinem irdischen Sterben-Müssen und also seiner Sterblichkeit. Vgl. auch BERG, Jenseitsvorstellungen, 51–52.

Gen 3 das Böse nicht nur personifiziert, sondern auch individualisiert wird, ist eingangs bereits hingewiesen worden wie auch darauf, dass sein Wirken nicht Teil des göttlichen Schöpfungsplanes ist. Das Böse als *der* Böse erhält somit eine Eigenmächtigkeit, die in Konkurrenz tritt zur Herrschaft Gottes über die Welt. Allerdings sieht der Verfasser die absolute herrscherliche Souveränität Gottes dadurch gewahrt, dass die Herrschaft dieser Macht als Herrschaft über das Nichts identifiziert wird. Sie ist das Los, das auch von Gott her denen zukommt, die er selbst von der Gabe der den Menschen erlösenden Weisheit ausschließt.

An diesem theologischen Knotenpunkt wird der schillernde Charakter der Anthropologie der Sapientia Salomonis deutlich. Denn auch wenn ihr Verfasser dem Menschen grundsätzlich die Möglichkeit zubilligt, dem Willen Gottes entsprechend zu leben, und wenn er das Streben nach Gerechtigkeit mit erhobenem Finger einfordert, so geschieht dies stets im Wissen darum, dass die Erlangung der Gerechtigkeit nur dem möglich ist, dem Gott Weisheit verliehen und damit Anteil an seinem Geist gegeben hat. Es bleibt also ein Vorbehalt im Blick auf den eigentlich zum Guten geschaffenen Menschen, ein Vorbehalt, der letztlich im Erwählungshandeln Gottes gründet. Da der Verfasser aber dasselbe nicht explizit zum Gegenstand der Reflexion macht, bleibt im Blick auf das Böse eine Leerstelle,[39] die auszufüllen erst gelingt, wo Erwählungs- und Schöpfungshandeln Gottes korreliert werden, und zwar unter gleichzeitig individuellem und universellem Aspekt, d.h. ausgerichtet auf die Frage nach dem eschatologischen Geschick der Heidenvölker.[40]

6 Resümee

Das Bild des Menschen, wie es die Sapientia Salomonis zeichnet, ergibt sich aus der Summe der Einzelteile. Dies hat beispielhaft die Analyse der Eingangskapitel 1 und 2 gezeigt. Allerdings lassen sich in der Gegenüberstellung von Gott und Satan und des ihnen jeweils zugeordneten Teils der Menschheit die Einzelteile nicht an jeder Stelle passgenau in das Bild einfügen. Man kann daher die An-thropologie der Weisheitsschrift nicht als einen in sich geschlossenen Entwurf verstehen,

---

39 Interessant und immer wieder Gegenstand von Spekulationen ist auch die Tatsache, dass der Verfasser der Weisheitsschrift an keiner Stelle sagt, wie Satan selbst in die Welt gekommen ist; vgl. HÜBNER, Weisheit Salomos, 47–48.
40 Den Versuch einer solchen Korrelation unternimmt eine andere Weisheitsschrift aus dem Umfeld des ägyptischen Diasporajudentums: Joseph und Aseneth; dazu ausführlich MITTMANN-RICHERT, Joseph und Aseneth.

sondern muss die Brüche wahrnehmen, die sich bei der Einordnung des Bösen in das Schöpfungsganze und bei der Bestimmung seiner Rolle im Verhältnis von Gott und Mensch ergeben. Der Entwurf, den der Verfasser hier bietet in Auseinandersetzung mit den Strömungen seiner Zeit und in Abgrenzung zu allem, was den jüdischen Glauben an den einen Gott und Schöpfer des Menschen gefährdet, tendiert hin zu einer dualistischen Sicht auf die Welt und den Menschen, ohne schon eigentlich dualistisch durchformt zu sein. Er lässt aber das Ziel erkennen, zu dem man gelangt, wenn man den Gedanken individueller Erwählung kosmologisch verankert. Dieses Ziel ist erkennbar auch in der pointierten Rede vom „Los" (κλῆρος) und „Anteil" (μερίς) des Menschen am göttlichen oder satanischen Herrschaftsbereich. Denn gerade diese Begriffe begegnen in anderen Kontexten als Leitmotive einer prädestinatianisch ausgeformten Anthropologie, wie sie sich etwa strikt systematisiert in der weisheitlichen Zwei-Geister-Lehre nach 1QSIII 13–IV 26[41] Ausdruck verschafft oder, im christlichen Bereich, im Johannesevangelium. Nicht von ungefähr reflektiert das vierte Evangelium das Problem der Grenzziehung zwischen jüdischer und christlicher Gemeinschaft im vielfältigen motivischen Rückgriff auf das Gedankengut der Sapientia Salomonis. Ihr Anliegen bleibt nach Sap 2,23–24 die tröstliche Erkenntnis, dass der, der nach Gen 1–3 den Menschen schuf, diesem von jeher die Gottesgemeinschaft zugedacht und ihn zur Anteilhabe am ewigen Leben Gottes zugerüstet hat.

Bibliographie

AMIR, Yehoshua, Die Gestalt des Thanatos in der "Weisheit Salomos", in: Ders. (Hg.), Studien zum Antiken Judentum (BEAT 2), Frankfurt a. M./Bern/New York 1985 = JJS 30 (1979) 154–178.
BARR, James, The Garden of Eden and the Hope of Immortality, Minneapolis, Minnesota 1993.
BERG, Werner, Jenseitsvorstellungen im Alten Testament mit Hinweisen auf das frühe Judentum, in: Gerhards, Albert (Hg.), Die größere Hoffnung der Christen. Eschatologische Vorstellungen im Wandel (QD 127), Freiburg i. Br./Basel/Wien 1990, 28–58.
BLOCHER, Henry, Original Sin. Illuminating the Riddle (New Studies in Biblical Theology 5), Leicester 1997.
BLUM, Erhard, Von Gottesunmittelbarkeit zu Gottähnlichkeit. Überlegungen zur theologischen Anthropologie der Paradieserzählung, in: Eberhardt, Gönke/Liess, Kathrin (Hg.), Gottes Nähe im Alten Testament (SBS 202), Stuttgart 2004, 9–29.
BREMMER, Jan N., Art. Hades, übers. von H. Kaufmann, in: DNP 5, Stuttgart/Weimar 1998, 51–53.

---

41 S. o. Anm. 24.

BRUEGGEMANN, Walter, Genesis (Interpretation. A Bible Commentary for Teaching and Preaching 1), Atlanta, Georgia 1982.
COLLINS, John J., The Root of Immortality. Death in the Context of Jewish Wisdom, in: HThR 71 (1978) 177–192.
COLLINS, John J., Before the Fall. The Earliest Interpretations of Adam and Eve, in: Najman, Hindy/Newman, Judith H. (Hg.), The Idea of Biblical Interpretations. Essays in Honor of James L. Kugel (JSJ.S 83), Leiden/Boston, Massachusetts 2004, 293–308.
ENGEL, Helmut, Das Buch der Weisheit (NSK.AT 16), Stuttgart 1998.
ENGEL, Helmut, Gerechtigkeit lieben oder den Tod. Die Alternativen der Lebensentscheidung nach dem Buch der Weisheit, in: JBTH 19 (2004) 173–193.
ENGEL, Helmut, Art., Weisheit Salomos, WiBiLex, http://www.bibelwissenschaft.de/weisheit-salomos (2005; abgerufen am 18. November 2014).
GEORGI, Dieter, Weisheit Salomos (JSHRZ III/4), Gütersloh 1980.
HARTENSTEIN, Friedhelm, „Und sie erkannten, dass sie nackt waren ..." (Gen 3,7). Beobachtungen zur Anthropologie der Paradieserzählung, in: EvTh 65 (2005) 272–293.
HÜBNER, Hans, Zur Ethik in der Sapientia Salomonis, in: Schrage, Wolfgang (Hg.), Studien zum Text und zur Ethik des Neuen Testaments. Festschrift zum 80. Geburtstag von Heinrich Greven, Berlin/New York 1986, 166–187.
HÜBNER, Hans, Die Weisheit Salomons (ATD Apokryphen 4), Göttingen 1999.
KEPPER, Martina, Hellenistische Bildung im Buch der Weisheit (BZAW 280), Berlin/New York 1999.
KRÜGER, Thomas, Sündenfall? Überlegungen zur theologischen Bedeutung der Paradiesgeschichte, in: Schmid, Konrad/Riedweg, Christoph (Hg.), Beyond Eden. The Biblical Story of Paradise (Genesis 2–3) and Its Reception History (FAT II 34), Tübingen 2008, 95–109.
LANGE, Armin, Weisheit und Prädestination. Weisheitliche Urordnung und Prädestination in den Textfunden von Qumran (StTDJ 18), Leiden 1995.
LEVIN, Christoph, Das verlorene Paradies (Genesis 2–3), in: Gehrig, Stefan/Seiler, Stefan (Hg.), Gottes Wahrnehmungen. Helmut Utzschneider zum 60. Geburtstag, Stuttgart 2009, 85–101.
MCKEOWN, James, Genesis (The Two Horizons Old Testament Commentary), Grand Rapids, Michigan/Cambridge, U.K. 2008.
MITTMANN-RICHERT, Ulrike, Die Dämonen und der Tod des Gottessohnes im Markusevangelium, in: Lange, Armin/Lichtenberger, Hermann/Römheld, K. F. Diethard (Hg.), Die Dämonen. Demons. Die Dämonologie der israelitisch-jüdischen und frühchristlichen Literatur im Kontext ihrer Umwelt. The Demonology of Israelite-Jewish and Early Christian Literature in Context of their Environment, Tübingen 2003, 476–504.
MITTMANN-RICHERT, Ulrike, Joseph und Aseneth. Die Weisheit Israels und die Weisheit der Heiden, in: Lichtenberger, Hermann/Mittmann-Richert, Ulrike (Hg.), Biblical Figures in Deuterocanonical and Cognate Literature (Deuterocanonical and Cognate Literature Yearbook 2008), Berlin/New York 2009, 239–279.
MITTMANN-RICHERT, Ulrike, Thesen zur offenbarungsgeschichtlichen Grundlegung der Christologie, in: Frey, Jörg/Krauter, Stefan/Lichtenberger, Hermann (Hg.), Heil und Geschichte. Die Geschichtsbezogenheit des Heils und das Problem der Heilsgeschichte in der biblischen Tradition und in der theologischen Deutung (WUNT 248), Tübingen 2009, 307–331.
MONRO, David B./ALLEN, Thomas W. (Hg.), Homeri Opera, Tom. I (Ilias) (OCT), Oxford 1902.
NEHER, Martin, Wesen und Wirken der Weisheit in der Sapientia Salomonis (BZNW 333), Berlin/New York 2004.

QUACK, Joachim Friedrich, Ein neuer ägyptischer Weisheitstext, in: WO 24 (1993) 5–19.
QUACK, Joachim Friedrich, Ein neuer prophetischer Text aus Tebtynis (Papyrus Carlsberg 399 + PSI Inv. D 17 + Papyrus Tebtunis Tait 13), in: Blasius, Andreas/Schipper, Bernd U. (Hg.), Apokalyptik und Ägypten. Eine kritische Analyse der relevanten Texte aus dem griechisch-römischen Ägypten (OLA 107), Leuven/Paris/Sterling 2002, 253–274.
QUACK, Joachim Friedrich, Zur Chronologie der demotischen Weisheitsliteratur. in: Ryholt, Kim (Hg.), Acts of the Seventh International Conference of Demotic Studies Copenhagen 23 – 27 August 1999, Kopenhagen 2002, 329–342.
QUACK, Joachim Friedrich/HOFFMANN, Friedhelm, Anthologie der demotischen Literatur (Einführungen und Quellentexte zur Ägyptologie 4), Berlin 2007.
QUACK, Joachim Friedrich, Einführung in die altägyptische Literaturgeschichte III. Die demotische und gräko-ägyptische Literatur (Einführungen und Quellentexte zur Ägyptologie 3), Berlin ²2009.
SCHMID, Konrad, Loss of Immortality? Hermeneutical Aspects of Genesis 2–3 and Its Early Receptions, in: Schmid, Konrad/Riedweg, Christoph (Hg.), Beyond Eden. The Biblical Story of Paradise (Genesis 2–3) and Its Reception History (FAT II 34), Tübingen 2008, 58–78.
SCHMITT, Armin, Komposition, Tradition und zeitgeschichtlicher Hintergrund in Weish 1,16–2,24 und 4,20–5,23, in: Gross, Walter/Irsigler, Hubert/Seidl, Theodor (Hg.), Text, Methode und Grammatik. Wolfgang Richter zum 65. Geburtstag, St. Ottilien 1991, 403–421.
SCHMITT, ARMIN, Wende des Lebens. Untersuchungen zu einem Situations-Motiv der Bibel, Berlin/New York 1996.
VON RAD, Gerhard, Das erste Buch Mose. Genesis (ATD 2/4), Göttingen ¹¹1981.
WINSTON, David, The Wisdom oft Solomon. A New Translation with Introduction and Commentary (AncB 43), Garden City, New York ⁴1984.
ZIEGLER, Joseph (Hg.), Sapientia Salomonis (Septuaginta. Vetus Testamentum Graece XII/1), Göttingen ²1980.

David A. deSilva
Human Experience and the Problem of Theodicy in 4 Maccabees

The editors of this volume have invited us together not to consider the arcane questions that often occupy the time of biblical scholars and those in related fields, but have given us an opportunity to explore, from the perspective of our own disciplines, the large questions that occupy—even plague—the minds of every person at some point, if not at many points, in his or her existence.

> What does it mean to be fully human?
> Whence does evil intrude upon human experience, and where does the responsibility for evil lie?
> Where is God in the midst of the experience of evil?
> How can "good" be restored?
> What is the meaning and significance of death?
> What role do convictions about life beyond death play in the confrontation of evil in human experience?

Professors Mittmann and Ego have thought very creatively and worked very hard to create this opportunity, and they are much to be thanked. I have the pleasure of exploring in this essay what the author of 4 Maccabees might contribute to a roundtable discussion of these essential questions.[1]

1 *Menschenbild* in 4 Maccabees

The author of 4 Maccabees gives explicit expression to his view of the human person: "When God fashioned humanity, he implanted humanity's passions and habits, and at that time enthroned the mind, the sacred governor, over all

---

[1] A slightly different version of this paper appeared in Bulletin for Biblical Research 13/1 (2013). The historical setting of 4 Maccabees remains somewhat contested, though all positions currently advocated fall within the period of the early Principate, between Augustus and Hadrian (see discussion in DESILVA, Introduction and Commentary, xiv–xvii), with a preference for the later half of that period (see DUPONT-SOMMER, Quatrième Livre, 75–85; KLAUCK, 4. Makkabäerbuch, 668–669). The provenance is also not certain, though VAN HENTEN, Jewish Epitaph, 44–69, has advanced a cogent argument for a provenance somewhere between Asia Minor and Syrian Antioch.

things through the power of discernment. And to this faculty he gave the Law. Governing one's life according to the Law, the mind will rule a kingdom that is self-controlled and just and good and courageous" (2:21–23). The image of God forming human beings, together with the image of God planting, immediately calls to mind the creation account in Gen 2:7–9, a story that our author appears to have shaped in ways similar to other Hellenistic Jewish philosophers. The starting point for the author's *Menschenbild* is his conception of God as creator, with the human being understood first and foremost as "creation," thus conceptualized entirely in relationship to God with a particular debt to God.[2] The "good" person understands and fulfills this debt, a foundational premise in the thinking of the martyrs throughout the narrative (see 13:13; 16:18–19). The "evil" person ignores or fails to understand this debt, and so acts unjustly toward his or her maker. All "evil" stems, in this regard, from a failure of reciprocity, a subset of "justice" in Greco-Roman discourse. This will be explicitly expressed in regard to Antiochus in 12:11–12.

As created beings, human beings possess an inherent, intelligent design—there is an inherent order in their creation and an ideal for their proper functioning. God planted both "passions" (πάθη)—a term including emotions, drives, and sensations[3]—and "inclinations" (or "character traits," ἤθη) in the human being, setting the mind over these other faculties as their governor.[4] The author's development of the creation story of Genesis (God as "planter") recalls Philo's insistence on reading it in terms of God's planting of the interior faculties of the human being rather than a physical garden spot (Leg. 1.43–55). From this model of the human being, it is clear why the author disagrees with the majority Stoic view that the πάθη are bad in and of themselves.[5]

---

[2] Greeks and Romans were well aware of the debt of gratitude owed to the gods for their sustenance of life. Aristotle (Eth. nic. 8,14,3 1163b15–18) writes that "requital in accordance with desert is in fact sometimes impossible, for instance in honoring the gods, or one's parents. No one could ever render them the honor they deserve, and people are deemed virtuous if they pay them all the regard they can" (translation RACKHAM).
[3] KLAUCK, 4. Makkabäerbuch, 688.
[4] The author takes as his theme a topic that is, indeed, "quintessentially philosophical" (1:1). Several authors regarded reason's ability to master the passions as the heart of ethical philosophy (see Let. Aris. 221–222, 256; Plutarch, Virt. mor. 1 [Mor. 440D]; Plato, Phaed. 93–94).
[5] TOWNSHEND, Fourth Book, 668. The classical Stoic goal was ἀπαθεία, no longer to experience emotion (Seneca, Ep. 116,1; Cicero, Tusc. 3,22; 4,57), though some Stoics, like Poseidonius, and the Peripatetics taught that the passions were to be controlled and moderated, not destroyed (RENEHAN, Background; STOWERS, 4 Maccabees, 846). The author of 4 Maccabees clearly aligns himself with the latter school, as would Plutarch, according to whom "mastery and direction" of the emotions by reason is the goal of the sage (Virt. mor. 4 [Mor. 442C; Mor. 443D]).

The ability to "feel" was created and pronounced "good" by God. These feelings have need, therefore, of being controlled so that they fulfill God's good purposes for them, but not eradicated.⁶ Thus, the glutton or the person who feasts alone is censured for not channeling the desire for food in such a way that it fulfills its divinely-appointed goal (2:7), but the person who sets a table for his compatriots and shares with the poor for the sustenance of life and the creation of community restrains the desire for food and funnels it toward God's better purposes. Rooting out the passions is neither expedient nor possible, for who can nullify God's design?

The author also does not affirm that the "evil inclination" of Jewish anthropology (see 4 Ezra 3:12–17) was planted in humanity by God or as a result of Adam's disobedience,⁷ as though the author has the *yetzer ha-ra᾽* in mind when he speaks of "inclinations." There is no agonizing over the power of the evil inclination and the futility of struggle against it, as in 4 Ezra. The odds are not stacked against human beings fulfilling their created design. "As many as attend to religion with their whole heart" are able to master the passions (7:18). Rather, God planted inclinations or character traits in the human being (for example, the proclivity of the young for sexual intercourse, as in 2:3 and Aristotle's discussions of age-related inclinations in Rhetoric 2.12) along with the passions which, like the passions, can be cultivated for good or perverted for evil depending on the possessor's cultivation of the same.

The critical point is for the mind to lead the passions and inclinations,⁸ and not the reverse. Again, this is similar to Philo (Leg. 3.118): "Scripture being well aware how great is the power of the impetuosity of each passion, anger and appetite, puts a bridle in the mouth of each, having appointed reason as their charioteer and pilot."⁹ The mind is thus charged with maintaining control over the "passions and inclinations" (τὰ πάθη, τὰ ἤθη) so that the person continues to walk in line with what is good and virtuous. The passions and inclinations are like plants, each having many offshoots; reason, or the mind, is "the chief

---

6 KLAUCK, 4. Makkabäerbuch, 688.
7 Versus HADAS, Third and Fourth Books, 156.
8 In this regard, it is significant that Jewish youths do *not* prove inferior to their passions, as Aristotle observes to be the tendency among youths (Rhet. 2,12,3), but rather are empowered by their observance of Torah to master any passions, whether the drive for intercourse (2,2–3) or pain (chapters 8–12, *passim*).
9 The author's vision of the mind enthroned as "governor" (ἡγεμόνα) over the "senses" (αἰσθητηρίων) is very similar to Zeno's psychology: "Zeno the Stoic claims the soul to consist of eight parts, dividing it into the governing principle, the five senses, the faculty of speech, and the procreative faculty" (cf. PEARSON, Fragments, 142; compare Philo, Opif. 30).

gardener, cleaning and pruning and binding and watering and irrigating in every manner, [and thus it] reclaims the forests of the inclinations and passions, for reason is the governor of the virtues, but it is the absolute master of the passions" (1:29–30). Again using agricultural imagery in a manner similar to Philo, the author charges reason with tending to every shoot with the appropriate treatment, eradicating some passions, cutting back the excess of some passions so that they can function more healthily within their natural bounds, "binding" others so that they incline in their proper direction rather than being perverted by malicious dispositions, and actually nurturing others,[10] another clue to the author's positive estimation of the value of some emotions and desires as aids to virtue. The garden is rank with weeds and thorns but it is also rife with potential for beauty and order.[11]

In the properly ordered person, reason (or the mind) keeps the passions in check so that the latter do not propel a person into the actions (the evils) that such drives as anger or malice promote (3:3–5). The consistent practice of virtue—of self-control, justice, courage, and prudence—promotes well-being in human experience. It is through vice—gluttony and lust, anger and malice, fear and pain—that evil breaks into human experience (1:3–4).

2 Torah and the Human Ideal

The Creator God has not left the human mind to its own devices, nor given it a role to fulfill without the proper guidance and empowerment. "To the mind, God gave the Law," and the mind must be subject to the divinely-given Torah if

---

10 TOWNSHEND, Fourth Book, 688, on the different nuances of ἐπάρδων and μεταχέων.
11 Such imagery was well-known. Plutarch conceives of the task of reason in strikingly similar terms: "The work of reason is not Thracian, not like that of Lycurgus—to cut down and destroy the helpful elements of the emotion together with the harmful, but to do as the god who watches over the crops and the god who guards the vine do—to lop off the wild growth and to clip away excessive luxuriance, and then to cultivate and to dispose for use the serviceable remainder" (Virt. mor. 12 [Mor. 451C], translation HELMBOLD). Philo, similarly, interprets Noah's work as a farmer to be a lesson that "like a good farmer, the virtuous man eradicates in the wild wood all the mischievous young saplings which have been planted by the passions or by the vices, but leaves untouched all those that bear fruit, and which may act as a wall and prove a firm defense for the soul. And, again, among the trees capable of cultivation he manages them in different ways, and not all in the same way: pruning some and adding props to others, training some so as to increase their size, and cutting down others so as to keep them dwarf" (Det. 105, translation YONGE; see Leg. 1,47).

it hopes to function properly and maintain proper governance over the passions. This was Plato's view of the function of all "law" and "convention" (Gorg. 504D), which the author now claims uniquely for the Jewish Law. The author speaks of Torah as, in effect, an operator's manual for the proper maintenance of the human being. Eleazar explains: "we do not eat unclean food, for, believing of God that he established the law, we know that the Creator of the world has shown sympathy toward us in accordance with nature (κατὰ φύσιν) by giving the law. On the one hand, he permitted us to eat the things that would be the best suited (τὰ οἰκειωθησόμενα) to our persons, but, on the other hand, he forbade us to eat the things that would be adverse" (5:25–26).

Eleazar uses a term here (τὰ οἰκειωθησόμενα) that recalls earlier Stoic discussions about living in accordance with nature. Diogenes Laertius (Lives of Eminent Philosophers 7,85), commenting on a saying of Chrysippus, writes: "nature in constituting the animal made it near and dear to itself; for so it comes to repel all that is injurious and give free access to all that is serviceable or akin (τὰ οἰκεῖα) to it."[12] The Law communicates to the Jewish sage what nature was held to implant in its creatures, namely knowledge of what is adverse and what is suitable.[13] Far from being in contradiction to the Stoic philosopher's goal of living "according to nature," as Antiochus criticizes (5:9), the giving of the Torah was itself done "in accordance with nature" as from a divine parent who makes provision for the child's education and upbringing. Adhering to Torah is a superior means to discovering what was truly in accordance with nature, being supplied by the God who also created the "world order" that was "nature."[14] The Torah had its origin in the mind of the Creator of nature itself; it is a God-given resource (5:25–26) to enable created beings to live in line with their creator's ordering of their persons (2:21–23).[15]

---

12 STOWERS, 4 Maccabees, 850.
13 In regard specifically to the dietary regulations of the Torah, the author appears to have embraced Philo's view that the Law forbids certain meats precisely because they are so succulent and apt to provoke gluttonous loss of self-control (1:31–35; Philo, Spec. 4,100).
14 REDDITT, Concept, 257. Torah's superiority to nature as a guide to virtue will be made even clearer in the narratives that follow, when the natural affections of sibling and maternal love would have led the martyrs to defect from the course of loyalty to God, were they not following a higher guide (see 13:27; 15:25). Those who follow nature, and not the creator of nature who has revealed the νόμος in Torah, may falter in attaining virtue at critical moments (7:18–19; 9:18).
15 Torah will be shown to be a more reliable guide to virtue than nature (15:25). When the author dramatizes the mother's internal struggle using the familiar image of the council chamber, "nature," the guiding principle of the Stoics (and the ultimate authority to which Antiochus appeals in 5:8–9), urges the mother to slacken in her courage, violate the demands of

The author gives extended consideration to how particular commandments within that Law assist reason to tame and master particular unruly passions (1:31–2:19) as evidence for his claims about the human potential for virtue and the value of the Torah in the pursuit of virtue. The ability of pious Jews to follow particular statutes of Torah provides the proof that reason can master the passions by the power of self-control (1:31–35; 2:1–6), but the Torah also provides the discipline—the exercise regimen—that trains and empowers a person's reason to overcome his or her inclinations and desires (2:7–9a, perhaps also 9b–14). Doing conscientiously what Torah stipulates makes one work against one's own greed or stinginess, or against one's feelings of dislike or enmity. The variegated commandments of Torah reflect the diversity of cultivating techniques envisaged by Philo and listed in 4Macc 1:29; following the particular commands is the way to prune excess and cultivate virtue according to the different requirements of each passion. Praising the value of the formative discipline (παιδεία) given by the Torah, Eleazar proclaims: "it thoroughly teaches us moderation so that we restrain all pleasures and desires, and it thoroughly teaches us courage so that we endure every pain willingly, and it instructs us in justice so that we render what is due in all our interactions, and it thoroughly teaches us piety so that we revere the only existing God in a manner befitting his greatness" (5:23–24).

The author of 4 Maccabees is entirely positive about the capacity of the human being to do what is good. The fact that the Law says "you will not covet" is, for him, sufficient proof that human beings are able not to covet. There is none of Paul's agonizing over how the commandment prohibiting coveting aroused all manner of covetousness in him (whether this is to be taken as a reflection of Paul's pre-Christian life, his post-conversion life, or the hypothetical struggles of the persona he adopts for a "speech in character"). Those who adopt this internal hierarchy (Torah guiding the mind; the mind controlling the passions and inclinations) and abide by it, the author avers, find themselves enjoying the position of the Greek ideal sage—kings and queens (see Diogenes Laertius, Lives

---

piety, and tell her sons to save themselves. REDDITT, Concept, 256, distinguishes between meanings of φύσις in 4 Maccabees' discussions of fraternal and parental affection from its meaning in chapter five as a "structure in harmony with which men [sic] ought to live." But that is the same φύσις that implants φιλοστοργία and φιλαδελφία into people's hearts. Redditt's distinction misses the significance of linking these meanings with regard to the claim being made in 4 Maccabees that nature itself is an insufficient guide to virtue, since the otherwise positive emotions of the parental and fraternal love that φύσις implants (as in Plutarch, Am. prol. 3 [Mor. 496A]), and for which it pleads, would have led the mother to perpetrate evil against God and, thus, her nation as well.

of Eminent Philosophers 7,122; SVF 3,617–619; Philo, Migr. 197) over a nobly governed domain that flourishes in every one of the cardinal virtues.[16]

The picture of Torah as training in virtue and exercise program for the rational faculty dominates the opening three chapters of 4 Maccabees. There is a second dimension to Torah, however, which comes to the fore alongside this first dimension once the author begins his "narrative demonstration" of his thesis. As we will explore shortly, this second dimension introduces some complications in what is otherwise a quite individual and potentially universal formulation of the problem of evil and its resolution. The Torah is also the covenant agreement with God, the terms of an alliance to which the ancestors of the Jews bound themselves by oath (5:29). As an agreement made between God and the *people*, not between God and individual persons, the problem of evil is complicated as a guilty *people* suffers the punishment stipulated in the covenant for breach thereof while innocent *persons* suffer as part of that people.

3 The Problem of Evil

Some definition of what is meant here by "evil" seems to be in order, although I will not pretend that it is a philosophically adept definition. I find that people are not so much concerned with the problem of "evil" as an abstract power or idea as much as with the problem of "evil" as the actual experience of undeserved misfortune, unhappiness, or loss. Questions about the problem of evil arise when what we would seek or choose for ourselves (the pleasant and happy future we envision for ourselves and ours, and towards which we strive) does not come about, but rather its opposite, or when what we would wish to avoid for ourselves and ours comes upon us from without. The problem also arises when we witness others falling into either of these situations through no fault of their own. In short, the problem of evil arises primarily when we inflict harm or harm is inflicted upon us, "harm" being broadly defined.

---

16 To what extent does the author of 4 Maccabees exhibit ethnocentrism in his formulation of the problem of human existence and its solution? On the one hand, there are some rather exclusivist claims made on behalf of Jews. "The children of the Hebrews *alone* are invincible on behalf of virtue" (9:18). On the other hand, Gentiles are not *intrinsically* debased *qua* Gentiles (as appears to be the case in Wisdom of Solomon's depiction of the Canaanites, who were beyond redemption, 12:10–11), but only insofar as they have not "attended to religion with a whole heart," a path that is theoretically open to all (7:18–19).

For the author of 4 Maccabees, with his theocentric view of human experience, evil is also—and especially—the violation of what God would seek or choose for human interaction and for human relating with Deity. Evil is that of which God does not approve. In the Jewish Scriptures, the constant refrain "he (or they) did what was evil in the sight of the Lord" shows that the regular reference point for "evil" as opposed to "good" was alignment with God's standards for human behavior (accessible in the Torah, the codification of the same). This dual perspective on evil—the human and the divine—may offer a way into the dual sources of evils breaking in upon human experience in 4 Maccabees: (1) the evil that results from individual humans, often large collections of individual humans, not living in alignment with their created ideal (i.e., with God-centered reason ruling the passions); and (2) the evil that results as the experience of divine punishment for violation of God's covenant (or God's claim upon the human being as creator and giver of life). The two exhibit a fundamental unity, however, since God's Torah (that is, living in line with Torah) is the path to avoid both evils, fulfilling both the human ideal and the covenantal ideal.

As 4 Maccabees opens, the problem of evil is presented as largely an interior issue. This will change somewhat in 3:19–18:24, when the issue of the consequences of covenant disobedience and divine punishment are raised, but even there evil's roots are interior to human beings. There is a striking absence of spiritual causes of evil in 4 Maccabees. After reading 1 Enoch, Daniel, Testaments of the Twelve Patriarchs, or even Tobit, with their presentations of fallen angels, demonic spirits, and spirits of error or truth taking possession of a human's will, 4 Maccabees seems to come from another world entirely—a highly rationalized and demythologized world. No evil angels, no giants, no forbidden knowledge, no spirits entering human being or enticing them away.[17] Angels themselves appear only once, at the end of the Apollonius episode (4:10–11), a

---

[17] There is one reference that might contradict this observation. In the mother's closing speech, viewed by many scholars as a secondary addition to the text (FREUDENTHAL, Flavius Josephus, 155–156; DEISSMANN, Makkabäerbuch, 175; DUPONT-SOMMER, Quatrième Livre, 152–154; ROST, Einleitung, 81; DESILVA, Introduction and Commentary, 256–257), the mother claims that she was not overcome by the "seducer or corruptor on a deserted plain" (18:8a), recalling the case law in Deut 22:25–27 which speaks of a man accosting a woman at some distance from an inhabited place, but here again it is a matter of another human being failing to master his own passions. In the next phrase, however, she adds that "the seducer, the snake of deceit" did not "defile the purity of [her] virginity" (18:8b). This appears to refer to a reading of Genesis 3 in which the serpent, possibly acting out the intentions of Satan, seduces or deceives the woman in the Garden (Gen 3:13).

narrative taken over and adapted from 2 Maccabees (where angels play a more prominent role).

The primary source of evil is a person's failure to maintain the God-ordained order within, as the author spelled this out in 1:29–30; 2:21–23. Evil enters the sphere of human experience from within, as a person allows the passions to overflow their bounds and to become the driving force in his or her decisions and actions. As the individual is overcome by a particular emotion, desire, or sensation, behavior that is destructive of well-being (one's own or that of others or both) is the result and "evil" is thereby experienced. The major battle is an internal one, as in 4 Ezra, where the whole point of life is to win the battle against the evil inclination (4 Ezra 7:89.92.127–129) or in Epictetus (Ench. 1.1) or Seneca (De constantia), where ultimately there is no evil that can be inflicted from without, as long as one's goals and expectations for life in this world are set just right.[18]

4Macc 2:15–20 provides a diptych of examples. When faced with a challenge to his authority, Moses does *not* respond out of his anger against Dathan and Abiram. He does *not* become an agent of self-motivated violence and harm. Levi and Simeon, on the other hand, allow their anger to gain the upper hand, and the result is the massacre of the males of Shechem. For the Shechemites, this was an experience of overwhelming evil—the violent end of many innocent lives (only Shechem himself, ostensibly, had been guilty of assault on Dinah), and the mourning of those lives by surviving wives, mothers, and children. "Cursed be their anger," indeed!

Where evil comes upon a person from without, it stems ultimately from another person's failure to discover and maintain this divine ordering of the inner person (often along with ignorance of *how* to achieve this ordering, seen, for example, in Antiochus IV's ignorance of the value of Torah—hence it is all "madness" or "stupidity" to him, 5:7; 8:5; 12:3). The rape of Dinah was an experience of evil born of Shechem's failure to master his lust (as opposed to Joseph's positive counter-example in 4Macc 2:2–4), allowing the passion to propel

---

18 The tortures, far from being experienced as an absolute evil, are turned into "splendid favors" because they give the martyrs the opportunity to show the depth of their dedication to the Torah-driven life and the mastery of the passions that this life has nurtured. The only real evil or injury that the martyrs can suffer is what they might do to themselves by breaking faith and yielding to the passions of fear, pain, and the like. As the brothers declare in unison, "Even if you kill us because of our godly character, don't think that you can truly harm us by these tortures. We will gain the awards of moral character through this suffering, and we will be with God, for whose sake we suffer" (9:7–8).

him to an impulsive act of violence against Dinah. But Levi and Simeon's response was of exactly the same kind from the same disordered source.

Ultimately, the same source drives Israel's enemies throughout the story of 4 Maccabees. Antiochus and his soldiers are "savage," "inhuman," driven by anger and rage to mistreat the Judean prisoners more and more brutally.[19] Antiochus is a placard example showing the vital importance of mastering the passions by portraying the horrific evils that can result where these are *not* mastered (and, in regard to *Menschenbild*, also the terrible consequences of failing to understand oneself as *creature* of the One God, the same God who created Antiochus's fellow human beings in Judea). He is himself driven by a particular passion afflicting the soul, namely "arrogance" (1:26; cf. 4:15). He lacks the humility that comes from acknowledging one's own fragility, and thus one's essential kinship with all other human beings who live within the limits of the same fragility (see 12:13), and therefore thinks it right to inflict physical harm in the extreme. He lacks the humility that comes from acknowledging that the will and rule of God is superior to one's own, and that one's own first duty and that of others is to God's will and rule. This is made explicit in 12:11, but emerges also earlier in 5:13 and 8:14, where Antiochus expects God to excuse transgression of God's own commands under compulsion while Antiochus enforces his own commands without giving room to the Jews for being "compelled" by a higher law to disobey his commands.

Antiochus is impelled to act by his own passions, which is a damning indictment of his fitness to rule. "In exceedingly violent passion he gave orders to bring others from the captives of the Hebrews" to be tortured, this anger coming from his defeat by Eleazar, his frustration at his own inability to coerce an elderly man to obey (8:2). It is Antiochus's passion (anger) that stands behind the order "to torture them still more cruelly" (8:2), as if to communicate that Antiochus's raw, unchecked passion was being translated into violence and evil enacted upon the bodies of other persons. He warns the seven brothers: "If you move me to anger by your disobedience, you will compel me to destroy each and every one of you with terrible punishments through tortures" (8:9). The brothers cannot be compelled to do evil by the fiercest tortures, but Antiochus can be compelled by his own anger (aroused by the imagined affront of people obeying their God rather than him) to have human beings like himself shred-

---

19 Thus, rightly, MOORE/ANDERSON, Taking It, 254; see also DESILVA, Using the Master's Tools, 108–110. Only the person who could rule himself or herself was deemed fit to rule over others (see Plato, Gorg. 491D; Xenophon, Oec. 21,12; Dio Chrysostom, Or. 62,1; MOORE/ANDERSON, Taking It, 253–254).

ded, dismembered, and killed. The brothers' declaration of loyalty to their own ancestral way of life and indictment of Antiochus for his ultra-violence against them leaves him "indignant" and "infuriated" (9:10). This fury becomes active in the tortures applied to the brothers (9:11). Antiochus's soldiers transform themselves to animals in their equipment and actions: they become "leopard-like beasts" (9:28), ripping and tearing into their prey. The torturers themselves are piqued by the third brother's freedom of speech and their embitterment fuels their violent treatment of the young man (10:5). In a world in which not everyone is committed to the mastery of the passions, to the regulation of one's own conduct by the cardinal virtues, and to living in awareness of one's creatureliness, it is sometimes ne-cessary to "die for the sake of virtue" (1:8) or "for the sake of nobility of character" (1:10).

The solution to the problem of evil, insofar as a solution lies in the hands of any individual, is entirely straightforward, namely ordering one's inner life/inner being through the discipline provided by Torah. The solution takes effect "as soon as a person adopts a way of life in accordance with the Law" (2:8), since the Torah at once constrains a person to act in ways that are just, generous, and so forth (2:9–14). Where people resist this solution, evils will still burst forth into human experience, but the solution lies ever close at hand, within the grasp of every person. The only way in which the individual can contribute to the solution, beyond appropriately ordering his or her life, is to witness to the value of Torah and the virtue of the Torah-guided life in the hope that others will be persuaded to become part of the solution rather than the problem.

The author of 4 Maccabees does not leave everything quite so simple, however. Within the narrative world, there is another source from which "evils" break into human experience—as divine punishment. Under Onias III, Judea enjoys the covenant blessings "because of their loyalty to the Law" (3:20–21). Onias's brother Jason, however, breaks the agreement: he "changed the nation's way of life and altered its form of government in complete transgression of the Law," and, therefore, exhibited scorn for the Law (4:19–21). This, in turn, provoked "divine justice," which "caused Antiochus himself to war against them." Antiochus specifically tries to destroy any remaining loyalty to the Law among the people (4:23–26). In stark opposition to the priestly elite, however, the "regular" people are disposed to be executed before breaking faith with the covenant agreement.

When are "evils" *evil*, and when are "evils" *justice*? When are they the consequences of one's own evil, or the evil (the injustice) in the decisions and actions of the people in whose midst one lives? The experience of persecution under Antiochus is, under the terms of the covenant, "just" as a consequence of the nation's departure from the covenant and forfeiture, therefore, of the protection of their divine Patron. A particular problem raised implicitly by the author, however, is the problem of the intense and brutal suffering of the most innocent Judeans, the ones most faithful to God and least deserving of being objects of divine punishment. Where is the justice in *their* experience of evils? Reading through 4 Maccabees, one must ask: Is God in Antiochus and Antiochus's horrific treatment of the Judeans? Is God behind the tortures? The author appears to be, again implicitly, aware of this problem, for he is at pains to demonstrate that their fate is not, in fact, an "evil." They are not overcome; they are not injured; they maintain their virtue intact. Here afterlife will play an important role: it is the ground for affirming, ultimately, that God is not unfair, that mastering the passions *is* ultimately advantageous (and *absolutely* so).

Where was God when these brothers were being twisted on wheels, burned over fires, and hacked into pieces? The author of 4 Maccabees would have an answer to offer, God was in the giving of the Torah (2:21–23), which allowed Eleazar, the seven brothers, and the mother of the seven to overcome the tyrant's attempts to compel them to act against the good, holding firm to their convictions and successfully maintaining the freedom of their wills. God was in the hope that each had of entering into life beyond death as the reward for a life well-lived, for ordering one's life in God's way and *not* becoming a source of evil and vice oneself.

The solution to this facet of the problem of evil, however, is closely compatible with the solution to the problem in regard to the individual. According to Deuteronomy 30:1–5, a revival of obedience would bring about a return of the covenant blessings. The martyrs offer representative obedience, but as it is complete obedience—obedience unto death—they cherish the hope that it will weigh more heavily in God's estimation than the disobedience of the priestly aristocracy (6:27–29; 17:20–21). Their extreme display of loyalty to the covenant, testifying to its value in the sight of their neighbors, reawakens commitment to such obedience in a broader public (18:4). Their individual commitment to maintain the divine ordering of their inward person, mastering the passions that would draw them away from the just path of loyalty to the covenant God, also contributes to the reversal of the experiences of evils plaguing the nation as a whole.

4 The Problem of Death

The author does not speak of the death of the rightly-ordered person as a tragic loss. Instead, he speaks of it positively as a "faithful" or "reliable seal" upon one's life. Praising Eleazar after recounting his martyrdom, he exclaims: "O man of blessed old age and respectable gray hair and life lawfully lived, whom the trustworthy seal of death perfected!" (7:15). The thought here is somewhat similar to the sober saying that closes Sophocles' Oedipus Tyrannus: "call no mortal happy until he is dead, free from pain." Just as tragedy may turn joy into sorrow in a single day, so some weakness of character may ruin a virtuous life in a single day and might well have that day before Antiochus. Life is a trial—a "noble contest" (16:16)—and one's virtue is always in jeopardy until death imprints its seal upon a completed life. Eleazar's virtue was not complete until it could no longer be threatened or assailed. Death removed him from the possibility of ever polluting himself. In this sense it placed a "seal" upon his virtue, a "trustworthy" one since nothing base would ever be able to creep in and defile Eleazar's virtue now that he was removed from this life. Indeed, in his particular circumstances, the fact that he died at all sealed his victory, for it meant that at no point did he yield to the feelings of pain being inflicted upon him. By dying honorably, the honor of his life would forever remain intact.[20]

The author opened his encomium on Eleazar expressing the same view of death, though using more colorful, nautical metaphors: "For just as an excellent navigator, the reason of our father Eleazar, steering the ship of piety in the open sea of the passions, assailed by the tyrant's threats and flooded by the high waves of the tortures, in no way turned the handles of the rudder of piety until it had sailed into the harbor of immortal victory" (7:1–14). The image of the pilot steering a ship was used to describe the activity of a political king (as in Sophocles, Oed. tyr. 689–696; Ant. 994–995). It was thus natural to apply the image, by extension, to the mind, or reason—the governing faculty "enthroned" among the senses (4Macc 2:21–23). Philo's use of the imagery is again illumining, showing how fully our author shares in the traditions of Hellenized Judaism:

---

20 A similar description of death as a "seal" is found in Thucydides 2,42, where Pericles speaks of the fallen soldiers' deaths as the seal upon their virtue, again completing it and removing it from the possibility of being assailed further (see also Epictetus on the death of Menoeceus in Diss. 3,20,4–6).

> As a ship holds on to her right course when the pilot has the helm in his hand and steers her, and she is obedient to her rudder, but the vessel is upset when some contrary wind descends upon the waves and the whole sea is occupied by billows; so when the mind, which is the charioteer or pilot of the soul, retains the mastery over the entire animal, as a ruler does over the city, the life of the person proceeds rightly (Leg. 3.223–224, translation Yonge; see also Leg. 3.118; Migr. 6).

Death was the only safe anchorage at the end of this rough voyage (7:3): any other ending would have meant that Eleazar yielded to the tyrant and made a shipwreck of his piety. For the author, however, Eleazar's death is also his transition to an immortal life with God, an eternal peace at the end of a harsh storm.

Death can be a "glorious" (10:1) or a "privileged" experience (10:15; cf. 12:1) when it is the result of maintaining virtue, keeping the proper ordering of oneself intact—even more, or at least in parallel, when it is the result of maintaining covenant loyalty with God, which is, for the author, the equivalent of ordering one's life properly by "pious reason" (cf. 1:15–17; 2:21–23). When death is the result of *not* breaking faith with God, it is a "noble death," since it is embraced as the means by which to give back to the creator God as one has received from God, namely life itself (12:14; 13:13; 16:18–19). Though the death is unjustly inflicted, dying itself is an act of justice (δικαιοσύνη). Death becomes a gift to God of the full measure of grateful response and covenant faithfulness.

The author also presents the possibility that death is a witness or a testimony. The seven brothers, says the mother, are called to bring forward evidence on behalf of the nation (the author uses a technical term from the Attic law courts, διαμαρτυρία, 16:16). It may be too refined to press the precise nuance of this term, "evidence given to prevent a case from coming to trial" (LSJ 403 col. 1), into this discourse. Nevertheless, the term shows that more than the martyrs' own lives are on trial. The martyrs' actions will testify to the nation's character and, in particular, to its covenant relationship with God. In this regard, and only in this regard, might the full sense of διαμαρτυρία be appropriate: the martyrs' faithfulness would prevent a covenant law suit in which God declares the covenant null and void on account of Israel's disobedience. Their obedience now would bring sufficient "evidence" to the contrary. In this regard, death becomes a testimony, a witness. On the one hand, it is a witness to other human beings (here, Antiochus) concerning the nobility and value of the Jewish way of life as a way in which to live and die in integrity, aligned with the created order and purpose of the human being. It is also, however, a witness to God, affirming the value that Jews placed upon the covenant and upon honoring the covenant, counter-evidence to be weighed against the acts of the priestly elite under Jason.

5 Life Beyond Death and the Contest Against Evil

The author's view of death depends entirely on his convictions about the afterlife. Death can be embraced as a harbor because this harbor lies on the shore of a new and deathless life. Death becomes the harbor gate through which one passes into immortality for those who die in a state of, and all the more on account of, covenant loyalty (16:13). Convictions about the afterlife play a major role for the author of 4 Maccabees in confronting evil, aligning oneself with the solution to evil rather than contributing to the problem through perpetrating injustice oneself (either against others or against the creator God). They become essential for properly weighing advantage and, thus, making one's decision in favor either of "pious reason" or of the direction in which the passions drive one.

Considerations of the afterlife play no part in the hypothetical responses that the author creates for the brothers and their mother (8:17–26; 16:6–11)—those "cowardly" responses that they did *not* make in their circumstances. In both hypothetical speeches, the situation facing the martyrs is seen and evaluated strictly from the perspective of this temporal life. Death means "removal from this most pleasant life" and "deprivation of this delightful world" (8:23). It means utter loss and the negation of all one's efforts on behalf of the deceased, poignantly expressed in the lament the mother *could* have uttered, but did not, speaking of giving birth "in vain," nurturing the boys "to no purpose," and ultimately "unfruitful" pregnancies (16:7[3x].8.9). Seeing death as the end of one's being, the author suggests, would have undermined the martyrs' commitment to virtue and their ability to master their passions for the sake of acting virtuously.

The author makes an explicit statement to this effect at the conclusion of his eulogy for Eleazar:

> Some people might say, perhaps, "Not all control the passions, because not all keep their reason prudent." But as many as have a care for piety from the whole heart—these alone are able to restrain the passions of the flesh, trusting that they do not die to God, just as neither our patriarchs Abraham and Isaac and Jacob did, but live to God. Therefore, for some people to be seen indeed to be ruled by the passions on account of the weakness of their reason contradicts this in no respect. For who, philosophizing with reference to the whole rule of philosophy, and trusting God, and knowing that it is blessed to endure every pain on account of virtue, would not control the passions on account of religion? (7:17–22).[21]

---

[21] See also 16:24–25: "the mother of the seven persuaded each one of the sons to die rather than disobey the commandment of God, but also, moreover, with them knowing these things—

The author shares with both Roman and Hellenistic Jewish authors the conviction that the removal of death's sting is a prerequisite to absolute commitment to virtue. Seneca writes: "If it is realized that death is not an evil and therefore not an injury either, we shall much more easily bear all other things—losses and pains, disgrace, changes of abode, bereavements, and separations" (Constantia 8,3; translation Basore). Similarly, Josephus acknowledges the importance of the belief for those who obey the Torah that "they shall come into being again, and at a certain revolution of things receive a better life than they had enjoyed before," and that it is precisely this conviction that enables martyrdom (C. Ap. 2,217–218; translation Whiston). This conviction transforms how people evaluate what is "advantageous" (or, in terms of a category invoked previously by Antiochus, "what is truly beneficial," τὴν τοῦ συμφέροντος ἀλήθειαν, 5:11). In light of the overwhelmingly greater value of a blessed eternity, enduring any temporary disadvantage in order to keep that eternal possession secure becomes the clear and prudent choice. Those who do not weigh advantages and disadvantages in light of eternity are susceptible to being mastered by their passions (7:20), but this is no objection to the author's thesis that human beings *can* live well-ordered lives and avoid perpetrating evil, since the element of "piety" is missing from the equation. Thinking about life according to the "*whole* canon of philosophy" (7:21) includes taking life beyond death into account in one's choices.

The promise of life with God beyond death, then, is an important incentive to dying in alignment with the Torah, the covenant agreement with God. It is this promise that provides the essential support for *absolute* mastery of the passions, since no breach of virtue (whether urged by the promise of pleasure or the compulsion/pressure of pain) would ever seem advantageous, while virtue (as alignment with the Torah) would always present itself as advantageous. Belief in life beyond death—and the possibility of securing the quality of that life beyond death in the here and now (whether good or ill)—redefines advantage and the weighing of relative advantages, as the author prominently displays throughout his narrative demonstration.

The brothers consider Antiochus's "pity, which offers safety at the cost of breaking our Law, to be more bitter than death" (9:4)—"more bitter than death," because transgression brings punishment worse than death, from which there is no release *in* death (see 13:15). Yielding to one's passions poses greater danger

---

that those dying on account of God continue to live to God, just as Abraham and Isaac and Jacob and all the patriarchs." Compare Mark 12:26–27//Matt 22:32//Luke 20:37–38. Both the author of 4 Maccabees and Jesus seem to presume a traditional exegesis of Exod 3:6.

to oneself (3:15; 13:14–15), since such yielding inevitably leads to provoking God, violating justice toward one's creator and one's covenant partner. On the basis of their assurance that they "will be with God, on whose account [they] are suffering," enjoying "the rewards given to moral character," the brothers tell Antiochus that, "even if you are able to kill us because of our godly character, don't think that you can truly harm us by these tortures" (9:8–9). But it is in his discussion of what was going on inside the mother's mind that the author gives fullest expression to the importance of a firm belief in life beyond death for mastering one's passions and remaining aligned with God's vision for the human being.

Weighing the respective advantages of two possible courses of action, both in terms of what makes for safety (providing "some plan or other for ensuring the avoidance of a present or imminent danger") and what leads to honor, is central to deliberation in classical rhetoric (see Rhet. Her. 3,2,3; Quintilian, Inst. 3,8,33), and is a primary arena in which the virtue of "wisdom" manifests itself (Rhet. Her. 3,3,4). Orators would be sensitive to contrasting short-term gain before long-term pain with its converse; it would fall mainly to philosophers (like Plato at the conclusion of the Gorgias) and to speakers in the Jewish and Christian minority cultures to transpose this to an otherworldly venue in which one might choose hardship in this life for the sake of security in the life of the world to come, or the afterlife (see, for example, Sus 22–23; 2Macc 6:26; 2Cor 4:16–18; Heb 11:24–26).

Verse	In favor of virtue	In favor of injustice against God
15:2–3	"piety that, according to divine promise, preserves to everlasting life"	"temporary preservation of her sons on the terms of the tyrant's promise"
15:8	"fear of God"	"temporary deliverance of her children"
15:26–27; 16:13	"one [ballot] bringing death," but "giving the full complement of her sons a new birth to life immortal" by urging them "on to death for the sake of piety"	"one [ballot bringing] deliverance that would preserve her sons for a short time"

Her conviction that death was not the end allowed her to exhibit proper "fear of God," in that she will not provoke God by treating Antiochus as more weighty and worthy of obedience than the Almighty (15:8; see also 13:14–15), in which she replicates the piety of "godfearing Abraham" (15:28), and "faith in/faithfulness toward God" (15:24), trusting God's promises of life for the righteous (15:3) and resolving to act loyally toward the Divine Patron for the sake both of past and future graces (see 16:18–19.22).[22]

This same conviction also empowered both the mother and her sons not to perpetrate evil upon their nation. Apostasy—the willful violation of the covenant—was, after all, the purported cause of the evils that had fallen upon the inhabitants of Jerusalem as a result of Antiochus's siege and attempt to stamp out their native way of life. Yielding to the passions, violating the divine order for the individual human being, would have meant participating in the systemic evils of further apostasy, further alienating the nation from God, inviting continued experience of the evils of the covenant curses.

The individual's refusal to perpetrate evil becomes, in the author's narrative, a principal cause of the reversal of the evils that had broken into the experience of their nation and victimized many. Their individual resistance to Antiochus's demands (11:24–25) encourages a resurgence of zeal for the covenant and the Torah throughout the nation, seen in the revival of covenant obedience throughout the land (18:4). Their individual commitment to maintain the integrity of their created ideal ultimately becomes the cause of the downfall of the imperial tyrant's hold on the nation (1:11).[23]

Conceptions of life beyond death also play an important role in solving the problems of theodicy raised by the author's introduction of the framework of Deuteronomistic theology into his narrative. The departures from the covenant on the part, essentially, of the priestly elite bring punishment upon the nation as a whole, innocent and guilty alike. The experience of the covenant curses spelled out in Deuteronomy 27–28 and lived out afresh under Antiochus is not the extent of punishment for transgression. There is the collective, this-worldly experience of the covenant curses, and the individual, other-worldly experience of (reward and) punishment. This is the threat of greater punishment ("everlasting torture") "awaiting those who transgress the commandment of God" (13:15). Divine justice is worked out at both levels, and the other-worldly level makes up

---

[22] On the topic of God as Divine Patron in 4 Maccabees, see DESILVA, 4 Maccabees (1998), 127–131.

[23] TOWNSHEND, Fourth Book, 667, insists that the Hasmonean family would be understood as the subject of the result clause at the end of 1:11: "The spirit roused by the martyrs led to the rising headed by Judas Maccabaeus and his brethren, and so was the *effectual* cause of the Temple being purified and its service re-established." This debate is renewed in connection with 18:4. Despite such special pleading, one should rather be struck by the complete silence of the author concerning the violent resistance movement. For all the historical problems involved, the author is intent on crediting the martyrs with the deliverance of their homeland (DUPONT-SOMMER, Quatrième Livre, 150; SEELEY, Noble Death, 93; O'HAGAN, Martyr, 111–112).

for the perceived injustices of the experiences of this life (e.g., the problem that God's provocation of Antiochus makes for the Torah-observant, covenant-loyal Judeans). Because of the existence of these two levels, the martyrs' deaths can have beneficial effects for the nation in this life (6:27–29; 9:24; 12:17–18; 17:21–22), becoming, as it were, an offering to God *on behalf of* others, while their *own* experience of divine reward as a result of covenant loyalty is also secured.

The author closes his oration with several assurances that the martyrs did, in fact, enter into their hoped-for immortality:

> The moon in heaven among the stars has not been made to stand nearly as revered as you, who lit the path toward piety for the seven star-like children, have been made to stand honored in God's presence and firmly set in the heavens together with them (17:5).

> They now stand before the divine throne and live throughout the blessed eternity. For indeed Moses says: "All those who have set themselves apart for you are under your hands" (17:18–19; see LXX Deut 33:3).

> The sons of Abraham together with their prize-winning mother have been joined with the chorus of their ancestors, having received pure and immortal souls from God (18:23).[24]

With such visual images, the author seeks to make the hope of immortality more real for his hearers, so that they, too, would "philosophize in line with the whole canon of philosophy," which includes living now as persons whose lives and, therefore, choices are not bounded by death. Thus they will be empowered to live fully in line with the ideal imprinted in their creation and encoded in their covenant.

6 Conclusion

The author of 4 Maccabees promotes a view of the human being and a set of convictions concerning death and the life beyond that nurture moral accounta-

---

24 Though quite possibly a secondary addition to the text, the summary of Scriptural teaching (as properly taught the seven boys by their father) reinforces these convictions. While indeed "many are the afflictions of the righteous" (18:15; the examples of Abel, Joseph, the three young men, and Daniel), affliction is not the final word in their story. They might indeed "pass through the fire" (18:14), but they are not ultimately extinguished by the fire. These bones shall indeed live" (18:17), because God has affirmed: "I will kill, and I will make alive; this is your life and the length of your days" (18:19). The order of actions here is of paramount importance: God "will make alive" on the far side of the experience of death.

bility beyond self-interest. Antiochus is an important figure as an exemplification of failure to understand this higher accountability. His authority and power is not given to him to serve his own interests, but to serve broader interests— what the author would call God's interests. He is accountable not within the artificial lines drawn between Greek and Judean, between ruling power and reluctant colonials, but to the larger bond and higher ideal of "humanity" that should connect him with his intended victims and guide his conduct much differently.

The conceptions of the human being as "creature" of God and of a life beyond death in which obedience or disobedience to these higher ideals are rewarded and punished are elements of a world view that nurtures a higher ethos than self-interest (with its objectification of the "other"), or even self-preservation. The proportionately greater temporal duration of life beyond death is a means of expressing the proportionately greater value of this higher ethos, and its proportionately greater demands on the individual person.

The author claims that people who hold firm to these convictions about an afterlife, the conditions of which are determined by the decision of the divine judge, are better able to choose the virtuous course of action, that is, choose for others or for a cause greater than themselves over and above choosing for self-interest or even self-preservation.[25] Those who lack such a hope, for whom death is truly the end, have a harder time rising above the passions (7:18–22). Indeed, according to the author of Wisdom of Solomon, the belief that *this* life is all that one has to enjoy can be a powerful inducement to self-centered living, to the intentional and programmatic indulgence of the passions, and to the perpetration of evil upon others for one's own satisfaction in this life (1:16–2:24).

There are ideals and values that are greater than our own preferences, inclinations, and desires for ourselves, ideals that call for our commitment and allow us to transcend ourselves by embodying them, even where this entails loss in terms of what we might otherwise desire for ourselves, for our own satisfaction. We might even *embrace* what we would not choose for ourselves—what from the perspective of our own desires or vision for a happy life could be accounted an "evil"—for the sake of a transcendent ideal. The deferral of self-interest and self-preservation to an arena beyond the historical sphere frees the individual from the domination of these instincts or drives for other-centered

---

25 The moral value of such convictions is seriously undermined by those who divorce eternal destiny from ethical action, something that Paul himself never did, but that many Christians have since done in the name of Paul.

moral action, and does enable moral actions that give us life, in a sense, beyond ourselves.

The author ascribes such moral power, then, to the belief in the transcendence of death since such a belief empowers the transcendence of "self" with its limitations (its self-protective and survival instincts, its fear of the loss that might ensue as the price of making the virtuous choice). I don't have to look after my own interests at the expense or to the neglect of others, as if my getting what I want out of this life is the highest priority. There is a life beyond *that* kind of life; there is One who is looking after my interests, who will ensure my ultimate fulfillment. Such convictions, in turn, empower one to resist interior inducements to perpetrate evil and the demands that systemic perpetrators of evil place on one, seeking to coerce compromise and cooperation. I am thereby freed to look after the interests of the other, or of the larger human community—truly to love my neighbor as myself.

Ultimately, such an approach to engaging the moral choices of life is in my own best interests as well, since it is a contribution to the creation of a community where others, acting in line with the same ideals, will also love *me* as they love themselves. It is an ethical ideal—and an ideal construction of the human being-in-community—that has rarely been enjoyed, it seems, in our history, but which the author of 4 Maccabees would affirm lies within the grasp of those who know themselves to have been created by God for more than the life of the self.

Bibliography

BASORE, John W. (Hg.), Seneca, Moral Essays I. With an English translation (LCL 310), Cambridge, Massachusetts 1970.
DEISSMANN, Adolf, Das vierte Makkabäerbuch, in: Kautzsch, Emil (Hg.), Die Apokryphen und Pseudepigraphen des Alten Testaments, Band II: Pseudepigraphen, Hildesheim 1900, 149–176.
DESILVA, David A., 4 Maccabees (Guides to Apocrypha and Pseudepigrapha), Sheffield 1998.
DESILVA, David A., 4 Maccabees. Introduction and Commentary on the Greek Text in Codex Sinaiticus (Septuagint Commentary Series), Leiden 2006.
DESILVA, David A., Using the Master's Tools to Shore Up Another's House. A Postcolonial Analysis of 4 Maccabees, in: JBL 126 (2007) 99–127.
DUPONT-SOMMER, André, Le Quatrième Livre des Machabées. Introduction, traduction et notes, Paris 1939.

FREUDENTHAL, Jacob, Die Flavius Josephus beigelegte Schrift über die Herrschaft der Vernunft (IV. Makkabäerbuch). Eine Predigt aus dem ersten nachchristlichen Jahrhundert, Breslau 1869.

HADAS, Moses, The Third and Fourth Books of Maccabees, New York 1953.

HELMBOLD, William (Hg.), Plutarch, Moralia, Vol. VI. With an English translation (LCL 337), Cambridge, Massachusetts 1969.

KLAUCK, Hans-Josef, 4. Makkabäerbuch (JSHRZ III/6), Gütersloh 1989.

MOORE, Stephen D./ANDERSON, Janice C., Taking It Like a Man. Masculinity in 4 Maccabees, in: JBL 117 (1998) 249–273.

O'HAGAN, Angelo, The Martyr in the Fourth Book of Maccabees, in: SBFLA 24 (1974) 94–120.

PEARSON, Alfred C., The Fragments of Zeno and Cleanthes, New York 1973.

RACKHAM, Harris (Hg.), Aristotle, Nicomachean Ethics. With an English translation (LCL 73), Cambridge, Massachusetts 1926.

REDDITT, Paul D., The Concept of *Nomos* in Fourth Maccabees, in: CBQ 45 (1983) 249–270.

RENEHAN, Robert, The Greek Philosophic Background of Fourth Maccabees, in: Rheinisches Museum für Philologie 115 (1972) 223–238.

ROST, Leonhard, Einleitung in die alttestamentlichen Apokryphen und Pseudepigraphen, Heidelberg 1971.

SEELEY, David, The Noble Death. Graeco-Roman Martyrology and Paul's Concept of Salvation, Sheffield 1990.

STOWERS, Stanley K., 4 Maccabees, in: Mays, James L. (Hg.), The Harper Collins Bible Commentary, San Francisco, California 2000, 844–855.

TOWNSHEND, Robert B., The Fourth Book of Maccabees, in: Charles, Robert Henry (Hg.), The Apocrypha and Pseudepigrapha of the Old Testament. Vol. II: Pseudepigrapha, Oxford 1913, 653–685.

VAN HENTEN, Jan Willem, A Jewish Epitaph in a Literary Text: 4 Macc 17:8–10, in: van Henten, Jan W./van der Horst, Pieter W. (Hg.), Studies in Early Jewish Epigraphy, Leiden 1994, 44–69.

VAN HENTEN, Jan Willem, The Maccabean Martyrs as Saviors of the Jewish People. A Study of 2 & 4 Maccabees, Leiden 1997.

WHISTON, William (Hg.), The Works of Josephus. With an English translation. New updated edition, Peabody, Massachusetts 1987.

YONGE, Charles Duke (Hg.), The Works of Philo. With an English translation. New updated edition, Peabody, Massachusetts 1993.

Ekaterina Matusova
The Post-mortem Divisions of the Dead in 1 Enoch 22:1–13

Against the Background of the Greek Influence Hypothesis

For more than 100 years, notions of Greek influence on several important aspects of the so-called journey of Enoch (1 Enoch 17-36) have been familiar to students of apocalyptic literature. There are a number of ideas of particular popularity. The rivers, and in particular the river of fire, in 1 En. 17:5–8 are often assumed to be a reference to the famous Greek rivers Kokytos, Styx, Acheron and Pyriphlegethon.[1] The description of the Garden of Eden in 1 En. 25:6 and 32:1–3 is often taken to reflect the Greek idea of the Isles of the Blessed.[2] The journey of Enoch to the realm of the dead, and in particular to the places of punishment, tends to be explained as being modelled on the Greek Nekyia.[3] Most notably, the Greek influence is used as a constant reference point by scholars seeking an explanation for the different destinies of the souls after death, even before the day of great judgement in 1 En. 22:1–13.[4]

First, I wish to show in this paper, using the first hypothesis referred to above as illustration, that quick and self-evident cross-cultural explanations of this kind are often based on insufficient premises. I will then outline the objections in terms of both methodology and the history of literature and religion that make the abovementioned approach highly problematic, particularly with regard to concepts of the post-mortem destiny of souls. Finally, I wish to discuss several principles followed by the author of 1 Enoch in presenting the post-mortem conditions of souls in 1 Enoch 22, which will emphasize the importance of interpreting this subject matter in terms of biblical thought.

---

[1] CHARLES, Book of Enoch, 38; GLASSON, Greek Influence, 12; BLACK, Book of Enoch, 156–157; NICKELSBURG, 1 Enoch, 283; BAUTCH, Geography, 83.85.
[2] DIETERICH, Nekyia, 30–33; GLASSON, Greek Influence, 12; WACKER, Weltordnung, 216–217.
[3] Dieterich used this term in a broad sense as a reference to various literary descriptions of the realm of Hades known in Greek literature; DIETERICH, Nekyia, 214–224; GLASSON, Greek Influence, 9–11; Nickelsburg, 1 Enoch, 280.
[4] GLASSON, Greek Influence, 12–18; WACKER, Weltordnung, 215; NICKELSBURG, 1 Enoch, 307.

1 The river topos

The discussion is provoked by 1 En. 17:4–8:

> 4 And they led me away to the waters and to the fire of the sunset (west), which provides all the sunsets. 5 And we came to *the river of fire*, in which fire flows down like water and discharges into the great sea of the sunset (west). 6 I saw *the great rivers*. And I arrived at the great river and the great darkness. And I departed (sc. went and came) where no flesh walks. 7 I saw the wintry winds of darkness and the gushing of all the waters of the abyss. 8 I saw the mouth of all the rivers of the earth and the mouth of the abyss.

As mentioned above, the interpretation most common until now assumes that the passage alludes to the four great rivers of Greek mythology, Pyriphlegethon among them. However, it is remarkable that the passage contains several formulaic expressions known from Ugaritic and Babylonian texts. The formulaic expressions familiar from Ugaritic texts have been recognized by Milik.[5] According to Ugaritic poems, the residence of Baal is situated "[…] at the sources of the rivers, in the middle of the channels of the two Deeps (abysses)", *mbk nhrm qrb apq thmtm*.[6] "The mouth of all the rivers" (v. 8) corresponds to *mbk nhrm*. Milik also argues that the expression "the gushing of all the waters of the abyss" (ἔκχυσιν ἀβύσσου πάντων ὑδάτων) in v. 7, picked up by "the mouth of the abyss" in v. 8., is equivalent to *apq thmtm*. Similar expressions are also found in biblical language (Gen 7:11; Deut 8:7; cf. also Ps 17[18]:16; Job 28:11).[7] Yet, the Ugaritic example is of greater importance because here the expressions are used as characteristics of a most unattainable place, the residence of a god, which is normally beyond human reach. In this context, the mention of the great river marking the border beyond which no human walks (v. 6) also indicates a certain typology. This river that separates the human world from the beyond is not only part of the image in the Ugaritic quotation above, but also a typical feature of a number of other Mesopotamian texts.[8] Against this background, the crossing of the ocean in Homer, Od. 10,508–515 proves to be a very clear echo of a wide-ranging ancient Mesopotamian tradition.[9] For instance, Gilgamesh traverses the great ocean through its most hazardous part, the Waters of Death, on his way to Ut-napishtim (Gilg. X 78–87; ed. George). Before doing so, he receives a warning that no human

---

5 MILIK, Books, 39.
6 Ed. GORDON, Ugaritic Textbook, 51 IV 19–22.
7 GORDON, Ugaritic Textbook, 441.
8 WEST, East Face, 155–156. See also GEORGE, Gilgamesh Epic, vol. I, 499–500.
9 See also WEST, East Face, 144–148.

can cross this line (X 79–82: "There never was, O Gilgamesh, a way across,//and since the days of old none who can cross the ocean"). This corresponds exactly to the idea conveyed by the expression "where no flesh walks" (v. 6). Tablet IX 80–81 of the Epic of Gilgamesh also stresses the same point, but, remarkably, like in 1 En. 17:6, here this statement is accompanied by a description of the great darkness that awaits the traveller beyond (X 82–83: "the darkness is dense and the [light is] there none"). The same sequence of notions is repeated in 1 En. 32:2. Enoch crosses the Red Sea and passes through darkness, before he comes to Paradise.[10]

From the second sentence of v. 6 onwards, we find a series of formulaic expressions and literary clichés, known from the Mesopotamian texts. They refer to some general characteristics of the beyond and to the idea of crossing the line. Even in our earliest Greek source, Homer, all these points, except the crossing of the ocean, have only a faint echo or have been significantly revised.[11] In the Greek sources of a later period, such as Plato, the motifs that we find united in the Mesopotamian sources and in 1 Enoch are dissociated from one another and some of them are absent altogether. In this light, it is evident that there is a direct connection between 1 En. 17:6–8 and the pre-Greek Oriental background.

This suffices to outline the main context of the passage in which the "great rivers" (v. 6) and "the river of fire" (v. 5) appear. The question arises as to whether we can still assume that both images originated under Greek influence. The most intriguing detail is naturally the "river of fire," which evokes the image of Pyriphlegethon by immediate association.

Etymologically, the name of the river consists of two roots: πῦρ, "fire," and φλέγω, "to burn." It is extremely tempting to interpret the river as consisting of a flood of burning fire. Yet, surprising as it is, the theology of this river as a stream of fire is not developed in the Greek sources. We find the only reference to such an image in Virgil (Aen. 6,550–551), i.e. in a late (compared to the date of the composition of 1 Enoch) and Latin author, whereas the authentic Greek sources remain surprisingly guarded and consistent on this point. Homer mentions the four great rivers of the underworld, but makes no distinction between the substance of Pyriphlegethon and the three other rivers (Homer, Od. 10,513–514). That

---

10 Cf. MILIK, Books, 15.38.
11 Thus, Odysseus upon being sent by Circe to Hades only complains that nobody has yet tried crossing the ocean *on a ship* (obviously alluding not only to the "normal" means of getting there, but also to the previous trip of Heracles, see Homer Il. 8,366–369). Presumably, a very faint echo of the motif of darkness appears in the description of the land of the Cimmerians, where there is no sunshine (Homer, Od. 11,14–18).

is consistent with the absence of any indication of the presence of fire in the Homeric underworld. A more detailed picture can be expected in Plato, whose descriptions of the underworld geography are much more elaborate. Indeed, in Phaedo he extensively speaks of the river in question. Pyriphlegethon is "dirty and muddy" (Phaed. 113a–b). Yet, like another river, Kokytos, it carries sinners from the inner area of Tartaros up to the Acherusian valley (114a). Plato does not suggest that those brought up by Pyriphlegethon are burnt by fire: both rivers act as floods and not as instruments of punishment. Nevertheless, he mentions that Pyriphlegethon passes through a place "burning with a great fire" (113a), where it forms a boiling lake. After this point its stream becomes dirty and muddy (but not fiery!). A scholion ascribed to Nonnus explains the difference between Kokytos and Pyriphlegethon, describing the former as the coldest river of the underworld, whereas the latter is the warmest.[12] The explanation of this mythographer accords with Plato's description: the characteristics of water in different floods are different, but there is no suggestion of flowing fire. It is highly significant that the late mythographers repeatedly attempt to explain the etymology of Pyriphlegethon. These explanations differ, but they have one feature in common: the general premise is that the substance flowing in the river is not fire. Thus, we encounter the idea that the name derives from the rite of burning corpses on a fire.[13] According to another metaphorical explanation, the name refers to the moral suffering of those who have lost a member of kin, because they are "burnt by grief."[14] This general tendency to find a plausible etymology that avoids the idea of a fiery flood sheds interesting light on Plato's description. It appears that by describing Pyriphlegethon as passing through the place "burning with fire" Plato offers another explanation—the earliest that has come down to us—of the provocative name, which is at odds with the Greek concept of this underworld river.

Apart from the river of Pyriphlegethon, Plato mentions "much fire and great rivers of fire" in Phaedo (111d). These rivers bear no relation to either the four mythological rivers of Hades or post-mortem punishment. They are, however, connected to the volcanic activity in Sicily (111e). By stressing this connection Plato subscribes to a very ancient Greek literary tradition. In Greek literature, any mention of the "rivers of fire" and lava has a precise geographical point of reference, namely the volcano of Etna in Sicily (Pindar, Pyth. 1,21–27; Aeschylus, Prom. 363–370; cf. also Ps.-Aristotle, De mundo 395 b 21–27). These literary images resulted from contemplating the geophysical landscape of Magna Graecia.

---

[12] Scholia mythologica 5,31.
[13] Apollodorus, Fr. 10,45–54 = Stobaeus, Flor. I 49–50; cf. Cornutus, Nat. d., 74,24.
[14] Galen, Gram. Allegoriae in Hesiodi theog. 324,6.

Yet, to the best of my knowledge, the Greek authors never go so far as to connect them with the traditional mythological geography of the beyond. On the contrary, if these rivers and sources evoke mythological connotations, they allude to the forge of the Olympic god Hephaistos.[15] Even Plato, who, as I mentioned above, seeks to give a coherent and complex cosmological description, keeps the areas separated.[16] He does not mention the rivers of fire in his description of the post-mortem wanderings of souls. In the Greek tradition, these rivers have a geographical rather than a mythological significance. It is not this kind of river that a human is supposed to see having crossed the invisible line between the worlds. That does not, however, exclude the possibility of the fiery mythology of Pyriphlegethon having developed in a later period somewhere beyond the sphere of our authoritative sources. However, the consistent picture drawn by the Greek mythographers casts doubt on the Greek character of this idea and suggests that we should view the development as also having been influenced by the neighbouring religious traditions.

I will now return to the "river of fire" in the text of 1 Enoch. Besides 1 En. 17:4–5, we find another mention of the rivers of fire in 1 En. 14:18–22. Here "the rivers of burning fire" (v. 19) are interwoven into the description of the shining Glory of God. One of the most peculiar features in this description is that it compares the Glory of God to the flame and splendour of the sun, rather than simply to the flame of fire (as is typical of other descriptions known to us [cf. Ezek 1-2]; Dan 7:9–10). The image of the sun predominates in this vision. Thus, all the images of burning fire in this passage are closely connected to the vision of the flaming sun.

This observation is in perfect accord with what we find lower in the text, in 1 En. 17:4–5. Here, starting from v. 4, the Greek text shows that the image of fire is strictly connected to the idea of the sun. The text speaks of the "fire of the sunset"[17] and then, even more precisely, stresses the connection between this fire and all the everyday sunsets (v. 4). In this context, the "river of fire" appears and transforms into "the great sea of the sunset." "The sea of the sunset" is not simply the sea of the west, but a kind of sea, possibly in a metaphorical sense, into which the evening sun disappears. Thus, "the river of fire, in which fire flows down like

---

15 Aeschylus, Prom. 363–370.
16 We can find a not very clear-cut attempt to connect the mythological underworld and geography in Phaedo 113b. This, however, does not have far reaching consequences in regard to the general picture presented by Plato.
17 One of the first meanings of the word δύσις is "the sunset", which can only indicate the west metonymically.

water," has strong astronomical connotations, symbolizing the fiery stream of the moving sun.[18]

The astronomical character of this image cannot be explained either by the influence of any of the rivers of Greek mythology (Pyriphlegethon being no exception despite its intriguing name), or by the volcanic rivers of the Sicilian landscape. However, it is again in perfect accord with the typology of crossing the line between the worlds in the Mesopotamian tradition. In the Epic of Gilgamesh cited above (X 79–82), where it is stressed that no human can go beyond the border, the sun appears as the only living being capable of doing so:

> There never was, O Gilgameš, a way across, //and since the days of old none who can cross the ocean. //The one who crosses the ocean is the hero Šamaš: //apart from Šamaš, who is there can cross the ocean?

The rising of the sun and the setting of the sun are mentioned in the same context in Gilg. IX 84–85,[19] in a Babylonian prayer, in the Ugaritic Keret Epic, and in a text of a Hittite ritual[20]. All these images are at work in 1 En. 17:4–8. This context makes it clear that the image of the (astronomical) river of fire does not essentially reflect the Greek ideas of the underworld. It can be explained from within another tradition that is active in every sentence of the passage.

Against this background, I see no justification for seeking Greek influence in the phrase "I saw the great rivers." The (great) rivers of the Greek tradition have widely known specific features, namely their number and names. In the absence of any indication of the characteristics inseparably connected with Greek mythology, the possibility remains that any other number or names can be alluded to. It should be recalled that in the Babylonian Epic of Gilgamesh Ut-napishtim dwells on the mouth of several rivers (*pi-i nārārti*—a description which is intended to stress the extreme remoteness of the place) (XI 205.206), and that the two streams of the abyss are alluded to in the Ugaritic text cited above. It may also be useful to keep in mind such passages as Gen 2:10–15 and Ps 23(24):2.[21]

Concluding this section of my argument I wish to stress the following. In the Greek text of 1 Enoch (1 En. 14:19) we find a collocation that may allude to the etymology of Pyriphlegethon: "and from beneath the throne issued rivers of flaming fire (ποταμοὶ πυρὸς φλεγόμενοι)." It is remarkable that, if it is a deliberate

---
[18] This is also the interpretation of MILIK, Books, 38, and NICKELSBURG, 1 Enoch, 282.
[19] Unfortunately, the text is corrupt there and the details remain obscure. The passage combines the idea of impossibility of crossing the line with that of the movement of the sun, of its movement across the river (the sea), and of its setting there.
[20] See WEST, East Face, 152–153.
[21] See also COBLENTZ BAUTCH, Geography, 71–72.

allusion, it refers to an image that has absolutely no point of contact with the Greek ideas of the underworld and its rivers and in which the presence of fire can be sufficiently explained from within the biblical tradition (cf. Ezek 1:27). Moreover, if it is an allusion, it is an etymological one. Etymological allusions in a Hebrew or Aramaic text to a foreign tongue would hardly be possible by definition. Yet, they can enter into a text during its translation from Aramaic (Hebrew) into Greek. Consequently, this case, which may exemplify many other cases, suggests the possibility that the problem of allusion to Greek material can be limited to the Greek translation and to the extent to which it could have influenced further translations.

2 Post-mortem justice in Greek sources in light of methodological problems

There is no doubt that the question of Greek influence on the extant Greek text of 1 Enoch is worth studying and deserves to be discussed in a separate paper.[22] Nevertheless, the hypotheses referred to above, according to which Greek religion and mythology at certain points influenced 1 Enoch as a Jewish apocalyptic work *tout court*, prompt many objections. These objections arise not only from a different view of how particular contexts of 1 Enoch should be interpreted (as demonstrated using the example of rivers), but also from a number of methodological premises and a different idea of the development of certain Greek traditions. I now wish to outline the methodological problems relevant to the subject of Greek-Oriental influences and related problems from the history of Greek literature. This discussion is all the more apposite because the arguments in question were set forth prior to the most important development in this field. The validity of the hypotheses outlined above should be questioned based on the following: a) methodology of the study of the Greek-Oriental connection studied from the Greek perspective, b) the literary and mythological context of 1 Enoch.

The scholars who developed or maintain the thesis that some important motifs in 1 Enoch are dependent in some manner upon Greek tradition have never taken into account an important direction of studies that deals with the Oriental roots and connections of Greek antiquity. Partly, this attitude can be explained. The works that significantly changed our ideas of the connection between Oriental and Greek cultures are those of Walter Burkert and Martin West. They were

---

22 The presence of Sirens in the Greek text (19:2) is eloquent proof of such an influence.

published in the last quarter of the 20th century. However, what Dieterich and Glasson were allowed to dismiss is impossible to ignore afterwards. The archaic period has been studied extremely systematically in the works of Burkert and West. These authors draw a wide picture of influences exercised by Mesopotamian cultures upon Greek mythology, literature and thought. One of the most important conclusions is that this influence cannot be reduced to one temporary, limited impact. It was a continuous process affecting different geographical and cultural areas.[23]

West ends his study at the middle of the 5th century B.C.E. Nevertheless, the declarative orientation of Plato and the Pythagorean tradition toward the Orient is at odds with the idea that the epoch of cultural influences drew to a close where the study of West ends. Even a general survey of the literary history of the Academy and the Lyceum testifies to the interest in different Oriental traditions on the part of Plato's followers.[24]

In speaking of the subjects relevant to 1 Enoch, we must stress that the study of West shows that in the Greek sources many aspects of the geography and conditions of the beyond[25], the Isles of the Blessed[26], the journey to Hades (known as *Nekyia*)[27] have strong parallels in the Mesopotamian tradition. The motif of the Greek Titans and of the Enochic bad angels, both imprisoned under the earth, can also be traced back to a common Mesopotamian prototype[28]. However, in the last case no attempts are made to explain the motif in 1 Enoch as being influenced by Greek culture, whereas the first three points are traditionally subject to this interpretation. Generally speaking, the idea of a common Mesopotamian prototype does not interfere with that of possible influences by Greek culture. Nevertheless, a common background makes it necessary for anybody setting out such a thesis to show that a given motif in the Jewish source was influenced not by what is common to both the Greek *and* Mesopotamian background, but by what is specifically typical of the development of a subject in the Greek tradition. This has never been attempted by those who support the idea of Greek influence. In seeking to define this influence, the scholars both before and after the important shift in our understanding of the Greek debt to Oriental sources have paid very little attention to distinguishing specifically Greek features of the given subject matter.

---

23 BURKERT, Babylon, 65; WEST, East Face, 493.585.
24 DIRLMEIER, Peripatos.
25 WEST, East Face, 137–165.
26 WEST, East Face, 166–167.
27 WEST, East Face, 415–417.
28 WEST, East Face, 297–299; KVANVIG, Roots, 295–318.

Following the principle of Burkert and West, if we do not find anything specific to Greek development in a subject supposedly influenced by Greek culture, it is more logical to assume a common source than an influence.[29]

2.1 Homer and 1 Enoch

I wish to illustrate this idea using the example of Odysseus' descent to Hades. In the eleventh song of the Odyssey Odysseus descends to Hades in order to question the soul of the prophet Teiresias. On his way he encounters many souls of his relatives and friends, as well as a number of other famous souls. He sees several great sinners, who are suffering eternal torments. The inference has been made by those studying intercultural influences that the specific feature of Odysseus' journey is that he travels to the places of punishment, which accords with the goal of Enoch's journey.

However, Homer's description of the netherworld contains both features inherited from an Oriental background and those that are specific to the Greek elaboration of this subject matter.

It is remarkable that among all the people seen by Odysseus only three figures are undergoing punishment: Titias, Tantalus and Sisyphus, all of them monstrous mythological offenders. West notes: "Apart from these latter individuals, there is no suggestion that different sorts of people receive different treatment in the Homeric underworld."[30] The punishment of Tantalus consists of thirst and hunger. He stands in a lake, but cannot drink because the water disappears when he tries to reach it. The same happens to the fruits that are hanging over his head.

When in the Epic of Gilgamesh Enkidu descends to the netherworld he sees a great variety of post-mortem situations. They vary from suffering to the highest well-being, according to different criteria. For instance, the man who did not respect the word of his father and mother "drinks water measured in a scale, he never gets enough."[31] The similarity with regard to the punishment is striking:

---

[29] A famous example would be the known parallel between Dan 2 and Hesiod's myth of the succession of generations. This close parallel could have been explained as an influence, but both Burkert and West deny this possibility, arguing for a common Mesopotamian source of Anatolian or Syrian provenance (BURKERT, Apokalyptik, 213–215; WEST, East Face, 218–219). Burkert specifies: "Dabei sind die Übereinstimmungen mit Daniel so speziell, dass unabhängige Entstehung so schwer zu verfechten ist wie eine Abhängigkeit Daniels von Hesiod" (BURKERT Apokalyptik, 214).
[30] WEST, East Face, 164.
[31] Bilgames 11,12 (GEORGE, Babylonian Gilgamesh Epic, vol. II, 776).

both have some contact with water and some access to it, but both remain thirsty. The kind of contact they have can be said to provoke thirst. Food is another feature known from the description of Enkidu that acts as a punishment/reward in the netherworld.[32]

Such rewards seem out of place in the Homeric underworld. The dead, emphatically described as shadows, are not supposed to maintain any bodily functions like eating or drinking or sexual intercourse (which is typical of the Epic of Gilgamesh). It is highly likely that the character of punishment to which Tantalus is subjected was borrowed from a non-Greek background together with the image of punishment itself. It should be stressed that Homer does not generalize the idea of rewards in the netherworld. Except for these three mythological figures, bad people are not punished (e.g. Thersites). Nor are good people rewarded. Even Achilles, who is addressed by Odysseus as "the most blessed" of all humans, famously laments his fate in Hades (Od. 11,488–491). The miserable destiny of all people indiscriminately is stressed in Od. 11,36–43. All the categories that are treated separately in the Netherworld of the Gilgamesh epic have a common and sad non-existence in the Homeric one.

The case of Menelaus, who receives a prediction that he will not die, but will be conveyed to the extremes of earth, where living is easiest for mortal people (Homer, Od. 6,561–569), only confirms the abovementioned statement. Menelaus is supposed to receive a blessed and eternal life *without dying*. The closest parallel to this is the situation of Ziusudra, Atra(m)hasis or Ut-napishtim in Sumerian texts and in the Epic of Gilgamesh.[33] All these heroes have likewise avoided death. The case of Menelaus is further eloquent testimony of the influence of an Oriental prototype. This prototype has been borrowed without being worked into the picture of post-mortem existence.

A very interesting illustration of the Homeric tendency not to explore the concept of post-mortem judgement and rewards is the representation of Minos. In the late tradition, for instance in Plato, Minos is one of the three famous judges in the netherworld. Legal functions in the netherworld are already assigned to him in Homer. However, it seems, here he exercises them only by judging cases *between* the dead and by having over-all legal charge of the dead (Homer, Od. 11,568–571). Thus, his post-mortem fate recalls less closely that attributed to him in Plato's

---

32 Bilgames a 2; j 2; k 3; n 2 (GEORGE, Babylonian Gilgamesh Epic, vol. II, 774–776); cf. Codex Hammurapi XXVII 40.
33 Gilg. XI 189–196; West, East Face, 166–167.

dialogues than that of a very "righteous" man in the Gilgamesh epic: "Among the junior deities he sits on a throne and listens to the proceedings."[34]

The Homeric picture can be summarized as follows. The number of the punished is reduced to three mythological figures, without the tendency to extrapolate the idea to ordinary people. One of the images particularly resembles a parallel in the Epic of Gilgamesh. The blessed eternal life predicted for Menelaus corresponds to the case of Ut-napishtim, who has not died, rather than referring to post-mortem rewards. The functions of Minos are interpreted not in the sense of post-mortem judgement, but in that of the legal order and legal proceedings of the beyond, which again has a parallel in the Mesopotamian sources. All these motifs have been borrowed from the Mesopotamian background, whereas a specifically Homeric elaboration of the picture of the beyond consists in elimination of the idea of the rewards and emphasis on the idea of sombre and hopeless parity.

This is precisely the most important divergence between the Homeric beyond and that of the Gilgamesh epic. In the latter, the idea of post-mortem rewards and punishments is treated most extensively. For instance, in Enkidu's description the category of sexuality/fecundity is discussed so extensively as to embrace almost all kinds of people who descend to the netherworld. At the same time this criterion is not the only one applied to the defunct in order to determine their post-mortem situation: there are many other criteria, such as various circumstances of death, as well as categories including disobedience to parents, perjury or incorrect behaviour toward the gods. The cases of lepers and stillborn babies are discussed separately. It is not correct to say that none of these criteria are ethical. Though many of them bear no relation to either Judeo-Christian or Greek philosophical ethics, many of them, including the criterion of sexuality, can be regarded as aspects of ancient morality. The picture drawn in the Epic of Gilgamesh implies that the post-mortem destiny of *all* people is defined either by how they conducted their lives or by the events of their lives.

Focusing on this principle, we should note that the idea, reflected in the journey of Enoch, that all people after death will be classified according to certain circumstances of their lives even before the last eschatological judgement, with some of them receiving punishment and others being treated well, corresponds to the Mesopotamian principle and contradicts the Homeric one.

---

34 Bilgames, 268 (GEORGE, Babylonian Gilgamesh Epic, vol. II, 774).

2.2 Plato and 1 Enoch

However, the argument of those assuming Greek influence does not draw on Homer only. Odysseus' descent to Hades only serves as a prototype, a pattern story, which they assume was later developed in the image of the underworld presented in Plato's dialogues. It is this alleged continuity of the Homeric and Platonic underworld tradition that serves as a starting point of the arguments concerning the influence of Greek religion.

However, the continuity of the tradition between Homer and Plato that appears to be self-evident to many students of non-classical antiquity is anything but certain. It cannot be denied that Plato was educated on Homer. He was not only familiar with Homer and with the broad range of the traditions around him, but also consciously explored Homer, alluded to him, and commented on him, trying to superimpose on him his own vision of post-mortem punishments and rewards.[35] However, one of the most intriguing questions of the history of Greek culture is where—given an evident discontinuity with the Homeric worldview—these ideas come from.

In an edition of Aeschylus, Wilamowitz stresses the non-Greek origin of the ideas of post-mortem judgement that are alluded to by the tragedian. In particular, he points to Egyptian influence when remarking: "judicium inferorum potius e religione Aegyptica quam Graeca."[36] West correctly notes that the ideas of the blissful "life after death" came from the same source.[37] Both these aspects are present in Orphic teaching (explicitly correlated with the Egyptian religion as early as in Herodotus' History [Hist. 2,81,5]). The Orphics promised a blessed existence after death to all those who have purified themselves by certain cathartic rites as practised by them. According to them, a very dreary destiny awaited all other people. Nevertheless, Plato sharply criticizes the Orphics for this essentially magic scheme, in which morality, responsibility and justice have no place (Plato, Resp. 364e–365a).

In his own scheme these three notions play a key role. They establish that absolutely every human soul will be justly rewarded after death according to a fair judgement received at their post-mortem trial.

The dialogues of Plato show that in his time the idea of absolute moral responsibility and the picture of the post-mortem conditions he draws was by no

---

35 Thus, Plato explains why Homer did not refer to the punishment of an undoubtedly bad figure of Homeric epic, Thersites (Plato, Gorg. 525e).
36 WILAMOWITZ, Aeschyli tragoediae, 343.
37 WEST, East Face, 537.

means common in Athenian society. Socrates always introduces these ideas as his personal and strong beliefs rather than alluding to them as familiar to his interlocutors. Nor are these ideas popular in the tradition after Plato. The genre of the vision of the underworld disappears in the Academic sources very soon after Plato and his more remote followers even allow themselves to mock at such descriptions and the fears they convey.[38]

Consequently, the question of what led Plato to develop these ideas, which were so important to him, but became relatively unimportant to his following, is all the more pressing, as is the question of the background to the ideas.[39]

It is impossible to explore this extremely difficult subject in any depth within the limits of this article. Nevertheless, some interesting points can be highlighted. It is remarkable that in The Republic Plato stresses the barbarian descent of a certain Er, who relates his vision of the post-mortem judgement and destiny of the souls, saying that he was Pamphylian in origin (Resp. 614a).[40] He is even more explicit in Phaedo, a dialogue that contains a very detailed description of Hades and post-mortem conditions, which are often compared to those found in 1 Enoch. When persuading his friends of the immortality of souls and inevitability of post-mortem justice and answering the question of what supports such a conviction, Socrates says (Plato, Phaed. 78a 3–7):

> "Hellas, Cebes," he replied, "is a large country, in which there are many good men, and there are many foreign people also (πολλὰ δὲ καὶ τὰ τῶν βαρβάρων γένη). You ought to search through all of them in quest of such a charmer, sparing neither money nor toil, for there is no greater need for which you could spend your money" (Transl. Fowler).

Plato's interest in barbarian sources accords with our knowledge of another important component of his background: the Pythagorean tradition. A remarkable feature of the Pythagorean doxography (systematized by the followers of Aristotle) is the tendency to trace the origin of Pythagorean teaching back to Oriental roots. The Babylonian component (referred to using the ethnonym *chaldaioi*) plays an important role here.[41] This information cannot simply be dismissed as a later invention. To mention only evident and widely known facts, the famous theorem, attributed to Pythagoras, is applied in cuneiform texts long before this philosopher.[42] The Mesopotamian influence on Greek astronomy, another favoured

---

38 Cf. BURKERT, Apokalyptik, 206; see Plutarch, Adol. poet. aud. 17 b–f.
39 Cf. BURKERT, Apokalyptik, 206–207.
40 Pamphylia was located on the Near Eastern coast, in the territory of present-day Turkey.
41 MATUSOVA, Philon, 47.
42 BURKERT, Lore and Science, 405, n. 10.

subject of the Pythagoreans, is also well known.[43] One of Pindar's odes contains a clear allusion to the Pythagorean teaching of the post-mortem destiny of souls (Pindar, Ol. 2,72–74). Those souls who have succeeded in passing three blameless lives enter paradise, a garden where flowers of gold blaze, some of them growing on trees and others in the water. Again, the closest parallel to this peculiar description is found in the Epic of Gilgamesh: the description of the garden that Gilgamesh and Enkidu enter behind mount Mashu (IX 171–176; 184–194).[44] Remarkably, we find a typologically cognate description of the "true earth", which is also the post-mortem dwelling of the righteous in Plato's Phaedo (109e-111c), though the details of this description are closer to one also preserved in Enoch's journey (1 En. 18:6–8.24–32; 24:4–5).[45] This makes it very reasonable to assume a common, in this case evidently Mesopotamian, background to these passages.[46]

Thus upon consideration of the evidence described above, the question of the correspondence between the picture drawn in Plato's Phaedo, the dialogue most often referred to when speaking of Greek influence, and 1 Enoch appears to be highly complex. It is possible that the parallels result not from the influence of any allegedly Greek tradition upon 1 Enoch, but from the fact that the two texts (Phaedo and 1 Enoch) are somehow rooted in a common background. The presence of Oriental, and in particular Mesopotamian patterns in Plato's description of the underworld is possible as
- a reworking of the archaic Greek tradition that had already absorbed something of this subject matter at a very early stage;
- the influence of the Pythagorean tradition, which to some extent drew on Oriental traditions and sources, in particular (as Pindar shows) in descriptions of post-mortem existence;
- his own special interest in Oriental wisdom, explicitly testified in connection with this subject matter in Phaedo.

Keeping this in mind we can compare the picture of post-mortem divisions in Phaedo and 1 Enoch in order to highlight their common points and differences.

It seems that both in Plato (Phaed. 113a–114b) and 1 Enoch 22 the souls are divided into four groups. In Plato, besides very good and utterly bad ("incurable") souls, there are "curable" souls, who despite being offenders and murders can expiate their sins by undergoing temporary punishment and by obtaining the

---

[43] VAN DER WAERDEN, Science Awaking; BURKERT, Lore and Science, 299–301.428–430.
[44] WEST, East Face, 538.
[45] GLASSON, Greek Influence, 20–22.
[46] Regarding the connection between the descriptions in 1 Enoch and the Epic of Gilgamesh see KVANVIG, Roots, 247–253.

forgiveness of their victims (114b), and those intermediate souls that receive both rewards and punishments in the measure and proportion as deserved by each individual soul (113d). Thus, the Platonic picture implies that one's condition can be changed in the beyond, a possibility that is absent from the picture presented in 1 Enoch. Also, in the Platonic vision the division of the fourth group of intermediate souls, every one of which is treated in the beyond individually, implies that in the Platonic underworld circumstances after death in fact range as widely as there are conditions among humans (which corresponds to the picture of multiple subdivisions and particular situations drawn in the 12th song of the Epic of Gilgamesh). Thus, the souls in the Platonic beyond can be placed into four groups only roughly and for the sake of systematization. In 1 Enoch, unlike in Plato's picture, the number of categories seems to be precise and invariable. The coincidence in the number of the groups appears to be incidental and conceals substantial differences. It is also evident that the criteria of division differ (except for a very general, almost archetypal, differentiation between the righteous and utter sinners): in 1 Enoch we find also "the companions with the lawless" and "unjustly murdered", who are absent from the Platonic picture. This makes it very problematic to assume the influence of the picture preserved in one author upon that developed by another.

Nevertheless, we can recognize that there is also a substantial similarity between the two visions. Plato and 1 Enoch have in common the idea that everybody has a particular condition after death according to their actions in life. Thus, they share the idea of *a moral code* (though the moral codes themselves differ), which inevitably determines the place of a soul in the beyond. Both pictures have in common the broad diversity of post-mortem conditions (good, very bad, bad and neutral[47]). This is certainly indicative of a common typology. However, this common typology cannot be inspired by the Orphic tradition (or by any other religious tradition of a mystery type), as the traditions which are focused on cathartic rites/initiations emphasize the salvational meaning of their acts and consequently are essentially concerned with only two states in the beyond, that of the rescued and that of the non-rescued. The typology that unites Plato and 1 Enoch results from the idea of using a moral code as the only criterion of post-mortem conditions. This is, however, what distinguishes Plato from the Orphics rather than associating him with them. The question of whether Plato borrows this important idea together with some other minor elements from the Near Eastern substratum (in which it is certainly present) or develops it independently cannot be

---

[47] Cf. the third and fourth hollows in 1 Enoch.

discussed in this article, and possibly, cannot be univocally answered at all. However, the discussion above shows that the attractive, but partly also deceptive resemblance between Phaedo and 1 Enoch can hardly allow us to interpret them as parallel elaborations on the Orphic principles.

2.3 Mesopotamian background and 1 Enoch

It was not until the second half of the 20th century that several studies appeared, independently of one another, that extensively developed and reinforced the arguments concerning the Mesopotamian background of Enochic literature.[48] In particular, Helge Kvanvig argued against the thesis of Enoch originating from a mixture of motifs occurring in a broad spectrum of sources of different origin and for the Mesopotamian background of practically *all* important mythological traditions underlying 1 Enoch. According to Kvanvig, the journey of Enoch in 17–36 is no exception to this rule. He believes that, when composing this part of the text, the author of 1 Enoch used a wide range of mythical Babylonian traditions and adopted them using the form of a visionary journey: "He could disclose the far recesses of cosmos, the heavens and the underworld as portrayed in ancient [Mesopotamian] myths, but in a visionary journey."[49] Kvanvig himself elaborated only on some of the themes of the journey.[50] However, it seems that there is no lack of particular evidence confirming the typology proposed by him with regard to 1 En. 22 either. As said, in accord with Mesopotamian tradition reflected in the Gilgamesh epic, in 1 Enoch souls after death are subject to different circumstances even before the last judgement. They are assigned to different compartments: with a spring of water in the first one only, in that of the righteous. If we can trust the Greek translation in 1 En. 22:9, the characteristic of brightness directly refers here to the spring: οὗ ἡ πηγὴ τοῦ ὕδατος ἐν αὐτῷ φωτινή. This can hardly be overestimated in light of the importance of this image in the Mesopotamian underworld. The access to water and quality (clearness, taste) of water play such an important role in the rewards and punishments in the description of Enkidu that the reference to *abundant* water of *perfect* quality in the hollow of the

---

[48] VanderKam, Enoch; Kvanvig, Roots, in particular 319–342; Stuckenbruck, Book of Giants.
[49] Kvanvig, Roots, 339.
[50] See Kvanvig, Roots, 250–253.261–270.

righteous in 1 En. 22:9 (as opposed to the absence of water in the other compartments) should be viewed as a direct echo of this tradition.[51]

3 Biblical tradition and 1 Enoch

Nickelsburg, when mentioning the Mesopotamian patterns that may underlie some motifs in the journey of 1 Enoch, notes that a number of corresponding elements "could have derived directly from the Bible."[52] He stresses that the Bible has been studied insufficiently in this regard. He himself, breaking with the tendency of focusing on the thesis of Greek influence mentioned above, demonstrates how the description of life in Paradise can be explained using only biblical, and in particular prophetic, texts.[53] Agreeing with these tendencies in his thought, I wish to stress that the perspectives of intracultural studies have not been fully explored with regard to the post-mortem destiny of the souls in 1 Enoch.

There are numerous studies showing that many subjects and motifs in 1 Enoch came to be through interpretation of and reflection on earlier biblical texts, though it has also been demonstrated that the author of 1 Enoch in some cases also drew from more ancient Mesopotamian prototypes.[54] One of the most telling examples is the angels story, in which the use of some Mesopotamian traditions is combined with elaboration on the biblical narrative. Yet, to the best of my

---

[51] For awards, s. Bilgames, 260 (limited, but reasonable access to water for a man who has one son); s 2 (clean water is available to a man who died a natural death); MS nn from Ur 9, 16 (Gilgamesh, performing mourning rites, wishes for his parents to have clear water in the netherworld). For "punishments," s. Bilgames i 2 (a leper is separated from water); l 2 (a man who did not respect the word of his parents is always thirsting); n 2 (bitter water for the injurer of the name of god), MS ll from Ur v 2; x 2 (the sons of Sumer and Akkad drink dirty water from the place of massacre); y 2 (the same regarding the parents of Gilgamesh; GEORGE, Babylonian Gilgamesh Epic, vol. II,774-777). On the contrary, the reference to some "Greek, and especially Orphic, sources" (NICKELSBURG, 1 Enoch, 307; cf. ibid. 304; cf. BLACK, Book of Enoch, 167) seems to imply a remote and highly inexact parallel. The idea of the division between those who have/do not have access to water, and the quality of the water that the dead drink is not attested in the Orphic sources.
[52] NICKELSBURG, 1 Enoch, 279.
[53] NICKELSBURG, 1 Enoch, 315–328.
[54] See, in particular, ALEXANDER, Enochic literature; see also the general overview in VANDERKAM, Biblical Interpretation in 1Enoch, 96–125; VANDERKAM, Interpretation of Genesis, 129–148; KVANVIG, Roots, 280–286; KVANVIG, Watchers Story, 17–21; STUCKENBRUCK, Genesis 6:1-4, 99–106.

knowledge no attempt has been made to apply this strategy to the conditions preceding the last judgement. However, as we can see on the basis of many texts from Qumran, in the period of the formation of apocalyptic literature, interpretative study of the Bible was considered to be the main source of knowledge about the future.[55] Thus, we may suspect that the difference between what we read in the Bible and in 1 Enoch concerning the post-mortem situation may be explained not only by the fact that some other extra-biblical tradition underlies the narrative, but also by the fact that we take into consideration the "un-interpreted" Bible, overlooking the possibility that the contexts of the Bible were interpreted correspondingly with regard to the idea of the last judgement. Therefore, in my opinion, the biblical contexts that refer to the judging activity of God or those which, by virtue of certain keywords used, can be understood as referring to this activity are of primary importance to our discussion.

The description of the last judgement in 1 En. 1:3–9 has been found to allude to many prophetic passages dealing with the issue of judgement.[56] I will show that this allusion to the biblical tradition is also evident in the main themes in chapter 22. First of all, we can demonstrate this using the idea of pits (hollows), in which souls are confined during the waiting time before the last judgement.

The chapter begins as follows (1 En. 22:1–4):

> 1 From there I travelled to another place. And he showed me to the west a great and high mountain and hard rocks. 2 And there were four hollow places (τόποι κοῖλοι) in it, deep and very smooth. Three of them were dark and one illuminated; and the fountain of water was in the midst of it. And I said, "why these hollows are smooth and altogether deep and dark to view?" 3 Then Raphael answered, one of the holy angels who was with me, and said to me, "These hollow places (τόποι κοῖλοι) (are intended) that the spirits of the souls of the dead might be gathered into them. To this they were judged[57], here the souls of all the sons of men should be gathered. 4 And behold these are the pits (τόποι, Aram.: פחתיא) for the place of their confinement. Thus they were made until the day on which they will be judged, and until the time of the day of the end of the great judgement, which will be exacted from them."[58]

The prophet Isaiah says in 2:10: "Enter into the rock (בוא בצור), and hide thee in the dust (והטמן בעפר) from before the terror of the Lord, and from the glory of His majesty" (KJV). This pair of notions, rock and dusty earth, appears again in connection with the announcement of the universal judgement in Isa 2:19: "And they

---

55 BETZ, Offenbarung, 3–59.82–87.
56 VANDERKAM, Theophany, 129–150; HARTMAN, Asking, 23–25.
57 Unlike NICKELSBURG, 1 Enoch, I have left the Greek verb ἐκρίθησαν, because I think that the subject can be "souls of men" rather than "pits."
58 MILIK, Books, 229.

shall go into the holes of the rocks (מערות צרים) and into the caves of the earth (מחלות עפר) for fear of the Lord, and for the glory of his majesty, when he ariseth to shake terribly the earth." מחלות עפר corresponds to עפר in 2:10 and literally means "the holes in the soil," while מערות צרים corresponds to צר and refers to some rocky caves. This interesting notion of hollows is found in another description of the great day in Isa 24:17–18: "Fear, and the pit (פחת), and the snare are upon thee, O inhabitant of the earth. And it shall come to pass that he who fleeth from the noise of the fear shall fall into the pit (יפל אל־הפחת)." Here, the idea of dug earth is resumed using the word פחת, pit (cf. the verb פחת—"to hollow out"), which has obviously been chosen to phonetically fit in the line: "Fear (פחד), and the pit (ופחת), and the snare (ופח) are upon thee, O inhabitant of the earth." Several verses lower down it is repeated that all the kings will be "gathered together, as prisoners are gathered in the dungeon (בור), and shall be shut up in the prison (וסגרו על־מסגר), and after many days shall they be punished" (Isa 24:22).

As in Isa 2:10.19–21, in these lines of chapter 24 we find the idea of seclusion in a hollow or pit when waiting for the judgement. However, the wording of 1 En. 22:3-4 is closer to that found in Isa 24. בית עגנון in the Aramaic text (4QEnᵉ 1XXII) corresponds to מסגר in Isa 24:22[59] and the idea of people waiting there for the day of judgement ("[they will be fashioned in this manner] until the day they will be judged and until the time of the Day of the End of the Great Judgement which will be exacted of them"[60]) is exactly that of Isa 24:22 ("and after many days shall they be punished [judged]"). Moreover, even the word used in the Aramaic text for "pits," פחתיא, is identical with the term used by Isaiah in 24:18: פחת. Nevertheless, the stressed combination of rock with hollows (the hollows being an echo of the pit mentioned in Isa 24:17–18, as the term shows) in 1 En. 22:1–2 (ὄρος μέγα καὶ ὑψηλόν, πέτρας στερεάς. καὶ τέσσαρες τόποι ἐν αὐτῷ κοῖλοι [...] καὶ λίαν λεῖοι) points to the allusion to Isa 2:10.19 and refers to Isa 2:19.21, where the *plurality* of hollows is stressed. The conclusion lies close at hand that the author of 1 Enoch adapted these eschatological contexts of the prophet Isaiah when drawing the picture of waiting for the judgement in pits like in a prison. This observation highlights the important part played by biblical contexts that touch upon the issue of judgement in elaboration of the picture of the post-mortem waiting time before the Judgement in 1 Enoch. I will give some further examples of this below.

Another passage of interest for our discussion is 1 En. 22:8–13:

> [...] Then I asked about all the hollow places, why they were separated one from the other. And he answered me and said, "These three were made that the spirits of the dead might be

---

59 Observed by NICKELSBURG, 1 Enoch, 305.
60 Transl. MILIK.

separated. 1 And this has been separated for the spirits of the righteous, where the bright fountain of water is. 2 And this has been created [for the spirits] of the sinners, when they die and are buried in the earth, and judgement has not been executed on them in their life. Here their spirits are separated for this great torment, until the great day of judgement, of scourges and tortures of the cursed forever: there was a recompense for their spirits. There he will bind them forever. 3 And this has been separated for the spirits of those who plead, who report their destruction, when they are murdered in the days of the sinners. 4 And this was created for the spirits of the men who will not be pious, but sinners, and will be companions with the lawless. And their spirits will not be punished (to death, afflicted) on the day of judgement, [because those who suffer affliction there are punished less; nor will they be raised] from there."

a. *Those confined in the second hollow and the Book of Qoheleth*—The first two hollows refer to the opposite categories of people who are either righteous (1), or utter sinners (2) with the latter being severely punished on the day of judgement and remaining in the second hollow forever. It is said of these wicked people that "when they die and are buried in the earth, and judgement has not been executed on them in their life [...] there was a recompense for their spirits." This is a highly interesting remark. The mention of the absence of "judgement" during their lifetime and of the "rewarding of the spirits" suggests that the author attempted to work other biblical texts touching upon the problem of divine judgement and recompense into his picture. Unlike many other biblical texts of the Second Temple period alluding to the execution of divine justice during the lifetime of the suffering and afflicted,[61] the Book of Qoheleth is known for its more pessimistic approach. Although it says that "for every matter there is time and judgement (משפט), for the evil of man is great upon him" (Qoh 8:6), in the same context the author of Qoheleth lists examples of wicked people prospering all their lives long while multiplying their evil doing (Qoh 8:10–14). This idea of evil prospering is generally typical of the Book of Qoheleth (Qoh 4:1; 7:15). In combination with the idea of inevitability of judgement for every human being and deed, it suggests the conclusion that these wicked people have not received "judgement" in their lifetime,[62] which makes clear the allusion of 1 Enoch to those wicked people in regard to whom "judgement has not been executed on them in their life." In accordance with Qoh 3:17, where it is said that "The righteous and the wicked God will judge; for there is a time *there* for every purpose and for every work," 1 Enoch asserts that

---

61 Sir 5:6; 12:6; 16:13–14; 32:14–17; 29:19; 33:11–15; 35:11–24; Wis 3:10–17; 4:18–20.
62 About the idea of "judgement" of a man at the end of his life cf. Sir 38:16.

these wicked people will receive a very severe judgement "there." Qoheleth asserts that "the dust returneth to the earth as it was, and the spirit (הרוח) returneth unto God who gave it" (Qoh 12:7). This suggests that the emphatic assertion of 1 Enoch that "there was a recompense for their spirits (ἣν ἀνταπόδοσις τῶν πνευμάτων)"[63] is another elaboration on the ideas inspired by the Book of Qoheleth.

b. *The murdered in the third hollow and Ps 37*—The third hollow is destined for the murdered. The reference to them having been slain "in the days of the sinners" obliquely shows that they were murdered by the sinners while being innocent. Nevertheless, they are still waiting for judgement in order to get satisfaction and be acquitted. Remarkably, we find an interesting parallel to this picture in Ps 37:32–33. It is said here that "(32) the wicked watcheth the righteous and seeketh to slay him. (33) The Lord will not leave him in his hand, nor condemn him when he is judged" (KJV; ולא ירשיענו בהשפטו). It is absolutely clear that the psalmist is speaking of the judgement of the murdered (or of one in danger of being murdered), which this person has to undergo. The other question is what kind of judgement the psalmist meant. Though he certainly explores the eschatological perspective in referring to the inheritance of the land by those who are blessed of God (37:9–22), it seems that he is speaking about the justice that has to be executed in this world during the lifetime of the oppressed. Nevertheless, we know that in the late second Temple period the psalms, among other prophetic writings, were interpreted eschatologically. By chance, an interpretation of Ps 37 has been preserved among the *pesharim* from Qumran (4Q171 [pPs37,45]). In it, the wicked and the righteous are interpreted as the wicked Priest and the Teacher of Righteousness and the time that has to pass before the Trial is said to be forty years (4Q171 II,7,18). The interpretation that we find in the *pesharim* from Qumran was offered by a group with concrete eschatological expectations, so it had to fit their historical vision. The purpose of the author of 1 Enoch was different, namely to draw a universal picture of the post-mortem circumstances of all souls in the waiting time before the last judgement. Consequently, he could use an eschatological interpretation of the psalms (in accordance with the tendency attested in the texts from Qumran) adapting it to his aims. Thus, by this reading,

---

[63] As NICKELSBURG ad loc. notes, the word πνεῦμα "undoubtedly translates Aram. רוח to judge from the preserved Aramaic text 4QEnᵉ 1 22:3–4 (1 En 22:5)."

he must have interpreted the judgement of the murdered as the great universal judgement, for which all the slain (from Abel onwards) wait, which is the situation presented in 1 En. 22:12. As our discussion below will show, it is difficult to say whether the interpretation offered in 1 Enoch was influenced in some manner by interpretation of the psalm or whether both texts independently reflect a common tendency in Jewish thought that connects lawless murder with a kind of divine trial of the murdered. The important point is that the combination of the idea of murder with the idea of the trial executed upon the victim of murder in 1 Enoch does not seem to be unparalleled in Jewish thought, which elaborated on the idea of judgement.

c. *The principle of division into the four groups in 1 Enoch and legislative context of Exodus*—With this in mind, we can turn to the principle according to which 1 Enoch divides the four groups. It is widely known that the prophets when elaborating on the subject of the last judgement traditionally allude to the Sinai theophany, which has become part of the prophetic eschatological language.[64] Even the expression נקרות הצרים in Isa 2:21 (which will serve as abodes [or prisons] for people hiding themselves from [and waiting for] divine wrath) is also attested in Ex 33:22 (it refers to the place where Moses hides when waiting for the appearance of God). The presence of the imagery of Exodus has also been attested in the introductory chapter of 1 Enoch, which introduces the main subject of the book, the announcement of the great judgement. Contrary to the comments of Black and Nickelsburg and in accordance with an earlier article by VanderKam[65], I would stress that the text of 1 Enoch not only shows acquaintance with the common prophetic language of theophany, but also contains direct allusions to the Book of Exodus.[66]

---

64 JEREMIAS, Theophanie.
65 VANDERKAM, Theophany, 129–150.
66 For instance, speaking of the appearance of God on the day of judgement, the prophets speak of Him as coming from the desert and mountain (Isa 21:1; Hab. 3:3) and from Sion (Amos 1:2; Joel 4:16; Isa 2:3) or, in one case, upon Sion (Isa 31:4), but never on mount Sinai. The prophet Micah, whose wording is considered to be close to 1 Enoch, also speaks vaguely of the "heights of the earth" without mentioning Sinai (Mic 1:3). The wording of 1 En. 1:4 (καὶ ὁ θεὸς τοῦ αἰῶνος ἐπὶ γῆν πατήσει ἐπὶ τὸ Σεινὰ ὄρος καὶ φανήσεται ἐκ τῆς παρεμβολῆς αὐτοῦ) directly alludes to Ex 19:11: "The Lord will come down in the sight of all the people upon mount Sinai;" and Ex 19:20: "And the Lord came down upon mount Sinai, to the top of the mount." The expression ἐκ τῆς παρεμβολῆς αὐτοῦ, "from His camp," can also be indicative of an interpretation of Ex 19:17,

This compels me to pay special attention to the wider context of Exodus. I wish to draw attention in particular to Ex 23:7:

> Keep thee far from a false matter; and the innocent and righteous slay thou not; for I will not justify the wicked (KJV; כי לא־אצדיק רשע).

The expression כי לא־אצדיק רשע is missing in the LXX, but is attested both in the MT and in the Paleo-Hebrew manuscript of Genesis-Exodus from the Qumran cave IV (Ex 23:5–16[67]). The presence of this subordinate clause in the Hebrew text and its absolute absence in the text of the LXX suggests two possible explanations. One possibility is that there were two parallel ancient textual traditions of Ex 23:7, one of which is reflected in the Greek text, while the other is preserved in the Paleo-Hebrew manuscript and MT. In this case, the importance of the *unique* use of the verb "to justify," צדק, in the first person as referring to God cannot be overestimated, particularly if we remember that the Sinai theophany serves the author of 1 Enoch as a pattern of the picture of the last judgement and that the general context defining ethical bans, orders, and restrictions strongly invites them to be rethought in the light of human responsibility at the last judgement. In this case, we accept the possibility that the author of 1 Enoch could reinterpret the expression "I will not justify the wicked" in terms of the judging activity of God at the last judgement. However, the second possibility is that the initially uniform text of Ex 23:7 suffered changes in the Hebrew tradition after it was translated into Greek. In this case the *terminus post quem* would be the early third century B.C.E., and the *terminus ante quem* would be the first half or first three quarters of the first century B.C.E.—the period to which the Paleo-Hebrew script of the parchment is dated[68]. This period, however, coincides with the time of formation of the apocalyptic literature and in particular with the approximate dating of 1 Enoch (which is believed to have been written in the third or early second century B.C.E.). If the phrase was inserted into the earlier text of Exodus, we have reason to think that this addition is eloquent testimony of the context being rethought from the viewpoint of the final judgement executed by God Himself. Neither of the possibilities can be excluded, but both invite us to look at this context of Exodus in terms of its relevance to 1 En. 22.

---

where the word המחנה (rendered in the LXX using the word παρεμβολή) is used with the preposition מן: ויצא משה את־העם לקראת האלהים מן־המחנה. If we assume that מן־המחנה was understood by the author of 1 Enoch as part of the collocation האלהים מן־המחנה (cf. the unnatural word order of the LXX: εἰς συνάντησιν τοῦ θεοῦ ἐκ τῆς παρεμβολῆς), we can explain why God appears ἐκ τῆς παρεμβολῆς αὐτοῦ.

67 DJD IX, 42.
68 DJD IX, 21.

Starting from chapter 20 of Exodus we find the ten commandments and additional prescriptions of ethical and legal nature. It is logical to suppose that execution of the moral code, given at mount Sinai as the law of the Jewish people, should be regarded as the condition of righteousness. The moral code, though its description in the Bible consists of many points, was given to the Jewish people to be fulfilled in its entirety. This idea makes it unnecessary for the author of 1 Enoch to specify any particular elements of righteousness or gradation of righteousness. From this point of view, the righteous should be those who fulfil (in the direct meaning of the word) the law. Those who do not acknowledge or do not fulfil the code are in the opposite category of those who are assigned to the first dark hollow.

The section of Exodus specifying the commandments and moral orders, which starts with Ex 20, contains the following words addressed by God to his people at the end of chapter 22: "And ye shall be holy men unto Me" (ואנשי־קדש תהיון לי; ἄνδρες ἅγιοι ἔσεσθέ μοι; Ex 22:30). In 1 En. 32:3, the characteristic of ἅγιοι (a usual translation of the Hebrew and Aramaic קדש) refers to people who enjoy a new life in the paradise of righteousness. This is an exceptional use of the epithet in 1 Enoch, as in the rest of the book this characteristic only refers to God and His angels. However, this accords with the prophet Isaiah, in whose book this epithet is applied to the saved "rest" of Israel (Isa 4:3). At the same time, unlike this context of Isaiah, "the holy ones" in 1 En. 32:3 are placed in the paradise of righteousness, which directly associates the idea of holiness with that of righteousness and thus with the "righteous" in 1 En. 22:9.

In Ex 22:30, the phrase "And ye shall be holy men unto Me" is placed in a context which admits double interpretation. On the one hand, it can be understood in the light of the following ban on eating impure food, but, on the other hand, it can be associated with the preceding text and understood as a description of the effect produced by the observance of all the orders of God. It is remarkable that the early books of the Bible testify to both possibilities. Holiness is connected to the observation of food restrictions in Lev 11:44 and 20:26, but to the fulfillment of all the divine commandments in Num 15:40. However, the texts from Qumran testify to the immense importance that the interpretation preserved in Num 15:40 had acquired in that period. The Qumran scrolls show that human holiness was strictly connected to the idea of fulfilment of all the divine commandments.[69] If we accept that this idea was familiar to the author of 1 Enoch (and it is highly probable, taking into consideration the strict connection of these notions in 1 En. 32:3), the conclusion lies close at hand that the line "And ye shall

---

[69] 4Q266 VII,4,5; XX,2,5,7; 1QS II,25; V,18,20; VIII,5,11,17,20–22; IX,4–6.

be holy men unto Me" at the end of Ex 22 drew his attention as an explicit formulation and recapitulation of this thought. Thus, we have reason to think that this line could have served him as a certain line of demarcation in the text, which he was rethinking.

It is not surprising, therefore, that at the beginning of the next chapter Ex 23, in the passage immediately preceding the phrase "for I will not justify the wicked," we can find indications of the two remaining groups: the "companions of the lawless" and the unjustly murdered.

Ex 23:1–2 starts with the following prescriptions: "Thou shalt not raise a false report; put not thy hand with the wicked (עִם־רָשָׁע; LXX: μετὰ τοῦ ἀδίκου) to be an unrighteous witness. Thou shalt not follow a multitude (אַחֲרֵי־רַבִּים; LXX: μετὰ πλειόνων) to do evil; neither shalt thou speak עַל־רִב (which is usually translated as "in a cause," "in a dispute," "in a lawsuit," but could be interpreted as "to the many") to decline after many (אַחֲרֵי רַבִּים; LXX: μετὰ πλειόνων) to wrest judgement" (KJV). We find in these lines the emphatic repetition of the idea of acting *together* with the sinners, *after* their example and *under* their influence. In two verses this thought is repeated four times using various Hebrew prepositions, all of which have been rendered into Greek using one preposition μετά. This corresponds to the way in which the idea of companionship is expressed in the Greek translation: μετὰ τῶν ἀνόμων ἔσονται μέτοχοι (cf. Ethiopic: "and with the wrongdoers they will be like them"). Thus, the idea of involvement in a crime with the perverse multitude could prompt our author to segregate into a different group those who "will be companions with the lawless," "the lawless" being identified with the perverse multitude.

The idea of cooperation with evil and acting together with the wicked, which makes a person or the whole Jewish nation guilty, important and old as it is in earlier biblical texts,[70] seems to acquire new and acute applicability in the period of formation of apocalyptic literature. Taking into consideration the early dating of the Book of Watchers together with the fact that the sectarian character of 1 Enoch cannot be considered as proven,[71] I think that we should look at the implications of the word "lawless," focusing on the legislative context in which we place the division. The word should refer to a category of people, directly indicated by the etymology of the word: those without the law, i.e. non-Jews (the inhabitants of the second hollow).

---

[70] Isa 2:6; 65:3–5; Jer 3:1–3; Ezek 6:9; 11:12.21; 14:5–11; 16:15; Ps 18(17):26; 26(25):4–5.9; 28(27):3.
[71] HIMMELFARB, Jubilees; ANDERSON, Denouncement; MATUSOVA, 1Enoch.

It is generally accepted that the development of apocalyptic and eschatological ideas took place amidst the political and cultural changes that followed the conquests of Alexander the Great. All over the Middle East, the Jews were confronted with the necessity of sharing the political and cultural field with newcomers, who had absolutely no experience of dealing with the religious habits of the Jews, which resulted both in bitter confrontations and in close companionship and common practices.[72] In this regard, I think that the brief comment of Matthew Black on the group in the fourth hollow is generally correct: "a probable reference to the 'fellow travelers,' the 'quislings' in Israel under the Seleucids and Roman oppressors,"[73] though the meaning of companionship can be broader, implying individual participation in cult practices. Thus, those contained in the forth hollow are not identical with non-Jews, yet behave or act according to the standards of the latter.

It should also be noted that although the Greek version explicitly speaks of a less severe punishment than that allotted to those in the second hollow (1 En. 22:13: οἱ ἐνθάδε θλιβέντες ἔλαττον κολάζονται αὐτῶν [sc. τῶν ἀνόμων]), on the day of judgement they will neither be justified, nor receive new life (1 En. 22:13: οὐδὲ μὴ μετεγερθῶσιν ἐντεῦθεν). This is in absolute accord with the prophetic words, predicting no forgiveness for the apostates (Isa 65:11–16; Jer 8-13; Ezek 6:11–14), as well as with the threats pronounced upon them in the texts of the Qumran community (4Q171 II,2-4; III,12; IV,18).

The last category of the innocently murdered is referred to in Ex 23:7: "Keep far from the false matter; and the innocent and righteous slay thou not (ונקי וצדיק אל־תהרג); for I will not justify the wicked." It is said in Exodus that God will not justify the wicked, though the context describes a situation in which the epithet "wicked" can only refer to the judge, while the innocent person stands trial and is judged. Exodus admits that an innocent person can be judged and murdered unjustly and, in this case, God promises justice will be done to the corrupt judge. Attentive reading suggests the conclusion that the phrase "I will not justify the wicked" refers to a kind of divine trial (judgement) that will come after the trial at which the innocent is condemned. This makes clear why the unjustly murdered are longingly waiting for divine judgement in 1 En. 22:12 and are also subjected to divine judgement in Ps 37:33.

The idea that the legislative context of the Sinai theophany plays a part in the formation of the picture of the conditions preceding the last judgement not only provides a key to understanding the principle of the segregation, but also draws

---

72 Sir 7:16; 12:14; 1 Macc 1:11–15; 2 Macc 2:27–29; 7:15.
73 BLACK, Book of Enoch, 17, cf. IBID., 168.

our attention to the roots of the idea of righteousness and suggests why the unjustly murdered are not placed together with the righteous (yet are not being punished either). In the legislative context the concept of righteousness, as mentioned above, would imply fulfilment of the entire law. In the eyes of all those who share this idea an unjust murder obviously does not imply that an unjustly murdered person was righteous in the sense of inviolable observance of all the commandments and prescriptions written in law. Nor would this interpretation interfere with the direct meaning of Exodus. Although Ex 23:7 speaks of "innocent and righteous," this characteristic is applied to a person facing an unjust trial and thus is strictly connected to his position in a concrete juridical case. According to the interpretation of the author of 1 Enoch this person has to wait until the day of the great judgement for justice to be done completely: the murderer is punished, but the murdered is judged with regard to his whole life.

4 Conclusion

In the first part of the article, I have questioned the idea that "the great rivers" and "the river of fire" in 1 En. 17:5–6 bear relation to the four rivers of the Greek underworld. In the second part, I have emphasized that the idea of multiple differentiations after death is related in a complex way to Greek thought. In a developed form, it can only be found in Plato. This picture is strictly connected to the idea that morality (a moral code) is the only criterion that determines the post-mortem destiny of souls. Whatever provenance this idea has in Plato, it was certainly present in the Mesopotamian substratum, to which many motifs in 1 Enoch can be traced back. In the third part, I have shown that the idea of the places (hollows) where the souls are confined after death in expectation of the last judgement and the principle according to which the souls are categorized draw on the biblical interpretation, particularly on the prophet Isaiah and on those contexts where the moral code is given. I have also suggested that the themes connected with the post-mortem circumstances in 1 Enoch should be interpreted in the biblical context, encompassing the broad spectrum of Second Temple texts concerned with themes of divine judgement. This significantly reduces the plausibility of the hypothesis of the eclectic character of the description found in 1 Enoch 22 and makes it unnecessary to turn to Greek philosophical sources in search of an explanation for the picture drawn there.

Bibliography

ALEXANDER, Philip S., The Enochic Literature and the Bible. Intertextuality and its Implications, in: Herbert, Edward D./Tov, Emanuel (Hg.), The Bible as Book. The Hebrew Bible and the Judaean Desert Discoveries, London/New Castle, Delaware 2002, 57-69.

ANDERSON, Jeff S., Denouncement Speech in Jubilees and Other Enochic Literature, in: Boccacini, Gabriele (Hg.), Enoch and Qumran Origins. New Light on a Forgotten Connection, Grand Rapids, Michigan 2005, 132–136.

BETZ, Otto, Offenbarung und Schriftforschung in der Qumransekte (WUNT 6), Tübingen 1960.

BLACK, Matthew, The Book of Enoch or 1 Enoch. A New English Edition, Leiden 1985.

BURKERT, Walter, Lore and Science in Ancient Pythagoreanism, Cambridge, Massachusetts 1972.

BURKERT, Walter, Apokalyptik im frühen Griechentum. Impulse und Transformationen, in: Hellholm, David (Hg.), Apocalypticism in the Mediterranean World and the Near East. Proceedings of the International Colloquium on Apocalypticism, Uppsala, August 12–19, 1979, Tübingen 1983, 235–254 (= Graf, Fritz [Hg.], Walter Burkert, Kleine Schriften IV. Mythica, Ritualia, Religiosa 1, Göttingen 2011, 204–224).

BURKERT, Walter, Babylon, Memphis, Persepolis. Eastern Contexts of Greek Culture, Cambridge, Massachusetts 2004.

CHARLES, Robert H. (Hg.), The Book of Enoch or 1 Enoch. Translated from the editor's Ethiopic text and edited with the introduction, notes, and indexes of the first edition wholly recast, enlarged, and rewritten. Together with a reprint from the editor's text of the Greek fragments, Oxford 1912.

COBLENTZ BAUTCH, Kelley, A Study of the Geography of 1 Enoch 17–19. "No One Has Seen What I Have Seen" (JSJSupp 81), Leiden 2003.

DIETERICH, Albrecht, Nekyia. Beiträge zur Erklärung der neuentdeckten Petrusapokalypse, Darmstadt ³1969 (1893).

DIRLMEIER, Franz, Peripatos und Orient, in: Antike 14 (1938) 120–136.

FOWLER, Harold North et al. (Hg.), Plato with an English Translation, 5 vols. (LCL), Cambridge, Massachusetts 1914-1935.

FRIEDRICH, Johannes, Hethitisches Elementarbuch, 2 vols., Heidelberg, 2. verb. und erweiterte Aufl. 1967.

GEORGE, Andrew R. (Hg.), The Babylonian Gilgamesh Epic. Introduction, Critical Edition and Cuneiform Texts, 2 vols., Oxford et al. 2003.

GLASSON, Francis T., Greek Influence in Jewish Eschatology. With Special Reference to the Apocalypses and the Pseudepigrapha (Biblical Monographs 1), London 1961.

GORDON, Cyrus H., Ugaritic Textbook. Grammar, Texts in Transliteration, Cuneiform Selections, Glossary, Indices (AnOr 38), Rom 1965.

GRELOT, Pierre, La géographie mythique d'Hénoch et ses sources orientales, in: RB 65 (1958) 33–69.

HARTMAN, Lars, Asking for a Meaning. A Study of 1Enoch 1-5 (Coniectanea biblica. New Testament Series 12), Lund 1979.

HIMMELFARB, Martha, Jubilees and Sectarianism, in: Boccacini, Gabriele (Hg.), Enoch and Qumran Origins. New Light on a Forgotten Connection, Grand Rapids, Michigan 2005, 129–131.

JEREMIAS, Jörg, Theophanie. Die Geschichte einer alttestamentlichen Gattung (WMANT 10), Neukirchen-Vluyn 1965.

KVANVIG, Helge S., Roots of Apocalyptic. The Mesopotamian Background of the Enoch Figure and the Son of Man (WMANT 61), Oslo 1988.

KVANVIG, Helge S., The Watchers Story, Genesis and Atra-Hasis. A Triangular Reading, in: Boccaccini, Gabriele (Hg.), The Origins of Enochic Judaism. Proceedings of the First Enochic Seminar, University of Michigan, Sesto Fiorentino, Italy, June 14-23, 2001, Torino 2002 (= Henoch 24,1.2 [2002]), 17–21.

MATUSOVA, Ekaterina D., Philon Alexandrijskij I grecheskaja doxographia, in: Vestnik Drevnej Istorii 2001 (1) 40–52.

MATUSOVA, Ekaterina D., 1Enoch in the context of Philo's writings, in: Lange, Armin et al. (Hg.), The Dead Sea Scrolls in Context, vol. 1, Leiden/Boston, Massachusetts 2011, 385–398.

MILIK, Józef T., The Books of Enoch. Aramaic Fragments of Qumrân Cave 4. With the collaboration of Matthew Black, Oxford 1976.

NICKELSBURG, George W.E., 1 Enoch. A Commentary on the Book of 1 Enoch. Chapters 1–36.81–108 (Hermeneia), Minneapolis, Minnesota 2001.

SKEHAN, Patrick W. et al. (Hg.), Qumran Cave 4. Paleo-Hebrew and Greek Biblical Manuscripts (DJD IX), Oxford 1992.

STUCKENBRUCK, Loren T., The Book of Giants from Qumran. Text, Translation and Commentary (TSAJ 63), Tübingen 1997.

STUCKENBRUCK, Loren T., Genesis 6:1–4 as Basis for Divergent Readings during the Second Temple Period, in: Boccaccini, Gabriele (Hg.), The Origins of Enochic Judaism. Proceedings of the First Enochic Seminar, University of Michigan, Sesto Fiorentino, Italy, June 14–23, 2001, Torino 2002 (= Henoch 24,1.2 [2002]), 99–106.

VANDERKAM, James C., The Theophany of Enoch I 3b–7,9, in: VT 23 (1973) 129–150.

VANDERKAM, James C., Enoch and the Growth of an Apocalyptic Tradition (CBQMS 16), Washington, D.C. 1984.

VANDERKAM, James C., Biblical Interpretation in 1Enoch and Jubilees, in: Charlesworth, James H./Evans, Craig A. (Hg.), The Pseudepigrapha and Early Biblical Interpretation (JSPSup 14), Sheffield 1993, 96–125.

VANDERKAM, James C., The Interpretation of Genesis in 1Enoch, in: Flint, Peter et al. (Hg.), The Bible at Qumran. Text, Shape, and Interpretation (Studies in the Dead Sea Scrolls and Related Literature), Grand Rapids, Michigan et al. 2001, 129–148.

VAN DER WAERDEN, Bartel L., Science Awakening, New York 1961.

WACKER, Marie Theres, Weltordnung und Gericht. Studien zu 1 Henoch 22 (FB 45), Würzburg 1982.

WEST, Martin, The East Face of Helicon. West Asiatic Elements in Early Poetry and Myth, Oxford 1997.

WILAMOWITZ-MOELLENDORFF, Ulrich von (Hg.), Aeschyli tragoediae, Berlin ²1958 (¹1914).

Hermann Lichtenberger
„Dem Tode verfallen war ich wegen meiner Sünden" (11QPs^a XIX,1–18)

> Dem Tode verfallen war ich wegen meiner Sünden, und meine Übertretungen hatten mich an die Scheol verkauft (11QPs^a XIX,9–10).[1]

Die Titelzeile mit dem dazu gehörenden Parallelismus membrorum steht in der Psalmenhandschrift 11QPs^a in einem Lied, das in der DJD-Edition von James A. Sanders „Plea for Deliverance" genannt wurde, das aber, wie Ingo Kottsieper[2] betont, nur in den Zeilen 13–16 Bitten enthält. Trotz der gewählten Gattungsbezeichnung hatte James A. Sanders diesen Psalm als „Danklied"[3] eines Einzelnen bezeichnet.[4]

Die Handschrift ist nicht vollständig erhalten, ihr Schluss ist durch eine Leerkolumne sicher, der Beginn dagegen völlig offen. Wie viele Kolumnen dem erhaltenen Text vorangingen, lässt sich nur vermuten, jedenfalls begann die Handschrift sicher nicht erst mit Ps 101.[5]

Das Lied steht in einer Sammlung von Psalmen, die kanonische (ab Ps 101) – z. T. in anderer Reihenfolge gegenüber MT –, deuterokanonische (Ps 151; Sir 51,13–20 [...] 30), nichtkanonische Psalmen und einen Prosatext („David's Compositions") bietet.[6]

Die Handschrift 11QPs^a ist auf ca. 50 n. Chr. zu datieren, die Sammlung mag in die Mitte des 2. Jahrhunderts v. Chr. zurückgehen. Ob es sich dabei um eine von MT abhängige oder unabhängige Sammlung handelt, ist umstritten. Die vor- bzw. außerqumran-essenische Herkunft erscheint mir zweifelsfrei. Wenn die Aussagen des Liedes im zweiten Teil unserer Ausführungen in Bezug zu qumran-essenischen Texten gebracht werden, so hat dies vor allem zwei Grün-

---
1 SANDERS, Psalms Scroll, 76–79.
2 KOTTSIEPER, Plea, 125–150.
3 SANDERS, Psalms Scroll, 76. SANDERS with CHARLESWORTH and RIETZ, Non-Masoretic Psalms, 193, kombiniert: "a prayer for deliverance from sin and Satan with a praise of thanksgiving for past experiences of salvation embedded within the prayer."
4 KOTTSIEPER, Plea, 147, bestreitet mit Recht den Gesamtcharakter als „Plea", will aber auch die Bezeichnung als „Lobpsalm" nicht gelten lassen. Eine genauere Gattungsbestimmung erfolgt freilich nicht, wohl aber eher allgemeine Umschreibungen wie „liturgischer Gebrauch [...] im Rahmen eines gemeinschaftlichen Gebets, was auch seine implizite Ausrichtung auf eine Gemeinschaft widerspiegelt" (148).
5 LANGE, Handbuch, 397–398.
6 Siehe LANGE, Handbuch, 395–400, mit Literatur 445–450.

de: die zeitliche Nähe zu den Hodayot und zur Gemeinderegel 1QS und die Überlieferung des Psalters 11QPs^a in der Gemeinschaft vom Toten Meer.

1 11QPs^a XIX,1–18: „Plea for Deliverance"

1.1 Ort in der Handschrift

Die „Plea for Deliverance" wird gerahmt vom 2. syrischen Psalm (Ps 154) Kolumne 18 und Ps 139, von dem in Kolumne 20 die Verse 8–24 erhalten sind; es folgt Ps 137. Ps 139 ist ein Davidpsalm, und im Gefolge der „Davidisierung"[7] von 11QPs^a ist es durchaus möglich, dass das Lied David zugeschrieben wurde.[8]

Klaus Seybold[9] macht darauf aufmerksam, dass in 11QPs^a – wenn auch z.T. in abweichender Reihenfolge – alle Psalmen des vierten Davidpsalters (Ps 138–145) enthalten sind. Seybold bestimmt den Sitz im Leben dieses Davidpsalters im Gerichtsverfahren wohl am Tempel: Die Beter sind in Untersuchungshaft und warten auf ihr Urteil. Die Feinde und Ankläger bedrängen sie, sie aber vertrauen auf JHWH.

Ob diese konkrete Situation auch bei der Aufnahme dieser Davidpsalmen in die Sammlung 11QPs^a eine Rolle spielt, kann dahingestellt bleiben. Weiterführend ist der Hinweis von Ingo Kottsieper[10], dass sowohl die Psalmen des 4. Davidpsalters als auch 11QPs^a XIX zur Situation in der Makkabäerzeit passen.

Die Handschrift 11Q6 bietet sehr fragmentarisch ebenfalls den Text der „Plea", fügt am Anfang dabei noch drei Worte einer vorhergehenden Zeile hinzu: ודל אנוכי כי („und ich bin schwach, denn"). Für die Interpretation wird das Leitwort דל wichtig werden.

Kurz soll auf jeweils auf den Psalm eingegangen werden, welcher der „Plea" vorausgeht und folgt.

Vorhergeht in der Sammlung/Handschrift 11QPs^a der sogenannte 2. syrische Psalm (Ps 154), dessen Schlusssequenz für den Zusammenhang mit der „Plea"

---

7 FLINT, Psalms Scrolls, 192–195; DAHMEN, Psalmentext, 109–126; DAHMEN, Psalter-Versionen, 127–146. LANGE, Handbuch, 439–444, bespricht sorgfältig die verschiedenen Möglichkeiten, die der „Davidisierung" innewohnen.
8 Die „Davidisierung" findet ihren deutlichsten Ausdruck in Kol. XXVII,4–11 („David's Compositions"), wo David 4050 Lieder zugeschrieben werden.
9 SEYBOLD, Geschichte, 368–390.
10 KOTTSIEPER, Plea, 148.

von Bedeutung sein wird: „Aus der bösen Zeit rettet er ihr Leben" – „יהוה erlöst (גואל) den Armen aus der Hand der Fremden" (11QPsᵃ XVIII,16–17). Dies führt direkt hinüber zur „Plea". Ps 139 andererseits, der direkt folgt, weiß um die allumfassende Gegenwart Gottes beim Beter. Dabei ist nichts verborgen, implizit eben auch nicht jene inneren Zusammenhänge zwischen Sünde und Tod, wie sie in der „Plea" zum Ausdruck kommen („JHWH du erforschst mich und kennst mich").

1.2 Text[11] und Gliederung des Psalms[12]

Nur der Lebende preist JHWH[13]

>] gering bin ich, denn [...] (11Q6,1)
> (1) denn keine Made[14] preist dich,
> und ein Wurm[15] erzählt nicht deine Gnade.
> (2) Wer lebt, wer lebt, der preist dich,[16]
> es preisen dich alle, deren Füße taumeln,
> wenn du ihnen deine (3) Gnade kundtust
> und mit deiner Gerechtigkeit belehrst.
> Denn in deiner Hand ist das Leben eines jeden (4) Lebenden,[17]
> den Atem allen Fleisches hast du gegeben.

Anrufung JHWHs

> Handle mit uns, יהוה, (5) nach deiner Güte,
> nach der Fülle deines Erbarmens
> und nach der Fülle deiner Gerechtigkeit.[18]

---

11 Zur Übersetzung siehe KOTTSIEPER, Plea, 130–132, dessen Übersetzung herangezogen, aber nicht übernommen wurde; die dort aus literarkritischen und metrischen Gründen als sekundär bezeichneten Kola werden in der vorliegenden Übersetzung lediglich benannt, ohne weiter diskutiert zu werden.
12 Siehe KOTTSIEPER, Plea, 126.
13 Dass in der Handschrift für das Tetragramm althebräische Schrift verwendet wurde, soll im Text durch die hebräische Wiedergabe des Tetragramms angedeutet werden.
14 Jes 14,11 רמה und חולענה.
15 Vgl. Ps 22,7.
16 Enges Zitat von Jes 38,19.
17 Vgl. Hiob 12,10.
18 Nach KOTTSIEPER, Plea, 131, sekundär von „Handle" bis „Gerechtigkeit".

JHWH hörte

Gehört hat (6) יהוה auf die Stimme derer, die seinen Namen lieben,[19]
und nicht hat er seine Güte von ihnen abgelassen.

Lobpreis

(7) Gelobt sei יהוה, der Gerechtigkeitstaten tut,
der seine Frommen mit (8) Güte und Barmherzigkeit krönt.[20]

Rückblick auf Not

Meine Seele (= ich) brüllte, deinen Namen zu preisen,
zu preisen mit Jubel (9) deine Hulderweise,
um kundzutun deine Treue/Wahrheit
zu einem Lobpreis ohne Ende.[21]
Dem Tod (10) war ich (verfallen) wegen meiner Sünden,
und meine Übertretungen hatten mich an die Scheol verkauft.
Du aber rettetest mich, (11) יהוה,
nach der Fülle deines Erbarmens
und nach der Fülle deiner Gerechtigkeitstaten.

Bekenntnis

Auch ich habe (12) deinen Namen geliebt,
und in deinem Schatten mich geborgen.
Wenn ich deiner Stärke gedenke, erstarkt (13) mein Herz,
und auf deine Gnadengaben habe ich mich gestützt.[22]

Anrufung und Bitte

Vergib doch, יהוה, meine Sünde,
(14) und reinige mich von meiner Übertretung.
Mit einem Geist der Treue und der Erkenntnis begnade mich,
nicht möge ich zu Fall kommen (15) durch Zerstörung.[23]
Lass nicht Satan über mich herrschen
und einen unreinen Geist,

---

19 Vgl. Ps 69,37; 119,132.
20 Vgl. Ps 103,4.
21 Nach KOTTSIEPER, Plea, 131, ist sekundär „um kundzutun deine Treue/Wahrheit zu einem Lobpreis ohne Ende".
22 Vgl. Ps 71,6; nach KOTTSIEPER, Plea, 132, ist sekundär von „Auch ich habe" bis „mich gestützt."
23 Nach KOTTSIEPER, Plea, 132, Zeile sekundär.

Schmerz und ein böser Sinn/Trieb
(16) mögen nicht in meinem Gebein herrschen.[24]

Vertrauensaussage

Denn du, יהוה, bist mein Lob,
und auf dich habe ich gehofft (17) täglich.
Es mögen sich freuen die Brüder meines Volkes
und das Haus meines Vaters, die verstört sind.
Wenn du gnädig bist [
(18)] ihnen
Ich will mich freuen an dir.

1.3 Zur Interpretation

Die Interpretation muss sich auf die engeren Zeilen beschränken; der Gesamtzusammenhang macht deutlich: Der Beter wurde aus dem sicheren Tod gerettet. Er bringt sein Todesverhängnis mit seinen Sünden, seinen Übertretungen, in Verbindung. Warum rettet ihn JHWH (trotzdem)? Einzig aufgrund seiner Barmherzigkeit. Denn „dem Tod war ich verfallen wegen meiner Sünden, und meine Übertretungen hatten mich an die Scheol verkauft" (XIX,9–10) entspricht „vergib JHWH (im Blick auf) meine Sünden, und reinige mich von meiner Übertretung".[25] Die Dramatik der Todverfallenheit wird deutlich in dem ungewöhnlichen „meine Seele *brüllte*, deinen Namen zu preisen", weiß sie doch, dass wer an die Scheol verkauft ist, nicht mehr loben kann. Damit wird an die Anfangszeilen angeknüpft:[26]

(1) denn keine Made preist dich,
und ein Wurm erzählt nicht deine Gnade.[27]

Nur ein Lebender kann preisen, auch wenn seine Füße taumeln (Z. 2–3).
Der zweite Passus in dem Lied, der für unsere Fragestellung von Bedeutung ist, ist die eigentliche Bitte in Z. 13–16:

---

24 Nach Kottsieper, Plea, 132, sekundär von „Schmerz" bis „herrschen".
25 Sprachlich auffällig die Variation zwischen 9–10 und 13–14: „meine Sünden" – „meine Sünde" – „meine Übertretungen" – „meine Übertretung".
26 Siehe Kottsieper, Plea, 138–139.
27 Siehe in Janowski, Konfliktgespräche, 243–250.

> Vergib doch, יהוה, meine Sünde,
> (14) und reinige mich von meiner Übertretung.
> Mit einem Geist der Treue und der Erkenntnis begnade mich,
> nicht möge ich zu Fall kommen (15) durch Zerstörung.
> Lass nicht Satan über mich herrschen
> und einen unreinen Geist,
> Schmerz und ein böser Sinn/Trieb
> (16) mögen nicht in meinem Gebein herrschen.

Der Zusammenhang zwischen Reinigung und Sünde wird für die Qumrantexte bestimmend (1QS III,4–12; IV,20–21). Auch dass die „Glieder" der Sitz von Unreinheit und Sünde sind, ist dort vertraut. Eschatologisch wird Gott „jeden Geist des Frevels aus den Gliedern seines Fleisches vernichten" (1QS IV,20–21). „Satan" (שטן), „unreiner Geist" (רוח טמאה), „böser Trieb" (יצר רע) und „Schmerz" (מכאוב) stehen parallel als personifizierte feindliche Sündenmächte, die in den „Gliedern" zur Herrschaft kommen möchten.[28]

1.4 Sünde und Tod

> Dem Tode verfallen war ich wegen meiner Sünden,
> und meine Übertretungen hatten mich an die Scheol verkauft.

Diese Aussagen gehen über den vierten Davidpsalter hinaus (vielleicht Vorstufen in Ps 143) und auch über alles, was sonst in 11QPs[a] überliefert ist. Die Drastik der Zugehörigkeit, des Ausgeliefertseins an den Tod (למות הייתי) und des Verkauftseins an die Scheol durch die Sünden (Z. 10) sprengen allen Rahmen. Zwar gibt Jes 50,1 Sprache und Vorstellung: „Ihr seid um eurer Sünden willen verkauft" (בעונתיכם נמכרתם), aber der Text geht einen Schritt weiter: Der Verkauf geschieht an die Scheol. Beteuert der Beter in den meisten Psalmen seine Unschuld, so weiß er hier um seine Todverfallenheit aufgrund der eigenen Sünden. Eine derart starke Sprache wird erst Paulus wieder finden: „verkauft unter die Sünde", die in den Tod führt (Röm 7,14.24).[29]

Die Datierung der Entstehung der Sammlung führt ins 2. Jahrhundert v. Chr. Es stellt sich die Frage, ob 11QPs[a] in einem Bezug zu den Ereignissen der seleukidischen Religionsverfolgung 167–164 v. Chr. stehen könnte.[30] 2Makk 7 bringt

---

28 Gegen KOTTSIEPER, Plea, 143, könnte man auch von einer „Dämonisierung" sprechen.
29 Vgl. auch Röm 6,23: „das Entgelt (ὀψώνια) der Sünde ist der Tod."
30 Von einem solchen Zusammenhang spricht KOTTSIEPER, Plea, 148, ohne ihn explizit zu machen.

das Leiden der Märtyrer mit den eigenen Sünden in Verbindung.[31] Ein vergleichbares Sündenbewusstsein könnte auch in der „Plea" leitend sein. Die Rettung aus dem Tod erfolgt freilich nicht, wie in 2Makk, postmortal in der Auferstehung, sondern ist jetzt bereits geschehen.

Der Psalm lebt aus der Sprache insbesondere des Jesajabuches, der Psalmen und des Hiobbuches.[32] Er nimmt aber nicht nur Sprache auf, sondern auch Erfahrungen und Einsichten, die sich in den genannten Büchern niedergeschlagen haben. Das ist einerseits das Todesgeschick des Gottesfeindes (Jes 14; siehe 2Makk), andererseits sind es wunderbare Rettungen (Jes 38, Hiob, Psalmen).

2 Kreatürlichkeit, Sünde und Tod in den Hodayot und in der Gemeinderegel 1QS

2.1 Die Kreatürlichkeit des Menschen und seine Sündhaftigkeit (1QH IX,23–29 [Suk. I,23–29])

Nach einem deutlich abgesetzten Schöpfungshymnus, aber in ausdrücklichem Bezug zu diesem, spricht der Beter davon, dass Gott ihn seine Schöpfungsgeheimnisse dank der ihm geschenkten Einsicht hat erkennen lassen, denn Gott hat sein Ohr geöffnet für „die wunderbaren Geheimnisse" (Z. 21). Es folgt eine Elendbetrachtung, in der Niedrigkeit und Sündhaftigkeit verbunden sind:

> Und ich
> (bin) ein Gebilde aus Lehm,
> und in Wasser Geknetetes,
> eine Gründung der Schande
> und eine Quelle der Unreinheit,
> ein Schmelzofen (oder: Ausbund) des Frevels
> und ein Bauwerk der Sünde (IX,21–22).

---

[31] Ganz deutlich in den Voten des sechsten und siebten Märtyrerbruders: „Wir leiden dies um unserer selbst willen, da wir gegen Gott gefrevelt haben" (7,18); „denn wir müssen unserer eigenen Verfehlungen wegen leiden" (7,32), und „mit mir aber und meinen Brüdern möge er den Zorn des Allmächtigen zum Stillstand kommen lassen, den er mit Recht auf unser ganzes Volk geworfen hat" (7,38). Auch die kommentierenden Erläuterungen des Autors von 2Makk nehmen den Topos auf: „er verlässt sein Volk nicht, auch wenn er es unter Leiden erzieht" (6,16); Übersetzung nach HABICHT, 2. Makkabäerbuch.
[32] Die meisten Bezüge sind bereits bei SANDERS, Psalms Scroll, 79, verzeichnet.

Wichtige und in den Hodayot wiederkehrende Begriffe sind dabei „Lehmgebilde" (יצר חמר), „Staubgebilde" (יצר עפר), „in Wasser Geknetetes" (מגבל ב/המים). Dies bewegt sich ganz im Rahmen der alttestamentlichen Kreatürlichkeitsaussagen. Doch dann gibt es einen ersten Übergang zu Unreinheitsbegriffen: „Gründung der Schande" (סוד הערוה) und „Quelle der Unreinheit" (מקור הנדה). Ein weiterer Schritt führt zu Aussagen der Sündhaftigkeit: „Ausbund des Frevels" (כור העון) und „Gebäude der Sünde" (מבנה החטאה). Dem korrespondiert die Aussage:

> ein Geist der Verirrung,
> und verkehrt ohne Einsicht,
> und erschreckt durch die gerechten Gerichte (22–23).

Diese Niedrigkeitsdoxologie beschreibt den Menschen in seiner kreatürlichen Beschaffenheit und Niedrigkeit. Doch nicht allein seine Kreatürlichkeit bestimmt ihn, sondern auch elementare Unreinheit und Sündhaftigkeit; Erschrecken erfasst ihn angesichts des Gerichts. Dem korrespondiert die Unfähigkeit, von sich aus zu reden und Erkenntnis zu gewinnen:

> Was kann ich reden,
> ohne dass es erkannt wäre?
> Und was vernehmen lassen,
> das nicht berichtet wäre?
> Alles ist vor dir eingeritzt mit dem Griffel des Gedächtnisses
> für alle ewigen Zeiten (23–24).

Der Mensch ist nicht einmal in der Lage, seine Sünde aufzuzählen und sich ihretwegen im Gericht zu verteidigen:

> Wie soll ein Mensch seine Sünde aufzählen,
> und wie sich verteidigen wegen seiner Übertretungen?
> Und was kann der Frevler antworten auf die gerechten Gerichte?
> Bei dir, Gott der Erkenntnis,
> sind alle Werke der Gerechtigkeit
> und Rat der Wahrheit,
> aber bei den Menschenkindern sind
> Tun des Frevels und Werke des Trugs (25–27).

Wir müssen uns vor Augen halten, wer so redet: Es ist der, der eben noch von der gottgegebenen Einsicht in die Schöpfungswerke sprach (21).

2.2 Kreatürlichkeit, Sünde und Tod (1QS XI,2–22)

Zunächst preist der Beter Gott als den Geber des Heils, des vollkommenen Wandels und der Sündenvergebung. Dann spricht er von der besonderen Einsicht, derer Gott ihn gewürdigt hat und die vor den (anderen) Menschen verborgen ist. Seinen Erwählten hat er Anteil an seinen Heilsgütern gegeben und sie vereint mit den Engeln. Sie sind in der Gemeinde als einer ewigen Pflanzung für alle künftigen Zeiten. Gerade der, der eben noch von seiner besonderen Erkenntnis und seinem Heilsstand gesprochen hat, bekennt in Z. 9–11 seine totale Sündenverfallenheit, Rettungslosigkeit und Todverfallenheit:

> Aber ich gehöre zur frevlerischen Menschheit
> und zur Gemeinschaft (סוד) des Sündenfleisches.
> Meine Sünden, meine Übertretungen,
> meine Verfehlungen zusammen mit der Verkehrtheit meines Herzens
> gehören zur Gemeinschaft des Wurms (רמה)
> und derer, die in Finsternis wandeln.

Hier werden ganz explizit Sündhaftigkeit, Sünden und Todesgeschick verbunden. Das heilvolle Handeln Gottes ist darum auch als „Retten aus der Grube" (13: ומשחת יחלץ נפשי) verstanden.

Dies soll noch an einem weiteren Beispiel aus den Hodayot erläutert werden.

2.3 1QH XI,19–22 (Suk. III,19–22)

> Ich preise dich, Herr,
> denn du hast mein Leben (נפשי) aus der Grube (שחת) gerettet,
> und aus der Scheol des Untergangs/Totenreichs (שאול אבדון)
> hast du mich emporgehoben zu einer ewigen Höhe.
> Und ich kann wandeln auf einer grenzenlosen Ebene
> und weiß, dass es Hoffnung gibt für den, den du aus Staub zur ewigen Gemeinschaft geschaffen hast (19–21).

Der Beter preist Gott für die Rettung vom Tod: שחת, שאול, אבדון stehen für das Totenreich, aus dem Gott befreit hat. Dort hinein hatte ihn seine Sünde geführt, von der er gereinigt wurde:

> Und den verkehrten Geist hast du von großer Sünde gereinigt,
> so dass er mit den Engeln im gemeinsamen Jubel Gott preisen kann:
> dass er sich stelle in die Reihe mit dem Heer der Heiligen
> und zu kommen in die Gemeinschaft mit der Gemeinde der Söhne des Himmels (21–22).

Diese Engelgemeinschaft findet im Lobpreis statt. Weil Gott den Menschen von Sünde gereinigt und für seinen Dienst geheiligt hat, kann er – wie die Priester im Heiligtum – vor Gott mit den Engeln stehen.[33]

Diese Gegenwärtigkeit des Heils,[34] die in der Engelgemeinschaft kulminiert, steht für die schon jetzt erfahrene Gottesgemeinschaft. Explizite Aussagen über Totenauferstehung finden sich daher nicht in diesen Texten.[35] Noch immer ist George W.E. Nickelsburg zuzustimmen: "He belongs to the eschatological community of the holy. He need not contemplate further death and resurrection because he is already participating in the blessings and privileges of the new life."[36]

2.4 Auferweckung der Toten in Qumran?

Unbestreitbare Belege für Totenauferweckung finden sich in 4Q521 und wohl in PsEz (4Q385–4Q388). Ganz gleich, ob diese Texte der engeren Gruppe der Qumrantexte zugeordnet werden, sind sie doch Belege für das Nebeneinanderbestehen von präsentischer und endzeitlicher Eschatologie.[37]

In 4Q385 und 4Q386 findet sich gegenüber Ez 37,10 eine aufschlussreiche Änderung. Heißt es dort von den durch Gottes Geist Belebten, sie seien ein „sehr großes Heer", so wird daraus in 4Q385 und 4Q386 „ein großes Volk von Menschen". Hier scheint ein Schritt in größere Konkretheit getan worden zu sein.[38]

Der wichtigste Text ist in diesem Zusammenhang 4Q521. Der fragmentarisch erhaltene Text ist ein dichter Teppich, gewebt aus dem Psalter und vornehmlich dem Jesajabuch, ein vollständiges Zitat findet sich von Ps 146,7–8 in Z. 8 unter Auslassung des Tetragramms. Der entscheidende Passus lautet 4Q521, fragm. 2,II,12: „Dann wird er Durchbohrte heilen, und Tote wird er lebendig machen (ומתים יחיה), und Armen wird er Frohbotschaft verkünden." Dazu

---

33 Engelgemeinschaft hat in den Qumrantexten noch andere Ausprägungen gefunden: als Segenszusicherung (11Q14,1,II,14–15) oder als Ausschlussbestimmungen aus der endzeitlichen Ratsversammlung (1QSa II,4–9), vom endzeitlichen Krieg (1QM VII,4–6) und aus der Gemeinde überhaupt (CD XV,15–17).
34 Kuhn, Enderwartung.
35 Gegen Puech, La croyance; siehe Lichtenberger, Studien, 219–224.
36 Nickelsburg, Resurrection, 156.
37 Der Bericht des Josephus über den essenischen Glauben der Unsterblichkeit der Seelen (Bell 2,154; Ant 18,18) bezeugt zumindest eine Heilserwartung über den Tod hinaus, auch wenn diese in der Vorstellungswelt griechischer Seelenvorstellungen geboten wird.
38 Der Text ist wegen des freien Gebrauchs des Tetragramms mit großer Sicherheit vor- bzw. außerqumranisch.

gehört 4Q521, fragm. 7,6: „[...] der die Toten seines Volkes lebendig macht [...]" (המחיה את מתי עמו). Ganz offensichtlich wird der klassisch gewordene Topos, dass Gott die Toten lebendig macht (siehe Jes 26,19 „*deine* Toten", über Röm 4,17 bis hin zur vielfältigen Verwendung in Liturgie und Gebet), aufgenommen. Spricht dieses Textstück also eindeutig von *Gottes* Lebendigmachen der Toten, so bleibt doch fraglich, ob der Text als authentisch qumran-essenisch gelten kann. Wohl könnte das Weglassen des Tetragramms im Zitat von Ps 146,7–8 dafür sprechen, so rät doch die ganz ungewöhnliche Aufnahme eines längeren Psalmzitats in einer poetischen Komposition gegen die Annahme einer genuin qumran-essenischen Herkunft von 4Q521. Sollte es sich bei 4Q521 um einen von der qumran-essenischen Gemeinde verfassten Text handeln, so wäre er das einzige zweifelsfreie Zeugnis für den Glauben der Qumran-Essener an die Auferstehung, genauer: die Lebendigmachung der Toten.[39] Unbeschadet einer Zuordnung zu einer bestimmten Gruppe innerhalb des Judentums der Zeit des Zweiten Tempels ist der Text dennoch ein wichtiger Beleg für die im 2. Jahrhundert v. Chr. zum Durchbruch kommende Hoffnung auf die Auferstehung der Toten. Dan 12,1–3 und 2Makk 7,6.9.11.14.23.29.36; 14,46 sind dafür wichtige Zeugnisse, und es scheint, dass die Frage der Theodizee dabei eine entscheidende Rolle gespielt hat. Wenn nach Lev 18,5 der leben soll, der die Gebote hält, was ist dann mit den Tätern der Gebote, die um deren Einhaltung sterben müssen? Die Martyrien der seleukidischen Religionsverfolgung haben hier als Katalysator für die Ausprägung der Auferstehungshoffnung gewirkt. Diese Tradition ist von der pharisäischen Frömmigkeit begierig aufgenommen worden und in die jüdische Apokalyptik und ins Urchristentum eingeströmt. Eher konservative Gruppen konnten hier zurückhaltender sein, wie die Sadduzäer (Mk 12,18–27parr; Act 23,8; Josephus, Bell 2,165) oder auch eine dem Wesen nach noch konservativere Gruppe wie die Qumran-Essener. Das schließt nicht aus, dass Heils- und Unheilsvorstellungen auch über die Lebenszeit des Einzelnen hinaus lebendig waren.

3 1QS III,13–IV,26: Der Mensch als Kampfplatz bis zum Eschaton

Aus dem berühmten Traktat über die beiden Geister sollen uns hauptsächlich die Tugend- und Lasterkataloge sowie die ihnen zugeordneten Heils- und Un-

---

39 Siehe dazu LICHTENBERGER, Auferstehung, 79–91.

heilsaussagen mit der eschatologischen Vollendung interessieren; die Texte werden hier in eigener Übersetzung vorangestellt.[40]

3.1 Texte

1QS IV,2–8: Der Geist der Wahrheit

(2) Und dies sind ihre Wege auf dem Erdkreis: das Herz des Menschen zu erleuchten und vor ihm alle Wege der Gerechtigkeit der Wahrheit zu ebnen und sein Herz fürchten zu machen die Gerichte (3) Gottes; und ein Geist der Demut und Langmut und Fülle des Erbarmens und ewige Güte und Einsicht und Verständnis und mächtige Weisheit, die vertraut auf alle (4) Werke Gottes und sich stützt auf die Fülle seiner Gnade; und ein Geist der Erkenntnis in allem Planen der Tat und Eifer für die gerechten Gerichte und (5) heiliges Denken mit festem Sinn und Fülle der Gnade für alle Söhne der Wahrheit und herrliche Reinheit, die alle Götzen der Unreinheit verabscheut, und demütiger Wandel (6) in Klugheit von allem, und zu verbergen für die Wahrheit die Geheimnisse der Erkenntnis. Dies sind die Ratschläge (oder: Grundlagen) des Geistes für die Söhne der Wahrheit auf dem Erdkreis, und die Heimsuchung aller, die darin wandeln, ist zur Heilung (7) und Fülle des Friedens in Länge der Tage und Fruchtbarkeit des Samens mit allen ewigen Segnungen und ewiger Freude im ewigen Leben und Krone der Herrlichkeit (8) mit dem Gewand des Glanzes im ewigen Licht.

1QS IV,9–14: Der Geist des Frevels

(9) Und dem Geist des Frevels kommt zu: Habgier und Lässigkeit der Hände im Tun der Gerechtigkeit, Frevel und Lüge, Stolz und Hochmut des Herzens, Trug und grausame Täuschung (10) und Fülle der Ruchlosigkeit, Jähzorn und Fülle der Torheit und Eifer des Übermuts, Werke des Gräuels im Geist der Hurerei und Wege der Unreinheit im Tun der Unreinheit (11) und Zunge der Lästerung, Blindheit der Augen und Schwere (Taubheit) des Ohrs, Starrheit des Nackens und Härtigkeit des Herzens, zu wandeln auf allen Wegen der Finsternis, und böswillige Hinterlist; und die Heimsuchung (12) aller, die in ihm wandeln, ist zur Fülle der Plagen durch alle Engel der Nichtigkeit zum ewigen Verderben durch den Zornesgrimm Gottes, Rache zum ewigen Abscheu und (13) ewige Schmach mit endgültiger Vernichtung im Feuer der Finsternisse. Und alle ihre Zeiten sind für ihre Generationen in Traurigkeit des Kummers und Unheil der Bitternisse im Verderben der Finsternis bis (14) zu ihrer Vernichtung, ohne Rest und Rettung für sie.

---

40 Siehe Lichtenberger, Gemeinderegel, 122–123.

1QS IV,20–23: Die endzeitliche Vollendung

> (20) Und dann wird Gott durch seine Wahrheit alle Taten des Menschen läutern, und er wird sich reinigen den Bau (d.h. Leib) des Menschen (oder: von den Menschensöhnen), um zu vernichten jeden Frevelgeist aus den Gliedern (21) seines Fleisches und um ihn zu reinigen mit heiligem Geist von allen Freveltaten. Und er wird auf ihn den Geist der Wahrheit sprengen wie Reinigungswasser von allen Abscheulichkeiten der Lüge und dem sich Wälzen (22) im Geist der Unreinheit, damit die Rechtschaffenen die Erkenntnis des Höchsten verstehen und die Weisheit der Söhne des Himmels, um zu unterweisen, die vollkommen wandeln. Denn sie hat Gott zum ewigen Bund erwählt, (23) und ihnen kommt die Herrlichkeit Adams zu. Und es wird keinen Frevel geben, und zu Schanden werden alle Werke des Trugs.

3.2 Der Mensch als Kampfplatz bis zum Eschaton 1QS III,13–IV,26[41]

Der grundsätzlichen Aussage, dass Gott den Menschen zum Herrscher über den Erdkreis eingesetzt habe (1QS III,17–18), folgt sogleich die Einschränkung, dass dieser Mensch selbst beherrscht sei:

> Und er schuf den Menschen zur Herrschaft über den Erdkreis, und er hat ihm zwei Geister gesetzt, darin zu wandeln bis zur Zeit seiner Heimsuchung[42]. Dies sind die Geister der Wahrheit und des Frevels.

3.3 Was sind die beiden Geister und wie ist ihr Verhältnis zum Menschen zu bestimmen?

Zunächst ist die Aussage wichtig, dass Gott die beiden Geister dem Menschen gesetzt hat. Damit wird von vornherein jede Annahme eines Gott gleichgeordneten bösen Prinzips zurückgewiesen. Die beiden Geister bilden die Grundmöglichkeiten menschlicher Existenz und des Verhaltens, sie haben jedoch ihre zeitliche Begrenzung in Gottes endzeitlichem Eingreifen. An dieser Stelle wird weder geklärt, ob der Mensch die Möglichkeit hat zu wählen, nach welchem Geist er leben möchte, noch ob die beiden Geister jeden Menschen gleichzeitig bestimmen; die letztere Frage wird erst IV,15–26 beantwortet. Im Folgenden

---

41 Zur älteren Literatur siehe LICHTENBERGER, Studien, 123–141; siehe weiter LANGE, Weisheit, 121–170; FREY, Antithese, 45–77.
42 Das ist, wenn Gott endgültig eingreift.

wird dann die Herkunft von Wahrheit und Frevel aus Licht und Finsternis hergeleitet, sie werden in Verbindung gebracht mit dem „Fürsten der Lichter" und dem „Engel der Finsternis": „Durch den Fürsten der Lichter geschieht die Herrschaft über alle Söhne der Gerechtigkeit, sie wandeln (dementsprechend) auf Wegen des Lichts; durch den Engel der Finsternis geschieht alle Herrschaft der Söhne der Finsternis, und auf den Wegen der Finsternis wandeln sie (demgemäß)" (1QS III,20–21). Die strikte Zuordnung der Gerechten zum Lichtfürsten und der Frevler zum Finsternisengel wird durchbrochen in der Möglichkeit der Verführung der „Söhne der Gerechtigkeit" durch den Finsternisengel: Die Sünden der Gerechten geschehen allein aufgrund seiner in Gottes unerforschlichem Geheimnis begründeten Verführung. „Aber der Gott Israels und der Engel seiner Wahrheit (kommen zu) Hilfe für alle Söhne des Lichts" (1QS III,24–25). Bewältigt wird so das Problem, dass auch die Gerechten sündigen, obwohl sie unter der Herrschaft des Lichterfürsten stehen. Mit dem Bezug auf die Geheimnisse Gottes wird dieses Faktum einerseits dem menschlichen Begreifen entzogen und mit Gottes Plan begründet; andererseits wird sichergestellt, dass dem Bösen nicht freier Lauf gewährt ist.

3.4 Der Geist der Wahrheit und der Geist des Frevels

In ausführlichen Tugend- (1QS IV,2–6) und Lasterkatalogen (1QS IV,9–11) werden dann die Wirkungen der jeweiligen Geister benannt.

Wirkungen des Geists der Wahrheit

> Das Herz des Menschen zu erleuchten und vor ihm alle Wege der Gerechtigkeit der Wahrheit zu ebnen und sein Herz fürchten zu machen die Gerichte Gottes; und ein Geist der Demut und Langmut und Fülle des Erbarmens und ewige Güte und Einsicht und Verständnis und mächtige Weisheit, die vertraut auf alle Werke Gottes und sich stützt auf die Fülle seiner Gnade; und ein Geist der Erkenntnis in allem Planen der Tat und Eifer für die gerechten Gerichte und heiliges Denken mit festem Sinn und Fülle der Gnade für alle Söhne der Wahrheit und herrliche Reinheit, die alle Götzen der Unreinheit verabscheut, und demütiger Wandel in Klugheit von allem, und zu verbergen für die Wahrheit die Geheimnisse der Erkenntnis (1QS IV,2–6).

Wirkungen des Geists des Frevels

> Habgier und Lässigkeit der Hände im Tun der Gerechtigkeit, Frevel und Lüge, Stolz und Hochmut des Herzens, Trug und grausame Täuschung und Fülle der Ruchlosigkeit, Jähzorn und Fülle der Torheit und Eifer des Übermuts, Werke des Greuels im Geist der Hure-

rei und Wege der Unreinheit im Tun der Unreinheit und Zunge der Lästerung, Blindheit der Augen und Schwere (= Taubheit) des Ohrs, Starrheit des Nackens und Härtigkeit des Herzens, zu wandeln auf allen Wegen der Finsternis, und böswillige Hinterlist (1QS IV,9–11).

3.5 Dem jeweiligen Verhalten entspricht dann Heil bzw. Unheil

Für die, die nach dem Geist der Wahrheit wandeln

> Heilung und Fülle des Friedens in Länge der Tage und Fruchtbarkeit des Samens mit allen ewigen Segnungen und ewiger Freude im ewigen Leben und Krone der Herrlichkeit mit dem Gewand des Glanzes im ewigen Licht (1QS IV,6–8).

Für die, die nach dem Geist des Frevels wandeln

> Fülle der Plagen durch alle Engel der Nichtigkeit zum ewigen Verderben durch den Zornesgrimm Gottes, Rache zum ewigen Abscheu und ewige Schmach mit endgültiger Vernichtung im Feuer der Finsternisse. Und alle ihre Zeiten sind für ihre Generationen in Traurigkeit des Kummers und Unheil der Bitternisse im Verderben der Finsternis bis zu ihrer Vernichtung, ohne Rest und Rettung für sie (1QS IV,12–14).

3.6 Zusammenfassung

Hier wird wieder ganz prinzipiell geredet: Je nachdem, welchem Geist der Mensch folgt, ist sein endzeitliches Geschick. Aber verhält sich ein Mensch nur nach dem einen Geist, also entweder ganz gerecht oder ganz frevelhaft? Und ist er frei, hier eine Wahl zu treffen?

Darauf antwortet der abschließende Abschnitt 1QS IV,15–26: Gott hat die jeweiligen Geistanteile im Menschen festgelegt, und dementsprechend verhalten sich die Menschen. Sie haben also nicht eine Wahl, sondern sie sind durch die ihnen zugeteilten jeweiligen Geistanteile von Wahrheit und Frevel in ihrem Tun determiniert, zu Heil oder Unheil prädestiniert. „Denn Gott hat sie (d.h. die Geistanteile) zu jeweiligen Teilen gesetzt bis zur letzten Zeit" (1QS IV,16–17). „Bis dahin kämpfen die Geister der Wahrheit und des Frevels im Herzen des Menschen" (1QS IV,23). „Entsprechend dem Erbe (= Anteil) eines Menschen an der Wahrheit ist er gerecht, und so hasst er den Frevel, und entsprechend seinem Besitz am Los der Bosheit frevelt er dadurch, und so verabscheut er die Wahrheit" (1QS IV,24–25).[43]

Der Abschnitt spricht vom Streit der beiden Geister im Menschenherzen. Diesen Kampf führt also nicht der Mensch gegen den Geist des Frevels oder den Geist der Wahrheit, sondern diese beiden Geister kämpfen im Menschenherzen gegeneinander. Je nach der Größe des Anteils an den beiden Geistern handelt der Mensch überwiegend gut oder böse. Die Größe des jeweiligen Anteils kann vom Menschen nicht verändert werden, sondern ist in Gottes Schöpfung festgelegt. Dies gilt bis zum Ende der Zeit, wenn Gott die Gerechten von allem Frevelgeist befreien wird und sie die verlorene „Herrlichkeit Adams" wiedererlangen. Dies wird als ein Akt der Neuschöpfung verstanden (1QS IV,20–26). Während der jetzigen Zeit der „Herrschaft Belials (= des Teufels)" (1QS II,19) aber ist der Mensch Kampfplatz der beiden widerstreitenden Geister, die ihn je nach dem von Gott zugeteilten Maß beherrschen. Diese Determination kann durch keine Paränese oder Askese überwunden werden, sondern findet erst in der endzeitlichen Restitution zur „Herrlichkeit Adams" (1QS IV,23) ihr Ende.

4 Abschließende Überlegungen

Das Menschenbild, das uns in den Texten aus den Qumranfunden begegnet, ist nicht einheitlich; auch die Texte, die wir auf eine bestimmte Gemeinschaft vom Toten Meer zurückführen („Qumran-Essener"), sprechen keineswegs übereinstimmend über den Menschen und seine Freiheit oder Unfreiheit zum Tun des Guten, seine Sünde und sein Todesgeschick. In Texten aus Qumran, die wir im weitesten Sinn den Psalmen zurechnen können, spricht sich das Staunen darüber aus, dass Gott den vergänglichen und sündigen Menschen des Heils und seiner Gemeinschaft – oft verstanden als Gemeinschaft mit den Engeln – würdigt. In dem lehrmäßigen Traktat 1QS III,13–IV,26 wird in argumentativem und sich gedanklich entwickelnden Stil Gottes Determinieren zu Wahrheit und Frevel, Licht und Finsternis und sein Prädestinieren zu Heil und Unheil ausgebreitet. Zunächst wird in dualistischen Gegenüberstellungen argumentiert, die sich selbst aber rasch als unzureichend erweisen. Denn auch die Gerechten, die unter der Herrschaft des Fürsten der Lichter stehen, sündigen. Die sich daraus entwickelnde Lösung kann nur deterministisch erklären, warum Gut und Böse im Menschen zusammen auftreten: In den Anteilen des Geistes der Wahrheit

---

43 Vgl. die Anteile an Licht und Finsternis in 4Q186 (Hor) 1 II,7(6:3); II,5–6(1:8); 2 II,7(8:1).

einerseits und denen des Geistes des Frevels andererseits, die Gott in den Menschen gegeben hat. Der Mensch wird zum Kampfplatz der widerstreitenden Mächte und wird erst endzeitlich aus diesem Dilemma befreit werden. In dieser Zeit der „Herrschaft Belials" (1QS I,18.23; II,19; vgl. III,21–23) herrschen auch für den Frommen die Bedingungen von Sünde und dem daraus resultierenden Tod. Nur durch Gottes Barmherzigkeit und Gerechtigkeit geschieht Rettung aus dem Tod.

Wir müssen heute sagen, dass dies, trotz aller mythologischen Vorgaben, ein beeindruckend realistisches Bild des Menschen zeichnet. Das Böse ist eben strukturell in der Welt und ist nicht bloß ein Mangel an Gutem, der durch guten Willen aufgehoben werden könnte. Dies Menschenbild der Qumrantexte ist radikaler als die späteren rabbinischen Modelle, die wohl auch von einem Kampf der Triebe des Guten und des Bösen im Herzen des Menschen wissen, die aber dem Menschen dabei eine wichtige Rolle einräumen, für welchen der Triebe er sich entscheiden möchte. Es ist auch radikaler als die aus sokratisch-stoischer Tradition erwachsene Auffassung, dass der Mensch, wenn er nur wisse, was das Gute ist, dies auch tue. Qumran steht hier sehr viel näher an Paulus, der eben von der verzweifelten Erfahrung spricht, dass er verkauft sei unter die Sünde (Röm 7,14), dass er wie ein Kriegsgefangener an die Sünde in seinen Gliedern gefesselt sei (Röm 7,23), dass er das Gute, das er will, nicht tue (Röm 7,15.19) und darum dem Tod verfallen sei (Röm 7,24), aus dem er sich nicht selbst retten könne (Röm 7,25a).[44]

Bibliographie

CHARLESWORTH, James H./RIETZ, Henry W. L., Non-Masoretic Psalms, in: Charlesworth, James H. et al. (Hg.), The Dead Sea Scrolls. Hebrew, Aramaic, and Greek Texts with English Translations, Vol. 4A: Pseudepigraphic and Non-Masoretic Psalms and Prayers, Tübingen/Louisville 1997, 155–215.
DAHMEN, Ulrich, Psalmentext und Psalmensammlung. Eine Auseinandersetzung mit P.W. Flint, in: Ders./Lange, Armin/Lichtenberger, Hermann (Hg.), Die Textfunde vom Toten Meer und der Text der Hebräischen Bibel, Neukirchen-Vluyn 2000, 109–126.
DAHMEN, Ulrich, Die Psalter-Versionen aus den Qumranfunden. Ein Gespräch mit P.W. Flint, in: Frey, Jörg/Stegemann, Hartmut (Hg.), Qumran kontrovers. Beiträge zu den Textfunden vom Toten Meer, Paderborn 2003, 127–146.

---

44 Siehe LICHTENBERGER, Ich Adams, 143–150.

FLINT, Peter W., The Dead Sea Psalms Scrolls and the Book of Psalms (StTDJ 17), Leiden/New York/Köln 1997.
FREY, Jörg, Die paulinische Antithese von „Fleisch" und „Geist" und die palästinisch-jüdische Weisheitstradition, in: ZNW 90 (1999) 45–77.
HABICHT, Christian, 2. Makkabäerbuch (JSHRZ I/3), Gütersloh 1979.
JANOWSKI, Bernd, Konfliktgespräche mit Gott. Eine Anthropologie der Psalmen, Neukirchen-Vluyn 2003.
KOTTSIEPER, Ingo, 11Q5 (11QPsª) XIX – A Plea for Deliverance?, in: García Martínez, Florentino/Steudel, Annette/Tigchelaar, Eibert (Hg.), From 4QMMT to Resurrection. Mélanges qumraniens en hommage à Émile Puech, Leiden/Boston, Massachusetts 2006, 125–150.
KUHN, Heinz-Wolfgang, Enderwartung und gegenwärtiges Heil. Untersuchungen zu den Gemeindeliedern von Qumran mit einem Anhang über Eschatologie und Gegenwart in der Verkündigung Jesu (StUNT 4), Göttingen 1966.
LANGE, Armin, Weisheit und Prädestination. Weisheitliche Urordnung und Prädestination in den Textfunden von Qumran (STDJ 18), Leiden/New York/Köln 1995.
LANGE, Armin, Handbuch der Textfunde vom Toten Meer, Band 1: Die Handschriften biblischer Bücher von Qumran und den anderen Fundorten, Tübingen 2009.
LICHTENBERGER, Hermann, Studien zum Menschenbild in Texten der Qumrangemeinde (StUNT 15), Göttingen 1980.
LICHTENBERGER, Hermann, Die Gemeinderegel, in: Charlesworth, James H. (Hg.), The Dead Sea Scrolls. Rule of the Community. Photographic Multi-Language Edition, Philadelphia, Pennsylvania 1996, 120–131.
LICHTENBERGER, Hermann, Auferstehung in den Qumranfunden, in: Avemarie, Friedrich/Lichtenberger, Hermann (Hg.), Auferstehung – Resurrection (WUNT 135), Tübingen 2001, 79–91.
LICHTENBERGER, Hermann, Das Ich Adams und das Ich der Menschheit (WUNT 164), Tübingen 2004.
NICKELSBURG, George W.E., Resurrection, Immortality, and Eternal Life in Intertestamental Judaism (HThS 26), Cambridge, Massachusetts/London 1972.
PUECH, Émile, La croyance des Esséniens en la vie future. Immortalité, résurrection, vie éternelle? Histoire d'une croyance dans le judaïsme ancien, Vol. I: La résurrection des morts et le contexte scripturaire; Vol. II: Les données qumraniennes et classiques (Études bibliques N.S. 21.22), Paris 1993.
SANDERS, James A., The Psalms Scroll of Qumran Cave 11 (11QPsª) (DJD IV), Oxford 1965.
SEYBOLD, Klaus, Zur Geschichte des vierten Davidpsalters (Pss 138-145), in: Flint, Peter W./Miller, Patrick D. (Hg.), The Book of Psalms. Composition and Reception (VT.S 99), Leiden/Boston, Massachusetts 2005, 368–390.

Part II: **New Testament**

Ian H. Henderson
The Child, Death and the Human in Mark's Gospel

When Martin Kähler described Mark's Gospel and then later all four canonical gospels as "Passionsgeschichten mit ausführlicher Einleitung,"[1] he raised for all future narrative criticism the question whether and how the "extensive introduction" actually supports the plot of the Passion narrative. Specifically, Mark's audience faces a real challenge to relate the characterisation of manifold human suffering, failure, evil, and death in the disparate episodes of the introduction to the climactic narrative of Jesus' own particular mortality. The following discussion will insist on the deliberate importance to the Marcan *Menschenbild* of the extended narrative introduction and of its most minor, most mortal characters: anonymous children.

Writing about the non-human characters in Mark, from a point of view which he might call "post-human," Stephen Moore criticizes most narrative approaches to human character in Mark for after all sliding back into abstract conceptual Christology. Moore laments that, even in the most adventurous narrative criticism,

> [a]s the roundest character in Mark, Jesus is also the model and measure of the human in Mark. Other characters attain to roundness—complexity, interiority, unpredictability, full humanity—on the basis of their respective closeness to or distance from Jesus.[2]

Perhaps less radically than Moore, I will experiment here with finding the Marcan *Menschenbild* in the first place in the characters other than Jesus and, indeed, other than Jesus' officially designated inner circle of adult, Jewish, non-slave, male "disciples."

1 Finding Humans in Mark

Focusing on issues of narrative characterisation, Elizabeth Struthers Malbon has recently compared David Rhoads' and Donald Michie's great 1982 *Mark as Story* with the equally influential 1999 revised edition completed in collabora-

---

[1] KÄHLER, Jesus, 60.
[2] MOORE, Humans, 83.

tion with Joanna Dewey. Malbon particularly notes one paragraph that appears, differently contextualised, in both editions:

> Just as Jesus puts forth children and servanthood as models for the disciples and later summons them to notice the self-giving of the poor widow, so the narrator puts forth the minor characters for the readers to notice and to learn from—so that they will be remembered wherever the good news is proclaimed. In fact, it is only by seeing the rule of God in the characters who are "least" that the reader has fully grasped the extent to which the rule of God turns the world upside down.[3]

What follows here will be centrally concerned with the implications of "Jesus put[ting] forth children [...] for the disciples" inside Mark's story and "the narrator put[ting] forth the minor characters for the readers" as the readers perform and interpret Mark's story in actual human existence.

The first edition of Rhoads and Michie goes on to say that

> the narrative enables the reader to see, through surprising twists and turns, just who the central characters are. Appropriately to Mark's story, the characters are led in the end to a crisis over the issue of death [...] and it is in the presence of death that the characters become fully known.[4]

In the second edition, those last sentences are replaced by something quite different:

> the narrative enables the reader to see, through surprising twists and turns, just what discipleship entails. Can the reader see the rule of God breaking in through Jesus' words and actions? [...] Can the reader be willing to live and die for the good news, trusting God enough to lose one's life for others? For this is what the Gospel of Mark is calling readers to do.[5]

Certainly, Mark's Gospel is interested in "what discipleship entails" and in those few who are specifically called to it by Jesus, yet it is on many levels unclear how Mark was designed to relate its *audience* to the construct "discipleship." I argue elsewhere that Mark's Gospel was historically not at all designed to persuade its whole audience to become "disciples" of Jesus.[6] Mary Ann Tolbert claims that Mark's choice of complex narrative form was intended to persuade a

---

3 MALBON, Characters, 57, citing RHOADS/DEWEY/MICHIE, Mark, 135.
4 MALBON, Characters, 57, citing RHOADS/MICHIE, Mark, 135–136.
5 RHOADS/DEWEY/MICHIE, Mark, 136.
6 HENDERSON, Reconstructing.

broad audience to trust Jesus and to spread the story about him.[7] Yet in Mark, trusting Jesus and spreading his story, even "following" him are not at all the same thing as becoming formally his "disciple."

In Mark's usage, the word "disciple" is not yet, as it would become in Matthew and in Luke-Acts, a universal (increasingly metaphoric) designation for Jesus-devotees.[8] Without the hermeneutical "correction" of being canonised together with Matthew and Luke-Acts, Mark's Gospel would not inspire its audience with a desire or an expectation of becoming Jesus' "disciple," any more than they would expect to be able to join the "Twelve." In Mark—I suspect in Mark's audience—the noun "disciple" quite narrowly designates a very few chosen specialists within Jesus' entourage, not automatically every ideal adherent of the movement. Prior to Mark 8:34, no one can become a disciple or even individually "follow" Jesus without direct appointment by him—though one who is expressly denied permission to *follow* Jesus becomes *ipso facto* Jesus' first emissary to non-Jews (5:18–20)! After Mark 8:34, admirers and suppliants can, indeed, opt to take up their crosses and "follow" Jesus, but such "followers" are not named "disciples." There is no suggestion that Jesus is appointing any new disciples. Similarly, it is possible to be an exorcist in Jesus' name without "following" his core disciples (9:38–41); Marcan disciples do not make disciples (contra Matt 28:19). The Marcan Jesus-movement thus consists of a very few carefully designated "disciples" (largely Simon "Rock", James and John, the "Boanerges," and the rest of the Twelve [3:13–19]), some individual followers (Levi and company [2:13–17]; BarTimaeus [10:46–52]; Mary Magdalene and company [15:40–41]), and wider circles of hosts, admirers, "family" (3:31–35), and suppliants.

On this reading, the majority of Mark's audience are still meant to relate to Jesus as the majority of Mark's characters relate to him: as suppliants, perhaps followers, but not disciples. Moreover, those explicitly named in Mark as "disciples" are so negatively portrayed that they cannot credibly be said to "represent the best human reaction" to Jesus.[9] "Disciple" in Mark is thus not a good index of this Gospel's general *Menschenbild*. "Disciple" in Mark is not a synonym for "believer" (9:42) or "Christian," still less for "ideal human person."

The question of "discipleship" aside, however, the older edition of Rhoads and Michie rightly suggests that "the narrative enables the reader to see,

---

[7] TOLBERT, Sowing, 302–304; GUNDRY, Children, 144–146, assumes a strongly apologetic motive for the Marcan composition, in my opinion losing sight of much Marcan irony.
[8] TREBILCO, Self-designations, 241–242.
[9] Quoting SHINER, Follow, 292.

through surprising twists and turns, just who the central characters are"[10] and, indeed, to find those central figures surprisingly in the little characters. It should not be self-evident to Mark's audience who the central characters of Mark's story must be. Certainly it is not the Jewish religious specialists who oppose Jesus; pretty clearly also not those other religious specialists who Jesus himself appoints as disciples. Surely, Jesus himself is Mark's central character, or that elusive Marcan character "God."[11] In another sense, however, it is all those other characters whose abject mortality and demonic oppression constitute the persuasive necessity, the narrative premise, for the whole plot by which Jesus' death ironically evacuates the tomb. At this point, Rhoads and Michie, first edition, note something which Rhoads, Dewey and Michie, revised edition, displace, that in Mark all "the characters are led in the end to a crisis over the issue of death" and that "it is in the presence of death that" all "the characters become fully known."[12]

Most discussions of characters in Mark's narrative process share Rhoads' and Michie's division among "Jesus," "The Authorities," "The Disciples," and "The Little People."[13] On such a division, "Jesus" and "The Disciples" are presumably "the Good Guys," "The Authorities" are "the Bad Guys," and in the conflict between them it is "The Little People" who are at stake. In place of this prejudicial duality, however, I propose dividing Mark's characters (and potentially its audience) into three morally more ambiguous categories: In one category are Jesus and John the Baptiser, together with Moses and Elijah; in another are specifically designated, in some sense official, religious-political specialists, the scribes, Pharisees, priests, and Sadducees, but also Jesus' own specifically designated disciples, the Twelve, especially Peter, James and John, along with the two morally problematic Jewish kings, Herod and David, perhaps even Pilate and his centurion; that still leaves "The Little People," but marked off from the other characters as those without either divine charisma or religious-political office.

These rather Weberian, morally ambiguous, categories (charismatic leaders; official leaders; other people) may help us sense some of Mark's complex ironies. Putting Jesus together with John, Moses, and Elijah may help us understand the prominence and some salient features of the last three. Lumping the office-holders and religious specialists all together highlights their shared am-

---

10 RHOADS/MICHIE, Mark, 136.
11 DRIGGERS, God; BORING, Mark, 3; see MALBON, Characters, 63, n. 69.
12　RHOADS/MICHIE, Mark, 136.
13 RHOADS/MICHIE, Mark, 103; MALBON, Characters, 49; MOORE, Humans, 84.

biguity of legitimacy and dysfunction in relation to God's sovereignty. Above all, the salient lack of authority of the "little people" is exposed: I share Stephen Moore's impatience with assumptions that the "little people" are dignified in Mark by their romantic qualities of "childlike humility" and "capacity for sacrificial service."[14] Instead, the "little people" in Mark compellingly represent some pretty desperate and miserable conditions not easily romanticized by any imaginable early Marcan audience.[15]

Mark's Gospel does not, however, rely entirely on characterisation to express its understanding of the human condition; inside the Marcan narrative, Jesus himself frequently discourses about categories of persons, either in parables or, occasionally, in direct representation. Although Mark's frontier, ethnic setting may have appeared exotic to some audiences, the Gospel presents a realist, non-utopian and non-fictional aesthetic: in the Marcan *Menschenbild* the audience should recognise the real human condition. For a reading which seeks to combine literary-narrative sensitivity and social-cultural realism, several bundles of episodic characterisation and discursive reflection suggest themselves within Mark as possible paradigms for outlining the text's normative representation of humanity:

> Slave-imagery: Mark's first audiences like other proto-Christian groupings presumably included slaves and freed men and women, some of whom held office and exercised cult leadership in some tension with their civic status. (The pre-Marcan Jesus movement even includes legally free religious specialists who openly self-identify as "slave of Christ" [Rom 1:1; Gal 1:10; Phil 1:1] and slave of those under their leadership [2 Cor 4:5]). Mark's Jesus tells parables about grandees who can send slaves as agents or leave them as housekeepers (Mark 12:2.4; 13:34). In the Marcan narrative, however, rather pointedly only the High Priest is actually described as using slaves (14:47). At the argumentative centre of Mark's Gospel, Jesus declares that leadership in his community will be marked by voluntary enslavement to those who being led (9:35; 10:43–45). Yet, while pre-Marcan Jesus-devotion can imagine the universal human condition in its ambiguity as enslavement (Rom 6:16; Q Matt 6:24 par. Luke 16:13), in Mark slave-imagery is reserved ironically for would-be leadership.

> Disciple-imagery: As we have seen, Jesus actually names some individuals as his disciples in Mark (and denies others); disciple-language figures both narratively and discursively in Mark; but "disciple" was not a proto-Christian official self-designator until later (as office-holders in the post-Easter movement Jesus' actual disciples were preferentially redesignated "apostles"). There were no actual people in Mark's audience who were regarded as Jesus' "disciples."

---

14 MOORE, Humans, 84, quoting RHOADS/MICHIE, Mark, 130.
15 HENDERSON, 'Salted With Fire.'

Child-imagery: Child-language is linked closely and emphatically by the Marcan Jesus with his slave-leader discourse (9:33–37); it is not possible to overlook the importance of Jesus' symbolic uses of children, yet actual children also appear narratively in Mark's story; surely, Mark's projected audiences included or had children. Child-language is unusual in that it functions discursively in Jesus' symbolism, narratively in Mark's anecdotes, *and* socially in Mark's audience.

Pauper-imagery: Responding to an earlier version of this paper, Georg Steins pointed out that the poor/destitute were surely socially present in Mark's projected audience (14:7). They are significantly represented inside Mark by the "poor widow" in the Temple (12:42). In Jesus' own speaking, however, "the poor" appear only as the potential beneficiaries of charity (10:21; 14:5.7): In contrast with the Q tradition, where, indeed, the destitute may be constitutive of a generalized *Menschenbild*, Mark does not have Jesus identify his followers, Israel, or humanity in general symbolically as "the poor." In Q, Jesus solemnly blesses the poor (Luke 6:20 par. Matt 5:3); in Mark Jesus blesses only the children (Mark 10:16).

Woman-imagery: several of the most compelling "minor" characters in Mark's narratives are women; two are discursively singled out by Jesus as key signifiers of his own death (12:41–44; 14:6–9). Perhaps most important, it is a group of Jesus' women followers who are present at the Empty Tomb (16:1–8; recall 15:40–41). In hindsight, it is clear they had "followed" and "served"[16] Jesus all along (15:40–41). These women, however, who are so central in Mark as hermeneutical keys to the death of Jesus are such ironically, as foils to the fecklessness of the official disciples. Despite their centrality for the Marcan narrative and for the Marcan Jesus' discursive self-imagination, the women in Mark function more to expose the nature of followership than to reveal universally the human condition.

Each of these fields of imagery and characterisation in Mark is clearly important and complex enough to focus the problems of method in any attempt to derive the Marcan *Menschenbild*.

The hypothesis of the present essay is that alone among these imagery-characterisation sets in Mark child-language refers to a universal human experience shared by all in Mark's historically projected, intended audience. The handling of children by Mark's Jesus and by the narrator is subtly but significantly more universal in its implications than the treatment of (other) categories of the marginalised (paupers, widows, tax-collectors, cripples). Thus I am proposing child-language in Mark as the best available paradigmatic link both internally between Jesus' discourse and the narrator's story inside Mark, and also between Mark's imagined human world and the perceived real world of Mark's intended audiences. It is essential that the category selected for such an experiment be not only thickly represented in the Marcan literary thought- and

---

[16] In Mark, only angels (Mark 1:13), women (1:31; 15:41), and the Son of Man (10:45) "serve," though aspiring leaders may become "servants" (9:35; 10:43).

story-worlds, but also deeply present in the experienced social worlds of the intended Marcan audience.

In his methodologically careful comparison of Mark's Gospel with *Menschenbilder* of Mediterranean antiquity, Carsten Jochum-Bortfeld discusses social constructions of slavery, womanhood, and discipleship extensively. By contrast, Jochum-Bortfeld discusses social evaluations of children and childhood almost cursorily, as a conceptual category which, by the standards of modern developmental theories or even by the standards of ancient social discourses, remained inchoate in antiquity.[17] Margaret MacDonald notes that "there have been great advances especially in the study of children in the Roman world in recent years and a growing body of literature on children in early Christianity."[18] In what follows, however, no highly-developed ideology of childhood will be assumed, either in Mark's literary portrayal or in the social consciousness of Mark's earliest audiences. Marcan treatment of slavery, womanhood, and discipleship may usefully be seen as deliberately subverting current Greco-Roman and Jewish social constructions as it invites "transformation through self-denial,"[19] through *Selbststigmatisierung*[20] or the like. Marcan portrayal of children is not so evidently a rejection of prevenient social discourses of childhood. The present essay thus differs from Jochum-Bortfeld's work in that I do not methodically foreground (especially contrastive) relevance of retrievable Greco-Roman or Jewish *Menschenbilder*. Moreover, without in principle denying the social-historical rootedness of Marcan discourse, I am much less committed than Jochum-Bortfeld to any particular reconstruction of the historical provenance of Mark's Gospel[21] or of the social processes in post-70 Judaism.[22]

In terms of method, the present study proposes a narratological bridge between Jochum-Bortfeld's global study of Marcan social language over against a wide range of reconstructed contemporary *Menschenbilder* and Peter Spitaler's "close reading of Mark 10.13–16." Where Jochum-Bortfeld offers a wide-angle

---

[17] JOCHUM-BORTFELD, Die Verachteten, 154–156; cf. GUNDRY, Children, 162–163; STEGEMANN, Kinder, 117–125; MEISER, Anthropologie.
[18] MACDONALD, Identification, 87; MACDONALD, Introduction; see also SPITALER, Welcoming, 424 and n. 3; AASGAARD, Paul, 131–132, n. 11; GUNDRY, Children, 164, n. 79. Generally, see DIXON, Childhood; BAKKE, Children; RAWSON, Children; HORN/MARTENS, Children; DASEN/SPÄTH, Children; LAES, Children; HARLOW/LOVÉN, Families; RAWSON, Companion.
[19] ROCHESTER, Anthrōpos, 28; cf. STEELE, Root.
[20] JOCHUM-BORTFELD, Die Verachteten, 198–215, in relation to discipleship.
[21] Ibid. 165–171, Syrian, urban, closely implicated in the catastrophe of the Second Temple; contra GUNDRY, Children, 143–146, Roman and largely Gentile.
[22] Ibid. 212–215.

contrastive study, Spitaler focuses narrowly, but with compensating focal depth, on "grammatical, syntactical, structural and contextual markers" inside one unit of Marcan narration/discourse (10:13–16).[23] While endorsing Spitaler's conclusions, the present essay will argue, however sketchily, for the centrality of child-language to the Marcan social-human portrait based on a wider discussion of the relation between Marcan episodic narratives and discourse attributed directly to Jesus (not least in Mark 10:13–16).

In otherwise excellent discussions of the Marcan child, Judith Gundry and Peter Müller both subordinate Marcan narrative to interpretation of Mark 10:13–16.[24] What follows will strongly emphasize the persuasive impact of Mark's narrative sequence;[25] Mark carefully prepares its audience to welcome correctly Jesus' gestures and declarations in Chapter 10.

2 Child-Episodes in Mark: Narrated Children

Narratively, there are four accounts in Mark in which someone is explicitly designated with one of several terms for non-adults (5:21–24; 6:14–29; 7:24–30; 9:14–29). They are all major, highly-elaborated episodes within Mark's narrative chain. These stories involving child characters, or at least persons under parental control, all precede the two contexts in which Mark's Jesus refers to children discursively to talk about leadership (9:33–37; 10:13–16). The turn is therefore quite noticeable *from* stories about Jesus involving children *toward* comments by Jesus relating childhood to leadership ideals.

2.1 Woman-Child and Child-Woman (Mark 5)

The first story (5:21–24.35–43) tells of an important religious leader (εἷς τῶν ἀρχισυναγώγων, v. 22) who approaches Jesus to heal his daughter. Jesus is delayed, the girl dies and Jesus resuscitates her. Her father calls her his θυγάτριον; both Jesus and the narrator call her παιδίον; when Jesus raises her, the narrator begins referring to her as κοράσιον. We are told, gratuitously it seems, that "the child" is twelve years old, but the child's age is intriguingly liminal, on the

---

23 SPITALER, Welcoming, 425.
24 GUNDRY, Children, 149; MÜLLER, Mitte, 33–80.
25 FARR, References.

threshold of adulthood.²⁶ Moreover, the period of twelve years relates her to the character of the woman who touches Jesus in the crowd and is healed from twelve years' of illness. Jesus addresses the adult woman as θυγάτηρ, whereas he will address the actual child mysteriously and intimately in Aramaic as ταλιθα.

The stories of Jairus' daughter and of the woman in the crowd are one of half a dozen pairs of stories in Mark where one story narratively interrupts the other. Such narrative sandwiches emphasize and connect the entwined stories by ironies which are hidden to the characters, but central to Mark's narrative.²⁷ The woman-child and the child-woman do not know each other, but they are linked by the double irony that the woman's salvation from chronic sickness ensures that the girl will die before Jesus comes—yet Jesus does arrive amid deep grieving only to pronounce the child's death, sleep, and then raise her back to full life. The twelve-year-old is brought to Jesus' attention by the agency of her important adult father; the grown woman approaches Jesus on her own, shyly and incognito. In this double story of two daughters it is not youth or childishness per se, but rather infirmity, mortality, and non-agency which seem to be stressed.

2.2 Dancing Girl, Kings and Revenants (Mark 6)

Mark's second story featuring an explicitly "child"-designated character is even less invested in a sentimental ideal of naive infancy. Neither Jochum-Bortfeld nor Spitaler seems even to mention the tale of a girl-daughter (θυγάτηρ and κοράσιον) dancing between king and prophet (Mark 6:14–29) as relevant to the Marcan *Menschenbild* or "reports about children."²⁸ The story of the beheading of the prophet John the Baptist is another instance of Marcan narrative sandwiching; the drama of John's death is wrapped in the sending out and return of the Twelve (6:7–44). Framing the story of John's death are the two places in Mark where Jesus' official disciples are actually successful as they act as Jesus' commissioned agents. No matter how dysfunctional Jesus' disciples become in the course of the narrative (and they, in fact, plumb the depths of dysfunc-

---

26 BOLT, Death, 159 and n. 94.
27 SHEPHERD, Function.
28 Quoting SPITALER, Welcoming, 424, also 430, n. 17 for the probability that Mark's use of child-language "is indiscriminate of age;" GUNDRY, Children, 172–174, at least tries.

tionality) it cannot be taken away from them that in Mark 6 Jesus uses them as his agents in miraculously feeding his sheep (6:30–44).

The narrative embedding of the decapitation story is even more complex than that of the raising of Jairus' daughter: the account of John's death is formally introduced as a narrative flashback recounted to explain why the Jewish Galilean king, Herod (foil to Jesus' true kingship [15:2.9.12.18.26.32]), apprehends Jesus as John the Baptist redivivus (6:14–16).

Narratively the flashback to John's death through Herod's guiltily paranoid viewpoint is strongly linked to the later story of Peter's Satanic attempt to distract Jesus from his destiny (8:31–33). Herod and Peter are both ambiguous office holders who threaten the destiny of the charismatics who challenge them. The stories of John's death and of Jesus' first prophecy of his own impending death both refer to popular perceptions of Jesus as John, Elijah or one of the prophets come back again (6:14–16; 8:27–30). The allegedly popular and speculative discourse which interprets Jesus as one of these charismatic figures, revenant, is not entirely repudiated in Mark: the association among John, Elijah, Jesus, Moses and the prophets is established at the very beginning of Mark (1:2–8) and reinforced in the Transfiguration story and its aftermath (9:2–13). In a more doctrinal or conceptual discussion with Sadducees about the resurrection of the dead, Mark's Jesus solemnly affirms the resurrected though altered life of Abraham, Isaac, and Jacob. In relation to John and Jesus, however, such talk is ironically undercut by insistence on the harsh corporeality of decapitation and crucifixion (15:33–37).[29]

This is, therefore, an interesting moment for our concern with Marcan anthropology, even if it has required a digression from our primary interest in the story's strangely adult "daughter-girl." The popular speculation about continuity between Elijah, John, and/or Jesus has to have some effect on how Mark's audience experience the narrative's strange sudden ending at the empty tomb (16:8). The eschatologically ambiguous individuation of Elijah, John, and Jesus should also influence the audience's perception of the mysterious deferred identity in Mark between Jesus and his eschatological alter ego, the Son of Man. In the Marcan story, Jesus both is and is not yet that Son of Man of whom he so often speaks, who has come to serve and die (10:45), but who will become God's judge over humanity (14:62). This Marcan way of narrating human destinies implies a conscious as well as complex *Menschenbild*. Yet the narrator declines in these matters to be drawn out of his narrative posture into any doctrinal, theoretical, or systematic formulation.

---

29 KRAEMER, Herodias, 343, n. 62.

Alan Culpepper correctly identifies Mark 6:17–29 as an episode which real readers, both scholarly and unschooled, have experienced as interrupting the Gospel's story.[30] The episode is an unusually intense "weave of plain sense, embellishments, asides, connections, and implications,"[31] but it doesn't even mention Jesus. The story was designed and placed to conduct its audience briefly into a different story-world of royal marriages and divorces, conspicuous consumption and foolish oaths, a world of glamour, horror, and fairy tale with just a touch of historical reference. Anyone raised in the culture-worlds of antiquity would experience in this story a shock of folkloric familiarity with its legal issues and stock characters; anyone literate in biblical or classical narrative would add a refinement of intertextuality to that impression.

It has always been hard to agree which character is the central character and what narrative genre to hear the story through: the story is apparently the martyrology of the true prophet, the tragedy of the duped king, or even the comedy of the wicked queen. Yet it is the girl who emerges as the dominant character in the story.[32] It is the girl who lends her frustrated mother agency; the mother, the king, even the prophet, lack full agency. The girl is referred to by the narrator more than the other characters (once as θυγάτηρ, three times as κοράσιον); moreover, the narrator designates this shocking girl in the same terms used before for the twelve-year-old and for the adult woman who touches Jesus. It is the girl who gets to speak the most direct discourse. It seems to be the girl's initiative to dance and then to ask her mother's advice. It is certainly the girl's macabre fancy to place the prophet's head, as it were, on the royal menu. The story-teller may also be emphasising the girl's agency by down-playing the implicit erotic possibilities in the narrative, in contrast, for example, with similar moments in the Esther tales. The narrator does not tell us how old the girl actually is or what kind of dance she danced; the emphasis is not on choreography, but on the dance's rhetorical effect.[33]

Culpepper and others note very well that this odd story, in fact, does important narrative work for Mark, foreshadowing Jesus' own death, establishing an expectation of homology between Jesus' coming death and the death that can be expected by his followers, anticipating also the shifted commensality of the Last Supper where Jesus, bizarrely like the dancing girl, will hijack expected food ritual. The whole story reinforces Mark's pivotal contrast between modes of

---

30 CULPEPPER, Mark 6:17–29, 146–148; BOLT, Defeat, 191.
31 CULPEPPER, Mark 6:17–29, 153.
32 On the intentionality of the Marcan narrative, see KRAEMER, Implicating.
33 CULPEPPER, Mark 6:17–29, 157–158.

kingship and discipleship (10:35–45). John dies because he takes a prophetic stand against the marital practices of the royal family; the Marcan Jesus also intervenes in issues of marriage and divorce, virtually the only issue of law in which he takes any coherent interest (10:1–12). The narrator ends the episode by having John's disciples behave in shocking contrast with Jesus' vagrant disciples (6:29; 15:42–47). The Marcan author has carefully crafted this interruption and its delinquent child at the centre of a key chapter on Jesus commissioning his official disciples.

2.3 Children and Dogs (Mark 7)

The third "child"-story in Mark abruptly and without stated motivation begins a series of incidents in which Jesus repeatedly crosses the borders of biblical Israel (7:24–30). In this instance, he goes into Tyrean territory where he is trying to pass unrecognized, but is confronted by the mother of a θυγάτριον affected by a πνεῦμα ἀκάθαρτον. The mother in this story is the only one of Jesus' conversation partners who is so emphatically labelled as ethnically and religiously not Jewish. Jesus is accordingly flagrantly rude to her as he labels Israel as τέκνα at God's table and the woman and her kind as κυνάρια. In a flash of metic wit, the mother accepts the label κυνάρια and claims for her daughter the children's table-scraps. Jesus relents and tells her that the demon has been expelled from her θυγάτηρ. The woman goes home to find her παιδίον well. The "little pagan girl" here is "the absent and passive actant who still caused all the actions and statements" in the episode.[34] For our purposes, this story superbly raises the question how it is possible to be fully human outside the community of Israel's covenant with God and, indeed, how it is possible to become fully human in the situation of demonic control, a situation which in Mark also infects Israel. The story's metaphors also presuppose that domestic dogs are the epitome of the non-human in human community; the story wouldn't work if Jesus had selected a different non-human species. No other Marcan story poses so starkly the question whether dogs, demons, Jews and Greeks constitute one, two or more species.

---

34 POKORNÝ, Puppy, 337.

2.4 Boy-Child and Human Threshold (Mark 9)

The last episode to be considered before turning to Jesus' discursive speeches about children is the story, this time, of a father and his demon-possessed son (9:14–29). In this carefully-wrought story, Jesus and his inner group of disciples descend from the mountain of Transfiguration where the chosen disciples have witnessed Jesus' epiphanic glorification and dialogue with Moses and Elijah. As they rejoin the main group of disciples waiting down below, they are greeted by a chaos of conflict and failure. While Jesus was away a man has brought his son, affected by a πνεῦμα ἄλαλον, to Jesus' disciples, who fail to help the child; the man then approaches Jesus in a passionate dialogue and persuades him to deliver the boy. Both father and narrator emphasize how violent and dangerous the possessing spirit is. Jesus expressly asks how long the son had been affected and the father answers "from childhood" (ἐκ παιδιόθεν, v. 21). Thereafter, the narrator refers to the son as a παιδίον. Jesus and the father enter into an extended dialogue, culminating in the man's characteristically paradoxical Marcan prayer: "I do believe! Help my unbelief!" Jesus then commands the spirit to leave the boy. In the process, the boy appears so like a corpse that onlookers declare him dead. Jesus then raises him back to life. Jesus' official disciples privately ask why they had failed to deal with the case. Jesus replies unhelpfully that "this kind" needs prayer.

As in earlier stories, the παιδίον here seems infantile in status more than in age: he is old enough to have been suffering "since childhood."[35] The demonic influence is clearly portrayed as physically life-threatening, but even more clearly the πνεῦμα ἄλαλον has chronically deprived its victim of his proper human, indeed adult, communicativity. Once again, it is the faith of a parent which moves Jesus to act; our notions of the individual subjectivity of faith do not hold in the Marcan story-world. The father in the story, like the women in the earlier stories, models a desperate resourcefulness evidenced in a style of dramatically unschooled, non-cultic faith and prayer. This exorcism intriguingly modulates the *Menschenbild* expressed in some Greco-Roman notions of the ideal boy-child ("puer sanus, incolumis, ingeniosus, decorus") as an optimally receptive oracular/magical medium between human and divine/demonic natures, permitting skillful trance-state manipulation.[36] The Marcan child is a

---

35 SPITALER, Welcoming, 430, n. 17.
36 Superbly formulated c. 160 in APULEIUS, Apologia pro se de magia, 43 (quoting 43.7), against a charge of using a boy in black magic (ed. HUNINK).

similarly liminal human individual, desperately vulnerable to demonic depersonalization, but it is the faith of his father in Jesus' authority which exposes the child to the divine.

3 Child-Oracles: Welcoming God Humanely (Mark 9:33–37; 10:13–16)

We now turn, presupposing Spitaler's detailed study, to consider briefly the Marcan Jesus' use of children in his discourses in the third quarter of Mark's story. The foregoing comments on the earlier episodes are meant to suggest the general claim that Mark is narratively interested in children as paradigmatic for understanding the human condition. Thus far, the Marcan audience has been carefully, decisively, and unsentimentally reminded that the human condition is that of children and parents. The Marcan child is abject under the determination of death and demonic power and yet also spontaneously able to initiate contact with the divine in an economy where faith and despair seem formally indistinguishable. Children and their relatives are hostages to mortality and demonic evil, yet surprisingly able to assert real agency in a world where Jesus is present.

Surveying what can be known about high rates of mortality, disease, and affective loss in the Greco-Roman world, Peter Bolt shows clearly that Mark's representations of child mortality were essentially realistic.[37] Everyone in any historically imaginable Marcan audience had watched a child die. Yet Mark's narrative focuses on parents and their *older* children, on the verge of the next stage in life, rather than on the whole range of infant mortality. Mark's selection of older children suggests that the narrative is not just constructed within a social realist aesthetic. I do not see that Jesus' remarkable embrace (ἐναγκαλισάμενος) of children (9:36; 10:16) indicates, as Gundry argues, "that the little children brought to Jesus become his own children and heirs by his adoptive embrace and blessing."[38] The children with whom Jesus interacts are not foundlings; they are "normally" socialised persons with fully engaged parents, especially vulnerable only because as children they are especially human; even the dancing girl is (pathologically) well-connected. Mark thus intentional-

---

[37] BOLT, Defeat, 26–34.155–167.
[38] GUNDRY, Children, 158 (though see 159 for nuance).

ly constructs a narrative anthropology, not in conceptual abstraction, but in a kind of ideal sample of human (and demonic) relationships centred on children.

It is in the larger narrative context, then, of a whole series of noteworthy incidents involving children that Mark's Jesus twice (9:33–37; 10:13–16) relates the sovereignty of God to the symbol of a child. Moreover, just as the sequence of child-episodes has prepared Mark's audience for the pair of Jesus' enacted child-sayings, so also Mark 9:33–37 prepares Jesus' and the narrator's shared audience shortly to hear Mark 10:13–16. Both Jesus' words challenge his hearers to welcome the humane sovereignty of God revealed in the one who will soon be crucified, but illustrated already in the child.

So in Mark 9:33–37, Jesus has just predicted for the second time the coming death of the Son of Man. Jesus' disciples miss the point so totally that they begin arguing about each other's status. Jesus then actually takes a παιδίον and sets it up among his disciples and followers. In Mark's story-world (and audience?), παιδία were on hand to serve as visual aids when needed.

A little later, in Mark 10:13–16 the narrative frame of Jesus' saying is that people "were bringing him children so that he might touch them." In Mark, people bring others to Jesus or pray to Jesus for others, because those being brought are in desperate, radical states of helplessness.[39] Similarly, in Mark when Jesus and others touch, it is in order to transfer spiritual power from Jesus to the desperate people he encounters.[40] Jesus' saying in Mark 10:15 is then given formulaic oracular emphasis as a climactic oracle: "Amen, I say to you, whoever does not welcome the sovereignty of God as a child, may not enter it."

Jesus' two sayings, about the one who welcomes a child for his sake and about the one who welcomes the sovereignty of God ὡς παιδίον, have been immensely influential. Usually, however, the Marcan Jesus' child-sayings have exercised their influence in deep hermeneutical isolation from the long Marcan narrative context established above. Indeed, discussion of Mark 9:33–37 and 10:13–16 has often understated the (redactionally deliberate[41]) importance and complexity of the medium-scale "narrative unit (9:33–10:16)" which Jesus' child-pronouncements "bracket."[42] The "two sections concerning the child frame one concerning divorce"[43] (10:2–12) and one concerning abuse of "little believers" (9:42–50).[44] Shortly after this narrative unit, Jesus will speak again of

---

39 Mark 1:32; 2:1–5; 7:32; 9:14–29.
40 Mark 1:41; 3:10; 5:27–31; 6:56; 7:33; 8:22; see LINDEMANN, Kinder, 179.
41 STEGEMANN, Kinder, 128–135; MÜLLER, Mitte, 54.
42 SPITALER, Welcoming, 436, n. 36, 441.
43 CROSSAN, Kingdom, 85.
44 HENDERSON, 'Salted With Fire.'

an experience of social re-orientation which links pre- and post-Easter followership: no one who abandons social relationships (including τέκνα) for the gospel will fail to receive new relations in anticipation of the eschaton (10:28–31).

What is it about παιδία in the Marcan story-world, then, that makes them attractive to Jesus as tenors of figurative meaning? Rhoads and Michie typify a powerful current in Marcan reception when they assume that it is the qualities of "childlike, often persistent faith," "childlike humility" and "capacity for sacrificial service" which interest Jesus in children and other "little people."[45] On this (reception-historically dominant) tradition, welcoming the kingship of God ὡς παιδίον, means welcoming God's sovereignty the way a child intuitively welcomes God's sovereignty. "The children are only defined by an attitude (although a passive one) toward the relation between holy and profane."[46] On such readings, the Marcan *Menschenbild* climaxes with Jesus urging the audience to become spiritually, subjectively childlike. Against this tradition of childlike discipleship, however, stands the whole narrative of Mark's Gospel, in which children are narrated as symbols of the human condition, but are *not* narrated as examples of naive (perhaps Torah-free[47]) trust.

Child-like attitude is, of course, canonised in the redaction of Mark 10:15 in Matthew 18:3: "Unless you [plural] turn and become as children (ὡς τὰ παιδία)."[48] Likewise, Matthaean redaction turns the "poor" whom Jesus blesses in Q (Luke 6:20) into an inner spiritual condition of ideal disciples (Matt 5:3; cf. 1Cor 14:20). Redactional interest in childhood as a metaphor of spiritual attitude (Matt 21:15–16) coheres with that specific Matthaean eschatological nomism in which "the righteousness of the disciples is a result of an internal quality, a pure heart."[49] Many texts in the Jesus tradition explore the idea that ideal discipleship or ideal humanity are like childhood or, indeed, babyhood (for example, Gos. Thom. 4; 22; 1Thess 2:7[50]; Q Luke 10:21–22 par. Matt 11:25–27; John 3:1–21[51]; Luke 18:15[52]); still other texts are more interested in the ironically revelatory

---

45 RHOADS/MICHIE, Mark, 130, 133, quoted in MOORE, Humans, 84.
46 PATTE, Pronouncement, 28.
47 GUNDRY-VOLF, The Least, 39–40; GUNDRY, Children, 168–172.
48 SPITALER, Welcoming, 428, n. 13.
49 GRINDHEIM, Ignorance, 325.
50 AASGAARD, Paul, 147–148.
51 DUNDERBERG, Secrecy, 232, n. 28.
52 LINDEMANN, Kinder, 180, n. 50.

presence of Jesus as a child/infant (Gos. Sav. 107:5–60; Gos. Judas 33[53]; Matt 1:18–23; Luke 1:5–52).[54]

In a valuable, but still partial correction to this received, post-Marcan understanding of the child, socially sensitive interpretation has increasingly pointed away from the romanticised spiritual qualities of children toward their allegedly low social status in ancient societies, analogous to the social status of other oppressed categories, slaves, women, the diseased or ritually impure.[55] Especially in Jewish settings,[56] it is not always clear that the social status of children was low in anything like the servile sense (notwithstanding Paul's interest in their limited, ambiguous, temporary similarity [Gal 4:1-7]). In any case, however, making the child in Mark 10:15 essentially an example of low social standing or marginality does not explain either Jesus' or Mark's special interest in children. The child in Mark is a symbol not just of the relatively marginalised, but of the human condition of universal dependence, fragility and powerlessness.

In Mark 9:37, Jesus commends anyone who actually welcomes a child, not anyone who behaves like a child. In Mark 10, when he solemnly declares that no one who does not welcome God's sovereignty ὡς παιδίον will himself enter it, Jesus is saying again that Mark's audience must urgently welcome God's kingship as they would welcome a dependant, vulnerable child—and as Jesus has in fact just done (v. 14).[57] For Gundry, with breath-taking candour, the option of reading ὡς παιδίον as an accusative "can be rejected since the kingdom of God in Mark has connotations of power and is unlikely to be compared with something so weak as a little child." It is, however, precisely the Marcan Jesus, who declares that power should be held by those willing to be slaves of all (10:41–45), who also urges that God's power should be welcomed as someone else's child.

Sometimes it is claimed that the immediate context of Mark 10:13–16 imposes a nominative reading of ὡς παιδίον: "Im vorliegenden Zusammenhang wird man ihn mit großer Sicherheit als Vergleich zum Subjekt nominativisch über-

---

53 KING, Images, 67 and lit. there for the philological problem.
54 KING, Images, 67–82.
55 SPITALER, Welcoming, 425, n. 5.
56 JOCHUM-BORTFELD, Die Verachteten, 258–260; GUNDRY-VOLF, The Least, 38–41; MÜLLER, Mitte, 67 69.
57 ROBBINS, Blessing, 59 and n. 28; CROSSAN, Kingdom, 84–87; SPITALER, Welcoming; STEGEMANN, Kinder, 133–135; FOCANT, Évangile, 380–381. For the dominant, "childlike attitude" tradition, see, e.g., COLLINS, Mark, 473; PATTE, Pronouncement, 28; RINGSHAUSEN, Kinder, 36.42–44; GUNDRY-VOLF, The Least, 39, n. 42.

setzen müssen."⁵⁸ With Spitaler,⁵⁹ I disagree, but in particular because the decisive preceding context should be the whole narrative of Mark's gospel, not only the immediately preceding phrase. This essay has, therefore, tried to show that at higher levels of Marcan narrative context, 9:33–10:16, and Mark as a whole, it is Jesus' and others' attitudes and behaviour toward children, not the child's attitude or behaviour, that is determinative.

4 Conclusion

The παιδίον, then, is indeed a central figure of a deliberate narrative portrait of the human condition. The essential points of that figuration are not the qualities of romantic childhood, innocence, intuitive trust, humility and so on, but rather the relational, social, communicative traits of Marcan narrative children: objective powerlessness, desperate vulnerability to death and the demonic, profound dependence on God, Jesus and the sometimes unreliable faith and cunning of others. Spitaler warns against reducing the child to a simple metaphor of God's kingdom.⁶⁰ Rather it is the complex action of welcoming the child which is metonymic of God's sovereignty, a complexity of action which is not intelligible without the narrative preface of Jesus' epiphanic encounters with narrated children throughout Mark. Descriptively, the Marcan audience may well identify with children and their parents in desperate need of Jesus' intervention. Prescriptively, however, Mark's audience are commanded to welcome Jesus by welcoming children; on pain of fearful punishments, Marcan leaders are commanded by Jesus to safeguard "little believers" who must by synecdoche include, but cannot be limited to actual children (Mark 9:42–50).⁶¹ Eschatologically, Mark's audience are commanded to welcome God's own sovereignty paradoxically as they would (and actually do?) welcome those liminal, fragile, even demonized children. Only in this spirit can Jesus' imitators prepare for the coming of the Son of Man.

---

58 RINGSHAUSEN, Kinder, 36; FARR, References, 113–114.
59 SPITALER, Welcoming, 434–439.
60 SPITALER, Welcoming, 428–429 and n. 14, 436, n. 36, and 439.
61 HENDERSON, 'Salted With Fire.'

Bibliography

AASGAARD, Reidar, Paul as a Child. Children and Childhood in the Letters of the Apostle, in: JBL 126 (2007) 129–159.

BAKKE, Odd M., When Children Became People. The Birth of Childhood in Early Christianity, Minneapolis, Minnesota 2005.

BOLT, Peter G., Jesus' Defeat of Death. Persuading Mark's Early Readers (MSSNTS 125), Cambridge, U.K./New York 2003.

BORING, M. Eugene, Mark. A Commentary, Louisville, Kentucky 2006.

COLLINS, Adela Yarbro, Mark. A Commentary (Hermeneia), Minneapolis, Minnesota 2007.

CROSSAN, John Dominic, Kingdom and Children. A Study in the Aphoristic Tradition, in: Semeia 29 (1983) 75–96.

CULPEPPER, R. Alan, Mark 6:17–29 in its Narrative Context. Kingdoms in Conflict, in: Iverson, Kelly R./Skinner, Christopher W. (Hg.), Mark as Story. Retrospect and Prospect (Resources for Biblical Study 65), Atlanta, Georgia 2011, 145–163.

DASEN, Veronique/SPÄTH, Thomas (Hg.), Children, Memory, and Family Identity in Roman Culture, Oxford/New York 2010.

DIXON, Suzanne (Hg.), Childhood, Class and Kin in the Roman World, London/New York 2001.

DRIGGERS, Ira Brent, Following God through Mark. Theological Tension in the Second Gospel, Louisville, Kentucky 2007.

DUNDERBERG, Ismo, Secrecy in the Gospel of John, in: Bull, Christian H./Lied, Liv Ingeborg/Turner, John D. (Hg.), Mystery and Secrecy in the Nag Hammadi Collection and Other Ancient Literature. Ideas and Practices. Studies for Einar Thomassen at Sixty (Nag Hammadi and Manichaean Studies 76), Leiden/Boston, Massachusetts 2012, 221–243.

FARR, Eric Allen, The Narrative and Discursive References to Children and Audience Duality in the Gospel of Mark (MA Thesis, McGill University), Montreal 2011.

FOCANT, Camille, L'Évangile selon Marc (Commentaire biblique. Nouveau testament 2), Paris 2004.

GRINDHEIM, Sigurd, Ignorance Is Bliss. Attitudinal Aspects of the Judgment according to Works in Matthew 25:31–46, in: NT 50 (2008) 313–331.

GUNDRY, Judith M., Children in the Gospel of Mark, with Special Attention to Jesus' Blessing of the Children (Mark 10:13–16) and the Purpose of Mark, in: Bunge, Marcia J. (Hg.), The Child in the Bible, Grand Rapids, Michigan/Cambridge, U.K. 2008, 143–176.

GUNDRY-VOLF, Judith M., The Least and the Greatest. Children in the New Testament, in: Bunge, Marcia J. (Hg.), The Child in Christian Thought and Practice, Grand Rapids, Michigan/Cambridge, U.K. 2001, 29–60.

HARLOW, Mary/LOVÉN, Lena Larsson (Hg.), Families in the Roman and Late Antique World (Family in Antiquity 2), London/New York 2012.

HENDERSON, Ian H., 'Salted With Fire' (Mark 9.42–50). Style, Oracles and (Socio)Rhetorical Gospel Criticism, in: JSNT 80 (2000) 44–65.

HENDERSON, Ian H., Reconstructing Mark's Double Audience, in: Malbon, Elizabeth Struthers (Hg.), Between Author and Audience in Mark. Narration, Characterization, Interpretation, Sheffield 2009, 6–28.

HORN, Cornelia B./MARTENS, John W., "Let the little children come to me." Childhood and Children in Early Christianity, Washington, D.C. 2009.

HUNINK, Vincent (Hg.), Apuleius of Madauros. Pro se de magia (Apologia). Edited with a Commentary, 2 vols., Amsterdam 1997.

JOCHUM-BORTFELD, Carsten, Die Verachteten stehen auf. Widersprüche und Gegenentwürfe des Markusevangeliums zu den Menschenbildern seiner Zeit (BWANT 178 [=9. Ser. 18]), Stuttgart 2008.

KÄHLER, Martin, Der sogenannte historische Jesus und der geschichtliche, biblische Christus, Leipzig 1892 (revised ²1896, reprinted München 1956).

KING, Karen L., "In your midst as a child"—"In the form of an old man." Images of Aging and Immortality in Ancient Christianity, in: Seim, Turid Karlsen/Økland, Jorunn (Hg.), Metamorphoses. Resurrection, Body and Transformative Practices in Early Christianity (Ekstasis 1), Berlin/New York 2009, 59–82.

KRAEMER, Ross S., Implicating Herodias and Her Daughter in the Death of John the Baptizer. A (Christian) Theological Strategy, in: JBL 125 (2006) 321–349.

LAES, Christian, Children in the Roman Empire. Outsiders Within (original title: Kinderen bij de Romeinen [2006]), Cambridge, U.K./New York 2011.

LINDEMANN, Andreas, ... ἐκτρέψετε αὐτὰ ἐν παιδείᾳ καὶ νουθεσίᾳ κυρίου (Eph 6.4). Kinder in der Welt des frühen Christentums, in: NTS 56 (2010) 169–190.

MACDONALD, Margaret Y., Beyond Identification of the Topos of Household Management. Reading the Household Codes in Light of Recent Methodologies and Theoretical Perspectives in the Study of the New Testament, in: NTS 57 (2011) 65–90.

MACDONALD, Margaret Y., Editorial Introduction. Special Issue on Children and Childhood in Early Judaism and Early Christianity, in: Studies in Religion/Sciences Religieuses 41 (2012) 341–349.

MALBON, Elizabeth Struthers, Characters in Mark's story. Changing Perspectives on the Narrative Process, in: Iverson, Kelly R./Skinner, Christopher W. (Hg.), Mark as Story. Retrospect and Prospect (Resources for Biblical Study 65), Atlanta, Georgia 2011, 45–69.

MEISER, Martin, Anthropologie im Markusevangelium, in: Rothschild, Clare K./Thompson, Trevor W. (Hg.), Christian Body, Christian Self. Concepts of Early Christian Personhood (WUNT 284), Tübingen 2011, 125–148.

MOORE, Stephen D., Why there are no Humans or Animals in the Gospel of Mark, in: Iverson, Kelly R./Skinner, Christopher W. (Hg.), Mark as Story. Retrospect and Prospect (Resources for Biblical Study 65), Atlanta, Georgia 2011, 71–93.

MÜLLER, Peter, In der Mitte der Gemeinde. Kinder im Neuen Testament, Neukirchen-Vluyn 1992.

PATTE, Daniel, Jesus' Pronouncement about Entering the Kingdom like a Child. A Structural Exegesis, in: Semeia 29 (1983) 3–42.

POKORNÝ, Petr, From a Puppy to the Child. Problems of Contemporary Biblical Exegesis Demonstrated from Mark 7.24–30/Matt. 15.21–28, in: NTS 41 (1995) 321–337.

RAWSON, Beryl, Children and Childhood in Roman Italy, Oxford/New York 2003.

RAWSON, Beryl (Hg.), A Companion to Families in the Greek and Roman Worlds, Chichester, U.K./Malden, Massachusetts 2011.

RHOADS, David M./MICHIE, Donald, Mark as Story. An Introduction to the Narrative of a Gospel, Philadelphia, Pennsylvania 1982.

RHOADS, David M./DEWEY, Joanna/MICHIE, Donald, Mark as Story. An Introduction to the Narrative of a Gospel (Revised edition), Minneapolis, Minnesota 1999.

RINGSHAUSEN, Gerhard, Die Kinder der Weisheit. Zur Auslegung von Mk 10.13–16 par., in: ZNW 77 (1986) 34–63.

ROBBINS, Vernon K., Pronouncement Stories and Jesus' Blessing of the Children. A Rhetorical Approach, in: Semeia 29 (1983) 43–74.
ROCHESTER, Stuart, The Eschatological Anthrōpos in Mark's Gospel, in: Kaleidoscope 3 (2009) 25–34.
SHEPHERD, Tom, The Narrative Function of Markan Intercalation, in: NTS 41 (1995) 522–540.
SHINER, Whitney Taylor, Follow me! Disciples in Markan Rhetoric (SBL Dissertation 145), Atlanta, Georgia 1995.
SPITALER, Peter, Welcoming a Child as a Metaphor for Welcoming God's Kingdom. A Close Reading of Mark 10.13–16, in: JSNT 31 (2009) 423–446.
STEELE, Denise, Having Root in the Self. Human Fruition and the Self-in-Relation in the Gospel of Mark (Ph.D Dissertation, University of Glasgow), Glasgow 2004.
STEGEMANN, Wolfgang, Lasset die Kinder zu mir kommen. Sozialgeschichtliche Aspekte des Kinderevangeliums, in: Schottroff, Willy/Stegemann, Wolfgang (Hg.), Traditionen der Befreiung. Sozialgeschichtliche Bibelauslegungen, Vol. I. Methodische Zugänge, München 1980, 114–144.
TOLBERT, Mary Ann, Sowing the Gospel. Mark's World in Literary-Historical Perspective, Minneapolis, Minnesota 1989.
TREBILCO, Paul, Self-Designations and Group Identity in the New Testament, Cambridge/New York 2012.

Rouven Genz
Reversal of Fate after Death?

Reflections on the Account of the Rich Man and Lazarus (Luke 16:19–31)

It is well known that, compared to the other Synoptic Gospels, the Gospel of Luke comes up with many peculiarities due to its extensive *Sondergut* traditions. One of the most striking examples is the account of the rich man and Lazarus in Luke 16:19–31. With regard to the subject of the present volume, "Evil and Death in Light of Present and Future Existence. Conceptions of the Human in Biblical, Early Jewish, Early Christian, Greco-Roman and Egyptian Literature," this passage may boldly be called the most suitable and significant New Testament text for any assessment in this field of study since the main issues are uniquely displayed here: Not only is human life in this world contrasted to diverging fates after death, but the question of good and bad in relation to present and future existence is addressed as well. In addition, the depiction of the hereafter is featured in an unusually detailed manner and the account ends with the discussion of a possible resurrection. Finally, as if there were not already enough reasons to engage in a closer examination of this remarkable passage, it is this text which has often been linked with Egyptian, Jewish and Greco-Roman traditions and which can therefore be considered a promising and enlightening test case of the interdisciplinary dialogue in demand. However, it has to be stated as well that generations of exegetes have been puzzled exactly by those contents of the text which make it so suitable for the discussion, and various approaches have been used in order to grasp the theological crux of the Lukan story.[1] In the following, attention will first of all be drawn to the text itself (section 1), before the relevance of the extrabiblical parallels and the significance of the Lukan context are investigated (sections 2 and 3) in order to arrive at some concluding theses for an adequate interpretation of the passage (section 4).

---

[1] Many dissertations testify to the permanent debate. Cf. SELLIN, Gleichniserzählungen; HINTZEN, Verkündigung; OJOK, Parable; and more recently LEHTIPUU, Afterlife Imagery; HAUGE, Tour of Hell. For a history of research on Luke 16:19–31, see especially LEHTIPUU, Afterlife Imagery, 11–38.

1 The Text and Its Structure

The account is not explicitly labelled as parable, and, based on a definition of a parable as a comparison of everyday life drawing on repeated phenomena, it might be conceded that the account of an afterlife scenario does not fit in this category. Still, the illustrative and parabolic character of this story is clear enough. In Luke, the Gospel which comprises most of the New Testament parables and comparisons, many of these are defined as such,[2] whereas others are not.[3] Furthermore, the introductory formula "a certain man" (ἄνθρωπός τις) is typical Lukan style and is mostly used in the "undefined" parables, where the comparative character is easily discernible.[4] Some of the less important manuscripts[5] even add the explicative phrase "And he (i.e. Jesus) told another parable" (Εἴπεν δὲ καὶ ἑτέραν παραβολήν) to Luke 16:19. So after all, it remains appropriate to classify the passage at least as an example story or as a didactic narrative.[6] Nevertheless, to accept that the passage is parabolic in character does not mean *a priori* that what is said about the afterlife is to be esteemed exclusively symbolic since doctrinal aspects can be conveyed in exceedingly figurative texts, too.[7]

A structural analysis reveals a coherent and elaborate scheme.[8] The text can neatly be divided into two parts (vv. 19–22 and vv. 23–31), each of which contains a parallel arrangement:

---

[2] Cf. Luke 6:47; 7:31; 8:4; 12:16.35–36; 13:6.18.20; 14:7; 15:3; 18:1.9; 19:11; 20:9; 21:29.
[3] Cf. Luke 7:41; 10:30; 11:5; 14:16.28; 15:8.11; 16:1; 17:7. See also Luke 11:24; 12:39.42.58; 13:24–25.
[4] See Luke 10:30; 14:16; 15:11; 16:1. The formula also appears in "defined" parables: see Luke 12:16; 19:12. Cf. LEONHARDT-BALZER, Abrahams Schoß, 647–648.
[5] Most notably Codex Bezae Cantabrigiensis (D).
[6] Cf. BOCK, Parable, 64–65; IDEM, Luke, vol. 2, 1362–1363; and KREMER, Lazarus, 112–113.
[7] The general correlation of content and form of presentation is also recognized by BOCK, Parable, 64–65.
[8] On the question of structure see also KNIGHT, Luke 16:19–31, 278; and SCHNIDER/STENGER, Tür.

I.	A	*Description* of the rich man (v. 19)	B	*Description* of Lazarus (vv. 20–21)
	B'	*Death* of Lazarus and transition to the otherworld, i.e. Abraham's bosom (v. 22ab)	A'	*Death* of the rich man and transition to the otherworld, i.e. Hades (v. 22c)
II.	A	*Demand 1* of the rich man: Abatement through Lazarus (vv. 23–24)	B	*Denial 1* of Abraham: Irreversible reversal of fate and unbridgeable chasm (vv. 25–26)
	A'	*Demand 2* of the rich man: Warning of his kin through Lazarus (vv. 27–28)	B'	*Denial 2* of Abraham: Listening to Moses and the Prophets instead (v. 29)
	A"	*Demand 3* of the rich man: Resurrection of Lazarus would out-weigh Moses and the Prophets (v. 30)	B"	*Denial 3* of Abraham: Resurrection of the dead would not be more convincing (v. 31)

The first part can be understood as a diptych, initially contrasting the main characters in their inner-worldly living conditions and subsequently in their death and postmortem fate. The chiastic parallelism (rich man—Lazarus/Lazarus—rich man) demonstrates the reversal of fortunes also on a formal level. Moreover, the description of the rich man is at first more succinct than that of Lazarus, while after death, his situation is portrayed in more detail.[9] In the second part, which is essentially a postmortem dialogue between the rich man and Abraham induced by the diverging fates, three demands of the rich man alternate with Abraham's denials. While the first demand—abatement of his torment—concerns the person of the rich man himself, the second—warning of his kin—expands to his family and poses the question of an enduring connection to the living. Finally, the third plea repeats the second demand more rigorously and is in itself a response to the preceding denial, taking up the phrase "Moses and the Prophets." It is worth mentioning that in each demand Lazarus plays the central role although he himself is decidedly a passive character during the whole story.[10]

---

[9] Cf. KREMER, Lazarus, 111.
[10] Yet, GLOMBITZA, Der reiche Mann, 172, rightly remarks that Lazarus is depicted "als eigentlich unüberhörbarer und doch übersehener Anruf Gottes zur Liebe [...] also als das verachtete Wort Gottes, als verachteter Gottesknecht." GLOMBITZA, then, regards as the core message of the passage the fact that there is a "too late" for man's response, an estimation which has to be kept in mind.

Looking at Abraham, it becomes clear that his first denial points out the finality and irrevocability of the situation, whereas the second and third denial concern the revelation of God's will, indicating that people can be convinced of its truth basically through listening, not by witnessing a miracle.[11] This last point can be considered the climax of the account.[12]

What is generally striking is the fact that, in contrast to every other New Testament parable, one of the main characters bears a name. Λάζαρος is the shortened Greek form of the Hebrew name Eleazar (אלעזר or אליעזר; LXX: Ελεαζαρ resp. Ελιεζερ), meaning "(My) God has helped." Therefore, the name can be understood as highlighting the very content of the story regarding the fate of the destitute man and is surely not coincidental.[13] In fact, it may be crucial for understanding the text correctly. Now, Lazarus has often been associated with Abraham's servant Eliezer, a Gentile by birth (cf. Gen 15:2).[14] This would raise the question whether the Lukan account might hint at the calling of the Gentiles into the faith of Abraham, a question which has to be borne in mind. However, more predominant is the observation that there is another character within the New Testament bearing the same name: Lazarus of Bethany, who, according to the Gospel of John, was raised from the dead by Jesus and personifies the major miraculous sign of the latter (John 11:1–45; 12:1-2.10–11). The shared name, the topic of suffering, death and resurrection as well as the appearance of the sisters Martha and Mary also in the Gospel of Luke (Luke

---

11 On that point, LUTHER commented that God obviously did not want the dead to preach, for otherwise he would not have appointed pastors (see WA 41:300).

12 JÜLICHER, Lc 16,19–31, 638–641, decidedly argued that vv. 27–31 were a later *addendum* by a Christian writer in the face of the experience that the majority of the Jews remained unbelieving even though Jesus had been raised from the dead. According to JÜLICHER, the conjunction of the original section (vv. 19–26) with the substantially different second part resulted in the fact that the text was transmitted "eben blos in vergewaltigtem Zustande." Especially since this line of argument was brought up the question of textual coherence has had some weight in scholarly debate, but unnecessarily so, for the text as such is a complete and nicely designed literary entity which *as a whole* conveys the narrative purpose of Luke (see the subsequent exposition). Besides, the suggested division breaks the parable in the middle of the conversation. Cf. FITZMYER, Luke, 1127; HOCK, Lazarus and Micyllus, 454–455; KREITZER, Luke 16:19–31, 140; SCHNIDER/STENGER, Tür.

13 Similarly KREITZER, Luke 16:19–31, 139. Yet, JÜLICHER, Lc 16,19–31, 622, concluded that the significance of the name lay merely in the more convenient reference to the poor man during the following dialogue. But this does not sufficiently explain why exactly *this* name was chosen. Cf. WOLTER, Lukasevangelium, 558.

14 Cf. DERRETT, Fresh Light, 371–372; and CAVE, Lazarus, 323–325, who also claims Isa 1:5 as the predominant reference for the depiction of Lazarus. HOCK, Lazarus and Micyllus, 454, remains critical and stresses that the etymology of the name is not provided as it is, for example, in the case of "Immanuel" in Matt 1:23.

10:38–42) have provoked scholarly investigation of the relation between, and possible interdependence of both texts with different results.[15] It has to be stated, though, that in John, Lazarus is not described as poor and lonely but primarily as dear to Jesus and as being actually raised from the dead, the latter aspect being the main point of the narration which is anchored in real locale and appears to take up rather authentic material. In Luke, on the other hand, the account is parabolic and deals with the question of eschatological reversal of *two* different fates; a possible resurrection of Lazarus is denied. So despite the similarities, the assumption that a fictional story manufactured out of the Lukan parable was preserved in John[16] is as questionable as the attempt to historicize the accounts as if Jesus told the parable on the way to raising Lazarus.[17] Rather, the parable could be based on, or have been connected with an incident later elaborated in John.[18] If, however, John wrote his Gospel in knowledge of the Lukan passage, the raising of Lazarus could be understood as excelling *one* aspect of Luke 16. In any case, what can be inferred is that in both texts, the name "Lazarus" emphasizes the key idea that especially in light of forsakenness and death, man is entirely dependent on an intervention of God on his behalf to be saved. Hence, in each case etymology might be more essential than the question of literary tradition, even though historically there may have existed a connecting factor.

With regard to the rich man, the early tradition provided a name as well. According to the papyrus ⁀P⁷⁵, he is called "Neues" (ὀνόματι Νευης) which the Sahidic tradition has as "Nineues."[19] Also, the Latin translation of the adjective

---

[15] An early example is Origen, Fr. Jo. 77 (cf. PREUSCHEN, GCS 10, 543–544), who rejects an identification of both figures. In a different way, Tertullian, in his argument for the corporality of the soul, assumed that Luke 16 related a real incident (An. 7; cf. the edition of WASZINK in CCSL 2).
[16] Cf. PEARCE, Raising of Lazarus, who assumes that Luke 7:11–17.36–50; 10:38–42; 16:19–31 and 19:41–44 lie behind the Johannine story.
[17] Thus DUNKERLEY, Lazarus, according to whom Jesus told the parable with relation to Lazarus after having received the news of the latter's illness. At his arrival in Bethany, however, he was apparently led to perform a deed that exceeded the parable.
[18] Cf. KREMER, Lazarus, in whose opinion the only satisfying explanation for the affinity of the Lukan and Johannine texts is a reworking of the parable, maybe by Luke himself, in light of the resurrection of a certain Lazarus.
[19] See the discussion of the textual variants including the further name "Finaeus" in METZGER, Textual Commentary, and HARNACK, Name, who opts for the originality of the name and, in light of Num 25:7, connects Φινεες with Eleazar, i.e. Lazarus, and therefore interprets Lazarus as the rich man's father. Cf. also LEFORT, Le nom du mauvais riche; FITZMYER, Luke, 1129–1130; CADBURY, Proper Name; and ID., Name, where an interesting erasure in ⁀P⁷⁵ is discussed. GROBEL, Name, argues for a textual development on the basis of the Egyptian and Jewish parallels (see section 2 below) with the result that, in the Sahidic form, a detail of the original pre-Lukan story would have been preserved (see especially the graph on p. 377).

"rich" by *dives* led to an understanding of this term as a proper name ("Dives"). However, that the rich man was originally nameless only enhances the significance of the naming of Lazarus.[20]

Still, different and difficult questions arise: Is Lazarus comforted because of his poverty or because of his piety and is the rich man punished because of his richness or because of a deficient piety? Is the description of a twofold hereafter a normative one and is it meant to confer a valid eschatological image? If the latter is the case, do Abraham's bosom and Hades stand for definitive and distinguished eternal spaces or do they symbolize two different habitable rooms until the Last Judgment?

These questions are best evaluated by exploring two perspectives: One is the possible contribution of Egyptian, Jewish, and Greco-Roman parallels to explaining the special traits of the text. On the other hand, the broader context of Luke has to be investigated in order to perceive how this text fits in with the Lukan conception of anthropology.

2 The Egyptian, Jewish, and Greco-Roman Parallels

Nearly a century ago, Hugo Gressmann published an important study in which he procured interesting extrabiblical parallels to the Lukan account. His approach was received with various degrees of approval but has been influential ever since.[21] First of all, there is the Egyptian tale of Setme Khamuas and his son Si-Osiris.[22] The account is extant in a Demotic text written almost certainly in the second half of the first century C.E., but is likely a close descendant of an older story.[23] This so-called second tale of Khamuas comprises two main parts and is quite extensive; the relevant passage, however, can be summarized as follows.

---

20 Other accounts in Luke's Gospel contrast two figures as well (cf. 7:36–50; 10:38–42; 18:9–14). There is one further instance where only one of two main characters receives a name: Cleopas in Luke 24:13–35. On the connection of Luke 16 with the Emmaus story in Luke 24, see section 3 below.

21 GRESSMANN, Lazarus. Regarding its impact on research, HOCK, Lazarus and Micyllus, 450, notes: "Indeed, it is difficult to imagine a more influential study of the parable than Gressmann's."

22 Although J.F. QUACK has discussed this text in his contribution to the present volume, also pointing to the question of interdependence with Luke 16, it is not superfluous to look at it from the Lukan perspective, as it were, and to recapitulate shortly the main issues.

23 The Demotic tale is known from a papyrus manuscript in the British Museum and written on the back of two Greek business documents one of which is dated in the seventh year of Claudius

Setme Khamuas, the son of Pharaoh Usermara, and his wife Meh-wesekht are a childless couple until they have a miraculous offspring, Si-Osiris; the way of conception and the naming have been announced to each of them in advance in a dream.[24] One day, Setme and Si-Osiris observe two funerals: one of a rich man who is carried to the necropolis in glorious condition, the wailing being exceedingly loud; the other of a poor man who is carried to the cemetery wrapped only in a mat and without ceremony or mourning. Setme declares he would rather have the lot of the rich man than the pauper, but Si-Osiris wishes that his father's fate in Amente, the realm of the dead, would be that of the pauper rather than that of the rich man. In order to justify his wish and demonstrate the reversal of fortunes in the afterlife, Si-Osiris takes his father on a tour of the seven halls of Amente. The account of the first three halls is lost. In the fourth hall, some dead are plaiting ropes while donkeys are chewing them up; others have provisions of water and bread hung over them but are hindered to reach them. In the fifth hall, noble spirits and those accused of crimes are met and a man is found with the pivot of the door of the hall fixed in his eye and his mouth opened in great lamentation. In the sixth hall, gods and attendants are standing in their places, and in the seventh hall, a scene of judgement before Osiris is witnessed with Anubis to his left and Thoth to his right. Before them is a balance, which weighs a person's evil deeds against his or her good deeds. If the evil deeds outweigh the good deeds, soul (*ba*) and body are destroyed and one is not permitted to live again forever. If the good deeds are more numerous, however, the *ba* goes to heaven with all the noble spirits. Finally, those whose good deeds equal their evil ones are taken amongst the spirits that serve Sokar-Osiris. Now, a man can be seen, clothed in raiment of byssus and elevated to high rank near Osiris. To Setme's amazement, Si-Osiris explains afterwards what they had seen in Amente, namely that the man clothed in garments of royal linen was the pauper who had been

---

(46–47 C.E.). As to the description of the papyrus as well as for a transcription and translation, see GRIFFITH, Stories, 41–68.142–207, and more recently LICHTHEIM, Book of Readings III, 125–127.138–151; HOFFMANN/QUACK, Anthologie, 118–137.340–343. MASPERO, Contes populaires, presumably was the first to point out the similarities between the Egyptian tale and Luke 16. In his estimation, the Egyptian tale borrowed from the Lukan parable (!) and was dramatized to fit another popular conception, i.e. the descent of a living person into hell (see op. cit., XI; text on pp. 154–181).

24 Si-Osiris, then, rivals the scribe that had been appointed to teach him, amazes the scribes at the House of Life, and by the age of twelve, no learned man in Memphis is found comparable to him in reciting spells and performing magic. In the end, it becomes clear that Si-Osiris is Horus-son-of-Paneshe, who was dead but was allowed to return from Amente to earth in order to deal with a Nubian magician who was proving too powerful for the magicians of Egypt. Having done what he came for, Si-Osiris passes away as a shadow.

buried without mourning, and that the man with the pivot in his eye was the previously rich man. As to the pauper, it is said that his good deeds were more numerous than his evil deeds in relation to the lifetime which Thoth had assigned to him, and relative to his luck on earth, and that it was commanded to give unto him the burial outfit of the rich man and to place him near Osiris amongst the noble spirits. As to the rich man, his evil deeds were found to be more numerous than his good deeds and he was commanded to requital. The final résumé is that "he who is good upon the earth, to him one is good in the netherworld," while "he who is evil, to him one is evil."[25]

Before evaluating this parallel, the related Jewish stories to which Gressmann also drew attention should be mentioned.[26] It must suffice to outline the earliest version which occurs in the Palestinian Talmud (y. Hag. 77d = y. Sanh. 23c):[27] In Ashkelon, two pious men habitually eat and drink together and study the Torah. One of them dies but goes unmourned. A tax collector named Bar Ma'yan[28] also dies and the whole town mourns him. The surviving of the two holy men is perplexed by this contrast until he has two visionary dreams. In the first, the reason for the different burials is given: The pious man sinned once in his life (he put on the phylactery of his head before that of the hand). The punishment for this was that he was disregarded in his death. On the other hand, the tax collector performed one good deed (he hosted a banquet for the councillors of his town and when no one came, he said, "Let the poor come and eat the food, so that it not go to waste").[29] The reward for this was the splendid funeral. In the second dream, the companion sees the deceased pious man walking among gardens, orchards, and fountains of water, and the tax collector tormented: With his tongue hanging

---

25 On the topic of death and the netherworld in Egypt in general, see Assmann, Tod und Jenseits.
26 Cf. Gressmann, Lazarus, 70–86 (texts A-G). His thesis is that the Jewish story in its main form goes back to the Egyptian tale. See n. 33 below.
27 See Wewers, Hagiga; id., Sanhedrin; and Neusner, Hagigah and Moed Qatan, where the numeration is y. Hag. 2:2 V. The story is only part of the answer to the question whether a certain Simeon ben Shatah was patriarch. The Egyptian and the following Jewish tale can also be found in abridged form in Berger/Colpe, Textbuch, 141–143.
28 The etymology of Bar Ma'yan is ambiguous. Gressmann, Lazarus, 21–22, considered ὁ Μιναῖος as origin. Since the Minaeans were important in trading between the Arabian Peninsula and Palestine, this could explain the paradigmatic role in representing a rich man. Cf. Lefort, Le nom du mauvais riche, 66.
29 Also, he is said to have travelled with a loaf of bread under his arm which fell onto the road, but when a poor man came to take it, Bar Ma'yan said nothing so as not to embarrass him. It is discernible, then, that Bar Ma'yan is thought of as being comparatively rich.

out he continually tries to drink from a river but is not able to.³⁰ Therefore, the different funerals apparently served to make possible only eternal bliss for the pious man and only punishment for the other.

The storyline shared by all three accounts is this: A rather rich and a rather poor man³¹ die and their fates are reversed in the hereafter. This reversal of fates is revealed to internal witnesses or to Jesus' audience respectively. Apart from that, there are just too many differences³² to assume that an Egyptian or Jewish tale is to be seen as the direct source of the Lukan parable.³³ Rather, it is more

---

30 Subsequently, a certain Miriam is said to be punished in hell, too, hanging by the nipples of her breasts or having the pin of the gate of the Gehenna fastened to her ear. Some see in this last aspect a further parallel to the Egyptian story where the rich man is described as having the pivot of the door in his eye. For dubious reasons, GRESSMANN, Lazarus, 22–26, interprets this figure as Mary, the mother of Jesus, assuming a later anti-Christian polemic.
31 In the Jewish story, the pious man is not explicitly labelled as poor; Bar Ma'yan, however, is clearly distinct from the poor since he can afford to host a banquet. Cf. also n. 29 above.
32 For example, in contrast to the parable which lays emphasis on the different living conditions of the two characters, the Egyptian and the Jewish stories stress that the diverging fates after death are to be seen in light of the diverging burials. Secondly, there is no internal witness in the parable as there is in the parallels, and the revelation of the disparate fates is treated quite differently: The possibility of the brothers' witnessing is denied. Furthermore, in the parallels the reason for the reversal is mainly seen in the good and bad deeds, while in the parable only the disparity in the receiving of "good things" (τὰ ἀγαθά) and "evil things" (τὰ κακά) is highlighted explicitly. Other distinct features are the dogs, Abraham's bosom, the dialogue between the rich man and Abraham as well as the naming of the *poor* man. Cf. the appendix.
33 To be sure, GRESSMANN, Lazarus, 46 and 59–62, admitted that the parable is not as close to the Egyptian tale as is the Jewish story. Nonetheless, he hypothetically deduced a lost form of the Egyptian story which served as the "Urfassung" for all three "recensions," and argued along the following line: In pre-Christian times, Egyptian Jews brought the story to Palestine where it was translated into Aramaic. This version, too, has been lost. The Lukan parable, then, is to be understood as the oldest tangible "Jewish" version and at the same time as a special recension with a different essence. The underlying Jewish legend, however, evolved into the several variants of later date. Basically following Gressmann, JEREMIAS, Gleichnisse Jesu, 181–186, assumed that Jesus himself was familiar with the Palestinian tale and added a new ending in the second part, which is why the punch line of the parable was neither the problem of rich and poor nor any instruction about the hereafter, but a warning against the impending fate. GRESSMANN, ibid., 59–60, as well as JEREMIAS, ibid., 182, also connected the Bar Ma'yan story with the passage of the great banquet in Luke 14:16–24: In each case, the initially invited do not appear; instead, the poor partake in the feast. Still, this does not necessarily imply a direct literary dependence. On the other hand, BULTMANN, Geschichte, 212–213, claimed another Jewish legend as the source for the parable. According to this legend, an impious woman is cast into hell. Since her husband is faint-hearted, a young boy volunteers to undertake a tour in order to check on the wife. He brings back her ring together with her plea that the husband repent. This suggestion of origin, however, has not met with approval, mainly since the reference is of a far later date.

adequate to speak of a common folkloric motif within the various cultural contexts, represented more in the first part of the parable than in the second.[34] This can be verified by the incorporation of Greco-Roman traditions into the comparative net,[35] whereby further analogies are manifested.

Apart from the Homeric description of the descent of Odysseus into Hades (Od. 11.1–640),[36] which shows similarities to Luke 16 in some details,[37] and the story of Er, the Pamphylian, which was preserved by Plato,[38] the most important reference is Lucian of Samosata.[39] In his dialogue *Cataplus*,[40] Lucian depicts a journey of the dead to Hades—conducted by Hermes, rowed across the Styx by Charon, judged and consigned to their destinies of punishment or bliss by Rhadamanthus. The dialogue focuses on a Cynic philosopher, the poor shoemaker Micyllus, and the rich tyrant Megapenthes ("Greatwoe"). Whereas Megapenthes is reluctant to die and bargains for a return to life because he has so much to lose, Micyllus welcomes death because he has nothing to lose and states that now "we paupers laugh while the rich are distressed and lament." Examined for sins, which means being searched for stigmata that result from wicked deeds, the philosopher and Micyllus are both found spotless and are sent to the Isles of the Blessed. The tyrant, however, is convicted of uncountable evil things and found deserving of a punishment which is designed especially for his case: He is not allowed to drink the water of oblivion of the river Lethe and so condemned to remember all he once had and did.[41] According to Lucian, then, Megapenthes is damned for his lack of self-control while Micyllus is blameless because his poverty has protected him from the corrupting opportunities for self-indulgence.[42]

---

34 It should also be remembered that a reverse direction of influence between the Egyptian, the Jewish and the Lukan stories cannot be excluded. See nn. 22 and 23 above. For the evaluation, cf. BAUCKHAM, Rich Man, 227–230; FITZMYER, Luke, 1127; GRIFFITHS, Eschatology; and HOCK, Lazarus and Micyllus, 449, n. 7, who supplies a list of those who followed Gressmann's assertion.
35 Expression of HOCK, Lazarus and Micyllus, 455, who calls for a paradigm shift and for an investigation of the Greco-Roman traditions.
36 Cf. the edition of MURRAY, Odyssey, vol. 1.
37 E.g. in Homer, Od. 11.582–592, one of the tortures of Tantalos consists in the constant craving to quench his thirst while he is unable to do so: Whenever he reaches down to cool his tongue with the water of the pond he is standing in, the water disappears. For an extensive treatment of Od. 11.1–640, see GILMOUR, Hints of Homer; and HAUGE, Tour of Hell, who presents the thesis that the Lukan parable is an imitation of the Homeric passage.
38 Republic 10.615–621. Cf. the edition of SHOREY, Plato in Twelve Volumes, vol. 6.2.
39 On Lucian see also the study of W. SPICKERMANN in the present volume.
40 Cf. HARMON, Lucian, vol. II.
41 Cf. the summary of BAUCKHAM, Rich Man, 234–235.
42 HOCK, Lazarus and Micyllus, 457–461, tries to establish many further analogies which are not truly convincing and which are also the result of a synoptic reading of the *Cataplus* and of *Gallus*,

Again, the similarities to the Lukan narrative are obvious, but the dissimilarities are even more evident.[43]

Regarding the topic of the return of a dead person or a message to the living alone, there exist many separate examples.[44] Again within the Jewish context, one of these is also most interesting, namely the Book of Jannes and Jambres, although neither the question of Jewish or Christian origin nor the question of date is easily decided. Strands of this story, however, may have been current in pre-Christian Judaism.[45] Only the relevant part of the account must be presented here. In Jewish tradition, Jannes and Jambres appear as the Egyptian magicians who opposed Moses. Once Jannes dies, Jambres uses a book of magic to call upon his brother's shade from Hades. The soul of Jannes, then, acknowledges that his death was a just punishment for his opposition to Moses and Aaron. He is now in the underworld where there is great burning and the pit of perdition, from which no ascent is possible. He urges Jambres to lead a good life so as not to share in his fate in Hades where no good exists, where gloom, darkness and torment prevail, and where not even kings are shown favour due to their social status.[46]

So after all, the comparison of the Lukan story with extrabiblical parallels reveals certain common ideas,[47] but it seems that, really to grasp its meaning, one has to look at the wider Lukan context.

---

texts of much greater length than the Lukan parable. According to HOCK, each time the poor Micyllus is compared to different rich men: Micyllus is not a beggar, but also socially marginal. As Lazarus is situated at the door of the rich man, Micyllus is the neighbour of the rich men. As Lazarus desired what fell from the rich man's table, Micyllus has a desire to share in the rich man's banquet. Lazarus has sores and Micyllus dreads winter's cold and sickness. The garments of the rich men are described similar to those of the rich man in Luke 16.

43 Cf. the synoptic view of the parable and the parallels in the appendix.
44 Collected by BAUCKHAM, Rich Man, 236–242. Others establish different links with Greco-Roman literature. Cf. HUGHES, Parable, who focuses on Greco-Roman rhetoric and infers that the parable gives the readers the writer's reason why Christian evangelization of Jews fails so miserably in Acts, and why the Jewish opposition to Jesus is so strong in Luke: because of their unfaithfulness to the former revelation of God in the Torah and the Prophets. For HUGHES, this disobedience is exemplified by the attitude of the rich man towards the poor.
45 Cf. PIETERSMA/LUTZ, Jannes and Jambres, OTP 2; and BAUCKHAM, Rich Man, 241–242.
46 In addition, another comparative constituent has been procured, namely the passage 33.1–5 of the pseudo-philonic Liber Antiquitatum Biblicarum. This passage reports the farewell address of the judge Deborah who deals with the denial of a postmortem repentance and with the intercession for the righteous dead and admonishes that one live according to the Law. Cf. REINMUTH, Liber Antiquitatum Biblicarum 33,1–5.
47 Cf. the conclusion of LEHTIPUU, Afterlife Imagery, 300: "On the whole, it is doubtful whether there are any particular stories circulating around that the teller of the story must have known.

3 The Significance of Context: Luke 16:19–31 within the Lukan Oeuvre

There is a vast number of passages that shed light on different aspects of the parable, namely the theme of rich and poor, the figure of Abraham, the concept of judgment and the hereafter, the importance of Scripture, and the question of resurrection. Taken together, they help to clarify the Lukan concept of the human.

To begin with, it is in the *Magnificat* (Luke 1:46–55) that God's salvific intervention in the sending of his Messiah is praised in terms relevant to the present investigation. This hymn proclaims God as one who …

> … has brought down the mighty from their thrones and exalted those of humble estate; he has filled the hungry with good things (ἐνέπλησεν ἀγαθῶν), and the rich he has sent away empty. He has helped his servant Israel, in remembrance of his mercy, as he spoke to our fathers, to Abraham and to his descendants forever (Luke 1:52–55).[48]

Right at the beginning of the Gospel, the reversal of fates is linked exemplarily with the hungry and the rich[49] as well as with Abraham (cf. Luke 1:73), and at the same time with Jesus as Israel's Messiah. God's intervention in the person of Jesus is of such nature that common patterns are turned upside down. However, the accompanying idea of judgment is emphasized in the preaching of John the Baptist in Luke 3. In a general way, his audience is confronted with the impending wrath and it is made explicit that for the Israelites there is no use saying "We have Abraham as our ancestor"—only fruits of repentance will demonstrate a valid kinship (vv. 7–8). In addition, John uses the picture of a tree that, when it does not bear good fruit, is cut down and thrown into the fire. He uses the image of the separation of wheat and chaff as well, the latter also being burned with unquenchable fire (vv. 9 and 17). The relation to the burning flame in Luke 16 is obvious. Moreover, John's ethical paraenesis that "whoever has two coats must share with him who has none; and whoever has food must do likewise" (v. 11) shows a further comparable element since it may be said that exactly this is missing in the rich man's treatment of Lazarus.

The story is simply based on the common cultural intertexture that prevailed around the Mediterranean and the Near East."
48 On the *Magnificat* in general, see Mittmann-Richert, Magnifikat und Benediktus.
49 For a further explication of these terms, see the subsequent observations.

Apart from the *Magnificat* and the preaching of John the Baptist, it is most important how Luke introduces the public ministry of Jesus in chapter 4, namely with the citation of Isa 61:1–2, complemented with Isa 58:6:

> The Spirit of the Lord is upon me, because he has anointed me (ἔχρισέν με) to bring good news to the poor (εὐαγγελίσασθαι πτωχοῖς). He has sent me to proclaim release to the captives and recovery of sight to the blind, to set at liberty those who are oppressed, to proclaim the year of the Lord's favor (Luke 4:18–19).[50]

After reading this passage aloud, Jesus states that this prophetic text has been fulfilled "today" (σήμερον; v. 21). It must be said that Isa 61:1–2 pertains to the Servant of JHWH tradition usually known from the more familiar text Isa 53, where the vicarious suffering and atoning death of the Servant figure is described as bringing about a new and sinless existence for both Israel and the heathens.[51] Recent study has shown that this tradition as a whole is crucial for Luke's depiction of Jesus.[52] Thus, the programmatic inaugural speech of the Lukan Jesus manifests a christological anchoring of the poverty theme that warns against joining too easily the choir of those who classify Luke too simply as the "social Gospel."[53]

---

50 The citation basically follows Isa 61:1–2 LXX, but instead of ἰάσασθαι τοὺς συντετριμμένους τῇ καρδίᾳ (Isa 61:1c), Luke has ἀποστεῖλαι τεθραυσμένους ἐν ἀφέσει, a phrase taken from Isa 58:6 LXX. It is not unlikely, then, that other elements of Isa 58:6–7—namely to share the bread with the hungry, bring the homeless poor into the house, cover the naked, and to hide not from one's kin—are alluded to in Luke 16. This would connect Luke 16 even more closely to Luke 4. Cf. SECCOMBE, Possessions, 176; HAYS, Wealth Ethics, 157. An echo of Luke 4:18–19 is found in Acts 10:38 where Jesus is again described as "anointed with the Holy Spirit and with power" (ἔχρισεν αὐτὸν ὁ θεὸς πνεύματι ἁγίῳ καὶ δυνάμει. Cf. also Acts 4:27 (τὸν ἅγιον παῖδά σου Ἰησοῦν ὃν ἔχρισας).
51 On Luke 4:16–30 as well as on the character of the citation and on the relation of Isa 61 especially to the first Servant Song in Isa 42, see MITTMANN-RICHERT, Sühnetod, 252–285. The literature on Isa 53 is abundant. See particularly JANOWSKI/STUHLMACHER, Isaiah 53, and BELLINGER/FARMER, Isaiah 53.
52 In addition to MITTMANN-RICHERT, Sühnetod, see JOHNSON, Jesus Against the Idols; KOET, Isaiah in Luke-Acts; MALLEN, Reading and Transformation of Isaiah.
53 Cf. ESLER, Community, who relies mainly on the socio-economic levels in "the Lukan community" and reckons that Luke's "this-worldly dimension" of salvation was influenced by the realities of life for the urban poor in the Roman East. Likewise LENTZEN-DEIS, Arm und reich, who concludes that "Lukas ist der Evangelist der wirklich Armen, die sich Gott öffnen" (p. 40). Similarly PRIOR, Jesus the Liberator, and KLEIN, Lukasstudien, 27–29, according to whom Luke was himself a man like Zacchaeus or, more likely, a poor man. BORNHÄUSER's rejection of the theory of a "Lukan pauperism," i.e. that God generally was *for* the poor and *against* the rich (Gleichnis, 138), needs to be heard as well. In addition, see SCHMITHALS, Lukas, who finds the reason for the Lukan emphasis in the actual situation of persecution of the Lukan community; and DE VOS,

Instead, the main concern of Luke is brought to the fore: to picture Jesus as the Suffering Servant whose ministry and death make possible a reversal of the individual fate in the first place. This is the good news that Israel and man as such needs to hear as one who is poor, blind, and kept in the bondage of sin.[54] Only because of this general view of the human condition do the poor play such an essential and exemplary role in Luke's Gospel as is made clear by Jesus' summary of his ministry in Luke 7:22 where he repeats and amplifies the Isaianic words:

> The blind receive their sight, the lame walk, the lepers are cleansed and the deaf hear, the dead are raised, the poor have good news brought to them (πτωχοὶ εὐαγγελίζονται).[55]

Taken together, an *inclusio* can be detected in the cited verses since the bringing of good news to the poor is the primary (Luke 4:18) and the last element (Luke 7:22), each time carrying programmatic weight.[56] It is noteworthy that so far in the Gospel, Luke has described Jesus in accordance with Luke 7:22 as healing people from unclean spirits and illnesses (Luke 4:33–41; 6:6–11.18–19), cleansing lepers (Luke 5:12–14), making the lame walk (Luke 5:17–26) and raising the dead (Luke 7:11–17; cf. 8:40–42.49–56). But apart from the Beatitudes (see below), there is no

---

Meaning, who employs a certain socio-economic perspective on the problem of poverty in antiquity to arrive at his conclusion that, for Luke, the good news which the gospel offers the poor (cf. Luke 4:18) is "that they now belong to a kinship (or kin-like) network" (p. 82); therefore, the reversal in Luke 16 is not one of belongings but of belonging since the formerly rich man now needs to beg, whereas Lazarus is received as a kinsman of Abraham. Although there is a certain truth to this viewpoint, it misses to reflect Luke 16 as well as Luke 4:18–19 on a more theological and especially on a christological level.

54 Therefore, STEYN, Perspectives, 96, is right in calling Luke 4:18–19 a key element in understanding Luke's soteriology. In 11QMelch (cf. ROBERTS, Melchizedek), the motif of Isa 61:1–2 is used in a similar sense. It is added to Lev 25:13 and Deut 15:2—verses that deal with the year of jubilee resp. the remission of debts—and is understood to address the last days: It is Melchizedek who "will proclaim liberty to the captives" which here equals "release them from the burden of all their iniquities." Also "the year of favor" is ascribed to Melchizedek. Subsequently, Isa 52:7 is quoted as well, a passage which is closely connected to Isa 61:1 in that it speaks of a messenger of peace (εὐαγγελιζόμενος ἀκοὴν εἰρήνης) and good news (εὐαγγελιζόμενος ἀγαθά). In 11QMelch, this double phrasing is taken to denote two figures: The messenger of peace is the "anointed of the spirit" about whom Daniel wrote (cf. Dan 9:25b), and the messenger of good news who announces salvation also seems to have been written about, but the explanatory text is not extant in the fragment.

55 Apart from Luke 4:18–19 resp. Isa 61:1–2, cf. Isa 26:19; 29:18; 35:5–6; 42:18.

56 In Luke 6:20–22; 14:13 and 14:21, the poor are also listed first which is why this phrase is to be understood as a generic term denoting all cases of neediness that are assigned to it in the mentioned references (the hungry, blind, deaf, lame etc.). This is rightly recognized by BUSSE, Nazareth-Manifest, 33 and 78.

example for a special encounter with the poor, a fact which corroborates the comprehension of the "poor" as a more general depiction of the human condition.[57] Furthermore, the addressees of the Beatitudes are not described as being particularly needy in a material sense.[58] An example for the healing of the blind is delivered subsequently in Luke 18:35–43, but a wider understanding is elucidated in many instances: In Luke 6:39, the phrase "the blind cannot lead the blind" is used in a parabolic sense; the beatitude in Luke 10:23–24 calls blessed the eyes that see what the disciples see and what many prophets and kings did not witness before; in Luke 19:42, Jesus weeps over Jerusalem, saying that the things that make for peace are "hidden from your eyes;" and in Luke 24, the eyes of the disciples have to be opened (v. 31: αὐτῶν δὲ διενοίχθησαν οἱ ὀφθαλμοί).[59] Regarding the deaf, Luke 4:16–30 (compare v. 21: "fulfilled in your hearing" [ἐν τοῖς ὠσὶν ὑμῶν] with the resulting intent to kill Jesus) and the apparent inability of the disciples to understand Jesus' announcement of his suffering in Luke 9:45 are fairly self-explanatory. Certainly other references could be added which demonstrate man's essential struggle for a right discernment towards the revelation of God.[60]

---

[57] This is not to say that substantial poverty is not in view and to proclaim merely a spiritualizing tendency. Rather, the term should be understood to comprise both aspects and yet to convey especially a fundamental anthropological insight. Similarly SECCOMBE, Possessions, who understands the term πτωχοί on the basis of its usage in Isaiah and the Psalms mainly as the "characterization of Israel in her need of salvation" (p. 23); TURNER, Power from on High, 250–251 with n. 116; and KVALBEIN, Jesus and the poor, who highlights the transferred sense of the term as describing man's fundamental position before God.
[58] The addressees are primarily the twelve apostles (cf. Luke 6:12–17), but also a great multitude of people (cf. Luke 6:17–20.27; 7:1) who are confronted as well with the Woes and with the challenge to give to everyone without demanding it back (Luke 6:30.34–35.38). Thus, the fact that Simon, James and John left everything in order to follow Jesus (Luke 5:11) and the plucking of some heads of grain by Jesus' disciples in order to satisfy their hunger (Luke 6:1) do not outweigh the more general depiction of the audience. Cf. also Levi in Luke 5:28–29 who leaves everything in order to follow Jesus and is nevertheless able to provide a great feast.
[59] On the Emmaus pericope, see also the observations below. On the topic of "blindness and (in-)sight," cf. as well Luke 2:30 and 8:10. As to Acts, the conversion of Paul, too, is most instructive since it combines "real" blindness with the gaining of sight in a deeper sense (Acts 9:17–18). Similarly to Jesus' ministry according to Luke 4, Paul's commission "to open the eyes of the heathens, so that they may turn from darkness to light and from the power of Satan to God" (Acts 26:18) is rooted in the Servant of JHWH tradition, especially in Isa 42:6–7 and 61:1 LXX. Finally, the ending of Acts again highlights the significance of the blindness and deafness motif for Luke: He quotes Isa 6:9–10 and hints at the underlying problem of the hardening of hearts (Acts 28:25–28). Cf. the treatment in MITTMANN, Polemik.
[60] See especially Luke 8:10; 11:28; Acts 28:25–27 and the preceding footnote.

Consequently, also the Lukan Beatitudes and the ensuing Woes in Luke 6:20–26 have to be conceived against this background when Jesus affirms:

²⁰ Blessed are you who are poor (οἱ πτωχοί),	Cf. Luke 16:20 (πτωχός)
for yours is the kingdom of God.	Cf. Luke 16:22b (εἰς τὸν κόλπον Ἀβραάμ)
²¹ Blessed are you who are hungry now (νῦν),	Cf. Luke 16:25 (νῦν)
for you will be filled (χορτασθήσεστε).	Cf. Luke 16:21 (ἐπιθυμῶν χορτασθῆναι)
[...]	
²⁴ But woe to you who are rich (τοῖς πλουσίοις),	Cf. Luke 16:19 (πλούσιος)
for you have received your consolation	
(τὴν παράκλησιν ὑμῶν).	Cf. Luke 16:25 (παρακαλεῖται)
²⁵ Woe to you who are full now (νῦν),	Cf. Luke 16:21 (τῶν πιπτόντων ἀπὸ τῆς τραπέζης);
for you will be hungry.	16:25 (νῦν)
[...]	

These sharp and contrasting words have close parallels in the last chapters of 1 Enoch where in opposition to the righteous the sinners are portrayed as ungodly men who gain their wealth in wrongful ways.[61] The latter aspect, however, is not mentioned in Luke, where these words can be seen as a commentary on the *Magnificat* and as a complementary text to Luke 16, the main thrust being: Those who, especially because of their wealth, do not realize their true human condition, that is their physical and spiritual dependence on God, cannot partake in his kingdom which is dawning with the coming of Jesus.[62] The individual fate is being reversed, and woe to those for whom God is not their help in this life and the next.[63]

---

61 Cf. 1 Enoch 94:8–10 (references to 1 Enoch follow Isaac, 1 [Ethiopic Apocalypse of] Enoch, OTP 1): "Woe unto you, O rich people! For you have put your trust in your wealth. You shall ooze out of your riches, for you do not remember the Most High. In the days of your affluence, you committed oppression, you have become ready for death, and for the day of darkness and the day of great judgment. Thus I speak and let you know: For he who has created you, he will also throw you down upon your own righteousness! There shall be no mercy (for you)." For a detailed comparison of 1 Enoch and Luke, see Aalen, St. Luke's Gospel, and Nickelsburg, Riches.

62 Therefore, it is noteworthy that the Beatitudes include a spiritualizing tendency not in Luke, but in the Gospel of Matthew. Cf. Matt 5:3: "Blessed are the poor *in spirit*;" 5:6: "Blessed are those who hunger and thirst *for righteousness*." See again n. 57. Cf. also the conclusion of Seccombe, Possessions, 92, that the Lukan Beatitudes and the Woes are a challenge to the disciples and to the crowds "to stand with the Son of man, and so to be a part of the true suffering Israel which will inherit the Kingdom."

63 Against this background, also the similarities of 1 Enoch 103:5–8 to Luke 16 should be noticed. Here, the sinners are associated with wealth and with an unproblematic earthly life. In the hereafter, however, judgment, evil, and great tribulation in Sheol are to be expected, i.e. darkness, nets, and burning flame.

In view of the foregoing observations, the question if Lazarus is comforted because of his poverty or because of his piety, and if the rich man is punished because of his richness or because of a deficient piety, has found its answer. It is actually neither. More specifically, Lazarus' fate symbolizes the true human condition before God and God's saving grace,[64] whereas the rich man is a portrait of man's failure to recognize his utter dependence upon God, a failure which can indeed be boosted by affluence.

Further illustrations of this principle could be added. One could cite, for example, *(a)* Jesus' interpretation of the parable of the sower, which lists riches and pleasures amongst the reasons for not acting according to the word of God and not bearing fruit (Luke 8:14). One could refer to *(b)* the warning against possessions followed by the parable of the rich man (Luke 12:15–21).[65] One could also point to *(c)* the account of the rich young man who is asked to sell everything, give it to the poor and follow Jesus in order to partake in God's kingdom (Luke 18:18–27)—including the famous word that it is easier for a camel to go through the eye of a needle than for a rich person to enter the kingdom of God (v. 25). And one must certainly not forget *(d)* the encounter of Jesus and the tax collector Zacchaeus (Luke 19:1–10) which is also remarkable because of the exclamation "Today salvation has come to this house, because he, too, is a son of Abraham" (v. 9).[66] Similarly, Abraham is called "father" by the rich man in Luke 16 and he himself addresses the rich man as "child" (τέκνον).[67] This corresponds to the general portrayal of Abraham as the forefather par excellence[68] and to the emphasis on the Jews as his children.[69] However, it becomes clear that the assumed Abrahamic kinship does not ensure

---

64 This is why the name Lazarus ("God has helped") is not haphazard. Cf. n. 13 above.
65 Again, cf. 1 Enoch 97:8–10, where the unjust accumulation of goods and a life led according to the principle "Let us do whatever we like" are damned and a great curse is predicted. See also the following remarks in Luke 12:22–34 on not worrying about clothes, eating and drinking, but selling possessions and giving alms in order to gain treasure in heaven.
66 Other references for the motif of wealth or money comprise Luke 8:1–3; 9:3; 10:29–37; 11:41; 14:12–14 (see the subsequent exposition); 14:33; 16:1–9; 19:11–27; 20:22–25.46–47; 21:1–4; 22:4–5.35–36; Acts 2:44–45; 4:32–37; 5:1–11; 6:1–7; 8:18–24; 9:36; 10:2–4; 11:29–30; 12:25; 20:33–35; 24:26. On the topic as such, see SECCOMBE, Possessions; PETRACCA, Gott; MINESHIGE, Besitzverzicht; and HAYS, Wealth Ethics.
67 KREITZER, Luke 16:19–31, 141, notes that, since the rich man and Lazarus are both related to Abraham as his children and can in this sense be understood as brothers, the parable may be an attempt to reinforce the penetrating question of Gen 4:9: "Am I my brother's keeper?"
68 See Luke 1:55.73; 3:8.34; 13:28; Acts 3:25; 7:2.16–17 and the formula "God of Abraham, Isaac and Jacob" in Luke 20:37; Acts 3:13; 7:32.
69 See Luke 13:18; 19:9; Acts 13:26; and DAHL, Abraham.

salvation, and that Jesus himself represents God's salvific intervention on which man as such is utterly dependent.

In this regard, it is necessary to highlight another passage connected with Abraham and eschatological expectations, namely Luke 13:28–29. Answering the question whether only a few will be saved, Jesus urges to strive to enter through the "narrow door" and says:

> There will be weeping and gnashing of teeth when you see Abraham and Isaac and Jacob and all the prophets in the kingdom of God, but you yourselves thrown out. And people will come from east and west, and from north and south, and will recline at table in the kingdom of God.[70]

Again, a dichotomous picture is established: There are those who participate in God's kingdom and those who are not allowed to do so. Read as a complementary text to Luke 16, the eating in the kingdom of God corresponds ironically to the feasting of the rich man, and the weeping and gnashing of teeth parallel the torments in Hades.

Now, Abraham in Luke 16 surely represents the faithfulness and the covenant of God. According to Old Testament tradition, he is a model of faith and trusting in God's promises (Gen 15:6; 22:1–19) as well as of wealth (Gen 13:2.6) and hospitality (Gen 18:1–8).[71] But it is early Jewish tradition which helps further understand Luke 13 and 16, namely the depiction of Abraham as the guarantee of an existence in the realm of God, his association with angels and also the quite unique expression "bosom of Abraham" (κόλπος Ἀβραάμ).[72] According to 4 Macc 7:18–19 and 16:25, those who make piety their first concern and even die for the sake of God "live unto God, as do Abraham and Isaac and Jacob."[73] Furthermore, in 4 Macc 13:17, the martyrs proclaim:

---

70 In the parallel Matt 8:11–12, the wording is slightly different: The "weeping and gnashing of teeth" is the final remark, not the first, and it is related to the heirs of the kingdom, not to "you;" only east and west are mentioned and the reclining at table in the "kingdom of heaven" (not "kingdom of God") is linked more directly with Abraham, Isaac and Jacob.
71 Cf. Philo, Abr. 107–118 (see COLSON, Philo in Ten Volumes, vol. VI); Josephus, Ant. 1.196 (see THACKERAY, Josephus in Nine Volumes, vol. IV). In this respect, Abraham serves as a contrasting figure to the rich man who did not show any hospitality to Lazarus.
72 Κόλπος is also used in Luke 6:38 ("a good measure will be poured into your lap;" cf. Isa 65:7; Jer 32:18; Ruth 3:15) and in Acts 27:39, where it denotes a bay. In the Gospel of John, it signifies the closest relation of Jesus to God (John 1:18: ὁ ὢν εἰς τὸν κόλπον τοῦ πατρός) and the position of the disciple whom Jesus loved and who is reclining next to him (John 13:23).
73 On 4 Maccabees, see also DAVID DESILVA's study in the present volume.

After our death in this fashion Abraham and Isaac and Jacob will receive us [in their bosoms], and all our forefathers will praise us.⁷⁴

And according to the Testament of Abraham,⁷⁵ not only is Abraham's soul escorted to the heavenly realm by angels (T. Ab. [A] 20:10.12),⁷⁶ but also the voice of God says:

> Take, then, my friend Abraham into paradise, where there are the tents of my righteous ones and (where) the mansions of my holy ones Isaac and Jacob are in his bosom, where there is no toil, no grief, no moaning, but peace and exultation and endless life (T. Ab. [A] 20:14).⁷⁷

Thus, not only for Luke does the bosom of Abraham represent everlasting life in proximity to God and can therefore be used interchangeably with the eternal kingdom.⁷⁸

However, the question remains if a twofold hereafter is the final eschatological picture in Luke or if Luke 13 and 16 are meant to convey the idea of intermediate states. This question, which Augustin considered quite unfathomable,⁷⁹ can

---

74 The *varia lectio* adds εἰς τοὺς κόλπους αὐτῶν. Cf. ANDERSON, 4 Maccabees, OTP 2. See also T. Levi 18:14; T. Jud. 25:1; T. Benj. 10:6, where Abraham, Isaac and Jacob are connected with the resurrection; and T. Benj. 10:8, where the resurrection of some men to glory and of others to dishonour is described. Cf. KEE, Testament of the Twelve Patriarchs, OTP 1.
75 Cf. SANDERS, Testament of Abraham, OTP 1.
76 This idea is also present in T. Ab. (A) 13:12–13; 14:8 and in T. Job 47:11; 52:2.5 (see SPITTLER, Testament of Job, OTP 1). According to Apoc. Mos. 37:3–6, Adam, too, is guided by an angel and then led to paradise by the archangel Michael. For the text and a thorough discussion of this passage, see DOCHHORN, Apokalypse, 456–457.487–504. Cf. as well Apoc. Mos. 33:2–5; 35:2 and T. Ash. 6:4–6. While other passages in Luke's work manifest his general interest in angels, Luke 16:22 is the only reference to angels escorting the dead. Cf. LEHTIPUU, Afterlife Imagery, 198–199.
77 In addition, see T. Ab. (A) 4:5, where linen, purple and byssos are mentioned, and T. Ab. (A) 13, where judgement after death is illustrated with angels and fire plays a crucial role. See also WARD, Abraham Traditions.
78 Cf. STRACK/BILLERBECK, Kommentar 2, 225–227; PLANAS, Seno de Abrahan; HAUPT, Abraham's Bosom; the analysis of the semantic aspect of the Lukan phrase by VAN DER HORST, Abraham's Bosom; and the remark of KNIGHT, Luke 16:19–31, 277, that in Luke 16, Abraham is more than Jewish tradition: He is the voice of God.
79 Augustin, Epistola 187.6 (PL 33:834): Utrum autem sinus ille Abrahae, ubi dives impius cum in tormentis esset inferni, requiescentem pauperem vidit, vel paradisi censendus vocabulo, vel ad infernos pertinere existimandus sit, non facile dixerim ("But whether that 'bosom of Abraham' in which the impious [sic] rich man, when he was in the torments of Hell, saw the pauper resting is to be accorded to the term Paradise, or whether it is to be regarded as belonging to the regions below, I could not easily say;" translation by GROBEL, Name, 378).

only be answered by including all other Lukan passages that are of importance in this respect. In Luke 14:13–14, Jesus declares:

> But when you give a banquet, invite the poor, the crippled, the lame, and the blind. And you will be blessed, because they cannot repay you, for you will be repaid at the resurrection of the just (ἐν τῇ ἀναστάσει τῶν δικαίων).

Again, these words can be understood as a comment on Luke 16, and they are also best understood in light of Luke 4 or Isa 61 respectively: Jesus summons to follow his example as the Servant of JHWH who has a special concern for the poor since they ultimately exemplify the true human condition before God. Regarding the resurrection of the righteous, which is here described in terms of a reward, Jesus also insists on it as a matter of fact elsewhere in Luke's Gospel. In a dispute with the Sadducees, Jesus announces that …

> … those who are considered worthy to attain to that age and to the resurrection from the dead (οἱ δὲ καταξιωθέντες τοῦ αἰῶνος ἐκείνου τυχεῖν καὶ τῆς ἀναστάσεως τῆς ἐκ νεκρῶν) neither marry nor are given in marriage. Indeed, they cannot die anymore (ἀποθανεῖν ἔτι δύνανται), for they are like angels and are children of God, being children of the resurrection (υἱοί εἰσιν θεοῦ τῆς ἀναστάσεως υἱοὶ ὄντες). But that the dead are raised (ὅτι δὲ ἐγείρονται οἱ νεκροί), Moses himself showed, in the story about the bush, where he calls the Lord the God of Abraham, the God of Isaac, and the God of Jacob. Now, he is God not of the dead, but of the living, for all live unto him (Luke 20:35–38).

This instance presents Abraham as indeed being alive in the realm of God,[80] a conception also underlying Luke 13 and 16. Moreover, Abraham is connected to the resurrection of the dead which seems to await no one but the "children of God." As for the rest, their fate is not elucidated more precisely; if anything, they are literally left in the dark.

In a more generalized way, the idea of a resurrection is taken up in Acts 23:6–8. Here, Paul, according to his own words, is on trial "with respect to the hope and the resurrection of the dead" (περὶ ἐλπίδος καὶ ἀναστάσεως νεκρῶν [ἐγὼ] κρίνομαι; v. 6), thereby provoking an argument between the Sadducees and the Pharisees. Subsequently, Paul reiterates towards Festus and Agrippa that God surely and without doubt raises the dead (Acts 26:8: τί ἄπιστον κρίνεται παρ' ὑμῖν εἰ ὁ θεὸς νεκροὺς ἐγείρει;). Interestingly enough, another statement by the Lukan Paul in Acts 24:15 is more specific and reveals a dual perspective:

---

80 The wording "all live unto God" (πάντες γὰρ αὐτῷ ζῶσιν) in Luke 20:38 is distinct from the synoptic parallels (Matt 22:32; Mark 12:27) and explicitly underlines the idea that the patriarchs are alive.

I have a hope in God [...] that there will be a resurrection of both the just and the unjust (ἀνάστασιν μέλλειν ἔσεσθαι δικαίων τε καὶ ἀδίκων).

This concept of a twofold resurrection is also attested elsewhere in the New Testament[81] and most probably draws on Dan 12:2 where it is said that ...

> ... many of those who sleep in the dust of the earth shall awake, some to everlasting life, and some to shame and everlasting contempt.[82]

According to an alternative interpretation, however, Dan 12:2 does not convey the idea of a full resurrection for those destined to shame and contempt; instead, they are solely meant to be left unraised in the dust of the earth. In any case, it is apparent that only the righteous are seen to benefit from resurrection in a positive manner.[83]

A further illustration of a dual perspective is 1 Enoch 22, a passage which has often been linked with Luke 16 and which depicts the gathering place of the souls of the dead until the great judgment: There are three dark hollows with torment for the sinners and one hollow illuminated and containing a fountain of water for the righteous. It is made clear that the process of retribution already begins at the

---

81 See John 5:28–29; Rev 20:12–15; cf. also Matt 25:31–46; Rom 2:5–10; 2Cor 5:10.
82 Cf. T. Benj. 10:8 (see n. 74 above). Other important references for the idea of a resurrection are *(a)* the statement in 1Sam 2:6 that "JHWH kills and brings to life, he brings down to Sheol (LXX: Hades) and raises up;" *(b)* the short phrase in Isa 26:19 "Your dead shall live; their bodies shall rise;" *(c)* the hope of being raised again by God in contrast to those for whom there will be no resurrection to life according to 2Macc 7:14; *(d)* the fact that Judas Maccabaeus provides a sin offering for the dead, taking account of the resurrection (2Macc 12:43–45); and *(e)* the conviction of 4 Ezra 2:23 that burying the dead qualifies for the first place in the resurrection (cf. the edition of METZGER in OTP 1). See also Isa 25:8; Ezek 37:1–14; Hos 6:1–3; 13:14; T. Jud. 25:4; and PERKINS, Resurrection, 37–56, who compiles and examines the early Jewish references for the idea of resurrection and immortality.
83 For a thorough discussion of Dan 12:1–3, see HARTMAN/DI LELLA, Daniel, 307–309; and CHESTER, Resurrection, 59–64. On Acts 24:15, see BRUCE, Acts, 444, n. 25; and BOCK, Acts, 693. The description of the Pharisees' view by Josephus also manifests the tendency of being more explicit in regard to a "positive resurrection." See Bell. 2.163: "Every soul, they maintain, is imperishable, but the soul of the good alone passes into another body, while the souls of the wicked suffer eternal punishment" (cf. THACKERAY, Josephus in Nine Volumes, vol. II) and Ant. 18.14: "They believe that souls have power to survive death and that there are rewards and punishments under the earth for those who have led lives of virtue or vice: eternal imprisonment is the lot of the evil souls, while the good souls receive an easy passage to a new life" (cf. FELDMAN, Josephus in Ten Volumes, vol. IX).

time of the individual death. Yet, while the author presumes some sort of resurrection, he provides no *minutiae* about it.[84] Again, it must be asked: Is this concept of intermediate states the dominant idea in Luke as well?

The last important Lukan passage seems to complicate the matter even more. In the scene of Jesus' crucifixion, Luke alone of all Gospel authors includes a dialogue between Jesus and the two villains hanging next to him (Luke 23:39b–43). While Jesus does not respond to the mocking one, he replies to the contrite villain's request that he be remembered by Jesus in his kingdom by saying (v. 43):

> Truly I tell you, today you will be with me in paradise (ἐν τῷ παραδείσῳ).

There are many who reckon that, for Luke, "paradise" is the complementary term to Hades designating an interim abode until the resurrection.[85] Sure enough, Luke 23:43 is one of only three references for παράδεισος in the whole New Testament (cf. 2Cor 12:4; Rev 2:7), and Hades (ᾅδης) occurs as sparsely in Luke's work as in the remaining writings. In addition to Luke 16:23, it is found in Luke 10:15 (par. Matt 11:23), where Jesus predicts that instead of being exalted to heaven, Capernaum will be brought down to Hades because it ignored God's revelation in the person of Jesus. The context is unmistakably one of eschatological judgment (cf. v. 14: ἐν τῇ κρίσει) and all the more so because the wording echoes the judgment against the king of Babylon described in Isa 14:11.13.15.[86] In other words, there is no indication that intermediate states *until* the judgment are in view. In each case, the contrast is

---

84 See NICKELSBURG, 1 Enoch 1, 300–309, especially p. 302. The thought that the disembodied shades of the dead were taken to the gloomy regions of Sheol is widespread in Old Testament traditions (cf. Num 16:30.33; Job 14:13; 17:16; Ps 16:10; 30:4; 139:8; Prov 9:18; Isa 14:9; 38:18; Ezek 32:21). However, in 1 Enoch 22, the place is a mountain in the west and it is not a final residence. Cf. GRENSTED, Use; STANDEN, Parable; and KREITZER, Luke 16:19–31, who lists as comparative features in 1 Enoch 22 and Luke 16 the geographical division of area, the deep and dark void, the spring of water, and the idea of a final judgment of those who escaped judgment in their earthly lives, concluding that in 1 Enoch 22, a traditional oral account or legend can be found which was "commonly known in Jesus's day and which formed the basis for his relation of the parable" (p. 141). On the other connections of 1 Enoch and Luke, see AALEN, St. Luke's Gospel, and NICKELSBURG, Riches.

85 E.g. BORNHÄUSER, Wirken des Christus, 229–230; OSEI-BONSU, Intermediate State; and BOCK, Luke, vol. 2, 1857–1858, for whom the term is also synonymous to "Abraham's bosom." This last aspect is also the tendency of JÜLICHER, Lc 16,19–31, 623.

86 Luke 10:15: μὴ ἕως οὐρανοῦ ὑψωθήσῃ; ἕως τοῦ ᾅδου καταβήσῃ; cf. Isa 14:11: κατέβη δὲ εἰς ᾅδου ἡ δόξα σου; v. 13: εἰς τὸν οὐρανὸν ἀναβήσομαι; v. 15: νῦν δὲ εἰς ᾅδου καταβήσῃ.

between heaven and Hades as the two spheres of the divine or else of greatest possible remoteness from God.[87] The same holds true for Ps 16:10 (LXX: Ps 15:10), a quotation of which is found in Acts 2:27. According to this Davidic verse, the abandonment of the soul to Hades is paralleled with corruption (διαφθορά) and there is hope that God may prevent both.[88] Within Peter's speech in Acts 2, the Old Testament text is understood as an oracular statement and the subsequent christological explanation in Acts 2:31 considers it fulfilled in light of Jesus' bodily resurrection.[89] Furthermore, there is but one occurrence of the corresponding term "Gehenna" (γέεννα) in Luke's Gospel and it is also best understood as depicting an eternal realm apart from God: In Luke 12:4–5, Jesus admonishes his disciples not to fear those who can kill the body but can do nothing more; instead, they should fear God who, "after he has killed, has authority to cast into hell."[90] Finally, the overall picture is corroborated by the remaining Lukan phrase describing human existence in the hereafter, namely the "eternal tents" (τὰς αἰωνίους σκηνάς) mentioned in Luke 16:9.[91]

All in all, the dichotomy is apparently not one of two intermediate states but one of belonging to the eternal realm of God and debarment from it. Therefore, Jesus' words in Luke 23:43 rather describe the realization of the eschatological reopening of paradise as a definitive stage facilitated through his atoning death in

---

[87] A further parallel is Gk. Apoc. Ezra 4:32, where it is said that the Antichrist was exalted to heaven but will descend as far as Hades. Cf. STONE, Greek Apocalypse of Ezra, OTP 1.
[88] PETERSON, Acts, 148, rightly notes: "The impotence of death to destroy his relationship with God is David's confidence."
[89] The last part of Ps 16:10 is also found in Acts 13:35 and serves again as reference text for the explanation of Jesus' resurrection. For the shift in meaning of Ps 16:10 in the LXX compared to the Masoretic Text, a shift which made possible an eschatological interpretation, see SCHMITT, Ps 16,8–11; and SCHNEIDER, Apg I, 260–261. The only other New Testament instances of ᾅδης are Matt 16:18; Rev 1:18; 6:8; 20:13. Yet, LEHTIPUU, Afterlife Imagery, 270–271, detects different nuances in Luke's use of the term "Hades." In her estimation, it is employed to depict either a place of torment (Luke 16) or a neutral abode of all the dead (Acts 2), while its connotation can also remain ambiguous (Luke 10:15).
[90] Cf. WOLTER, Lukasevangelium, 442, who lists early Jewish references for γέεννα that convey the same idea. BÖCHER, Art. ᾅδης, 73, does not see a clear difference between Hades and Gehenna in the case of Luke 12:5 and 16:23, either. Meanwhile, γέεννα is a typical expression of Matthew: see Matt 5:22.29–30; 10:28; 18:9; 23:15.33. Beyond that, it is only found in Mark 9:43.45.47 and James 3:6.
[91] Cf. also the more general concept of "eternal life" (Luke 9:24; 10:25–28; 17:33; 18:18.30; cf. 20:38; also Acts 13:46.48) and the picture of the eschatological feast (Luke 12:35–38; 13:28–29; 14:15–24; 22:16.18.30).

Jerusalem: Unhindered by sin, man can encounter the eternal God "today."[92] This interpretation is substantiated by the fact that in Isa 51:3 the idea of paradise is connected with Jerusalem which is compared to "Eden" and to the "garden of the Lord" (LXX: παράδεισος).[93] Since this verse is found in the context of the Isaianic Servant of JHWH passages, and because of the notable adoption of Isaiah by Luke in general,[94] this observation cannot be easily dismissed. Besides, the connection of the reopened paradise with Jerusalem in eschatological perspective is detectable in early Jewish texts as well.[95] At the same time, the relational character of the saying in Luke 23:43 must be recognized, for the affiliation with Jesus is crucial here ("you will be *with me*" = μετ' ἐμοῦ).[96] Hence, Ambrose rightly explains: "Vita est enim esse cum Christo; ideo ubi Christus, ibi vita, ibi regnum."[97] Moreover, the use of "today" (σήμερον) is equally programmatic: Luke thereby links the crucifixion scene not only with the angelic proclamation of Jesus' birth (Luke 2:11), but also with the already mentioned inaugural speech of Jesus in Nazareth (Luke 4:21) and his encounter with Zacchaeus (Luke 19:5.9), each time highlighting the immediate character of messianic salvation through the person of Jesus.[98] If this

---

92 Thus, SCHWEIZER, Lukas, 240, is correct in rejecting the idea of intermediate states and in concluding: "Vermutlich soll betont werden, daß der 'mit Christus' Lebende schon teilhat an dem in ihm gegenwärtigen Reich und so in die Christusgemeinschaft des Paradieses hinein stirbt." This is also the firm view of DUPONT, L'après-mort, 376. Similarly GIESEN, Zur individuellen Eschatologie, 173–175, for whom Jesus' accession to power takes place immediately after his death and who comprehends paradise in this case not as an intermediate state, but as the status of salvific consummation. FITZMYER, Luke the Theologian, 219, likewise stresses the specific Lucan notion of the term as distinct to most of the intertestamental literature: "For the evangelist 'in paradise' is merely a biblical way of phrasing what he otherwise refers to as the entrance of Christ 'into his glory' (24:26) or as the exaltation to God's right hand (Acts 2:33; 5:31)."
93 Cf. the detailed treatment in MITTMANN-RICHERT, Sühnetod, 106–107 and 151–153, where also the relation between the βασιλεία τοῦ θεοῦ resp. Ἰησοῦ (cf. Luke 23:42) and παράδεισος is discussed.
94 See n. 52 above.
95 See 4 Ezra 8:52; T. Levi 18:10–11; T. Dan 5:10, 12; 2 Bar. 4 (cf. the edition of KLIJN in OTP 1). Cf. also Rev 22:1–5 and LEHTIPUU, Afterlife Imagery, 277–284, especially 278, n. 46. General references for paradise as the postmortem abode of the righteous in early Jewish thought can be found in WOLTER, Lukasevangelium, 761; and HULTGÅRD, Paradies, 32–39, where Luke 23:43 is again classified as indication of an intermediate state.
96 This aspect is observed and elaborated by GRELOT, "Aujourd'hui," 205–210. Cf. also Luke 23:46 and Acts 7:58 as well as Acts 14:22.
97 "Indeed, life means being with Christ, for where Christ is, there is life, there is the kingdom" (Expos. Luc. 10.121; see PL 15:1834).
98 Cf. Luke 5:26; 13:32–33 and also the remark of STEYN, Perspectives, 94: "The *kairos* of God's salvation takes place in the present, in the presence of Jesus" (italics original).

interpretation is correct, the bosom of Abraham in Luke 16 can indeed be understood as an equivalent for the relational concept of paradise in Luke 23, the difference being that paradise is defined by the relation with Jesus, not with Abraham. In each case, however, Luke does not refer to interim states but to a final status. In this regard, the association of Abraham's bosom and paradise in T. Ab. (A) 20:14 (cf. above) is noteworthy, as is the fact that the also mentioned "tents of my righteous ones" bear resemblance to the "eternal tents" of Luke 16:9.

Having said this, the question arises how the concepts of the Parousia, the Last Judgment, and the resurrection of the dead, all of which are present in Luke's work as well, fit into the picture.[99] While some hold that, in Lukan perspective, after an immediate postmortem punishment or reward the wicked are sent to hell and the righteous to paradise from where they are resurrected with Jesus at the time of his coming,[100] one should be cautious not to schematize the different passages too rigidly.[101] After all, Luke reflects anthropological questions in an eschatological and at the same time christological and soteriological horizon which apparently transcends common time and space connotations. This is why, on some occasions and as an admonition to lead a different life right *now*, the emphasis can be on the dichotomy of the here*after*, and why, on other occasions, salvation through Jesus is described in *eternal* perspective but also as being *already* valid because the focus is on the relational dimension, which means being "with Jesus." Therefore, it might be said that to some extent Luke does take over traditional concepts of the hereafter understandable to his audience,[102] but he ultimately focuses on the cross as the decisive pivot of anthropological and eschatological issues. For Luke, God indeed has power to throw into the Gehenna (Luke 12:5) or Hades (Luke 10:15; 16:23; Acts 2:27.31), but Luke 23 proves that this need not be any more: Man is being saved once and for all. In other words: The great reversal of fate has already taken place on Calvary.[103]

---

99 For the Parousia see Luke 9:26; 12:40; 17:22–37; 18:8; 21:25–28; Acts 1:11; 3:20–21; 17:30–31. For the Last Judgment see Luke 10:12–15 (ἐν τῇ ἡμέρᾳ ἐκείνῃ); 11.30–32 (ἐν τῇ κρίσει); 21:33–36 (ἡ ἡμέρα ἐκείνη). Cf. 3:9.17; 9:24–25; 12:5.8–9; 17:26–27.32–35; 18:6–8; 19:11–27.36; 22:30; Acts 7:55–56; 10:42; 17:31. For the resurrection of the dead see again Luke 14:13–14; 20:33.35–38; Acts 24:15 and also Acts 4:2; 17:18.32; 23:6.8; 24:21.
100 Cf. MILIKOWSKY, Which Gehenna?, 244.
101 Cf. JÜLICHER, Lc 16,19–31, 623.
102 Cf. REGALADO, Background, 346.
103 This main aspect is missing in the otherwise comprehensive and profound analysis of LEHTIPUU, Afterlife Imagery, according to whom the juxtaposition of different "eschatologies" is due to the fact that Luke did have neither a coherent theology concerning the fate of the dead nor a consistent eschatological doctrine. In LEHTIPUU's estimation, Luke uses several different

Nevertheless, it is precisely this message that needs to be universally spread within the dimension of time and space until the consummation of the world which is, in fact, still turning. This is the reason why Luke can also retain the concept of the Parousia of the now exalted Jesus, of judgment, and of resurrection without being paradoxical. The juxtaposition of what has often been called "individual" and "universal" eschatology, "present" and "future" eschatology or "vertical-transcendent" and "horizontal" eschatology is due to the fact that with the person of Jesus, the incorporation of the heavenly dimension into history has ultimately been accomplished and participation in the eschatological salvation has become present-day reality. For Luke, it is because of Jesus that both aspects—the eternal and the historical, the transcendent and the immanent—are complementary; he does not abandon one facet at the expense of the other since they are essentially interdependent and present the same belief, only in different perspectives.[104] Still, it is but for God's self-revelation in Jesus which has already taken place that the reshaping of the individual fate and of the universal future is guaranteed.[105] With this in mind, and particularly in light of Luke 23:43, it is not wrong to say that Lukan eschatology is "less a definition of chronology and more one of quality."[106]

---

images when describing the fate of the dead which should simply not be pressed into one, harmonious whole. While there is some truth in this, to say that eschatology is not the key for understanding Luke's work and that it serves primarily his paraenetic teaching is to miss Luke's christological and soteriological anchoring of eschatological themes (cf. ibid. 41–42.303). Lukan eschatology is, in fact, subject to ongoing debate. Of the manifold studies see particularly DUPONT, L'après-mort; SCHNEIDER, Parusiegleichnisse; ERNST, Herr der Geschichte; WILSON, Lukan Eschatology; MICHEL, Heilsgegenwart und Zukunft; ELLIS, Funktion der Eschatologie; SCHNACKENBURG, Eschatologie; and more recently BAUSPIESS, Gegenwart des Heils; WOLTER, Eschatology; BUSSE, Eschatologie.

104 Thus, SCHNACKENBURG, Eschatologie, 264–265, rightly notes: "Das 'Durchlässigwerden' der lukanischen Theologie für die 'individuelle' Eschatologie (den Eingang nach dem Tod in die himmlische Welt) darf nicht den Blick dafür trüben, daß Lukas [...] nach wie vor den Blick auf die Vollendung der Zeiten, das Kommen Christi als Retter und Richter wendet." Similarly, GIESEN, Zur individuellen Eschatologie, 177. According to BAUSPIESS, Gegenwart des Heils, 144–146, this juxtaposition of thoughts is due to Luke's distinction between the historical reality and the reality of salvation. Meanwhile, it is not unprecedented in the New Testament: Paul, who is looking forward to be with Christ immediately after his death (Phil 1:23: σὺν Χριστῷ εἶναι), also speaks of the eschatological judgment (cf. Rom 14:10; 2Cor 5:10) and of the Parousia and the resurrection of the dead (cf. 1Cor 15:20–26; 1Thess 4:13–18).

105 Cf. ELLIS, Funktion der Eschatologie, 397, who notes that, whether in life or death, the individual completion is present only in fellowship with Jesus.

106 NIELSEN, Until it is Fulfilled, 280. Similarly WOLTER, Eschatology, 106.

One final aspect needs to be mentioned fully to grasp the meaning of Luke 16:19–31: the significance of "Moses and the Prophets." It is noticeable that in the immediate context[107] not only the problem of wealth is addressed (Luke 16:1–9.10–13), but also the validity of the Law and the Prophets is stressed (Luke 16:14–18). Indeed, Jesus specifically refers to "the Law and the Prophets" (ὁ νόμος καὶ οἱ προφῆται) that were in effect until John the Baptist came; now the good news of the kingdom of God is proclaimed (v. 16) and yet, no stroke in the law will be dropped (v. 17). Now, when the parable highlights that the living should listen to Moses and the Prophets in order to be spared the torments of Hades, this phrase proves two things. Firstly, it demonstrates that man as such is in need to become right with God. This is why the rich man demands the re-surrection of Lazarus in order that his brothers may *repent*.[108] The drama is that man is apparently not able truly to listen to and understand God's revelation (Luke 16:30).[109] Secondly, and to put the final verse differently, a miraculous resurrection is denied since it would be helpful only if man had listened to Moses and the Prophets in the first place. Again, the problem of understanding God's revelation is emphasized. And it is this problem which Luke illustrates over and again in his Gospel.

In Luke 4, the effect of the inaugural speech of Jesus, which has already been considered and which is plainly referring to a prophetic passage, is not that people understand the words "fulfilled in their hearing" (v. 21) but that they want to kill Jesus (vv. 28–30). The human inability to grasp the divine revelation could not be presented in a more dramatic way. Moreover, Jesus is portrayed both in continuity with Moses and the prophets and as the ultimate revelation of God at his transfiguration in Luke 9:28–36: According to the heavenly voice, it is neither Moses nor Elijah, the representative of the prophets, to whom the disciples should listen (cf. Luke 16:29: ἀκουσάτωσαν αὐτῶν), but Jesus as God's chosen son (Luke 9:35: αὐτοῦ ἀκούετε).[110] And in the last chapter of his Gospel, Luke

---

107 The question of context, i.e. the arrangement of material in Luke 16 and the relation between Luke 15 and 16, has been investigated in several studies: cf. DERRETT, Fresh Light; FEUILLET, Parabole; PIPER, Background; BALL, Parables; KILGALLEN, Luke 15 and 16; ROOSE, Umkehr.
108 Cf. HAYS, Wealth Ethics, 156–158, who recognizes the significance of "Moses and the Prophets" and concludes that "Dives is punished for neglecting the Law, insofar as he fails to extend food, clothing, and alms to Lazarus, who is starving, naked, and impoverished" which equals breaking "a covenant condition" (p. 158). According to HAYS, then, the Lukan context shows how the rich man should have acted and the recourse to Scripture makes the Lukan position all the more theologically imposing.
109 In this sense, the remark of JÜLICHER, Lc 16,19–31, 641, that the six brothers together represent the unbelieving part of the twelve tribes of Israel, is noteworthy.
110 For details of the transfiguration account, cf. MITTMANN-RICHERT, Sühnetod, 222–223; and MITTMANN-RICHERT, Erinnerung, 246–250.

twice connects the person of Jesus with Scripture and also with human disbelief while surpassing the denial of a possible resurrection of Lazarus: To the disciples on the road to Emmaus who are "slow of heart to believe all that the prophets have declared" (Luke 24:25), the actually resurrected Jesus has to explain his death and resurrection and ...

> ... beginning with Moses and all the Prophets, he interpreted to them the things about himself in all the Scriptures (Luke 24:27).[111]

And later on, Jesus testifies ...

> "... that everything written about me in the Law of Moses, the Prophets, and the Psalms must be fulfilled." Then he opened their minds to understand the Scriptures, and he said to them, "Thus it is written, that the Messiah is to suffer and to rise from the dead on the third day, and that repentance and forgiveness of sins is to be proclaimed in his name to all nations" (Luke 24:44–47).[112]

Unsurprisingly then, it is exactly this message of redemption through the death and resurrection of Jesus as explicitly fulfilling the Scriptures which runs like a golden thread through the second part of Luke's work (cf. Acts 2:22–32; 3:18.22–26; 7:37.52–53; 8:28–35; 10:43; 13:15.29–39; 17:2–3; 18:28; 24:14; 26:22–23; 28:23). The most impressive illustration in this regard is the account of the Ethiopian official (Acts 8:26–40) who is at first unable to understand the full meaning of a passage of Isa 53 (v. 31: "How can I, unless someone guides me?") and to whom Philip proclaims Jesus, starting with this Scripture. The passage in question demonstrates again the importance of the Servant of JHWH tradition for Luke and links this text with Luke 4 and Luke 24. And one might add that, since the Ethiopian is in charge of the treasury (v. 27) and therefore clearly represents wealth, he can be seen as a counterexample of the rich man in Luke 16: His fortune is changed in a positive way even here and now.

---

[111] On the Emmaus passage, see MITTMANN-RICHERT, Sühnetod, 210–238.

[112] JEREMIAS, Gleichnisse Jesu, 185, therefore rightly notes that the phrase "Moses and the Prophets" in Luke 16:29.31 has to be read in connection with Luke 24 and includes obedience to the final revelation in the person of Jesus since the latter "bringt ja doch die Offenbarung in Gesetz und Propheten auf das Vollmaß." The connection of Luke 16:29–31 and Luke 24:46 is also highlighted by REINMUTH, Liber Antiquitatum Biblicarum 33,1–5, 37–38.

4 Conclusion

It is hoped that the preceding observations have helped to appreciate the account of the rich man and Lazarus on different levels. On a literary level, the passage is without question one of the most elaborate examples of the Lukan storytelling. Besides, the fact that in Luke 16 various ideas and motifs are present which occur, to some extent, also in Egyptian and Hellenistic writings, both Jewish and pagan, is a reminder to read biblical Scriptures within their historical and cultural context, to search for shared patterns as well as for the respective particularities. On a theological level, the illumination of the immediate literary context has shown that within the Lukan Gospel the account of the rich man and Lazarus is best understood as a contrasting foil that depicts human fate without Jesus. And as such it manifests Luke's struggle for man, taking seriously the idea that life is not without eternal consequences. Luke's work as a whole, however, transcends this view and presents Jesus as the one who, precisely through his death and resurrection, fulfils the Scriptures to which the living are admonished to listen and who makes possible the reversal of the individual fate "today." Therefore, Jesus himself ensures what is deliberately missing in Luke 16: the certainty of a present and future existence in relation with and not in remoteness of God.[113]

---

[113] Hence, one might say that Luke 16 presents the pre-Easter situation in all its severity, as it were. In post-Easter perspective, however, the question arises what happens to those who still do not accept the gospel. Within Luke's work, this question is mainly illustrated by the repeated rejection of Jesus and his disciples by the Jews. For a further discussion of this issue, which is beyond the scope of this essay, see MITTMANN-RICHERT, Sühnetod, 265–280.

Table 1: The Parable and the Parallels – A Synoptic View

	Luke 16:19–31	Egyptian Story: Setme and Si-Osiris	Jewish Story: Bar Ma'yan and the Pious Man	Greco-Roman Story: Lucian of Samosata, Cataplus
Characters	Rich man (anonymous) Poor man = Lazarus + Abraham + the rich man's brothers	Rich man (anonymous) Poor man (anonymous) + Setme (father) + Si-Osiris (son)	Rich man = Bar Ma'yan Pious man (anonymous) + companion	Rich man = Megapenthes Poor man = Micyllus + philosopher Cyniscus (among others)
Details of description 1 (rich man)	Purple and fine linen (Byssos) Making merry daily	(Fine linen/Byssos at the funeral)	Tax collector	Tyrant, rich, splendour, purple clothing, hedonistic, unjust
Details of description 2 ("poor" man)	Hungry, covered with ulcers, dogs licking the wounds		Habitually eating, drinking and studying the Torah with his friend	Poor shoemaker, neighbour of the rich man
Details of death 1 (rich man)	Burial of the rich man	Funeral in sumptuous clothing, with mourning	Mourned by the whole town	Journey to Hades (unwillingness to die)
Details of death 2 ("poor" man)	Poor man taken away by angels	Funeral without ceremony, wrapped in a mat	Not properly mourned	Journey to Hades (willingly)
Further elements		Tour of the seven halls of Amente	Two visionary dreams of the companion (appearance of the deceased pious man)	Judgment: uncountable bad deeds (Megapenthes) / blameless (Micyllus)

	Luke 16:19-31	Egyptian Story: Setme and Si-Osiris	Jewish Story: Bar Ma'yan and the Pious Man	Greco-Roman Story: Lucian of Samosata, Cataplus
Details of afterlife 1 ("poor" man)	Abraham's bosom Comforted	7th hall of Amente, close to Osiris, with garments of the rich man	"Paradise": gardens, orchards, and fountains of water	Micyllus (and Cyniscus) sent to the Isles of the Blessed
Details of afterlife 2 (rich man)	Haces Torment: flame; wants to have his tongue cooled with water Unbridgeable chasm	5th hall of Amente Torment: pivot of the door in his eye	"Hell" Torment: wants to drink from a river but cannot reach it	Hades Punishment: no drinking of the water of Lethe; has to remember what he did in life
Reason for the reversal of fate	Receiving of good and bad things during life is equated	Good and bad deeds are weighed (with regard to the poor man: in relation to the lifetime and relative to the luck on earth)	The righteous are punished in this world for their few sins to enjoy only bliss in the next world; the wicked receive reward for their few good deeds in this world, so that in the next world they receive only punishment	Bad deeds that leave dark spots on the soul are investigated and determine the eternal fate
Dialogue	Dialogue between the rich man and Abraham: Abatement and warning of the living brothers through Lazarus?	Dialogue between Si-Osiris and his father Setme: Which fate is more favourable?	Dialogue between the deceased and the surviving companion: Unjust inequality of burials?	Bargaining of Megapenthes with Clotho
Reference to resurrection?	Denial of the raising of Lazarus	(Cf. Si-Osiris as temporarily raised from the dead and incarnated)		Return to life denied

Bibliography

AALEN, Sverre, St. Luke's Gospel and I Enoch, in: NTS 13 (1966) 1–13.
AMBROSE, Expositio Evangelii secundum Lucam, in: PL 15 (1845) 1527–1850.
ANDERSON, Hugh, 4 Maccabees, in: OTP 2 (1985) 531–564.
ASSMANN, Jan, Tod und Jenseits im alten Ägypten, München 2003.
AUGUSTIN, *Epistola* 187, in: PL 33 (1865) 832–848.
BALL, Michael, The Parables of the Unjust Steward and the Rich Man and Lazarus, in: ExpTim 106 (1995) 329–330.
BAUCKHAM, Richard, The Rich Man and Lazarus. The Parable and the Parallels, in: NTS 37 (1991) 225–246.
BAUSPIESS, Martin, Die Gegenwart des Heils und das Ende der Zeit. Überlegungen zur lukanischen Eschatologie im Anschluss an Lk 22,61–71 und Apg 7,54–60, in: Eckstein, Hans-Joachim/Landmesser, Christof/Lichtenberger, Hermann (Hg.), Eschatologie—Eschatology, The Sixth Durham-Tübingen Research Symposium, Tübingen, September 2009 (WUNT 272), Tübingen 2011, 125–148.
BELLINGER, William H., Jr./FARMER, William R. (Hg.), Jesus and the Suffering Servant. Isaiah 53 and Christian Origins, Eugene, Oregon 2009 (1998).
BERGER, Klaus/COLPE, Carsten, Religionsgeschichtliches Textbuch zum Neuen Testament (Texte zum Neuen Testament 1), Göttingen/Zürich 1987.
BOCK, Darrell L., Luke, Vol. 2: 9:51–24:53 (BECNT 3B), Grand Rapids, Michigan [8]2008 (1996).
BOCK, Darrell L., The Parable of the Rich Man and Lazarus and the Ethics of Jesus, in: SwJT 40.1 (1997) 63–72.
BOCK, Darrell L., Acts (BECNT), Grand Rapids, Michigan [3]2009 (2007).
BÖCHER, Otto, Art. ᾅδης, in: EWNT I, Stuttgart [3]2011 (1980), 72–73.
BORNHÄUSER, Karl, Das Wirken des Christus durch Taten und Worte (BFCT II/2), Gütersloh [2]1924 (1921).
BORNHÄUSER, Karl, Das Gleichnis vom reichen Mann und armen Lazarus. Luk. 16,19–31, in: id., Studien zum Sondergut des Lukas, Gütersloh 1934, 138–160.
BRUCE, Frederick F., The Book of the Acts, Revised Edition (NICNT), Grand Rapids, Michigan 1988.
BULTMANN, Rudolf, Die Geschichte der synoptischen Tradition. Mit einem Nachwort von Gerd Theißen (FRLANT 29 = N.F., H. 12), Göttingen [10]1995 (1921).
BUSSE, Ulrich, Das Nazareth-Manifest Jesu. Eine Einführung in das lukanische Jesusbild nach Lk 4:16–30 (SBS 91), Stuttgart 1978.
BUSSE, Ulrich, Eschatologie in der Apostelgeschichte, in: Watt, Jan G. van der (Hg.), Eschatology in the New Testament and Some Related Documents (WUNT II 315), Tübingen 2011, 141–178.
CADBURY, Henry J., A Proper Name for Dives. Lexical Notes on Luke-Acts VI, in: JBL 81 (1962) 399–402.
CADBURY, Henry J., The Name of Dives, in: JBL 84 (1965) 73.
CAVE, C. H., Lazarus and the Lukan Deuteronomy, in: NTS 15 (1969) 319–325.
CHESTER, Andrew, Resurrection and Transformation, in: Avemarie, Friedrich/Lichtenberger, Hermann (Hg.), Auferstehung—Resurrection, The Fourth Durham-Tübingen Research Symposium, Tübingen, September 1999 (WUNT 135), Tübingen 2001, 47–77.

COLSON, Francis Henry, Philo in Ten Volumes, Vol. 6 (LCL 289), London/Cambridge, Massachusetts 1966 (1935).

DAHL, Nils A., Story of Abraham in Luke-Acts, in: Keck, Leander E./Martyn, J. Louis (Hg.), Studies in Luke-Acts, Essays presented in honor of Paul Schubert, Nashville 1966, 139–158.

DERRETT, J. Duncan M., Fresh Light on St. Luke XVI. II. Dives and Lazarus and the Preceding Sayings, in: NTS 7 (1961) 364–380.

DOCHHORN, Jan, Die Apokalypse des Mose. Text, Übersetzung, Kommentar (TSAJ 106), Tübingen 2005.

DUNKERLEY, Roderic, Lazarus, in: NTS 5 (1959) 321–327.

DUPONT, Jacques, L'après-mort dans l'œuvre de Luc, in: id., Nouvelles études sur les Actes des Apôtres (LD 118), Paris 1984, 358–379.

ELLIS, E. Earle, Die Funktion der Eschatologie im Lukasevangelium, in: ZTK 66 (1968) 387–402.

ERNST, Josef, Herr der Geschichte. Perspektiven der lukanischen Eschatologie (SBS 88), Stuttgart 1978.

ESLER, Philipp F., Community and Gospel in Luke-Acts. The Social and Political Motivations of Lucan Theology (SNTSMS 57), Cambridge 1987.

FELDMAN, Louis H., Josephus in Ten Volumes, Vol. 9: Jewish Antiquities, Books XVIII-XIX (LCL 433), London/Cambridge, Massachusetts 1981 (1965).

FEUILLET, André, La parabole du mauvais riche et du pauvre Lazare (Lc 16,19–31) antithèse de la parabole de l'intendant astucieux (Lc 16,1–9), in: NRTh 101 (1979) 212–223.

FITZMYER, Joseph A., The Gospel According to Luke (X-XXIV), Introduction, Translation, and Notes (AB 28A), Garden City, New York 1985.

FITZMYER, Joseph A., Luke the Theologian. Aspects of His Teaching, New York/Mahwah 1989.

GIESEN, Heinz, „Noch heute wirst du mit mir im Paradies sein" (Lk 23,43). Zur individuellen Eschatologie im lukanischen Doppelwerk, in: Müller, Christoph G. (Hg.), „Licht zur Erleuchtung der Heiden und Herrlichkeit für dein Volk Israel". Studien zum lukanischen Doppelwerk. Josef Zmijewski zur Vollendung seines 65. Lebensjahres am 23. Dezember 2005 (BBB 151), Hamburg 2005, 151–177.

GILMOUR, Michael J., Hints of Homer in Luke 16:19–31, in: Did 10 (1999) 23–33.

GLOMBITZA, Otto, Der reiche Mann und der arme Lazarus. Luk. xvi 19–31. Zur Frage nach der Botschaft des Textes, in: NovT 12 (1970) 160–180.

GRELOT, Paul, "Aujourd'hui tu seras avec moi dans le paradis" (Luc, XXIII, 43), in: RB 74 (1967) 194–214.

GRENSTED, Laurence W., The Use of Enoch in St. Luke xvi. 19–31, in: ExpTim 26 (1915) 333–334.

GRESSMANN, Hugo, Vom reichen Mann und armen Lazarus. Eine literargeschichtliche Studie. Mit ägyptologischen Beiträgen von G. Möller (Abhandlungen der Preußischen Akademie der Wissenschaften. Philosophisch-Historische Klasse 1918/7), Berlin 1918.

GRIFFITH, F. Llywellyn, Stories of the High Priests of Memphis. The Sethon of Herodotus and the Demotic Tales of Khamuas, Oxford 1900 (repr. Osnabrück 1985).

GRIFFITHS, J. Gwyn, Cross-cultural Eschatology with Dives and Lazarus, in: ExpTim 105 (1993) 7–12.

GROBEL, Kendrick, "... whose name was Neves", in: NTS 10 (1964) 373–382.

HARMON, Austin Morris, Lucian in Eight Volumes, Vol. 2 (LCL 54), London/Cambridge, Massachusetts 1968 (1915).

HARNACK, Adolf, Der Name des reichen Mannes in Luc. 16,19, in: TUGAL 13.1 (1895) 75–78.

HARTMAN, Louis F./DI LELLA, Alexander A., The Book of Daniel (AB 23), Garden City, New York 1977.

HAUGE, Matthew Ryan, The Biblical Tour of Hell (Library of New Testament Studies 485), London et al. 2013.
HAUPT, Paul, Abraham's Bosom, in: AJP 42 (1921) 162–167.
HAYS, Christopher M., Luke's Wealth Ethics. A Study in Their Coherence and Character (WUNT II 275), Tübingen 2010.
HINTZEN, Johannes, Verkündigung und Wahrnehmung. Über das Verhältnis von Evangelium und Leser am Beispiel Lk 16,19–31 im Rahmen des lukanischen Doppelwerkes (BBB 81), Frankfurt a.M. 1991.
HOCK, Ronald F., Lazarus and Micyllus. Greco-Roman Backgrounds to Luke 16:19–31, in: JBL 106 (1987) 447–463.
HOFFMANN, Friedhelm/QUACK, Joachim Friedrich, Anthologie der demotischen Literatur (Einführungen und Quellentexte zur Ägyptologie 4), Berlin 2007.
HORST, Pieter W. van der, Abraham's Bosom, the Place Where He Belonged. A Short Note on ἀπενεχθῆναι in Luke 16:22, in: id., Jews and Christians in Their Graeco-Roman Context. Selected Essays on Early Judaism, Samaritanism, Hellenism, and Christianity (WUNT 196), Tübingen 2006, 164–166.
HUGHES, Frank W., The Parable of the Rich Man and Lazarus (Luke 16.19–31) and Graeco-Roman Rhetoric, in: Porter, Stanley E./Olbricht, Thomas H. (Hg.), Rhetoric and the New Testament. Essays from the 1992 Heidelberg Conference (JSNTSup 90), Sheffield 1993, 29–41.
HULTGÅRD, Anders, Das Paradies: vom Park des Perserkönigs zum Ort der Seligen, in: Hengel, Martin/Mittmann, Siegfried/Schwemer, Anna Maria (Hg.), La Cité de Dieu. Die Stadt Gottes, 3. Symposium Straßbourg, Tübingen, Uppsala, 19.–23. September 1998 in Tübingen (WUNT 129), Tübingen 2000, 1–43.
ISAAC, Ephraim, 1 (Ethiopic Apocalypse of) Enoch, in: OTP 1, New York et al. 1983, 5–89.
JANOWSKI, Bernd/STUHLMACHER, Peter (Hg.), The Suffering Servant. Isaiah 53 in Jewish and Christian Sources, Transl. by D.P. Bailey, Including bibliographical references, Grand Rapids, Michigan 2004 (original title: Der leidende Gottesknecht. Jesaja 53 und seine Wirkungsgeschichte. Mit einer Bibliographie zu Jes 53 [FAT 14], Tübingen 1996).
JEREMIAS, Joachim, Die Gleichnisse Jesu, Göttingen [8]1970 (ATANT 11, Zürich 1947).
JOHNSON, Dennis E., Jesus Against the Idols. The Use of the Isaianic Servant Songs in the Missiology of Acts, in: WTJ 52 (1990) 343–353.
JÜLICHER, Adolf, Vom reichen Mann und armen Lazarus. Lc 16,19–31, in: id., Die Gleichnisreden Jesu, Zweiter Teil: Auslegung der Gleichnisreden der drei ersten Evangelien, Freiburg/Leipzig/Tübingen 1899, 617–641.
KEE, Howard C., Testament of the Twelve Patriarchs, in: OTP 1, New York et al. 1983, 775–828.
KILGALLEN, John J., Luke 15 and 16: a Connection, in: Bib 78 (1997) 369–376.
KLEIN, Hans, Lukasstudien (FRLANT 209), Göttingen 2005.
KLIJN, Albertus Frederik Johannes, 2 (Syriac Apocalypse of) Baruch, in: OTP 1, New York et al. 1983, 615–652.
KNIGHT, George W., Luke 16:19–31. The Rich Man and Lazarus, in: RevExp 94 (1997) 277–283.
KOET, Bart J., Isaiah in Luke-Acts, in: Moyise, Steve/Menken, Maarten J.J. (Hg.), Isaiah in the New Testament (The New Testament and the Scriptures of Israel), London/New York 2005, 79–100.
KREITZER, Larry, Luke 16:19–31 and 1 Enoch 22, in: ExpTim 103 (1992) 139–142.
KREMER, Jacob, Der arme Lazarus. Lazarus, der Freund Jesu. Beobachtungen zur Beziehung zwischen Lk 16,19–31 und Joh 11,1–46, in: id., Die Bibel beim Wort genommen. Beiträge zu

Exegese und Theologie des Neuen Testaments, hg. v. Roman Kühschelm u. Martin Stowasser, Freiburg 1995, 108–118.
KVALBEIN, Hans, Jesus and the Poor. Two Texts and a Tentative Conclusion, in: Them 12 (1987) 80–87.
LEFORT, Louis Théophile, Le nom du mauvais riche (Lc 16,19) et la tradition copte, in: ZNW 37 (1938) 65–72.
LEHTIPUU, Outi, The Afterlife Imagery in Luke's Story of the Rich Man and Lazarus (NovTSup 123), Leiden 2007.
LENTZEN-DEIS, Fritzleo, Arm und reich aus der Sicht des Evangelisten Lukas, in: Kamphaus, Franz et al. (Hg.), „…und machen einander reich". Beiträge zur Arm/Reich-Problematik, reflektiert am Lukasevangelium, Annweiler 1989, 17–68.
LEONHARDT-BALZER, Jutta, Wie kommt ein Reicher in Abrahams Schoß? (Vom reichen Mann und armen Lazarus)—Lk 16,19–31, in: Zimmermann, Ruben (Hg.), Kompendium der Gleichnisse Jesu, Gütersloh 2007, 647–660.
LICHTHEIM, Miriam, Ancient Egyptian Literature. A Book of Readings, Vol. 3: The Late Period, London/Berkeley, California/Los Angeles, California ²2006 (1980).
LUTHER, Martin, Predigt am 2. Sonntag nach Trinitatis (6. Juni 1535), in: WA 41, Weimar 1910, 293–300.
MALLEN, Peter, Reading and Transformation of Isaiah in Luke-Acts (LNTS 367), London/New York 2008.
MASPERO, Gaston, Les contes populaires de l'Égypte ancienne, Paris ⁴1911 (1882).
METZGER, Bruce M., The Fourth Book of Ezra. With the Four Additional Chapters, in: OTP 1, New York et al. 1983, 517–560.
METZGER, Bruce M., A Textual Commentary on the Greek New Testament. Second Edition. A Companion Volume to the United Bible Societies' Greek New Testament (Fourth Revised Edition), Stuttgart ⁸2007 (1994).
MICHEL, Hans-Joachim, Heilsgegenwart und Zukunft bei Lukas, in: Fiedler, Paul/Zeller, Dieter (Hg.), Gegenwart und kommendes Reich, Schülergabe Anton Vögtle zum 65. Geburtstag (SBB 6), Stuttgart 1975, 101–115.
MILIKOWSKY, Chaim, Which Gehenna? Retribution and Eschatology in the Synoptic Gospels and in Early Jewish Texts, in: NTS 34 (1988) 238–249.
MINESHIGE, Kiyoshi, Besitzverzicht und Almosen bei Lukas. Wesen und Forderung des lukanischen Vermögensethos (WUNT II 163), Tübingen 2003.
MITTMANN-RICHERT, Ulrike, Magnifikat und Benediktus. Die ältesten Zeugnisse der judenchristlichen Tradition von der Geburt des Messias (WUNT II 90), Tübingen 1996.
MITTMANN-RICHERT, Ulrike, Erinnerung und Heilserkenntnis im Lukasevangelium. Ein Beitrag zum neutestamentlichen Verständnis des Abendmahls, in: Barton, Stephen C./Stuckenbruck, Loren T./Wold, Benjamin G. (Hg.), Memory in the Bible and Antiquity, The Fifth Durham-Tübingen Research Symposium (WUNT 212), Tübingen 2007, 243–276.
MITTMANN-RICHERT, Ulrike, Der Sühnetod des Gottesknechts. Jesaja 53 im Lukasevangelium (WUNT 220), Tübingen 2008.
MITTMANN, Ulrike, Polemik im eschatologischen Kontext. Israel und die Heiden in der Apostelgeschichte des Lukas, in: Wischmeyer, Oda/Scornaienchi, Lorenzo (Hg.), Polemik in der frühchristlichen Literatur. Texte und Kontexte (BZNW 170), Berlin/New York 2011, 517–542.

MURRAY, Augustus Taber, Homer. The Odyssey, Vol. 1: Book 1–12, Revised by G.E. Dimock (LCL 104), London/Cambridge, Massachusetts 1995 (1919).

NEUSNER, Jacob, Hagigah and Moed Qatan. The Talmud of the Land of Israel, Vol. 20 (CSJH), Chicago 1986.

NICKELSBURG, George W.E., Riches, the Rich, and God's Judgement in 1 Enoch 92-105 and the Gospel According to Luke, in: NTS 25 (1979) 324–344.

NICKELSBURG, George W.E., 1 Enoch 1. A Commentary on the Book of Enoch, Chapters 1–36; 81–108, Edited by Klaus Baltzer (Hermeneia: A Critical and Historical Commentary on the Bible), Minneapolis 2001.

NIELSEN, Anders E., Until it is Fulfilled. Lukan Eschatology Accordig to Luke 22 and Acts 20 (WUNT II 126), Tübingen 2000.

OJOK, Vincent A., Parable of the Rich Man and Lazarus. Literary and Semiotic Analysis of Lk 16:19–31, Rom, Diss. Pont. Univ. Urbaniana 1993.

OSEI-BONSU, Joseph, The Intermediate State in Luke-Acts, in: IBS 9 (1987) 115–130.

PEARCE, Keith, The Lucan Origins of the Raising of Lazarus, in: ExpTim 96 (1985) 359–364.

PERKINS, Pheme, Resurrection. New Testament Witness and Contemporary Reflection, London 1984.

PETERSON, David G., The Acts of the Apostles (The Pillar New Testament Commentary), Grand Rapids, Michigan/Cambridge, U.K. 2009.

PETRACCA, Vincenzo, Gott oder das Geld. Die Besitzethik des Lukas (Texte und Arbeiten zum neutestamentlichen Zeitalter 39), Tübingen 2003.

PIETERSMA, Albert/LUTZ, R. T., Jannes and Jambres, in: OTP 2, New York et al. 1985, 427–442.

PIPER, Ronald A., Social Background and Thematic Structure in Luke 16, in: Segbroeck, Frans van et al. (Hg.), The Four Gospels, Festschrift Frans Neirynck, Vol. 2 (BETL 100), Leuven 1992, 1637–1662.

PLANAS, Francisco, En el seno de Abrahan, in: CB 15 (1958) 148–152.

PREUSCHEN, Erwin, Origenes Werke, Vierter Band: Der Johanneskommentar (GCS 10), Leipzig 1903.

PRIOR, Michael, Jesus the Liberator. Nazareth Liberation Theology (Luke 4.16–30) (The Biblical Seminar 26), Sheffield 1995, 163–181.

REGALADO, Ferdinand O., The Jewish Background of the Parable of the Rich Man and Lazarus, in: AJT 16 (2002) 341–348.

REINMUTH, Eckart, Ps.-Philo, *Liber Antiquitatum Biblicarum* 33,1–5 und die Auslegung der Parabel Lk 16:19–31, in: NovT 31 (1989) 16–38.

ROBERTS, Jimmy J. M., Melchizedek (11Q13 = 11QMelchizedek = 11QMelch), in: Charlesworth, James H. et al. (Hg.), The Dead Sea Scrolls. Hebrew, Aramaic, and Greek Texts with English Translations, Vol. 6B. Pesharim, Other Commentaries, and Related Documents (The Princeton Theological Seminary Dead Sea Scrolls Project), Tübingen/Louisville, Kentucky 2002, 264–273.

ROOSE, Hanna, Umkehr und Ausgleich bei Lukas. Die Gleichnisse vom verlorenen Sohn (Lk 15.11–32) und vom reichen Mann und armen Lazarus (Lk 16.19–31) als Schwesterngeschichten, in: NTS 56 (2009) 1–21.

SANDERS, Ed P., Testament of Abraham, in: OTP 1, New York et al. 1983, 871–902.

SCHMITHALS, Walter, Lukas—Evangelist der Armen, in: ThViat 12 (1973/74) 153–167.

SCHMITT, Armin, Ps 16,8–11 als Zeugnis der Auferstehung in der Apg, in: BZ 17 (1973) 229–248.

SCHNACKENBURG, Rudolf, Die lukanische Eschatologie im Lichte von Aussagen der Apostelgeschichte, in: Gräßer, Erich/Merk, Otto (Hg.), Glaube und Eschatologie. Festschrift für Werner Georg Kümmel zum 80. Geburtstag, Tübingen 1985, 249–265.
SCHNEIDER, Gerhard, Parusiegleichnisse im Lukas-Evangelium (SBS 74), Stuttgart 1975.
SCHNEIDER, Gerhard, Die Apostelgeschichte. Erster Teil. Einleitung. Kommentar zu Kap. 1,1–8,40 (HTKNT 5), Freiburg/Basel/Wien 1980.
SCHNIDER, Franz/STENGER, Werner, Die offene Tür und die unüberschreitbare Kluft. Strukturanalytische Überlegungen zum Gleichnis vom reichen Mann und armen Lazarus (Lk 16,19–31), in: NTS 25 (1979) 273–283.
SCHWEIZER, Eduard, Das Evangelium nach Lukas (NTD 3), Göttingen 1993.
SECCOMBE, David P., Possessions and the Poor in Luke-Acts (SNTSU B:6), Linz 1982.
SELLIN, Gerhard, Studien zu den großen Gleichniserzählungen des Lukas-Sonderguts. Die ἄνθρωπός τις-Erzählungen des lukanischen Sonderguts—besonders am Beispiel von Lk 10,25–37 und 16,14–31 untersucht, Diss. masch., Münster 1973.
SHOREY, Paul, The Republic. With an English Translation, Plato in Twelve Volumes, Vol. 6.2 (LCL 276), London/Cambridge, Massachusetts 1970.
SPITTLER, Russell P., Testament of Job, in: OTP 1, New York et al. 1983, 829–868.
STANDEN, A. O., The Parable of Dives and Lazarus, and Enoch 22, in: ExpTim 33 (1922) 523.
STEYN, Gert J., Soteriological Perspectives in Luke's Gospel, in: Watt, Jan G. van der (Hg.), Salvation in the New Testament. Perspectives on Soteriology (NovTSup 121), Atlanta 2008, 67–99.
STONE, Michael E., Greek Apocalypse of Ezra, in: OTP 1, New York et al. 1983, 561–579.
STRACK, Hermann L./BILLERBECK, Paul, Kommentar zum Neuen Testament aus Talmud und Midrasch, Bd. 2: Das Evangelium nach Markus, Lukas und Johannes und die Apostelgeschichte, München ⁸1983 (1924).
THACKERAY, H. St. John, Josephus in Nine Volumes, Vol. 2: The Jewish War, Books I-III (LCL 203), London/Cambridge, Massachusetts 1967 (1927); Vol. 4: Jewish Antiquities, Books I-IV (LCL 242), London/Cambridge, Massachusetts 1978 (1930).
TURNER, Max, Power from on High. The Spirit in Israel's Restoration and Witness in Luke-Acts (JPTSS 9), Sheffield 2000.
VOS, Craig S. de, The Meaning of 'Good News to the Poor' in Luke's Gospel. The Parable of Lazarus and the Rich Man as a Test Case, in: Hagedorn, Anselm C. (Hg.), In Other Words. Essays on Social Science Methods and the New Testament in Honor of Jerome H. Neyrey (SWBA 2.1), Sheffield 2007, 67–86.
WARD, Ray Bowen, Abraham Traditions in Early Christianity, in: Nickelsburg, George W.E. (Hg.), Studies on the Testament of Abraham, Revised papers of the Society of Biblical Literature Pseudepigrapha Seminar held at the International Congress of Learned Societies in the Field of Religion (1972) (SBLSCS 6), Missoula, Montana 1976, 173–184.
WASZINK, Jan Hendrik, De anima, in: Tertulliani Opera. Pars 2 (CCSL 2), Turnholti 1954, 779–869.
WEWERS, Gerd A., Sanhedrin. Gerichtshof (Übersetzung des Talmud Yerushalmi IV/4), Tübingen 1981.
WEWERS, Gerd A., Hagiga. Festopfer (Übersetzung des Talmud Yerushalmi II/11), Tübingen 1983.
WILSON, Stephen G., Lukan Eschatology, in: NTS 16 (1970) 330–347.
WOLTER, Michael, Das Lukasevangelium (HNT 5), Tübingen 2008.
WOLTER, Michael, Eschatology in the Gospel According to Luke, in: Watt, Jan G. van der (Hg.), Eschatology in the New Testament and Some Related Documents (WUNT II 315), Tübingen 2011, 91–108.

Ellen Bradshaw Aitken
Death and *Cultus* as Constitutive of the Human in the Epistle to the Hebrews

"And someone somewhere has borne witness, saying, 'What is the human that you remember him, the son of the human that you care for him?'" (διεμαρτύρατο δέ πού τις λέγων τί ἐστιν ἄνθρωπος ὅτι μιμνήσκῃ αὐτοῦ, ἢ υἱὸς ἀνθρώπου ὅτι ἐπισκέπτῃ αὐτόν; Heb 2:6). The first-century discourse that we have come to know as the Epistle to the Hebrews poses this explicitly anthropological question early in its argument about the identity of Jesus, the "Son," and about Jesus' cosmic and earthly relation to God, the angels, the audience and, by extension, humankind. Hebrews is coy in its setting of this quotation of Psalm 8:5, "Someone somewhere has borne witness." The "you" in the quotation, "What is the human (ἄνθρωπος) that you remember him," is of course God; this address accounts for the fact that, unlike most of the other quotations of scripture in Hebrews, these words are not placed directly (without a quotation formula) on the lips of God, Jesus, or the Spirit in a semblance of divine ventriloquism.[1] Hebrews' deployment of the psalm verse, moreover, specifies that "the human" and "the son of the human" are to be understood as Jesus, and not *in the first place* as humankind in general. This specificity is, I would note, lost in many recent English translations, which in the laudable interests of gender-inclusive language move the translation of this verse and the subsequent verses into the plural, as for example the New Revised Standard Version does, "What are human beings that you are mindful of them, or mortals that you care for them? You have made them a little lower than the angels, you have crowned them with glory and honor" (Heb 2:6–7). To understand the verse in the plural in reference to human beings generally is to get ahead of the argument in Hebrews, and to miss the flow of the rhetoric, namely, that the point here is to say something crucial about who Jesus is and about God's regard for Jesus; the more general anthropological exploration that the verse proposes is not yet underway. Yet, the presence of the verse does initiate within Hebrews an interest in the anthropological, "What is the human?" which underlies the unfolding of the argument and explores the question as a consequence of what Hebrews has to say about Jesus.

Before I turn to the matter of how the anthropological question unfolds in Hebrews, a few words about Hebrews and my working presuppositions are in

---

[1] ATRRIDGE, Giving Voice, 107–110.

order.² First, I approach Hebrews as a highly multivalent text that contains numerous interwoven ways of constructing and defining the identity and ethic of its audience, as is not uncommon in texts that are homiletical in character. Hebrews is generally acknowledged as one of the more complex texts contained within the New Testament; it has been characterized as "the most elegant and sophisticated, and perhaps the most enigmatic text of first-century Christianity"³ and as drawing upon esoteric, advanced theological reflection. The discursive practices of Hebrews have been connected most frequently to philosophical circles specializing in allegorical interpretation of scripture and other authoritative texts. Second, Hebrews is ultimately a parenetic text, aimed at shaping the community's way of life.⁴ Hebrews is best understood as utilizing many of the rhetorical conventions of the hellenistic Jewish sermon, and indeed it characterizes itself not as a letter but as a "word of exhortation" (ὁ λόγος τῆς παρακλήσεως, Heb 13:22).⁵ Although it has been handed down within the New Testament canon as a "letter," Hebrews lacks any thorough-going epistolary character. It is not a sermon, but it is composed out of the interpretive practices and rhetorical conventions of homilies as experienced within a worshipping community. It may be the case that such material was reworked into this elegant and coherent piece of rhetoric both for internal use and for sending to other communities. Hebrews calls at every turn upon the resourcefulness and versatility of its hearers and readers, certainly in the modern period, and I suspect it did so also for its ancient audiences. Although the specific content of the ethical instruction in Hebrews is one of the enigmas of the text, we can recognize the text's concern to exhort its audience with such appeals as "let us hold fast to the confession" (Heb 4:14) and "let us run with perseverance the race that is set before us" (Heb 12:1).

---

2 A fuller discussion of these issues can be found in AITKEN, Jesus' Death, 130–133.
3 ATTRIDGE, Hebrews, 1.
4 The alternation of exposition and exhortation in Hebrews is widely recognized and informs most attempts to outline the structure of Hebrews; see the discussion in ATTRIDGE, Hebrews, 14–21. Attridge also identifies (p. 21) the two types of exhortation found in the text, "let us hold fast" and "let us approach" (both found in Heb 4:14–16). On the pastoral dimension of Hebrews, see KUSS, Verfasser, 1–12.65–80.
5 On the homiletic character of Hebrews, see WILLS, Form, 280–283; BLACK, Form, 1–18; ATTRIDGE, Paraenesis, 211–226. See also MACRAE, Heavenly Temple, 179–199. ATTRIDGE, Hebrews, 14.408, points out that this designation is used in Acts 13:15 for Paul's synagogue address in Pisidian Antioch. More recently, deSilva accepts the position that Hebrews is a sermon, but one that makes significant use of the conventions of hellenistic epideictic rhetoric; see DESILVA, Perseverance, 58.514.

Hebrews is commonly dated to the Flavian period, most broadly between 70 and 96 C.E., and its composition situated in the city of Rome. In other contexts,[6] I have argued that Hebrews should be read in close connection with the imperial ideological and monumental program of the Flavian rulers as visible and accessible within the city of Rome, most particularly in the years immediately following the death and apotheosis of the emperor Titus. I shall not repeat this social-historical argument in detail, although I shall mention one dimension of it in my conclusion. Suffice it here to say that I approach Hebrews as cultivating the arts of resistance in its audience, teaching them to view and interpret the ideological monumental cityscape of imperial rule through an alternative and contrasting understanding of divine sovereignty and of their own identity and character.[7]

Because Hebrews is concerned with the cultivation of character and identity, as well as with encouraging its audience to distinct social practices, I take up the anthropological question in Hebrews, "What is the human?" but do not look for a static definition, a given upon which Hebrews builds. Rather, I look for the ways in which Hebrews has an idea of the human—the ideal human, perhaps—as one who exists in potential, as something to be shaped and constituted, to be brought into being. On the one hand, the human may be brought into being—cultivated—through the practices, affiliations, and interpretive orientation that the discourse encourages; in other words, the ideal human is brought into being by adopting that to which the rhetorical strategies of parenesis are directed. On the other hand, if the text is also performative, as a ritual practice, then we may ask how it in itself functions to constitute the human: how does it *bring the human into being*? Or to put it more precisely and to anticipate what we shall see, how does the discourse function to *complete* (*perfect, sanctify*) the human? To answer this question, I inquire particularly into the place of death (and we should properly say death and suffering) and the role of *cultus* in constituting or enacting the human. Examining these questions with regard to Hebrews requires starting with Jesus and his relation to both death and *cultus*.

The first two chapters of Hebrews are intricately concerned with establishing the place and identity of Jesus in relation to the cosmic hierarchy, his relationship as Son to the Father, and the itinerary of his coming to share in the Father's sovereignty in heaven. Much of this argument is articulated through chains of quotations from the psalms, including the quotation of Psalm 8 with which I began. Here is the larger passage in which this quotation occurs:

---

6 AITKEN, Portraying the Temple, 131–148.
7 AITKEN, Wily, 294–305.

> For it was not to angels that he [scil. God] subjected the *oikoumenē* to come, of which we are speaking. And someone somewhere has borne witness, saying, "What is the human that you remember him, or the son of the human that you care for him? You have made him for a little while lower than the angels; you have crowned him with glory and honor; you have subjected all things under his feet." For in putting everything in subject to him, he left nothing unsubjectable to him. As of now we do not yet see all things subjected to him; but we do see the one who was made for a little while lower than the angels, Jesus, because of the suffering of death crowned with glory and honor, so that by God's grace he might taste death for everyone (Heb 2:5–9).

Hebrews implies an itinerary in which Jesus travels from the heavens to earth and back again, to sit down "on the right hand of the Majesty on high" (Heb 1:3).[8] The story of divine Wisdom which underlies the exordium of the discourse in Heb 1:1–4 is here used to establish the journey of the Son, the radiance of God's glory, through whom God "created the universe," to a place lower than the angels where he shares in the sufferings of humanity and, as we will see, makes purification for sins.[9] Thereupon he makes the journey of return to the heavenly home, where he is now enthroned and crowned with glory and honor (Heb 2:9).[10] Attridge, among others, has pointed out that this sequence of preexistence, incarnation, descent, humiliation, and exaltation belongs to a classic early christological pattern,[11] which appropriates various ancient mythical soteriologies, including the plot of the hellenistic hero such as Herakles or Orpheus who descends to the underworld.[12] The concluding phrase, "that he might taste death for everyone" is particularly significant for Hebrews's Christology and anthropology. On the one hand, Jesus' experience of death is the transactional moment for his triumphal return to the heavens to share sovereignty. On the other hand, Jesus' experience of death is a key moment of *solidarity* with "everyone," that is, all humans.

This solidarity is developed further in the next verses (Heb 2:10–13):

> For it was fitting for him, for whom and through all things exist, in bringing many sons and daughters to glory, to perfect (τελειῶσαι) through sufferings the *archēgos* who leads the way to salvation. For the one who sanctifies and the ones who are sanctified are from a single source, for which reason he is not ashamed to call them brothers and sisters, say-

---

8 AITKEN, Hero, 179–188.
9 On the role of a story about divine Wisdom (especially Wis 7:26) in informing the exordium of Hebrews, see ATTRIDGE, Hebrews, 42–45; KOESTER, Hebrews, 187–188.
10 SCHENCK, Appointment, 91–117.
11 ATTRIDGE, Hebrews, 41.
12 ATTRIDGE, Hebrews, 79, with particular reference to Heb 2:10–18. See also IDEM, Liberating Death's Captives, 103–115; AITKEN, Hero, 179–188.

ing, "I shall proclaim your name to my brothers and sisters; in the midst of the assembly I shall sing your praise," (Ps 21:23) and again, "I shall trust in him," (Isa 8:17) and again, "Behold I and the children whom God gave me" (Isa 8:18).[13]

The verb τελειῶσαι, "to perfect," might be better translated "to complete" or "to bring full circle," in order to preserve the imagery of the itinerary of return.[14] Death for Jesus is the "turning post" of this itinerary, necessary to bring him home. Jesus, however, has company on this return, namely, the "sons and daughters" whom God is bringing to glory. They are enabled to share in this heavenly journey by virtue of Jesus' solidarity with them in "the suffering of death;" this solidarity is expressed here in language of kinship—in keeping with the emphasis on Jesus' status as Son—these are Jesus' brothers and sisters. The language of kinship, however, quickly switches to language of the cultic assembly, due to the parallelism in Jesus' utterance of the psalm verse, "in the midst of the assembly I sing your praise" (Heb 2:12). The argument in Hebrews has covered a lot of ground in a short space: the heavenly realm is both the place of the shared sovereignty of Father and Son and the place of cultic worship, anticipating the more extended depictions of heavenly *cultus* later in the discourse. In addition, the other two quotations on Jesus' lips in this passage, both from Isaiah 8, each function as speech acts in the context of we may call a ruler cult or an imperial *cultus*. First is Jesus' profession of fidelity to the ruler, "I shall trust in him" (Heb 2:13a), which is an oath of loyalty to the co-emperor. The second is the act of announcement and presentation in the heavenly court, "Behold I and the children whom God gave me" (Heb 2:13b). The passage presents, I argue, the event of *apotheosis*; it is striking that this *apotheosis* includes not only Jesus, but also his "brothers and sisters" who share in the glory and participate in the *cultus*.

The following verses (Heb 2:14–18) return to death as a key element in developing the theme of Jesus' solidarity with humankind:

> Now since the children share in blood and flesh, he too likewise partook of the same things so that through death he might break the power of the one who holds sway over death, that is, the devil, and might release those who by fear of death were subject to slavery through all of their lives. For he does not take hold of angels, but he does take hold of the seed of Abraham. Wherefore, he had to be likened to his brothers and sisters in every respect, so that he might become a merciful and faithful high priest in matters pertaining

---

13 Translation adapted from ATTRIDGE, Hebrews, 78.
14 NAGY, Greek Hero, 542–545.

to God, in order to make expiation for the sins of the people. For inasmuch as he himself was tested and suffered, he is able to give aid to those who are being tested.[15]

The motif of kinship is expanded here to take in bodily existence—sharing in blood and flesh—and makes it clear that the solidarity of Jesus with all humanity is in view. Mortality is necessarily part of such existence, and it is Hebrews' argument that Jesus' participation changes the power relations around death, removing the "devil's" power over death. This is one indication of Hebrews' capacity to include apocalyptic motifs in its argument.[16] Death is not abolished; Hebrews indeed is silent on the ramifications of its continued existence and regards it, I suggest, as a given of human existence. The relationship of humans to death, however, is transformed: they are liberated from "the fear of death," not from death itself, and from a life-long condition of slavery. Attridge has described this action as "liberating death's captives," interpreting the passage in terms of the heroic story of Herakles.[17] The metaphor also resonates within from the social world of manumission, freed-persons, and imperial clemency toward enslaved prisoners of war. As I have argued elsewhere, Jesus is depicted here as returning in triumph with his freed-persons in procession after him.[18]

At this point Hebrews introduces two further concepts that will motivate later lines of its argument and which assist its parenetic aims as grounds for encouragement: first, that Jesus makes expiation for the sins of the people, and second, that Jesus' solidarity in suffering and temptation is a help for those (i.e., all humanity) who are being tested. These two concepts look ahead to Hebrews' use of Psalm 95 and the foundational legend of the Israelites in the wilderness and their entry into the land of promise. Hebrews uses this scriptural material to distinguish between the "ancestors" who died in the wilderness because of disobedience and disloyalty and the addressees of the discourse, "you," addressed throughout and to whom the possibility of entering the promised land is opened because of Jesus' work.[19] In making this distinction, Heb 3:11 cites God's oath in Psalm 95:11, "They shall not enter into my rest," with reference to failure of the Israelites to enter the promised land. Hebrews, however, retains the motif of entry into the promised "rest" to characterize parenetically the goal of the journey for the audience ("rest" and "the promised land" are narrative

---

15 Translation from ATTRIDGE, Hebrews, 78.
16 See, e.g., MACKIE, Eschatology; NONGBRI, Condemnation.
17 ATTRIDGE, Liberating Death's Captives, 103.
18 AITKEN, Portraying the Temple, 144.
19 On the importance of the wilderness journey to the promised land as a structural narrative for Hebrews, see particularly KÄSEMANN, Wandering People.

metaphors equivalent in Hebrews to the heavenly court and sanctuary). In order for the audience to be able to "enter," a different situation has to pertain for them than did for the wilderness generation; the "sin" of the wilderness generation has to be addressed and expiated in order for the way to be opened. Once it has been opened, through Jesus' death understood thus in terms of expiatory sacrifice, the audience has an opportunity—almost literally a window of opportunity—of entering as part of Jesus' processional entry. Again using the language of Psalm 95, this opportunity is named as "today": "Today, if you hear his voice, do not harden your hearts as in the rebellion" (Heb 3:15, citing Ps 95:7–8). Hebrews similarly recognizes the dimension of trial and temptation from the wilderness story, and aims at encouraging the audience not to give way to the temptation of disobedience and "falling away." To this end, Jesus' ability in solidarity to "help" those who are being tested (Heb 2:18) is also crucial encouragement. Without it, they are more apt to fall away, to lose the opportunity of entrance, and to "die" in the wilderness (Heb 3:17). Here, "death" appears to function as a metaphor derived from the narrative of the wilderness story, and not about physical mortality; it is certainly social death in terms of the community of Jesus' followers addressed by the discourse. Such social death also means, implicitly, exclusion from the heavenly *cultus* and abandonment of the solidarity that Jesus has initiated.

We have seen in Heb 2:10 that one of the consequences of Jesus' itinerary is that he is "made complete." Such "completion" is also understood as the goal of the audience's journey. In Heb 6:1, they are exhorted, "let us go on to τελειότης (perfection, completion)," and in 10:1 and 14, Jesus' expiatory work is understood as "perfecting" (τελειῶσαι) the audience. Within the framework of the anthropological question, I propose that this "completion" been seen in terms of what may be called the fullness of humanity, coming into the ideal of the human, as Hebrews understands it. The human has frailty, fallibility, and weakness, as well as being affected by sin, whether their own or the sins of the ancestors. As a result, the human has the capacity of "falling away" and not "holding fast." These characteristics recur often throughout Hebrews (e.g., 4:11; 6:6) in its construction of the present susceptible condition and proclivities of the audience. They are also conditions of the human addressed by Jesus' faithful actions, his itinerary, and his solidarity with humanity. Presumably, they are not the proclivities of the "completed" or "perfected" humans whom Jesus presents as his brothers and sisters in the heavenly court.

From the perspective of Hebrews' rhetoric, the audience has not yet reached the goal; they have not yet entered into the place of "rest," the promised land, or the heavenly sanctuary, and they are not yet made complete. In terms of the inscribed narrative of the wilderness journey, we may say that they are standing on Mount Pisgah (Deut 34:1), overlooking the promised land and having the opportunity to enter.[20] The rhetorical goal of the text is to instruct and encourage them so that they have the capacities and orientations to enter and to be made complete. Thus, fundamental to Hebrews' argument is a notion of the human as having potential. The question that follows from this conclusion is what, according to Hebrews, does the human have the potential to be?

One of the answers to this question is supplied by the extended quotation of Jer 31:31–34 in Heb 8:8–12. This quotation structurally answers the similarly extended quotation of Psalm 95 in Heb 3, in that it declares in Jeremiah's words the "fresh covenant" that God makes with the people, which is not like the covenant that God made with their ancestors in the wilderness (Heb 8:9, quoting Jer 31:32). Its placement functions to define "completion" in covenantal terms: such is the life open to the audience through their holding fast to Jesus. The declaration of the covenant relationship in Heb 8:10 with the words of Jer 31:33, "I shall be their God and they shall be my people," also defines the potential of humanity to be the people of God in covenantal relationship.[21] We may note too the close parallelism between this covenant formula concerning the people and the use of an adoption formula for Jesus in Heb 1:5, "I will be his father, and he shall be my son," utilizing the words of 2Sam 7:14; it is for this that Jesus is brought full circle through his suffering and solidarity. In both cases, the relationship of belonging to God is the goal of the journey and what being completed entails.

We have observed the role that death and *cultus* play in terms of Hebrews' understanding of Jesus; accordingly we ask what death and *cultus* have to do with the completion of humanity. How are death and *cultus* constitutive of the human in Hebrews? I turn first to *cultus* and its depiction in Heb 12:22–24 where we find Hebrews' fullest description of the heavenly sanctuary. In terms of parenetic rhetoric, the splendor of this place is here displayed to attract the audience to it as a goal. Its capacity as a place for festal worship is emphasized as is also the means for the cultic assembly's restored relationship. The inscribed audience is told that they have come "to Mount Zion and to the city of the living God, the heavenly Jerusalem, and to innumerable angels in festal gathering, and to the assembly of the first-born who are enrolled in heaven, and to a judge who is God of all, and to the spirits of the just made perfect, and to

---

[20] In other words, just as in the final chapter of Deuteronomy Moses is portrayed as ascending Mount Nebo "to the top of Pisgah," from where God shows him the entire promised land before he dies and before the Israelites enter the land, so too the audience of Hebrews is given a vision of the promised "rest," from the vantage point of being on the verge of entering.
[21] BALTZER, Covenant Formulary, 28; AITKEN, Jesus' Death, 136–140.

Jesus the mediator of a new covenant, and to the sprinkled blood that speaks more graciously than the blood of Abel" (12:22–24).[22]

This place of cultic assembly is explicitly contrasted with another—that to which the audience has *not* come: "For you have *not* come to what may be touched, a blazing fire and darkness and gloom and a tempest and the sound of a trumpet and a voice whose words made the heavens entreat that no further messages be spoken to them" (Heb 12:18–19).[23] The characterization of this place is drawn directly from the description of Mount Sinai in Exodus 19 and 20. Although this mountain is—in Exodus—the site for encountering God, Hebrews does not employ it allegorically as an earthly counterpart of a heavenly reality. Rather, it functions in tandem with the picture of God's fiery judgment in Hebrews 10 to create an apocalyptic picture of an end to be avoided.

This terrifying image of fire is combined with earthquake in Heb 12:25–26, and Heb 12:26 quotes Haggai 2:6, "[God's] voice then shook the earth; but now he has promised, 'Yet once more I will shake not only the earth but also the heaven.'"[24] This image contrasts with the picture of restoration and the true lasting cult site. The exhortation to perseverance in Hebrews 12 ends with the statement "for our God is a consuming fire." I propose that this axiom, quoting Deuteronomy (4:24; 9:3), functions not simply as a warning to the audience against rejecting God (12:25) but also as a critique of those whom the text casts as "enemies" (10:30), much as it does in Deut 9:3 in reference to the enemies of the people of God. Thus Hebrews identifies fire and earthquake as aspects of God, but does not locate them in the heavenly cult site. Instead, fire and earthquake serve to indicate both divine judgment and the destructibility of all that does not participate in the true cult. In this way, *cultus* is constitutive of the human made perfect.

The inscribed audience is to find their way into the heavenly sanctuary, maintaining solidarity with Jesus and one another, by means of πίστις, which I translate, following Dieter Georgi's suggestion, as loyalty, with attention to its

---

22 ἀλλὰ προσεληλύθατε Σιὼν ὄρει καὶ πόλει θεοῦ ζῶντος, Ἰερουσαλὴμ ἐπουρανίῳ, καὶ μυριάσιν ἀγγέλων, πανηγύρει καὶ ἐκκλησίᾳ πρωτοτόκων ἀπογεγραμμένων ἐν οὐρανοῖς καὶ κριτῇ θεῷ πάντων καὶ πνεύμασι δικαίων τετελειωμένων καὶ διαθήκης νέας μεσίτῃ Ἰησοῦ καὶ αἵματι ῥαντισμοῦ κρεῖττον λαλοῦντι παρὰ τὸν Ἄβελ.
23 οὐ γὰρ προσεληλύθατε ψηλαφωμένῳ καὶ κεκαυμένῳ πυρὶ καὶ γνόφῳ καὶ ζόφῳ καὶ θυέλλῃ καὶ σάλπιγγος ἤχῳ καὶ φωνῇ ῥημάτων, ἧς οἱ ἀκούσαντες παρῃτήσαντο μὴ προστεθῆναι αὐτοῖς λόγον.
24 οὗ ἡ φωνὴ τὴν γῆν ἐσάλευσεν τότε, νῦν δὲ ἐπήγγελται λέγων· ἔτι ἅπαξ ἐγὼ σείσω οὐ μόνον τὴν γῆν ἀλλὰ καὶ τὸν οὐρανόν.

Latin equivalent *fides* and its socio-political uses.²⁵ It is important to ask, however, what are the techniques whereby such loyalty is depicted and displayed for the audience of Hebrews. We have already noted Jesus' declaration of loyalty when he enters the heavenly court in Heb 2:13, expressed in terms of his solidarity with humanity. In addition, Hebrews 11 plays a crucial role in displaying such loyalty, with its long catalogue of heroes, those scriptural ancestors who by πίστις, "were attested" (ἐμαρτυρήθησαν, Heb 11:2). These figures form "the cloud of witnesses" (Heb 12:1) surrounding the inscribed audience and functioning as their encouragement as they look to Jesus and are thus enabled to enter the heavenly sanctuary. They also provide a portrayal of human solidarity with one another.

Jesus' solidarity with humankind was in the suffering of death; death was also a critical dimension of his itinerary and coming full circle. The question that follows from this aspect of Hebrews' argument is the following: In what way is death also constitutive of the human made complete, the "perfected" human? In this respect, Hebrews undertakes an unusual twist to its argument and places the emphasis on solidarity, indeed solidarity in suffering, rather than death per se.²⁶ Of the few indications of ethical practice in this discourse most are marked by the practice of solidarity with those who are suffering. In Heb 10:32–34, the audience is urged to recall "those earlier days, when after you had been enlightened, you endured a hard struggle with sufferings, sometimes being publicly exposed to abuse and persecution, and sometimes being partners (κοινωνοί) with those so treated. For you had compassion for those who were in prison, and you cheerfully accepted the plundering of your possessions, knowing that you yourselves possessed something better and more lasting." Similarly, in Heb 13:1–3 the audience is exhorted to "let love within the community (φιλαδελφία) continue. Do not neglect to show hospitality to strangers, for by doing so some have entertained angels without knowing it. Remember those who are in prison, as though you were in prison with them; those who are being tortured as though you yourselves were in [their] body." Important in these passages is the ethic of adopting the situation of another as one's own. It is an ethic of crossing a boundary, into the world of another, and in particular, into a situation of imprisonment, torture, abuse, and persecution. In this sense, it may be characterized more specifically as an ethic of crossing an important civic

---

25 GEORGI, Theocracy, 83–84.
26 It would be fair to say that Hebrews de-emphasizes individualization. That is, Hebrews thinks of the human in terms of the social body. Even though the choice to enter into solidarity may in practice be that of an individual, Hebrews consistently addresses not the individual human, but rather the social body of its audience.

boundary from the world of perceived honor into the world of shame—all in the service of solidarity in suffering. As the audience makes this journey, they learn a new language: they learn to call what is shameful the vehicle of receiving honor, even as Jesus' shame enabled him to be crowned with honor (Heb 2:9).[27] It is, I suggest, an ethic of being πολύτροπος, multiform or protean, capable of shifting into identity with the suffering and persecuted (as if you yourself were in their body), and sufficiently versatile to negotiate the crossing of civic boundaries. Such an ethic may indeed be signaled by the use of the adverb πολυτρόπως in the opening verse of Hebrews (1:1), in given its resonance in the Greek poetic tradition.[28]

In the concluding paraenesis, Hebrews urges the audience, "let us go out (ἐξερχώμεθα) to Jesus outside the camp and bear the disgrace he bore" (Heb 13:13). This exhortation "to go out" stands in stark contrast to the language of "go in" which has marked the rest of Hebrews (e.g., 4:1; 10:19). Suddenly, it seems that the audience is not to go in, but to go out. But Jesus' suffering "outside the [city] gate" (Heb 13:12) identifies his suffering—his solidarity with humanity—as an act of crossing civic boundaries. In order to maintain this solidarity with Jesus, so that they too might enter in the heavenly sanctuary and participate in the heavenly *cultus*, the audience must also cross these civic boundaries. They do so by their practices of solidarity with those who are suffering and bearing abuse. In other words, they can "go in" only by "going out."[29]

In advocating these practices, Hebrews seeks to develop and encourage a certain way of being in its audience. By these practices of shape-shifting,

---

27 DeSilva, Perseverance, uses the cultural polarities of honor and shame as his primary interpretive framework for the discourse as a whole. I do not adopt honor and shame as a thoroughgoing motif for reading Hebrews, but rather recognize these as one set of markers for the community's journey.
28 πολύτροπος is the epithet used of Odysseus in the opening line of the Odyssey, denoting, in the words of Gregory Nagy, his "prodigious adaptability in myth," as the "ultimate multiform;" see Nagy, Greek Hero, 312; I discuss Hebrews's use of πολυτρόπως at greater length in Aitken, Homerizon.
29 Koester, Outside the Camp, 301–303, argues that the exhortation to "go outside the camp" is a call "neither to lead an unworldly life as a member of a heavenly city, nor to escape from this world and life as soon as possible." Rather, according to Koester's reading, it is an appeal to a "radical openness to the challenges and sufferings that necessarily result from the existence 'outside the camp,'" that is, in "the acceptance of the secular reality." This is an anti-cultic interpretation, which contrasts cultic performances with acts of "thanksgiving and charity." My argument builds on Koester's emphasis on "outside the camp" as a place of profound engagement with the sufferings that come as a result of living in the world. I stress, however, that this ethic is one of movement into solidarity with the situation of the other who is suffering and "bearing reproach."

boundary-crossing, traveling into solidarity with the suffering, the audience may initiate an alternative culture, take on different social relations, and create a new identity for themselves[30]—which is defined also as being in solidarity with Jesus whose journey was itself marked with suffering and struggle.[31] It is an *askēsis* suitable for travel and travail on the journey; it is an *askēsis* of being πολύτροπος, multiform, shape-shifting, and versatile. These capacities are part of the potential of the human being, as Hebrews develops its anthropology.

Death—Jesus' death—is constitutive of the human according to Hebrews' logic. As though in covenantal response, humans' solidarity with one another in suffering, which "going to Jesus outside the camp and bearing the abuse he bore" signals, is likewise constitutive of the fullness of humanity—being the people of God. The circle of Hebrews' argument brings its audience to this recognition; it is one of its central parenetic goals. Moreover, Jesus' cultic action—his expiatory offering (indicated in Hebrews 2 and developed in great detail in Hebrews 9–10) and his triumphal entry into the heavenly assembly, there to declare his fidelity and present his "brothers and sisters"—is also constitutive of the human according to Hebrews' logic. And again in covenantal response, humans' participation in the *cultus* (both outside the city gate and in the heavens) comes to constitute their full humanity and their participation in Jesus' apotheosis.

At the outset of this discussion I posed the following question: If we understand Hebrews not only as parenesis, but also as performative, as a ritual practice, then how does it in itself function to constitute the human? At this point, I can only sketch a way of exploring this question. Humankind, according to Hebrews' logic, needs the capacities to be faithful, to maintain *pistis*, "to see Jesus," and to hold fast to Jesus. Humankind needs to cultivate the capacities for solidarity and for being the people of God. It is helpful, following Gregory Nagy's approach to the Homeric *ainoi* or enigmatic stories,[32] to think of these capacities in three categories: the affiliative, the ethical, and the intellectual. Or in Greek terms, humans need to be *philoi*, *agathoi*, and *sophoi* in order to be fitting, "meet and right," for participation in the *cultus* (including receiving the cultic narrative). The ethic of solidarity in Hebrews aims at constituting humanity with the proper affiliative and ethical capacities; the effect of the rhetoric itself and the occasion of performance may also contribute to the development

---

[30] VALANTASIS, Social Function, 548.550; AITKEN, Hero, 179–188.
[31] On the ethic of solidarity within the community as a stance of resistance to the imperial Flavian triumphal ideology and theology, see AITKEN, Portraying, 141–146.
[32] NAGY, Greek Hero, 69.

of affiliative bonds. As speech acts or performative utterances, the declaration of covenant partnership, the words of presentation in the heavenly court, and the statement "But you have come to Mount Zion" to the cultic assembly all have the potential to constitute the audience as humans made complete, as the holy people of God, *philoi* to God and one another. Such solidarity also defines the ethical, that is, what it takes to be *agathoi*.

This performative approach to Hebrews would also consider how the practices of scriptural interpretation performed throughout the text constitute the audience as *sophoi*, that is, how Hebrews creates within its audience the capacity for reading scripture "aright" so that they see Jesus at every turn. That is, through following the discourse they learned to read the scriptures of Israel in terms of Jesus and with reference to their own covenantal relationship made possible through Jesus. I would also suggest, based on arguments that I have made elsewhere, that through similar means Hebrews creates within its audience the capacity for reading the monumental cityscape of Flavian Rome "aright" so that there too they see Jesus at every turn.[33] In other words, as a performative discourse as well as in its parenetic dimensions Hebrews cultivates arts of resistance and arts of memory within its audience as part of what it takes to become human, to maintain fidelity, to share in the sufferings of others, and thus to participate in the *cultus* of heaven.

Bibliography

AITKEN, Ellen Bradshaw, Portraying the Temple in Stone and Text. The Arch of Titus and the Epistle to the Hebrews, in: Gelardini, Gabriella (Hg.), Hebrews. Contemporary Methods—New Insights (Biblical Interpretation Series 75), Leiden/Boston, Massachusetts 2005, 131–148 (originally published in 2001).

AITKEN, Ellen Bradshaw, The Hero in the Epistle to the Hebrews. Jesus as an Ascetic Model, in: Warren, David/Brock, Ann Graham/Pao, David (Hg.), Early Christian Voices. In Texts, Traditions, and Symbols. Essays in Honor of François Bovon (Biblical Interpretations Series 66), Leiden/Boston, Massachusetts 2003, 179–188.

AITKEN, Ellen Bradshaw, Jesus' Death in Early Christian Memory. The Poetics of the Passion (NTOA/SUNT 32), Göttingen/Fribourg 2004.

AITKEN, Ellen Bradshaw, An Early Christian Homerizon? Decoy, Direction, and Doxology, in: Armstrong, Richard/Dué, Casey (Hg.), The Homerizon. Conceptual Interrogations in Homeric Studies, in: Classics@: An Online Journal 3 (2006), http://chs.harvard.edu/wa/pageR?tn=ArticleWrapper&bdc=12&mn=1309.

---

33 AITKEN, Portraying the Temple.

AITKEN, Ellen Bradshaw, Wily, Wise, and Worldly. Instruction and the Formation of Character in the Epistle to the Hebrews, in: Henderson, Ian/Oegema, Gerbern S. (Hg.), The Changing Face of Judaism. Christianity and Other Greco-Roman Religions in Antiquity (Jüdische Schriften aus hellenistisch-römischer Zeit, Studien 2; Studies in Christianity and Judaism 10), Gütersloh 2006, 294–305.

ATTRIDGE, Harold W., The Epistle to the Hebrews (Hermeneia), Philadelphia, Pennsylvania 1989.

ATTRIDGE, Harold W., Liberating Death's Captives. Reconsideration of an Early Christian Myth, in: Goehring, James E. et al. (Hg.), Gnosticism and the Early Christian World. In Honor of James M. Robinson, Sonoma, California 1990, 103–115.

ATTRIDGE, Harold W., Paraenesis in a Homily (λόγος παρακλήσεως), in: Semeia 50 (1990) 211–226.

ATTRIDGE, Harold W., Giving Voice to Jesus. Use of the Psalms in the New Testament, in: Attridge, Harold W./Fassler, Margot Elsbeth (Hg.), Psalms in Community. Jewish and Christian Textual, Liturgical, and Artistic Traditions (SBLSS 25), Atlanta, Georgia 2003, 101–112.

BALTZER, Klaus, The Covenant Formulary in Old Testament, Jewish, and Early Christian Writings (Original title: Das Bundesformular [1964]), Philadelphia, Pennsylvania 1971.

BLACK, C. Clifton, The Rhetorical Form of the Hellenistic Jewish and Early Christian Sermon. A Response to Lawrence Wills [77:277–299 1984], in: HTR 81 (1988) 1–18.

DESILVA, David A., Perseverance in Gratitude. A Socio-Rhetorical Commentary on the Epistle "to the Hebrews", Grand Rapids, Michigan 2000.

GEORGI, Dieter, Theocracy in Paul's Praxis and Theology, Minneapolis, Minnesota 1991.

KÄSEMANN, Ernst, The Wandering People of God. An Investigation of the Letter to the Hebrews (Original Title: Das wandernde Gottesvolk. Eine Untersuchung zum Hebräerbrief [1957]), Minneapolis, Minnesota 1984.

KOESTER, Craig R., Hebrews. A New Translation with Introduction and Commentary (AB 36), New York 2001.

KOESTER, Helmut, "Outside the Camp". Hebrews 13:9-14, in: HThR 55 (1962) 299–315.

KUSS, Otto, Der Verfasser des Hebräerbriefes als Seelsorger, in: TTZ 67 (1958) 1–12.65–80.

MACKIE, Scott, Eschatology and Exhortation in the Epistle to the Hebrews (WUNT II 223), Tübingen 2007.

MACRAE, George W., Heavenly Temple and Eschatology in the Letter to the Hebrews, in: Semeia 12 (1978) 179–199.

NAGY, Gregory, The Ancient Greek Hero in 24 Hours, Cambridge, Massachusetts/London 2013.

NONGBRI, Brent, A Touch of Condemnation in a Word of Exhortation. Apocalyptic Language and Graeco-Roman Rhetoric in Hebrews 6:4–12, in: NovT 45 (2003) 265–279.

SCHENCK, Kenneth, Keeping His Appointment. Creation and Enthronement in Hebrews, in: JSNT 66 (1997) 91–117.

VALANTASIS, Richard, A Theory of the Social Function of Asceticism, in: Wimbush, Vincent/Valantasis, Richard (Hg.), Asceticism, New York/Oxford 1995, 544–552.

WILLS, Lawrence, The Form of the Sermon in Hellenistic Judaism and Early Christianity, in: HTR 77 (1984) 280–283.

Part III: **Greco-Roman and Egyptian Literature**

Wolfgang Spickermann
Trauer und Tod in der 2. Sophistik am Beispiel des Lukian von Samosata[1]

„Es sollte [beim Sterben] nämlich dabei der Reihe nach vorgegangen werden, der ältere vorher sterben und hernach jeder nach seinem Alter, keineswegs es umgekehrt sein, nicht, während die schönsten und kräftigsten Jünglinge sterben, der übermäßig alte Mann weiter leben, der nur mehr drei Zähne übrig hat, nur mit Mühe sieht, auf vier Diener gestützt gebückt geht, die Nase voller Rotz, die Augen voller Augenbutter hat, der kein Vergnügen mehr kennt und von den jungen Leuten als lebender Leichnam verlacht wird; da könnte es wirklich heißen: Die Flüsse fließen aufwärts!" So beschwert sich der schon mit 30 Jahren gestorbene Terpsion beim Totengott Pluto in den Totengesprächen des Lukian von Samosata.[2] Dieser hat darüber hinaus eine kleine satirische Lehrrede für ein breiteres Publikum (Diatribe) über Tod und Trauer verfasst (*De luctu*), welche einen wichtigen Beitrag zur intellektuellen Beurteilung von Trauerriten im 2. Jahrhundert n. Chr. darstellt. Im Folgenden soll 1. zunächst Lukian kurz vorgestellt werden, dann 2. auf seine Adressaten, sein Publikum eingegangen werden, 3. wird versucht, seine Kritik an den Vorstellungen vom Totenreich zu skizzieren, 4. soll seine Einstellung zu einem grausamen Tod und dessen Inszenierung durch den Scharlatan Peregrinos analysiert werden, um dann 5. seine Auffassung zu Trauer und Totenkult, besonders am Beispiel seiner gleichnamigen Rede, darzustellen.

1 Leben und Werk

Geboren zwischen 115 und 125 n. Chr., bezeichnet er sich selbst in der *Dea Syria* als Assyrer,[3] während er sich anderenorts „Syrer" oder sogar „Barbar" nennt.[4] Ein hellenisierter Syrer kann zugleich Ethnographie des eigenen Territoriums

---

[1] Mein Beitrag „Tod und Jenseits am Beispiel des Lukian von Samosata", in: Gordon, R./Spickermann, W./Waldner, K. (Hg.), Burial and Afterlife, Stuttgart (in Vorbereitung), ist in einigen Abschnitten identisch, zielt aber auf Jenseitsvorstellungen und den Vergleich mit dem frühchristlichen Apologetiker Tatian.
[2] D.Mort. 16[6]. Übersetzung MRAS. Diese und alle folgenden Zitationen aus dem Werk Lukians richten sich nach dem Abkürzungsverzeichnis NESSELRATH, Lukianos, 495.
[3] Syr.D. 1,8.
[4] LIGHTFOOT, Lukian, 205.

betreiben und, gleichsam in den Fußstapfen des Herodot, in der *Dea Syria* als Tourist aus hellenischer Sicht die „barbarischen" Riten in Hierapolis beschreiben. Letztlich wissen wir aber nicht ganz genau, wie es sich mit den Ich-Erzählern der lukianischen Schriften genau verhält und inwieweit sich hier Fiktion und Biographisches vermischen.[5] Sicher ist jedoch, dass Lukian in Samosata am Ufer des Euphrats am östlichen Rand des römischen Syrien geboren wurde. Er erhielt in Ionien seine rhetorische Ausbildung[6] und kam dann als Wanderredner nach Italien und Gallien.[7] Im Jahre 163/164 hielt er sich vielleicht in Antiochia auf, wo er um die Gunst des sich von 161–166 auf dem Partherfeldzug befindlichen Kaisers Lucius Verus geworben zu haben scheint. Möglicherweise war er zuvor 161/162 n. Chr. in Samosata gewesen.[8] Bald darauf spielt die von ihm selbst geschilderte Auseinandersetzung mit dem Orakelpropheten Alexander von Abonuteichos (*Alexander oder der Lügenprophet*). Die von ihm ebenfalls beschriebene Selbstverbrennung des pythagoreischen Kynikers Peregrinos in Olympia datiert 165 n. Chr. Um diese Zeit bis in die 70er Jahre muss sich Lukian in Athen aufgehalten haben, wo er zahlreiche Schriften verfasste. Später scheint er in der Provinzialbürokratie Ägyptens tätig gewesen zu sein.[9] Da er die Divinisierung Marc Aurels im *Alexander* noch erwähnt, muss er nach 180 gestorben sein.[10]

Die Vorrede (Prolalia) *Herakles* lässt ihn als alten Mann erscheinen, sie nimmt die erneute Aufnahme einer Redetätigkeit zum Anlass. Als alter Mann erscheint er auch in den Vorrede *Dionysos* (Bacch.) sowie in seinen autobiographischen Essays *Apologia* (Apol.) und *Zur Verteidigung eines Fehlers in der Anrede* (Laps.). Insgesamt kennen wir von ihm acht Vorreden, mit denen er seine Vortragsdarbietungen zu eröffnen pflegte: *Der Geschichtsschreiber Herodot* oder *Der Maler Aetion* (Herod.), *Der Aulos-Spieler Harmonides* (Harm.), *Der Skythe* (Skyth.), *Über die Dipsas-Schlangen* (Dips.), *Über Bernstein* (Electr.), *Der Maler Zeuxis* oder: *Der König Antiochos* (Zeux.). Hinzu kommen einige kleine Schriften, bei denen es sich um geistreich-paradoxe Spielereien handelt. Anders stellt die *Dea Syria* eine Schrift zu einem zeitgenössischen Phänomen dar, wenn man so will die erste systematische religionshistorische Schrift. Zu den erzählenden Schriften gehören ebenfalls die *Wahren Geschichten*, in denen der Ich-Erzähler

---

5 Ebd.
6 Bis Acc. 27.
7 Bis Acc. 27; ferner Apol. 15.
8 LIGHTFOOT, Lukian, 208.
9 Apol. 12.
10 NESSELRATH, Lukianos, 493.

münchhausenhafte Reisen zu märchenhaften Orten schildert, was sich vor allem gegen die zeitgenössischen utopisch-abenteuerlichen Reiseromane richtete.

Teilt man das umfangreiche Oeuvre Lukians systematisch ein, so kann man zwischen rhetorischen Schriften, Dialogen, menippischen Schriften (satirische Dialoge mit dem Kyniker Menippos von Gadara aus dem 3. Jahrhundert v. Chr.), erzählenden Schriften und Pamphleten über zeitgenössische Phänomene unterscheiden. Unter letzteren befinden sich die schon erwähnte Schilderung der Selbstverbrennung des Peregrinos, *Alexander oder der Lügenprophet*, *Über die, die für Lohn Unterricht halten*, die Beschreibung der unwürdigen Existenz griechischer Philosophen in den Häusern reicher Römer, *Gegen den Ungebildeten, der viele Bücher kauft* oder aber *Wie man Geschichte schreiben soll*, eine Auseinandersetzung mit der zeitgenössischen Historiographie zum gerade tobenden Partherkrieg.[11]

Die Diatriben *De luctu* (Über die Trauer) und *De sacrificiis* (Über die Opfer) sind in hellenistischer Tradition abgefasste kleine unterhaltsame Belehrungen für ein größeres Publikum. Da Lukian sich zu allem und jedem häufig satirisch und in einem gefälligen, schon feuilletonistischen Stil geäußert hat, waren seit der zweiten Hälfte des 19. Jahrhunderts konservative Altphilologen und Althistoriker, deren Disziplinen sich in dieser Zeit etablierten, lange Zeit geneigt, einem solchen Autor jedwede Glaubwürdigkeit abzusprechen.[12] Unterstützt wird dies dadurch, dass er von seinen Zeitgenossen so gut wie nicht zitiert ist und sich auch nicht bei Philostrat (* um 165/170; † zwischen 244 und 249 n. Chr.) findet, der die wichtigen Vertreter der zweiten Sophistik behandelt.[13] Diese Verurteilung ist heute einer differenzierteren Auffassung gewichen, wobei die Intention des lukianischen Oeuvres nach wie vor umstritten bleibt. Während die einen in Lukian einen Kritiker politischer, kultureller und sozialer Zustände seiner Zeit sehen wollen, relativieren andere die Aktualität seiner Schriften und stellen eher seinen Klassizismus in den Vordergrund. Graham Anderson bezieht hier eine vermittelnde Position.[14]

---

11 NESSELRATH, Lukianos, 497.
12 Hierzu besonders HELM, Lucian und Menipp; vgl. DERS., Lukianos, 1771–1773, über die Charakterschwäche Lukians. Auch BETZ, Lukian und das Neue Testament, 6, nimmt diese Wertung auf, wenn er schreibt, dass man bei Lukians Charakter nicht erwarten dürfe, dass er sich um genauere Informationen über die Christen bemüht habe.
13 Philostr. soph. Vgl. dazu NESSELRATH, Vorwort, VIII.
14 ANDERSON, Lucian. Tradition, mit einem Überblick über die bisherigen Forschungskontroversen.

2 Lukian und sein Publikum

Es ist in der Tat ein Problem, wenn Lukian seine Leser immer wieder in die Irre führt, eben noch als sicher Geglaubtes in Frage stellt und man immer begründete Zweifel haben muss, ob es sich bei dem Ich-Erzähler tatsächlich um den Autor handelt.

Wenden wir uns zunächst einmal dem literarischen Genre zu, in welchem sich Lukian bewegt. Die „zweite Sophistik"—der Begriff stammt von Philostrat— war mit einer Wertschätzung der Gelehrsamkeit verbunden, die nicht auf einen bestimmten Themenkreis beschränkt war. Es war dem „Viel-Wissen", der πολιμάθεια, förderlich, sich gelegentlich mit einer scheinbar beiläufigen Literatur zu beschäftigen, und so kam es zu der sogenannten „Buntschriftstellerei", zu Werken, die ihren Stoff in einer bewusst unterschiedslosen Reihenfolge präsentierten. Vor diesem Hintergrund ist man versucht, angesichts seines großen Themenspektrums das gesamte Oeuvre des Lukian als Vielschreiberei zu charakterisieren. Dennoch ist das Primat der Rhetorik durchaus erkennbar, die er aber immer mit anderen Formen zu verbinden versteht. Sein griechischer Stil ist exzellent, ja er schafft mit der menippischen Satire oder der geschickten Verbindung von Formen philosophischer Dialog-Komödien Neues.[15] Im Vordergrund scheint ihm aber zu stehen, mit dem klassischen Bildungsgut kunstvoll zu spielen und der Gesellschaft im römischen Reich den Spiegel vorzuhalten: einer Gesellschaft, die sich immer wieder selbst wie in einer öffentlichen Theateraufführung inszeniert, die Formen eines hierarchisch gelenkten öffentlichen Diskurses entwickelt, der wie im Theater an ein Publikum gerichtet ist. So muss man vor allem die satirischen Schriften Lukians nach Tim Whitmarsh gleichsam als im theatralen Raum an ein imaginäres Publikum gerichtet sehen. Im Theater repräsentiert sich die lokale Gesellschaft in ihrer Hierarchie allein schon durch die Sitzordnung. Die Darbietung ist entsprechend ausgerichtet und trifft entweder den Zeitgeschmack oder nicht. Lukian scheint seine Themen für diese Art der Kommunikation im Rahmen eines Schauspiels ausgewählt zu haben.

Seine Themen mussten in das Bildungsideal eines kultivierten Umfeldes, welches literarische Formen pflegt, passen, aber gleichzeitig auch ein größeres Publikum ansprechen. Wie im Theater geht es aber nicht um die bloße Darstellung der Fakten. Es geht vielmehr um das Erzählen von Geschichten sowie Dialoge und das Vortragen von Reden auf hohem Niveau. Nicht alles muss buchstabengetreu der Wahrheit entsprechen, aber es muss doch glaubwürdig

---

15 Prom. Es. 5–6.

bleiben. Auch wenn Lukian mit seinem *Nigrinus* den Konflikt zwischen dem frei lebenden, wahrheitsliebenden Philosophen und der wirtschaftlichen und sozialen Macht Roms darstellt, welche die griechischen Philosophen von den Reichen abhängig macht, stellt er dieses System doch nicht grundsätzlich infrage. Rom ist aufgrund seiner Macht das neue Athen, das Zentrum der Patronage für Philosophen. So ist es ein reichsrömisches Publikum, welches angesprochen werden muss und das auch die Sujets bestimmt.[16] Lukian war ein Meister darin, Belehrendes und Unterhaltendes zusammenzubringen.

3 Das Bild vom Hades

In der Necyomanteia, die den Abstieg des kynischen Wanderphilosophen Menippos in die Unterwelt beschreibt und die an den Hadesbesuch des Odysseus angelehnt ist, macht Menippos in Babylon die Bekanntschaft des Chaldäers Mithrobazanes, den er mit einem Honorar beliebiger Höhe dazu bewegen kann, ihn auf seine Katabasis vorzubereiten. Es folgen zahlreiche Reinigungsriten und das Anlegen magischer Gewänder, bis die beiden ein Boot mit den magischen Requisiten beladen, ein Sumpfgebiet am Euphrat durchqueren und dort wie einst Odysseus eine Opfergrube graben und das Blut der mitgebrachten Opfertiere darin auffangen. Dann beginnt die Show des Magiers: „Während dieses Opfers rief der Magus mit einer brennenden Fackel in der Hand, nicht mehr mit leiser Stimme, sondern so laut, als er aus voller Brust zu schreien vermochte, alle Götter der Hölle auf, die Poinen und die Erinnyen, die nächtliche Hekate und die furchtbare Persephone, denen er noch verschiedene barbarische Namen beifügte, die ich nicht verstehen konnte."[17]

Eine ähnliche Episode schildert der Gastgeber Eukrates in der Schrift *Die Lügenfreunde oder der Ungläubige* (Philopseudes sive Incredulus). In dieser besucht Tychiades, der in mehreren Schriften Lukians als sein Alter Ego auftritt, den gichtkranken Eukrates an seinem Krankenbett und trifft dort außer dem behandelnden Arzt Antigonos mehrere bekannte Philosophen, den Peripathetiker Kleodemos, den Stoiker Deinomachos und den Platoniker Ion, an. Da es dem Eukrates schon besser geht—die Gicht ist in die Füße gerutscht—entwickelt sich ein lebhaftes Gespräch. Als Tychiades, der Skeptiker, die von den Philosophen empfohlenen völlig abstrusen Vorschläge zur Heilung des Gichtanfalls als abergläubisch entlarvt, ja ins Lächerliche zieht, wird er von dem Arzt Antigonos

---

16 Vgl. WHITMARSH, Greek Literature, 265–270.
17 Nec. 6,17–8,6.

zunächst unterstützt. Um Tychiades dann aber von der Tatsache zu überzeugen, dass Magie und Zauberwissen wirksam sind, erzählen die Philosophen und der Hausherr Wundergeschichten, die Tychiades stets mit spöttischen Kommentaren versieht und als offensichtliche Lügengeschichten entlarvt. Selbst die Gespenstergeschichte des später hinzukommenden Pythagoräers Arignotos, den man den Heiligen nennt, und auch die Geschichte von einer wandelnden Statue des Hippokrates, die der Arzt zum Besten gibt, vermag ihn nicht zu überzeugen. Tychiades verlässt schließlich die Gesellschaft, als der Hausherr in Anwesenheit seiner hinzugekommenen beiden jungen Söhne immer unglaublichere Geschichten erzählt. Eine wichtige Rolle spielt darin sein Hadeserlebnis. Eukrates erlebt während der Weinlese auf dem Lande ein Erdbeben und steht plötzlich der Hekate gegenüber, die ihn mit ihren Hunden, die größer sind als Elefanten, bedroht. Durch das Drehen eines Zauberrings mit einer Gemme, den er von einem Araber erhalten hat, stampft Hekate mit ihrem Schlangenfuß auf. Es bildet sich ein Loch zum Tartarus, durch das sie verschwindet. Während Eukrates sich an einem Baum festhält, kann er in den Hades sehen: „Dann sah ich alles im Hades, den Pyriphlegeton, den See, den Kerberos und die Toten, so dass ich einige von ihnen erkannte, z.B. meinen Vater sah ich, genau noch mit jenen selben Kleidern angetan, mit denen wir ihn bestattet haben."[18] Im weiteren Verlauf seiner Schilderung beschreibt Eukrates, dass die Seelen (ψυχαί) gesondert nach Stämmen und Verbänden mit ihren Verwandten verkehren und auf der Asphodeloswiese liegen, nach der Überlieferung dem Platz für die normalen Seelen. Der Platoniker Ion bemerkt dazu, dass dann die Epikureer die Platoniker in Bezug auf die Seelen korrigieren müssten, und fragt den Hausherrn, ob er auch Sokrates und Platon gesehen habe. Dieser kann das nur im Falle des an Bauch und Glatze deutlich erkennbaren Sokrates bejahen.[19] Lukian bemüht in seiner Schilderung alle gängigen Klischees vom Hades und verbindet sie wie so oft in seinen Schriften mit einer Spitze gegen die Philosophen. Der Hades wird so beschrieben, wie ihn Homer, Hesiod und die Autoren der klassischen Tragödien ausmalen, die Toten gelangen genau so in die Unterwelt wie sie bestattet werden. Eukrates, der zu Beginn des Dialoges als sechzigjähriger Mann von hoher Glaubwürdigkeit beschrieben wird, der sich außerdem viel mit Philosophie beschäftigt hat,[20] macht sich mit einer solchen naiven Schilderung ohne jede Originalität völlig unglaubwürdig. Doch er trägt noch dicker auf, als der Zweifler Tychiades über diese Geschichte lacht. Als er einmal an einem ho-

---

18 Philops. 24.
19 Philops. 22–24.
20 Philops. 5.

hen Fieber gelitten und der Arzt Antigonos am siebenten Tag alle Besucher weggeschickt habe, sei ein schöner weiß gekleideter Jüngling zu ihm gekommen und habe ihn durch einen Schlund in den Hades geführt. Dort habe er sofort den Tantalos, Tityos und Sisyphos gesehen, die drei großen Sünder der griechischen Mythologie. Er sei dann zum Unterweltsgericht gekommen, welches von Pluto – so glaubt er – präsidiert wird und bei dem auch Aiakos, Charon, die Moiren und die Erinnyen anwesend gewesen seien. Pluto las die Namen derer vor, die sterben sollten, weil ihre Lebensfrist überschritten war. Als der Jüngling als Psychopompos des Eukrates diesen vor den Richter führte, stellte sich heraus, dass eine Verwechslung mit dem Schmied Demylos vorlag. Unser Hausherr durfte wieder zurück in sein Krankenzimmer, war vom Fieber genesen und konnte allen melden, dass der kranke Schmied aus der Nachbarschaft sterben werde, was auch geschah.[21] Die Schilderung des Totengerichts ist wieder so nah an Platons Gorgias (523a) angelehnt, dass dem gebildeten Hörer dies sofort auffallen musste, was die Glaubwürdigkeit unseres Hausherrn nicht gerade erhöht. Doch übt diese Geschichte bis in die heutigen Tage ihren Reiz auf diejenigen aus, die sich mit Nahtod-Erlebnissen beschäftigen. Obwohl ein Kunstprodukt, findet sie sich in einer im Jahr 2000 herausgegebenen Anthologie mit Erfahrungen Wiederbelebter in der Weltliteratur.[22] Es fehlt hier allerdings die anschließende Bekräftigung des Arztes Antigonos, der die Geschichte seines Patienten bestätigt, indem er sagt, dass er einen Menschen vor seinem Tod und, nachdem er nach dem zwanzigsten Tag wieder auferstanden sei, erneut behandelt habe. Unser Zweifler Tychiades fragt ihn daraufhin, warum sein Leib in zwanzig Tagen entweder nicht verwest oder er verhungert sei, wenn er nicht gerade Epimenides sei, der nach der Sage 58 Jahre lang geschlafen habe.[23] Der dadurch völlig unglaubwürdige Zusatz des Arztes stützt damit nicht die Geschichte des Eukrates, sondern diskreditiert sie vielmehr.

Auch die Schattenexistenz des Herakles im Hades und seine gleichzeitige Präsenz im Olymp werden bei Lukian hinterfragt und ad absurdum geführt.[24] Herakles ist daher auch unter den Göttern nur Metöke, da ein Teil von ihm sterblich ist. Momos, dem Gott des Tadels, wird in der Schrift *Die Götterversammlung* von Zeus untersagt, den Herakles und Asklepios als nicht rechtmäßige olympische Götter zu tadeln, weil sie seine Söhne sind.[25] Schließlich streiten sich in den Göttergesprächen die beiden Halbgötter, die beide durch Feuer um-

---

21 Philops. 25.
22 CZYCHOLL, Als ich am gestrigen Tag entschlief, 281.
23 Philops. 26.
24 D.Mort. 11[16].
25 Iupp. Trag. 32; Deor. Conc. 6.

kamen, wer den Vorsitz an der Tafel habe, den Zeus Asklepios zugesteht, weil der früher gestorben sei.[26] Herakles wird von dem Tadler Lukian/Momos als ehemaliger Sklave des sterblichen Eurystheus bezeichnet: Während letzterer sterben musste, wurde der Sklave divinisiert.[27]

In seinen schon zitierten Totengesprächen benutzt Lukian die gängigen Hadesvorstellungen als fiktiven Hintergrund, vor dem er seine Protagonisten agieren lässt, die sich im realen Leben mit einigen Ausnahmen nicht hätten treffen können. Vielfach wird dabei auch die unbefriedigende Situation der Toten in der Schattenwelt selbst aufs Korn genommen. Auf die Spitze getrieben wird dies aber jeweils in den menippischen Satiren. Die schon erwähnte Hadesfahrt des Menippos (*Necyomanteia*) beschreibt eine *Ekklēsía* der Toten im Hades. Hier wird die gesamte Verfahrensordnung der attischen Volksversammlung satirisch verzerrt dargestellt. Die Prytanen des Koinons der Toten berufen eine *Ekklēsía* ein, um die gemeinsamen Dinge zu entscheiden.[28] Ein Tagesordnungspunkt geht um die Reichen, die man der Gewalttätigkeit, der Verachtung der Gesetze des Wohlstandes und der Ungerechtigkeit beschuldigt. Einer der Demagogen liest dann sein *Psephisma* vor, die *Boule* und die *Ekklēsía* sollten für gut befinden, dass der Leib der Reichen wie alle sterbe, ihre Seelen aber für 250000 Jahre verurteilt werde, Esel zu sein und von Armen getrieben zu werden.[29] Der Antrag ist abgefasst von Kraneion, Sohn des Skeleton aus der *Deme Nekysia* und der *Phyle* Alibantis (also Kahlschädel, Sohn des Skeletts aus der *Deme* Leichenstatt von der *Phyle* der Abgestandenen). So kommt es zu einem *Psephisma* der Versammlungsleiter und des Volkes, welches dem Antrag des Kranion entspricht. Hier wird das Totengericht mit der athenischen Volksversammlung verbunden und damit zu einer Groteske.

4 Der grausame Tod und seine Inszenierung

Zu Anfang seiner Schrift *Der Fischer oder die Auferstandenen* wird Lukian unter dem Pseudonym „Freimund (*Parresiades*)" von den berühmten auferstandenen Philosophen Sokrates, Empedokles, Platon, Aristoteles, Chrysippos und Diogenes gefangengesetzt. Wegen seiner angeblichen ständigen Lästerungen der Philosophie will ihm Sokrates die Zunge herausschneiden und die Augen aus-

---

[26] D.Deor. 15[13].
[27] Deor. Conc. 7; vgl. OLIVER, Actuality, 306.
[28] Nec. 19,7–10.
[29] Vgl. auch HALL, Lucian's Satire, 230.

stechen lassen, danach soll er gegeißelt und gekreuzigt werden. Empedokles will ihn lieber in den Ätna werfen, wo er selbst ja verstarb, und Platon will ihn gar wie Pentheus und Orpheus zerreißen, damit jeder sich ein Stück mitnehmen könne.[30] Letztlich verlangt Lukian ein Gerichtsverfahren, bei dem er dann freigesprochen wird. Die Todesarten sind hier überzeichnet, um den Freispruch umso mehr herauszustellen, doch geben sie wieder, was man sich im 2. Jahrhundert n. Chr. unter einem grausamen, schändlichen Tod vorstellte.[31]

Auch der ehrenvolle Tod in der Schlacht hat nach Lukian nichts wirklich Schönes. Dem schon bejahrten persischen Satrapen Arsakes wird beispielsweise die Sarissa eines thrakischen Peltasten in den Unterleib gestoßen, mit der dieser zuvor auch sein Pferd durchbohrt hatte.[32]

Hat man nämlich ein gewisses Alter und Erben, ist der Tod durch Gift nicht selten.[33] Ja, der Totengeleiter Hermes beschwert sich bei Charon, dass früher eher mit Wunden bedeckte, in der Schlacht gestorbene (junge) Männer in die Unterwelt gekommen seien, heutzutage würden diese (alt geworden) durch Kinder und Ehefrauen vergiftet oder zögen sich Krankheiten wie Wassersucht und Gicht zu; die meisten müssten aber um des Geldes willen sterben.[34]

Ein vorbildlicher Tod ist der des Kynikers Demonax aus Athen, der am Ende seines Lebens die Nahrung verweigert und nicht begraben werden will, damit er den Hunden und Vögeln zur Nahrung diene. Dennoch wurde er von der gesamten athenischen Bürgerschaft auf das prächtigste bestattet.[35] Die Verweigerung der Nahrung galt besonders den stoischen Philosophen als ehrenvoller Tod.[36] Eine würdevolle Bestattung war dabei aber unabdingbar und nur die Kyniker konnten sich auch dieser Tradition verweigern.

Lukian nimmt in seinen beiden Satiren Phalaris auch die Überlieferung über das Musterbild eines grausamen Tyrannen, Phalaris von Akragas, auf. Mit diesem ist die Sage von einem bronzenen (ehernen) Stier verbunden, den der Künstler Perilaos für Phalaris hergestellt haben soll, um Fremdlinge und ihm verhasste Personen in seinem Bauch auf einem Feuer langsam zu rösten, wobei ihre Schmerzensschreie durch eine besondere Vorrichtung wie das Brüllen eines Stieres klangen. Als erstes Opfer soll Phalaris den Künstler selbst in den Leib des Stieres gesperrt haben und ihn dann sterbend herausgezogen und über

---

30 Pisc. 2
31 Der halbverkohlte Empedokles findet sich beispielsweise auch im Hades: D.Mort. 6[20].
32 D.Mort 27.4.
33 D.Mort. 17[7],2,1–9 (Zenophantes und Kallidemides) und 14[4], 2 (Hermes und Charon).
34 D.Mort. 14[4],2,4–13.
35 Demonax 66–67.
36 Vgl. z.B. Ps.-Lukian, Makrobii 19 (zu Zenon).

die Klippen geworfen haben.³⁷ Lukian greift dieses auf und lässt dabei in seiner ersten Rede namens Phalaris Abgeordnete des Tyrannen in Delphi auftreten, welche Apollon jene Höllenmaschine zum Geschenk antragen und den grausamen Tyrannen als einen gerechten Mann darstellen; woraufhin in der zweiten Rede namens Phalaris die Priester die Gabe des Wüterichs als gottgefälliges Opfer erklären. Die grausame Tötungsmaschine charakterisiert hier den Unmenschen Phalaris.

Der Feuertod gilt im gesamten lukianischen Oeuvre als die grausamste Todesart. Der Tod der Herakles auf dem *Oita* und seine Aufnahme in den Olymp ist dabei das klassische Vorbild. Umso schändlicher gilt Lukian die freiwillige Nachahmung durch den Scharlatan Peregrinos, den er auch Proteus nennt. Schon in den Meergöttergesprächen zweifelt Menelaos daran, dass die mythische Meeresgestalt Proteus sich in Feuer verwandeln kann. Er sieht dies als Taschenspielertrick an und hat dabei sicher auch Peregrinos im Auge.³⁸

In seiner in Form eines Briefes an einen Kronios dargebotenen Schrift *Peregrinos* berichtet Lukian über die inszenierte Selbstverbrennung dieses Kynikers anlässlich der Olympischen Spiele wahrscheinlich des Jahres 165 n. Chr., bei der er selbst Augenzeuge gewesen sein will.³⁹ Lukian kommt es von Anfang an darauf an, den Peregrinos als Scharlatan zu entlarven und seinen Freitod als Ergebnis seiner unermesslichen Ruhmsucht darzustellen.⁴⁰ Er schildert uns mit satirischer Häme dessen wechselvolle Karriere vom Ehebrecher, Knabenschänder und Vatermörder zum Leiter einer christlichen Gemeinde in Palästina, dann zum kynischen Philosophen und selbst stilisierten Märtyrer bis zum gottgleichen Heros, dessen Apotheose auch noch von Zeugen bestätigt wird.⁴¹

Schließlich verbrennt sich Peregrinos 165 n. Chr. anlässlich der Spiele öffentlich, um endlich die ihm gebührende Aufmerksamkeit zu bekommen. Interessant wird die Darstellung Lukians aber besonders da, wo er die direkten Umstände des Todes beschreibt. Die Selbstverbrennung vollzog sich offenbar in

---

37 Der Stier ist überliefert bei Pindar, P. 1,95; Aristot. pol. 5,10,1310b 28; rhet. 2,20,1393b 5–8; Polyain. 5,1,1; Diod. 9,30; Cic. rep. 1,28,44; off. 2,7[26]; Att. 7,12,2; 7,20,2. Die Geschichte der Übergabe des Stieres an den Tyrannen ist bei Ov. Trist. 3,11. beschrieben.
38 D.Mar. 4.
39 Vgl. zum Folgenden auch SPICKERMANN, Der brennende Herakles, und DERS., Philosophical Claim.
40 Grundlegend dazu GERLACH, Die Figur des Scharlatans.
41 Lukian spottet dabei auch über die Einfalt der Christen, die einen solchen Betrüger sogar zum Gemeindeleiter machten, vgl. ausführlich BAUMBACH/HANSEN, Karriere, 111–128. Seine Beurteilung des Christentums ist aber milde zu nennen: Er nennt Christus einen am Kreuz gestorbenen Sophisten und sieht in dessen Anhängern in erster Linie harmlose Verrückte, vgl. Peregr. 11–16; vgl. BETZ, Lukian und das Christentum, bes. 231–232.

einem kleineren Kreise von Kynikern erst nach Beendigung der Olympischen Spiele, als die große Masse der Leute schon gegangen war, außerhalb der Spielstätten. In seiner einige Tage zuvor in der hinteren Halle des Zeustempels von Olympia gehaltenen Rede über sich selbst verweist Peregrinos auf die Gefahren, die er überstanden hatte, und was er der Philosophie wegen ertragen hatte. Er wolle nun einem goldenen Leben eine Krone aufsetzen, denn wer wie Herakles gelebt habe, müsse auch wie Herakles sterben und sich mit dem Äther vereinen. Im Vordergrund steht also das Vorbild des Herakles, nicht nur im Leben, sondern auch im Tod. Dies macht auch der glühende Verehrer des Peregrinos, Theagenes aus Patras, in seiner Rede zu Anfang der Schrift deutlich.[42] Er nennt Herakles Patroos, also Ahnherrn und Vorbild der Kyniker in Entsagung und Kampf gegen die Lust.[43] Und er benutzt ihn als Vorbild für seinen Meister Peregrinos, wenn er darauf verweist, dass Herakles auf diese Weise starb, Dionysos und Asklepios durch Blitze umkamen und Empedokles in den Krater des Ätna sprang.[44] Lukian will durch diese nicht ganz richtige Darstellung den Redner lächerlich machen, denn Asklepios starb nicht ganz freiwillig und Dionysos wurde nicht vom Blitz erschlagen.[45] Das Beispiel des Empedokles wird bei Lukian an anderer Stelle ausdrücklich negativ gewertet. Menippos wirft ihm in den Totengesprächen nämlich im Hades vor, er habe sich aus Eitelkeit, Ruhmsucht und Narrheit in den Ätna gestürzt und nicht, wie Empedokles behauptet, aus Melancholie.[46] Wenn nun Peregrinos schon die herakleische Todesart wähle—so der Gegenredner des Theagenes—, dann solle er sich nicht, wie geplant, in Olympia vor der Festversammlung braten, sondern sich still und leise einen Berg suchen und sich dort allein verbrennen.[47] Ja, wenn Theagenes seinem Lehrer und dem Herakles nacheifern wolle, solle er selber auch ins Feuer springen, denn nicht Ranzen, Stab und Mantel, also die äußeren Zeichen des Kynikers, zeigen seinen Eifer, sondern seine innere Einstellung und seine Taten. Außerdem sei Herakles, wie es in der Tragödie heiße, durch Kentaurenblut

---

42 Ob mit diesem Namen auf den Olympiasieger angespielt werden soll, dessen Statue als wundertätig galt, oder ob Theagenes mit einem von Galen erwähnten Kyniker identisch ist, lässt sich nicht ausmachen; vgl. PILHOFER, Anmerkungen, 52, Anm. 18. Jedenfalls war die gedankliche Verbindung mit dem Heros in Olympia sicherlich gewollt.
43 Peregr. 4,3; vgl. dazu PILHOFER, Anmerkungen, 51, Anm. 14.
44 Peregr. 4,9-12: οὐ γὰρ Ἡρακλῆς οὕτως; οὐ γὰρ Ἀσκληπιὸς καὶ Διόνυσος κεραυνῷ; οὐ γὰρ τὰ τελευταῖα Ἐμπεδοκλῆς εἰς τοὺς κρατῆρας (ed. HARMON, vol. 5).
45 Peregr. 5,4; v.gl. PILHOFER, Anmerkungen, 51-52, Anm. 17, und SZLAGOR, Verflochtene Bilder, 107.
46 D.Mort. 6[20], 4; vgl. dazu SZLAGOR, Verflochtene Bilder, 109.
47 Peregr. 21,10.

gezwungen gewesen, ins Feuer zu springen, dies sei aber bei Peregrinos nicht der Fall.[48] Der unbekannte Gegenredner—wohl eine literarische Kunstfigur des Lukian—führt im Weiteren das Beispiel der indischen Brahmanen an, die sich ebenfalls ruhmsüchtig, allerdings auf qualvollere Art als Peregrinos, verbrennen.[49] Er erwähnt dabei die Verbrennung des Kalanos, der der Geschichtsschreiber und Steuermann Alexanders des Großen, Onesikritos, beigewohnt habe, was aber nicht stimmen kann. Kalanos, ein indischer Weiser, der Alexander einige Zeit begleitet hatte, hatte sich 325 v. Chr. in Persis selbst verbrannt und Onesikritos hat später lediglich hierüber berichtet, ohne selbst Augenzeuge gewesen zu sein.[50] Lukian erwähnt nur diese Geschichte, obwohl ihm auch ein jüngerer Fall der Selbstverbrennung eines Brahmanen 20 v. Chr. aus Athen bekannt gewesen sein dürfte,[51] und benutzt sie als Beispiel für seine eher negative Wertung der Selbstverbrennung, die bei Randvölkern zwar üblich ist, im kultivierten Mittelmeerraum aber ein deviantes Verhalten darstellt, zumal der Feuertod generell ja als unehrenhaft galt. Dass die Brahmanen oder Gymnosophisten—ganz anders als Peregrinos, der nur in eine Grube mit Feuer springt—regungslos neben und dann auf dem Scheiterhaufen verharren, wird auch noch einmal in Lukians Schrift *Von den entlaufenen Sklaven* betont.[52] Zu Beginn dieses Dialoges berichtet Zeus seinem Sohn Apollo, wie er vor der Selbstverbrennung des Peregrinos Proteus aus Olympia bis nach Arabien fliehen musste und dass ihn immer noch Brechreiz überkomme, wenn er daran denke.[53]

---

48 Peregr. 24,9–25,2. Vgl. den Kommentar von Pilhofer, Anmerkungen, 73–74, Anm. 87.
49 Peregr. 25,5–20: νὴ Δί', ὅπως τὴν καρτερίαν ἐπιδείξηται καθάπερ οἱ Βραχμᾶνες ἐκείνοις γὰρ αὐτὸν ἠξίου Θεαγένης εἰκάζειν, ὥσπερ οὐκ ἐνὸν καὶ ἐν Ἰνδοῖς εἶναί τινας μωροὺς καὶ κενοδόξους ἀνθρώπους. ὅμως δ'οὖν κἂν ἐκείνους μιμείσθω ἐκεῖνοι γὰρ οὐκ ἐμπηδῶσιν ἐς τὸ πῦρ, ὡς Ὀνησίκριτος ὁ Ἀλεξάνδρου κυβερνήτης ἰδὼν Κάλανον καόμενον φησιν, ἀλλ' ἐπειδὰν νήσωσι, πλησίον παραστάντες ἀκίνητοι ἀνέχονται παροπτώμενοι, εἶτ' ἐπιβάντες κατὰ σχῆμα καίονται, οὐδ' ὅσον ὀλίγον ἐντρέψαντες τῆς κατακλίσεως. Οὗτος δὲ τί μέγα εἰ ἐμπεσὼν τεθνήξεται συναρπασθεὶς ὑπὸ τοῦ πυρός; οὐκ ἀπ' ἐλπίδος μὴ ἀναπηδήσασθαι αὐτὸν καὶ ἡμίφλεκτον, εἰ μή, ὅπερ φασί, μηχανήσεται βαθεῖαν γενέσθαι καὶ ἐν βόθρῳ τὴν πυράν.
50 Arr. an. 7,3; Plut. Alexander 69,6–7.
51 Im Jahre 20 v. Chr. hatte Augustus nach den Berichten des Nikolaos von Damaskus, des Plutarch und des Cassius Dio in Antiochia oder auf Samos eine indische Gesandtschaft empfangen, deren einer, ein Weiser namens Zarmanochegas oder Zamaros, sich später in Athen verbrannt habe, um sich—so Nikolaos—nach väterlicher Sitte der Inder in die Unsterblichkeit zu versetzen: Nikolaos von Damaskos bei Strab. 15,1,73 (p. 719) = FgrHist90 F 100; leicht abweichend Cass. Dio 54,9,10. Dazu Pilhofer, Anmerkungen, 74–76, Anm. 90, und Plut. Alexander 69,6. Vgl. auch Hall, Lucian's Satire, 180–185, und Szlagor, Verflochtene Bilder, 110, Anm. 49.
52 Fug. 7,1–3.
53 Fug. 31,8.

Lukian beschreibt das theatralische Sterben in negativer Weise, was nicht unbedingt einem literarischen Muster entspricht. Verwiesen sei in diesem Zusammenhang beispielsweise auf Tacitus' Schilderung des Todes des Petronius im Jahre 66 n. Chr., die eher positiv zu bewerten ist.[54] Ganz anders als in dieser negativen Sicht der Inszenierung des Freitodes des Peregrinos durch die Götter wird dieser von seinen Anhängern gedeutet. So fliegt angeblich ein Geier aus den Flammen, der mit menschlicher Stimme sagt, er steige nun zum Olymp auf, und ein alter, seriös aussehender Mann bezeugt, den Peregrinos nach seinem Feuertod in ein weißes Gewand gehüllt, strahlend und mit einem Ölzweig bekränzt herumwandeln gesehen zu haben.[55] Dies erinnert sehr an die Elemente der kaiserlichen Apotheose in Rom. So wundert es Lukian denn auch nicht, dass dem neuen Heroen Proteus/Peregrinos bald von den Eleern selbst und anderen Griechen Statuen aufgestellt werden, ja er habe selbst noch dafür gesorgt, dass Totenboten verschiedenen Städten Verfügungen über seine postumen Ehren überbrächten.[56] Dass dies zumindest teilweise tatsächlich geschah, scheint die schon genannte Erwähnung einer Statue in Parion, seiner Heimatstadt, durch Athenagoras zu belegen. So kann man Lukians Bericht als ein Vaticinium ex eventu deuten.[57] Schon der fiktive Gegenredner des Theagenes hatte ja prophezeit, dass sich Peregrinos durch seine Divinisierung wie Phönix aus der Asche erheben werde.[58]

5 Trauer und Totenkult

Die zentrale Schrift, in der sich Lukian mit dem Umgang mit dem Tod auseinandersetzt, ist seine Diatribe *De luctu* (Über die Trauer um die Verstorbenen). Grundtenor der Schrift ist, die Vorstellungen der gemeinen Menschen vom Totenreich, die auf Homer, Hesiod und anderen Mythopoioi fußen, ad absurdum

---

54 Tac. ann. 16,19,2–3; vgl. dazu BINDER, PALLIDA MORS, 221–222.
55 Peregr. 39 und bes. 40: Ἀπελθὼν δὲ ἐς τὴν πανήγυριν ἐπέστην τινὶ πολιῷ ἀνδρὶ καὶ νὴ τὸν Δί᾿ ἀξιοπίστῳ τὸ πρόσωπον ἐπὶ τῷ πώγωνι καὶ τῇ λοιπῇ σεμνότητι, τά τε ἄλλα διηγουμένῳ περὶ τοῦ Πρωτέως καὶ ὡς μετὰ τὸ καυθῆναι θεάσαιτο αὐτὸν ἐν λευκῇ ἐσθῆτι μικρὸν ἔμπροσθεν, καὶ νῦν ἀπολίποι περιπατοῦντα φαιδρὸν ἐν τῇ ἑπταφώνῳ στοᾷ κοτίνῳ τε ἐστεμμένον. εἶτ᾿ ἐπὶ πᾶσι προσέθηκε τὸν γῦπα, διομνύμενος ἦ μὴν αὐτὸς ἑωρακέναι ἀναπτάμενον ἐκ τῆς πυρᾶς, ὃν ἐγὼ μικρὸν ἔμπροσθεν ἀφῆκα πέτεσθαι καταγελῶντα τῶν ἀνοήτων καὶ βλακικῶν τὸν τρόπον.
56 Peregr. 41.
57 Vgl. SZLAGOR, Verflochtene Bilder, 121.
58 Peregr. 27–30.

zu führen.⁵⁹ Lukian will mit seinen Diatriben *De luctu* und *De sacrificiis* seinem Publikum die Absurditäten der traditionellen Mythen von Göttern und insbesondere dem Hades vor Augen führen, indem er sie lächerlich macht.⁶⁰ Beispielsweise wird der Brauch, die Toten mit Libationen und Speiseopfern zu nähren, auf sarkastische Weise kommentiert, dass diejenigen, die auf Erden keine Freunde oder Verwandten hinterlassen, als Tote Hunger leiden müssen.⁶¹ Paradox ist auch der Rahmen der Geschichte: Ein Sohn stirbt jung, die Trauer des Vaters und seiner Familie wird beschrieben und nun wird die Möglichkeit eröffnet, dass der Sohn von Aiakos und Pluto die Erlaubnis erhält, ihm aus der Unterwelt zu antworten, um ihm die Absurdität seiner Art der Trauer und der Begräbnisriten in einer kunstvollen Gegenrede vor Augen zu halten.⁶² Hier finden sich genau diejenigen Beschreibungen des Hades wieder, welche auch den Beteiligten seines mehrfach zitierten Dialogs *Die Lügenfreunde*—insbesondere dem gebildeten Gastgeber Eukrates—in den Mund gelegt werden. Nur dass in *De luctu* ausdrücklich gesagt wird, dass nur die große Masse der Ungebildeten, von den Weisen (σοφοί) als ἰδιῶται bezeichnet, an einen tief unter der Erde befindlichen, großen und weiten Raum, *Hades* genannt, glaube: Kein Sonnenstrahl dringe in diese Finsternis, und doch soll er auf unerklärliche Weise hell genug sein, um alles, was darin ist, deutlich unterscheiden zu können.⁶³ In den folgenden Abschnitten (2–9) werden die Vorstellungen der gemeinen Leute vom Hades beschrieben, wobei Lukian insbesondere auf Homer und Hesiod zurückgreift. Dann aber wendet er sich den sich aus diesen Vorstellungen ergebenden Begräbnisbräuchen und ihren Widersprüchlichkeiten zu:

> Diese Vorstellungen sind es, welche bei den Leuten allgemein im Umlauf sind. Wenn daher einer ihrer Angehörigen gestorben ist, so sind sie sogleich mit einem Obolus bei der Hand, den sie ihm in den Mund stecken, damit er dem Fährmann die Überfahrt bezahlen könne. Welches Geld dort unten kursiere, ob der attische, der makedonische oder der aeginetische Obolus, danach fragt man nicht, ebenso wenig bedenkt man, dass es viel klüger wäre, gar kein Fährgeld bei sich zu haben; denn so würde der Tote, wenn der Fährmann ihn nicht einnähme, zurückgeschickt und könnte wieder ins Leben heraufkommen.⁶⁴

---

59 Luct. 2; vgl. HALL, Lucian's Satire, 204.
60 Vgl. HALL, Lucian's Satire, 196–197, und JONES, Culture and Society, 33.
61 Luct. 9; vgl. JONES, Culture and Society, 33.
62 Luct. 16–19; vgl. dazu ANDERSON, Lucian. Theme, 105.
63 Luct. 2.
64 Luct. 10.

Dieser Brauch wird auch an anderer Stelle des lukianischen Oeuvres noch einmal in besonderer Weise lächerlich gemacht, wenn nämlich der Habenichts Menippos sein Fährgeld nicht zahlen kann und Charon dies vom Psychopompos Hermes einfordert, der sich natürlich weigert, worauf Menippos zurückgebracht werden will, was zu einem völligen Dilemma führt.[65] Lukian widmet dem Charon auch eine eigene Schrift, in der er, aus der Unterwelt hinaufgestiegen, sich von Hermes die Menschenwelt erklären lässt und erstaunt ist von dem Gewimmel und ihrem Streben nach Ehre, Macht und Geld, ohne an den sicher bevorstehenden Tod zu denken (*Charon oder die [Welt]betrachter*).

Während in *De luctu* der Vater des jung gestorbenen Sohnes alle konventionellen Trauerriten vollzieht—Waschen, Salben und Bekränzen des Leichnams, Anlegen der besten Kleider, Aufbahren des Toten, Geheul der Klagefrauen, Bejammern des frühen Todes durch die Eltern (11–14)—, wird im Folgenden kritisiert, dass viele sogar die Pferde, die Beischläferinnen, ja die Mundschenken ihrer Toten abgeschlachtet hätten und deren Kleider und den übrigen Schmuck mit verbrannt oder begraben hätten, als ob sie alles dieses dort unten noch gebrauchen und genießen könnten.[66] Hier scheint Lukian besonders auf ägyptisches Brauchtum anzuspielen, das er auch an anderer Stelle ablehnt. Darauf wird kritisch angemerkt, dass dem Vater wohl bewusst sei, dass der Sohn sein „Geschwätz" nicht höre. Er mache dies nur wegen der Anwesenden und weil er nicht wisse, was seinem Sohn eigentlich widerfahren sein. Auch mache er sich keine Gedanken darüber, ob dieses Leben es überhaupt wert sei, sein Ende zu beklagen.[67] Die folgenden im Irrealis gehaltenen Ausführungen des Sohnes, der seine Gegenrede aus dem Hades hält, gehen auf dieses unnütze Totenbrauchtum ein und führen es ad absurdum, wie das oben genannte Beispiel der Speise- und Trankopfer am Grab zeigt. Die Lebenden sollen die Toten in Ruhe lassen, der Tote hat keine Bedürfnisse mehr und befindet sich damit in einer ungleich besseren Situation als die Lebenden. Die Lebenden können folglich für die Toten nichts tun (16–19). Hier nimmt Lukian eine epikureische Haltung ein: „Der Tod geht uns nichts an!"[68] Dennoch muss er konstatieren, dass die Menschen sich durch eine solche Rede, käme sie auch aus dem Hades, nicht

---

65 D.Mort 2 [22]. Die Sitte, Toten eine Münze in den Mund zu legen, lässt sich archäologisch übrigens in Griechenland vom 5. Jahrhundert v. Chr. an und später auch im Westen des Römischen Reiches von der Iberischen Halbinsel bis nach Britannien nachweisen. Ebenso ist dies in Polen und bei den germanischen Völkern des Nordens zu belegen; vgl. STEVENS, Charon's Obol, 225.
66 Luct. 14.
67 Luct. 15.
68 Epik. Sent. Vat. (gnom.); vgl. dazu Lucr. 3,830: Nil igitur mors est ad nos.

von dem Wehklagen um die Verstorbenen abbringen ließen. Die Wehklage sei bei allen Völkern dieselbe, nur in der Art der Bestattung unterschieden diese sich, ob es sich um Grabhügel, Pyramiden oder Denkmäler mit Inschriften handelte.[69] Lukian betont hier gerade die Absurdität und Lächerlichkeit der Vorstellungen fremder Völker.[70] Er bedient in vielen seiner Schriften allgemeine Klischees, um die griechische Kultur von denen der Randvölker abzugrenzen. Ganz in diesem Sinne werden auch die unterschiedlichen Opferpraktiken von Assyrern, Lydern und Skythen dargestellt,[71] ja die Skythen wegen ihrer Menschenopfer für Artemis diskreditiert.[72] Auch der Topos, die Skythen würden ihre Toten essen, wird gerne aufgenommen, wenn er die verschiedenen Bestattungssitten vergleicht: „Die Griechen verbrennen ihre Toten, die Perser beerdigen sie, die Inder glasieren sie, die Skythen essen sie auf, die Ägypter pökeln sie ein."[73] Zum Schluss werden dann noch die manchmal stattfindenden Kampfspiele und das Leichenmahl erwähnt, bei dem die Eltern nach dreitägigem Hungern wieder etwas zu sich nehmen. Dabei werden die Hungernden absurderweise von den anwesenden Verwandten mit einem Iliasspruch, den Lukian wörtlich zitiert, aufgefordert, doch etwas zu essen.[74] Auch die Rede des Toten endet übrigens mit einem Iliaszitat.[75]

Es geht Lukian in dieser Diatribe wohlgemerkt nicht um die Verteidigung einer epikureischen Position, sondern wieder einmal um die Diskrepanz, die zwischen dem Handeln und der Überzeugung gebildeter Menschen liegt. Jemand, der Bildung, *Paideia*, für sich in Anspruch nehmen will, muss doch das gängige Totenbrauchtum abstoßend finden, da er zugeben muss, über das, was nach dem Tod kommt, nichts zu wissen.

---

69 Luct. 22.
70 Vgl. COENEN, Zeus tragodos, 123, der glaubt, dass Lukian hier eine skeptisch-akademische Quelle verfolgt.
71 Sacr. 14.
72 Iupp. Trag. 44; Sacr. 13; D.Deor. 3[23],1; 18[16],1. Auch dies ist ein gängiger Topos; vgl. COENEN, Zeus tragodos, 129–130.
73 Luct. 21; vgl. Hdt. 3,24, und Diod. 2,14–15; hierzu BETZ, Lukian und das Neue Testament, 73. Die im 2. Jahrhundert in verschiedenen Regionen des Römischen Reiches häufiger vorkommende Körperbestattung wird von Lukian nirgendwo angesprochen, auch der erwähnte Sohn wird verbrannt.
74 Luct. 24; vgl. Hom. Il. 24,602: καὶ γάρ τ' ἠΰκομος Νιόβη ἐμνήσατο σίτου, und Hom. Il. 19,225: γαστέρι δ' οὔ πως ἔστι νέκυν πενθῆσαι Ἀχαιούς—Denn auch die schönhaarige Niobe gedachte der Speise; mit dem Magen aber können nicht einen Toten beklagen die Achaier (Ed. ALLEN; Übersetzung SCHADEWALDT).
75 Luct. 19,20; vgl. Hom. Il. 16,502: ὣς ἄρα μιν εἰπόντα τέλος θανάτοιο κάλυψε – Als er so gesprochen hatte, umhüllte ihn das Ende des Todes.

Lukian zeigt dies noch einmal in aller Deutlichkeit in einer Episode über den untröstlichen Herodes Atticus, einen der berühmtesten Redner seiner Zeit und Lehrer des Kaisers Marc Aurel: Als ebendieser Herodes sich aus Verzweiflung über den Tod seines Sohnes in ein finsteres Gemach einschloss, um seinem Schmerz desto ungestörter nachhängen zu können, ließ sich der bereits erwähnte Demonax unter dem Namen eines Magos bei ihm anmelden und versicherte, er sei imstande die abgeschiedene Seele seines Sohnes wieder zurückzubringen, wenn er ihm drei Menschen nennen könne, die in ihrem ganzen Leben um niemanden hätten trauern müssen. Da nun jener sich lange besann und vermutlich, weil er keinen solchen zu nennen wusste, um die Antwort verlegen war, sagte Demonax: „Ist es nun nicht lächerlich, dass du allein etwas Unerträgliches zu leiden glaubst, da du doch siehst, dass dein Schicksal etwas Allgemeines ist?"[76]

6 Schluss

So schwierig es ist, Lukian von Samosata auf eine philosophische Richtung festzulegen, so klar ist sein moralischer Anspruch, beruhend auf dem Ideal der *Paideia*. Wenn eine Wahrheit einmal erkannt ist, so muss sie Einfluss auf das Handeln nehmen. Anspruch und Wirklichkeit müssen in Einklang miteinander stehen. Gebildete müssen daher Spekulationen über ein Weiterleben nach dem Tode, ja die Divinisierung von Menschen grundsätzlich ablehnen.

Lukian ist ausgerichtet auf das Hier und Jetzt dieser Welt und verneint jede transzendente Spekulation. Über ein Leben nach dem Tod kann man nichts Sicheres wissen, Totenbrauchtum nützt daher nur den Lebenden. Die Wirksamkeit jedweder magischen Praktiken (*Nekromantia*) wird konsequent bestritten und lässt sich mit dem Ideal der *Paideia* nicht verbinden. Mit seiner Schrift *Lügenfreunde* wendet er sich gerade gegen diejenigen Zeitgenossen, die sich selbst als gebildete Philosophen bezeichnen, aber Wundergeschichten für wahr halten, und entlarvt sie damit als irrational und wundergläubig. Im gesamten Schrifttum Lukians offenbart sich eine fundamentale Verteidigung der *Paideia*. Athen ist dabei das Zentrum der gebildeten Welt; von hier gingen und gehen alle kulturellen Impulse aus. Selbst die Römer hätten keine eigenständige Kultur, sie kopieren, wenn sie gebildet sind, nur die griechische.[77]

---

76 Demonax 25.
77 Vgl. z.B. Nigr. 15.

Der grausamste und schändlichste Tod ist für ihn der Feuertod, den Herakles, Empedokles und in deren Nachahmung zuletzt auch sein Zeitgenosse Peregrinos erlitten haben. Während Herakles sich durch seine durch Kentaurenblut erlittenen Schmerzen auf den Scheiterhaufen begibt, wird schon Empedokles für sein vorschnelles Handeln kritisiert, wobei die Selbstverbrennung des Peregrinos, den Lukian sogar ironisch Proteus nennt, als ruhmsüchtige Tat eines abgehalfterten Betrügers charakterisiert wird, der am Ende seines Lebens noch einmal großen Applaus bekommen will. Dies ist nun gar nicht zur Nachahmung empfohlen, selbst wenn am Ende die Divinisierung steht.

Bibliographie

ALLEN, Thomas William (Hg.), Homeri Ilias, 3 vols., Oxford 1931.
ANDERSON, Graham, Lucian. Theme and Variation in the Second Sophistic (Mnemosyne/Supplementum 41), Leiden 1976.
ANDERSON, Graham, Lucian. Tradition versus Reality, in: Temporini, Hildegard/Haase, Wolfgang (Hg.), Aufstieg und Niedergang der Römischen Welt, Teil 2, Vol. 34,2, Berlin/New York 1994, 1422–1447.
BAUMBACH, Manuel/HANSEN, Dirk Uwe, Die Karriere des Peregrinos Proteus, in: Pilhofer, Peter et al. (Hg.), Lukian. Der Tod des Peregrinos. Ein Scharlatan auf dem Scheiterhaufen (SAPERE 9), Darmstadt 2005, 111–128.
BETZ, Hans Dieter, Lukian von Samosata und das Christentum, in: NT (1959) 226–237.
BETZ, Hans Dieter, Lukian von Samosata und das Neue Testament. Religionsgeschichtliche und paränetische Parallelen. Ein Beitrag zum Corpus Hellenisticum Novi Testamenti (TU 76; 5. Reihe, Vol. 21), Berlin 1961.
BINDER, Gerhard, PALLIDA MORS. Leben und Tod, Seele und Jenseits in römischen und verwandten Texten, in: Binder, Gerhard/Effe, Bernhard (Hg.), Tod und Jenseits im Altertum (Bochumer Altertumswissenschaftliches Colloquium 6), Trier 1991, 203–247.
COENEN, Jürgen, Lukian. Zeus tragodos. Überlieferungsgeschichte, Text und Kommentar (Beiträge zur klassischen Philologie 88), Meisenheim am Glan 1977.
CZYCHOLL, Dietmar (Hg.), Als ich am gestrigen Tag entschlief ... Erfahrungen Wiederbelebter in der Weltliteratur – eine Anthologie aus drei Jahrtausenden, Oberstaufen 2003.
GERLACH, Jens, Die Figur des Scharlatans bei Lukian, in: Pilhofer, Peter et al. (Hg.), Lukian. Der Tod des Peregrinos. Ein Scharlatan auf dem Scheiterhaufen (SAPERE 9), Darmstadt 2005, 151–197.
HALL, Jennifer, Lucian's Satire (Monographs in Classical Studies), New York 1981.
HARMON, Austin M. (Hg.), Lucian. In Eight Volumes, with an English translation, Vol. 5 (LCL 302), Cambridge, Massachusetts 1936 (ND 2001).
HELM, Rudolf, Lucian und Menipp, Leipzig 1906 (ND Hildesheim 1967).
HELM, Rudolf, Art. „Lukianos", in: RECA 13,2, Stuttgart 1927, 1725–1777.

JONES, Christopher P., Culture and Society in Lucian, Cambridge, Massachusetts 1986.
LIGHTFOOT, Jane L. (Hg.), Lucian. On The Syrian Goddess, Ed. with Introduction, Translation and Commentary, Oxford 2003.
MRAS, Karl (Hg.), Die Hauptwerke des Lukian. Griechisch und Deutsch (Sammlung Tusculum), München 1954.
NESSELRATH, Heinz-Günther, Vorwort, in: Lucians Werke, übersetzt von August Pauly, Stuttgart/Weimar 1997 (^{2}1929).
NESSELRATH, Heinz-Günther, Art. „Lukianos", in: DNP 7, Stuttgart 1999, 493–501.
NESSELRATH, Heinz-Günther, Lukian und die Magie, in: Ebner, Martin (Hg.), Lukian. Philopseudeis ē apistōn, Die Lügenfreunde oder: Der Ungläubige, eingeleitet, übersetzt und mit interpretierenden Essays versehen (SAPERE 3), Darmstadt 2002, 153–166.
OLIVER, James H., The Actuality of Lucian's *Assembly of the Gods*, in: American Journal of Philology 101 (1980) 304–313.
PILHOFER, Peter, Livius, Lukas und Lukian: Drei Himmelfahrten, in: Ders. (Hg.), Die frühen Christen und ihre Welt. Greifswalder Aufsätze 1996–2001 (WUNT 145), Tübingen 2002, 166–182.
PILHOFER, Peter, Anmerkungen, in: Ders. et al. (Hg.), Lukian. Der Tod des Peregrinos. Ein Scharlatan auf dem Scheiterhaufen (SAPERE 9), Darmstadt 2005, 48–93.
SCHADEWALDT, Wolfgang, Homer. Ilias (Insel Taschenbuch), Frankfurt 1975.
SEEL, Otto (Hg.), Lukian. Gespräche der Götter und Meergötter, der Toten und Hetären. In Anlehnung an Christoph Martin Wieland übersetzt und herausgegeben (Reclam Universal-Bibliothek 1133), Stuttgart 1967.
SPICKERMANN, Wolfgang, Der brennende Herakles—Lukian von Samosata und Proteus/Peregrinos, in: Fuhrmann, Sebastian/Grundmann, Regina (Hg.), Martyriumsvorstellungen in Antike und Mittelalter. Leben oder sterben für Gott? (AJEC 80), Leiden/Boston, Massachusetts 2012, 111–132.
SPICKERMANN, Wolfgang, Philosophical Claim and Individual Lifestyles. Lucian's Peregrinus/Proteus—Charlatan and Heros, in: Rüpke, Jörg/Woolf, Greg (Hg.), Religious Dimensions of the Self in the Second Century CE (Studien und Texte zu Antike und Christentum 76), Tübingen 2013, 175–191.
STEVENS, Susan T., Charon's Obol and Other Coins in Ancient Funerary Practice, in: Phoenix 45 (1991) 215–229.
SZLAGOR, Barbara, Verflochtene Bilder. Lukians Porträtierung „göttlicher Männer" (Bochumer Altertumswissenschaftliches Colloquium 63), Trier 2005.
WHITMARSH, Tim, Greek Literature and the Roman Empire. The Politics of Imitation, Oxford 2001.

Veit Rosenberger
Privatdeifikationen in der römischen Kaiserzeit – Tod, Trauer und Memoria

> Hier liegt in süßer Ruh
> Erdrückt von seiner Kuh
> Franz Xaver Maier.
> Daraus sieht man,
> Wie kurios man sterben kann.
> *(Alpiner Grabspruch aus Tirol)*

Trimalchio, ein Protagonist in den um die Mitte des 1. Jahrhunderts n. Chr. entstandenen „Satyrica" des Petronius, ist ein ehemaliger Sklave, der es zu beträchtlichem Reichtum gebracht hat. Im Laufe eines verschwenderischen Festmahls legt Trimalchio die Pläne für sein Grabmal dar. Die gesamte Anlage soll überdimensional groß sein, mit Obstbäumen und einem Weingarten, mit Statuen von Trimalchio, seiner Frau und seines Lieblingshundes. Damit niemand am Grabmal seine Notdurft verrichtet, soll ein Freigelassener Trimalchios Wache schieben. Eine Sonnenuhr wird direkt über der Inschrift mit seinem Namen angebracht, so dass jeder, der wissen will, wie spät es ist, Trimalchios Namen lesen muss. Auch seine Grabinschrift hat der Neureiche bereits verfasst:

> Hier liegt Gaius Pompeius Trimalchio Maecenatianus. Ihm wurde das Amt des Sevir Augustalis (Kaiserpriester) in seiner Abwesenheit übergeben. Obwohl er alle Beamtenposten in Rom hätte haben können—er wollte es nicht. Fromm, stark und treu wurde er aus kleinen Verhältnissen reich. Er hat 30 Millionen Sesterzen hinterlassen und hat nie einen Philosophen gehört. Lebe wohl—du auch.[1]

Petronius hat Trimalchio als grotesk verzerrte Gestalt angelegt. Gleichwohl sind viele Aspekte von Trimalchios Grabmal aus anderen Grabanlagen bekannt, etwa Statuen der Verstorbenen, Defäkationsverbote[2] sowie die Gefahr, dass der Name auf einer Inschrift weggeschlagen oder überschrieben wurde.[3] Doch dem sozialen Aufsteiger Trimalchio fehlen Stil und Maß. Die Anlage ist zu groß, der eigene Aufseher nicht nötig, die Inschrift angeberisch, die Sonnenuhr egoistisch.

---

1 Petron. 71: C. Pompeius Trimalchio Maecenatianus hic requiescat. Huic seviratus absenti decretus est. Cum posset in omnibus decuriis Romae esse tamen noluit. Pius fortis fidelis ex parvo crevit. Sestertium reliquit trecenties nec unquam philosophum audivit. Vale—et tu.
2 CIL VI 8899.
3 CIL III 6082; CIL VI 24799: Inschrift weggehackt (*deasciare*); CIL VI 29942: inscriptor, rogo te ut transeas hoc monumentum – Überschreiber, bitte geh an diesem Monument vorüber.

Bei aller Maßlosigkeit plant Trimalchio keine Privatdeifikation, also die kultische Verehrung seiner selbst oder seiner Frau als Gottheit. Nun ist der Begriff der „Privatdeifikation" ebenso plastisch wie problematisch. Zum einen sind in der Antike die Sphären des „Privaten" und des „Öffentlichen" nicht sauber zu trennen; „Privatdeifikation" soll besagen, dass die Vergöttlichung einer Person nicht durch ein Gemeinwesen oder einen Priester, sondern durch eine Einzelperson vorgenommen wurde. Doch durch die Veröffentlichung dieses Aktes—wir wissen durch Inschriften von den „Privatdeifikationen"—war schon wieder der Charakter des „Privaten" aufgegeben. Zum anderen ist die Frage, inwieweit die römischen Vorstellungen von Gottheiten mit den Konzepten des Göttlichen im 21. Jahrhundert übereinstimmen. Dennoch soll in Ermangelung einer Alternative der Begriff „Privatdeifikation" verwendet werden.

Eine Privatdeifikation, so die im Folgenden vertretene These, stellte keinen Tabubruch dar, sondern war lediglich eine Zuspitzung der Rituale zum Umgang mit Trauer und Tod. In einem ersten Schritt sollen einige Inschriften vorgeführt werden, um zugleich die Komplexität der Situation zu verdeutlichen. Im zweiten Schritt soll der Versuch unternommen werden, die Privatdeifikation im Rahmen der römischen Jenseitsvorstellungen zu deuten.

1 Inschriften

Grabinschriften machen schätzungsweise 60 Prozent des epigraphischen Bestandes der römischen Kaiserzeit aus; die Zahl dieser Texte geht in die Zehntausende. Daher erlauben Grabinschriften belastbare Aussagen. Die meisten Belege stammen aus den ersten beiden Jahrhunderten der Kaiserzeit; bis etwa 160–180 n. Chr. nimmt die Zahl der Inschriften stets zu, danach fällt sie stark ab, um in der Mitte des 3. Jahrhunderts auf relativ niedrigem Niveau stabil zu bleiben; mit regionalen und lokalen Abweichungen von dieser Entwicklung ist stets zu rechnen.

Wenn Althistoriker über die Zahl der inschriftlichen Belege nachdenken, fügen sie—fast schon in einem Pawlow'schen Reflex—stets eine Einschränkung hinzu: Es könnte sein, dass Inschriften auch auf vergänglichem Material, vor allem Holz, hergestellt worden waren, die heute verloren sind, und mit diesem Argument schränken wir die Aussagekraft der Inschriften auf Stein ein.[4] Auch wenn dieser Gedanke nicht ganz von der Hand zu weisen ist, sollten wir die

---

4 Cf. ALFÖLDY, Sozialgeschichte, 190, n. 405; ECK, Inschriften auf Holz, 203–217.

Bedeutung eines Materials nicht unterschätzen. Wer auf Holz schrieb und den Text im Freien aufstellte, wusste von der Vergänglichkeit des Denkmals. Texte auf Holz waren nicht für die Dauer geschaffen, Texte auf Stein hingegen schon: Das Medium—oder besser: das Material—war ein Teil der Botschaft.[5]

Beginnen wir mit dem einzigen genau datierbaren Beispiel einer Privatdeifikation. Im Jahr 169 n. Chr. errichtete Aulus Plutius Epaphroditus, aufgrund seines griechischen Cognomen mit einiger Wahrscheinlichkeit ein ehemaliger Sklave, in Gabii, also im näheren Umfeld von Rom, einen Tempel der Venus Vera Felix Gabina. Aulus Plutius Epaphroditus stattete das Heiligtum mit einer goldenen Statue der Venus, einem goldenen Altar und allerhand weiteren kostspieligen Gegenständen aus. Seine Stiftung verband er mit der Auflage, dass am Geburtstag seiner Tochter Plutia Vera die Stadträte und Kaiserpriester der Gemeinde in der Öffentlichkeit ein Göttermahl abhielten. Die Zinsen, die aus dem gestifteten Kapital anfielen, sollten die Finanzierung des Rituals in der Zukunft absichern. Nun wird die Tochter nicht als Gottheit bezeichnet, aber die Rituale und der Beiname Vera der Göttin bringen die verblichene Tochter in die Nähe des Göttlichen. Hervorhebung verdient, dass der neugestiftete Tempel nicht auf dem Landgut des Geldgebers stand, sondern mitten in der Stadt; das Stück Land hatte Aulus Plutius Epaphroditus durch einen Beschluss des Stadtrats erhalten.[6] Es war also eine Bestimmung, die in Absprache mit den Honoratioren der Stadt Gabii getroffen worden war; man unterstützte den trauernden Vater – zugleich bot der Tod der Tochter eine Gelegenheit, sich durch die Bautätigkeit zu präsentieren.

Von den zahlreichen stadtrömischen Inschriften sind 70 Prozent der Grabinschriften von Freigelassenen. Dieser Befund lässt zwei Deutungen zu. Zum einen mag dieses Zahlenverhältnis durch die große Zahl von Sklaven und Freigelassenen in der Stadt Rom bedingt sein – doch es scheint wenig plausibel,

---

5 Cf. MATHIEU, L'épitaphe; DONATI/POMA, L'officina Epigrafica; DAVIES/ WILKES, Epigraphy.
6 CIL XIV 2793: Veneri Verae Felici Gabinae / A(ulus) Plutius Epaphroditus accens(us) velat(us) negotiator sericarius templum cum / signo aereo effigie Veneris, item signis aeries n(umero) IIII dispositis in zothecis, et / balbis aereis et aram aeream et omni cultu a solo sua pecunia fecit. Cuius ob / dedicationem divisit decurionibus sing(ulis) (denarios) V, item VIvir(is) Aug(ustalibus) sing(ulis) (denarios) III, item taber / nariis intra murum negotiantibus (denarios) I, et (sestertium) X m(ilia) n(ummum) reipubl(icae) Gabinor(um) intulit, ita ut ex / usuris eiusdem summae quodannis IIII k(alendas) Octobr(es) die natalis Plutiae Verae / filiae suae decur(iones) et VIvir(i) Aug(ustales) publice in triclinis suis epulentur; quod si / facere neglexserint, tunc ad municipium Tusculanor(um) (sestertium) X m(ilia) n(ummum) pertineant, / quae confestim exigantur. Loc(o) dato decreto decur(ionum). / Dedicata idibus Mais L(ucio) Venuleio Aproniano II L(ucio) Sergio Paullo co(n)s(ulibus); cf. RÜPKE, Gestiftete Religion, 73–79.

dass die Freigelassenen rund 70 Prozent der Bevölkerung ausmachten. Zum zweiten kann dies bedeuten, dass einfach nicht jeder freie Bewohner der Stadt Rom das Bedürfnis nach einer Grabinschrift für sich oder seine Angehörigen hatte. Wenn dies zutrifft, so sind zahlreiche Aussagen über die epigraphische Kultur der Römer zu überdenken.

Die Freilassung war das wichtigste Ereignis im Leben eines Sklaven. Auch wenn nach wie vor Abhängigkeiten zum ehemaligen Herrn bestanden haben mögen, auch wenn die unfreie Vergangenheit oft als Makel galt, war die Freilassung ein sozialer Aufstieg. In vielen Epochen der Geschichte lässt sich zeigen, wie Aufsteiger die Werte ihrer neuen Gruppe inhalieren, imitieren und internalisieren: Cato und Cicero, beide *homines novi*, identifizierten sich mehr mit den Werten des Senats als ihre Kollegen mit einem langen senatorischen Stammbaum. Daher ist es nicht verwunderlich, wenn die vielen Freigelassenen in Rom das kopierten, was sie von den Freigeborenen, vor allem aber von ihren ehemaligen Herren, kannten. Das Grabmal mit der Inschrift des eigenen Namens sicherte nicht nur die *memoria* in der Nachwelt, sondern war für eine Person, die über eine lange Zeit ihres Lebens nur Sklavenstatus hatte, auch eine Gelegenheit das eigene Selbst und die eigene Individualität zu dokumentieren. Möglicherweise lässt sich jede Freilassung eines Sklaven als persönlicher Individuierungsprozess verstehen; hochgerechnet auf den hohen Anteil von Sklaven und Freigelassenen in der Stadt Rom ergibt sich ein breiter Individualisationsprozess, der vom 1. bis zur Mitte des 3. Jahrhunderts n. Chr. durch den großen Vorrat an Sklaven und ihre Freilassung—Sklaven in der Stadt hatten weitaus bessere Chancen als auf dem Land—in Gang gehalten wurde. Danach schlägt sich, zumindest in den Inschriften, eine De-Individualisierung nieder. Dieser Anstieg und Niedergang in der Häufigkeit von Inschriften wurde von Ramsay MacMullen in einem berühmten Aufsatz als Teil des *epigraphic habit* beschrieben.[7] Nun verwendete MacMullen mit *habit* einen Terminus, der wohl erst in den folgenden Jahren durch Pierre Bourdieus Habitus-Begriff Karriere machte: Das symbolische Kapital, um bei der Begrifflichkeit Bourdieus zu bleiben, der Inschriften war offensichtlich nicht immer gleich hoch. Im Übrigen ist zu bezweifeln, dass es einen einheitlichen epigraphischen Habitus im Römischen Reich gab. Selbst bei den Grabinschriften von Angehörigen des Heeres, das einen beträchtlichen Anteil am Prozess der Romanisierung hatte, finden sich starke regionale Unterschiede.[8]

---

[7] MACMULLEN, Epigraphic Habit, 233–246.233: "My central question, why people inscribed some facts on stone, I cannot answer".
[8] FEUCHT, Uniformity, 147–183.

Bei der Privatdeifikation imitierten die Freigelassenen den Habitus des Kaiserhauses, die verstorbenen Familienangehörigen zu divinisieren.⁹ Auf einen ähnlichen Befund verweist der Archäologe Henning Wrede, der bei einer Untersuchung der bildlichen Angleichung, Gleichsetzung oder gar Identifikation von Verstorbenen mit einer Gottheit auf etwa 300 Beispiele kam, vor allem im lateinischen Westen. Ein Großteil stammt von Freigelassenen aus dem Umfeld des Kaiserhauses;¹⁰ Belege finden sich ab der Mitte des 1. Jahrhunderts v. Chr. bis in die Zeit um 200 n. Chr.¹¹

Die weiteren Beispiele für Privatdeifikation auf Inschriften lassen sich nicht genau datieren, dürften aber alle in das 1. oder 2. Jahrhundert n. Chr. gehören. Lucius Cocceius Apthorus, mit einiger Wahrscheinlichkeit ein freigelassener Sklave, setzte seiner verstorbenen Frau in Rom eine Grabinschrift, in der er sie als „meine ehrwürdige Göttin" (*dea sancta mea*) bezeichnete.

> Deae Sanctae meae / Primillae Medicae / L(uci) Vibi Melitonis F(iliae) / vixit annis XXXXIIII / ex eis cum L(ucio) Cocceio / Apthoro XXX sine / querella fecit / Apthorus coniug(i) / opti[mae] cast[a]e / et sibi.

> Meiner ehrwürdigen Göttin Primilla Medica, der Tochter des Lucius Vibius Melito, sie hat 44 Jahre gelebt, von diesen zusammen mit Lucius Cocceius Apthorus 30 ohne Zank. Aphtorus hat dies für die beste und keusche Gattin und für sich gemacht.¹²

Besonders durch die Formulierung „meine Göttin" wird deutlich, dass Primilla Medica für ihren Gatten als Göttin galt; dies war eine persönliche Entscheidung des Apthorus. Im nächsten Beispiel, ebenfalls aus Rom, wird explizit auf die Freilassung verwiesen. Publius Clodius Amomus widmete dies seiner Frau, mit der er viele Jahre verheiratet gewesen war:

> Dis Manibus [et memoriae aet]ernae P. Clodius Amomus consacr(avit) / Clodiae Pontic[ae feminae opt]imae conlibertae fidelissimae / uxori dulciss[imae omnibus comm]endatissimae, cum qua multis annis sine / ve[rbo s]cabro vi[xi ...]a immoverissima dea memor beneficior(um) / tuorum.

> Den Totengöttern und dem ewigen Angedenken. Publius Clodius Amomus hat es der Clodia Pontica geweiht. Der besten Frau, treuesten Mitfreigelassenen, der süßesten Gattin,

---

9 ALFÖLDY, Rolle des Einzelnen, 38–49; ALFÖLDY, Sozialgeschichte, 190, n. 405.
10 WREDE, Consecratio, 160–164.
11 WREDE, Consecratio, 170; cf. KRANZ, Herakles Hope, 393–409; WAELKENS, Privatdeifikation, 259–307.
12 CIL VI 7581.

> vor allen ausgezeichnet, mit der ich viele Jahre ohne bitteres Wort gelebt habe [...] unbeweglichste Göttin, eingedenk deiner Wohltaten.[13]

Zwischen der Nennung der Gattin und den Worten, in denen von der „unbeweglichsten Göttin" die Rede ist, besteht eine Lücke. Aufgrund des Aufbaus der Inschrift ist es allerdings zwingend, dass nicht irgendeine Gottheit gemeint ist, sondern die Verstorbene. Clodia Pontica hatte sich nie mit ihrem Gatten gestritten; wahrscheinlich bedankte er sich dafür mit dem Epitheton „unbeweglichste". *Beneficia* erhielt man von sozial höhergestellten Personen. Wenn Publius Clodius Amomus seiner Frau für die *beneficia* dankte, so betonte er auch damit ihre göttliche Stellung. Das nächste Beispiel unterscheidet sich von den drei vorhergehenden in zwei Aspekten: Zum einen ist es nicht aus der Nähe von Rom, zum anderen gehört es—soweit der Name dies erkennen lässt—nicht in das Milieu der Freigelassenen. Die Inschrift stammt aus Millingen (Niederlande). Mucronia Marcia weihte ihrer jung verstorbenen Tochter Rufia Materna einen Hain, richtete also ein Heiligtum ein, und bestimmte, an welchen Tagen die Tote Opfer erhalten sollte.

> Deae Dominae Rufiae / [M]aternae aram et / [l]ucum consacravit / [?] Mucronia Marcia / ubi omnibus annis sacrum / instituit XVI K(alendas) Aug(ustas) / et natal(i) Maternae f(iliae) suae / [?] in Octob(ri) et Parental(ibus) / I[X] K[alendas] Martias Rufi(i)s Simil[i] / patri et [S]imili [f]il(io) [et] Maternae [fil(iae)]

> Der Göttin und Herrin Rufia Materna hat Mucronia Marcia einen Altar und einen Hain geweiht, wo sie für jedes Jahr ein Opfer festgelegt hat: Am 16. Tag vor den Kalenden des August (= 17. Juli), beim Geburtstag ihrer Tochter Materna am (?) im Oktober und während der Parentalia am 9. Tag vor den Kalenden des März (= 20. Februar). Dem Vater Rufius Similis, dem Sohn Similis und der Tochter Materna.[14]

Die Verstorbene wird nicht nur als *dea* (Göttin) angesprochen, sondern auch als *domina* (Herrin). Dass die Mutter ihre Tochter als „Herrin" apostrophierte, ist eine seltsame Verkehrung der sozialen Rollen. Allerdings sollte die Inschrift nicht nur aus der Perspektive der Mutter gelesen und gedeutet werden: Allein durch ihre aufwendige Herstellung wurde die Inschrift für eine breitere Gruppe von Rezipienten, welche viele Jahre danach noch die Worte lesen sollten, konzipiert. Damit wurde die Tochter zur „Herrin" für viele andere. Opfer für die Dea Domina Rufia Materna waren am 17. Juli und an ihrem Geburtstag im Oktober vorgesehen; die Opfer im Rahmen der zumindest in Rom über neun Tage gefei-

---

13 CIL VI 15696.
14 CIL XIII 8706; cf. EGELHAAF-GAISER, Totenkult, 232–233.

erten Parentalia im Februar, in denen der Vorfahren gedacht wurde, könnten auch dem verstorbenen Vater Rufius Similis gelten.

Neben diesen unbestreitbaren Vergöttlichungen von verstorbenen Familienmitgliedern finden sich auch weniger deutliche Verbindungen der Verstorbenen mit der Sphäre des Göttlichen. So war es möglich, einen Grabstein zugleich zum Altar für eine Gottheit zu machen, wie dies aus einer Inschrift aus Iuvanum in Mittelitalien geschehen ist: „Der Diana geweiht. Servandus, der Vater, für Obidia Maxima".[15] Durch die Kombination aus einer Weihinschrift für die Gottheit und dem Grabstein wurde Obidia Maxima zwar nicht zur Göttin, aber in einem Atemzug mit einer Gottheit genannt. Weiter geht die folgende Inschrift, in der die Eltern, der kaiserliche Freigelassene P(ublius) Aelius Asclepiacus und Ulpia Priscilla, ein Monument für Diana und die Erinnerung an die verstorbene Tochter Aelia Procula aufstellten.[16] In diesem Beispiel lässt sich schön zeigen, wie die Monumente—soweit möglich—als Ganzes betrachtet werden müssen. Auf dem Relief ist Diana auf der Jagd, mit Bogen und einem Hund dargestellt; die verstorbene Frau fehlt—es sei denn, das Bild zeigt Aelia Procula als Diana. Wie ist die Diana zu interpretieren? Einerseits war sie eine Göttin der Jagd, was wohl keine Beziehung zu Aelia Procula bildet. Andererseits galt Diana als eine jungfräuliche Gottheit; dieser Aspekt würde zur früh verstorbenen Aelia Procula gut passen: Es war in der Antike stets möglich, nur ein Charakteristikum einer Gottheit hervorzuheben. Doch bei aller Trauer um die Tochter lag dem Vater noch eine andere Sache am Herzen. Die Buchstaben AVG LIB (= *Augusti libertus*; Freigelassener des Kaisers) sind größer als die anderen und füllen eine ganze Zeile aus. Der ehemalige Sklave Asclepiacus, seit seiner Freilassung Publius Aelius Asclepiacus, legte größten Wert darauf, dass er vom Kaiser selbst, wahrscheinlich Hadrian, seine Freiheit erhalten hatte.[17] Die Weihinschrift für Livilla Dea im Museum von Avenches dürfte mit einiger Wahrscheinlichkeit auch als Privatdeifikation zu deuten sein. Stifter war Genialis, der Freigelassene eines Flavius Eros—aufgrund seines Namens wohl ebenfalls ein Freigelassener.[18]

Auch im griechischen Osten des Römischen Reiches finden sich ähnliche Fälle. Aus Acheloi (Mesambria) stammt die Grabstele einer Frau namens Ioulia, datiert in die erste Hälfte des 3. Jahrhunderts n. Chr. Eine weibliche Figur sitzt

---
15 CIL IX 6314: Deanae sacr(um) / Servandus Ob/idiae Maximae pater.
16 CIL VI 10958, um 140 n. Chr., Louvre, Kat. 123, Abb. 73; Maße: 99x72x40: D(is) m(anibus) sacrum. Deanae et memoriae Aeliae Proculae. P(ublius) Aelius Asclepiacus Aug(usti) lib(ertus) et Ulpia Priscilla filiae dulcissimae fecerunt.
17 WREDE, Consecratio, 226, Nr. 91, Taf. 12,2; FERAUDI-GRUÉNAIS, Grabbauten, 102, Nr. 123, Abb. 73.
18 FREI-STOLBA, Livilla dea, 125–132; SPICKERMANN, Germania Superior, 52–53.

auf einem Wagen, wobei sich nicht bestimmen lässt, ob es die Verstorbene oder die Gottheit ist. Auch der Text ist von Ambiguität geprägt: „Hier liege ich, die Göttin Hekate, wie du siehst. / Einst war ich sterblich, nun bin ich unsterblich und alterslos, / Ioulia, des Neikios Tochter, des vielbesitzenden Mannes."[19] Durch die Charakterisierung als „unsterblich und alterslos" wurde die Verstorbene zur Göttin Hekate. Wie dieser Vorgang zu konzeptualisieren ist, muss unklar bleiben.[20]

Gleich mehrere Inschriften mit einer Privatdeifikation galten bereits bei der Publikation des Corpus Inscriptionum Latinarum im späten 19. Jahrhundert verschollen und fehlen daher in dieser Sammlung, die bis heute die Standards setzt. Gaius Turranius Phalix stellte eine Inschrift für die 45jährige *mater sanctissima et dea* Callicla Pyrras auf.[21] Hervorhebung verdient, dass die Geehrte nicht eine junge Frau war, sondern der Sohn das Grabmal für die Mutter finanzierte. In einer weiteren Inschrift aus Rom wird die Tochter Gemina für die Eltern zur *dea* Gemina.[22] Eine detaillierte Interpretation dieser Stücke erübrigt sich aufgrund der schlechten Überlieferung. Gleichwohl erhebt sich ein Verdacht: Die relative Häufung von verschollenen Inschriften, die also verloren gegangen sind oder im Lauf der Zeit nicht weiter beachtet wurden, mag durch ihren unglaubwürdig erscheinenden Inhalt begründet sein. Möglicherweise hielt man sie für Fälschungen.

2 Versuch einer Deutung

Spätestens zu diesem Zeitpunkt stellt sich die Frage, wie die Privatdeifikationen einzuordnen sind. Der große Philologe Ulrich von Wilamowitz-Moellendorff etwa urteilte 1932 in seinem von stupender Gelehrsamkeit zeugenden und immer noch lesenswerten Alterswerk „Der Glaube der Hellenen" folgendermaßen über die Praxis, die gewöhnlichen Toten als Heroen zu verehren: „Hinz und

---

19 PEEK, Vers-Inschriften, 438a; WREDE, Consecratio, 238, Nr. 120: ἐνθάδε ἐγὼ κεῖμε Ἑκάτη / θεός, ὡς ἐσορᾷς, ἤμην τὸ / πάλαι βροτός νῦν δὲ ἀθάνα / τος καὶ ἀγήρως.
20 Cf. WREDE, Consecratio, S. 197, Nr. 6: Grabstele des Lysimachos 3. Jh. n. Chr. (?) Aurelios Iulianos hat den Sohn Lysimachos aufgestellt εἰς θεὸν Ἀλέξανδρον.
21 MURATORI, Novus thesaurus, 1246, Nr. 9: Calliclae Pyrradi vix(it) ann(os) XLV. C(aius) Turranius Phalix f(ilius) matri sanctissimae et deae.
22 Johann Caspar von ORELLI, Inscriptionum latinarum amplissima collectio, Zürich 1828, Nr. 4587: Deae Geminae virgini sanctissimae filiae dulcissimae piissimi parentes; cf. WREDE, Consecratio, 230, Nr. 103. In einem verschollenen Grabaltar aus dem Codex Pighianus (16. Jh.) heißt es: coiugi sanctae; 295, Nr. 264.

Kunz wird nun erhöht." Während die Helden der homerischen Epen zu Recht posthumen Heroenkult erhielten, diagnostizierte Wilamowitz-Moellendorff spätestens für das 4. Jahrhundert v. Chr.: „Alles ist doch nur Ausartung des alten ernsten Glaubens".[23] Wilamowitz-Moellendorff argumentierte im Rahmen eines Dekadenzparadigmas, das zu seiner Zeit galt und teilweise bis heute nachwirkt. Dies gilt auch für die römische Religionsgeschichte; für Georg Wissowa befand sich die römische Religion ebenfalls seit dem 4. Jahrhundert v. Chr. in einem Verfallsprozess, der durch das Einsickern „unrömischer" Kulte bedingt war. Solche Bewertungen entstanden mit dem Wissen um den Sieg des Christentums über die „heidnischen" polytheistischen Kulte. Allerdings besteht die Schwäche dieses Dekadenzparadigmas darin, dass die paganen Religionen trotz ihres vermeintlichen Niedergangs über viele Jahrhunderte praktiziert wurden. Seit einiger Zeit ist das Dekadenzparadigma abgelöst durch die Erkenntnis, dass Religion, wie Kultur überhaupt, vielfältigen Veränderungsprozessen unterliegt.[24]

In den antiken Grabinschriften begegnen unterschiedliche Emotionen und Einstellungen. Besonders stark ist dies bei den griechischen Grabinschriften vertreten, von denen stellvertretend einige Beispiele aus Kleinasien genannt sein sollen. So wird oft über das Übel des Todes geklagt: „hinweggerafft vom Neid des Hades".[25] Das Grab kann als ein Siegesdenkmal der Totengöttinnen[26] gedeutet werden. In einer Inschrift des ehemaligen Festspielleiters Capella aus Kleinasien heißt es: „Spiele und lache, solange du lebst; denn wenn du hierher gekommen bist, wirst du nichts anderes mehr sehen können als lange Nacht und Schweigen."[27] Einige Grabtexte sind hoffnungsvoller, so heißt es etwa auf dem Sarkophag des Dichters Boethos aus Telmessos, ins 1. Jahrhundert v. Chr. zu datieren: „Er schläft den Schlaf der Ewigkeit, in süßem Honig liegend." Ein verstorbener Rechtsgelehrter verkündet durch seine Inschrift: „Meine gute Seele befindet sich auf der Insel der Seligen."[28] In christlichen Grabinschriften, die von anderen Jenseitsvorstellungen ausgehen, konnte man zur Mäßigung in der Trauer auffordern: „Darum ermahne ich alle Menschen, die vorübergehen, nicht zu viel in Leid über die Gestorbenen zu weinen; denn der selige Schöpfer der Welt hat in seinem starken Plan und seiner Kraft und Macht gegeben, wieder

---

23 WILAMOWITZ-MOELLENDORFF, Glaube der Hellenen, Vol. II, 19.
24 ROSENBERGER, Religion, 8–12.
25 MERKELBACH/STAUBER, Steinepigramme, 3,204; 3,390: Da kam die bittere Moira und hat ihn rasch hinweggerafft.
26 MERKELBACH/STAUBER, Steinepigramme, 3,411: Μοιρῶν τρόπαιον.
27 MERKELBACH/STAUBER, Steinepigramme, 2,231.
28 MERKELBACH/STAUBER, Steinepigramme, 4,12 und 4,167.

aufzuerstehen." Unsterblichkeit war einerseits nur Gott vorbehalten: „Denn keiner ist unsterblich außer der eine Gott selbst, der Erzeuger von allen, der allen alles zuteilt."[29] Andererseits wurde der Christ Diomedes aus Lykaonien alterslos und unsterblich im Paradies[30]: Auch das Christentum war keineswegs monolithisch.

Trost spenden konnten auch populärphilosophische Schlussfolgerungen nach dem Muster: „Tot bin ich hier und bin Asche, diese Asche ist Erde, wenn die Erde eine Göttin ist, bin ich eine Göttin, bin ich nicht tot."[31] Hier werden spielerisch die Grenzen zwischen Tod und Leben, zwischen Sterblichen und Göttern aufgehoben. Das „Ich", das aus diesen Inschriften spricht, ist eine erste Person Singular innerhalb einer literarischen Konvention; daher muss das Gedicht nicht von dem Verstorbenen verfasst sein.[32]

Dass Menschen, vor allem Verstorbene, als Götter verehrt wurden, war in der Antike nicht verwunderlich. In der Mythologie gab es Gestalten wie Herakles oder Castor und Pollux, die in die Reihe der Götter aufgenommen wurden. Ähnliches geschah—wohl auf lokaler Ebene und daher stark variierend—mit den mythischen Gründern einer Stadt, wobei es sich oft auch um späte Konstruktionen handeln mochte. Als Beispiele mögen Theseus für Athen und Romulus für Rom genügen. Göttlichkeit beschränkte sich nicht nur auf Personen einer weit entfernten Vergangenheit, sondern konnte auch lebenden Menschen zugeschrieben werden. Der Herrscherkult entwickelte sich in der hellenistischen Zeit und wurde im Römischen Reich fortgesetzt.[33] Ob Alexander der Große zu Lebzeiten als Gott verehrt wurde, ist nicht zu belegen. Auf den Münzen zumindest verschwimmen die Grenzen zwischen Alexander und Herakles: Ist es Herakles mit den Zügen Alexanders oder Alexander mit den Attributen des Herakles? 291 v. Chr. wurde Demetrios Poliorketes in Athen als Gottheit empfangen, als Gottheit, die sogar präsenter sei als die namensähnliche Demeter. Im Römischen Reich begann nach dem Tod Caesars die göttliche Verehrung des Kaisers. Mit der *lex Rufrena* des Jahres 42 v. Chr. installierte sein Erbe Octavian einen Kult für Caesar. Augustus selbst wurde nach seinem Tod zum *Divus*, zum Vergöttlichten, viele weitere Kaiser und ihre Angehörigen folgten, vorausgesetzt, sie hatten sich als gute Herrscher erwiesen und ihre Nachfolger waren daran interessiert sie zu divinisieren. Nicht jede Nennung eines „Unsterblichen"

---

29 MERKELBACH/STAUBER, Steinepigramme, 3,277 und 3,245.
30 MERKELBACH/STAUBER, Steinepigramme, 3,61: ἀθάνατον καὶ ἀγήραον ἐν Παραδίσσῳ.
31 CLE 1532: mortua heic ego sum et sum cinis, is cinis terrast, sein est terra dea, ego sum dea, mortua non sum.
32 Sammlungen von Versinschriften bieten ARENA EVRE, Carmina; CRINITI, Lege nunc viator.
33 Cf. FLORY, Deification, 127–134.

bezeichnet einen Gott. So rückte 313/14 n. Chr. Epitynchanus aus Phrygien, Priester der Hekate, des Manes-Zeus und des Apollon-Helios, durch ein nicht mehr greifbares Ritual in den Rang eines „Unsterblichen" auf.[34]

In der polytheistischen Antike war die Trennlinie zwischen Menschen und Göttern keineswegs so ausgeprägt wie im Christentum.[35] Es gab keine allgemeingültige Definition einer Gottheit. Ein möglicher Aspekt ist die Unsterblichkeit. Allerdings kursierten über viele Götter Abstammungsmythen, sie waren also gezeugt und nicht schon seit dem Anfang der Welt vorhanden. Götter einer niedrigeren Kategorie, wie etwa Pan, konnten nach einem Jahrtausend sterben; in der Regierungszeit des Kaisers Tiberius (14–37 n. Chr.) soll der Hirtengott Pan gestorben sein.[36] Waren die Götter allmächtig? Kaum ein Gott wurde als „Schöpfer" bezeichnet; Allmacht besaßen vielleicht Zeus oder Iuppiter, aber die anderen Götter nicht; überdies waren die Götter dem Schicksal weitgehend untergeordnet. Waren die antiken Götter allgegenwärtig? Zeus und Apollon konnten als Orakelgötter an vielen Orten gleichzeitig auftreten; zugleich gab es Gottheiten, die nur lokale Wirksamkeit beanspruchten. Daher gilt: Wer göttliche Ehren, also Opfer, erhielt, konnte als Gottheit angesehen und bezeichnet werden.[37]

Mit dieser sehr offenen Definition lassen sich die Toten schnell in den Bereich des Göttlichen verweisen, da an den Gräbern Rituale abgehalten wurden.[38] Zu den regelmäßig für die Toten durchgeführten Ritualen gehörten die Feralia am 21. Februar; hier erhielten die *Di Manes*, zumeist als „Totengötter" übersetzt, Opfer an den Gräbern: Weizen, Salz, Weizenfladen und Veilchen. Die Formel *Dis Manibus*, „den Totengöttern", steht auf Zehntausenden von Grabinschriften

---

34 MERKELBACH/STAUBER, Steinepigramme, 3,237: [Ἀ]θάνατος Ἐπιτύγχανος Πίου, τιμηθεὶς ὑπὸ Ἑκάτης πρώτης, δεύτερον ὑπὸ Μάνου Δάου [ἡ]λιοδρόμου Διός, τρίτον Φοίβου ἀρχηγέτο[υ] χρησμοδότου. ἀληθῶς δῶ[ρ]ον ἔλαβ[ο]ν χρησ[μ]οδοτῖ[ν] ἀλη[θεί]ας ἐν πατρίδι κὲ (ἐ)ν ὅ[ρ]οις χρησμοδοτῖν νόμους τιθῖν, ἐν ὅροις [χρ]ησμοδοτῖν [π]ᾶσιν τοῦτο ἔχω δῶ[ρ]ον ἐξ ἀθανάτων πάντων—Der unsterbliche Epitynchanos, Sohn des Pios, geehrt—erstens von Hekate, zweitens von Manes Daos, dem Heliodromos des Zeus, drittens von Phoibos (= Apollon), dem Gründer und Orakelgeber. Wahrlich, ich habe die Gabe erhalten, Orakel über die Wahrheit zu geben in meinem Heimatort und innerhalb der Grenzen Orakel zu geben, Gesetze zu geben, innerhalb der Grenzen allen Orakel zu geben; ich habe diese Gabe von allen Unsterblichen. Generell zur Inschrift 235–241.
35 RÜPKE, Religion der Römer, 72; BENDLIN, Vergöttlichung, 68–69, meint, dass sich die Götter von den Menschen durch zwei Eigenschaften unterscheiden: Unsterblichkeit und Macht; Menschen, die eine besondere Machtposition innehaben, können daher göttliche Ehren erhalten.
36 Plut. mor. 419 a–d.
37 CLAUSS, Kaiser, passim.
38 OBRYK, Unsterblichkeitsglaube, 94–115.

seit etwa dem Beginn des 2. Jahrhunderts n. Chr.; sehr häufig wird nur die Abkürzung DM benutzt. Beide Varianten werden zumeist mit „den Totengöttern" übersetzt. Doch trotz der großen Anzahl von Belegen bleibt es unklar, wie diese Formulierung zu verstehen ist. Wir wissen nicht viel über diese *Di Manes*, die immer im Plural genannt wurden. Es kann sein, dass durch *Dis Manibus* die Toten den Bewohnern der Unterwelt übergeben und ihrem Schutz unterstellt wurden.[39] Es mag sein, dass die Verstorbenen selbst zu diesen *Di Manes* gehörten. Es ist tröstlich, dass auch für Griechen *Dis Manibus* ein Rätsel darstellten. In griechischen Grabinschriften, die lateinisches Formular imitierten, finden sich unterschiedliche Übersetzungen: den „unterirdischen Göttern" (θεοῖς καταχθονίοις), den „göttlichen Daimonen" (θεοῖς δαίμοσι) und den „göttlichen Heroen" (θεοῖς Ἥρωσι).[40]

Weitere Opfer wurden Mitte Mai bei den Lemuria dargebracht, unter anderem auch schwarze Bohnen.[41] Bei den Rosalia wurden die Gräber mit Rosen geschmückt. Ob diese Rituale im gesamten Römischen Reich und über Jahrhunderte hinweg stabil blieben, ist stark zu bezweifeln. Entsprechend der Ausdehnung des Römischen Reiches existierten regionale und lokale Traditionen; so wurden im römischen Ägypten in vielen Fällen die Leichen mumifiziert; aufwendige Grabkammern wurden nach wie vor im ägyptischen Stil ausgestattet; umgekehrt finden sich auch in Rom einige wenige Belege für die Mumifizierung. Das *testamentum Lingonis*, ein im 19. Jahrhundert in einer Baseler Bibliothek entdecktes Manuskript aus dem 10. Jahrhundert, enthält ausführliche Anweisungen eines unbekannten Mannes aus dem Gebiet der Lingonen (Langres), wohl aus dem 2. Jahrhundert n. Chr. Der anonyme Autor legte schon zu Lebzeiten fest, was an seinem Grabmal geschehen sollte. Auf der Außenseite des Grabmonuments sollten mehrere Dinge notiert werden, unter anderem das Alter des Verstorbenen. Einmal im Jahr sollten die zahlreichen Freigelassenen— es kann sich also nur um einen sehr reichen Mann handeln—Geld sammeln und damit vor dem Grab ein Mahl abhalten. Im Unterschied zur Situation in Rom sind hier deutlich mehr Termine für Rituale genannt: Opfer waren zu Beginn der Monate April, Mai, Juni, Juli, August und Oktober geplant.[42]

Die *di parentes* und die *lemures* gehörten zu den im Haus verehrten Göttern; sie waren möglicherweise in irgendeiner Form von den Vorfahren abgeleitet. In der antiken Literatur finden sich noch deutlichere Aussagen: Nach Varro waren

---

39 WAELKENS, Privatdeifikation, 283, mit Verweis auf CAGNAT, Cours d'épigraphie, 281–282; RÜPKE, Religion der Römer, 70, „gute Götter".
40 WAELKENS, Privatdeifikation, 294–295, n. 75.
41 Ov. fast. 2,533–570; 5,419–661.
42 CIL XIII 5708 = ILS 8379; cf. EGELHAAF-GAISER, Totenkult, 225–257.

die Toten Götter.⁴³ Cicero äußerte sich ähnlich: „Die verstorbenen Guten sollen als Götter verehrt werden."⁴⁴ Auch wenn an dieser Stelle Ciceros Bruder alte Sakralgesetze aus dem Kopf zitiert, ist unbestritten, dass die guten Toten—gemeint sind wohl alle, die sich für Rom einsetzten—als Götter betrachtet wurden. Auch aus dem griechischsprachigen Raum lassen sich vergleichbare Aussagen finden, wobei oft nach Regionen zu unterscheiden ist; in Boiotien und auf Thera etwa wurden die Toten als Heroen verehrt.⁴⁵

In den Briefen Ciceros an Atticus schlägt sich die Trauer um die Anfang 45 v. Chr. verstorbene Tochter Tullia nieder. Durch die Pläne für ihr Grabmal sollte die Trauer ausgedrückt und überwunden werden. Cicero bemühte sich in den Wochen nach Tullias Tod darum, ein angemessenes Grundstück für ihr Grabmal für sie zu finden. Er trat mit mehreren Personen in Kontakt und sinnierte über die Grundstückspreise sowie vor allem über die Lage der Parzellen. Eine Zeitlang trug er sich mit dem Gedanken, eine Villa am Meer zu erwerben, um dort die Tochter zu bestatten, nahm aber Abstand davon: Villen in Küstenlage mochten von großer Schönheit sein, aber zugleich bestand bei einer solchen Anlage immer die Gefahr, dass spätere Besitzer das Grabmal ignorierten; überdies war die Öffentlichkeit eines solchen Ortes begrenzt. Daher suchte Cicero einen belebten Ort, am besten an einer Straße. Auch über die Form diskutierte er mit Atticus. Cicero wollte kein einfaches Grabmal, sondern ein *fanum*, also ein Heiligtum.

> Fanum fieri volo, neque hoc mihi erui potest. Sepulcri similitudinem effugere non tam propter poenam legis studio, quam ut maxime adsequar ἀποθέωσιν.

> Ich möchte, dass es ein Tempel wird; und nichts kann mich davon abhalten. Die Ähnlichkeit mit einem üblichen Grabmal scheue ich nicht aufgrund der Gesetzeslage, sondern weil ich so nahe wie möglich an eine Apotheose kommen will.⁴⁶

In dieser Passage legte Cicero die Karten auf den Tisch. Er wollte seine Tochter in die Nähe der Vergöttlichung bringen. Dies war nicht nur ein Ausdruck seiner Vaterliebe, sondern zeigt auch die Möglichkeiten, die denjenigen offen standen, die es sich leisten konnten. Tullia wurde nicht als Göttin bezeichnet, war aber

---

43 Plut. qu.R. 14A(267B); Aug. civ. 8,26. Cf. WAELKENS, Privatdeifikation, 270–271.
44 Cic. leg. 2,22.
45 WREDE, Consecratio, 249, Nr. 144, nennt einen Sarg mit Heraklesdarstellung aus Thessalonike: „Γ. Ἀντωνίῳ Ἀττικῷ νέῳ ἥρῳ, gewidmet von den Eltern Antonios Attikos und Fabia Sambo." WILAMOWITZ-MOELLENDORFF, Glaube der Hellenen, Vol. II, 19: „In Böotien ist das aphheroizein gewöhnlich, in Thera heißt der Tote einfach heros."
46 Cic. Att. 12,38.

durch das *fanum* und die Apotheose nahe am Bereich des Göttlichen. Damit verband Cicero die Hoffnung, dass ein solches Gebäude durch die *religio* (Scheu) der Menschen auch in kommenden Generationen respektiert werde. Auch an anderer Stelle berichtete Cicero von seinem Plan für einen Tempel und zur Apotheose der Tochter; er forderte Atticus auf, die für den Tempel nötigen Säulen zu kaufen.[47] Letztlich verliefen Ciceros ehrgeizige Pläne für das Grabmal im Sand, da ihm die finanziellen Mittel fehlten.[48] Der Bau wurde nie vollendet.

In der Antike war die *memoria*, das Gedenken an die Verstorbenen, von zentraler Bedeutung. Daher waren so viele Grabmäler am Straßenrand errichtet. Die Nachwelt sollte das Grabmal sehen, an ihm vorbeigehen und die Inschrift lesen. Viele Grabinschriften beginnen mit der Aufforderung an die Passanten, stehen zu bleiben und den Text zu lesen: *Siste viator*—„Bleib stehen, der du vorbeikommst". Im Wettbewerb um die Aufmerksamkeit der Nachwelt erhöhten sich die Chancen, wenn man als Gottheit angesprochen wurde. Wenn nun ein Kult eingerichtet wurde, wenn festgelegt wurde, an welchem Tag Rituale abgehalten werden sollten und wenn ihre Finanzierung geregelt war, so war die *memoria* der Verstorbenen dauerhaft gesichert. Dies war der große Vorteil einer Privatdeifikation. Zugleich muss es doch eine gewisse Scheu gegeben haben, die eigenen Toten in einer Inschrift als Gottheit anzusprechen; anders ist die geringe Zahl der Belege nicht zu erklären. Wie lange solch ein Kult aufrechterhalten wurde, lässt sich nicht sagen. Wahrscheinlich geriet er in Vergessenheit, sobald die nächsten Verwandten nicht mehr vor Ort oder verstorben waren.

3 Zusammenfassung

Hinter dem vermeintlich einfachen und „lapidaren" Latein der römischen Inschriften verbergen sich auf Schritt und Tritt semantische Untiefen; als Beispiel mag die im Detail unklare Bedeutung der Formel *Dis manibus* genügen. Die hier

---

47 Cic. Att. 12,19 und 22. Cf. CIL X 7566, das Grabmonument in der Gestalt eines Tempels aus Carales in Sardinien, das M. Cassius Philippus für seine verstorbene Gattin Atilia Pomptilla erbaute: Quod credis templum, quod saepe viator adoras, / Pomptillae cineres ossaq(ue) parva tegit – Was du für einen Tempel hältst, was du, Reisender, oft anbetest, das bedeckt die Asche und die Gebeine der Pomptilla; CIL X 7576: [I]unonis sedes infernae cerni[te cu]ncti: / Numine mutato fulget Pomptilla per aevom – Seht alle den Wohnsitz der unterirdischen Iuno, / mit gewandeltem *numen* glänzt Pomptilla auf ewig.
48 Zu den Trauerbriefen Ciceros cf. CARCOPINO, Correspondence, 169–175; JÄGER, Briefanalysen, 290–336.

vorgeführten Fälle von Privatdeifikation weisen vier Gemeinsamkeiten auf. 1. Zeit: Die Beispiele sind wohl ausnahmslos ins 1. und 2. Jahrhundert n. Chr. zu datieren. 2. Raum: Die Belege kommen bis auf einen aus Rom oder der näheren Umgebung der Stadt. 3. Soziale Schicht: Die meisten Fälle stammen aus dem Bereich der Freigelassenen. 4. Geschlecht: Stets erhalten Frauen diese göttlichen Ehren. Aufgrund der geringen Anzahl der Belege müssen alle Deutungen dieses Befundes im Spekulativen bleiben. Alle Privatdeifikationen sind in die Zeit zu datieren, in der ohnehin die meisten Inschriften hergestellt wurden; ebenso kommt ein Großteil der Inschriften aus Rom und seinem Umland. Eher signifikant scheinen Schichtenzugehörigkeit und Geschlecht. Freigelassene zeigten nach Maßgabe ihrer Kräfte ihren neuen Status und finanzierten sich und ihren Familienangehörigen Grabmonumente mit Inschriften. Für Senatoren wäre es kaum ratsam gewesen, ihre toten Familienmitglieder zu deifizieren; dies hätte man leicht als Herausforderung gegenüber dem Kaiser werten können. Über die Frage, warum nur Frauen der Ehre einer Privatdeifikation teilhaftig wurden, lassen sich aufgrund des Fehlens von Aussagen in der antiken Literatur lediglich Spekulationen anstellen. Möglicherweise bietet der unterschiedliche Status von Frauen und Männern einen Schlüssel. Bei Männern aus derselben sozialen Schicht konnte man den Beruf oder die erreichten Ämter angeben. Diese Option fehlte bei den Frauen fast gänzlich; für sie blieb immer nur der Verweis darauf, dass sie ihre gesellschaftliche Rolle gut gespielt hatten.

Über die Entstehung und das Verschwinden der Privatdeifikation lassen sich kaum Aussagen machen. In der römischen Religion war es stets möglich, in einer Form von *bricolage* Rituale neu zusammenzusetzen. Dies gilt auch für den rituellen Umgang mit Tod. Eine kultische Verehrung der Toten war in der gesamten Antike—sicherlich in vielen Brechungen und Varianten—üblich. Tote erhielten Opfergaben und waren damit auch in den Bereich des Göttlichen verwiesen. Und da die Zahl der Götter in einem polytheistischen System nie abgeschlossen sein kann, bestand die Option, durch die Privatdeifikation eine Familienangehörige zur Göttin zu machen. Damit war die Privatdeifikation nur eine Zuspitzung der üblichen Praxis. Dies implizierte nicht, dass man den Kult für alle Einwohner einer Stadt einforderte, sondern die Verehrung fand im engen Rahmen der Familie und *familia* statt, umfasste also Verwandte, Freunde und die mehr oder weniger unfreien Mitglieder eines Hauses oder eines Gutshofes. Gerade das Beispiel Ciceros zeigt, in welchem Maß die Privatdeifikation auch ein Ausdruck besonderer Trauer war; ob dabei „echte" Emotionen der Angehörigen im Spiel waren oder ob es sich um eine Inszenierung handelte, können wir nicht entscheiden.

Am Ende seines rauschenden Festes ist Trimalchio vollständig betrunken und will seine eigene Beerdigung inszenieren. Trompeter spielen eine Trauer-weise, ohrenbetäubender Lärm entsteht und Feuerwehrleute, die eine Katastrophe vermuten, crashen die Party.[49] Warum Trimalchio weder für sich noch für seine Frau eine Privatdeifikation vorsieht, darüber lässt sich nur spekulieren: War diese Praxis zur Abfassungszeit des Textes in der Mitte des 1. Jahrhunderts n. Chr. noch nicht so verbreitet? Lag es daran, dass Trimalchio und seine Frau noch am Leben waren? Oder war eine Privatdeifikation einfach nicht so grotesk, wie sie uns Monotheisten manchmal scheinen mag?

Bibliographie

ALFÖLDY, Géza, Die Rolle des Einzelnen in der Gesellschaft des Römischen Kaiserreiches. Erwartungen und Wertmaßstäbe (SHAW.PH 1980, 8), Heidelberg 1980.

ALFÖLDY, Géza, Römische Sozialgeschichte (Wissenschaftliche Paperbacks Sozial- und Wirtschaftsgeschichte 84), Stuttgart ⁴2011.

ARENA EVRE, Marigrazia, Praeteritae carmina vitae. Pietre e parole di Numidia (Numidia meridionale) (PRSA 28), Rom 2011.

BENDLIN, Andreas, Art. „Vergöttlichung. Griechenland und Rom", in: DNP 12/2, Stuttgart/Weimar 2002, 68–69.

CAGNAT, René, Cours d'épigraphie latine, Paris ⁴1914.

CARCOPINO, Jérôme, Cicero. The Secrets of his Correspondence, London 1951.

CARROLL, Maureen, Spirits of the Dead. Roman Funerary Commemoration in Western Europe (Oxford Studies in Ancient Documents), Oxford 2006.

CLAUSS, Manfred, Kaiser und Gott. Herrscherkult im römischen Reich, Stuttgart 1999.

CRINITI, Nicola et. al. (Hg.), "Lege nunc, viator ..." vita e morte nei carmina Latina epigraphica della Padania centrale, Parma 1996.

DAVIES, John/WILKES, John, Epigraphy and the Historical Sciences. 13th International Congress of Greek and Latin Epigraphy (PBA 177), Oxford 2012.

DONATI, Angela/POMA, Gabriella (Hg.), L'officina Epigrafica Romana. In ricordo di Giancarlo Susini. Papers Presented at a Conference Held in Bertinoro, Italy, Sept. 16–18, 2010 (Epigrafia e antichità), Faenza (Ravennna) 2012.

ECK, Werner, Inschriften auf Holz. Ein unterschätztes Phänomen der epigraphischen Kultur Roms, in: Kneissl, Peter/Losemann, Volker (Hg.), Imperium Romanum. Studien zu Geschichte und Rezeption. Festschrift für Karl Christ zum 75. Geburtstag, Stuttgart 1998, 203–217.

EGELHAAF-GAISER, Ulrike, Träger und Transportwege von Religion am Beispiel des Totenkultes in den Germaniae, in: Spickermann, Wolfgang/Cancik, Hubert/Rüpke, Jörg (Hg.), Religion in den germanischen Provinzen Roms, Tübingen 2001, 225–257.

---

49 Petron. 78.

FERAUDI-GRUÉNAIS, Francisca, Inschriften und „Selbstdarstellung" in stadtrömischen Grabbauten (Libitina 2), Rom 2003.
FEUCHT, Birgit, Uniformity up to the Grave? Funerary Inscriptions of Roman Legionaries in Western Europe, in: AncSoc 41 (2011) 147–183.
FLORY, Marleen B., The Deification of Roman Women, in: The Ancient History Bulletin 9 (1995) 127–134.
FREI-STOLBA, Regula, Livilla dea, in: Jahrbuch der Schweizerischen Gesellschaft für Ur- und Frühgeschichte 73 (1990) 125–132.
JÄGER, Wolfgang, Briefanalysen. Zum Zusammenhang von Realitätserfahrung und Sprache in Briefen Ciceros (Studien zur klassischen Philologie 26), Frankfurt a. M. et al. 1986.
KOLB, Anne/FUGMANN, Joachim, Tod in Rom. Grabinschriften als Spiegel römischen Lebens, Darmstadt 2008.
KRANZ, Peter, Der sogenannte Herakles Hope. Frühwerk des Skopas oder neuerlicher Fall kaiserzeitlicher Privatdeifikation?, in: Römische Mitteilungen 96 (1989) 393–409.
MACMULLEN, Ramsay, The Epigraphic Habit in the Roman Empire, in: The AJP 103 (1982) 233–246.
MATHIEU, Nicolas, L'épitaphe et la mémoire. Parenté et identité sociale dans les Gaules et Germanies romaines (Histoire: Histoire antique), Rennes 2011.
MERKELBACH, Reinhold/STAUBER, Josef (Hg.), Steinepigramme aus dem griechischen Osten, 5 Vols., München et al. 1998–2004.
MURATORI, Lodovico Antonio, Novus thesaurus veterum inscriptionum, Mailand 1740.
OBRYK, Matylda, Unsterblichkeitsglaube in den griechischen Versinschriften (UALG 108), Berlin et al. 2012.
PEEK, Werner, Griechische Vers-Inschriften aus Thessalien (SHAW.PH 1974,3), Heidelberg 1974.
ROSENBERGER, Veit, Religion in der Antike (Geschichte Kompakt), Darmstadt 2012.
RÜPKE, Jörg, Die Religion der Römer. Eine Einführung, München 2001.
RÜPKE, Jörg, Gestiftete Religion in der römischen Kaiserzeit, in: Piegeler, Hildegard/Pohl, Inken/Rademacher, Stefan (Hg.), Gelebte Religion. Untersuchungen zur sozialen Gestaltungskraft religiöser Vorstellungen und Praktiken in Geschichte und Gegenwart. Festschrift für Hartmut Zinser zum 60. Geburtstag, Würzburg 2004, 73–79.
SPICKERMANN, Wolfgang, Germania Superior (Religion der römischen Provinzen 2), Tübingen 2003.
von ORELLI, Johann Caspar, Inscriptionum latinarum amplissima collectio, Zürich 1828.
WAELKENS, Mark, Privatdeifikation in Kleinasien und in der griechisch-römischen Welt. Zu einer neuen Grabinschrift aus Phrygien, in: Donceel, Robert/Lebrun, René (Hg.), Archéologie et religions de l'Anatolie ancienne. Mélanges en l'honneur du professeur Paul Naster (HoRe 10), Louvain-la-Neuve 1983, 259–307.
WILAMOWITZ-MOELLENDORFF, Ulrich von, Der Glaube der Hellenen, 2 Vols., Berlin 1931/32.
WREDE, Henning, Consecratio in formam deorum. Vergöttlichte Privatpersonen in der römischen Kaiserzeit, Mainz 1981.
ZUCCA, Raimondo, Il complesso epigrafico rupestre della "Grotte delle Vipere", in: Gasperini, Lidio (Hg.), Rupes loquentes. Atti del convegno internazionale di studio sulle iscrizioni rupestri in età romana in Italia, Rom 1992, 503–540.

Christiane Kunst
Tod auf der Latrine—
Zum Ende von Caracalla und Elagabal

Nach der brutalen Ermordung Caligulas im Jahr 41 n. Chr. erklärte dessen Prätorianerpräfekt Arrecinus Clemens, der als oberster Personenschützer des Princeps selbst in die Tat verwickelt war[1]: ein Herrscher, der die Gesetze nicht achte und ermordet werde, sei an seinem Tod selber schuld.[2] Eine ähnliche Haltung nahm auch der Kaiser Marc Aurel in der Vita des Avidius Cassius nach dem Tod des aufständischen Statthalters ein und wies nach, „dass kaum je ein guter Herrscher von einem Gegenkaiser (*tyrannus*) besiegt oder getötet worden sei."[3] Der gewaltsame Tod eines Princeps war also Hinweis auf seine Untauglichkeit als Herrscher.

Diese Sichtweise ist eng mit der sich allmählich entwickelnden Praxis beim Herrscherwechsel verknüpft. Zum einen bestand die Möglichkeit, die *memoria* des Vorgängers zu befestigen, indem man ihn per Senatsbeschluss konsekrierte.[4] Dieses Verfahren eignete sich für diejenigen, die als Erben des Vorgängers gelten wollten; besonders natürlich für die Söhne verstorbener Kaiser, die auf diese Weise selbst Gottessohnschaft erwarben. Das zweite Verfahren war die sogenannte *damnatio memoriae*, die Entehrung der *memoria* des Vorgängers durch einen Senatsbeschluss, der in erster Linie die Auslöschung des Namens in öffentlichen Monumenten vorsah.[5]

---

1 Zu seiner Verwicklung cf. Cass. Dio 59,29.
2 Cf. Josephus, Ant 19,1,19<155–156>: τυραννίδα γὰρ εἰς ὀλίγον μὲν ἀνθεῖν ἡδονῇ τοῦ ὑβρίζειν ἐπαρθεῖσαν, εὐτυχεῖς δ' οὐκ ἄρα ποιεῖσθαι τὰς ἀπαλλαγὰς τοῦ βίου, μίσει τῆς ἀρετῆς πρὸς αὐτὴν χρωμένης, ἀλλὰ μετὰ τοιαύτης δυστυχίας ὁποία δὴ Γάιον συνελθεῖν πρὸ τῶν ἐπαναστάντων καὶ συνθέντων τὴν ἐπίθεσιν αὐτὸν ἐπίβουλον αὑτῷ γενόμενον, καὶ διδάξαντα οἷς ὑβρίζων ἀφόρητος ἦν, ἀφανίζων τοῦ νόμου τὴν πρόνοιαν, πολέμῳ πρὸς αὐτὸν χρῆσθαι τοὺς φιλτάτους, καὶ νῦν λόγῳ μὲν εἶναι τούτους οἳ ἀνῃρήκασι Γάιον, ἔργῳ δ' αὐτὸν ὑφ' ἑαυτοῦ κεῖσθαι διολωλότα (Ed. BEKKER, Opera, Bd. 4).
3 SHA Avid. 8,3: nec quemquam facile bonum vel victum a tyranno vel occisum (Ed. HOHL).
4 Cf. RICHARD, Funérailles, 1121–1134; CHANTRAINE, Herrscher, 67–88; GRADEL, Apotheosis, 186–199; DAVIES, Death, 10–11; ENGELS, Entrückung, 79–133.
5 Cf. SABLAYROLLES/PAILLER, Damnatio, 11–55; zuletzt FLOWER, Art, 115–159, und KRÜPE, Damnatio, 140–176.

Die Praxis der Erinnerungsächtung eines verstorbenen Princeps war eine bewusst inszenierte Handlungskette,[6] die das Regiment des Vorgängers diskreditierte und diesen als Feind des Staates und seiner Freiheit stigmatisierte. Damit bot sich die Chance zum politischen Neuanfang. Das Verfahren diente dazu, politische Diskontinuität zu propagieren und den neuen Herrscher vom Vorgänger abzugrenzen, ohne dabei das monarchische System selbst in Frage zu stellen.

Nach dieser Lesart gab es entweder den *caesar* oder aber den *tyrannus*, der früher oder später sein verdientes gewaltsames Ende fand. Kein so definierter *tyrannus* ist friedlich gestorben. Da ein römischer Princeps zu Lebzeiten immer auch göttlich verehrt wurde, bestand die Notwendigkeit, den Tyrannen zumindest symbolisch in die menschliche Sphäre zurückzuholen.[7] Die Zurschaustellung der verstümmelten Porträts war ein wirkungsvoller Akt, die Entehrung der Gescheiterten zu kommunizieren und die menschliche, sterbliche Natur des gefallenen Gegners herauszustellen. Dies galt umso mehr, als dem Bildnis zuvor göttliche Ehren erwiesen worden waren und es als tatsächlicher Vertreter des Herrschers galt.[8] Sinnesorgane der Bildnisse waren daher auch das bevorzugte Ziel von Angriffen.[9] Bis zur Severerzeit erhielt die überwiegende Zahl der entehrten Kaiser ein privates Begräbnis und ihre Leichen wurden nicht geschändet.[10] Es genügte, die Statuen zu verstümmeln und damit den Leichnam des Kaisers symbolisch zu profanieren.[11]

Am Beispiel der beiden severischen Herrscher Caracalla[12] und Elagabal[13] will ich im Folgenden zeigen, dass dieses Verfahren im frühen 3. Jahrhundert punktuell verschärft und dem Entehrten auch seine menschlichen Eigenschaften abgesprochen wurden. Das änderte jedoch nichts an der Tatsache, dass der Umgang mit der *memoria* des Verstorbenen ein rein politischer Akt war, der von seinem jeweiligen Nachfolger nach Bedarf inszeniert wurde.

Die severische Zeit rehabilitierte erstmals bereits verfemte Kaiser, was vermutlich der Hauptgrund für die extreme Brutalisierung im Umgang mit dem politischen Konkurrenten auf dem Kaiserthron war, so dass eine einfache Rückholung in die menschliche Sphäre nicht mehr genügte. Beide hier zu behandelnden Prin-

---

6 Cf. KNIPPSCHILD, Destrucción, 57–88.
7 Aus diesem Grund wurden gerade Edelmetallbildnisse beseitigt (cf. Cass. Dio 74,14,2a).
8 Cf. PEKÁRY, Kaiserbildnis, 134.
9 Cf. VARNER, Mutilation, 3.
10 Cf. KUNST, Leichnam, 79–100.
11 Cf. Plin. paneg. 52,4–5 (Domitian); Cass. Dio 74,2,1 (Commodus).
12 Eigentlich: Marcus Aurelius Antoninus; vor 195 n. Chr.: (L.) Septimius Bassianus.
13 Eigentlich: Marcus Aurelius Antoninus; vor 218 n. Chr.: Varius Avitus.

cipes starben eines gewaltsamen Todes, wobei die *memoria* Caracallas nach seinem Tod ambivalent behandelt wurde,[14] die des Elagabal aber vorbehaltlose und dauerhafte Entehrung erfuhr. Zunächst will ich kurz auf die Funktion von Todesdarstellungen in der antiken Historiographie eingehen, um anschließend auf der Grundlage von jeweils drei relativ ausführlichen Berichten die Todesdarstellungen[15] beider Herrscher zu analysieren. Zwei der Autoren, die Historiker Cassius Dio und Herodian, waren Zeitgenossen; die dritte Quelle, die hoch umstrittene Biographiensammlung der Historia Augusta, stammt nach eigener Aussage aus der Zeit Constantins, greift aber zumindest für die Vita Caracallas auch auf die zeitgenössische verlorene Biographiensammlung des Marius Maximus zurück.[16]

Die antike Literatur hat den Tod eines berühmten Menschen immer wieder dazu benutzt, ein Schlaglicht auf seine Persönlichkeit zu werfen. Dies geschah durch die mit Todesszenen verbundenen allgemeinen Nachrufe,[17] vor allem aber durch die Darstellung des Sterbens selbst. Eusebios macht das beim Tod Konstantins explizit: „Denn es hat das schmähliche Lebensende eines jeden von diesen [Konkurrenten um den Thron] den augenscheinlichen Beweis erbracht, dass sie Gott verhasst waren, wie hingegen das allen offenbare Ende Konstantins die Bürgschaft bot, dass er bei Gott in Gnaden stand."[18] Und der Autor in der Historia Augusta formuliert mit Blick auf die entehrenden Hinrichtungen der Anhänger Elagabals, „dass ihr Tod [= die Todesart] ihrer Art zu leben entspreche".[19]

Spätestens seit Livius waren Todesdarstellungen pointierte Zusammenfassungen des vorangegangenen Lebens eines Individuums.[20] Gerade in Hinblick auf die Herrscher handelt es sich um hochgradig konstruierte Texte. Das lässt sich besonders deutlich am Beispiel des Julian Apostata ablesen, dessen Sterben in der paganen und christlichen Historiographie jeweils gegensätzlich beschrieben wird.[21]

---

14 Cf. zuletzt SIMELON, Caracalla, 792–810.
15 Cf. TIMONEN, Cruelty, 176–190.
16 Cf. HOHL, Ende, 276–293; HEINEN, Tendenz, 421–435.
17 Etwa das Totengericht des Augustus (Tac. ann. 1,9–10; Cass. Dio 56,43–46); Sen. suas. 6,17–21. Cf. POMEROY, Death Notices, 120–125.; SCHUNCK, Sterben, 16–49.
18 Eus. vita Const. 74: τῆς ἐφ' ἑκάστῳ τοῦ βίου καταστροφῆς ἐναργῆ τὸν ἔλεγχον τῆς αὐτῶν θεοεχθρίας ἐνδειξαμένης, ὥσπερ οὖν τῆς θεοφιλίας τὰ ἐχέγγυα τὸ Κωνσταντίνου τοῖς πᾶσι φανερὸν κατέστησε τέλος (Ed. SCHNEIDER). Laktanz' gesamte Schrift *de mortibus persecutorum* hat den Gedanken entsprechend systematisiert und auf die Todesdarstellungen der Christenverfolger angewandt.
19 SHA Elag. 16,5: ut mors esset vitae consentiens.
20 Cf. RONCONI, Exitus, 1257–1268; POMEROY, Death Notices, 146–168.
21 Dazu ARAND, Ende, 234–236.

Caracalla starb am 8. April 217 n. Chr. durch die Hand des Iulius Martialis, eines Angehörigen der Prätorianergarde, der noch auf der Flucht getötet wurde. Alle Darstellungen sind sich einig, dass sein Nachfolger, der Prätorianerpräfekt Opellius Macrinus, der eigentliche Drahtzieher der Ermordung seines Herrn war. Mit ihm bestieg der erste Ritter den Thron, was—nach Aussage Cassius Dios—nur in Folge der schlimmen Verfehlungen Caracallas vom Senat sanktioniert wurde.[22]

Die drei Hauptquellen haben sehr unterschiedliche Gewichtungen in der Bewertung der Ereignisse. Für Cassius Dio ist Caracalla ein Despot, der die Ordnung der römischen Gesellschaft infrage stellt, indem er seine Vertrauten im Militär und nicht im Stand der Senatoren sucht. Für ihn steht daher der Strafcharakter des Todes im Vordergrund. Der Kaiser wird von jenen getötet, denen er am meisten vertraut, den Prätorianern. Aus diesem Grund räumt Cassius Dio auch den Motiven des Verrats von Seiten ihres Kommandanten Macrinus breiten Raum ein: Jener handelt in Notwehr und offenbart die Boshaftigkeit Caracallas. Das Leben des Präfekten war in Gefahr, nachdem Prophezeiungen aufgetaucht sein sollen, dass er der nächste Kaiser sein werde.[23]

Die Verletzung der Ordnung durch Caracalla wird im Zusammenhang mit der Todesdarstellung zeichenhaft an drei Indizien festgemacht: 1. dem Mord an seinem Bruder Geta zu Beginn der Herrschaft, der die Zerstörung der natürlichen, durch Familienbande gegebenen Ordnung bedeutet; 2. der Förderung seiner skythisch-germanischen Leibwache. Sie symbolisiert die Vernichtung der gegebenen gesellschaftlichen Ordnung durch die Bevorzugung von Barbaren gegenüber Römern und sie entfremdet dem Kaiser die Soldaten, die angeblich ungerührt zusehen, als ihn die Prätorianer beseitigen;[24] 3. der Haltung von (zahmen) Löwen als Bett- und Tischgenossen. Die Inversion besteht darin, dass Caracalla seinen Lieblingslöwen öffentlich küsst,[25] was nur einem gleichrangigen Freund, also einem Senator, zukommen dürfte. Gleichzeitig liest sich gerade die Gemeinschaft mit den Löwen[26]—seine barbarischen Leibwächter nennt er übrigens ebenfalls Löwen—als Indiz für die Barbarisierung und Entmenschli-

---

22 Cf. Cass. Dio 79(78),14,4. Obwohl er formal dem Senatorenstand angehörte, erkannten die Senatoren ihn nicht als gleichrangig an. Cf. FLAIG, Usurpation, 190, mit Hinweis auf CIL XV 7505. Zur Darstellung Herodians cf. ZIMMERMANN, Kaiser, 214–216; zu Cassius Dio cf. DAVENPORT, Cassius Dio, 796–815.
23 Cf. Cass. Dio 79(78),5.
24 Cf. Cass. Dio 79(78),6,1.
25 Cf. Cass. Dio 79(78),7,2–3.
26 Cf. WELWEI, Löwen, 231–239.

chung des Kaisers, die in seinem grausamen Charakter vielfältig thematisiert wird.

Herodian stellt die Reaktion des Militärs gänzlich anders dar. Für ihn ist die Tat des Martialis wie die des Macrinus persönlicher Natur. Die gesamte Darstellung ist von Versatzstücken aus anderen Berichten von Herrschertoden durchsetzt, die ich hier nicht ausführlich besprechen kann. Zwei Beispiele: 1. Caracalla wirft Macrinus Unmännlichkeit vor wie Caligula seinem Mörder Chaerea.[27] 2. Macrinus erfährt zufällig von der Prophezeiung seiner eigenen Kaisererhebung. Ein ebenso zufällig entdecktes Todesurteil kommt beim Untergang Domitians und des Commodus vor.[28]

Herodians Darstellung ist virtuos komponiert. Hatte Cassius Dio noch behauptet, Martialis sei enttäuscht gewesen, weil Caracalla ihm ein Centurionenamt verweigert habe, so ist Herodians Martialis über solch kleinlichen Ehrgeiz erhaben. Er ist Centurio und wird von zwei Motiven bewegt: Zum einen will er seinen Bruder rächen, der ungerechtfertigterweise kurz zuvor von Caracalla hingerichtet worden war; zum anderen hatte der Kaiser ihm wiederholt persönlich gedroht.[29] Mit Blick auf Caracallas Brudermord waltet höhere Gerechtigkeit: Der Brudermörder Caracalla wird für den Mord am Bruder eines anderen zur Rechenschaft gezogen. Martialis' Tat lässt sich also sittlich legitimieren. Auch die Sterbeszene gewinnt an Dramatik. Cassius Dio erwähnt die Notdurft des Kaisers nur beiläufig.[30] Herodians Caracalla hat Blähungen, alle treten schamhaft zur Seite und der Mörder stößt von hinten mit dem Dolch zu, als der Kaiser sich gerade entblößt hat.[31]

Der wichtigste strukturelle Unterschied besteht meines Erachtens darin, dass Herodian Caracallas Tod als Resultat persönlicher Konflikte betrachtet und ganz anders als Cassius Dio die kollektive Loyalität des Heeres gegenüber dem toten Kaiser konstatiert: seine Trauer, Wut und Kopflosigkeit, „denn nach ihrer Vorstellung hatten sie weniger einen Befehlshaber verloren als vielmehr einen Mitsoldaten und Lebenskameraden; und sie hegten keinerlei Verdacht gegen Macrinus, sondern glaubten, dass Martialis aus persönlicher Feindschaft heraus

---

27 Cf. Josephus, Ant 19,1,3.
28 Cf. Cass. Dio 67,15,3; Hdt. 1,17. Beide Male stehen Frauen (Domitia Longina bzw. Marcia) im Mittelpunkt und das „Opfer" wird als heimtückischer Täter entlarvt.
29 Cf. Hdt. 4,13,1–2.
30 Cass. Dio 79(78),5,3.
31 Hdt. 4,13,5.

seine Rache vollzogen habe".[32] Damit wird die Soldateska zur eigentlichen Bedrohung der Freiheit des Staates.

Für die Historia Augusta ist dagegen der sechs Jahre zurückliegende Untergang des Präfekten Papinian im Zusammenhang mit der Ermordung Getas durch Caracalla ausschlaggebend für den Tod des Herrschers. Der Mord macht das persönliche Versagen des Kaisers bereits zu Beginn seiner Alleinherrschaft deutlich und zeigt seine animalische Blutrünstigkeit. Papinian soll, so die Historia Augusta, auf dem Weg zur Richtstätte gesagt haben, „sein Nachfolger würde ein Dummkopf sein, sofern er den brutalen Angriff auf das Präfektenamt nicht räche".[33] Caracallas moralische Verfassung, seine Unberechenbarkeit und Grausamkeit, wird zum Ausgangspunkt für seinen Tod. Für die Historia Augusta stehen nicht mehr konkrete historische Umstände im Vordergrund, sie stigmatisiert Caracalla auch im Sterben zeichenhaft als tierischen Charakter. Caracalla wird als maßlos aufgefasst, was sich etwa in übermäßigem Essen und Trinken zeigt, und als allen verhasst dargestellt: „den Seinen zuwider und in allen Heerlagern mit Ausnahme der Prätorianer verhasst".[34] Allerdings besaß er Anlagen zu einem besseren Menschen, denn die Historia Augusta streicht heraus, dass er als Knabe von anderem Charakter[35] war. Tierische Züge verleiht ihm die Historia Augusta schließlich durch den angeblichen Inzest mit seiner Mutter Iulia Domna,[36] während ausgerechnet der Brudermord erstaunlich unprofiliert bleibt.

Elagabal, der sich 118 n. Chr. als Vierzehnjähriger mit Hilfe seiner Großmutter, der Tante Caracallas, an die Macht putschte, konnte sich nur knapp vier Jahre als Augustus halten. Neben Geld überzeugte die aufständischen Legionen, dass Elagabal angeblich der illegitime Sohn Caracallas sei.[37] Daneben versuchte er sich intensiv religiös durch seine besondere Beziehung zu *sol Elagabalus*, dem unbesiegbaren Gott, dessen Priester er war, zu legitimieren.[38] Als die allgemeine Akzeptanz des jungen Herrschers zu schwinden begann, bereitete die

---

32 Herod. 4,13,7: ἤνεγκε τὸ πραχθέν· συστρατιώτην γὰρ καὶ κοινωνὸν τοῦ βίου, ἀλλ' οὐκ ἄρχοντα ᾤοντο ἀποβεβληκέναι. καὶ οὐδεμίαν πω ἐπιβουλὴν ὑπώπτευον ἐκ τοῦ Μακρίνου, ᾤοντο δὲ τὸν Μαρτιάλιον οἰκείαν ἔχθραν ἀμύνασθαι (Ed. STAVENHAGEN).
33 SHA Carac. 8,8: dicens eum stultissimum fore qui in suum subrogaretur locum, nisi adpetitam crudeliter praefecturam vindicaret.
34 SHA Carac. 9,3: Fuit male moratus et patre duro crudelior. Avidus cibi, vini etiam adpetens, suis odiosus et praeter milites praetorianos omnibus castris exosus.
35 Cf. SHA Carac. 1.
36 Cf. SHA Carac. 10,1–4,11,5.
37 Cf. Cass. Dio 79(78),31.
38 Ab 220 n. Chr. fügte er seiner Titulatur *sacerdos amplissimus dei invicti Solis Elagabali* hinzu. Cf. ICKS, Priest, 330–341; SOMMER, Elagabal, 95–110; FREY, Untersuchungen, 76–86; PIETRZYKOWSKI, Religionspolitik, 1806–1825.

einflussreiche Großmutter Iulia Maesa die Machtübertragung auf ihren zweiten Enkel, den Vetter Elagabals, Severus Alexander, vor. Im Juni 221 n. Chr. wurde Alexander adoptiert und zum Caesar erhoben. Das Gerücht wurde gestreut, Severus sei der eigentliche Sohn Caracallas.[39] Ein dreiviertel Jahr später, am 11. oder 12. März 222 n. Chr., wurde Elagabal zusammen mit seiner Mutter und einigen Anhängern im Lager der Prätorianer in Rom ermordet.[40]

Elagabal wurde von der antiken Historiographie als bösartig und verkommen dargestellt: ein „unwürdiger Kaiser", eine „Pest", „Geißel", „einer, der nichts tat, was nicht böse und gemein war", „die verworfenste aller Kreaturen auf zwei und vier Beinen".[41]

Unisono wird als Auslöser für seinen Tod genannt, er habe dem Caesar Alexander nach dem Leben getrachtet, weshalb die Soldaten ihn töteten und damit nur ihre Pflicht gegen Severus Alexander erfüllten, den zu schützen sie geschworen hatten. Geta war von Caracalla aus dem gleichen Grund getötet worden. Während man die Anschuldigung bei Geta für haltlos hält, wird sie bei Elagabal vorbehaltlos geglaubt. Cassius Dio, selbst zum zweiten Mal Konsul (229 n. Chr.) unter Alexander Severus, macht Elagabal konsequent zum Orientalen, der Rom mit seinem fremden, abstoßenden Kult zu pervertieren sucht und gänzlich nach dem Prinzip seiner schändlichen Lüste lebt. Wiederholt nennt er ihn Sardanapalus, jener mythische assyrische König, der dem Luxus verfallen unter seinen Frauen lebte. Überhaupt wird die Geschlechtertransgression stark betont: Elagabal ist durch und durch Frau.[42] Als er die Feindseligkeit der Prätorianer spürt und um sein Leben fürchtet, springt er feige in eine Kiste, um zu entfliehen, wird jedoch entdeckt und ermordet. Wie das genau vor sich ging, lässt Cassius Dio im Dunkeln, bis auf das Detail, dass der Princeps im Tod von seiner Mutter fest umschlungen gehalten wird, die ebenfalls sterben muss. Das Bild verdichtet die Unwürdigkeit als Herrscher: Der Kaiser klammert sich wie ein Kind an seine Mutter.

Cassius Dio berichtet weiter, dass beide Leichen enthauptet und durch die Stadt geschleift wurden. Während man sich der Leiche der Soemias irgendwo entledigte, warf man Elagabal in den Tiber.[43] Das war der Ort, in den die Millio-

---

39 Cf. Cass. Dio 80(79),19,4. Zur Adoption und Caesarernennung cf. Cass. Dio 80(79),17–18.
40 Cf. SHA Heliog. 18,2; 33,7; Cass. Dio 80(79),20,1–2; Hdt. 5,8,8.
41 Herod. 5,8,8: ἀσχημονοῦντα βασιλέα; SHA Heliog. 10,1: pestem; SHA Heliog. 34,1: haec clades; Cass. Dio 79(78),29,3: ὑφ' οὗ οὐδὲν ὅ, τι οὐ κακὸν καὶ αἰσχρὸν ἐγένετο (Ed. DINDORF); SHA Alex. 9,4: omnium non solum bipedum sed etiam quadrupedum spurcissimus.
42 Etwa in seinem Sexualverhalten (Cass. Dio 80[79],13), aber auch in seinen Körpergesten und Beschäftigungen (Cass. Dio 80[78],14,3–4).
43 Cf. Cass. Dio 80(79),20,2.

nenstadt ihren Unrat spülte, dort endeten die gemeinen Verbrecher.[44] Offenbar genügte es für Elagabal nicht, stellvertretend nur das Bildnis zu schänden. Seine Existenz musste gänzlich ausgelöscht werden. Explizit verweist die Historia Augusta darauf, dass ein auf diese Weise entsorgter Leichnam nicht mehr bestattet werden könne.[45]

Wieder ist Herodians Version die dramatischere.[46] Im Fahnenheiligtum erschlagen die Prätorianer den Kaiser, nachdem sie sich lange genug von ihm haben zum Narren halten lassen. Sie bestrafen die Treu- und Maßlosigkeit des Kaisers, der keine Minute Abstand von seinem Plan nimmt, den Caesar zu töten. Der Tatort macht den Mord zur heiligen Handlung: Am Ort des Kaiserkults wird der Kaiser abgeschlachtet. Herodian lässt die Leichen von Mutter und Sohn nicht nur schänden und durch die Stadt schleifen, sondern in die zum Tiber führenden Abwasserkanäle werfen.[47] Was Cassius Dio metaphorisch beschreibt, wird explizit gemacht.

Auch die Historia Augusta sieht Severus Alexander als Lichtgestalt, Elagabal dagegen als dunklen Herrscher, der nicht davor zurückschreckt, die Erzieher des Prinzen als Mörder zu dingen. Eine erste Krise gibt es, als er angeblich Leute ausschickt, um, wie bei Gegenkaisern üblich, die Inschriften der Statuen des Caesars mit Kot zu beschmieren.[48] Nur durch einen Kompromiss entgeht er dem bevorstehenden Tod, setzt sein frevlerisches Handeln jedoch fort und stellt dem Caesar weiter nach. Als er das Wohl des Staates aktiv zu bedrohen beginnt, indem er sich am Neujahrstag weigert, öffentlich mit Severus Alexander den Konsulat anzutreten, und die notwendigen Opfer und Supplikationen durch einen Stellvertreter vollziehen lässt, ist sein Schicksal besiegelt. Seine Missachtung der religiösen Tradition wird ihm zum Verhängnis.[49] Völliger Realitätsverlust spiegelt sich schließlich in der Ausweisung der Senatoren aus Rom,[50] was die Soldaten in ihre Rolle als Verteidiger der Republik drängt.

---

44   Cf. Plin. nat. 8,145; Tac. ann. 6,19,2–3. Zum Tiber als Ort der Reinigung cf. KYLE, Spectacles, 212–214.
45   Cf. SHA Heliog. 17,2: ne umquam sepeliri posset. Für Elagabal war es daher unmöglich den Prozess der Erinnerungsächtung später umzukehren, wie bei Commodus, Pertinax und Caracalla geschehen.
46   BOWERSOCK, Herodian, 229–236.
47   Cf. Hdt. 5,8,9.
48   Cf. SHA Heliog. 13,7.
49   Cf. SHA Heliog. 15,5–7.
50   Cf. SHA Heliog. 16,1.

Zunächst beseitigte man auf bestialische Weise seine Vertrauten.[51] Einigen wurden lebenswichtige Organe aus dem Leib gerissen, wieder andere wurden rektal durchbohrt zum Zeichen ihrer angeblichen sexuellen Beziehung mit Elagabal. Darauf nahm man sich den Kaiser vor, der sich auf eine Latrine geflüchtet hatte, wo er erschlagen wurde.[52]

Die Historia Augusta lässt die Leiche durch die Straßen und anschließend durch den Circus schleifen: „Ihr wollten die Soldaten auch noch Schmach antun, sie in eine Kloake werfen. Da aber zufällig die Kloake nicht genügend Raum bot, so hängte man der Leiche ein Gewicht an, damit sie nicht im Wasser treiben sollte, und warf sie über die aemilische Brücke in den Tiber, um eine ehrliche Bestattung für immer unmöglich zu machen."[53] Der Bestrafungsaspekt wird durch den Hinweis auf den Circus weiter erklärt. Die Leichen der Verbrecher wurden zum Tor des Circus hinaus geschleift, aber auch die der getöteten Tiere.[54] Das Motiv, Elagabal als ein Stück Dreck zu sehen, wird ebenfalls drastischer zum Ausdruck gebracht: Nicht einmal die Kloake will den verkommenen Kaiser haben. Der Autor bemerkt dazu: „Er [Elagabal] ist der einzige von allen Kaisern, der durch die Straßen geschleift, in die Kloake gezwängt und in den Tiber geworfen wurde. Dieses Los bereitete ihm der allgemeine Hass der Öffentlichkeit, vor dem sich namentlich die Herrscher in Acht nehmen müssen, verdient doch kein Grab, wer von ihnen nicht die Liebe des Senats, des Volkes und des Heeres verdient."[55] Die Einzigartigkeit der Ermordung Elagabals wird so betont. Zuvor genügte eine symbolische Entsorgung des toten Kaisers im Abflusskanal oder in der Latrine: In Ostia wurde ein Bildnis des Otho (gest. 69 n. Chr.) in einem Abwasserkanal beim Herkulestempel gefunden[56] und eine Ehreninschrift des Diadumenianus (Mitaugustus des Macrinus) in der Latrine der Vigilen.[57] Elagabal aber wurde selbst in die Kloake gestoßen.[58]

---

51 Cf. SHA Heliog. 16,5.
52 Cf. SHA Heliog. 17,1.
53 SHA Heliog. 17,1-2: Addita iniuria cadaveri est, ut id in cloacam milites mitterent. Sed cum non c[a]episset cloaca fortuito, per pontem Aemilium adnexo pondere, ne fluitaret, in Tiberim abiectum est, ne umquam sepeliri posset.
54 Cf. Kyle, Spectacles, 156.
55 SHA Heliog. 17,6-7: Solusque omnium principum et tractus est et in cloacam missus et in Tiberim praecipitatus. Quod odio communi omnium contigit, a quo speciatim cavere debent imperatores, si quidem nec sepulchra mereantur, qui amorem senatus populi ac militum non merentur.
56 Cf. Varner, Mutilation, 108.
57 Cf. ILS 465; Varner, Mutilation, 188.
58 Cf. SHA Heliog. 17,1.

Die Umkehrung der Geschlechterordnung wird unmittelbar als Grund genannt, den Kaiser den Unterweltsgottheiten auszuliefern.[59] Seine Pervertiertheit wird schließlich noch einmal ausgeführt, indem der Todesnachricht eine minutiöse Beschreibung von Elagabals Luxusleben angehängt wird—freilich nicht ohne den Kommentar, dass man sich schäme, davon zu berichten. Die Aneinanderreihung seiner Ausschweifungen lässt den Kaiser als einen einzigen Frevler erscheinen, der Gräber am vatikanischen Feld planieren ließ, um Elefantenquadrigen darauf zu weiden, oder im Sommer in seinen Gärten einen Schneeberg aufschichten ließ: „Sein einziger Lebensinhalt bestand im Aufspüren neuer Genüsse."[60] Selbst den eigenen Selbstmord[61] habe er versucht luxuriös zu gestalten, mit Purpurstricken oder einem goldenen Schwert. Stärker konnte der Kontrast wohl kaum sein zwischen dem Luxusleben und dem Leichnam im Schmutz der Latrine.[62]

Während Herodian und Cassius Dio den Fremden in Elagabal zur Wurzel des Übels machen, repräsentiert in seinem orientalischen Luxus, seiner Pervertierung der Geschlechterrollen und seinem fremden Gott, akzentuiert die Historia Augusta anders. Auch hier verdreht Elagabal die Ordnung der Geschlechter und Ränge. Seine sexuellen Perversionen sowie der unendliche Luxus zeigen das.[63] Aber sie sind nicht Taten eines vermeintlich Fremden, sondern Teil des egomanischen Anspruchs, seinen einen Gott zum obersten römischen Staatsgott zu machen und alle traditionellen Götter darin aufgehen zu lassen.[64] Elagabals Monotheismus ist sein eigentlicher Fehler und wird zur Gottlosigkeit gestempelt. Dagegen stilisiert die Historia Augusta Alexander Severus zum Polytheisten, der auch Christus unter seinen Hausgöttern verehrt habe.[65]

Betrachten wir die historiographische Tradition zum Tod beider Kaiser, sind beide zweifellos böse und gemein. Dennoch wird nur Elagabal dauerhaft zum Unmenschen, zur Inkarnation des Schlechten. Bezogen auf Caracalla lautet die Bilanz der Historia Augusta: „Und doch wurde dieser Allergrausamste, um es mit einem Wort zu sagen, ein Brudermörder und Blutschänder, der Feind seines Vaters, seiner Mutter und seines Bruders, von seinem Mörder Macrinus aus Furcht vor der Soldateska und namentlich vor der Garde unter die Götter ver-

---

59 Cf. SHA Heliog. 18,3.
60 SHA Heliog. 19,6: Nec erat ei ulla vita nisi exquirere novas voluptates.
61 Cf. SHA Heliog. 33,2-6.
62 Cf. SHA Heliog. 33,7.
63 Cf. SHA Heliog. 4,1-3; 5; 8,6; 12,1; 20,1-2.6; 21; 23,2-5; 25; 28,2.5; 31,7.
64 Cf. SHA Heliog. 3,4; BRANDT, Mortibus, 65-72; ICKS, Heliogabalus, 477-488.
65 Cf. SHA Alex. 29,2.

setzt."⁶⁶ Das widerspricht der Version des Zeitgenossen Cassius Dio, der von einem angeblich allgemeinen Hass gegen den Kaiser ausgeht und ausdrücklich vermerkt: „Denn er [Macrinus] wagte es nicht, ihn [Caracalla] zum Halbgott oder Landesfeind zu erklären; meinem Dafürhalten nach zögerte er wegen der Freveltaten seines Vorgängers und des verbreiteten Hasses gegen ihn, den ersten Weg zu beschreiten. Den zweiten Weg verbot die Rücksicht auf die Soldaten. Einige argwöhnten jedoch als Grund seinen Wunsch, dass die *damnatio memoriae* des Tarautas [= Caracalla] mehr vom Senat und vom Volk als von ihm ausgehen solle, zumal er sich doch mitten unter den Legionen befand."⁶⁷

Zunächst ist gar nicht sicher, ob Macrinus tatsächlich der eigentliche Mörder Caracallas war und es nicht vielmehr darum ging, seine Herrschaft durch ein solches Gerücht zu diskreditieren. Ihn für den Mörder zu halten brandmarkte Macrinus als herrschsüchtig und treulos. Seine Karriere⁶⁸ lässt hingegen ein enges Vertrauensverhältnis zu Caracalla vermuten. Philippus Arabs, Prätorianerpräfekt Gordians III., wurde ebenfalls unterstellt, er habe seinen Herrn ermordet und den Leichnam feierlich nach Rom überführt. Neuere Forschungen belegen jedoch, dass Gordian bei Kampfhandlungen mit den Persern getötet wurde.⁶⁹ Während Philippus Arabs sich eindeutig für die Anknüpfung an den Vorgänger entschied,⁷⁰ blieb Macrinus in seiner Erinnerungspolitik ambivalent: Er verbrannte den toten Herrscher feierlich im Angesicht seiner Truppen.⁷¹ Die sterblichen Überreste ließ er zwar nach Rom überführen, nicht aber offiziell im Mausoleum der Antonine beisetzen. Gegenüber den Soldaten wurde durch eine feierliche Verbrennung Kontinuität betont;⁷² gegenüber dem Senat, der Caracalla mehr als distanziert gegenüberstand, propagierte Macrinus durch seinen

---

66 SHA Carac. 11,5: Hic tamen omnium durissimus et, ut uno conplectamur verbo, parricid[i]a et incestus, patris, matris, fratris inimicus, a Macrino, qui eum occiderat, timore militum et maxime praetorian<or>um inter deos relatus est.
67 Cass. Dio 79(78),17,2-3: οὔτε γὰρ ἥρωα οὔτε πολέμιον ἀποδεῖξαι ἐτόλμησεν, ὡς μὲν ἐγὼ δοκῶ, ὅτι τὸ μὲν διά τε τὰ πραχθέντα αὐτῷ καὶ διὰ τὸ πολλῶν ἀνθρώπων μῖσος, τὸ δὲ διὰ τοὺς στρατιώτας ὤκνησε πρᾶξαι, ὡς δέ τινες ὑπώπτευσαν, ὅτι τῆς τε γερουσίας καὶ τοῦ δήμου τὴν ἀτιμίαν αὐτοῦ ἔργον γενέσθαι μᾶλλον ἢ ἑαυτοῦ, ἄλλως τε καὶ ἐν τοῖς στρατεύμασιν ὄντος, ἠθέλησε.
68 Er wird im Krisenjahr 212 n. Chr., also nach der Ermordung Getas, Prätorianerpräfekt und erhält kurz vor Caracallas Tod die *ornamenta consularia*.
69 Cf. MACDONALD, Gordian, 502-508; zum Gerücht der Ermordung cf. SHA Gord. 30,8; zur Überführung der Leiche nach Rom cf. Eutr. 9,2,3.
70 Cf. SHA Gord. 31,7.
71 Cf. Cass. Dio 79(78),9; SHA Carac. 9,12.
72 Der Autor der Historia Augusta (SHA Carac. 11,5; SHA Opil. 5,9) geht sogar von der Konsekration Caracallas durch Macrinus aus.

Verzicht auf ein *funus publicum* in Rom Diskontinuität. Er verfolgte einen bewusst offenen Kurs, ohne sich eindeutig festzulegen: Er selbst nahm den Namen „Severus" an und gab seinem Sohn den offiziellen Namen Caracallas, Antoninus.[73] In einem Geheimdekret befahl er dagegen—so Cassius Dio—, bestimmte Standbilder Caracallas in Rom zu entfernen.

Anders als uns Cassius Dio glauben machen will, war die allgemeine Anhänglichkeit an Caracalla offenbar ungebrochen. Elagabal, sein vorgeblicher Sohn, vollzog schließlich die Divinisierung.[74] Dass es nicht einmal eine routinemäßige Vernichtung der Erinnerung Caracallas nach seinem Tod gab, belegt der archäologisch-epigraphische Befund. Es kam zu keinen nennenswerten Eradierungen.[75] Nicht nur Elagabal, sondern auch dessen Nachfolger Severus Alexander knüpfte an Caracalla an, indem er sich offiziell ebenfalls als Sohn des Divus Magnus bezeichnen ließ.[76] Stattdessen muss man wohl davon ausgehen, dass der gewaltsame Tod des Herrschers den Historikern die Gelegenheit bot, umfänglich mit ihm abzurechnen. Sowohl die Historia Augusta als auch Cassius Dio bezeugen, dass man den Kaiser in bestimmten Kreisen durch Belegung mit Spottnamen einer inoffiziellen *damnatio* unterwarf.[77] Die Verwendung solcher Spottnamen ist auch für Elagabal literarisch belegt, wie das schon erwähnte „Sardanapalus" oder „der Falsche Antoninus" bei Cassius Dio.[78] Weitere Spottnamen sind „Tiberinus", „Tractatius", „Inpurus".[79] Alle verweisen auf das furchtbare Ende des Kaisers und sein unwiderrufliches Ausscheiden aus dem Kreis der menschlichen Gemeinschaft. Das entspricht dem allgemeinen Verständnis der Historia Augusta vom Umgang mit einem schlechten Kaiser, „insofern die einen nach langer Herrschaft ein natürliches Ende nahmen, während die anderen ermordet, (am Haken) geschleift und Tyrannen genannt wurden, deren Namen man nur ungern nennt".[80]

Elagabals *memoria* wurde komplett verfemt. An den tatsächlichen Herrschaftsverhältnissen in Rom änderte sich indessen wenig. Sein Nachfolger legi-

---

73 Cf. SHA Opil. 2,5; Cass. Dio 79(78),19,2.
74 Cf. Cass. Dio 80(79),2,6; GESCHE, Divinisierung, 387; BENARIO, Titulature, 9–14.
75 Cf. VARNER, Mutilation, 184.
76 Cf. Elagabal: RIT 84 (Tarragona); AE 1990,654 = AE 1997,882 (Tarragona); Severus Alexander: AE 1937,33 (Lambaesis), CIL VIII 711 (El Khima).
77 Cf. Cass. Dio 79(78): Tarautas. Bassianus; SHA Carac. 9,7.
78 Cf. Cass. Dio 80(79),1,1. Hinzu kommen „Assyrer" oder auch die pejorative Verwendung seines Geburtsnamens „Avitus".
79 Cf. SHA Heliog. 17,5.
80 SHA Heliog. 1,3: quod illi et diu imperarunt et exitu naturali functi sunt, hi vero interfecti, tracti, tyranni etiam appellati, quorum nec nomina libet dicere.

timierte sich genau wie Elagabal selbst über Caracalla. Nach wie vor hielt Iulia Maesa die Fäden in der Hand, statt Soemias ging ihr nun Maesa, die Mutter des Severus Alexander, zur Hand. Allenfalls äußere Formen wurden verändert. Für das neue Regiment war die glaubwürdige Abgrenzung von Elagabal überlebensnotwendig. Analog hatte Caracalla unter den Anhängern seines Bruders ebenfalls ein riesiges Blutbad angerichtet und mit Hilfe des Militärs die Erinnerungsmonumente beseitigt.[81] Das vergleichbare Blutbad unter Elagabals Anhängern betonte dagegen deren Komplizenschaft des Bösen. Severus Alexander hielt sich immerhin dreizehn Jahre an der Macht, blieb aber während dieser Zeit weitestgehend von seiner Mutter abhängig, die schließlich während eines Militärputsches bei Mainz 235 n. Chr. mit ihm zusammen ermordet wurde. Unsere Quellen, die ein sehr positives Bild dieses Kaisers zeichnen, allenfalls die Abhängigkeit von der Mutter rügen, berichten nicht von irgendwelchen Schändungen oder Erinnerungsächtungen. Im Gegenteil, nach Ausweis der Historia Augusta war die allgemeine Trauer überbordend, so dass der Senat den Toten unter die Götter versetzte und ihm in Gallien ein Kenotaph und in Rom ein prachtvolles Grabmal errichtet wurde.[82] Diese Aussage steht ebenfalls in deutlichem Widerspruch zum archäologisch-epigraphischen Befund. Die Porträts und Inschriften von Mutter und Sohn wurden zielgerichtet verstümmelt oder zerstört.[83] Eine spätere absichtliche Wiedereinsetzung der Namen zeigt vielmehr, dass eine *damnatio* aufgehoben wurde, vermutlich unter Gordian III., der wieder den Namen „Antoninus" führte.[84]

Beide Kaiser wurden entmenschlicht und die Art und Weise, wie das geschah, lässt auch einige Schlüsse auf das Menschenbild der Kaiserzeit zu. Beiden wurde, wie schon den vorangegangenen tyrannischen Principes Caligula, Nero oder Domitian, rationales Verhalten abgesprochen. Die Rationalität, darin war man sich einig, unterschied den Menschen vom Tier, rückte ihn stattdessen in die Nähe der Götter.[85] Allerdings kreisten derartige Anthropologien weniger um eine Definition des Menschen in Abgrenzung zum unsterblichen Gott[86] oder dem vernunftlosen Tier,[87] sondern im Mittelpunkt stand stets die Frage, wie der Mensch zum wahren Menschsein oder besser zur wahren Mannhaftigkeit ge-

---

81 Cf. KRÜPE, Damnatio, 202–215.
82 Cf. SHA Alex. 63,2–3.
83 Cf. VARNER, Mutilation, 196–197.
84 CIL VIII 27432; XI 5269. Cf. VARNER, Mutilation, 18, Anm. 3.
85 Cf. Sen. epist. 76,9–11; 66,12.
86 Festzuhalten bleibt die Transformation.
87 Cf. DIERAUER, Mensch, 37–85.

langt.⁸⁸ Vor diesem Hintergrund bleibt ein universales Menschenbild vergleichsweise unkonturiert.⁸⁹ Grundsätzlich war es möglich, als übermenschlich, ja göttlich, betrachtet zu werden (wie der Herrscher) oder in den Kategorien von Effeminierung und sozialer Inferiorität das wahre Menschsein zu verfehlen. Am unteren Rand standen dabei die Sklaven, denen trotz ihrer grundsätzlichen Teilhabe am biologischen Menschsein⁹⁰ diese Teilhabe an der sozietären *virtus* abgesprochen wurde. Zwar gestehen Anhänger der Stoa, wie Seneca, auch Sklaven zu, ihren Charakter (*mos*) bilden zu können,⁹¹ aber allein die Tatsache, dass der schlechte Mensch im gleichen Text in den Kategorien des Sklavenstatus beschrieben wird, zeigt deren Rand- und Grenzsituation.

Trotz punktuell emotionaler Beziehungen zwischen Sklaven und ihren Herren galten erstere als minderwertig und kaum mehr als beseelte Werkzeuge.⁹² Im realen Leben war der Gegensatz zwischen den Menschen tief in die Körper und deren Sprache eingeschrieben. Das war nicht nur eine Frage der Erziehung, die den Gebildeten eine verfeinerte Körper- und Gebärdensprache⁹³ vermittelte und sie so deutlich von den ihnen sozial Unterlegenen unterschied. Die realen sozialen Gegebenheiten selbst schrieben diese Dichotomie körperlich fest. Hierfür sei auf die Ergebnisse von anthropologischen Untersuchungen aus Pompeii verwiesen, wo ein Herr und sein etwa gleichaltriger Sklave beim Vesuvausbruch etwa sechsundvierzigjährig ums Leben kamen.⁹⁴ Der Herr war bei seinem Tod wohlgenährt und durch regelmäßiges Training körperlich fit, der Körper seines zehn Zentimeter kleineren Sklaven war dagegen aufgrund von Arbeit und Mangelernährung deformiert, der Mund voller Abszesse. Zu dieser täglichen Erfahrung gesellte sich die feste Überzeugung, dass die Physiognomie Rückschlüsse auf den Charakter eines Individuums zuließe.⁹⁵ Aus dieser Perspektive musste

---

88 Cic. leg. 1,30. Bezugsgröße ist dabei stets der erwachsene (zeugungsfähige) Mann der Elite, der sich abgrenzt gegen alles Weibliche und in seiner Männlichkeit zudem bedroht wird von den Kräften der Natur wie Altersverfall und angeborener Triebhaftigkeit.
89 Cf. Sen. epist. 5,48,4.
90 Cf. Dig. 50,17,32 (Ulpian), wonach Sklaven nach bürgerlichem Recht nicht als Personen gelten, nach dem Naturrecht schon.
91 Cf. Sen. epist. 76. Auch Cicero geht von einer *facultas discendi* aus (Cic. leg. 1,30).
92 Arist. pol. 1,1253b: ὀργάνων [...] ἔμψυχα (Ed. Ross). Der Gutsbesitzer Varro (Varro rust. 1,17,1) bezeichnet seine Sklaven als *instrumenta vocalia*, seine Nutztiere als *instrumenta semivocalia*, Geräte und Werkzeuge als *instrumenta muta*; cf. Iuv. 6,222: ita servus homo est? (Ed. Clausen); zur Entmenschlichung von Sklaven cf. Flaig, Grenze, 639–662.
93 Cf. Rouselle, Gestes, 231–269; Corbeill, Nature, 1–11.
94 Cf. Butterworth/Laurence, Pompeii, 66–67.
95 Zur antiken Physiognomielehre cf. Barton, Power, 95–113.

der Sklave in der allgemeinen Wahrnehmung mehr einem Tier als einem Menschen ähneln.

Caracalla und Elagabal werden beide als Sklaven ihres Körpers entlarvt. Beherrschend für Caracalla ist seine Grausamkeit[96] und für Elagabal ungezügelte sexuelle Begierde.[97] Beide beherrscht ihr Körper, nicht ihr Geist. Das ist auch zeichenhaft gemacht in Caracallas stets finsterer Miene[98] und Elagabals völliger Verwandlung in eine Frau, die als unbeherrscht und triebgesteuert gilt. Elagabal wie Caracalla lassen sich von Zorn hinreißen, statt diesen, wie erzieherisch angestrebt, zu beherrschen.[99]

Der Zeitgenosse Aelian hat Tiergeschichten zusammengestellt, in denen er darlegt, dass auch Tiere im Einzelfall Qualitäten eines vernunftbegabten Menschen erreichen. In der Einleitung heißt es: „Dass der Mensch weise und gerecht ist, dass er für seine Kinder die höchste Aufmerksamkeit hegt, dass er seinen Eltern gebührende Sorge widmet, dass er Nahrung für sich sucht und Nachstellungen vermeidet und was ihm sonst für Gaben der Natur eigen sind, darin ist vielleicht nichts Seltsames. Denn der Mensch ist mit Vernunft begabt, der Gabe von Allem, und ist der Überlegung fähig, die für ihn höchst förderlich und ersprießlich ist. Außerdem hegt er Scheu gegen die Götter und weiß sie zu ehren."[100] Nicht nur die Vernunft, auch die Gottesfurcht scheidet den Menschen vom Tier, aber weder Caracalla noch Elagabal sind wahrhaft fromm. Elagabal ehrt nur seinen Gott und verweigert damit den übrigen Göttern den notwendigen Kultus, schlimmer, er entehrt den Vestakult durch die erzwungene Ehe mit der *virgo maxima*.[101] Sein Tod im Fahnenheiligtum macht ihn schließlich zeichenhaft zum (Opfer)tier. Caracallas Religiosität wird als vorgeschoben und pervers dargestellt; auch er vergeht sich an einer Vestalin, schlachtet unkontrolliert Opfertiere ab, neigt der Nekromanie zu.[102]

Das für die Mehrheit unserer literarischen Überlieferung gängige, stoisch geprägte Menschenbild geht von der Bildbarkeit des Individuums aus, misst

---

96 Die Historia Augusta (Carac. 9) betont zudem seine maßlose Fressgier und Weinliebe.
97 SHA Elag. 5,2.
98 Cf. Cass. Dio 78(77),11.
99 Zur Forderung der Zornkontrolle cf. HARRIS, Rage, 80–87.
100 Ail. nat. Proömium: ἄνθρωπον μὲν εἶναι σοφὸν καὶ δίκαιον καὶ τῶν οἰκείων παίδων προμηθέστατον, καὶ τῶν γειναμένων ποιεῖσθαι τὴν προσήκουσαν φροντίδα, καὶ τροφὴν ἑαυτῷ μαστεύειν καὶ ἐπιβουλὰς φυλάττεσθαι καὶ τὰ λοιπὰ ὅσα αὐτῷ σύνεστι δῶρα φύσεως, παράδοξον ἴσως οὐδέν· καὶ γὰρ λόγου μετείληχεν ἄνθρωπος τοῦ πάντων τιμιωτάτου, καὶ λογισμοῦ ἠξίωται, ὅσπερ οὖν ἐστι πολυαρκέστατός τε καὶ πολυωφελέστατος· ἀλλὰ καὶ θεοὺς αἰδεῖσθαι οἶδε καὶ σέβειν (Ed. GARCIA VALDÉS). Dazu auch HÜBNER, Mensch, 154–176.
101 Cf. Cass. Dio 80(79),9,3.
102 Cf. Cass. Dio 78(77),15–16.

dem Menschen die Fähigkeit zu, sich zu entscheiden, Gutes oder Schlechtes zu tun, die Natur des Körpers in Schach zu halten.[103] Cassius Dio charakterisiert Caracalla vor diesem Hintergrund als minderwertig, bildungsfeindlich, sich gemein machend mit den einfachen Soldaten, deren Speise und Strapazen er teilt.[104] Caracalla strebt nicht nach dem Göttlichen im Menschen. Aus diesem Grund—so Cassius Dio—lehnt er es ab, wie Commodus als Herkules bezeichnet zu werden, denn er will nichts eines Gottes Würdiges tun.[105]

Die genauere Betrachtung der Todesumstände von Caracalla und Elagabal zeigt, dass unsere historiographischen Quellen das Böse jeweils neu definieren. Konsens ist die Infragestellung der gegebenen tradierten Ordnung, die in Chiffren von angeblichen Extremen verhandelt wird. Hierzu gehört die *imago* des Fremden (Orientale oder Barbar), des sexuell Perversen oder des religiösen Fanatikers—jeweils aufgeladen durch Bilder von Maßlosigkeit, Grausamkeit, sozialer Inferiorität und Irrationalität. Daraus ergibt sich eine Stilisierung der gescheiterten Herrscher als Kreaturen, die sich den gängigen Anforderungen ihrer Standesgenossen im Hinblick auf ihre Menschenbildung entzogen haben. Während Caracalla nicht dazu bereit war, wird Elagabal durch seine angeblich orientalische Herkunft daran gehindert. Als Kategorie dient in beiden Fällen körperbezogenes Verhalten, das als animalisch stigmatisiert wird. Caracalla und Elagabal handeln beide impulsiv und nicht vernunftbezogen.

Die politische Funktionselite Roms führte jedoch mittels der historiographischen Tradition ihren eigenen Wertediskurs, der mit der offiziellen Erinnerungspolitik der Herrscher oder ihrer tatsächlichen Beliebtheit nicht notwendigerweise kongruent ist, das Gedächtnis der Nachwelt jedoch tief geprägt hat. Gelegenheit hierzu verschaffte ihr in einzigartiger Weise die Praxis der *damnatio memoriae*, mit deren Hilfe römische Herrscher sich legitimierten. Wer eines gewaltsamen Todes starb, wurde offiziell verfemt und konnte entsprechend instrumentalisiert werden.

Die von den Severern wiederholt praktizierte Rehabilitierung geächteter Kaiser zwang in der Folge zu einer wirkungsvolleren Demonstration beim Tod eines Kaisers als zuvor.[106] Elagabals brutales Ende und seine Stilisierung zum Monster waren weniger Resultat seiner Verfehlungen als vielmehr Instrument, um die severische Herrschaft durch einen neuen Repräsentanten fortsetzen zu können und somit die Fehlentwicklung zu personalisieren. Gleichzeitig eröffne-

---

103 Cf. Sen. epist. 113,18.
104 Cf. Cass. Dio 78(77),13; Hdt. 4,7.
105 Cf. Cass. Dio 78(77),5.
106 Wahrscheinlich wurden schon die Leichen von Macrinus und seinem Sohn wieder durch Enthauptung geschändet. Cf. SHA Diad. 9,4; Hdt. 5,4,11.

te sein Ende der folgenden Historiographie einen Weg, aktuelle Missstände im Kaisertum am Beispiel dieses Herrschers zu diskutieren, war er doch zum Symbol des Bösen geworden.

Bibliographie

ALFÖLDY, Géza, Die Römischen Inschriften von Tarraco, Berlin 1975.
ARAND, Tobias, Das schmähliche Ende. Der Tod des schlechten Kaisers und seine literarische Gestaltung in der römischen Historiographie (Prismata 13), Frankfurt a.M. et al. 2002.
BARTON, Tamsyn S., Power and Knowledge. Astrology, Physiognomics and Medicine in the Roman Empire, Ann Arbor, Michigan 1994.
BEKKER, Immanuel (Hg.), Flavii Iosephi opera, Bd. 4, Leipzig 1856.
BENARIO, Herbert W., The Titulature of Julia Soaemias and Julia Mamaea. Two Notes, in: Translations and Proceedings of the American Philological Association 90 (1959) 9–14.
BONFANTE, Pietro et al. (Hg.), Digesta Iustiniani recognoverunt et ediderunt, Mailand 1960.
BORZSÁK, Stephanus (Hg.), Cornelii Taciti libri qui supersunt 1,1. Ab Excessu Divi Augusti libri I-VI, Stuttgart/Leipzig 1992.
BOWERSOCK, Glen W., Herodian and Elagabalus, in: YCS 24 (1975) 229–236.
BRANDT, Hartwin, De mortibus principum et tyrannorum. Tod und Leichenschändung in der Historia Augusta, in: Paschoud, Francois/Bonamente, Giorgio (Hg.), Historiae Augustae Colloquium Perusinum, Edipuglia 2002, 65–72.
BUTTERWORTH, Alex/LAURENCE, Ray, Pompeii. The Living City, London 2005.
CHANTRAINE, Heinrich, Der tote Herrscher in der Politik der römischen Kaiserzeit, in: Geschichte in Wissenschaft und Unterricht 39 (1988) 67–88.
CLAUSEN, Wendell V. (Hg.), A. Persi Flacci et D. Ivni Ivvenalis Satvrae (Oxford Classical Texts), Oxford 1992.
CORBEILL, Anthony, Nature Embodied. Gesture in Ancient Rome, Princeton, New Jersey 2004.
DAVENPORT, Caillan, Cassius Dio and Caracalla, in: CQ 62 (2012) 796–815.
DAVIES, Penelope J. E., Death and the Emperor. Roman Imperial Funerary Monuments from Augustus to Marcus Aurelius, Cambridge 2000.
DIERAUER, Urs, Mensch und Tier im griechisch-römischen Denken, in: Münch, Paul (Hg.), Tiere und Menschen. Geschichte und Aktualität eines prekären Verhältnisses, Paderborn 1998, 37–85.
DINDORF, Ludwig, Dionis Cassii Cocceiani historia Romana, Bd. 4, Leipzig 1864.
ENGELS, David, Cum non comparuisset deorum in numero conlocatus putaretur. Entrückung, Epiphanie und Consecration. Überlegungen zur Apotheose des römischen Kaisers, in: Groß, Dominik/Grande, Jasmin (Hg.), Objekt Leiche. Technisierung, Ökonomisierung und Inszenierung toter Körper, Frankfurt/New York 2010, 79–133.
FLACH, Dieter (Hg.), Marcus Terentius Varro. Über die Landwirtschaft (Texte zur Forschung 87), Darmstadt 2006.
FLAIG, Egon, Den Kaiser herausfordern. Die Usurpation im Römischen Reich (Historische Studien 7), Frankfurt 1992.

FLAIG, Egon, An der sozialen Grenze des Menschseins in der griechischen Klassik. Wie man Sklaven zu Untermenschen macht, in: Stagl, Justin/Reinhard, Wolfgang (Hg.), Grenzen des Menschseins. Probleme einer Definition des Menschlichen (Veröffentlichungen des Instituts für Historische Anthropologie 8), Wien et al. 2005, 639–662.

FLOWER, Harriet I., The Art of Forgetting. Disgrace and Oblivion in Roman political Culture, Chapel Hill, North Carolina 2006.

FREY, Martin, Untersuchungen zur Religion und zur Religionspolitik des Kaisers Elagabal (Historia. Einzelschriften 62), Stuttgart 1989.

GARCIA VALDÉS, Manuela (Hg.), Claudius Aelianus. De natura animalium, Berlin 2009.

GESCHE, Helga, Die Divinisierung der römischen Kaiser in ihrer Funktion als Herrschaftslegitimation, in: Chiron 8 (1987) 376–390.

GRADEL, Ittai, Roman apotheosis, in: Thesaurus cultus et rituum antiquorum, Vol. II, Los Angeles, California 2004, 186–199.

HARRIS, William V., Restraining Rage. The Ideology of Anger Control in Classical Antiquity, Cambridge, Massachusetts 2001.

HEINEN, Heinz, Zur Tendenz der Caracalla-Vita in der Historia Augusta, in: Chiron 1 (1971) 421–435.

HOHL, Ernst (Hg.), Scriptores Historiae Augustae, Bd. 1, Leipzig 1927.

HOHL, Ernst, Das Ende Caracallas, in: Miscellanea Academica Berolinensia 1950, 276–293.

HÜBNER, Wolfgang, Der Mensch in Aelianus' Tiergeschichten, in: Antike und Abendland 30 (1984) 154–176.

ICKS, Martijn, Heliogabalus. A Monster on the Roman Throne. The Literary Construction of a "Bad" Emperor, in: Sluiter, Ineke/Rosen, Ralph M. (Hg.), Kakos. Badness and Anti-Value in Classical Antiquity, Leiden 2008, 477–488.

ICKS, Martijn, From Priest to Emperor to Priest-Emperor, in: Turner, Andrew et al. (Hg.), Private and Public Lies. The Discourse of Despotism and Deceit in the Graeco-Roman World, Leiden 2010, 330–341.

KNIPPSCHILD, Silke, ¡Abja el tirano! Destrucción de símbolos imperiales como representación del cambio de poder, in: Heimann, Heinz-Dieter et al. (Hg.), Ceremoniales, ritos y representación del poder (Universitat Jaume I. Publicacions, Humanitats 15), Castellon 2004, 57–88.

KRÜPE, Florian, Die Damnatio memoriae. Über die Vernichtung von Erinnerung. Eine Fallstudie zu Publius Septimius Geta (189–211 n. Chr.), Gutenberg 2011.

KÜHN, Werner (Hg.), Plinius der Jüngere, Panegyrikus. Lobrede auf den Kaiser Trajan (Texte zur Forschung 51), Darmstadt ²2008.

KUNST, Christiane, Der Leichnam des Princeps zwischen *consecratio* und *damnatio*, in: Potestas 1 (2008) 79–100.

KYLE, Donald, Spectacles of Death in Ancient Rome, London/New York 1998.

MACDONALD, David, The Death of Gordian III – Another Tradition, in: Historia 31 (1981) 502–508.

MÜLLER, Friedhelm L. (Hg.), Eutropii breviarium ab urbe condita—Eutropius, Kurze Geschichte Roms seit Gründung (753 v. Chr.–364 n. Chr.) (Palingenesia 56), Stuttgart 1995.

PEKÁRY, Thomas, Das römische Kaiserbildnis in Staat, Kult und Gesellschaft, dargestellt anhand der Schriftquellen (Das römische Herrscherbild 3,5), Berlin 1985.

PIETRZYKOWSKI, Michael, Die Religionspolitik des Kaisers Elagabal, in: ANRW II 16,3 (1986) 1806–1825.

POMEROY, Arthur J., The Appropriate Comment. Death Notices in the Ancient Historians (Studien zur klassischen Philologie 58), Frankfurt 1991.

POWELL, Jonathan G.F. (Hg.), M. Tvlli Ciceronis De re pvblica. De legibvs. Cato maior de senectvte. Laelivs de amicitia (Oxford Classical Texts), Oxford 2006.

PRÉCHAC, François (Hg.), Sénèque. Lettres à Lucilius, 2 vols., Paris 1963–1964.

RICHARD, Jean-Claude, Recherches sur certaines aspects du culte impérial. Les funérailles des empereurs Romains aux deux premiers siècles de notre ère, in: ANRW II 16,2 (1978) 1121–1134.

RONCONI, Alessandro, Exitus illustrium virorum, in: RAC 6 (1966) 1257–1268.

ROSS, William D. (Hg.), Aristoteles Politica (Oxford Classical Texts), Oxford 1957.

ROUSELLE, Aline, Gestes et signes de la famille dans l'Empire romain, in: Burguiere, André/Segalen, Martine (Hg.), Histoire de la famille, Vol. I, Paris 1986, 231–269.

SABLAYROLLES, Robert/PAILLER, Jean Marie, Damnatio memoriae. Une vraie perpétuité, in: Pallas 40 (1994) 11–55.

SCHNEIDER, Horst (Hg.), Eusebius von Caesarea. De Vita Constantini (Fontes Christiani 83), Turnhout 2007.

SCHUNCK, Peter, Römisches Sterben. Studien zu Sterbeszenen in der kaiserzeitlichen Literatur, insbesondere bei Tacitus, Heidelberg 1955.

SIMELON, Paul, Caracalla. Entre apothéose et damnation, in: Latomus 69 (2010) 792–810.

SOMMER, Michael, Elagabal – Wege zur Konstruktion eines schlechten Kaisers, in: Scripta Classica Israelica 23 (2004) 95–110.

STÄDELE, Alfons (Hg.), Laktanz. De mortibus persecutorum. Die Todesarten der Verfolger (Fontes Christiani 43), Turnhout 2003.

STAVENHAGEN, Kurt, Herodiani ab excessu divi Marci libri octo, Leipzig 1922 (Nachdruck Stuttgart 1967).

TIMONEN, Asko, Cruelty and Death. Roman Historians' Scenes of Imperial Violences from Commodus to Philippus Arabs (Turun yliopiston julkaisuja/Annales Universitatis Turkuensis B 241), Turku 2000.

VARNER, Eric, Mutilation and Transformation. Damnatio Memoriae and Roman Imperial Portraiture, Leiden 2004.

WELWEI, Karl-Wilhelm, Die „Löwen" Caracallas, in: Bonner Jahrbücher 192 (1992) 231–239 (nachgedruckt in: Welwei, Karl-Wilhelm, Res publica und Imperium. Kleine Schriften zur römischen Geschichte [Historia Einzelschriften 177]), Stuttgart 2004, 281–289.

ZIMMERMANN, Martin, Kaiser und Ereignis. Studien zum Geschichtswerk Herodians (Vestigia 52), München 1999.

Darja Šterbenc Erker
Der Religionsstifter Numa im Gespräch mit Jupiter
Menschenbild in der römischen Religion

Im Rahmen der Analyse der Menschenbilder in verschiedenen Religionen und Kulturen ist die Frage nach dem Verhältnis zwischen Menschen und Göttern von großer Bedeutung.[1] Die Repräsentationen, seien es literarische oder bildliche Darstellungen, sagen viel über die Stellung des Menschen in Bezug auf die Götter aus. In der polytheistischen Religion des antiken Roms lassen sich viele sehr unterschiedliche Auffassungen dieses Verhältnisses beobachten. In diesem Aufsatz werde ich untersuchen, wie die Autorität des Gottes in Bezug auf die Autorität des Menschen in einem literarischen Werk imaginiert wurde. Dazu werde ich ein literarisches Beispiel des Umgangs eines Menschen mit einem Gott in Ovids elegischem Gedicht *Fasti* analysieren.[2]

1 Einige Charakteristiken der römischen Religion

Einen wichtigen Kontrastpunkt zur heutigen Auffassung von Religion stellt die antike Vorstellung dar, dass die Götter in der Gemeinschaft anwesend sind. Für die Griechen und Römer standen die Götter nicht außerhalb der Welt, sie waren keine transzendenten Wesen, sondern griffen stets in das Leben der Menschen ein.[3] Die republikanische Kultausübung beruhte auf dem Glauben, dass die Götter Zeichen (Prodigien) schicken und stets auf die Befragung der Auguren, z.B. ob ein Tag für den Kriegsbeginn oder eine Abstimmung geeignet ist, positive oder negative Antworten geben.[4]

---

[1] Roland Baumgarten danke ich für die inhaltlich konstruktive Lektüre.
[2] Der Dichter Ovid verfasste sechs Bücher der *Fasti* zwischen 2 v. Chr. und 8 n. Chr., bevor er aus Rom verbannt wurde; im Exil in Tomi am Schwarzen Meer redigierte er einige Passagen des Werkes.
[3] BRUIT ZAIDMANN/SCHMITT PANTEL, Religion, 9–10.
[4] Beispielsweise war *obnuntiatio* ein Terminus technicus in der Augurensprache für eine Meldung über Vorbedeutungen; aufgrund ungünstiger göttlicher Zeichen hatten Auguren das Recht, die Volksversammlung zu vertagen, s. SCHEID, Religion, 49–51. Zu den Prodigien in der Republik s. ROSENBERGER, Prodigienwesen; RASMUSSEN, Portents; ENGELS, Vorzeichenwesen.

Der Rahmen der öffentlichen Religion in Rom war die Polis bzw. Civitas, die politische Gemeinschaft. Das zentrale Anliegen der öffentlichen Religion war die Erhaltung der *res publica* und ihrer sozialen Gruppen. Von der öffentlichen Religion, die im Namen der politischen Gemeinschaft durch ihre Repräsentanten ausgeübt wurde, unterscheidet sich die private Religion,[5] die als Hauskult, Totenkult oder private Verehrung der Götter der *res publica* zelebriert wurde. Zwischen den beiden Sphären waren verschiedene religiöse Vereine und Mysteriengemeinden angesiedelt (z.B. Bacchus- und Isiskult), an denen Menschen nicht aufgrund ihrer sozialen Stellung, sondern auf eigenen Wunsch teilnahmen. Unabhängig davon, ob es sich um den Umgang mit den Toten handelt oder um die Verehrung der höchsten Götter der politischen Gemeinschaft, waren die grundlegenden Regeln für alle Ebenen der Religionsausübung gleich: Die genaue Einhaltung ritueller Vorschriften ermöglichte eine gelungene Kommunikation mit den Göttern, die einen guten Ausgang sichern sollte.[6] Die Toten wurden als *Di Manes*, die guten Götter, verehrt und erhielten von den Mitgliedern ihrer Gemeinschaft an bestimmten Tagen (Parentalia im Februar sowie am Todestag) Opfer.[7]

Eine Besonderheit der römischen Religion war, dass die rituellen Fehler berichtigt werden konnten. So suchten Magistrate und Priester stets nach neuen Ritualen, mit denen sie Handlungen, die als fehlerhaft wahrgenommen wurden, korrigierten. Die eventuellen Transgressionen der religiösen Vorschriften korrigierten Priester und Magistrate durch Wiederholung des Rituals; diesen Mechanismus kennen wir als *instauratio*.[8] Deshalb herrschte im Normalfall keine Angst, dass Menschen Frevel begehen könnten, die die Götter zur Todesstrafe bewegen würden. Nur wenn einem Individuum bewiesen werden konnte, dass es willentlich gegen die sozialen oder rituellen Regeln verstoßen hatte, wurde es als *impius*, als Gottloser und Frevler, gebrandmarkt und musste mit der göttli-

---

5 Dion. Hal. ant. 2,65,2.
6 LINDER/SCHEID, Croire, 54–55; s. u. die Legende über das verkehrte Ritual des Tullus Hostilius.
7 ŠTERBENC ERKER, Totenkult; DIES., Gender/Funeral, 50–58.
8 Cic. har. esp. 23: An si ludius constitit, aut tibicen repente conticuit, aut puer ille patrimus et matrimus si tensam non tenuit, si lorum omisit, aut si aedilis verbo aut simpuvio aberravit, ludi sunt non rite facti, eaque errata expiantur, et mentes deorum immortalium ludorum instauratione placantur—Wenn der Tänzer innehält oder der Flötenspieler plötzlich verstummt oder wenn der Junge, dessen Vater und Mutter noch leben, den Wagen nicht hält und die Zügel loslässt oder wenn der Ädil beim Aufsagen der Formel oder mit der Schöpfkelle einen Fehler macht, dann sind die Spiele nicht ordnungsgemäß abgehalten, und man korrigierte die Fehler und stellte die unsterblichen Götter durch eine Wiederholung der Spiele zufrieden (Ed. FUHRMANN). Cf. SCHEID, Religion, 35.

chen Rache, dem Tod, rechnen.⁹ Die rechtliche Formel *sacer esto!* im Zwölftafelgesetz setzte die Annahme voraus, dass die Götter selbst solche Menschen bestraften. Ein Patron, der seinen Schützling betrogen hat, hat beispielsweise ein Grundgebot des gegenseitigen Vertrauens (*fides*) verletzt, deshalb solle er laut einem Gesetz der achten Tafel *sacer* werden.¹⁰ Das Adjektiv *sacer* deckt zwei in unseren Augen diametral entgegengesetzte Eigenschaften ab, „heilig" und „einer Gottheit zur Vernichtung geweiht", ihr als Opfer verfallen; diese Nuance wird als „verflucht" oder „verwünscht" übersetzt.¹¹ Einer Person, die *sacer* ist, wird der menschliche und göttliche Schutz entzogen. Die überlieferten Anschuldigungen der Gottlosigkeit sind meist Ausnahmefälle, die einen Gegensatz zur täglichen effektiven Kommunikation darstellen. Die Anklagen der Gottlosigkeit, wie z.B. in Ciceros Rede *Über die Antwort der Haruspices*, verraten uns nicht viel über das dahinter stehende Menschenbild, sondern eher über die Art und Weise, wie man politische Gegner durch Unterstellung einer Freveltat (*scelus*), der Transgression der religiösen Regeln, disqualifiziert.

In diesem Aufsatz werde ich das Verhältnis zwischen Göttern und Menschen anhand von Ovids Nacherzählung einer Legende über Numa und Jupiter untersuchen, um feststellen zu können, welches Menschenbild der Text Ovids beinhaltet.

2 Menschenbilder in der römischen Religionsgeschichte

Die Frage nach dem Menschenbild, das hinter der antiken römischen Religionsausübung steckte, wurde in der Religionsgeschichte des antiken Roms selten explizit gestellt. Hier werde ich zwei religionsgeschichtliche Auffassungen des Menschenbildes ansprechen, die zu ihrer Zeit die Religionsgeschichte wesentlich geprägt haben. Einige Altertumswissenschaftler des 18. und 19. Jahrhunderts verstanden die römische Religion als eine „wenig Sinn für Religiosität verratende einseitig juristische Betrachtungsweise", der gegenüber sie sich sehr

---

9 Liv. 29,8–9: das *sacrilegium* des Pleminius; cf. SCHEID, Religion 35–45; LINDER/SCHEID, Croire, 50.
10 Serv. Aen. 6,609: AVT FRAVS INNEXA CLIENTI ex lege XII tabularum venit, in quibus scriptum est „patronus si clienti fraudem fecerit, sacer esto". Die Wendung „oder Betrug, um einen Schützling gegarnt" erklärt sich aus einer Bestimmung der Zwölf Tafeln, auf denen geschrieben steht: „Wenn ein Patron an einem sich an ihn anlehnenden Schützling Betrug verübt, soll er verflucht werden!" (Ed. und Übersetzung FLACH).
11 Oxford Latin Dictionary, 1674.

kritisch äußerten.[12] John Scheid und nach ihm Andreas Bendlin haben herausgestellt, dass vor allem für die protestantischen Gelehrten wie Georg Wilhelm Friedrich Hegel und Theodor Mommsen nur eine „innere" oder „subjektive" Religiosität die Grundlage einer Religion darstellen konnte.[13] Georg Wissowa, der Autor des Handbuches über die antike römische Religion, verteidigte deshalb die Ansicht, dass „Religiosität kein völlig feststehender und für alle Zeiten und Völker konstanter Begriff" ist.[14] Diese—richtige—Erkenntnis über die Variabilität des religiösen Empfindens widersprach jedoch dem in seiner Zeit verbreiteten Religionsbegriff.[15]

James Frazers Interpretationen antiker Kulte und Mythen bedienten umso besser den damaligen Zeitgeist. Frazer schrieb das Werk *The Golden Bough* im Sinne der anthropologisch orientierten Vergleichenden Religionswissenschaft;[16] seine Bücher über antike Kulte und Mythen übten einen großen Einfluss auf die populärwissenschaftliche und wissenschaftliche Wissensvermittlung seiner Zeit aus.[17] Frazer interpretierte antike Religionen durch Parallelen mit „wilden" Völkern aus den britischen Kolonien, die er lediglich aus zweiter Hand (aus Berichten von Geschäftsreisenden, Beamten, Missionaren) kannte.[18] Er glaubte, eine genaue Entsprechung zwischen antiken Ritualen, die ihm zufolge den natürlichen Rhythmus der Jahreszeiten darstellten, und Mythen über Tod und Wiedergeburt der Götter zu erkennen. Das Menschenbild, das sich Frazer von einem antiken Zelebranten ausmalte, war sehr reduktionistisch und beruhte auf der Annahme seiner exzessiven Emotionalität und Furcht. Der antike Mensch sei ein Bauer gewesen, der mit zitternder Hand das Saatgut aussäte, ohne zu wissen, ob er sich überhaupt eine Ernte erhoffen konnte. Die Götter hätten Frazer zufolge für die primitiven Völker, zu denen er auch die Römer zählte, die Vegetation repräsentiert. Sie feierten in „dramatischen" Ritualen, die in ihrer Substanz „magisch" gewesen seien, den traurigen Tod des Vegetationsgottes (sei es Osiris, sei es Persephone, sei es Dionysos) mit Lamentationen und die

---

12 WISSOWA, Religion, VIII.
13 WISSOWA, Religion, VIII; SCHEID, Polytheism; BENDLIN, Sinn. SCHLESIER, Leiden, hat Friedrich Schleiermachers (1768–1834) Rezeption des griechischen Dionysos-Kultes analysiert: Schleiermacher war ein stark vom Pietismus geprägter Theologe und Philosoph.
14 WISSOWA, Religion, VIII.
15 BENDLIN, Sinn, 229–230, stellt heraus, dass der schlesische Katholik Wissowa die Suche nach einer (protestantisch geprägten) inneren Religiosität ablehnte und eine grundsätzliche Alterität der römischen Kultur und Religion postulierte.
16 1. Auflage in zwei Bänden 1890, 3. Auflage mit bezeichnendem Untertitel: A Study in Magic and Religion I-XII, London 1907–1915.
17 GRAF, Mythologie, 33.
18 KIPPENBERG/VON STUCKRAD, Einführung, 64.

Wiedergeburt des Gottes, die er mit dem Wachstum der Pflanzen interpretiert, mit Fröhlichkeit. Diese rituellen Tätigkeiten hätten nach Prinzipien der sympathetischen Magie gewirkt, so dass antike Menschen glaubten, sie hätten die Regeneration der Vegetation im Frühling gesichert.[19] Da die primitiven Völker nichts über den regelmäßigen Wechsel der Jahreszeiten gewusst hätten, hätten sie eine vollkommene Illusion der Wirkung von „magischen" Ritualen und Verehrung der („orientalischen") Vegetationsgottheiten gehabt.[20] Nach Frazer wurde der natürliche Zyklus des Jahresablaufes in eine genaue Parallele zwischen Mythos und Ritual transponiert.[21] Frazer übernahm somit Wilhelm Mannhardts Erklärungsmuster, nach dem die Landwirtschaft und die Sorge um Fruchtbarkeit im Mittelpunkt der Rituale stünden.[22] In der Religionsgeschichte des antiken Roms führte Kurt Latte Frazers Religionsbegriff in seinem Handbuch zur römischen Religionsgeschichte fort.[23] So interpretierte Latte zahlreiche römische Kulte durch verallgemeinernde Paradigmen wie „Die Religion der Bauern", „Agrarmagie und magische Abwehr von Dämonen". Frazers Religionsbegriff und Menschenbild kritisierte und berichtigte Jane Ellen Harrison in ihrem im Jahr 1912 erschienen Buch, indem sie auf die Ansätze des Soziologen Émile Durkheim zurückgriff.[24]

Heute interpretieren Religionswissenschaftler die Anfänge der Religionswissenschaft aus der Feder Frazers als „koloniale" Vergleichende Religionswissenschaft. David Chidester versteht solche Deutungen als ein „koloniales Diskursfeld", in dem es nicht nur um historische Rekonstruktionen der Religion ging, sondern um die Absicherung von territorialen Eingriffen in Afrika.[25] Die Rolle der kolonialen Vergleichenden Religionswissenschaft sieht Chidester und mit ihm Hans G. Kippenberg und Kocku von Stuckrad als rhetorische Absicherung der Internierung und Reservation der indigenen Bevölkerung in Afrika. Den indigenen Stämmen wurde das Vorhandensein einer Religion—solange sie nicht militärisch und politisch besiegt waren—abgesprochen.[26] Frazers Auffas-

---

19 FRAZER, Adonis, 3–5.
20 FRAZER, Adonis, ebd.
21 Zum Adonis-Mythos und -Kult s. FRAZER, Adonis, 3–33.
22 WALDNER, Geburt, 12–13.
23 Im fünften Kapitel untersucht Latte „Die Religion des Bauern", indem er unter anderem den Larenkult, Geburts- und Bestattungsriten diskutiert, s. LATTE, Religionsgeschichte, 64–107.
24 Cf. WALDNER, Geburt, 13.
25 KIPPENBERG/STUCKRAD 2003, 65, weisen auf die Abhängigkeit der Missionare und Reisenden von den Geldgebern und Organisatoren der Reisen hin. Nur die Informationen, die die Überlegenheit der westlichen Kultur bestätigten, brachten viel ein.
26 KIPPENBERG/VON STUCKRAD, Einführung, 64.

sung der Religion des primitiven Menschen war somit tief in koloniale Machtverhältnisse verstrickt. Seine Analysen dienten der Stärkung des europäischen Selbstbildes und des Gefühls der Superiorität im Vergleich mit den antiken Gesellschaften und den Völkern des britischen Commonwealths. Es ging wieder um ein Menschenbild, nämlich das Selbstbild des expandierenden Europäers.

Durch das Interesse für die Mentalitäts- und Alltagsgeschichte und den *cultural turn*, der Übertragung von kulturwissenschaftlichen Forschungsmethoden auf die Altertumswissenschaft, schwand die Notwendigkeit eines alles umfassenden und deutenden Paradigmas des Menschenbildes in anderen Kulturen und Religionen. Aus dem Blickwinkel der sozial- bzw. kulturwissenschaftlichen Religionsgeschichte wird

> Religion als soziales Phänomen gesehen, durch religiöse Rituale und die damit verbundenen symbolischen Systeme wird soziale Kohäsion hergestellt, der einzelne an eine bestimmte Gruppe gebunden, die sich ihrerseits wiederum über ihre Ordnung durch Rituale und mythische Texte verständigt.[27]

Im Mittelpunkt der Analyse stehen somit Rituale als kommunikative Vorgänge, die Performativität des Rituals und Analysen der diskursiven Strategien antiker Autoren vor dem kulturwissenschaftlich-geschichtlichen Hintergrund.[28] Kippenberg und von Stuckrad sprechen somit von der diskursiven Religionswissenschaft; die antiken Texte spiegeln die zeitgenössischen Diskurse wider, die das Verhältnis zwischen Göttern und Menschen immer wieder neu verhandeln.[29] Ich möchte noch hinzufügen, dass die Auffassung des Menschenbildes in der Literatur situativ zu verstehen ist, abhängig von den jeweiligen textuellen und historischen Zusammenhängen. So kann man weder verallgemeinernd vom Menschenbild in der augusteischen Epoche sprechen noch von einem einzigen Menschenbild in einem literarischen Werk. Autoren portraitieren verschiedene mythische oder historische Personen, um auf bestimmte Werte und Tugenden zu verweisen. Darüber hinaus ist die Positionierung des Autors gegenüber einer literarischen Person besonders wichtig. So zeigt sich Numa in den *Fasti* als Prototyp des Augustus und Ovids zugleich.

---

27 WALDNER, Geburt, 13.
28 Zum Ritual als Kommunikation s. RÜPKE, Religionen; zur Performativität des Rituals s. ŠTERBENC ERKER, Lupercalia.
29 Cf. VON STUCKRAD, Christen, 195–202.

3 Menschenkopf wird durch eine Zwiebel ersetzt: Vom Menschenopfer zu symbolischen Gaben

Ovid erzählt eine Legende aus der Zeit nach der Gründung Roms, die das Verhältnis zwischen Gott und Mensch thematisiert, weshalb sie sich für die Analyse des Menschenbildes besonders eignet.[30] Diese mythische Episode weist neue Elemente auf, die bei Livius, dessen literarische Behandlung der Erzählung älter ist, nicht vorkommt.[31] Das Gespräch zwischen Jupiter und Numa ist eine Erfindung Ovids, dieser hellenistischen literarischen Technik bedient er sich in den *Fasti* an mehreren Stellen. Meist fragt der Dichter einzelne Gottheiten nach mythischen Ursprüngen ihrer Feste oder einiger ritueller Gesten, Praktiken und Orte.

Zunächst zu den beiden Protagonisten des Gesprächs: Numa war laut Legende der zweite römische König; Romulus gründete die Stadt Rom, sein Nachfolger Numa galt als zweiter Gründer, der Recht, Gesetze und religiöse Institutionen etablierte. Numa war Friedensstifter und Symbol des guten Herrschers,[32] der Livius zufolge den Weg für Camillus und Augustus ebnete, die sich beide durch ihr besonders ehrwürdiges Verhalten gegenüber den Göttern der Gemeinschaft auszeichneten.[33] Sein göttlicher Gesprächspartner, Jupiter, war im polytheistischen Pantheon Roms der wichtigste Gott der *res publica*, zusammen mit Juno Regina und Minerva bewohnte er den Tempel auf dem Kapitol.

Die Unterhaltung zwischen Numa und Jupiter hat mehrere Erzählrahmen. Zunächst ist sie im dritten Buch der *Fasti* situiert, in dem Ovid die Feste im März, dem dritten Monat nach der neuen Kalenderordnung Roms, schildert.[34] Der März war dem Kriegsgott Mars gewidmet, dem göttlichen Vorfahren der Römer, wie ihn die augusteische Ideologie darstellte. Im Zusammenhang mit dem Anfang des archaischen Jahres erzählt Ovid die Legenden über die Stadt-

---

30 Ov. fast. 3,277–377; cf. Plut. Numa 15; Arnobius, Contra Gentiles 5,1–8. Prescendi, sacrifice, 189–198, diskutiert die Gemeinsamkeiten und Unterschiede dieser Erzählungen. Arnobius erwähnt einen älteren Gewährsmann für diese Episode, Valerius Antias, einen Historiker aus Sullas Zeit. Littlewood argumentiert, dass bereits Ennius die Legende in den Annalen erwähnt, indem er auf zwei Fragmente verweist (ann. 113 und 144 Sk.), die die Protagonistin und einen Gegenstand aus der Erzählung (Egeria und *ancilia*) thematisieren, s. Littlewood, *imperii*, 182.
31 Liv. 1,20,7.
32 Dion. Hal. ant. 2,60,4; Liv. 1,19,1–5.
33 Liv. 5,50,1: diligentissimus religionum cultor (sc. Camillus) (Ed. Convey); 4,20,7: (sc. Augustus) templorum omnium restitutorem ac conditorem; cf. Littlewood, *imperii*, 180.
34 Der Monat März stand nach dem archaischen Kalender Roms am Anfang des Jahres, s. Ov. fast. 3,75.

gründung und die mythischen Ereignisse danach, zunächst die Geburt von Romulus und Remus, der Sprösslinge von Mars und der Vestalin Rhea Silvia. Es folgt die Kalenderordnung des Romulus, die gleich nach seiner Stadtgründung in Kraft getreten ist, sowie die Erzählung, wie Romulus den politischen Körper unterteilte.[35] Anschließend thematisiert der Dichter das Fest Matronalia am 1. März, an dem römische Matronen zur Geburtsgöttin Juno Lucina beteten, damit sie den Frauen der *res publica* eine leichte Geburt ermögliche.[36]

Das Gespräch zwischen Numa und Jupiter kommt erst nach dem Besingen des Matronalia-Festes zustande.[37] Dieser Dialog erklärt ätiologisch, warum Jupiter die Schilde des Mars (*ancilia*) vom Himmel hinabwarf und dadurch einen Vertrag zwischen ihm und Numa besiegelte.[38] Am 1. März verehrten nicht nur Matronen die Geburtsgöttin Juno Lucina, sondern veranstalteten auch die Salier-Priester ihre Umzüge durch die Stadt Rom.[39] Zu Beginn und nach der Beendigung der Kriegszeit nach dem Kalender des archaischen Roms hielten die Salier ihre feierlichen Umzüge mit Waffentanz durch den stadtrömischen Raum ab.[40] Dabei trugen die Priester und ihre Diener achtförmige Schilde an Stangen aufgehängt durch die Stadt.[41] Die Schilde nennt Ovid „himmlische Waffen des Mars" oder *ancilia*, sie galten als Unterpfand der römischen Herrschaft und somit als Garanten für den Bestand der römischen Macht über die gesamte Welt.[42] In allen genannten Episoden stellt Ovid deutlich die Bezüge zur au-

---

35 Ov. fast. 3,131–133.
36 Es folgt das Aition der Matronalia, der Raub der Sabinerinnen. Die als rein männlich imaginierte Gemeinde der ersten Römer raubte der Legende zufolge die Frauen des Nachbarvolkes, die ihnen in der Ehe Kinder gebaren. Zum Matronalia-Fest s. Ov. fast. 3,243–258. PRESCENDI, Matralia, 126–127, stellt zu Recht fest, dass dieses Fest unter dem Aspekt der sozialen Rollen und Aufgaben der Mütter analysiert werden soll; zur Ätiologie s. ŠTERBENC ERKER, Tears, 135–160, und DIES., Matronage, 80–81.
37 Ov. fast. 3,300–354.
38 Ov. fast. 3,353–354.
39 Junge Patrizier, die ihre Ämterlaufbahn noch nicht angetreten hatten, konnten Salier werden, s. Varro ling. 5,85; Dion. Hal. ant. 2,70,4. SCHÄFER, Ikonographie, 370, argumentiert überzeugend zugunsten der These, nach der die Salier mit Erlangung des ersten öffentlichen Amtes aus der Priesterschaft ausschieden.
40 Die Salier haben am 1., 9., 14., 19. sowie 23. März ihre Tänze durchgeführt, was eine symbolische Eröffnung der Kriegssaison markierte, durch das Tanzen am 19. Oktober (Fest: Armilustrium, „Reinigung der Waffen") markierten sie ihr Ende.
41 Dion. Hal. ant. 2,71,1; SCHÄFER, Ikonographie, 364, Abb. 20 (Sardonyx mit Salierumzug aus Florenz).
42 Ov. fast. 3,259–261.346. Littlewood analysiert die literarischen Vorbilder, auf welche Ovid anspielt, vor dem Hintergrund der Verleihung des Tugendschildes an Augustus im Jahre

gusteischen Ideologie her. Auf den ersten Blick hat man den Eindruck, dass Ovid die Ätiologien verbindet, obwohl im historischen Alltag keine direkten Bezüge zwischen den Umzügen der Salier, dem Matronalia-Fest und dem Kult des Jupiter Elicius festzustellen sind. Der Dichter schafft es jedoch, indem er die Feste Anfang März schildert, der den Anfang des archaischen Jahres darstellt, mehrere historisierende Legenden über die Genese der politischen und religiösen Institutionen des archaischen Roms zu erzählen. Dabei wird deutlich, dass die Ereignisse rund um die Entstehung der politischen Gemeinschaft im Mittelpunkt stehen, Numa wird sich somit als Vertreter dieser Gemeinschaft mit Jupiter unterhalten.

Ovid führt den eigentlichen Grund für die Unterhaltung Numas mit Jupiter als Wunsch nach einem ruhigen Leben an, nachdem die Kriege mit den Nachbarvölkern beendet wurden:

> principio nimium promptos ad bella Quirites
>   molliri placuit iure deumque metu.
> inde datae leges, ne firmior omnia posset,
>   coeptaque sunt pure tradita sacra coli.
> exuitur feritas, armisque potentius aequum est,
>   et cum cive pudet conseruisse manus,
> atque aliquis, modo trux, visa iam vertitur ara
>   vinaque dat tepidis farraque salsa focis.[43]

> Zuerst beschloss man, die Quiriten, denen der Sinn all zu sehr nach Kriegen stand, durch Recht und Gottesfurcht zu bändigen. Daher gab man Gesetze, dass der Stärkere nicht alles durchsetzen könnte, und man begann, die überlieferten Rituale korrekt auszuführen. Wilde Sitten werden abgelegt, Recht ist stärker als Gewalt, es ist verpönt, sich mit dem Mitbürger zu schlagen, so manch einer, eben noch im Herzen wilden Trotz, schaut den Altar, ändert seine Haltung und spendet Wein und Mehl mit Salz am warmen Opferherd.[44]

Ovid thematisiert hier den Übergang von der Regierung des kriegerischen Romulus, der mit den Nachbarvölkern Krieg führte, zu Numa, der friedlich regierte. Numa stiftete laut Legende den Janusbogen, den er auch als erster schloss, um das Ende der Kriege symbolisch zu markieren.[45] Dem mythischen König Numa wurde die Stiftung zahlreicher archaischer Kulte und ritueller Vor-

---

27 v. Chr. und zeigt, dass Ovid in dieser Episode Augustus in die Tradition der großen Schildträger (Achilles, Aeneas, Numa) einordnet; siehe LITTLEWOOD, *imperii*, 188.
43 Ov. fast. 3,277–284 (Ed. ALTON).
44 Leicht veränderte Übersetzung von BÖMER, *Ovidius*.
45 Liv. 1,19,2.

schriften zugeschrieben.⁴⁶ Neben der Etablierung der Gesetze scheint auch die Angst vor den Göttern ein Instrument für die Besänftigung römischer Bürger zu sein. Hier spielt Ovid auf die antike Theorie über die staatspolitische Notwendigkeit bzw. den Nutzen der Gottesfurcht an, wodurch sich das Volk regieren lässt.⁴⁷ Numa sorgte dafür, dass die überlieferten und dabei wohl etwas „verkommenen" Rituale wieder korrekt ausgeführt wurden.

Spätestens an dieser Stelle fällt auf, dass Numas Charakterbeschreibung die Eigenschaften aufweist, die Augustus, dem ersten Kaiser Roms, zugeschrieben wurden. Nach der Beendigung der Bürgerkriege durch seinen Sieg über Marcus Antonius (31 v. Chr.) ließ sich Augustus als derjenige feiern, der dem römischen Volk die Gesetze zurückgegeben hat. Ebenfalls stellte sich Augustus als der Wiederhersteller zahlreicher Kulte, Priesterschaften und Heiligtümer dar.⁴⁸ Bereits der Anblick des Altars soll manchen Bürger von seinen mörderischen Absichten zur frommen Gottesverehrung durch Opfer bewegen. Hier ist die Panegyrik mit der Ideologie der Versöhnung der römischen Bürger nach dem Ende der Bürgerkriege verknüpft. Die Darbringung von Wein, Salz und Mehl, die Ovid am Ende dieser Textpassage erwähnt, weist auf die rituelle Kommunikation mit den Göttern hin: Das war entweder eine Supplikationsgeste, also eine Geste der bittflehenden Ehrung der Gottheit, oder ein Teil des Tieropfers. Bei jedem öffentlichen Opfer wurden die *mola salsa*, eine Mischung aus Speltschrot (*far*) und Salzlake, zusammen mit Wein über die Stirn der Opfertiere, den Altar und das Opfermesser gestreut bzw. gegossen.⁴⁹ Das friedliche Leben verdeutlicht Ovid—völlig im Einvernehmen mit Augustus' Selbstdarstellung—durch den Vollzug der Opferhandlungen. Augustus veranstaltete öffentliche Rituale, um die Bürger und Bürgerinnen Roms zur Teilnahme an Opferhandlungen unter seiner Ägide anzuregen.⁵⁰

Dieses friedliche Bild der ersten Römer trüben aber Jupiters Blitze, ausgiebige Regenfälle und die darauf folgende Trockenheit, was Numa und seinem Volk Angst einflößt.⁵¹ Blitze und Naturkatastrophen hielten die Römer für Prodigien, Zeichen des göttlichen Zorns, was die große Furcht verständlich macht. In Ovids Erzählung ergreift Numas Gattin Egeria das Wort und sagt dem

---

46 Liv. 1,19,1.
47 Cf. Cic. leg. 2,16; 2,27.
48 Suet. Aug. 30,2; 31,3–4.
49 Die Etablierung dieser Geste führen römische Autoren auf Numa zurück, s. Cic. div. 2,37: *immolare*; Fest. 125L s.v. *mola*; Serv. Aen. 2,133.
50 Zum Beispiel die *ludi saeculares*. Eine umfassende Studie der augusteischen Ritualerneuerung und Macht der Rituale ist nach wie vor ein Forschungsdesiderat.
51 Ov. fast. 3,285–288.

König, dass man Blitze „reinigen" bzw. „sühnen" (*piare*) kann. Picus und Faunus, zwei weissagende Götter, könnten Numa verraten, nach welchem Ritus Jupiters Blitze zu „sühnen" seien. Egeria weiß auch, mit welcher List Numa dieses Wissen den beiden Göttern entlocken könnte, nämlich indem er sie in Fesseln legt.[52]

Im Text ist kein Grund dafür zu finden, warum Jupiter in der Zeit von Numas Regierung seinen Zorn durch das Werfen von Blitzen zeigt. Allerdings ist hier ein historischer Bezug von Bedeutung; Littlewood zeigt zu Recht die Parallele zwischen Jupiters und Augustus' Zorn, auf die Ovid häufig anspielt.[53] Augustus stellte sich als Schützling des Jupiter Tonans dar, Sueton zufolge hat einmal ein Blitz Augustus' Sänfte gestreift und dabei einen Sklaven getötet, er selbst entkam jedoch dem Tod.[54]

Die Wörter für die „Entsühnung" der Blitze, *piaculum* und *piare*, decken die semantischen Felder von Reinigung, Besänftigung und Wiedergutmachung ab.[55] *Piaculum* bedeutet hier die Wiederherstellung des Friedens mit den Göttern (*pax deorum*), der Voraussetzung für das Wohlergehen der *res publica*. Im historischen Rom besaßen Auguren und Haruspices das nötige Wissen, um die Prodigien zu deuten, und bestimmten, mit welchen Ritualen die Götter zu besänftigen seien. Aber in der mythischen Zeit nach der Gründung Roms fehlte dieses Spezialistenwissen. Ovids Erzählung über das Gespräch zwischen Numa und Jupiter soll unter anderem den Ursprung der auguralen Lehre und der Autorität erklären,[56] die die Magistrate daraus schöpften.

Ovid visualisiert anschließend ein mythisches Bild vom Aventin zu Numas Zeit und einem Hain mit einer Quelle, an der nur Picus und Faunus getrunken haben. Numa handelt nach Egerias Anweisungen[57] und bereitet eine Falle für die beiden Götter vor: Er opfert der Quelle im Hain einen Schafsbock, die obligatorische Weingabe stellt er in Bechern um die Quelle herum auf und versteckt sich in einer Grotte.[58] Als die Waldgötter erscheinen, trinken sie nicht nur das Wasser der Quelle, sondern auch den Wein und legen sich auf der Stelle zur

---

52 Ov. fast. 3,289–294.
53 LITTLEWOOD, *imperii*, 190: „Bearing in mind the multilayered significance of the Virgilian intertext in the first part of the Salii passage and the ubiquitous dynastic undertones of the *Fasti*, we cannot ignore the connection between Jupiter's thunderbolts and imperial displeasure, which runs like a leitmotif through Ovid's *Tristia*."
54 Suet. Aug. 29,3.
55 Oxford Latin Dictionary, 1377 (s.v. *piaculum, piamen*), 1382 (s.v. *pio*).
56 Liv. 1,20,7.
57 Ov. fast. 3,289–296.
58 Ov. fast. 3,300–306. Zum Quellopfer s. Hor. carm. 3,13; Mart. 6,47; BÖMER, Kommentar, 166.

Ruhe. Numa fesselt ihre Hände und lässt sie weiter schlafen, erst als sie erwachen und sich nicht aus den Fesseln befreien können, zeigt sich Numa vor ihnen.[59] Zunächst entschuldigt sich Numa höflich bei den Göttern, dass er sie gefesselt habe.[60] Daraufhin bittet er sie, dass, wenn sein Herz ohne Frevel (*scelus*) sei, er also keine *impietas* begangen habe, sie ihm zeigen sollten, wie ein Blitzschlag gereinigt werden könne. Die Entschuldigung und der Verweis auf sein reines Herz stehen im Zusammenhang mit Numas Behauptung, er habe die Götter immer pflichtbewusst verehrt, was Picus (und später auch Jupiter) mit ihrem Entgegenkommen gegenüber Numas Wünschen bestätigen.[61] Ovid schildert Numa als einen besonders frommen und gottesfürchtigen Mann, eine mythische Präfiguration des Augustus und zugleich für Ovid selbst. Beide schöpfen ihre Inspiration von Egeria.[62] Eine der autobiographischen Aussagen Ovids in den *Fasti* stellt die Ähnlichkeit fest zwischen Numa, der von der Göttin Egeria die Weisungen für die Stiftung der Gesetze und Rituale erhielt, und dem Dichter, der von Egeria seine poetische Inspiration für die Gründung des römischen sakralen Jahrs im Gedicht bekommen habe.[63]

Faunus antwortet zunächst mit dem Verweis darauf, dass er und Picus eine begrenzte Wirkungsmacht hätten, da sie lediglich über den Wald sowie die hohen Gebirge herrschten.[64] Diese Antwort erinnert an die fest umrissene Amtsgewalt eines römischen Magistraten (oder auch eines heutigen Beamten), der sich in den Machtbereich seines Kollegen nicht einmischt. Die sozialen Verhältnisse zwischen den Menschen überträgt Ovid hier auf die Götter. Faunus bietet aber gleich seine Hilfe an, indem er vorschlägt, dass er und Picus den Jupiter

---

59 Das Vorbild für das Fesseln einer Gottheit, die Auskunft geben kann, ist der Seher Proteus, den z.B. Aristaeus nach dem Rat seiner Mutter gefesselt hat, siehe Ov. fast. 1,367–378; Verg. georg. 4,387–529; Hom. Od. 4,382–569; cf. Pasco-Pranger, Founding, 93. Die Erzählung von der Gefangennahme von Picus und Faunus ist bei Val. Ant. Frg. 6 HRR I 239–275 überliefert, wahrscheinlich kannte Ovid nur Varros Erzählung, s. Bömer, Kommentar, 165.
60 Ov. fast. 3,309.
61 Ov. fast. 3,335–336.
62 Pasco-Pranger, Founding, 90–91. Bereits Hinds erkannte in Numas verbaler Schärfe und Aufmerksamkeit, die er dem römischen Kult widmet, Ovids eigenen Prototyp. Cf. Littlewood, *imperii*, 190, Anm. 49: „Ovid's own ideological prototype".
63 Egeria als Numas Beraterin, s. Ov. fast. 3,276–284; Ovid als *vates*, der inspirierte Dichter, und Gründer des stadtrömischen Jahres, fast. 6,21; 1,25–26; Pasco-Pranger, Founding, 92. Ovid interpretiert seine poetische Inspiration durch das Trinken aus Egerias Quelle, allerdings in kleinen Schlucken, s. fast. 3,274. Die kleinen Schlucke verweisen auf die alexandrinische Dichtungstradition, in die sich Ovid einordnet, s. Pasco-Pranger, Founding, 91–92.
64 Ov. fast. 3,315–318.

vom Himmel herablocken.⁶⁵ Picus schwört bei Styx, dem unterirdischen Fluss, dass sie sich an das Versprochene halten würden. Die Bindung durch den Schwur ist so stark, dass Numa Picus und Faunus beruhigt von den Fesseln befreit. Picus und Faunus ziehen Jupiter mit Inkantationen, die geheim gehalten werden müssen, wie Ovid schreibt, von seinem Himmelsthron herab (*eliciunt*). Von *elicere*, herablocken, leitet Ovid die ätiologische Erklärung von Jupiters Epitheton ab.⁶⁶ Der Altar des Jupiter Elicius, den Numa als Folge seines Gesprächs mit Jupiter errichtete, stand auf dem Aventin. Livius zufolge deutete Numa die Blitze des Jupiter Elicius.⁶⁷

Livius thematisiert die Bedeutung der *pietas* und der genauen Durchführung der Rituale für Jupiter Elicius in der Legende über den König Tullus Hostilius. Hostilius war Numas Nachfolger, der seine Notizen mit Regeln zur Durchführung eines geheimen Rituals für Jupiter Elicius gefunden habe. Als Tullus Hostilius das Ritual im Geheimen vollzog, erhielt er vom Himmel kein Zeichen, sondern ist von dem erzürnten und wegen des verkehrten Rituals (*prava religione*) erbosten Jupiter Elicius durch einen Blitz erschlagen worden und samt seinem Haus verbrannt.⁶⁸ In dieser Legende soll Jupiter Elicius die rituellen Fehler des gottlosen Tullus Hostilius erkannt und bestraft haben, weshalb sich nur ein gottesfürchtiger und frommer (*pius*) Mensch wie Numa im Umgang mit ihm sicher fühlen könnte.

Ovid schildert Jupiters Ankunft und die Unterhaltung:

> constat Aventinae tremuisse cacumina silvae,
>   terraque subsedit pondere pressa Iovis:
> corda micant regis totoque e corpore sanguis
>   fugit et hirsutae deriguere comae.
> ut rediit animus, „da certa piamina" dixit
>   „fulminis, altorum rexque paterque deum,
> si tua contigimus manibus donaria puris,
>   hoc quoque quod petitur si pia lingua rogat."
> adnuit oranti, sed verum ambage remota
>   abdidit et dubio terruit ore virum.
> „caede caput" dixit; cui rex „parebimus" inquit;
>   „caedenda est hortis eruta cepa meis."
> addidit hic „hominis"; „sumes" ait ille „capillos."

---

65 Ov. fast. 3,318.
66 Ov. fast. 3,327–328. Nach einer anderen Version bezieht sich *elicere* auf *elicere aquam* beim Bittfest *aquaelicium*, s. BÖMER, Kommentar 165; cf. WISSOWA, Religion, 121.
67 Liv. 1,20,7. Jupiter Optimus Maximus war der Gott, der den Menschen Zeichen schickte, die von den Auguren interpretiert wurden, s. Cic. leg. 2,20.
68 Liv. 1,31,8.

> postulat hic animam; cui Numa „piscis" ait.
> risit, et „his" inquit „facito mea tela procures,
>   o vir conloquio non abigende deum.
> sed tibi, protulerit cum totum crastinus orbem
>   Cynthius, imperii pignora certa dabo."[69]

Es ist bekannt, daß die Berggipfel des Waldes auf dem Aventin erzitterten, die Erde senkte sich, vom Gewicht Jupiters erdrückt. Das Herz des Königs zitterte, aus seinem ganzen Körper wich das Blut, und rau sträubten sich seine Haare. Dann fasste er sich und sprach: „Gib ein sicheres Mittel zur Entsühnung für den Blitz, König und Vater der Götter im Himmel, wenn ich deinen Altar je mit reiner Hand berührte und auch diese Bitte eine fromme Zunge spricht." Er nickte ihm Gewährung für sein Gebet, verbarg aber die Wahrheit durch ein dunkles Rätsel und erschreckte Numa durch eine doppeldeutige Rede: „Opfere ein Haupt", sprach er; der König antwortete ihm: „Ich will gehorsam sein. Ein Zwiebelkopf, aus meinem Garten ausgegraben, soll geopfert werden." „(Den Kopf) eines Menschen (will ich)", fügte Jupiter hinzu. „Du sollst", sprach Numa, „sein Haar erhalten". (Doch Jupiter) forderte ein Leben. Numas Antwort lautete: „Das eines Fisches." Unter Lachen sagte Jupiter: „Mach, dass du damit meine Blitze sühnst, Mensch, der du dich (selbst) vor einem Wortwechsel mit Göttern nicht scheust. Doch will ich dir, wenn Kynthios morgen das ganze Rund der Sonne zeigt, ein sicheres Unterpfand des Reiches geben" (Übersetzung nach BÖMER).

Die Beschreibung von Jupiters Ankunft visualisiert die gewaltige Präsenz des Gottes auf der Erde und die Erschütterung, die Numa überwältigt. Verschiedene Götter wirken unterschiedlich auf Erde und Menschen; Vestas Ankunft hat zur Folge, dass sich die Erde freut, Janus erhellt Ovids Haus durch sein Erscheinen, der Dichter erschreckt sich so, dass ihm die Haare zu Bergen stehen.[70] Jupiter erschüttert Natur und Mensch. Durch dieses Bild wird die Größe des Gottes verdeutlicht und zugleich der Mut Numas, der sich doch schnell fasst und beginnt, Jupiter nach Entsühnungsmitteln zu befragen. Numa gelingt es, die hohen Ansprüche Jupiters nach wertvollen Opfergaben, beginnend mit dem Menschenopfer, zu vermindern, wobei er ihm Gaben anbietet, die nicht Bestandteile römischer Expiationsrituale waren (Zwiebel, menschliches Haar, Fische). Dabei verwendet er römisches juridisches Vokabular und Wortspiele, manipuliert geschickt mit der Ähnlichkeit der Worte (*caput/cepa/capilli*) und Syntax (anstatt Kopf auf den Menschen zu beziehen, bietet Numa ein neues Substantiv dazu, das Haar).[71]

Dieses Wortgefecht kam Franz Bömer, dem Kommentator der *Fasti*, schlicht respektlos vor. Die Vorstellung, dass Götter überlistet werden und dass ein

---

69 Ov. fast. 3,329–345.
70 Janus: Ov. fast. 1,94–98; Vesta: fast. 6,251–252.
71 DUMÉZIL, Religion, 57; PASCO-PRANGER, Founding, 97.

Mensch mit einem Gott um seine Ehre feilscht, hält er für fehl am Platz. So bezeichnet Bömer das Gespräch als „nicht römisch" und sieht hier einen hellenistischen Einfluss.[72] Das Gespräch passt somit weder zu Bömers Verständnis der römischen Religiosität noch zum Menschenbild, das er sich von einem Römer machte. Vor allem scheint Numas Mangel an Respekt gegenüber dem ihm übergeordneten Jupiter problematisch zu sein. Die Tatsache, dass Jupiter nicht beleidigt ist, beweist jedoch, dass es für Ovid denkbar war, dass die Beredsamkeit Numas den Gott erfreute, weshalb er Zustimmung Jupiters erntete.[73] Georges Dumézil interpretiert die Episode in diesem Sinne und vermutet, dass Jupiter Numas Kenntnisse des juridischen Vokabulars und der Syntax überprüft.[74] Diese mythische Erzählung nimmt Dumézil als Beispiel für die Sorge eines Römers im religiösen Alltag, ohne Fahrlässigkeit zu sprechen, keine rituellen Formeln anzuwenden, die der Gott oder ein menschlicher Interpret anders verstehen könnte.[75] Zu dieser Mentalität passt die Legende, die veranschaulicht, wie sehr der mythische König Numa den Göttern und seiner perfekten Kommunikation mit ihnen vertraut habe. Eines Tages, als man ihm gesagt hatte, dass sich Feinde der Stadt näherten, lächelte er und sagte: „Ich opfere."[76]

Ein weiteres Thema ist in dieser Erzählung von großer Bedeutung, die genaue Beachtung verschiedener Kompetenzräume bei der dichterischen Wissensvermittlung. Die Protagonisten der Erzählung und der Dichter selbst betonen, dass sie nur darüber sprechen, was ihnen nach dem göttlichen Recht (*fas*) erlaubt ist.[77] Ronald Syme macht darauf aufmerksam, dass in den letzten Jahren der Regierung des Augustus, als die politische Lage wieder angespannt war, der Kaiser die Redefreiheit einschränkte.[78] Denis Feeney vertritt somit zu Recht die Meinung, dass das Thema der Redefreiheit eines der wichtigsten der *Fasti* ist.[79]

---

72 BÖMER, Kommentar, 167.
73 PASCO-PRANGER, Founding, 98 (mit Anm. 47), deutet Jupiters Lachen als Zustimmung zu Numas Schlagfertigkeit und Numas poetischem Gebrauch von Sprache.
74 DUMÉZIL, Religion, 136; cf. PRESCENDI, sacrifice, 198. Prescendi ist der Meinung, dass Jupiter Numas Verständnis der Gerechtigkeit testet.
75 DUMÉZIL, Religion, 57.
76 Plut. Numa 15,11.
77 Der gefesselte Faunus erwidert Numa, der ihn nach Entsühnungsmitteln für den Blitzschlag fragt, dass er und Picus diese nach dem göttlichen Recht nicht nennen dürfen, s. Ov. fast. 3,314.
78 Im Jahr 12 n. Chr. verbannte der Senat Cassius Severus nach Kreta, weil er ranghohe Männer und Frauen in seinen Schriften verspottete, s. Tac. ann. 1,72,3; SYME, History, 13–20; FEENEY, *licet*, 4.
79 FEENEY, *licet*, 6, mit Verweis auf Dinge, die auszusprechen erlaubt sind, s. fast. 4,17–18. MASCIADRI, Geburt, 191, äußert sich pauschal gegen die Relevanz des Themas „Redefreiheit" für

Hier ist allerdings der Kontext zu beachten, um zu verstehen, welche Art von Redefreiheit gemeint ist. Ovid bittet in seinem im Exil redigierten Prooemium zum ersten Buch *Germanicus*, den er als *vates* anredet, er solle ihn, den ebenfalls vom Gott inspirierten Dichter, lenken, wenn es nach menschlichem und göttlichem Recht erlaubt ist.[80] Der Dichter betont in der Erzählung über Numa und Jupiter, dass es *nefas* für einen Menschen wäre zu wissen, wie Picus und Faunus Jupiter aus seinem erhabenen Sitz auf die Erde gelockt hätten, und versichert auf zweifache Weise, dass er nur das erzähle, was einem inspirierten Dichter erlaubt sei.[81] Ovid thematisiert somit die Frage, was ein Dichter, der einen engen Kontakt zu den Göttern pflegt, den Menschen verraten darf und was nicht, wodurch er auf die eng umrissenen Kompetenzräume der Götter und des *vates* verweist. Indem sich Ovid in der Erzählung durch seine Frömmigkeit, Gottesfurcht und dichterische Inspiration durch Egeria in Numas Bild erkennen lässt, stilisiert er sich als einen integren Dichter, der die Grenzen zwischen göttlicher und menschlicher Welt respektiert.

Wie ist nun Egerias beratende Rolle in dieser Erzählung zu deuten? Die Altertumswissenschaft schenkte Egeria kaum Aufmerksamkeit, obwohl sie die entscheidenden Anregungen für Numas Handlungen gibt.[82] Der Dichter wendet sich am Anfang der Erzählung an Egeria, die er als Quellnymphe und Geburtsgöttin charakterisiert, sie solle ihn über *ihre* Taten belehren.[83] Im Laufe der Erzählung wird sich herausstellen, dass Ovid die Nymphe Egeria als Numas Gattin und Beraterin in wichtigsten Angelegenheiten erwähnt.[84] Plutarch sieht Egeria sogar als Souffleuse im Gespräch mit Jupiter.[85] Dionysios von Halikarnass und Livius vermuten in rationalistischer Manier, dass sich Numa selbst eine göttliche Beraterin namens Egeria ausgedacht habe, damit das Volk, das Angst vor

---

die Interpretation der *Fasti*: „Deutungen, die Ovid zum Kritiker der Grundlagen eines augusteischen ‚Regimes' umprägen, projizieren mithin einen modernen Begriff von Freiheit auf die antiken Texte."
80 Ov. fast. 1,25–26.
81 Ov. fast. 3,323–326.
82 LITTLEWOOD, *imperii*, untersucht Numas Rolle in Ovids *Fasti*; Egeria erwähnt sie nur am Rande.
83 Ov. fast. 3,262: Nympha, Numae coniunx, ad tua facta veni.—Nymphe, Numas Gattin, komm, wenn ich deine Taten besinge!
84 Ov. fast. 3,276: illa Numae coniunx consiliumque fuit.—Sie war Numas Gattin und Ratgeberin. Ebenso lässt Ovid die Möglichkeit zu, dass Egeria (oder Pythagoras) Numa geraten habe, den zehn Monaten des römischen Kalenders, die Romulus etabliert hat, noch zwei fehlende hinzufügen, s. Ov. fast. 3,151–154: Egeria sua monente—auf den Rat seiner Frau Egeria hin.
85 Plut. Numa 15,9.

den Göttern hatte, Numas religiöse Gesetze akzeptieren würde.[86] Hier zeigt sich wieder die Vorstellung der Oberschicht, dass das Volk angeblich Angst vor den Göttern habe, die Magistrate und öffentlichen Priester jedoch freundschaftlich mit ihnen verkehrten.

Auffälligerweise nennen augusteische Autoren nicht nur archaische religiöse Institutionen als Numas religiöse Innovationen, sondern auch zahlreiche Neuerungen (die Rituale der Fetiales, die Aufnahme von Augustus' Namen in das Salier-Lied), die im engen Zusammenhang mit der Religionspolitik des ersten römischen Kaisers standen. Einige Altertumswissenschaftler betonen, dass Numa als eine historische Präfiguration des Augustus zu verstehen sei, wodurch die zahlreichen positiven Eigenschaften Numas (*pietas*, Gründung der Kulte und Priesterschaften, Nähe zu den Göttern) auf Augustus projiziert würden.[87] Augustus legitimierte seine Sonderstellung in der *res publica* durch zahlreiche religiöse Mechanismen, so stellte er sich als Schützling der Götter (Apollo, Jupiter Tonans) dar, erneuerte Tempel, Kulte und Priesterämter. Er übernahm—im Gegensatz zur republikanischen Tradition—zahlreiche öffentliche Priesterämter, womit er ein Vorbild für die religiöse Legitimation des Herrschers schuf.[88]

Egeria könnte als eine Präfiguration von Augustus' Gattin Livia verstanden werden. Ovid erwähnt zwar Livia in anderen Passagen der *Fasti* als treue Gattin, die dem Vorbild ihres Mannes folgt (z.B. als Stifterin der Tempel für weibliche Angelegenheiten) und seine Tätigkeiten ergänzt.[89] In Egerias listiger Beratungsrolle spiegelt sich jedoch ein Topos wider, dem zufolge Herrscherfrauen ihre Ehemänner beraten. Die römischen Historiographen konnten sich den weiblichen Einfluss auf den Kaiser lediglich innerhalb der *domus*, in der Verwandtschaft und in den sozialen Netzen von Freundschaft und Patronage vorstellen.[90] In diesem Punkt ähneln sich die Aussagen über den Einfluss der Kaisergattinnen auf ihre Ehemänner in der Historiographie mit denen über den Einfluss der mythischen Herrscherfrauen auf ihre Gatten in den elegischen Erzählungen.[91]

---

86 Dion. Hal. ant. 2,61,1; Liv. 1,19,5.
87 LITTLEWOOD, *imperii*, 188.
88 ŠTERBENC ERKER, Religion, 118–119, zu Neros Akkumulation der Priesterschaften nach Augustus' Vorbild.
89 Concordia-Tempel und Porticus Liviae, s. Ov. fast. 1,637–639; fast. 6,637–640; 5,150–158: Erneuerung des Bona Dea-Heiligtums. Cf. KUNST, Livia, 162–167.
90 SPÄTH, Herrscherin, 274.
91 Ovid, Livius und Dionysios von Halikarnass inszenieren die mythischen Herrscherfrauen als Beraterinnen ihrer Ehemänner in politischen und religiösen Belangen der *res publica*, s. ŠTERBENC ERKER, Matronage, 84–85.

4 Fazit

Ovids literarische Inszenierung eines Gesprächs zwischen Numa und Jupiter veranschaulicht die persönliche Auffassung des Dichters von einem guten Verhältnis zwischen einem römischen Magistraten und den Göttern. Numa wird als römischer Magistrat dargestellt und Jupiter als Gott, der sich in das Leben der römischen Bürger einmischt. Aus dieser literarischen Schilderung lese ich ein reziprokes Verhältnis zwischen dem Gott und Numa heraus. Der Gott Jupiter setzt seinen Willen nicht durch, sondern diskutiert mit Numa, welche Opfer er in der neuen religiösen Ordnung, die Numa geschaffen hat, bekommen solle. Es ist nicht nur der Gotteswille, der verkündet und umgesetzt wird, sondern es sind beim Verhandeln die List Egerias, der Gattin Numas, die Beredsamkeit Numas sowie seine Sorge um die Menschen in seiner Gemeinde ausschlaggebend. Numa hat als ein sehr frommer und gottesfürchtiger Mensch ein großes Vertrauen in seine Götterverehrung und unterhält sich unerschrocken mit dem höchsten Gott Roms. Numas Ziel ist es, durch die Verhandlung um die Art und Weise, wie Jupiters Blitze entsühnt werden, für seine politische Gemeinschaft ein furchtloses Zusammenleben mit den Göttern zu sichern. Obwohl Jupiter ausdrücklich ein Menschenopfer als Reinigungsmittel für seine Blitze verlangt, schafft es Numa, ein rein symbolisches Opfer durchzusetzen. Dieses Bild Numas ist eine idealtypische literarische Inszenierung eines vorbildlichen römischen Magistraten und seiner Haltung gegenüber den Göttern. So eignet sich dieser mythische König als Projektionsfläche für die Eigenschaften von Augustus und Ovid, die beide in den *Fasti* als fromm und sich ihrer Pflichten gegenüber den Göttern vollkommen bewusst fungieren.

Numas selbstbewusster Umgang mit Jupiter entspricht dem Menschenbild, das in Ritualen der römischen *res publica* immer wieder inszeniert wurde. Hinter der täglichen Ehrung für die Götter der politischen Gemeinde steckte die Idee, dass die römischen Priester und Magistrate das nötige rituelle Wissen besitzen und haargenau in Ritualen umsetzen, um die Gunst der Götter gegenüber ihrer politischen Gemeinde zu sichern. All die Leistungen Numas konnten antike Rezipienten auf Augustus projizieren, vor allem die *pietas*, die ein sehr wichtiger Teil der Selbstdarstellung des Kaisers war. Ovid schreibt eben diese Tugend sich selbst zu und betont häufig, dass er in den *Fasti* nur das erzählt, was erlaubt ist, womit er die zeitgenössischen Diskurse zum Ausdruck bringt, die über die Grenze zwischen dem Wissen, das nur den Göttern zugänglich ist, und dem Wissen, das man unter den Menschen verbreiten kann, reflektieren.

Welchen Religionsbegriff kann man aus Ovids Nacherzählung der Legende über Numa ableiten? Ein wichtiger Bestandteil der öffentlichen Religion war die genaue Befolgung traditioneller religiöser Vorschriften. Die Auswirkung der Orthopraxie auf das Menschenbild, in unserem Fall auf das Bild der römischen Magistrate, erweist sich nach der Lektüre Ovids als positiv und verrät das imaginierte gute Verhältnis zwischen den Vertretern der politischen Gemeinde und deren Göttern. Die Normen der römischen Religion beinhalteten also nicht ein Bild des Menschen, der Angst vor den Göttern hat, wie ihn Frazer ausmalte, sondern als das eines römischen Magistraten, der im Zweifelsfall sogar mit den Göttern verhandelt.

Bibliographie

ALTON, Ernst H. et al. (Hg.), P. Ovidi Nasonis Fastorum Libri Sex (BSGRT), Leipzig 1978.
BENDLIN, Andreas, „Ein wenig Sinn für Religiosität verratende Betrachtungsweise": Emotion und Orient in der römischen Religionsgeschichtsschreibung der Moderne, in: Archiv für Religionsgeschichte 8 (2006) 227–256.
BÖMER, Franz P. (Hg.), Ovidius Naso. Die Fasten I. Einleitung, Text und Übersetzung, Heidelberg 1957.
BÖMER, Franz P., Ovidius Naso. Die Fasten II. Kommentar, Heidelberg 1958.
BRUIT ZAIDMANN, Luise/SCHMITT PANTEL, Louise, Die Religion der Griechen. Kult und Mythos, München 1994 (Originaltitel: La religion grecque, Paris 1989).
CONWAY, Robertus Seymour/WALTERS, Carolus Flamstead (Hg.), T. Livius. Ab Urbe Condita Libri I–V (SCBO), Vol. 1, Oxford 1955.
DUMÉZIL, Georges, La religion romaine archaïque, Paris ²2000.
ENGELS, David, Das römische Vorzeichenwesen (753–27 v. Chr.). Quellen, Terminologie, Kommentar, historische Entwicklung (Potsdamer Altertumswissenschaftliche Beiträge 22), Stuttgart 2007.
FEENEY, Denis C., *Si licet et fas est*. Ovid's Fasti and the Problem of Free Speech under the Principate, in: Powell, Anthon (Hg.), Roman Poetry and Propaganda in the Age of Augustus, Bristol 1992, 1–25.
FLACH, Dieter (Hg.), Das Zwölftafelgesetz (TzF 83), Darmstadt 2004.
FRAZER, James G., The Golden Bough. A Study in Magic and Religion. Part 1: The Magic Art and the Evolution of Kings, 2 Vols., London 1890.
FRAZER, James G., The Golden Bough. A Study in Magic and Religion. Part 4: Adonis, Attis, Osiris, 2 Vols., London/New York 1906.
FUHRMANN, Manfred (Hg.), Marcus Tullius Cicero. Sämtliche Reden (BAW.RR), Band 5, Zürich/München 1978.
GLARE, Peter G.W. (Hg.), Oxford Latin Dictionary, Oxford 1982.
GRAF, Fritz, Griechische Mythologie. Eine Einführung, Düsseldorf ⁵1999.
KIPPENBERG, Hans G./STUCKRAD, Kocku von, Einführung in die Religionswissenschaft. Gegenstände und Begriffe (C.H. Beck: Studium), München 2003.
KUNST, Christiane, Livia. Macht und Intrigen am Hof des Augustus, Stuttgart 2008.

LATTE, Kurt, Römische Religionsgeschichte (HAW 5/4), München 1960.
LINDER, Monica/SCHEID, John, Quand croire c'est faire. Le problème de la croyance dans la Rome ancienne, in: ASSR 81 (1993) 47–62.
Lindsay, Wallace M. (Hg.), Sexti Pompei Festi De verborum significatu quae supersunt cum Pauli epitome, Leipzig 1913.
LITTLEWOOD, R. Joy, *imperii pignora certa*. The Role of Numa in Ovid's Fasti, in: Herbert-Brown, Geraldine (Hg.), Ovid's Fasti. Historical Readings at its Bimillenium, Oxford 2002, 175–197.
MASCIADRI, Virgilio, Die Geburt der Laren. Mythos und dichterische Erfindung in Ovids Fasti, in: Archiv für Religionsgeschichte 11 (2009) 179–207.
PASCO-PRANGER, Molly, Founding the Year. Ovid's Fasti and the Poetics of the Roman Calendar (Mnemosyne), Leiden/Boston, Massachusetts 2006.
PRESCENDI, Francesca, Matralia und Matronalia. Feste von Frauen in der römischen Religion, in: Späth, Thomas/Wagner-Hasel, Beate (Hg.), Frauenwelten in der Antike. Geschlechterordnung und weibliche Lebenspraxis, Darmstadt 2000, 123–131.
PRESCENDI, Francesca, Décrire et comprendre le sacrifice. Les réflexions des Romains sur leur propre religion à partir de la littérature antiquaire (Potsdamer altertumswissenschaftliche Beiträge 19), Stuttgart 2007.
RASMUSSEN, Susanne William, Public Portents in Republican Rome (ARID.S 34), Rom 2003.
ROSENBERGER, Veit, Gezähmte Götter. Das Prodigienwesen der römischen Republik (Heidelberger althistorische Beiträge und epigraphische Studien 27), Stuttgart 1998.
RÜPKE, Jörg, Antike Religionen als Kommunikationssysteme, in: Brodersen, Kai (Hg.), Gebet und Fluch, Zeichen und Traum. Aspekte religiöser Kommunikation in der Antike (Antike Kultur und Geschichte 1), Münster 2001, 13–30.
SCHÄFER, Thomas, Zur Ikonographie der Salier, in: JdI 95 (1980) 342–373.
SCHEID, John, Numa et Jupiter ou les dieux citoyens de Rome, in: ASSR 59 (1985) 41–53.
SCHEID, John, Polytheism Impossible; or the Empty Gods. Reasons behind a Void in the History of Roman Religion, in: History and Anthropology 3 (1987) 303–325.
SCHEID, John, Religion et piété à Rome (Sciences des religions), Paris ²2001.
SCHLESIER, Renate, Die Leiden des Dionysos, in: Kneppe, Alfred/Metzler, Dieter (Hg.), Die emotionale Dimension antiker Religiosität (FARG 37), Münster 2003, 1–20.
SPÄTH, Thomas, Skrupellose Herrscherin? Das Bild der Agrippina minor bei Tacitus, in: Späth, Thomas/Wagner-Hasel, Beate (Hg.), Frauenwelten in der Antike. Geschlechterordnung und weibliche Lebenspraxis, Darmstadt 2000, 262–280.
STUCKRAD, Kocku von, „Christen" und „Nichtchristen" in der Antike, in: Hutter, Manfred/Klein, Wassilios/Vollmer, Ulrich (Hg.), Hairesis. Festschrift für Karl Hoheisel zum 65. Geburtstag (JAC.E 34), Münster 2002, 184–202.
ŠTERBENC ERKER, Darja, Das Lupercalia-Fest im augusteischen Rom. Performativität, Raum und Zeit, in: Archiv für Religionsgeschichte 11 (2009) 145–178.
ŠTERBENC ERKER, Darja, Women's Tears in Ancient Roman Ritual, in: Fögen, Torsten (Hg.), Tears in the Graeco-Roman World, Berlin/New York 2009, 135–160.
ŠTERBENC ERKER, Darja, Der römische Totenkult und die Argei-Feier bei Ovid und Dionysios von Halikarnass, in: Rüpke, Jörg/Scheid, John (Hg.), Bestattungsrituale und Totenkult/Rites funéraires et culte des morts aus temps impériales (Potsdamer altertumswissenschaftliche Beiträge 27), Stuttgart 2010, 9–21.

ŠTERBENC ERKER, Darja, Gender and Roman Funeral Ritual, in: Hope, Val M./Huskinson, Janet (Hg.), Memory and Mourning in Ancient Rome. Studies on Roman Death, Oxford u.a. 2011, 40–60.

ŠTERBENC ERKER, Darja, Matronage in der augusteischen Aitiologie. Handlungsstrategien mythischer Herrscherfrauen, in: Kunst, Christiane (Hg.), Matronage—Handlungsstrategien und soziale Netzwerke von Herrscherfrauen im Altertum in diachroner Perspektive, Rahden 2013, 79–87.

ŠTERBENC ERKER, Darja, Art. „Religion", in: Dinter, Martin/Buckley, Emma (Hg.), A Blackwell Companion to Neronian Literature and Culture, Malden/Oxford 2013, 118–133.

SYME, Ronald, History in Ovid, Oxford ²1997.

WALDNER, Katharina, Geburt und Hochzeit des Kriegers. Geschlechterdifferenz und Initiation in Mythos und Ritual der griechischen Polis, Berlin/New York 2000.

WISSOWA, Georg, Religion und Kultus der Römer, München ²1912.

Marlis Arnhold
Narrating Meleager's Deeds and Death in Words and Images

1 Introduction: Conceptualizing "Evil"

Many studies concerned with evil forces focus on their origins and raise the question of definition. Attention is mostly drawn to what evil is, where it comes from, and if it is inevitable.[1] Evils have thus often been viewed from a Christian theologian perspective in which the issue of the theodicy dominates.[2] However, the famous words of Lactantius, asking for the existence of "the evil" in light of an almighty divine force, are of elder origin and reflect a question with a history of its own however hard it may be to trace the latter.[3] Debates on evil in Plato and Aristotle, for instance, illustrate that the issue is rooted in pre-Christian contexts and reveal moreover that there is not just one conception of evil. This becomes particularly apparent, when one calls to mind that the texts and images referring to an evil force presented media that were each composed with a specific intention and for a specific audience. In this regard, varying perspectives on what evil is, where it derives from, and which consequences result from it seem hardly surprising.

Understanding "evil" as a narrative device, this contribution aims to investigate how various conceptions of evil have been used by ancient authors and craftsmen to evoke particular sentiments and reactions in their audiences. The analysis of various versions of the myth of Meleager and the legendary events at Calydon will thus focus both on intentions and perceptions, but does not allow any insights into supposedly true beliefs. Viewed in this way, the discussion is not reduced to negative or indefinite answers on what evil actually is or could be, but presents a first, albeit tentative, step towards a historization by drawing attention to the conditions under which a certain conception of evil was applied. The length of an article will hardly allow for a full answer, but is meant as an invitation to follow and to broaden this perspective further. In which ways did Meleager die and what impact did various constructions of evil forces have on them?

---

1 For an overview, compare PIEPER, Gut und Böse.
2 The issue of the theodicy and the various arguments based on it have recently been summarized by DALFERTH, Malum.
3 Compare Lactantius, Ir. 13,19. The author attributes his arguments to Epicurus.

2 Meleager's Deeds and Death in Words and Text

From Homer onwards, the hunt of the Calydonian boar has been addressed by various authors throughout antiquity, such as Bacchylides, Diodorus Siculus, Ovid, Pseudo-Apollodorus, and Pseudo-Hyginus. The texts differ greatly as regards the space the narration is given, the course of events, the details mentioned, and the way the various agents are characterized. Consequently, not one single story of the events at Calydon exists despite occasional attempts at unification, but rather several versions, some of which attracted more attention than others. To illustrate these variations, the texts of three authors dealing with the events at Calydon and the death of Meleager will be analyzed in the following with regard to the ways in which evil forces are addressed in each of them and used to evoke positive and negative sentiments in the recipient of the texts.

The essential events of the myth as known from textual versions can be summarized in a few sentences: Oeneus, king of Calydon, omits a sacrifice to Artemis upon which the enraged goddess sends a boar to devastate the land. The king's son, Meleager, sets out together with others to hunt the beast. They eventually succeed, but a dispute arises over the trophy during which Meleager kills his uncles, who are the brothers of his mother Althaia. Consequently, the latter curses her son which results in his death.

The various textual versions of the tale differ on several elements, such as the exact cause of the dispute, the number of the uncles killed in its course (one or two) and the way Meleager himself dies at the end of the story. Many versions feature a woman, Atalante, who joins the hunters and with whom Meleager falls in love. When he grants her the trophy because it was she who wounded the boar first, the deathly dispute with his uncles arises. Although Althaia's impact on her son's death remains unaltered in all versions, death is brought on him in various ways. In some versions, he is slain by divine infringement,[4] whereas in others, Althaia throws a log of wood into the fire and thus allows the prophecy to be fulfilled, which the Moirai, goddesses of fate, had given at her son's birth: He dies as the log burns to ashes.[5]

---

4 For instance, in Homer's version, compare below.
5 This is the case, for instance, in Ovid's Metamorphoses.

2.1 Homer's Meleager: Sacrificing a Hero

Neither Atalante nor the log are mentioned in the Homeric version of the story, which is the oldest that has been preserved. In the ninth book of the Iliad, light is shed on the events of a war at Calydon, which broke out in consequence of the dispute over the trophy. The progress of the hunt, which plays a major role in many of the images and the later versions of the myth, is not dealt with. The text only relates that Meleager killed the boar with the help of fellow hunters and hounds from other cities which are not specifically named in the text.[6] The beast and the evils which it brought on Calydon as Artemis' revenge are referred to as:

> [...] χλούνην σῦν ἄγριον ἀργιόδοντα, ὃς κακὰ πόλλ' ἔρδεσκεν ἔθων Οἰνῆος ἀλωήν· πολλὰ δ' ὅ γε προθέλυμνα χαμαὶ βάλε δένδρεα μακρὰ αὐτῇσιν ῥίζῃσι καὶ αὐτοῖς ἄνθεσι μήλων.

> [...] a fierce wild boar, white of tusk, that wrought much evil, wasting the orchard land of Oeneus; many tall trees did he uproot and cast upon the ground, with root and apple blossom.[7]

Both the boar and the war breaking out over the trophy-dispute appear as part of the goddess's vengeance[8] that only terminates with Meleager's death. Artemis answers the omission of the sacrifice with a punishment that hits Calydon as a whole and does not differentiate between Oeneus and his people. However, the text does not allude to the lasting effects of the devastation of the land by the boar and the war, but concentrates on the essential elements of the narrative. As such, the father's misconduct and the fulfillment of the tragic prophecy suffice to construct the story, even though the text does not reveal which action is actually leading to which consequence. The prophecy given at Meleager's birth clearly antedates the omission of the sacrifice in the course of the events making the latter appear almost a mere pretext for its fulfillment. On the other hand, the goddess's enduring anger outright demands Meleager's death to be appeased. The narrative is construed in a way that characterizes every single action of the events as determined and inevitable.

The author of the verses nevertheless offers an assessment of these actions. Although Althaia's anger at her son is sufficiently motivated by Meleager killing a single uncle[9] in the Homeric version, her reaction is questioned to a certain

---

6 Homer, Il. 9,544–545.
7 Homer, Il. 9,539–542. Quoted according to GOOLD; translation ARNHOLD.
8 Homer, Il. 9,547–549.
9 Homer, Il. 9,567.

degree as the text implies the battleground as the site of her brother's death. It is thus left open, whether Meleager kills his uncle intentionally or by accident.[10] Since neither possibility can be ruled out, Althaia's cursing and betrayal of her son appear less foreseeable than in other versions of the tale. Her reaction has thus been marked as particularly passionate and strong. As the log does not feature in the Homeric version, she here prays to the gods to kill her son and the verses record that the Erinys hears her.[11] Meleager returns to the battlefield, which he had left when he heard of the curse, and only this context hints at the way he dies, as his death itself is not described.[12] His re-entrance into battle is, however, characterized as sacrifice in a broader sense in the last verse of the Homeric version:

> ὣς ὃ μὲν Αἰτωλοῖσιν ἀπήμυνεν κακὸν ἦμαρ εἴξας ᾧ θυμῷ.
>
> Thus he warded off the day of evil from the Aetolians, driven by his own spirit.[13]

The Homeric evil in the story on the events at Calydon is characterized as being entirely divine in origin. It takes the form of the boar sent by Artemis and is likewise apparent in Althaia's curse calling for the divinely determined destiny of her son to be fulfilled. Neither the question of intention nor the attempts at expiation undertaken by the human agents have any impact on the divine decisions. Evil is perceived here as the logical consequence of any human disturbance of a very static world order which is determined by the authority of the gods.

2.2 The Unfortunate Hero Presented by Bacchylides

A vengeful goddess that is only appeased by the hero's death can also be found in the 5th century B.C.E. victory ode for Hieron of Syracuse composed by Bacchylides. Here, the story is embedded in a song of praise for the winner of the horse race, who is imagined as blessed by a god, but likewise warned that his fortune may not be lasting.[14] Meleager's fate serves as an example in this case.

---

10 Compare Homer, Il. 9,567: κασιγνήτοιο φόνοιο—because of the killing of her brother.
11 Homer, Il. 9,566–572.
12 Homer, Il. 9,597–598.
13 Homer, Il. 9,597–598.
14 Compare SEGAL, Ovid, 309–310.

Heracles descends to the netherworld and meets the hero's shade. Astonished about the young age of the deceased he inquires about the circumstances of his death.[15] In Meleager's subsequent account, the narration of the events is not given the space of the Homeric version. Nevertheless it has been enriched with details that emphasize character attributes of the agents and stress temporal settings such as the duration of crucial actions. Particular intention is paid to the consequences which prove fatal for Meleager himself, from whom the recipient of the verses learns about the events.

According to the hero's account, the unforgiving and merciless goddess sends the boar after rejecting sacrifices which Oeneus offers to her as expiation for his earlier omission.[16] Whereas the beast in the Homeric version is only said to have devastated the land, Bacchylides has it kill livestock and people alike.[17] The harm it brings hits the people not in a slightly distant future leaving time and thus a chance for a better outcome, but it comes upon them immediately. The implicit wording of details like this one in the Homeric version does not exclude the full force of the consequences, but leaves the outcome slightly open. Bacchylides, on the other hand, is very specific and does not allow the recipient of his verses to wonder about the character or consequences of the various actions. His Meleager kills his uncles by accident and the author stresses the misfortune of this deed by letting it be two instead of only one uncle.[18] Althaia, in her fury, burns the log without hesitation and Meleager dies instantly and quickly on the battleground.[19] Like Artemis, who is marked as insatiable, Althaia acts rapidly and without thinking and demands the maximum penalty. Both female characters mirror each other in their rage and lust for revenge. The evil thus illustrated by Bacchylides only knows one form, which is the extreme. This also becomes evident in the many contrasts drawn throughout the narration: The boar is described as ἀναιδομάχαν, "ruthlessly fighting,"[20] and is sent ἐς καλλίχορον Καλυδῶν, "to Calydon with its beautiful places."[21] To hunt it down, it takes even the best of Greek men, Ἑλλάνων ἄριστοι,[22] six long days[23]

---

15 Bacchyl. Ep. 5,89.
16 Bacchyl. Ep. 5,100–106.
17 Bacchyl. Ep. 5,107–110.
18 Bacchyl. Ep. 5,127–135.
19 Bacchyl. Ep. 5,140–154.
20 Bacchyl. Ep. 5,105; quoted according to WERNER.
21 Bacchyl. Ep. 5,106–107.
22 Bacchyl. Ep. 5,111.
23 Bacchyl. Ep. 5,113.

and several of them are killed.[24] Meleager's impact on the course of events, his guilt, on the other hand, is neither obscured nor omitted but entirely negated, which the first-person narrative[25] still increases. All the same, the recipient of the verses cannot deny an undertone of ridicule when he learns that Meleager relates his account δακρυόεις, "in tears."[26]

Bacchylides draws a very clear picture, sketching the evils, irrespective of origin, as highly destructive, inevitable, and demanding the extreme. Those who it is brought upon have no chance to escape. Good and evil are thus imagined as two sides of one coin. The moment it is flipped, the course of events turns to the other extreme. Presenting the hero's tale in this particular way while praising the success of Hieron of Syracuse in the Olympic horse race adds a warning to the panegyric[27] and also somewhat entertaining verses. The author presents the winner as extraordinary lucky and a favorite of the gods, but expresses all the same hopes and fears when he speaks out:

> εὖ ἔρδων δὲ μὴ κάμοι θεός.
>
> May the god not tire of doing good.[28]

Evil forces are here employed to lend particular emphasis to this aspect. They communicate to the recipient of the ode that he may be at the height of success and filled with youth and life at one moment, but can be in despair at the very next. Bacchylides stresses how extremely close good and bad lie together. Where Homer leaves minor options and remains vague in terms of temporal settings and details, the author of the victory ode is very precise. If the gods are imagined in the Iliad as rulers of the world, their authority is perceived as even less questionable, their will as even less predictable in the version by Bacchylides. A reason for this pointed emphasis may be sought in the specific address of the verses to the victor of a sportive competition. For him in particular, they were intended as a warning; for the general audience, they served as entertainment.

---

24 Bacchyl. Ep. 5,115–124.
25 On the first person narrative in Bacchylides, compare SEGAL, Ovid, 308.
26 Bacchyl. Ep. 5,94.
27 Compare SEGAL, Ovid, 309–310.
28 Bacchyl. Ep. 5,36.

2.3 Meleager Responsible for his Own Destiny in Ovid

Ovid goes further than Homer or Bacchylides, including the issue of love into the narration by means of Atalante who, albeit a woman, joins the hunters. Fragments of a Euripidean tragedy show that this female character certainly was not an invention of Ovid. In the few 5th century B.C.E. verses of Euripides, Atalante, being unmarried, rather active, and keen to be outside the house, is presented in stark contrast to the expected ideal of female behavior.[29] It seems to have been this moralizing tone which once marked the entire play and is likewise apparent, when the issue is raised what sort of parentage is required for the ideal offspring.[30] Ovid may have gained his idea for the character of Atalante from Euripides, but certainly did not use it in this way. Although his Atalante does not behave differently from the Euripidean, the contrasting references to female virtue are missing in the Metamorphoses.[31] Instead, the text focusses strongly on the relationship between Atalante and Meleager. Furthermore, Ovid's account exceeds those of Homer and Bacchylides in length and the Augustan author put more weight on episodes which promise to be especially dramatic.

The frame of the events remains unaltered. The slighted goddess—here called by her Latin name Diana—sends the boar to devastate the land. Ovid's beast, however, is described in detail.[32] The author compares its size with that of Epirean bulls, stating that it likewise exceeded that of Sicilian brand,[33] and hence gives his audience references which must have been well known in Augustan time. The audience's sentiments are thus being prepared for a vivid description which must have recalled pictures from living beasts known from the arena:

> Sanguine et igne micant oculi, riget ardua cervix, et stantque velut vallum, velut alta hastilia saetae. Fervida cum rauco latos stridore per armos spuma fluit. Dentes aequantur dentibus Indis, fulmen ab ore venit, frondes adflatibus ardent.
>
> His burning, bloodshot eyes seemed coals of living fire, the neck soaring stiff, the bristles standing like a fortified wall, like high spears. Fervent and with hoarse grunts the foam

---

29 Euripides, Fragments, 521: ἔνδον μένουσαν τὴν γυναῖκ' εἶναι χρεὼν ἐσθλήν, θύρασι δ'ἀξίαν τοῦ μηδενός—A woman staying within the house is proclaimed virtuous; one out of doors is of nobody's value; quoted according to COLLARD/CROPP; translation ARNHOLD.
30 Euripides, Fragments, 520.
31 Ovid furthermore adds an erotic notion when describing his Atalante: SEGAL, Ovid, 313–314.
32 Compare SEGAL, Ovid, 312.
33 Ovid, Metam. 8,284.

ran down its broad shoulders. Its teeth were comparable to those of Indian elephants; lightning came out of its throat; the afflated leaves burned.[34]

This not enough, not only the setting of the hunt and its course—never related in the known earlier versions—is given in detail and even the various hunting methods are named with which the hunters went after the beast: They tried with nets, dogs, and tracking techniques before the boar is finally slain with spears and bows and arrows.[35] All the participants of the hunt are individually named, resulting in a "who is who" of well-known heroes, including Theseus, Telamon, and Nestor.[36] The reader literally joins them as the events of the story are narrated in the chronological sequence of the hunt. The names of those rescuing themselves on or behind trees interchange with the names of those less fortunate who are killed by the boar. The dramatic climax of the hunting scene is reached when Atalante finally manages to inflict the first wound, whereupon Meleager lands the lethal blow.[37] "Renuente deo", "against a god's will,"[38] he had secretly fallen in love with her the moment they had met[39] and therefore grants the trophy to her. Upset about this, his two uncles[40] take it from her, causing Meleager to slay them in anger. Here, the hero's impact on the outcome of the events is characterized as severe, as it is his disobedient preference of Atalante that drives him to give the trophy to her and provokes his uncles' rage in consequence of which he kills them. The severity of the deed is underlined by the doubling of their number.

Althaia, his mother, first learns about her brothers' death before she finally hears of her son's deed.[41] Her inner conflict between a sister's grief and a mother's feelings is broadly illustrated by Ovid who literally lets his audience live through Althaia's inner torment.[42] Having recalled the prophecy and the log of wood, she heavily rings with herself before her feelings overcome her in the end:

> Ergo impune feret vivusque et victor et ipso successu tumidus regnum Calydonis habebit, vos cinis exiguus gelidaeque iacebitis umbrae? Haud equidem patiar: Pereat sceleratus et

---

34 Ovid, Metam. 8,284–289; quoted according to MILLER; translation ARNHOLD.
35 Ovid, Metam. 8,331–381.
36 Ovid, Metam. 8,301–317.
37 Ovid, Metam. 8,380–381; 8,414–419.
38 Ovid, Metam. 8,325.
39 Ovid, Metam. 8,324–327.
40 Ovid, Metam. 8,434.
41 Ovid, Metam. 8,445–450.
42 Ovid, Metam. 8,449–514.

ille spemque patris regnumque trahat patriaeque ruinam! Mens ubi materna est? Ubi sunt pia iura parentum et quos sustinui bis mensum quinque labores? O utinam primis arsisses ignibus infans, idque ego passa forem! Vixisti munere nostro, nunc merito moriere tuo. Cape praemia facti bisque datam, primum partu, mox stipite rapto, redde animam vel me fraternis adde sepulcris!

What, shall he live, victorious and boasting with his success, reign over Calydon, and you, a small pile of ashes, lie there in cold darkness? How can I endure this: Shall the wicked perish and with him the hope of his father, his kingdom and homeland fall into ruins!— Where are now the motherly feelings? Where are the affectionate vows of the parents and the ten months that I carried him? Oh, if this child would have but been burnt in the first fire and if I had suffered it! You only lived through my kindness: now your death is my merit. Take what is yours, what I've been given to you twice, first when you were born and shortly afterwards, when I pulled the log from the fire, hand back your soul or bury me with my brothers![43]

Meleager dies; his slow and painful death[44] is paralleled with the burning of the log in the fire. Thus once more, the emotions of the audience are being addressed directly.

Acting for his own sake and giving preference to his own individual sentiments, it is above all Meleager who in the Ovidian version appears to direct the course of events which lead to his own death and to the despair of others: Unable to bear her grief, his mother commits suicide and all of Calydon is described as filled with lamentations.[45] Also the grief of Meleager's sisters seems infinite, moving Diana, the goddess, who at this moment of the story is active for the third[46] time, to relieve two of them by transforming them into birds.[47] Although it was Diana who sent the boar and initially caused the tragic events to unfold, she takes almost no share in their course and outcome, with the exception of these final verses. Though offended by having been neglected when the sacrifices were made, the Ovidian goddess reveals no further interest in any of the characters or events. Evil in Ovid, therefore, is in most cases of human origin. Even though the gods' share is not denied, it is reduced to a minimum;

---

[43] Ovid, Metam. 8,494–504.
[44] According to SEGAL also very unheroic: SEGAL, Ovid, 322.
[45] Ovid, Metam. 8,526–530.
[46] Diana actively appears three times in the course of events: Ovid, Metam. 8,279–280 (omission of the sacrifice); 8,353 (for a brief moment directing a spear); 8,542–546 (transforming Meleager's sisters into birds). She may thus be more present than the various goddesses in the other literary versions, but her comparatively frequent appearance throughout the Ovidian verses is limited to specific moments of the actions. The emphasis is thus on situations in which she is not involved.
[47] Ovid, Metam. 8,542–546.

an observation that also applies to their positive involvement. The human characters appear to be mostly left to themselves and in charge of their own destiny (albeit Meleager's fate is nevertheless determined). This is particularly apparent, for instance, in the processual character of the events which allows the reader to identify cause and effect of all actions at any time. Problems mainly result not from neglect, but rather from selfish and passionate behavior. Even sending the boar is displayed as answer of an affronted, even sulking goddess. Althaia, on the other hand, throws the log only when she cannot hold her rage back any longer. The moment is preceded by an inner torment covering more than 60 verses[48] which reveals that the mother did not act out of a momentary impulse. While she battles against her emotions, she even has the pyre built and lit,[49] into which she throws the log at the end. However emotional it was, her torment yet involved consideration. Ovid thus puts the responsibility for the various actions entirely into the hands of each of the characters involved. The author's social critique is evident. He communicates it by taking the recipients of his verses on the hunt alongside the heroes. He lets them experience the beast, dangers and tensions alluding to impressions known from the arena and makes the recipient suffer through the hunt, the dispute over the trophy and the mother's inner torment.

2.4 Evil in Homer, Bacchylides, and Ovid

None of the human or divine characters of the myth can per se be referred to as good or bad: Oeneus omits the sacrifice to Artemis, but already Homer wondered whether he did so intentionally or out of neglect.[50] Artemis behaves enraged, seeking for revenge, and acts insatiable as well as unforgiving. When it comes to Ovid, the goddess, however, shows little interest in the events. Here, she sends the boar not out of rage, but out of a sensation of offence to which she responds by sulking. Only at the very end of the story, the sisters' grief stirs her compassion and induces her to another active engagement into the actions.

Although Meleager plays a leading role in every version, he commits his wrongs in different ways and in varying contexts. Homer lets him slay an uncle in battle, leaving the aspect of intention open. Bacchylides marks the deed as a tragic accident, whereas Ovid has Meleager act in rage. Although in all of the

---

48 Ovid, Metam. 8,447–511.
49 Ovid, Metam. 8,460–461.
50 Homer, Il. 9,537.

versions the actions lead to the same result—one or two killed uncles—, the question of Meleager's guilt has been treated differently from author to author and also to varying degree. By locating the fatal deed on the battlefield, Homer at least implies that Meleager killed his uncle unintentionally. The hero certainly did so in Bacchylides' more pointedly emphasized version of the events. Ovid, however, has the hero commit homicide. By adding Atalante and her involvement in the quarrel over the trophy, the author furnishes his hero with a motive.

Althaia, Meleager's mother, curses her son and conjures his death in all of the versions, but also in her case the degree of her guilt is treated differently. In Homer and even more so in Bacchylides she acts impulsively and instantly, whereas Ovid has her experience an inner torment stretching over more than 60 verses. Even though she loses the battle against herself in the end, she does not act in an instant impulse, but in fact takes time for consideration. Evil is thus employed very differently from author to author, which results in small shifts of the narration but has major consequences for the message of the story.

3 Images of the Hero's Death — Standardized Representations and Varying Reference-Levels

What happens when this very differently narrated topic is transformed into images? What scenes and characters are chosen for the pictures? Which ones were added? In which contexts have they been employed? And how are, for instance, the boar, the hero, the latter's mother and his fate imagined? What role does evil play in light of the various contexts? Images of the events of the hunt and war at Calydon appear on various media throughout antiquity. Red and black figure Greek vases, box-shaped Etruscan ash urns as well as Roman sarcophagi are only the most important among many, all three of which belong to the funerary sector. Mosaics and wall paintings from the domestic context could be added among others. By taking a closer look at the sarcophagi, I shall now further explore the idea that evil features as a narrative device also in the images, a device that is used to articulate a specific intention, which can here be summarized as displaying grief and loss.

About 200 sarcophagi with images of the myth of Meleager are still preserved today which makes them the largest group among the sarcophagi decorated with mythological themes.[51] Around three quarters of these were produced

---

51 KOCH, Meleager, 3.

in the city of Rome, and present the broadest range of variances of the images.⁵² Whereas the examples from Attica as well as 70 of those from Rome reveal the general preference for images of the actual hunt,⁵³ the other examples from Rome also show how the dead hero is being carried home or laid out on a bed and mourned.⁵⁴ The banquet following the hunt, including its preparation, is also occasionally depicted on sarcophagus lids.⁵⁵ Already this overview of the depicted topics reveals that different parts and elements of the myth have been addressed. This also implies that evil was not a concern in the selection of motifs. In fact, the aspects that were discussed above only became visible when the images allow us to grasp a narrative level. Two cases shall illustrate how artists altered the message of the myth.

3.1 Grief in its Various Stages as Depicted on a Sarcophagus from Ostia: Ostia Mus. Inv. 101⁵⁶

The front of the sarcophagus from Ostia is divided into three panels by means of an architectural element as well as a statue base. The panels can be viewed as a narrative sequence starting from the right, even though the central scene of the relief is emphasized by means of its position and slightly larger width. From right to left the scenes start with the dispute over the trophy at the end of the hunt and continue with the dead hero being laid out and mourned as well as a scene with two mourners flanking a tomb.

The dispute over the trophy, that is, the skin and head of the boar, depicted in the right panel, is composed out of five figures including the statue of Artemis, as it is an agent in this case. Meleager forms the central figure of the composition, although Atalante next to him occupies the same amount of space as he does. These two are the largest figures of the panel. Holding the boar's skin in his left, the hero faces two male figures at the right edge of the panel. One of these has sunken down in front of his feet whereas the other one approaches him from behind the first one. Meleager has his sword drawn and has evidently just stabbed the man by his feet who is still clutching the boar's skin and can be identified as an uncle. The approaching second figure, presumably the second

---

52 KOCH, Meleager, 85, Cat. no. 1–132, Cat. no. 149.
53 LORENZ, Image, 311.
54 KOCH, Meleager, 106, Cat. no. 112–118, Cat. no. 111 (Meleager being carried home); 119, Cat. no. 112–125, Cat. no. 126 (death-bed scene).
55 KOCH, Meleager, 125, Cat. no. 127–129, Cat. no. 142; LORENZ, Image, 312.
56 Images: KOCH, Meleager, 119, Cat. no. 112; Tav. 95c.96a.97.

uncle, reaches for his own sword, which indicates that the dispute has not yet come to an end. Meleager is shown in the middle of an action.

The controversy is witnessed by Atalante sitting on a rock in the left half of the panel, directly behind the hero. The quiver over her shoulder allows the viewer to identify her. She covers her face with her right hand and pulls her clothes with her left as if to shield herself even more from the scene in front of her. Whereas her gestures could be interpreted as a sign of shock, her seating position appears rather calm and relaxed. Also the dog beside her seat gives no impression of being terrified. Rested next to the rock, the animal only raises its head to the huntress in curiosity. Her mixed emotional status—half shocked, half withdrawn into herself in grief—results from the application of a specific representation scheme for her illustration, which strongly resembles images of mourners. But in contrast to the grieving figures sitting by the tomb in the far left panel, for instance, Atalante does not rest the elbow of her raised right arm on her knee. Her posture appears less lasting and seems to have been adopted only moments before. A sudden outburst of emotions is thus indicated, a snapshot of which has been taken before the huntress calms herself again.

On a high base behind Atalante stands the statue of Artemis, functioning both as an element separating the panels as well as a character engaged in the depicted actions. Likewise turned towards the fighting hunters, the goddess pulls an arrow from her quiver and raises her bow in the direction of the fighting men. Her gesture, also shown as a snapshot of the motion, ought to be understood metaphorically as she would hardly shoot the arrow at one of the men. What hits them in the literary versions of the myths are not divine arrows but the goddess's desire for expiation and revenge. Bow and arrow can be understood here as a reference to the fate of the various characters involved in the dispute as well as to the inevitable outcome of the events in general.

Nevertheless, a further layer of meaning is applied to the scene by its compositional details. Whereas the goddess and the two uncles cover only comparatively little space towards the left and right margin of the panel, Atalante and Meleager fill the central part of the panel and are equals in the amount of space they occupy. Though seated, the huntress has the same height as the hero does. Again, the representation is not meant to be taken literally. Instead, the two figures are simply supposed to take pride of place within the panel. Atalante's mixed emotions about the fatal events are displayed directly next to their cause. Shocked, the huntress faces Meleager's dreadful deeds. Her presence in the image alone suffices to remind the viewer that the hero's action is caused by rage out of love in the Ovidian sense and that the death of his uncles is not an accident but homicide. Filled with grief, the figure of Atalante nevertheless contrasts with that of Meleager, who is depicted in the height of his youth and triumphing in the fight, and thus Atalante's grief hints at his sudden and unexpected death. Since her emotional outbreak and the dispute over the trophy are shown as having started only moments before and are shown as still ongoing actions, the scene can also be read as an allusion to sentiment, that is to the sudden shock, sense of bereavement, and absolute grief felt by those who ordered the sarcophagus. Again, the reference is not necessarily to real events. The intention behind such images was rather to communicate what kind of sentiments those left behind wanted to display about the death of their relative. It may not be without interest in this context that the small size of the Ostian sarcophagus reveals that it was intended for a child.[57]

Furthermore, it is striking that the Ovidian version of the legendary events at Calydon is being alluded to in the hunting scene of this panel without much assessment of the actions of the various characters. The critique of Meleager's deed takes second seat to details of the composition such as standardized representation formula and the varying sizes of figures as well as the amount of space occupied by the latter. The scene can be read differently. The additional layer of meaning is, therefore, not just a coincidental by-product, but has been intentionally added.

Shock and grief about what has happened are also communicated in the central panel, which depicts the death-bed scene. Again Meleager forms the center of the composition even though he is not depicted as acting but, being dead, laid out on a bed. The scene is set inside a house as is indicated by the pillar at its left margin and the arch on top of it bending towards the figures described in the following. A shield, helmet, and sword are shown lined up in front and below the death-bed. The hero lying on it is surrounded by four persons. Two women stand behind the bed, one holding the hero's head, the other one burying her cheek in her left hand. Another woman, stretching her arms towards the back in despair, approaches from the left side of the panel, whereas a bearded man stands in the foreground, in front of the bed's lower end. The four figures display various gestures and postures of grief, such as the hand at the cheek in case of one woman, loose clothes in case of the other two females as well as loose hair in case of all three of them. The bearded man simply stands next to the bed, the left foot raised on the bed's pedestal, the outstretched right arm supported by a walking stick. He can most likely be identified as Meleager's father Oeneus, who omitted the sacrifice, whereas the women must represent female members of the hero's family such as his mother Althaia, one or two sisters, and his wife Kleopatra, who is occasionally mentioned by the Greek and

---

[57] Measurements of the sarcophagus: length 1,37 m; width 0,36 m; height 0,40 m.

Latin authors, but invariably plays only a marginal role in the events of the myth.[58] Since the sarcophagus was made for a child, an identification of the deceased of the death-bed scene with the person buried in the sarcophagus seems out of question. Nevertheless, the illustrated topic of the father mourning his child, which passed before its time, appears well chosen. An allusion to the actual worldly—"everyday" in the wording of Katharina Lorenz[59]—circumstances for which the sarcophagus had been employed can therefore be recognized also for this panel.

The pillar at its left margin likewise separates the scene from the last panel of the relief, which is placed at the far left end of the sarcophagus. Two seated figures here flank a tomb formed out of a circular outer wall and a conical top which can be interpreted either as a roof structure or a small mound. A garland decorates the monument. The two mourners to its sides are both seated on rocks. Supporting their heads with one hand and with their elbows propped up on a knee, both are shown deeply withdrawn into themselves. Their sex is defined as female and male as one of them is bearded,[60] so that they can perhaps be understood as representations of the hero's grieving parents or rather of his father and a sister since his mother does not live long beyond her deed. However, the precise identification of the two is left to the imagination of the viewer, since the picture does not exclude the likewise possible allusion to the tomb of the child buried in the sarcophagus.[61] In light of the possible semantic plurality of the hunting scene, this reading cannot be excluded.

The evils that are addressed in the various literary versions are only partially alluded to in the image: The figure of Artemis raising her bow towards the fighting hunters refers to the outcome of the dispute as determined, even though Atalante's presence reminds the viewer of the scene of the negative characterization of Meleager's deed as homicide. The moralizing undertone, however, is secondary to the grief that dominates the huntress's appearance. And also in the other panels, the mourning of the deceased dominates the message of the images. The viewer gains the impression that the greatest evil in the mythological events is in fact the death of the hero.

---

[58] At least in some cases, she functions as a counterpart to Atalante in order to stress the immorality of Meleager's love for the huntress (compare Pseudo Apollodorus, Library 1,66).
[59] LORENZ, Image, 309.
[60] KOCH, Meleager, 119, Cat. no. 112.
[61] Compare LORENZ, Image, 327, for a similar interpretation, which, however, goes further since the author suggests regarding the left panel as a gateway into the picture.

3.2 Paris, Louvre Inv. MA 539: Meleager, Mourned by Everyone[62]

Likewise partitioned into three scenes, the sarcophagus in Paris presents several parallels to the composition of the example from Ostia, but also differs in several respects. First of all, here, the division into three scenes has not been realized by means of separating architectural elements or the like as in the first example, but through the arrangement of the various figures. Each scene has been composed symmetrically around a central vertical axis towards which the figures are oriented. The central scene stretches over about half of the total width of the sarcophagus' front, whereas the two flanking scenes are given almost the same amount of space, each covering approximately a quarter of the total width.

As in case of the Ostian example, the scene to the right depicts the dispute over the trophy and the one in the center the death-bed scene. To the far left, however, Althaia is shown throwing the log into the fire. The narrative sequence indicated by the scenes to the right and in the center is, therefore, interrupted. The death-bed scene in the center is rather framed by images of the two most prominent moments in the course of events that led to Meleager's death. If the viewer so desires, the sequence would start with the scene to the right, followed by the one to the left, and culminate with the central panel. The images of the dispute over the trophy and Althaia's desperate deed, however, also stand for themselves.

Meleager's conflict with his uncles repeats the formalized representation already known from the sarcophagus in Ostia. The hero faces his uncles with drawn sword in his right and the trophy in his left hand. Still clutching the boar's skin, one of the uncles has sunken to the ground in front of Meleager, whereas the second uncle approaches from the right, likewise ready to draw his sword. This group appears repeatedly on sarcophagi although variances in the details occur. Meleager and his approaching opponent here are represented with the same height, both covering equal amounts of the panel's space. Between them, the head, shoulders, and the right hand of another figure appear in the background, whose identity remains obscure. Since the figure is dressed in a *palla* that binds the right arm and hand to the chest, it appears to be female. Her hair is tied in a knot at the back of the head. In her right hand, she holds a thin, elongated object resembling a stick. Whether this is meant to represent a wooden measuring rod, a thin scroll, or a smaller version of the log—although the latter is depicted much larger in the left panel—cannot be said with certainty.

---

[62] KOCH, Meleager, 120–121, Cat. no. 116, Tav. 103b.106–111.113a.b.

Whereas the first two would refer to Lachesis or Atropos, two of the Fates, the latter would also allow an interpretation as Althaia, Meleager's mother. In any case, an allusion to the hero's fate seems to be indicated. Koch addresses the figure as representation of one of the Erinyes with a whip in her hand.[63] Since the Erinyes are generally far fiercer in images, as can be seen, for instance, in the left panel of the same sarcophagus relief, this interpretation seems unlikely.

In principle, the death-bed scene in the central panel again repeats the scene described for the sarcophagus in Ostia, but has been extended by including the figure of Atalante in her mourning posture. She is seated on a stool at the left margin of the scene, her right hand raised to her forehead, resting the elbow of the same arm on the back of her left hand, which is pulling at her clothes only very slightly. Next to the stool rests the dog raising his head to the huntress. Unlike its counterpart in the Ostian example, the figure gives a much calmer impression, all her limbs being rather relaxed. Rather than being under tension, she appears withdrawn into herself, not participating at all in the rest of the scene in front of her.

In the central and left part of the panel, the mourners at the death-bed of the hero can be seen. In addition to the shield, helmet, and sword below and in front of the bed, a spear is shown referring to Meleager's actual weapon as known from the textual versions of the myth. Of the four mourners, the three women form a row in the background. All three of them have been characterized by their loose clothes and hair and are only distinguished by their gestures. Whereas the one bending over Meleager's head is about to place an apple into the hero's mouth, the two others show the familiar gestures of grieving. Their arms are stretched to the back or, in one case, moved to the head. Only the bearded man accompanying them seems to remain calm in his grief. As in case of the sarcophagus from Ostia, he raises one foot onto the pedestal below the bed and supports his right hand on his walking stick while looking firmly at the dead hero. Displaying the feelings in various ways, the mourning figures have thus all been piled into a single panel, whereas in the Ostian example they were placed into various panels in order to stress different temporal stages of grief. This temporal notion is entirely lacking here, but also not required since the composition follows a different intention. The grieving is presented as the final stage and result of the events. In this context, the identity of the mourners is of interest. Whereas Atalante represents the mourning lover, the bearded man stands for the grief of a parent, in particular for a father's grief for his son. The three women in the background, who can hardly be distinguished in their rela-

---

63 KOCH, Meleager, 121.

tion to the deceased hero, may refer to the female members of a *familia* in general. Three different categories of grief, the lover's, the parent's and the *familia's*, represented in the females, are thus particularly emphasized in the panel.

Understood in this regard, the figure of Atalante hardly dominates the scene.[64] As in the case of the example from Ostia, her seating height should not be taken too literally, as the huntress is not meant to be standing up. The space of the relief covered by the figure—not just its height—rather counterbalances the space occupied by the figures on the opposite side of the scene where one of the female mourners bends over Meleager's head at the upper end of the bed.

The panel to the far left of the sarcophagus relief shows Althaia's deed as well as her inner torment. The scene is composed of three figures standing around an altar on which the fire is lit. The Fate Atropos, identified by the scroll in her left hand, is presented to the left, whereas Althaia flanks the altar on the opposite site of the panel. Between them, an Erinys hurls her torch upside down in direction of Althaia, who raises her left hand in a (weak) defensive gesture. With her outstretched right, Meleager's mother holds the log into the fire, while she turns her face away to the right, averting her eyes from her own deed. Her hesitation is also expressed by the posture of her feet, which are about a step apart, her left foot pointing to the side as though she was about to turn away in the last moment. Althaia's *palla* is only loosely held, hang over her upper arms and forms an agitated arch around her head. Her torment is furthermore emphasized by the Erinys, who is gripping her right shoulder. The agitated clothes of the latter, her hurling of the torch with the right hand, the small wings on her head, which is likewise surrounded by an arch of clothes, provide her with a fierce look. If Althaia expresses mainly hesitation, this impression is strongly contrasted by the Erinys and the force deriving from her. The mother's inner torment, as described by Ovid, is thus illustrated by means of two figures. However, the Erinys—mentioned in context of this myth by Homer alone—assumes a

---

[64] LORENZ refers to Atalante as the tallest figure in the panel (p. 319–320) arguing with the height the figure would reach when rising from the seat. Based on this extrapolation, she ascribes the huntress a particular role within the image, in that she sheds light on the male virtues represented by Meleager through a female perspective. The male virtues are said to become apparent in the hero's role as hunter and warrior, which LORENZ addresses as specifically Roman (p. 318). This, however, is an over-interpretation in my view, since the textual versions speak of both the hunt and a war breaking out following the dispute over the trophy. Discrepancies occur, indeed, in the armor and weapons of the hero, since, for instance, the spear mentioned by Ovid only appears lying on the floor in front of the death-bed, whereas sword, helmet, and shield do not feature in the verses of the *Metamorphoses* or those of the other authors.—Compare LORENZ, Image, 318–323.

different role here than in the Iliad. There, she alone brings death upon Meleager whereas the log does not feature. But also, even though the Ovidian torment of the mother is being alluded to, the scene does not present an illustration of Ovid's version. This is evident from the fire being lit on an altar, which refers to the idea of the hero being sacrificed and most certainly creates a sacred atmosphere. Whether this atmosphere can, however, be referred to as Roman, seems questionable.[65] But also the presence of Atropos, the third of the Fates, shows that not just Ovid is being alluded to, but that elements from various textual versions as well as images and conventions from visual language have been employed. With her left foot placed on a wheel, she makes the tragic note on the scroll in her left hand.

In the end, it is Althaia, driven by the Erinys, who kills Meleager in this version. The final interpretation in a more or less literal sense is nevertheless left to the observer. The Erinys can both be understood as an external force in the Homeric sense or as a representation of the two contrasting sentiments of the Ovidian Althaia. Fate, however, maintains a prominent position in either case, as Atropos observes the burning of the log.

If the figure which has been inserted between the fighters of the right panel likewise refers to the hero's fate as has been suggested above, the dispute over the trophy and its consequences can also be regarded as determined. The human agents of the legendary events of the myth are thus, at least in part, deprived of their guilt or the responsibility for their deeds. A feeling of lacking power in regard to the hero's death is thus articulated on behalf of all of those left behind: the partner in love, parent, and entire *familia*. It is in this sense that the reference to the person buried in the sarcophagus becomes apparent. Whereas an assessment of the actions was lacking in the example from Ostia, it evidently presents an issue here. The responsibility for the actions is, however, assigned to the divine agents. Death is thus regarded as particularly inevitable; the deceased is shown as being mourned by everyone.

---

65 Contra LORENZ, Image, 325.

3.3 Evil as an Expression of Grief — Displaying Utmost Grief as a Trend

The two examples for sarcophagi with scenes of the deeds and death of Meleager illustrate that the images discuss evil in terms of grief. The messages behind these can—despite the composition out of highly standardized figures and elements—be altered by means of minor modifications. The selection of certain figures and omission of others in a scene as well as the conscious employment of proportions in depicting the various characters present two major ways of achieving this. In the case of the sarcophagus at Ostia, grief is thus presented in its various stages, underlining the temporal progress. In the far left panel showing the two grieving figures at the tomb, the time after the burial is alluded to, which even displays the mourning as an ongoing, continuous action. The sarcophagus in Paris depicts grief not in a temporal manner, but sheds light on those mourning the deceased. In this case, the aspect of everyone, the partner, parent and *familia*, being struck by the death is addressed. For this, the responsibility of the evils in the story is placed within the divine sphere. Meleager's death is presented as determined by fate. His mother does not act on her own behalf.

The two sarcophagi discussed do not stand alone in illustrating these sentiments, but rather belong to a period of time in which the display of grief in tomb imagery was fairly common. The sarcophagus from Ostia was produced around A.D. 160; the one in Paris twenty to thirty years later.[66] They thus present two examples from the group of mythological sarcophagi of the Antonine and Severan periods, which were dedicated to images of this kind.[67] As Zanker underlined, these images served as means of a new and specific form of conversation about death, which evolved in close relation to changes in the appearance of the actual tombs.[68] Visually less distinct from another, both as regards architectural forms and decoration, the tombs of the 2nd century A.D. served to communicate with a select group of people rather than the general public.[69] They were equipped with tomb chambers for family burials, which often presented richly decorated rooms that contrasted with the relatively standardized outer appearance of the tomb architectures. The few cases in which the sarcophagi

---

[66] KOCH, Meleager, 119.121.
[67] Compare ZANKER, Ikonographie, 243–245.
[68] ZANKER, Sarkophagreliefs, 345.347–348.
[69] ZANKER, Sarkophagreliefs, 347–349; JUNKER, Sarkophage, 165.

have been preserved within their original context[70] illustrate that the tombs hosted several of these stone coffins, which were often positioned closely together. Access to the tomb chambers and thus also the visual access to the images of the sarcophagi must have been limited to specific occasions such as the regular festive celebrations at the tombs as well as funerals. The images and their specific messages were thus always intended for a small audience comprising members of the *familia* and friends.[71] The evils dealt with and grief displayed focused on the deceased persons buried in the sarcophagi and those related and befriended to them.

4 Conclusion

The analysis of three textual versions and two illustrations on Roman sarcophagi of the myth of Meleager has revealed a number of aspects: The legendary events centered around Calydon have been constantly retold over time revealing a multitude of alterations as well as influences in regard to characters, details, and scenes. Outlining a figure in a particular light and slightly changing its active involvement in the actions, as well as the relation of various characters to each other suffice to achieve major alterations of the overall message of the story. Evil, in this context, forms one narrative device among others as it generates a relational framework for the characters, as well as the causes and consequences of their actions. The answer to the question of who is responsible for and guilty of an action has in some cases been found in the divine, in others, such as Ovid, entirely in the human sphere. The victory ode by Bacchylides in particular illustrated to what degree the context of the narration could add to the way the events were related. The same can be said for the sarcophagus images discussed here, which addressed the aspect of evil in the context of death within lived reality, not myth. Used in tombs, the two pictoral versions presented two diverse forms of displaying grief which have been realized by means of a different handling of the evils featuring in the myth. The death and deeds of Meleager were thus constantly rewrapped in new meaning, that generally must have presented several layers, even though only in some of the cases the original situations for which the texts and images were produced are known.

---

70 Compare ZANKER, Betrachter, 8.
71 ZANKER, Sarkophagreliefs, 348; JUNKER, Sarkophage, 165–166.

Bibliography

COLLARD, Christopher/CROPP, Martin (Hg.), Euripides, Fragments, ed. and translated, Cambridge, Massachusetts 2008.
DALFERTH, Ingolf U., Malum. Theologische Hermeneutik des Bösen, Tübingen 2008.
GOOLD, George P. (Hg.), Homer, Iliad, Cambridge, Massachusetts 1999.
JUNKER, Klaus, Römische mythologische Sarkophage. Zur Entstehung eines Denkmaltypus, in: MDAI.R 112 (2005–2006) 163–188.
KOCH, Guntram, Die mythologischen Sarkophage 6. Meleager (Die antiken Sarkophagreliefs 12), Berlin 1975.
LORENZ, Katharina, Image in Distress? The Death of Meleager on Roman Sarcophagi, in: Elsner, Jaś/Huskinson, Janet (Hg.), Life, Death and Representation. Some New Work on Roman Sarcophagi (Millenium-Studien 29), Berlin 2011, 309–336.
MILLER, Frank Justus (Hg.), Ovid, Metamorphoses Books I-VIII, with an English translation, revised by G.P. Goold, Cambridge, Massachusetts ³1977.
PIEPER, Annemarie, Gut und Böse, München 1997.
SEGAL, Charles, Ovid's Meleager and the Greeks. Trials of Gender and Genre, in: HSCP 99 (1999) 301–340.
WERNER, Oskar (Hg.), Simonides—Bakchylides, Gedichte. Griechisch und Deutsch herausgegeben und übersetzt, München 1969.
ZANKER, Paul, Die mythologischen Sarkophagreliefs und ihre Betrachter, München 2000.
ZANKER, Paul, Die mythologischen Sarkophagreliefs als Ausdruck eines neuen Gefühlskultes. Reden im Superlativ, in: Hölkeskamp, Karl-Joachim et al. (Hg.), Sinn (in) der Antike. Orientierungssysteme, Leitbilder und Wertkonzepte im Altertum, Mainz 2003, 335–355.
ZANKER, Paul, Ikonographie und Mentalität. Zur Veränderung mythologischer Bildthemen auf den kaiserzeitlichen Sarkophagen aus der Stadt Rom, in: Neudecker, Richard/Zanker, Paul (Hg.), Lebenswelten. Bilder und Räume in der römischen Kaiserzeit. Symposium am 24. und 25. Januar 2002 zum Abschluss des von der Gerda Henkel Stiftung geförderten Forschungsprogramms „Stadtkultur in der Kaiserzeit", Wiesbaden 2005, 243–251.

Joachim Friedrich Quack

„Sage nicht: ‚Der Frevler gegen Gott lebt heute'; auf das Ende sollst du achten!"

Gedanken der spätägyptischen Literatur zum Problem des Bösen in der Welt

In meinem Beitrag soll es speziell um Ägypten in der Spätzeit gehen. Dabei konzentriere ich mich auf literarische und religiöse Texte, die in demotischer Sprache abgefasst sind. Dies ist einerseits diejenige Sprachstufe des Ägyptischen, welche zwischen Neuägyptisch und Koptisch liegt und grob von etwa 700 v. Chr. bis 300 n. Chr. angesetzt werden kann—wobei die genauen Grenzpunkte durchaus etwas willkürliche taxonomische Schnitte in einer oft eher kontinuierlichen Weiterentwicklung darstellen. Andererseits wird mit diesem Begriff auch ein Schriftsystem bezeichnet, das durch Reduktion des Zeichenbestandes und Vereinfachung der Linienführung aus der älteren ägyptischen Kursivschrift entstanden ist, die als hieratisch bezeichnet wird.

Aus dieser Zeit ist eine große Menge von wenigstens in weiterem Sinne literarischen Texten überliefert,[1] wobei in einigen Fällen die Abgrenzung zu den Kompositionen eher religiösen Charakters nicht ganz leicht ist bzw. Texte, die man üblicherweise als „literarisch" einstuft, nach Inhalt und Überlieferungsbefund besser als „religiös" zu verorten wären. Dies betrifft nicht zuletzt den unten herangezogenen Mythos vom Sonnenauge.

In manchen dieser Texte wird das Thema der Bestrafung von Vergehen angesprochen. Dabei ist es natürlich von der Textgattung abhängig, in welcher Intensität und aus welchem Blickwinkel heraus dies erfolgt. Infolgedessen sind auch manche Textgattungen für meine Darlegung erheblich wichtiger als andere. Die für die nachfolgende Analyse bedeutsamsten sind die Weisheitstexte. Dies ist eine derjenigen Gattungen, welche in Ägypten traditionell gut repräsentiert sind.[2] In ihnen geht es darum, dass eine Lehrautorität aus den eigenen

---

[1] Einen Überblick gebe ich in QUACK, Einführung; umfangreiche deutsche Übersetzungssammlung in HOFFMANN/QUACK, Anthologie; französische in AGUT-LABORDÈRE/CHAUVEAU, Héros.

[2] Die derzeit beste verfügbare Sammlung von Übersetzungen der vordemotischen Weisheitstexte dürfte VERNUS, Sagesses, darstellen. Für die demotischen Weisheitstexte vgl. die Spezialstudien von LICHTHEIM, Wisdom Literature; LAZARIDES, Wisdom; AGUT-LABORDÈRE, Le sage; einige schlecht erhaltene Fragmente ediere ich erstmals oder substantiell verbessert in QUACK, Fragmente.

Lebenserfahrungen heraus einem Schüler, meist seinem Sohn, angibt, wie man sich im Leben verhalten soll. Dies beinhaltet nicht selten auch die Frage, warum bestimmte Verhaltensweisen vermieden werden sollen. Dabei gibt es zwei relativ gut erhaltene Texte, welche im Folgenden besonders herangezogen werden. Dies ist zum einen das große demotische Weisheitsbuch, das in einer ganzen Reihe von Handschriften überliefert ist, von denen der Papyrus Insinger bei weitem die besterhaltene ist. Die Textzeugen stammen aus der spätptolemäischen und römischen Zeit, doch dürfte die Komposition an sich in die Saitenzeit zurückgehen. Dieser Text ist in durchnummerierte Lehreinheiten strukturiert, welche jeweils mit nur lose verbundenen Sprüchen ein spezifisches Thema umspielen. Das andere ist die Lehre des Chascheschonqi, deren Haupthandschrift aus der späten Ptolemäerzeit stammt, die aber auch auf etwas ältere Quellen zurückgehen dürfte. Sie besteht vorwiegend aus Einzelsprüchen mit nur loser, assoziativer Abfolge. Gelegentlich sind auch kleinere bzw. schlechter erhaltene Kompositionen herangezogen worden, deren Handschriften meist aus der Ptolemäerzeit stammen, in einem Fall (Brooklyner Weisheitstext) aber noch aus der Saitenzeit.

Gelegentlich können auch fiktionale narrative Erzählungen die praktische Umsetzung dessen zeigen, was in den Lehren theoretisch postuliert wird, gemessen an ihrer Menge innerhalb der demotischen Literatur sind sie jedoch relativ wenig ergiebig.

Prinzipiell sehr wichtig, allerdings wegen meist sehr schlechter Erhaltung weit weniger nutzbar sind diskursive theologische Traktate. Der für meine Fragestellung bei weitem wichtigste unter ihnen ist der sogenannte Mythos vom Sonnenauge bzw. genauer von der Rückkehr der Göttin.[3] In ihm geht es darum, dass die Tochter des Sonnengottes sich im Zorn von ihm getrennt hat und in Form einer Katze in Nubien haust. Der Sohn des Weisheitsgottes Thot zieht in Form eines Hundsaffen aus, um sie wieder zurückzuholen. Auf dem Weg führen sie tiefsinnige Gespräche, bei denen sowohl ethische und moralische Grundsätze geklärt als auch theologische Zuordnungen durchgesprochen werden. Die moralischen Diskurse werden dabei teilweise auch mit Tierfabeln erläutert.

Um diesen theologischen Traktaten etwas mehr Gewicht zu geben, sei einleitend aus einem noch unveröffentlichten Text zitiert, welcher dadurch, dass er die möglichen guten und schlechten Aktionen der Gottheit gegen die Menschen

---

3 QUACK, Einführung, 148–160; zusätzlich zur griechischen Version THISSEN, Translation, 126–163. Inzwischen hat sich eine internationale Forschergruppe konstituiert, welche eine vollständige Neuedition unter Einschluss etlicher bislang unpublizierter Quellen beabsichtigt.

als Folge von gutem oder schlechtem Verhalten thematisiert, immerhin für unsere Frage nicht irrelevant erscheint:

> Es gibt vier Ptahs in Memphis; siehe ihre Namen: Ptah, der Herr von „Unter seinem Ölbaum"; das ist Thot, der Herr der Lebenszeit. Ptah, der Herr des Platzes der Wahrheit; das ist Thot, der Herr des Sohnes. Ptah, der Herr von Chenti-Nen; das ist Thot, der Herr der Sättigung. Ptah, der Herr des ehrwürdigen Djed-Pfeilers; das ist Thot, der Herr des Festsetzens des Alters. Wer sich vor dem Gott in acht nimmt, dem wird Besitz zuteil. Wer nicht gewaltsam ist, dem gibt man einen Sohn. Wer nicht raubt, dem gibt man ein Begräbnis. Wer dem Gott gedient hat, dem gibt man Lebenszeit. Darüber hinaus gibt es den, dem man ein, zwei, oder drei davon gibt, oder den, dem man alle gibt. Die Wohltat, die der Gott für einen Menschen macht, ist Lebenszeit, Sohn, Bestattung und weise Frau. Die böse Tat, die der Gott für einen Menschen macht, ist, sein Auge fortzunehmen,[4] seinen [Besitz] fortzunehmen, das Leben fortzunehmen, seine Ehefrau fortzunehmen (pWien D 10014+10103a+b).[5]

Hier gilt also das Vermeiden bestimmter negativer Aktionen als Grund für die Gewährung bestimmter Glücksgüter durch die Gottheit. Umgekehrt kann man annehmen, dass die Verweigerung bzw. Entziehung durch die Gottheit eben darauf beruht, dass man negative Aktionen nicht vermieden hat – womit wir schon voll beim Thema sind, weil damit bereits einer der grundsätzlichen Punkte genannt wird, wie damals Strafe für Vergehen konzipiert wurde.

Die Entstehung des Bösen in der Welt wird von den Ägyptern relativ früh situiert, bereits in der Epoche der Schöpfung.[6] Bei der Erschaffung der Welt und der Entstehung der ersten Götter erscheinen auch schon negativ konnotierte Gestalten, insbesondere gibt es neben dem Sonnengott Re auch den schlangengestaltigen Apopis, welcher die negative Figur schlechthin ist. Hinsichtlich seiner Verbindung zum Sonnengott ist es ganz beachtenswert, dass die Ägypter seinen Ursprung in der Nabelschnur eben des Sonnengottes sahen, welche ins

---

[4] Das „Auge" könnte hier im Sinne von „Glück" gemeint sein, zumindest wird idiomatisch der Begriff „Größe des Auges" im Demotischen für „Glück" gebraucht. Eine andere Möglichkeit wäre allerdings, die Wendung als plötzliche Blindheit zu deuten und an das besonders auf Stelen der Ramessidenzeit nicht seltene Motiv der „Finsternis bei Tage" zu denken, welche Gottheiten den betreffenden Menschen sehen ließen; s. dazu GALAN, Darkness, 18–30; LUISELLI, Gottesnähe, 162–175.

[5] Hier zitiert nach einer Fotografie, die mir Herr Hofrat Hermann Harrauer zur Verfügung gestellt hat. Der Papyrus dürfte aus Soknopaiou Nesos stammen und datiert als Handschrift wohl ins 1. Jahrhundert n. Chr. Edition der griechischen Vorderseite des Papyrus MESSERI SAVORELLI, Registro, 81–92. Eine unzuverlässige Beschreibung des demotischen Textes in REYMOND, Literary Works, 57f.

[6] Vgl. KEMBOLY, Question of Evil.

Wasser geworfen wurde.[7] Wie die Menschen zum Bösen gekommen sind, ist weniger klar; eine Verführungsszene wie im biblischen Schöpfungsbericht (Gen 3,1–6) ist aus Ägypten nicht bekannt. Gut belegt ist allerdings die Idee, dass am Anbeginn der Geschichte Götter und Menschen gemeinsam gelebt haben, wobei der Sonnengott die Herrschaft innehatte. In dieser Situation wird vielfach von versuchter Rebellion durch die Menschen gesprochen.[8] Hier ist natürlich auch die reale Situation des potentiell durch Rebellion bedrohten ägyptischen Königs als vorhandene Erfahrung zu beachten.[9]

Auch wenn keine derart explizite „Abwerbung" der Menschen bezeugt ist, kann man doch zumindest feststellen, dass einige Kategorien von Menschen explizit den negativ bewerteten Gottheiten zugeordnet werden. So gibt es im Traumbuch des pChester Beatty III rt. eine Beschreibung von Typen, die Seth zugeordnet sind.[10] Im Buch vom Tempel gibt es eine Darlegung einiger Arten von Menschen, die nicht zum Tempeldienst zugelassen werden sollen und von denen es heißt, sie seien in der Art von Seth, Apopis und jenem Gott, gegen den in Memphis der Arm ausgestreckt würde.[11]

Für die Konsequenzen schlechter Handlungen im Sinne einer Bestrafung haben die Ägypter verschiedene Modelle entwickelt, die sich keineswegs gegenseitig ausschließen, sondern eher komplementär zueinander stehen. Als erstes anführen möchte ich das, was man sozusagen als den Erfolg des Rechtsstaates bezeichnen könnte. Der Verbrecher wird von den staatlichen Institutionen gefunden und seiner gerechten Strafe zugeführt.

Zweites Modell ist die göttliche Strafe im Diesseits, die relativ rasch nach der Tat erfolgt. Bei ihr sollte man zwei verschiedene Typen unterscheiden. Die eine erfolgt quasi direkt, weil das Verbrechen so grauenhaft erscheint, dass die Götter von sich aus aktiv werden. Der zweite Typ besteht in einem Appell an die göttliche Gerechtigkeit, die somit erst auf Antrag hin tätig wird. Die Unterscheidung dieser Typen scheint mir nicht irrelevant im Hinblick auf die in der Theo-

---

7 Vgl. QUACK, Apopis, 377–379; DERS., Geburt eines Gottes?
8 Vgl. zuletzt SMITH, P. Carlsberg, 462.95–112.
9 Vgl. die Zusammenstellung von LEITZ, „Unruhen", 852–858, die deutlich zeigt, dass es kaum je eine längere Periode ohne politische Unruhen in Ägypten gab. Speziellere Studien sind etwa MENU, Problématique, 55–70 = DIES., Recherches, 107–119; VERNUS, Affaires, 141–157; KANAWATI, Conspiracies; s. auch KÖTHEN-WELPOT, Haremsverschwörungen, 103–126.
10 Ediert in GARDINER, Hieratic Papyri, 20, Taf. 8,8a. Deutsche Übersetzung LEITZ, Traumdeutung, 244–245; Diskussion in FISCHER-ELFERT, Abseits von Ma'at, 55–58.
11 Vgl. QUACK, Kranke, 64.66–67.

logie ja intensiv diskutierte Frage, inwieweit es einen direkten Tun-Ergehen-Zusammenhang gibt.[12]

Im dritten Modell erscheinen das Lebensende und der Tod als der Punkt, an dem sich entscheidet, wie die Gesamtbilanz aussieht. Dies kann sowohl eine verzögerte Bestrafung des Schuldigen darstellen als auch eine Generationenverschiebung, bei welcher die Kinder die Folgen tragen müssen.

Das vierte Modell schließlich betrifft die nachtodliche Strafe, also ein Gericht im Jenseits.

Auf das erste Modell, also den funktionierenden Ordnungsstaat, möchte ich hier weniger eingehen, allenfalls auf Spezialbereiche. Dieses Modell ist das am wenigsten spektakuläre, aber dennoch wird es nicht nur stillschweigend vorausgesetzt, sondern als plausible Möglichkeit gelegentlich explizit ausgesprochen. Ganz elementar formuliert es die Lehre des Chascheschonqi: „Stiehl nicht; man wird es dir nachweisen!" (15,x+14); und sachlich ganz ähnlich heißt es im Papyrus Insinger: „Mancher nimmt sein Ende beim Diebstahl aufgrund von Gi[er]" (5,23). Letzteres steht dabei im Text im größeren Zusammenhang von verschiedensten Mahnungen, dass zu große Gier zum Verderben führt, wie es in der gesamten achten Lehreinheit des Textes entfaltet wird. Auch anderswo im selben Text findet sich der Gedanke „Der Frevler, der gierig ist, den bringt sein Herz zu Schaden" (4,13).

Ebenso dürften einige andere Wendungen in der Lehre des Chascheschonqi in dem Sinne zu verstehen sein, dass man durch problematische bzw. eindeutig rechtswidrige Handlungen mit Strafe zu rechnen hat, so „Bring nicht in Schuldhaft, wenn es dir gut geht, damit es dir nicht schlecht geht!" (6,x+11) oder „Schwör keinen Meineid, wenn es dir schlecht geht, damit es dir (danach) nicht noch schlechter geht!" (16,x+13).

Ein spezielles Augenmerk gilt dem Diebstahl, und zwar besonders der Bandenkriminalität. Die Lehre des Chascheschonqi gibt dazu an: „Mach dir keinen Dieb zum Gefähr[ten, damit] er [nicht] zur Ursache deines Todes wird!" (14,x+3). Etwas ausführlicher formuliert denselben Gedanken der Papyrus Louvre 2414: „Der Dieb der Stadt—der Reichtum ist sein Wunsch; mach ihn dir nicht zum Gefährten, damit er nicht bewirkt, dass man dich tötet!" (I,3).

Verschiedene Optionen scheinen durchgespielt in einer Passage des Brooklyner frühdemotischen Weisheitstextes: „Wenn man dich ertappt, nachdem du gestohlen hast, wird man dich [strafen]. Wenn man dich nicht ertappt, nachdem du gestohlen hast, ist Fieber an deinen Gliedern. Wer mit seinem Die-

---

12 KOCH, Vergeltungsdogma, 1–42; ASSMANN, Ma'at, 66–67.253–255.

ner gemeinsam stiehlt, kann ihn das Schicksal nicht erreichen lassen. Man gibt ihn auf den Hügel, wobei er festlich gestimmt ist, nachdem er dessen Besitz genommen und vor seinen Augen mit dessen Frau geschlafen hat, während er schweigt und nichts sagen kann" (5,3–5). Zunächst gibt es die Alternative, ob die direkte obrigkeitsstaatliche Bestrafung greift oder nicht. Für den letzteren Fall scheint es als Strafe die Krankheit (y'b.t) zu geben, was sich gut an eine größere Menge von Belegen anknüpfen lässt, dass Krankheit als Strafe einer Gottheit verstanden wurde.[13]

Schließlich gibt es noch die Frage eines Komplizen, der sein Wissen und damit die Erpressbarkeit des Straftäters ausnutzt, um sich dreist über dessen Besitz und dessen Frau herzumachen. Gerade für den letzten Punkt gibt es eine sehr gute Parallele in einem anderen, später überlieferten Weisheitstext, der es etwas knapper auf den Punkt bringt: „Stiehl mit einem gemeinen Mann, dann verkehrt er mit deiner Frau vor <deinen> Augen" (pLouvre N 2377,x+2, 12).[14]

Auch diese sozusagen rein strafrechtliche Aufarbeitung von Verbrechen kann in Ausnahmefällen verzögert und erst unter Spezialbedingungen ablaufen. Ein Beispiel dafür ist etwa die Erzählung im Papyrus Carlsberg 207.[15] Dort wird die Strafverfolgung erst dadurch in Gang gesetzt, dass der Prinz Setem Chaemwase einem Geist begegnet, der ihm davon erzählt, wie er und seine Familie von seinen Feinden umgebracht wurden. Der Prinz sorgt dann, nachdem sein königlicher Vater ihn dazu autorisiert hat, dafür, dass die Verantwortlichen mit ihrer ganzen Sippe überlistet, gefesselt und hingerichtet werden.

Gelegentlich kann die Suche nach Schuldigen und der Nachweis der Verbrechen fast schon detektivische Züge annehmen, und wenigstens ein demotischer Text, nämlich der Papyrus Saqqâra 1 (mit mutmaßlicher Parallele im Papyrus Saqqâra 1a) scheint genau in diese Richtung zu gehen.[16]

Zu erwähnen sind auch Fälle, die nicht als Justizvollzug zu bewerten sind, sondern mehr unter das Stichwort der „ausgleichenden Ungerechtigkeit" gehören. Einschlägig ist hier etwa aus der Lehre des Chascheschonqi der Spruch „Wer mit einer Frau auf (dem) Bett schläft, die einen Gatten hat, mit dessen Frau schläft man auf dem Boden" (21,x+9). Das ist zweifellos kein Strafvollzug und auch kaum eine eigentlich göttliche Strafe; darin zeigt sich eher die Über-

---

13 Vgl. BARDINET, Remarques, 3–36; QUACK, Rezension, 459.
14 Textedition WILLIAMS, Wisdom Texts, 266, wo der Sinn der Stelle nicht erkannt worden ist. Korrekte Deutung durch ZAUZICH bei DIELEMAN, Fear of Women?, 40–41.
15 Vgl. hierzu TAIT, P. Carlsberg 207.19–44, Taf. 2–3; QUACK/RYHOLT, Notes, 141–163, Taf. 24–26.
16 Vgl. SMITH/TAIT, Saqqâra Demotic Papyri, 1–64.65–69.

zeugung, dass man genau in dem Bereich, in dem man sich schuldig gemacht hat, letztlich selbst Schaden nimmt.

An der Grenze zwischen funktionierender Verbrechensaufklärung und göttlicher Gerechtigkeit liegt wohl ein Spruch im pAshmolean 1984.77: „Es scheint dem, der eine Bosheit begeht, dass der Gott am nächsten Tag nicht (zur Stelle) sein wird. Er denkt nicht an Gott, er denkt auch nicht an den Menschen. Eins sind die Gedanken des Gottes, ein anderes die Gedanken der Menschen" (x+4,7–9). Hier scheinen sowohl Gott als auch die Menschen als mögliche Akteure einer Vergeltung für Missetaten gesehen.

Damit kann man definitiv zum zweiten Modell übergehen, also der Vergeltung durch die Gottheit. Sie beruht auf einem Grundsatz der Vergeltung durch eine allwissende und allwahrnehmende Gottheit, wie es etwa in der Lehre des Chascheschonqi heißt: „(Jede) Tat geschieht wieder an dem, der sie begangen hat. Auf das Herz schaut der Gott" (26,x+10–11). Das hier erwähnte Herz dient als objektiv beurteilbarer Zeuge auch in einem Zweizeiler des Papyrus Insinger: „Der Gott legt das Herz auf die Waage gegenüber dem Gewicht. Er erkennt den Frevler und den Mann Gottes an seinem Herzen" (5,7–8). Für diese Passage bleibt allerdings angesichts der sonstigen ägyptischen Traditionen der Herzwägung noch die Frage, ob er sich auf den Zustand des Lebenden oder die nachtodliche Existenz bezieht. Ich werde darauf noch zurückkommen.

Ein besonders direkter Fall für das Eingreifen der Gottheit ist im Brooklyner Weisheitstext formuliert, nämlich: „Wer zur Verachtung für den Gott treibt, ist es, der seine Ehrwürde bekannt macht" (4,11). Man nimmt also an, dass gerade derjenige, der behauptet, man könne die Gottheit ungestraft missachten, durch das an ihm vollzogene Strafgericht der Gottheit selbst zum Exempel für deren Macht wird.[17] Gott ist hier sowohl der Geschädigte als auch der Vergelter, was eine Ausnahme darstellt, weil es normalerweise die Schädigung von Menschen ist, welche die göttliche Vergeltung auf den Plan ruft.

In Erzähltexten wird gelegentlich eine göttliche Intervention als konkrete Strafe angesprochen. Praktisch in direktem Anschluss an die Tat erfolgt dies in der Erzählung von Bes.[18] Ausgangslage ist, dass ein gewisser Bes sich mit seinem Freund Haryothes, mit dem er Eide der Freundschaft geschworen hat, zusammentut, um dessen Geliebte Tasis vor einem anderen Mann zu retten. Das

---

17 Wie das konkret aussehen kann, sieht man vielleicht am besten im sogenannten Gedicht vom verkommenen Harfner, in dem das göttliche Strafgericht breit ausgemalt wird, s. die Interpretation in QUACK, Einführung, 100–102.
18 Der demotische Text ist bislang noch nicht ediert, eine deutsche Übersetzung der betreffenden Passage findet sich in HOFFMANN/QUACK, Anthologie, 55–59.

gelingt zunächst, aber dann verliebt sich Bes selbst in die Frau und tötet deshalb seinen Freund. Die Frau gibt zum Schein vor, sich ihm hingeben zu wollen, wenn nur ihr Freund Haryothes zuerst bestattet würde, nutzt dann aber die Gelegenheit, um in dessen Grab Selbstmord zu begehen. Offenbar ist Bes dann sogar gewillt, Leichenschändung zu begehen.

> [Es(?)] gesch[ah], dass er kam, um mit ihr zu schlafen. Er sah eine Frauengestalt, (eine) *mnḫ.t*-Kleid-Trägerin,[19] die oben vor dem Grab, in(?) dem sie(?) lagen, stand, während sie [zu(?) ihm(?)] sagte: „Der Fluch des Atum, deines Gottes, sei auf dich geworfen! Du wirst nicht aus <dem> Grab hinaufkommen, bis du die Sache gemacht hast, die für(?) dich bestimmt(?) ist." Sowie er die Worte hörte, fand er keinen O[rt auf Erden], an dem er [war]. Die große Göttin Isis ließ [ein] Milch[...] auf ihn kommen. Es brachte Lepra. (In) der nämlichen Stunde (gab es) abscheuliche Wunde(n) [vo]m Scheitel seines Kopfes bis zu den Näge[ln] seiner Füße.

Hier sind offenbar die von Bes begangenen Verbrechen derart abscheulich, dass die Strafe der Göttin sofort kommt; und zwar nicht etwa ein rascher Tod, sondern die Infizierung mit Aussatz, die zunächst einmal den sozialen Tod mit sich bringt.[20] Von nun an muss Bes die menschliche Gemeinschaft meiden und sich in die nubischen Steppen zurückziehen.

Eventuell als direkte göttliche Strafe zu betrachten ist auch ein Vorgang am Anfang der Erzählung über den Streit um den Panzer des Inaros.[21] Dort springt Anubis auf die Erde und reißt dem Schreiber des Gottesbuches das Herz aus der Brust. Leider sind die Motive hierfür nur bedingt deutlich; es scheint vor allem darum zu gehen, dass der betreffende Priester die Geheimnisse der Götter erkunden wollte (und dadurch den von ihnen gehegten Plan, zwei Kriegersippen aufeinander zu hetzen, vereiteln könnte). Inwieweit der Schreiber des Gottesbuches sich bewusst schuldig gemacht hat, bleibt leider einstweilen relativ unklar.

Eine spontane Reaktion auf Frevel scheint auch eine gewichtige, wenngleich leider schlecht erhaltene Passage im sogenannten Mythos vom Sonnenauge zu implizieren. Dort heißt es (Mythus Lille A 32–37):

> Der Mensch mit seinem Geschick ist wie ein Boot, das im Fahrtwind [segelt]. Sein Geschick ist wie das sichere Ufer(?) [...] Bestattung. Der Wind zum Kentern(?), dessen Richtung, Farbe und [...] man nicht kennt [...] Die Änderungen des Windes sind wie die Schicksalsschläge. Der Gott ist wie der Schiffer, der es steuert. Sein Herz ist sein Steuerruder [...] sein [...] wiederum. Wer wohltätig ist in seinem Erfolg, den lässt er an das sichere Ufer kom-

---

19 Das bezieht sich wohl auf das traditionelle Gewand ägyptischer Göttinnen, das nicht mehr der aktuellen Mode bei Frauengewändern entsprach.
20 Vgl. FISCHER-ELFERT, Abseits von Ma'at, 33–90.
21 Vgl. hierzu HOFFMANN, Panzer des Inaros; RYHOLT, Inaros Story, 151–169, T. 19.

men. Wer aber grausam ist, der gleitet aus. Sein [...] ist sein [...] sofort. Der Gott ist der [...] der Fähre. Sein Werk ist, täglich zu leiten. Tägliche Leitung besorgt er. Derjenige, dem er zürnt, den wirft er hinaus; derjenige, dem er gnädig ist, den holt er herein.

In diesem Textstück gibt es vorderhand zwei verschiedene Motivierungen für das jeweilige Schicksal. In einem Falle sind es die guten oder bösen Taten eines Menschen, wobei die konkrete demotische Terminologie dieselbe ist wie in der 2. Setneerzählung. Das andere ist die Haltung der Gottheit, die zornig oder gnädig sein kann. So wie dies formuliert ist, könnte man zunächst auf einen freien Willen der Gottheit schließen. Die Frage ist allerdings, wie sehr damit gerechnet wird, dass dieser göttliche Wille in seiner Unergründlichkeit konträr zu den wahrgenommenen Verdiensten bzw. Vergehen des betroffenen Menschen liegt. Dies wirft letztlich ein Grundproblem der spätägyptischen Weisheit auf. Spätestens seit Helmut Brunners Forschungen spielt hier eine große Rolle, dass man in den späteren ägyptischen Lebenslehren einen freien Willen Gottes erkennt.[22] Zumindest im Papyrus Insinger am Schluss jeder Lehreinheit, in einer isolierten Passage auch innerhalb der Lehre des Chascheschonqi gibt es tatsächlich die Idee, dass die Regeln des Lebens nicht ausnahmslos gültig sind, sondern es auch Fälle geben kann, in denen genau das Gegenteil des Erwarteten eintritt.[23]

Eine andere Passage des Mythos vom Sonnenauge scheint in ihrer grundsätzlichen Formulierung zunächst auch den Automatismus des göttlichen Zorns anzusetzen, wenn der kleine Wolfsaffe der Katze sagt (Mythus Leiden, 2,2–6):

> Du sollst dir Zeugnis ablegen von jedem guten Werk. Wer sich zum Räuber macht, den wird man mit Raub berauben. Derjenige, welcher das Land bedrängt, hat keinen Wohnort auf Erden. Die Hyänen sind es, die sein Fleisch auf dem Hügel zerreißen. Wenn er auf dem Weg läuft, gibt es unversehens göttlichen Zorn gegen ihn, denn er hatte es sich nicht klargemacht; umso mehr (soll man es) in einer Erzählung darlegen(?).

Ein wenig subtiler sieht die Lage allerdings aus, wenn man sich die konkrete Exemplifizierung anschaut, die mit Hilfe der Fabel von der Katze und der Geierin vorgenommen wird. Diese ziehen in Nachbarschaft zueinander ihre Jungen groß und haben jeweils Angst, die eine könnte die Abwesenheit während der Futtersuche ausnutzen, um über die Jungen der anderen herzufallen. Deshalb leisten sie sich Eide, wechselweise die Jungen der anderen Partei zu verschonen. Diese Vereinbarung geht allerdings schief, wobei die Gründe wegen

---

[22] BRUNNER, Der Freie Wille, 103–120; wieder abgedruckt in BRUNNER, Das hörende Herz, 85–102.
[23] Vgl. LICHTHEIM, Late Egyptian Wisdom Literature, 138–150; QUACK, Einführung, 115–116.133–134; AGUT-LABORDÈRE, Le sage, 202–226.

schlechter Texterhaltung nur mäßig deutlich sind. Jedenfalls fällt die Geierin über die Jungen der Katze her und verspeist sie. Die Katze betet daraufhin zum Sonnengott und fleht um Gerechtigkeit.

Dieses Gebet wird auch erhört und ein strafender Dämon ausgeschickt,[24] der die Gestalt eines Syrers annimmt, der Fleisch röstet. Die Geierin raubt dieses Fleischstück, ohne die daran haftenden glühenden Kohlen zu bemerken, und zündet so ihr eigenes Nest an; ihre eigenen Jungen kommen dabei um. In dieser Fabel tritt die göttliche Strafe somit nicht etwa automatisch ein, sondern erst auf Appell. Insofern ist auch die knappere theoretische Formulierung vielleicht weniger im Sinne eines direkten Automatismus zu verstehen, sondern lediglich als Folge von Gebeten und Hilferufen der Opfer.

Die rechtliche Genehmigung der Aussendung eines strafenden Dämons findet sich auch in der ersten Setne-Erzählung.[25] Konkret hat sich dort Prinz Naneferkaptah das geheime Buch des Thot angeeignet und dessen Wächterschlange getötet. Thot richtet daraufhin seinen Appell an den Sonnengott Re, der ihm auch die Erlaubnis zur Bestrafung erteilt. Ein strafender Dämon wird ausgeschickt, der erst den kleinen Sohn und dann die Schwestergattin des Prinzen ertrinken lässt, woraufhin dieser an seinem Schicksal verzweifelt und Selbstmord begeht. Bemerkenswert daran ist, dass selbst Götter den korrekten Dienstweg einhalten müssen, d.h. eine Autorisierung durch den Götterkönig brauchen, bevor die Strafe vollzogen werden darf. Ebenso ist zu beachten, dass in diesen Fällen verzögerter Reaktion die großen Götter nicht selbst direkt agieren, sondern spezialisierte Untergebene ausschicken.

Die reale soziale Relevanz gerade derartiger Konzeptionen sollte unbedingt betont werden, gibt es doch aus der griechisch-römischen Zeit tatsächlich genügend Belege dafür, dass Personen, die sich ungerecht behandelt sahen, die Götter um Gerechtigkeit und Strafe an ihren Gegnern angefleht haben.[26]

Am besten vertraut sind aus dem demotischen Schrifttum Bitten an die Götter, dem Notleidenden und Bedrängten beizustehen, wie sie besonders in den sogenannten „Briefen an Götter" bezeugt werden.[27] Es gibt aber auch die andere Stoßrichtung, dass man den Gott vorrangig auffordert, Personen zu bestrafen. Ein sehr interessantes und substantielles Zeugnis findet sich in den Schlussge-

---

24 Zu diesen Gestalten vgl. LIEVEN, Himmel über Esna, 50–55.
25 Neubearbeitung von GOLDBRUNNER, Gelehrte.
26 VERSNEL, Beyond Cursing, 60–106; DERS., Prayers, 275–354; KIERNAN, Britische Fluchtafeln, 99–114; QUACK, Göttliche Gerechtigkeit, 141–145; DREHER, Gerichtsverfahren, 301–335; VÉLISSAROPOULOS-KARAKOSTAS, Gebete, 337–348.
27 MIGAHID, Demotische Briefe; DEPAUW, Demotic Letter, 307–313.

beten des Papyrus Rylands IX.[28] Zu ihrer Situierung sind einige Erläuterungen nötig. An sich ist der Text wie eine lange Eingabe an die Verwaltung stilisiert, und zwar konkret um 509 v. Chr., in der frühen Perserzeit Ägyptens. Der Text rollt die Geschichte einer Familie über etliche Generationen auf, konkret ab der frühsaitischen Zeit, als es dem Stammvater gelingt, durch gute Beziehungen zum Königshaus Anrechte auf substantielle Priestereinkünfte im Tempel von El-Hibe in Mittelägypten zu erhalten. Dadurch entsteht aber ein harter Sozialkonflikt, da er allein 20 Prozent der Einkünfte des Tempels erhält, während sich 80 weitere Priester den Rest teilen müssen. Die Spannungen entladen sich in Aktionen, die bis zu Mord und Totschlag gehen und letztlich in einer Situation gewandelter politischer Einflüsse dazu führen, dass die Priester die betreffenden Einkünfte wieder an sich bringen und teilweise unter sich aufteilen, teilweise dem Verwandten eines mächtigen Mannes zuschreiben, von dem sie auf Protektion hoffen.

Angeblich werden bei dieser Gelegenheit auch Stelen mit Inschriften ausgehackt, auf denen der Stammvater seine Aktionen zugunsten des Tempels geschildert hat. Eine hieratische Kopie dieser Inschriften wird quasi als Anlage dem Bericht beigegeben. Schließlich gibt es als letztes Element der Handschrift noch eine Reihe von demotischen Gedichten, die angeblich von Amun, dem Hauptgott des Tempels, inspiriert worden sein sollen. In ihnen wird teilweise von Amun in der dritten Person gesprochen, teilweise wird er auch direkt angerufen. Inhalt ist sowohl die Gewissheit, dass die Bösen vom Gott bestraft werden, als auch die konkrete Aufforderung an den Gott, diese Strafe jetzt zu vollziehen. Insofern stellen diese Texte auch einen bemerkenswerten Gegenpol zu den besser bekannten Bekenntnissen eigener Verfehlungen mit der Bitte um Gnade dar (pRylands IX,24,1–25,9).

> Kopie der Gesänge, die Amun inspiriert hat, als er zu diesen Stelen kam, die ausgemeißelt wurden, [a]ls er sich zum Allerheiligsten seines sakrosankten Schreines begab, als er sich hinab begab und dem Obersänger Zeichen gab:
>
> Die Zeugnisse(?) der Bösen sind an ihren Kindern.
> Wer unter ihnen Erfolg hat, nennt dich nicht Gott.
> Die von Abydos werden Steine(?) nach ihnen werfen,
> die von Achmim werden (sagen): „Bringt sie nicht hoch!"
> Die Hitzigen sind zahlreich im Verüben von Verbrechen,
> wobei sie denken: „Amun wird uns gegenüber stillhalten."

---

28 Erstbearbeitung GRIFFITH, Catalogue, 60–112.218–253; neue Untersuchung VITTMANN, Papyrus Rylands 9; letzte deutsche Übersetzung HOFFMANN/QUACK, Anthologie, 22–54.331–333; französische Übersetzung AGUT-LABORDÈRE/CHAUVEAU, Héros, 145–200.332–341.

Aber er hält ihnen gegenüber nicht still.
Sie sind wie Gänse, sie haben eine Kräuterweide gefunden,
sie haben sich keine Mäßigung vorgenommen.
Wehe dir, Mutter der Gänse!
Ihres Bauches wegen wird man sie fangen.

Ein anderer Gesang:

Amun, wenn man zu dir ruft,
dann wende dich nicht zur Gnade für die <Hit>zigen!
Ihre Herzen sind sündig,
ihre Augen sind böse,
ihre Sünder sind zahlreich.
Ihre Münder sind freundlich in (der) Not,
(doch) grausam sind sie, wenn sie entkommen sind.
Wer unter ihnen Erfolg hat, nennt dich nicht Gott.
Sie bauten sich ihre Häuser als Neubau,
während deines verfallen(?) ist.
Sie zerlegten das Deine in Einzelteile,
und jedermann raubt für sich.
Ihre Häuser, für die sie geraubt haben, wird man zerstören,
während deines feststeht.
Mögest du sie abschlachten wie alles Vieh, mit dem sie ausgestattet waren!
Wer von ihnen übrig bleiben wird,
den wirst du nur übrig lassen, um ihr Herz zu bedrücken.
Du hast sie ihren Fälligkeitstermin nicht wissen lassen(?),
Sie haben ihre Bäuche nicht im Zaum gehalten.
Das, worin sie gegen dich raubgierig waren,
das sollen ihnen die Dämonen zwangsweise abnehmen.
Was sie nicht für dein Opfergut gegeben haben,
das sollen die Dämonen verzehren(?).
Sie haben nicht für dich gehandelt, als es Zeit gewesen wäre.
Für was willst du sie erachten?
Sie haben nicht für dich gehandelt, als sie Erfolg hatten,
indem sie wie Rinderhirten ohne Sesam sind.
Sie haben nicht für dich gehandelt zu ihren Zeiten(?),
bevor die Dämonen sie knechteten.
Mögest du ihnen Dinge nach ihrem Herzen antun!
Mögest du die Dämonen auf sie loslassen!
Mögest du die Dämonen auf sie loslassen!
Mögest du die Dämonen auf sie loslassen!
Mögest du die Dämonen auf sie loslassen,
ohne dass sie für sie säumen,
indem sie ihnen täglich Schaden zufügen
als Entgelt für das, was sie getan haben!
Mögest du sie in ihren Übeln schlafen lassen!
Mögest du sie auch den Tag in ihnen verbringen lassen!

Mögest du sie bescheiden reden lassen zu denen, die geringer als sie sind!
Mögest du sie ihre Diener anflehen lassen!
Mögest du sie in ihren Handschellen schlafen lassen!
Mögest du sie den Tag in ihren Fallen verbringen lassen!
Mögest du sie täglich den Tod erflehen lassen
aufgrund dessen, was ihnen geschehen wird!
Mögest du sie im Gewahrsam der Wächter schlafen lassen!
Zum peinlichen Verhör erheben die sich,
ohne auf sie zu hören bei der Anklage.
Deine Macht ist es, die unter ihnen ist,
da sie dich nicht als Gott bezeichnen.
Sie bezeichnen dich erst als Gott,
nachdem du sie den Dämonen ausgeliefert hast.
Sie wenden sich um, um in deinem Namen zu flehen,
nachdem sie dem Bösen zugestimmt hatten.
Was du gesagt hast, ist es, was gekommen ist.
Was du angekündigt hast, ist es, was geschehen ist,
und man sagt: „Gerecht ist, was Amun getan hat."
Es dünkt ihnen, dass sie handeln würden,
aber es unterliegt dir, sie nicht handeln zu lassen.
Sie nähren das Fleisch, sie verschönern die Haut,
(doch) Amun ist der Herr des Gemetzels.
Sie halten sich selbst für wahrhaftige Menschen,
doch sie wandeln, indem das Unrecht in ihrem Schoß ist.
Sie haben den Schwachen vor dem Starken bedrückt,
sie begingen dein Tabu, das du hasst,
sie schmälerten dein Getreidemaß,
sie stahlen dein Opfergut,
sie gingen in ihre Häuser,
aber sie öffneten deine Kammer nicht.
Die in deinem Dromos standen,
von denen töteten sie jeden einzelnen,
ohne dass sie dich als Macht bezeichnet hätten.
Du zerschmetterst(?) ihre Kinder vor ihren Augen,
ohne dass sie sagen könnten: „Was haben wir getan?"
Sie werden sagen: „Gerecht ist, was Amun getan hat",
wenn der Berg an ihre eigenen Herzen gegeben wurde.

Ein anderer Gesang:

Die Vergeltung verbringt die Nacht nicht säumig,
Amun hört nicht auf zu vergelten.
Ein Räuber verzehrt sein Raubesgut nicht,
die Not säumt nicht, hart (zu ihm) zu sein.
Amun dauert, die Waage ist in seiner Hand.
Sie kreist unter seinen Dienern.
Er nimmt kein Opferrind vom Harten,

um ihm deshalb die Bedrückung nachzusehen.
Sein Opferrind stinkt mehr als Fische,
sein Kurzhornrind ist verfault.
Der Opferfladen des Gerechten ist es, auf den er schaut.
Komm zu uns, o Amun! Rette uns vor ihren Übeltaten und Verbrechen!

Eine komplexe Aufarbeitung der Frage der Vergeltung findet sich im Mythos vom Sonnenauge. Sie wird dort zunächst mit einer Fabel eröffnet, nämlich derjenigen von zwei Geierinnen, dem Sehvogel und dem Hörvogel. Diese beiden beobachten von ferne, wie ein Tier ein anderes frisst, um daraufhin selbst zur Beute zu werden, bis am Schluss sogar der Löwe von einem Greifen erlegt wird.[29] Dies löst bei ihnen eine Diskussion aus.

> Die beiden Geierinnen flogen zum Berg. Sie fanden alles, was sie beide gesagt hatten, indem es alles wahr war. Seherin sagte zu Hörerin {rufen}: „Nichts auf Erden geschieht außer dem, was der Gott anordnen wird im Horizont. Wer eine gute Tat vollbringt, den sucht sie heim, und eine schlechte Tat ebenso. Jedoch, o Hörerin, was soll geschehen angesichts der gewaltsamen Tötung des Löwen, über den der Greif hergefallen ist? Wo soll man das lassen?"

> Hörerin sagte zu Seherin: „So verhält es sich: Weißt du nicht, dass der Greif das Abbild [des Todes] ist? Er ist der Hirte von allem, was auf Erden ist. Er ist der Vergelter, dem man nicht vergelten kann. Sein Schnabel ist der eines Falken(?), seine Augen sind die eines Menschen, seine Glieder sind die eines Löwen, seine Ohren sind die Schuppen des [...] Fisches des Meeres, sein Schwanz ist der einer Schlange. Die fünf belebten Wesen, die auf [Erden] sind – wenn er sie in dieser Art darstellt, so deshalb, weil er Macht ausübt über alles, was auf Erden ist, wie der Tod, der Vergelter, welcher wiederum der Hirte von allem ist, was jetzt(?) auf Erden ist."

Hier schließt sich unmittelbar die Diskussion des kleinen Hundsaffen an, der sich an die nubische Katze wendet (Mythus Leiden 14,28–15,24):

> Heil dir! Wer tötet, den tötet man. Wer zu töten befiehlt, dessen Vernichtung [befiehlt] man. Ich habe die besagten Dinge gesagt, damit es dir verständlich wird, dass es keine [Angelegenheit] gibt, die vor dem Gott verborgen sein könnte. Re, das Licht, der Vergelter der Götter—Variante: Der Gott—, nimmt Rache für alles, was auf Erden ist, angefangen mit der Schmeiß(?)fliege, die das allergeringste Geschöpf ist, bis seine Strafe den Greifen erreicht hat, der wiederum das allergrößte Geschöpf auf Erden ist. Das heißt, die gute Tat und die böse Tat, die man auf Erden begehen wird, Re ist es, der es vergilt. So möge man sagen: „Ich bin kleiner an Statur als du, aber Re sieht mich ebenso, wie er dich sieht." Sein Geruch und sein Gehör sind in allem, was [...] auf Erden ist.

---

29 Vgl. TAIT, Fable, 27–44; QUACK, Animals, 345–346.

> Sie sagte ferner: Er schaut auf das, was im Ei ist, während es Schleim(?) ist. Wer ein Ei zerbrochen hat, ist wie einer, der getötet hat. Ihr Makel lässt sich niemals von ihnen abwaschen. Falls (du glaubst, dass) ich lüge, dann sieh auf dich. Sein Makel ist auf deinen Kleidern. Siehe, das Blut der Frevler, die getötet haben, denen man es nicht zu Lebzeiten erwidert hat! Als sie gestorben waren, suchte man nach ihren Knochen, um an ihnen nach ihrem Tod Vergeltung zu üben, wobei man die Kleider der Götter und der Menschen mit ihrem Blut markierte, um ihre Herzen damit zu erfreuen, dass die Vergeltung Rache nimmt an dem, dem es vergolten wurde. Wenn er ihre Kleider markiert, so deshalb, damit sich die Leute auf Erden von ihnen fernhalten, denn der Makel des Mordes lässt sich in Ewigkeit nicht abwaschen. Er verfolgt den, der ihn begangen hat, sei er lebend oder tot. Niemals, niemals ist er fern von ihm.

Die Schlusspassage dieses Abschnittes geht bereits zum Thema der Bestrafung nach dem Tod über und soll deshalb unten genauer behandelt werden.

Eine interessante, wenn auch sehr sophistische Verdrehung dieses Konzepts der direkten göttlichen Vergeltung für Fehltaten findet sich in der Lehre des Chascheschonqi. Der hochdekorierte königliche Leibarzt Harsiese, Sohn des Ramose, hat sich in ein Komplott gegen den Pharao verwickeln lassen. Als die Sache auffliegt und das Strafgericht ansteht, fragt ihn der König, warum er so gehandelt habe. Er antwortet darauf: „Mein großer Herr! An dem Tag, als Re anordnete, mir Gutes zu tun, gab er das gute Geschick Pharaos in mein Herz. An dem Tag, als Re anordnete, mir Schlechtes zu tun, gab er das Unglück Pharaos in mein Herz" (3,x+14–15). Hier wird also der göttliche Zorn gegenüber einem Menschen genau umgekehrt zur Ursache des Vergehens gemacht. Man kann nicht erwarten, dass dies allgemein anerkannte Sichtweise in Ägypten war. Ich muss allerdings gestehen, dass mir der Gedanke literarisch gefällt. Als ertappter Hochverräter hatte Harsiese ohnehin keinerlei Chance und wusste, was ihm blühte. Auf diese Weise kann er sich wenigstens einen starken Abgang verschaffen.

Eine andere Idee findet sich ebenfalls im Papyrus Insinger klar formuliert, nämlich die der bewusst verzögerten endgültigen Strafe, um den Frevler nur umso länger und intensiver bestrafen zu können. Dies kann auch mit dem komplementären Gedanken verbunden werden, dass der Fromme und Gerechte im Unglück letztlich doch die verdiente Belohnung findet. Mehrere Stellen behandeln dies in unterschiedlicher Ausführlichkeit:

> Der Frevler, der den Gott vergisst, ist es, der an Depression stirbt.
> Ein kurzer Tag im Unglück gilt im Herzen des Kleinmütigen wie Millionen.
> Die Stütze des Mannes Gottes im Unglück ist der Gott.
> Der Tor ruft ihn in der Gefahr nicht an, weil er frevlerisch ist.
> Wer in einer harten Lage hartnäckig ist, dessen Schicksal kommt und geht deshalb.

Das Schicksal und der Gott bringen Wohltat noch spätabends. (19,10–15)

Segle nicht mit dem Wind des Bösen, auch wenn das Schicksal ihm gewogen ist.
Der Frevler stirbt nicht in dem Geschick, das er wünscht. (20,2–3)

Der Gott nimmt die Lampe und das Fett nach dem Herzen an.
Er kennt seinen Geliebten und gibt dem Habe, der ihm gegeben hat.
Ein Gottloser verbringt die Zeit nicht in dem Verhalten, das er liebt. (30,7–9)

Das Werk des Gottes erweckt im Herzen des Toren den Eindruck von Scherz.
Das Leben des Toren jedoch ist eine Last im Herzen des Gottes.
Man gibt dem Gottlosen Lebenszeit, damit er die Vergeltung trifft.
Man gibt dem Bösen Habe, damit man ihm deshalb den Lebensodem nimmt. (30,21–24)

Der Gottlose allein bildet ein Pfand von Tausend zu Eins.
Der Gott lässt ihn aus dem Gemetzel entkommen, nachdem er gebunden wurde. (31,7–8)

Der Gottlose fürchtet sich nicht vor ihr, die Vergeltung wird nicht satt an ihm. (33,11)

Ähnlich ist der Gedanke auch in der Lehre des Chascheschonqi zu finden (11,x+21–23; danach Lücke):

Sage nicht: „Der Frevler gegen Gott lebt heute"; auf das Ende sollst du achten!
Du sollst erst im hohen Alter „gutes Geschick" sagen!
Überlass dein Geschick dem Gott!

Im Rahmen der Konzeptionen, die mit einer aufgeschobenen Bestrafung rechnen, nimmt eine Idee eine zentrale Stelle ein, nämlich die Überzeugung, dass unrecht Gut sich nicht vererben lässt. Dies ist eine Konzeption, die in Ägypten seit alters zu belegen ist.[30] Sie zieht sich auch durch eigentlich alle demotischen Weisheitstexte. Bereits im Brooklyner Weisheitstext, der auch seiner Niederschrift nach mutmaßlich noch aus der 26. Dynastie stammt, heißt es: „Der gerechte Besitz vergeht nicht, aber ein Räuber kann seinem Sohn nichts weitergeben" (4,10).

Besonders intensiv wird diese Frage wieder und wieder im Papyrus Insinger angesprochen. Dort heißt es etwa: „Der Frevler hinterlässt seine Ersparnisse bei seinem Tod, und irgendein anderer nimmt sie" (4,9), oder „Die Art der Bestrafung für diejenigen, die vom rechten Weg abgekommen sind, ist, ihre Ersparnisse einem anderen zu hinterlassen" (18,17).

Besonders komplex wird dieser Punkt in einer längeren Sequenz ausgearbeitet (18,5–14):

---

30 ASSMANN, Ma'at, 92–97.

Frevler und Mann Gottes kennen nicht die Art der Lebenszeit, die ihnen zugeschrieben wurde.
Wer vom Schicksal in seinen Tagen begünstigt wurde, ist es, der in ihnen an den Tod denkt.
Wer nur zum Sparen an ihn denkt, dem setzt die „Dämonin" ein Ende.
Der „Oberdämon"(?)[31] ist es, der ihm zuerst Strafe zufügt, nachdem man ihm den Lebensatem genommen hat.
Pech, Weihrauch, Natron, Salz und das „heiße Medikament" sind Heilmittel für seine Wunden.
Eine unbarmherzige Seefahrt ist es, die seinen Körper malträtiert(?).
Er kann nicht „Halt ein!" sagen bei der Bestrafung durch den, der examiniert hat.
Das Ende des Mannes Gottes ist, ihn mit seiner Grabausstattung in der Nekropole zu begraben.
Der Herr von Millionen, der sie durch Sparen erworben hat, wird sie nicht mit sich ins Grab nehmen.
Man gibt dem, der gespart hat, keine (weitere) Lebenszeit, damit er es einem anderen hinterlässt.

Ich hatte bereits früher vorgeschlagen, dass dieser Passus im Rahmen der Balsamierung zu verstehen ist und sich auf eine rituelle Seefahrt bezieht, die mit einem Totengericht verbunden ist.[32] Als Parallele habe ich auf die Schilderung bei Diodor I,92 verwiesen. Dort heißt es, dass nach der Balsamierung, wenn der Körper für die Bestattung bereit ist, eine Seefahrt mit rituellem Totengericht durchgeführt wird. Sofern Ankläger auftreten, die nachweisen können, dass der Verstorbene Unrecht begangen hat, würde ihm die Bestattung verweigert. Meine Deutung dieser Passage ist in wesentlichen Punkten bestritten worden.[33] Ich glaube aber an ihr festhalten zu müssen.[34] Zunächst sollte klar sein, dass die Erwähnung von Pech, Weihrauch, Natron, Salz und dem „heißen Medikament" sich nur auf die Balsamierung beziehen kann, wo dies ganz typisch verwendete Substanzen sind.[35] An der Lesung des entscheidenden Wortes _ḥne_ als „Seefahrt"

---

31 Wahrscheinlich ist aus dem problematischen Text der Handschrift vielmehr ein Priestertitel wiederherzustellen, was aber hier nicht vertieft werden soll.
32 QUACK, Balsamierung, 27–38.
33 STADLER, Aufführung des Totengerichts, 340–342; DERS., Zwei Bemerkungen, 186.189–196; SMITH, Traversing Eternity, 26–27.
34 Da eine ausführliche Darlegung sehr fachspezifisch ausfallen und zudem den verfügbaren Raum sprengen würde, begnüge ich mich hier mit den allerwichtigsten Punkten. Die Detailargumentation soll an anderer Stelle gebracht werden.
35 So richtig SMITH, Traversing Eternity, 26–27, während STADLER, Zwei Bemerkungen, 342, irrig behauptet, dass sich dies auf Höllenstrafen bezöge, ohne auch nur einen Beleg dafür zu nennen, dass diese Substanzen nach ägyptischer Konzeption bei den Höllenstrafen eine Rolle spielen. HORNUNG, Höllenvorstellung, führt nichts Derartiges an, und mir ist auch kein Beleg dafür bekannt. STADLER, Zwei Bemerkungen, 195–196, scheint wieder zur Interpretation auf die

kann nach der Originalschreibung nicht gezweifelt werden.³⁶ Somit bleibt die Kernaussage bestehen, dass nur der fromme und gerechte Mann erwarten kann, ein rituell korrektes Begräbnis zu erhalten und damit ein seliges Schicksal im Jenseits erfahren zu können. Wer dagegen ohne Skrupel nur auf die Vermehrung seines Besitzes aus war, muss nicht nur erleben, dass die angehäuften Reichtümer letztlich einem anderen zugute kommen, sondern auch noch darauf gefasst sein, dass ihm ein gutes Jenseitsgeschick vorenthalten bleibt.

Diese Passage enthält offensichtlich ein Gericht; das Leben wird untersucht. Insofern muss sich die Frage stellen, wie sich diese Konzeption zur oben bereits angesprochenen Stelle im Papyrus Insinger verhält, in welcher die Wägung des Herzens der Gottheit als Maßstab zur Begutachtung des Menschen dient. Schaut man sich die betreffende Passage allerdings im Ganzen an, so steht die Erwähnung der Waage, welche der Gott Thot auf die Erde gesetzt hat, um damit Ebenmaß zu erzeugen (Papyrus Insinger 4,16), sowohl der expliziten Formulierung „auf die Erde" nach als auch im größeren Zusammenhang der Argumentation, in dem es um das Schicksal der Menschen auf Erden geht, ganz eindeutig in einem diesseitigen Kontext, ist also vom Jenseitsgericht zu trennen.³⁷

Einen speziellen Aspekt göttlicher Strafe, nämlich die Bestrafung von Königen durch eine nur kurze Regierungsdauer oder eine Verweigerung der Nachfolge des Sohnes aufgrund eigener Verfehlungen, Sünden des Vaters oder genereller Gesetzlosigkeit der Zeit, spricht die sogenannte demotische Chronik an.³⁸ Sie mustert die ägyptische Geschichte der letzten indigenen ägyptischen Dynastien, wobei die meisten Herrscher schlecht eingestuft werden – ziemlich im Stil des deuteronomistischen Geschichtswerks.

In gewissem Sinne zu vergleichen ist hier ein Spruch in der Lehre des Chascheschonqi, nämlich: „Ein Fürst, der raubt—sein Sohn ist arm dran" (11,x+17). Allerdings könnte sich dies auch ganz simpel im Sinne der in Ägypten praktizierten „Sippenhaft"³⁹ darauf beziehen, dass der Sohn des vom Staat ertappten

---

Balsamierung zurückzukommen, ohne seinen früheren Ansatz allerdings explizit zu widerrufen.

36 Vgl. die gut übereinstimmende Form des Determinativs im Kanopus-Dekret A 15 und A 16 (s. SPIEGELBERG, Priesterdekrete, 177 Nr. 279), während der Versuch von STADLER, Zwei Bemerkungen, 191–194, unter den Schreibungen für „Freund" eine gleichartige Form des Determinativs zu finden, erfolglos bleibt; im Papyrus Insinger wird dieses Wort distinktiv anders geschrieben.

37 So schon in QUACK, Balsamierung, 35–37, argumentiert.

38 Übersetzung in HOFFMANN/QUACK, Anthologie, 204–213.353–354. Vgl. hierzu zuletzt QUACK, Kritik an ägyptischen Herrschern.

39 Vgl. etwa MÜLLER-WOLLERMANN, Vergehen, 184.187–188.199.

Verbrechers keinerlei Chancen mehr hat, eine Karriere im Staatsdienst zu machen.

Vielleicht kann man gerade in einen solchen Diskurs auch einen Spruch im Papyrus Ashmolean 1984.77 stellen, nämlich: „Verdirb nicht eine Familie wegen des Frevlers; kein Haus ist je <gewesen>, das keinen Sünder gehabt hätte. Sie entstanden (selbst) unter den Göttern am Anbeginn" (x+3,6–7). Einerseits wird hier die Frage der Sippenhaft angesprochen und problematisiert. Andererseits ist diese Aussage insofern interessant, als sie die Frage des Bösen in der Welt in eine größere Perspektive stellt und bis in die Götterwelt zurückführt.

Die bereits oben zitierte Passage aus dem Mythos vom Sonnenauge enthält bereits die Vorstellung, dass es auch Missetäter gäbe, die im Leben selbst nicht bestraft werden. Damit wird die Notwendigkeit geschaffen, eine Strafe nach dem Tod zu konzipieren, will man an Grundvorstellungen der Ethik festhalten. Im Falle des Mythos vom Sonnenauge ist es bemerkenswert, dass die Strafe, obgleich sie nach dem Tod erfolgt, scheinbar innerweltlich bleibt. Die Leichen der Frevler werden aufgespürt und dazu genutzt, Textilien rot zu färben.

Diese zunächst befremdlich scheinende Aussage muss vor dem Hintergrund ägyptischer Ritualszenen verstanden werden. In ihnen gibt es tatsächlich rot gefärbte Textilien, welche der Gottheit überreicht werden.[40] Im dazu gehörenden Rezitationsspruch wird im vorderen Teil gerade die Göttin thematisiert, welche u.a. als „Auge des Re", „Herrin der Wut" und „Herrin am Kopf dessen, der sie schuf" bezeichnet wird. Dies ist also einerseits genau diejenige mythologische Konstellation, welche im Mythos vom Sonnenauge die nubische Katze als Tochter des Sonnengottes einnimmt, andererseits die Rolle der gefährlichen, zornigen Göttin, welche gut zum Thema der Bestrafung der Frevler passt. Daraus erklärt sich auch, warum es von den Kleidern speziell heißt, die nubische Katze würde sie tragen. Was auf der naturalistischen Ebene zunächst befremdlich klingt, erklärt sich im Rahmen der mythologischen Rolle.

Ein weiterer Punkt gewinnt wohl ebenfalls erst im Rahmen ägyptischer Vorstellungen seine volle Relevanz: Die nachtodliche Bestrafung besteht hier im Aufspüren des Leichnams, der zur Einfärbung der Textilien verwendet wird. Das wirkt zunächst nach einer relativ geringfügigen Bestrafung für Verbrecher. Es klärt sich jedoch, wenn man sich klar macht, dass die Gewinnung des „Farbstoffes" Blut voraussetzt, dass man den Leichnam zerdrückt,[41] und somit von einer

---

40 Vgl. OTTO, Mundöffnungsritual, 117–118.
41 Den Vorgang kann man sich wohl ähnlich dem der Szenen von Köpfen und Menschenleichnamen in der Presse vorstellen, wie ihn SCHOTT, Keltergerät, 88–93, behandelt hat. Vgl.

Vernichtung der körperlichen Existenz die Rede ist. Dies impliziert für einen Ägypter auch den Verlust der Möglichkeit auf ein gutes Schicksal im Jenseits.

Gerade die Frage nach der Vergeltung im Jenseits findet sich in einer lange bekannten demotischen Erzählung, nämlich im vorderen Teil der Geschichte von Setne[42] und seinem Sohn Si-Osiris im Papyrus BM 10822.[43] Die Handschrift findet sich auf der Rückseite eines Papyrus, der auf der Vorderseite aus zwei sekundär zusammengeklebten griechischen Landregistern besteht, die ins siebte Jahr des Claudius (46–47 n. Chr.) datieren. Es ist in dieser Zeit durchaus üblich, dass demotische Erzählungen auf der Rückseite ausrangierter griechischer Akten niedergeschrieben werden, die quasi als Altpapier recycelt wurden. Nach allem, was man über die Ausmusterungsvorgänge von Akten weiß, dürfte der demotische Text somit in die Mitte bis zweite Hälfte des ersten Jahrhunderts n. Chr. gehören, und dazu passt auch die paläographische Beurteilung der Handschrift, die sich von gesichert ins zweite Jahrhundert gehörigen demotischen Texten doch deutlich unterscheidet.[44] Wohlgemerkt gilt dieses Datum nur für die aktuelle Niederschrift, nicht für die Genese des Textes als solchen,[45] auch wenn angesichts der allgemein instabilen Überlieferung demotischer narrativer Literatur[46] anzunehmen ist, dass die letzte Kopie noch gewisse Modifikationen im genauen Wortlaut eingebracht hat. Dass der Text an sich von einer älteren Vorlage übernommen ist, erkennt man schon daran, dass er mancherlei offensichtliche Textfehler enthält, in Einzelfällen sogar eindeutige Auslassungen von ganzen Sätzen.

---

auch Urk. VI, 143,13, wo es von den kämpfenden Göttern im Zusammenhang der Bestrafung des Aggressiven heißt, dass ihre Kleider von ihm rot würden; s. ALTMANN, Kultfrevel, 174–175.

42 Die Lautform „Setne" ist diejenige, welche den Ägyptologen am vertrautesten ist, weil sie im Papyrus Kairo 30604 auftritt, der als erster Text dieses Erzählzyklus bekannt geworden ist. Die meisten Handschriften, einschließlich der hier kommentierten, benutzen allerdings die Form „Setem", die auch historisch gesehen ursprünglicher ist. Sie wird deshalb im Folgenden verwendet werden.

43 Erstedition GRIFFITH, Stories, 41–66.142–207; neue deutsche Übersetzung HOFFMANN/QUACK, Anthologie, 118–137.340–343.

44 Die von HORNUNG, Höllenvorstellungen, 10, Anm. 1, gegebene Ansetzung zwischen dem 1. Jahrhundert v. Chr. und dem 2. Jahrhundert n. Chr., die von dort auch GRIFFITHS, Divine Verdict, 230, Anm. 113, übernommen hat, ist hinsichtlich der aktuellen Niederschrift unnötig unpräzise, die Frage des Alters der Komposition dagegen gar nicht eigens aufgegriffen.

45 Unzureichend ist allerdings die Argumentation von BAUCKHAM, Rich Man, 225, der demotische Text gehe vermutlich auf eine ältere ägyptische Geschichte zurück, weil der historische Chaemwese um 1250 v. Chr. gelebt habe.

46 Vgl. QUACK, Einführung, 13–14.

"Sage nicht: ‚Der Frevler gegen Gott lebt heute'; auf das Ende sollst du achten!" — **397**

Auf dem Papyrus sind zwei im Grunde separate Erzählungen überliefert, welche allein durch die Protagonisten, nämlich den Wunderknaben Si-Osiris und seinen Vater Setem Chaemwese, zusammengehalten werden, nicht durch andere Personen oder durchlaufende Handlungsstränge. Für die vorliegende Fragestellung wichtig ist nur die erste. In ihr geht es darum, wie Setem nach einer Traumoffenbarung an seine Frau einen Sohn erhält, der wunderbar schnell heranreift. Dieser Knabe unterhält sich eines Tages mit seinem Vater, während sie zwei verschiedene Bestattungen in Memphis beobachten. Die eine ist die eines reichen, die andere die eines armen Mannes. Dem Reichen folgt eine große Gesellschaft in Totenklage, während der Arme nur in eine Matte gewickelt ist und keinerlei Gefolge hat. Setem schätzt die Bestattung des Reichen als erheblich besser ein, sein Sohn dagegen wünscht ihm, ihm solle nicht widerfahren, was dem Reichen widerfährt. Um diese zunächst erstaunliche Aussage zu beweisen, nimmt er seinen Vater auf eine Besichtigung durch die Unterwelt mit, deren Anfang leider im schlecht erhaltenen unteren Teil der ersten Kolumne fast restlos verloren ist. Erst der Schlussteil ist zusammenhängend überliefert (pBM 10822,2,1–23).

> Sie gingen zu der fünften Halle. Setem sah die vornehmen Verklärten, wie sie gemäß ihrem Rang (da)standen, (und) die, welche Klage über Gewaltanwendung erhoben, wie sie an der Tür standen und klagten, indem der Zapfen der Tür der fünften Halle in dem rechten Auge eines Mannes befestigt war, der klagte und laut schrie. <Sie> gingen in das Innere der sechsten Halle. Setem sah die Götter (und) die Unterweltsfürsten, wie sie gemäß ihrem Rang (da)standen (und) wie die Diener(?) des Westens (da)standen, während sie Meldung machten.
>
> Sie gingen in das Innere der siebten Halle. Setem sah die geheime Gestalt des Osiris, des großen Gottes, wie er auf seinem Thron von schönem Gold saß; wie er mit [d]er Atefkrone gekrönt war; [wie] Anubis, der große Gott, zu seiner Linken und der große Gott Thot zu seiner Rechten war; wie die Götter (und) die Unterweltsfürsten zu seiner Linken (und) Rechten standen; wie die Waage in der Mitte vor ihnen aufgestellt war, indem sie die bösen (Taten) gegen die guten wogen, während Thot, der große Gott, schrieb und Anubis seinem Kollegen [Mi]tteilung machte; wie der, den sie finden würden, indem seine bösen (Taten) zahlreicher als seine guten waren, (indem) er der Fresserin des Herrn des Westens gegeben würde, indem man seinen Ba auf seinem Leib schlagen(?) würde—sie pflegt ihn niemals atmen zu lassen—; wie der, den sie finden würden, indem seine guten (Taten) zahlreicher sind als seine bösen, indem sie ihn unter die Götter (und) die Fürsten des Herrn des Westens bringen würden, indem sein Ba mit den vornehmen Verklärten zum Himmel gehen wird; wie der, den sie finden würden, indem seine guten (Taten) seinen bösen gleichkommen, indem sie ihn unter die trefflichen Verklärten, die Sokar-Osiris dienen, bringen werden. Setem sah einen reichen Mann, der mit einem Byssosgewand bekleidet war und dem Ort nahe war, an dem Osiris war, wobei der Rang(?), in dem er war, überaus groß war. Setne wunderte sich sehr über das, was er im Westen gesehen hatte.
>
> Si-Osiris ging vor ihm hinaus. Er sagte zu ihm: „Mein Vater Setem! Siehst du nicht diesen reichen Mann, der mit einem Byssosgewand bekleidet ist und dem Ort, an dem Osiris

ist, nahe ist? Er ist dieser arme (Mann), den du sahst, als man ihn aus Memphis herausbrachte, ohne dass ihm irgendjemand folgte, indem er (nur) in eine Matte eingewickelt war. Man brachte ihn in die Unterwelt. Man wog seine bösen (Taten) gegen seine guten, die er auf der Erde getan hatte. Man fand seine <guten> (Taten), indem sie zahlreicher waren als seine bösen im Verhältnis(?) zu seiner Lebenszeit, die Thot ihm zugeschrieben hatte, sie ihm zu geben, (und) im Verhältnis(?) zu seinem Glück auf der Erde. Es <wurde> vor Osiris befohlen, zu veranlassen, dass man die Begräbnis(aus-rüstung) dieses reichen Mannes, den du gesehen hattest, als man ihn [...] aus Memphis hinausbrachte, wobei die Ehre, die ihm zuteil wurde, zahlreich war, diesem nämlichen armen Mann anlegte und dass man ihn unter die vornehmen Verklärten brachte als Geist, der Sokar-Osiris dient, wobei er [dem Ort] nah ist, an dem Osiris ist.

Dieser reiche Mann, den du gesehen hattest: man brachte (auch) ihn in die Unterwelt. Man wog [seine] bösen (Taten) gegen seine guten. Man fand ihn, indem seine bösen zahlreicher als seine guten waren, die er auf der Erde getan hatte. <Man> befahl, es ihm im Westen zu vergelten. Er [ist dieser Mann, den du ges]ehen [hast], wie der Zapfen der Tür des Westens in seinem rechten Auge befestigt ist, indem man auf seinem Auge schließt und öffnet, während sein Mund in großem Geschrei geöffnet ist. Bei Osiris, dem großen Gott, dem Herrn des Westens! Ich habe dir auf der Erde gesagt: ‚[Man soll] dir gemäß dem [tun], was man diesem armen Mann tun wird. Man soll dir nicht gemäß dem tun, was man diesem reichen Mann tun wird', da ich wusste, was mit ihm geschehen würde".

Setem sagte: „Mein Sohn Si-Osiris! Zahlreich sind die Wunder, die ich im Westen sah. Aber lass mich [das] erfahren, [was] mit diesen Leuten [gescha]h, die Seile drehen, während die Eselinnen sie hinter ihnen (auf)fr[essen], während andere <(da) waren>, deren Nahrung, Wasser und Brot, über ihnen hängt, und sie laufen, sie herabzuholen, während andere unter ihren Füßen Gruben graben, um sie nicht zu ihnen gehen zu lassen?"

Si-Osiris sagte: „So verhält es sich, mein Vater Setem! Diese Leute, die du siehst, die Seile drehen, während die Eselinnen sie hinter ihnen (auf)fressen: Sie sind die Art der Menschen, die auf der Erde sind, die unter einem Fluch des Gottes sind, wobei sie in Tag und Nacht für den Lebensunterhalt arbeiten, während ihre Frauen es hinter ihrem Rücken stehlen, so dass sie nichts zu essen finden. Sie kamen auch in den Westen. Man fand ihre bösen (Taten), indem sie zahlreicher waren als ihre guten. Es wurde herausgefunden, [was] ihnen auf der Erde zugestoßen war, indem es ihnen im Westen zustößt, ihnen und diesen anderen Leuten, [die] du siehst, wie ihre Nahrung, Wasser und Brot, über ihnen hängt und sie laufen, sie herabzuholen, während andere unter ihren Füßen eine Grube gra[ben], um sie nicht [z]u ihnen gehen zu lassen: (Das ist) die Art der Menschen, die auf der Erde sind, deren Leben vor ihnen ist, während der Gott eine Grube unter ihren Füßen gräbt, um sie es nicht finden zu lassen. Sie kamen [auch] zum Westen. Man ließ das, was ihnen auf der Erde geschehen war, ihnen auch [im Westen] geschehen, um ihren Ba [ni]cht in der Unterwelt aufzunehmen. Erkenne in deinem Herzen, mein Vater Setem, dass man dem, der auf der Erde gut ist, im [W]es[ten] gut sein wird. Der, der böse ist, dem wird man böse sein. Dies, es ist festgese[tzt und(?) wird(?)] niemals [geä]ndert(?). Die Dinge, die du in der Unterwelt von Memphis siehst, sie geschehen in diesen 42 Gauen, in denen [die Gliede]r(?) des Osiris, des großen Gottes, sind. Ferner [geschieht(?) es(?) auch(?) in(?) A]bydos, der Stätte des Spazierengehens, den Wohnungen (des) Fürsten von [A]re[q]heh."

Dies ist genau genommen ein ziemlich erstaunlicher Text, der genauerer Aufmerksamkeit wert ist, schon allein aufgrund der seit Langem gesehenen motivischen Verwandtschaft mit der biblischen Geschichte vom reichen Mann und dem armen Lazarus (Lk 16,19–31).[47] Zunächst aber sollte eine Verortung innerhalb der ägyptischen Konzeptionen vom Totengericht versucht werden.

In Ägypten gibt es schon in sehr früher Zeit die Vorstellung, dass es einen jenseitigen Gerichtshof gibt, vor dem man Anklagen erheben kann. Hierfür gibt es bereits in den Pyramidentexten, dem ältesten umfangreichen religiösen Korpus Ägyptens, aus dem 3. Jahrtausend v. Chr. Zeugnisse, und in den Sargtexten, die aus der Wende vom 3. zum 2. Jahrtausend v. Chr. niedergeschrieben bezeugt sind, werden diese noch deutlich substantieller.[48] In den betreffenden Texten liegt der Hauptakzent darauf, dass der Verstorbene die Möglichkeit hat, seinen Tod als Verbrechen darzustellen, das ihm von jemand anderem angetan wurde, und gerechte Strafe dafür einzufordern.[49] Erst später fassbar wird die Idee, dass es ein generelles Totengericht gibt, dem sich jeder stellen muss. Hauptzeugnis dafür ist das berühmte Kapitel 125 des Totenbuches, das ab der 18. Dynastie, etwa ab der Mitte des 2. Jahrtausends v. Chr., in erhaltenen Textzeugen belegt ist.[50]

Für die aktuelle Frage wichtig ist besonders, in welcher Weise mit denjenigen umgegangen wurde, welche die Prüfung nicht bestanden. Der Text des Totenbuchkapitels ist dazu nicht übermäßig explizit, auch deshalb, weil er ja darauf angelegt ist, seinem Besitzer und Nutzer zu einem ungefährdeten Jenseitsschicksal zu verhelfen. Deutlich ist jedenfalls aus den Darstellungen der Gerichtsszene, dass es neben der Waage ein tierisches Mischwesen gibt, das aus Krokodil, Löwe und Nilpferd zusammengesetzt ist und als „Totenfresserin" oder einfach „Fresserin" bezeichnet wird.[51] Normalerweise sitzt oder steht sie nur einfach da, erst ganz spät, in der Römerzeit—also immerhin derjenigen Zeit, aus

---

47 Zuerst erkannt von MASPERO, Contes relatifs, 496; DERS., Contes populaires, XI. Ausführliche Studie GRESSMANN, Vom reichen Mann. An neueren Kommentaren zur biblischen Passage habe ich FITZMYER, Gospel, 1124–1136, und WOLTER, Lukasevangelium, 551–563, konsultiert. GROBEL, Name, 373–382, versucht, den biblischen Text noch etwas näher mit dem ägyptischen zu verbinden, seine Argumente sind jedoch problematisch. HOCK, Lazarus, 447–463, stellt Parallelen aus der griechischen Tradition in den Vordergrund, deren Pertinenz mir allerdings keinesfalls größer als die der von Gressmann angeführten erscheint. Neuere Detailstudie BAUCKHAM, Rich Man, 225–246.
48 Hierzu GRIESHAMMER, Jenseitsgericht.
49 ASSMANN, Tod, 89–100.
50 Vgl. zu diesem Text derzeit MAYSTRE, Déclarations; eine Neubearbeitung wäre ein Desiderat. Synoptische Edition des hieroglyphischen Textes (ohne Bearbeitung) LAPP, Totenbuch.
51 SEEBER, Totengericht, 163–192.

welcher die Handschrift der zweiten Setneerzählung stammt—wird sie auch in der konkreten Aktion des Verzehrens von Schatten oder zumindest mit im Kessel vor ihr kochenden Leichen dargestellt.[52] In jedem Fall ist es deutlich, dass ihre Aufgabe darin besteht, die Frevler zu verzehren, und zwar im Sinne einer endgültigen und vollständigen Vernichtung, nicht etwa einer dauerhaften Pein. Auch die eben zitierte Passage der Erzählung selbst nennt ja explizit die Fresserin mit dieser Aufgabe.

Damit ergeben sich in der Erzählung von Si-Osiris und Setem Chaemwese einige schwerwiegende Divergenzen zu den normalen ägyptischen Jenseitsvorstellungen. Weder die Konzeption verschiedenartiger dauerhafter Qualen oder sinnloser Mühen, noch die Weitergabe der Grabausstattung an einen tugendhaften Armen ergeben sich bruchlos aus den traditionellen Konzeptionen.

Man hat in der Forschung versucht, wenigstens einige innerägyptische Parallelen für die ungewöhnlicheren Details zu finden. Erik Hornung weist auf die 10. Stunde im Amduat hin.[53] Dort werden einerseits im unteren Register Regelungen für diejenigen getroffen, welche tot im Wasser treiben.[54] Horus sichert ihnen zu, dass ihre Seelen Luft erhalten sollen, dass sie rudern können und sich einen Weg im Gewässer bahnen können, um an Land zu kommen. Ihre Körper sollen nicht verwesen, ihre Seelen sollen atmen können. Andererseits gibt es im obersten Register der zehnten Stunde eine Gruppe von Göttern, von der gesagt wird: „Sie sind es, welche die Leichname entblößen und die Bandagen zusammenballen der Feinde, die zu bestrafen in der Unterwelt befohlen wurde."[55] Mir scheint die Ähnlichkeit der Konzepte nicht überwältigend zu sein. Die Bestrafung bzw. Vernichtung der Verbrecher ist ein gängiges Motiv der Jenseitsbücher und ebenso, dass für das Jenseitsschicksal derjenigen gesorgt wird, die sich in der Unterwelt befinden. Es ist auch mit keinem Wort davon die Rede, dass die Grabausstattung der Feinde den im Wasser treibenden Leichen zugute käme.

Mark Smith meint zunächst, es gäbe im sogenannten Thotbuch eine Parallele dafür, dass für diejenigen, welche keine finanziellen Möglichkeiten für Mumifizierung hätten, eine Gruppe wohlwollender höherer Wesen dies durchführen

---

[52] Fresserin mit Leiche im Maul auf dem Leichentuch Berlin 11652: SEEBER, Totengericht, 171.232 (Literatur), Photo in PARLASCA, Mumienporträts, Taf. 12/2; Diskussion MORENZ, Osiris, 414–427; wiederabgedruckt in MORENZ, Religion, 243; Kessel mit kochenden Leichen vor der Fresserin in Grabszene in Achmim: VON BISSING, Tombeaux, 568–576 und Taf. I.
[53] HORNUNG, Höllenvorstellungen, 12–13.
[54] Gegen die Auffassung von Hornung handelt es sich nicht spezifisch um Ertrunkene, vgl. VERNUS, Le mythe, 19–34.
[55] Ägyptischer Text in HORNUNG, Texte zum Amduat, 715–716; Übersetzung IDEM, Das Amduat, 165–166.

würde.⁵⁶ Dies beruht allerdings auf einem Missverständnis der betreffenden Stelle in der Erstedition. Dort erscheint ein Wort ḫꜣ (mit Determinativ des schlechten Pakets und des schlechten Vogels), welches die Herausgeber als ḫꜣ.t „Leichnam" aufgefasst haben,⁵⁷ obgleich altes ḫ im Demotischen nicht als ḫ erscheint und zudem das Genus nicht stimmt. Tatsächlich dürfte es sich hier vielmehr um eine demotische Schreibung für ḫꜣy „Kranker" (WB III,224,12) handeln.⁵⁸ Die Stelle lautet somit „während sie einen Leidenden heilen, für den es kein Buch gibt, indem sie Sünden mit ihren Aussprüchen abwischen, indem sie einen Mann vor seinem Schicksal retten, während sein Tod hinter ihm dasteht". Tatsächlich geht es hier also vielmehr um die wunderbare Heilung von Fällen, die so hoffnungslos sind, dass in den medizinischen Büchern kein wirksames Rezept gefunden wird. Ein Schlüssel ist dabei die göttliche Austilgung von Vergehen und Vergebung von Sünden, die sicher in dem Komplex zu sehen ist, dass Krankheit als göttliche Strafe verstanden wird. Dies ist von einer gewissen Relevanz für den oben diskutierten ersten Komplex der göttlichen Strafe für Verbrechen, für die Deutung der Unterweltsepisode in der zweiten Setne-Erzählung jedoch m.E. irrelevant.

Ein zweiter von Mark Smith vorgeschlagener Punkt betrifft die Idee, dass zwei Individuen in der Unterwelt die Position austauschen könnten.⁵⁹ Dafür beruft er sich auf einen Text, der auf dem Lederzelt der ägyptischen Königin Isis-em-Achbit überliefert ist und lautet: „Ein schönes Sitzen in den Armen des Chons. Er ist der Herr von Theben, der denjenigen, welchen er liebt, errettet, (auch) wenn er in der Unterwelt ist, der einen anderen als seinen Ersatz gibt."⁶⁰ Dieser Text erscheint mir ebenfalls nicht wirklich einschlägig. Dort geht es *de facto* keineswegs darum, dass zwei gleichermaßen im Jenseits befindliche Personen ihre Ausstattung bzw. ihr Geschick tauschen, sondern darum, dass ein eigentlich für die Unterwelt, also den Tod, Bestimmter dadurch am Leben bleibt, dass jemand anders als Ersatz dafür von den Göttern in die Unterwelt

---

56 SMITH, Traversing Eternity, 28–29.
57 JASNOW/ZAUZICH, Book of Thot, 324.
58 Für noch weitere Verbesserungen zu Lesung und Übersetzung der Stelle s. QUACK, Initiation, 286; Übersetzung DERS., Ägyptischer Dialog, 282 (dort noch mit der Bedeutung „Leiden", die angesichts des Genus des demotischen Wortes zu präzisieren ist).
59 SMITH, Traversing Eternity, 29. Die Bezeichnung dieses Textes als „Hymnus" ist nicht wirklich angemessen.
60 Originaltext STUART, Funeral Tent, 23–34 (Übersetzung und Kommentar, heute veraltet), Falttafel (Hieroglyphentext); vgl. ASSMANN, Sonnenhymnen, 283, Anm. b); JANSEN-WINKELN, Inschriften, 185.

geschickt wird—ein Motiv, das gerade aus der Zeit dieses Zeltes (21. Dynastie) auch sonst zu belegen ist.[61]

Ungewöhnlich erscheint auch das Motiv, dass das Auge des Sünders als Zapfenloch für die Tür verwendet wird. Schon Francis W. Griffith in seiner Erstbearbeitung, und ihm folgend Robert K. Ritner, hat hierfür eine Parallele in Form einer frühdynastischen Figur eines gefangenen Feindes vorgeschlagen, die als Drehzapfenloch diente, indem in ihren Rücken ein Loch eingelassen war.[62] Die Parallele erscheint nur mäßig treffend, da es sich dort nicht um einen innerägyptischen Sünder, sondern um einen politischen Feind handelt, und auch keineswegs ein klarer Jenseitskontext auszumachen ist. Da zudem zwischen diesen beiden durch etwa 3000 Jahre getrennten Zeugnissen keine Verbindungsglieder nachweisbar sind, keine der an Strafszenen doch nicht mangelnden ägyptischen Unterweltsschilderungen derartige Martern bezeugt, und auch der genaue Ort am Körper variiert, müssen andere Optionen gesucht werden.

Damit wird es Zeit, sich den außerägyptischen Parallelen zu stellen, die schon Hugo Gressmann in einer vielbeachteten Studie zusammengestellt und untersucht hat. Er weist bereits darauf hin, dass engere Parallelen des demotischen Textes nicht zum Evangelium bestehen, sondern zu den jüdischen Traditionen.[63] Während das Thema des Türzapfens im Kopfbereich (allerdings im Ohr, nicht im Auge) des Sünders in der Bibel ganz fehlt, ist es in den meisten der jüdischen Versionen präsent. Ebenso bieten viele von ihnen das Tantalos-Motiv, dass dem Sünder das Wasser zwar nahe ist, aber er doch nicht dazu gelangt, davon zu trinken. Gressmann hat angenommen, dass die jüdische Legende auf die ägyptische Erzählung zurückgeht. Wie gesichert ist diese Richtung?

Schon Gaston Maspero überlegte, ob die Motivik in Ägypten fremden Ursprungs sein und sich dort nicht aus sich heraus hätte entwickeln können, kam aber letztlich zu dem Schluss, die Behandlung sei in den Details rein ägyptisch.[64] Seitdem scheint dieser Punkt in der Ägyptologie als gesichert zu gelten

---

[61] Vgl. EDWARDS, Hieratic Papyri, 5, Anm. 34, wo bereits die Parallele zur Inschrift auf dem Zelt der Isis-em-Achbit gezogen wird; POSENER, Papyrus Vandier, 25, sowie QUACK, Ägyptische Dekane, Kapitel 1.3.2.
[62] GRIFFITH, Stories, 46; RITNER, Magical Practice, 117–118.
[63] GRESSMANN, Vom reichen Mann, 44–46. Auch BAUCKHAM, Rich Man, 227–229, betont, dass man in den jüdischen Versionen noch dieselbe Geschichte wie in der ägyptischen erkennen könne, während die biblische Parabel abweiche.
[64] MASPERO, Contes relatifs, 496–500.

und ist kaum mehr hinterfragt worden.[65] Einen Disput hat es lediglich hinsichtlich der Frage des Oknos- und Tantalos-Motivs gegeben. Galten diese lange Zeit über ganz selbstverständlich als Übernahme aus der griechischen Kultur, so hat Friedhelm Hoffmann versucht, die umgekehrte Entlehnungsrichtung nachzuweisen.[66] Sein Ansatz ist allerdings auf Kritik gestoßen, insbesondere Günter Vittmann hat gute Argumente für die Herkunft aus Griechenland aufgeführt.[67]

Dann muss sich aber die Frage stellen, ob ein Text, der in diesem Punkt definitiv fremde Elemente aufgenommen hat und dessen Kernpunkte nicht nahtlos in der ägyptischen Tradition stehen, wirklich die ursprünglichste Fassung des Stoffes bietet. Mehrere Details fordern zur Kritik auf, und zwar gerade solche Punkte, welche Gressmann angesetzt hat. Folgende Fragen stellt er: „Warum erhält gerade dieser Arme die Kleider jenes Reichen? Warum hat man den Reichen gerade in dieser Weise unter der Höllentür gemartert? Worin bestand die Sünde des Reichen?"[68]

Hier lässt einen die ägyptische Fassung tatsächlich im Stich, während die jüdischen Fassungen die Sünden klar angeben,[69] meist auch eine Beziehung zwischen dem Reichen und dem Armen im Leben oder spätestens im Tod explizieren, und die Strafen auch besser motiviert wirken. Dabei kann die ägyptische Geschichte so, wie sie von ihrem Startpunkt her angelegt ist, vom Ausgangspunkt her, nämlich der zufälligen Beobachtung zweier Bestattungszüge, kaum in der Exposition diese Punkte darlegen; man könnte allenfalls erwarten, dass Si-Osiris sie in seiner Erklärung aufführt,[70] was aber unterbleibt.

Ein Gesichtspunkt sei allerdings noch angemerkt. Die Kommentatoren des biblischen Textes haben betont, dass dort im Unterschied zu den beigebrachten Parallelen eben der Reichtum bzw. die Armut im Leben aus sich heraus die Motivation für das jeweilige Jenseitsschicksal sind und von Sünden überhaupt

---

[65] SERRANO DELGADO, Rhampsinitus, 104, scheint, allerdings ohne Detailargumentation, dieses Motiv als fremden Einfluss auf die demotische Erzählung zu bewerten.
[66] HOFFMANN, Seilflechter, 339–346.
[67] VITTMANN, Tradition und Neuerung, 68-69.
[68] GRESSMANN, Vom reichen Mann, 43.
[69] In der christlichen Fassung ist dagegen von expliziten Sünden gar nicht die Rede, vielmehr reicht das Faktum von Reichtum und Armut an sich aus, s. WOLTER, Lukasevangelium, 557–558.
[70] Gerade die Frage des prassenden Reichen, welcher den Armen (konkret sogar den eignen Bruder) nicht teilhaben lässt, könnte man in der ägyptischen Literatur übrigens gut mit einem anderen Text illustrieren, nämlich dem „Beistand der Isis" (HOFFMANN/QUACK, Anthologie, 178-180), wo die Lösung allerdings innerweltlich (wenngleich mit dem Eingreifen einer Gottheit) bleibt.

nicht die Rede ist.[71] Für die außerbiblisch-jüdischen Texte mit ihrer klaren Nennung von Sünden und guten Taten der betreffenden Menschen mag dies zutreffen, für den demotischen aber nur bedingt. Dort ist gerade nicht allein von den Taten die Rede (dabei in der aktuellen Handschrift sogar noch mit einem evidenten Textfehler), sondern auch noch speziell beim armen Mann von der ihm bestimmten Lebenszeit sowie seinem Glück auf Erden. Das ist sicher noch keine Beurteilung rein nach Reichtum oder Armut, aber es deutet doch darauf hin, dass die Messlatte hinsichtlich guter Taten für diejenigen, welche im Diesseits mit den Glücksgütern des Lebens gesegnet waren, deutlich höher gehängt wird als für die Armen und vom Leben Benachteiligten. Hier ginge der demotische Text also zumindest leicht in Richtung des biblischen.

Zu denken geben muss auch, dass der ägyptische Text gerade in denjenigen Elementen, welche engere Beziehungen zu den fremden Versionen aufweisen, nicht einfach in ägyptischer Tradition steht, ja der eigentlich ägyptischen Idee einer endgültigen Vernichtung der Frevler sogar diametral entgegengesetzt steht. Dies macht doch den Eindruck, als sei nicht nur das Oknos- und Tantalos-Motiv hier adaptiert und nicht ohne Brüche in einen ägyptischen Zusammenhang integriert worden,[72] sondern gerade die zentrale Idee vom Austausch der Grabausstattung und der ewigen Pein des Sünders entweder als innerägyptische Weiterentwicklung schlecht mit den weiterbestehenden Traditionen integriert worden oder tatsächlich ebenfalls eine Übernahme anderswo entwickelter Vorstellungen.[73] In jedem Falle scheint es mir schwer vorstellbar, dass die demotische Erzählung und die jüdische Tradition völlig voneinander unabhängig sind; und egal in welche Richtung man das Geben und Nehmen letztlich sehen will, gibt es im Rahmen der jüdischen Bevölkerung Ägyptens in Ägypten in der Ptolemäer- und Römerzeit (bis Hadrian) genügend Möglichkeiten der Begegnung.[74]

---

[71] So etwa BAUCKHAM, Rich Man, 228.232–233; WOLTERS, Lukasevangelium, 557–558.561.
[72] Zu den Schwierigkeiten dieser Motive in ihrer Umgebung vgl. QUACK, Einführung, 46–47.
[73] Man beachte, dass für die agierenden schwarzen Schattengestalten der späten Totenleinen, die MÖLLER bei GRESSMANN, Vom reichen Mann, 41–42, als mögliche Vergleiche für die Vorstellungen der zweiten Setnegeschichte genannt hat, GEORGE, Schatten als Seele, 104–106, mit Einflüssen hellenistischer Vorstellungen rechnet.
[74] Vgl. etwa MÉLÈZE-MODRZEJEWSKI, Juifs d'Égypte.

Bibliographie

AGUT-LABORDÈRE, Damien, Le sage et l'insensé. La composition et la transmission des sagesses démotiques, Paris 2011.

AGUT-LABORDERE, Damien/CHAUVEAU, Michel, Héros, magiciens en sages oubliés de l'Égypte ancienne. Une anthologie de la littérature en Égyptien démotique, Paris 2011.

ALTMANN, Victoria, Die Kultfrevel des Seth. Die Gefährdung der göttlichen Ordnung in zwei Vernichtungsritualen der ägyptischen Spätzeit (Urk. VI) (Studien zur spätägyptischen Religion 1), Wiesbaden 2010.

ASSMANN, Jan, Sonnenhymnen in thebanischen Gräbern (Theben 1), Mainz 1983.

ASSMANN, Jan, Ma'at. Gerechtigkeit und Unsterblichkeit im Alten Ägypten, München 1990.

ASSMANN, Jan, Tod und Jenseits im Alten Ägypten, München 2001.

BARDINET, Thierry, Remarques sur les maladies de la peau, la lèpre et le châtiment divin dans l'Égypte ancienne, in: RdE 39 (1988) 3–36.

BAUCKHAM, Richard, The Rich Man and Lazarus. The Parable and the Parallels, in: NTS 37 (1991) 225–246.

BEINLICH-SEEBER, Christine, Untersuchungen zur Darstellung des Totengerichts im Alten Ägypten (MÄSt 3), München/Berlin 1976.

VON BISSING, Friedrich W. Freiherr, Tombeaux d'époque romaine à Akhmim, in: ASAE 50 (1959) 547–576.

BRUNNER, Hellmut, Der freie Wille Gottes in der ägyptischen Weisheit, in: Les sagesses du Proche-Orient ancien. Colloque de Strasbourg, 17–19 mai 1962, Paris 1963, 103–120.

BRUNNER, Hellmut, Das hörende Herz. Kleine Schriften zur Religions- und Geistesgeschichte Ägyptens (OBO 80), Freiburg/Göttingen 1988.

DEPAUW, Mark, The Demotic Letter. A Study of Epistolographic Scribal Traditions against their Intra- and Intercultural Background (Demotische Studien 14), Sommerhausen 2006.

DIELEMAN, Jacco, Fear of Women? Representations of Women in Demotic Wisdom Texts, in: Studien zur Ägyptischen Kultur 25 (1998) 7–46.

DREHER, Martin, Gerichtsverfahren vor Göttern? – „Judicial Prayers" und die Kategorisierung der *defixionum tabellae*, in: Thür, Gerhard (Hg.), Symposion 2009. Vorträge zur griechischen und hellenistischen Rechtsgeschichte (Seggau, 25.–30. August 2009), Akten der Gesellschaft für Griechische und Hellenistische Rechtsgeschichte 21, Wien 2010, 301–335.

EDWARDS, Iorwerth E.S., Hieratic Papyri in the British Museum, Fourth Series. Oracular Amuletic Decrees of the Late New Kingdom, London 1960.

FISCHER-ELFERT, Hans-Werner, Abseits von Ma'at. Fallstudien zu Außenseitern im Alten Ägypten (Wahrnehmungen und Spuren Altägyptens 1), Würzburg 2005.

FITZMYER, Joseph A., The Gospel According to Luke (X-XXIV). Introduction, Translation, and Notes (AnchB 28), Garden City, New York ²1986.

GALAN, Jose M., Seeing Darkness, in: CEg 74 (1999) 18–30.

GARDINER, Alan H., Hieratic Papyri in the British Museum, Third Series. Chester Beatty Gift, London 1935.

GEORGE, Beate, Zu den altägyptischen Vorstellungen vom Schatten als Seele, Bonn 1970.

GOLDBRUNNER, Sara, Der verblendete Gelehrte. Der erste Setna-Roman (P. Kairo 30646) (Demotische Studien 13), Sommerhausen 2006.

GRESSMANN, Hugo, Vom reichen Mann und armen Lazarus. Eine literaturgeschichtliche Studie (APAW 1918/7), Berlin 1918.

GRIESHAMMER, Reinhard, Das Jenseitsgericht in den Sargtexten (ÄA 20), Wiesbaden 1970.
GRIFFITH, Francis Ll., Stories of the High Priests of Memphis. The Sethon of Herodotus and the Demotic Tales of Khamuas, Oxford 1900.
GRIFFITH, Francis Ll., Catalogue of the Demotic Papyri in the John Rylands Library (Manchester), Vol. III, Manchester/London 1909.
GRIFFITHS, John G., The Divine Verdict. A Study of Divine Judgement in the Ancient Religions, Leiden et al. 1991.
GROBEL, Kendrick, '...Whose Name was Neves', in: NTS 10 (1963–64) 373–438.
HOCK, Ronald F., Lazarus and Micyllus. Greco-Roman Background to Luke 16:19, in: JBL 106 (1987) 447–463.
HOFFMANN, Friedhelm, Seilflechter im Jenseits, in: ZPE 100 (1994) 339–346.
HOFFMANN, Friedhelm, Der Kampf um den Panzer des Inaros. Studien zum P. Krall und seiner Stellung innerhalb des Inaros-Petubastis-Zyklus (Mitteilungen aus der Papyrussammlung der Österreichischen Nationalbibliothek [Papyrus Erzherzog Rainer], Neue Serie 26), Wien 1996.
HOFFMANN, Friedhelm/QUACK, Joachim F., Anthologie der demotischen Literatur (Einführungen und Quellentexte zur Ägyptologie 4), Berlin 2007.
HORNUNG, Erik, Das Amduat. Die Schrift des verborgenen Raumes, Teil II: Übersetzung und Kommentar (ÄA 7), Wiesbaden 1963.
HORNUNG, Erik, Altägyptische Höllenvorstellungen (ASAW 59,3), Berlin 1968.
HORNUNG, Erik, Texte zum Amduat, Teil III. Langfassung 9. bis 12. Stunde (Aegyptiaca Helvetica 15), Basel/Genf 1994.
JANSEN-WINKELN, Karl, Inschriften der Spätzeit, Teil I: Die 21. Dynastie, Wiesbaden 2007.
JASNOW, Richard/ZAUZICH, Karl-Theodor, The Ancient Egyptian Book of Thot. A Demotic Discourse on Knowledge and Pendant to the Classical Hermetica, Wiesbaden 2005.
KANAWATI, Naguib, Conspiracies in the Egyptian Palace. Unis to Pepi I, London/New York 2003.
KEMBOLY, Mpay, The Question of Evil in Ancient Egypt, London 2010.
KIERNAN, Philip, Britische Fluchtafeln und „Gebete um Gerechtigkeit" als öffentliche Magie und Votivrituale, in: Brodersen, Kai/Kropp, Amina (Hg.), Fluchtafeln. Neue Funde und neue Deutungen zum antiken Schadenzauber, Frankfurt a.M. 2004, 99–114.
KOCH, Klaus, Gab es ein Vergeltungsdogma im Alten Testament?, in: ZTK 52 (1955) 1–42.
KÖTHEN-WELPOT, Sabine, Überlegungen zu den Haremsverschwörungen, in: Bröckelmann, Dirk/Klug, Andrea (Hg.), In Pharaos Staat. Festschrift für Rolf Gundlach zum 75. Geburtstag, Wiesbaden 2006, 103–126.
LAPP, Günther, Totenbuch Spruch 125, Basel 2008.
LAZARIDES, Nikolaos L., Wisdom in Loose Form. The Language of Egyptian and Greek Proverbs in Collections of the Hellenistic and Roman Periods (Mnemosyne Supplement 287), Leiden/Boston 2007.
LEITZ, Christian, Art. „Unruhen", in: LÄ VI, Wiesbaden 1986, 852–858.
LEITZ, Christian, Traumdeutung im Alten Ägypten nach einem Papyrus des Neuen Reiches, in: Karenberg, Axel/Leitz, Christian (Hg.), Heilkunde und Hochkultur I. Geburt, Seuche und Traumdeutung in den antiken Zivilisationen des Mittelmeerraumes, Münster 2000, 221–246.
LICHTHEIM, Miriam, Late Egyptian Wisdom Literature in the International Context. A Study of Demotic Instructions (OBO 52), Freiburg/Göttingen 1983.
LIEVEN, Alexandra von, Der Himmel über Esna. Eine Fallstudie zur Religiösen Astronomie im Alten Ägypten (ÄA 64), Wiesbaden 2000.

LUISELLI, Maria M., Die Suche nach Gottesnähe. Untersuchungen zur Persönlichen Frömmigkeit in Ägypten von der Ersten Zwischenzeit bis zum Ende des Neuen Reiches (Ägypten und Altes Testament 73), Wiesbaden 2011.
MASPERO, Gaston, Contes relatifs aux grands-prêtres de Memphis, in: Journal des Savants (1901) 473–504.
MASPERO, Gaston, Les contes populaires de l'Égypte Ancienne. Quatrième édition entièrement remanié et augmenté, Paris 1904.
MAYSTRE, Charles, Les déclarations d'innocence (Livre des Morts, chapitre 125), Kairo 1937.
MELEZE-MODRZEJEWSKI, Joseph, Les Juifs d'Égypte de Ramsès II à Hadrien, Paris 1991.
MENU, Bernadette, La problématique du régicide en Égypte ancienne, in: Méditerranées 2 (1994) 55–70 = Dies., Recherches sur l'histoire juridique, économique et sociale de l'ancienne Égypte II (Bibliothèque des Études 122), Kairo 1998, 107–119.
MESSERI SAVORELLI, Gabriella, Registro di pagamenti del Συνταξιμον (in un quartiere ebraico), in: Palme, Bernhard (Hg.), Wiener Papyri als Festgabe zum 60. Geburtstag von Hermann Harrauer (P. Harrauer), Wien 2001, 81–92.
MIGAHID, Abd-el-Gawad, Demotische Briefe an Götter von der Spät- bis zur Römerzeit. Ein Beitrag zur Kenntnis des religiösen Brauchtums im alten Ägypten, Diss. Würzburg 1986.
MORENZ, Siegfried, Das Werden zu Osiris. Die Darstellungen auf einem Leichentuch der römischen Kaiserzeit (Berlin 11651) und verwandten Stücken, in: Forschungen und Berichte 1 (1957) 414–427 = ID., Religion und Geschichte des Alten Ägypten. Gesammelte Werke, Weimar 1975, 231–247.
MÜLLER-WOLLERMANN, Renate, Vergehen und Strafen. Zur Sanktionierung abweichenden Verhaltens im Alten Ägypten (PÄ 21), Leiden/Boston, Massachusetts 2004.
OTTO, Eberhard, Das ägyptische Mundöffnungsritual. Teil II: Kommentar (ÄA 3), Wiesbaden 1960.
POSENER, Georges, Le papyrus Vandier, Kairo 1985.
QUACK, Joachim F., Balsamierung und Totengericht im Papyrus Insinger, in: Enchoria 25 (1999) 27–38.
QUACK, Joachim F., Rezension zu W. Westendorf, Handbuch der altägyptischen Medizin, in: OLZ 94 (1999) 455–462.
QUACK, Joachim F., Beiträge zu den ägyptischen Dekanen und ihrer Rezeption in der griechisch-römischen Welt, Habil. Berlin 2002.
QUACK, Joachim F., Einführung in die altägyptische Literaturgeschichte III. Die demotische und gräko-ägyptische Literatur (Einführungen und Quellentexte zur Ägyptologie 3), Berlin ²2009 (2005).
QUACK, Joachim F., Tabuisierte und ausgegrenzte Kranke nach dem „Buch vom Tempel", in: Fischer-Elfert, Hans-Werner (Hg.), Papyrus Ebers und die antike Heilkunde. Akten der Tagung vom 15.–16.3.2002 in der Albertina/UB der Universität Leipzig (Philippika 7), Wiesbaden 2005, 63–80.
QUACK, Joachim F., Apopis, Nabelschnur des Re, in: Studien zur Altägyptischen Kultur 34 (2006) 377–379.
QUACK, Joachim F., Ein ägyptischer Dialog über die Schreibkunst und das arkane Wissen, in: ARG 9 (2007) 259–294.
QUACK, Joachim F., Die Initiation zum Schreiberberuf im Alten Ägypten, in: Studien zur Altägyptischen Kultur 36 (2007) 249–295.
QUACK, Joachim F., Göttliche Gerechtigkeit und Recht am Beispiel des spätzeitlichen Ägypten, in: Barta, Heinz/Rollinger, Robert/Lang, Martin (Hg.), Recht und Religion. Menschliche

und göttliche Gerechtigkeitsvorstellungen in den antiken Welten (Philippika 24), Wiesbaden 2008, 135–153.

QUACK, Joachim F., The Animals of the Desert and the Return of the Goddess, in: Herb, Michael et al. (Hg.), Desert Animals in the Eastern Sahara (Colloquium Africanum 4), Köln 2010, 341–361.

QUACK, Joachim F., „Da er das Gesetz mißachtete, ersetzte man ihn zu Lebzeiten". Zur Kritik an ägyptischen Herrschern in der sogenannten Demotischen Chronik, in: Börm, Henning (Hg.), Antimonarchische Diskurse, im Druck.

QUACK, Joachim. F., Die Geburt eines Gottes? Papyrus Berlin 15765a, in: Nord, Rune/Ryholt, Kim (Hg.), Festschrift Paul Frandsen, im Druck.

QUACK, Joachim F., Fragmente demotischer Weisheitstexte, in: F. Haikal (Hg.), Mélanges offerts à Ola El-Aguizy (Bibliothèque d'Étude 165), Kairo 2015, 331–347.

QUACK, Joachim F./RYHOLT, Kim, Notes on the Setne Story. P. Carlsberg 207, in: Frandsen, Paul J./Ryholt, Kim (Hg.), The Carlsberg Papyri 3. A Miscellany of Demotic Texts and Studies (CNI Publications 22), Kopenhagen 2000, 141–163.

REYMOND, Eve A.E., Demotic Literary Works of Graeco-Roman Date in the Rainer Collection of Papyri in Vienna, in: Zessner-Spitzenberg, Josef (Hg.), Festschrift zum 100-jährigen Bestehen der Papyrussammlung der Österreichischen Nationalbibliothek Papyrus Erzherzog Rainer (P. Rainer Cent.), Wien 1983, 42–60.

RITNER, Robert K., The Mechanics of Ancient Egyptian Magical Practice (SAOC 54), Chicago, Illinois 1993.

RYHOLT, Kim, A Parallel to the Inaros Story of P. Krall (P. Carlsberg 456 + P. CtYBR 4513). Demotic Narratives from the Tebtunis Temple Library (I), in: JEA 84 (1998) 151–169.

SCHOTT, Siegfried, Das blutrünstige Keltergerät, in: ZÄS 74 (1938) 88–93.

SERRANO DELGADO, Jose M., Rhampsinitus, Setne Khamwas and the Descent to the Netherworld. Some Remarks on Herodotus II, 122, 1, in: Journal of Near Eastern Religions 11 (2011) 94–108.

SMITH, Mark J., P. Carlsberg 462. A Fragmentary Account of a Rebellion against the Sun God, in: Frandsen, Paul J./Ryholt, Kim (Hg.), The Carlsberg Papyri 3. A Miscellany of Demotic Texts and Studies (CNI Publications 22), Kopenhagen 2000, 95–112.

SMITH, Mark J., Traversing Eternity. Texts for the Afterlife from Ptolemaic and Roman Egypt, Oxford 2009.

SMITH, Harry S./TAIT, William J., Saqqâra Demotic Papyri I (P. Dem. Saq. I) (TE 7), London 1983.

SPIEGELBERG, Wilhelm, Der demotische Text der Priesterdekrete von Kanopus und Memphis (Rosettana) mit hieroglyphischen und griechischen Fassungen und deutscher Übersetzung nebst demotischem Glossar, Heidelberg 1922.

STADLER, Martin A., War eine dramatische Aufführung des Totengerichts Teil der ägyptischen Totenriten?, in: Studien zur Altägyptischen Kultur 29 (2001) 331–348.

STADLER, Martin A., Zwei Bemerkungen zum Papyrus Insinger, in: ZÄS 130 (2003) 186–196.

STUART, Villiers, The Funeral Tent of an Egyptian Queen together with the Latest Information Regarding other Monuments and Discoveries with Translations of the Hieroglyphic Texts and Explanatory Notices of the Various Emblems, London 1882.

TAIT, William J., The Fable of Sight and Hearing in the Demotic Tefnut Legend in the Demotic Kufi Text, in: AcOr 37 (1976) 27–44.

TAIT, William J., P. Carlsberg 207: Two Columns of a Setna-Text, in: Frandsen, Paul J. (Hg.), The Carlsberg Papyri 1. Demotic Texts from the Collection (CNI Publications 15), Kopenhagen 1991, 19–44.

THISSEN, Hans-Joachim, „Lost in Translation?" Von Übersetzungen und Übersetzern, in: Fischer-Elfert, Hans-Werner/Richter, Tonio S. (Hg.), Literatur und Religion im Alten Ägypten. Ein Symposium zu Ehren von Elke Blumenthal (ASAW 81/5), Stuttgart/Leipzig 2011, 126–163.

VÉLISSAROPOULOS-KARAKOSTAS, Julie, „Gebete um Gerechtigkeit". Réponse à Martin Dreher, in: Thür, Gerhard (Hg.), Symposion 2009. Vorträge zur griechischen und hellenistischen Rechtsgeschichte (Seggau, 25.–30. August 2009), Akten der Gesellschaft für Griechische und Hellenistische Rechtsgeschichte 21, Wien 2010, 337–348.

VERNUS, Pascal, Le mythe d'un mythe: la prétendue noyade d'Osiris. De la dérive d'un corps à la dérive du sens, in: Studi di egittologia e di antichità puniche 9 (1991) 19–34.

VERNUS, Pascal, Affaires et scandales sous les Ramsès, Paris 1993.

VERNUS, Pascal, Sagesses de l'Égypte pharaonique. Deuxième édition révisée et augmentée, Paris 2010.

VERSNEL, Hendrik S., Beyond Cursing. The Appeal to Justice in Judicial Prayers, in: Faraone, Christopher A./Obbink, Dirk (Hg.), Magika Hiera. Ancient Greek Magic and Religion, New York/Oxford 1991, 60–106.

VERSNEL, Hendrik S., Prayers for Justice, East and West. New Finds and Publications since 1990, in: Gordon, Richard L./Simón, Francisco M. (Hg.), Magical Practice in the Latin West. Papers from the International Conference held at the University of Zaragoza, 30 Sept.–1 Oct. 2005 (Religions in the Graeco-Roman World 168), Leiden/Boston, Massachusetts 2010, 275–354.

VITTMANN, Günter, Der demotische Papyrus Rylands 9 (Ägypten und Altes Testament 38), Wiesbaden 1998.

VITTMANN, Günter, Tradition und Neuerung in der demotischen Literatur, in: ZÄS 125 (1998) 62–77.

WILLIAMS, Ronald J., Some Fragmentary Demotic Wisdom Texts, in: Johnson, Janet H./Wente, Edward F. (Hg.), Studies in Honor of George R. Hughes (SAOC 39), Chicago 1976, 263–271.

WOLTER, Michael, Das Lukasevangelium (Handbuch zum Neuen Testament 5), Tübingen 2008.

Index of Names and Subjects (German)

Adam 3, 12ff., 18f., 84f., 102, 125, 129, 191, 194ff., 239
Ägypten 99, 276, 387, 399, 404f.
Aiakos 281, 288
Alexander der Große 174, 286, 304
Amun 387ff.
Anubis 227, 384, 397
Apollon 284, 286, 305, 349
Apostasie 121
Apostat 117
Apotheose 284, 287, 307f., 329
Aristoteles 282, 331
Arsakes 283
Artemis 290, 358f., 364, 366
Asklepios 281, 285
Asphodeloswiese 280
Atheismus 115
Athenagoras 287
Ätiologie des Todes 10
Ätna 283, 285
Auferstehung 185, 189, 196, 252, 256
Auferweckung der Toten 188
Augur, augural 333, 343, 345
Augustus 127, 256, 286, 304, 315, 318, 329, 338ff., 342ff., 347, 349ff.
Aussatz 384
Autonomie 105, 113, 117
Baum der Erkenntnis 4ff., 10, 102
Belial 194f.
Bes 383f.
Bestattung 13, 283, 290, 321, 379, 384, 393, 397
Böse 3f., 6, 10f., 16ff., 21, 42, 97ff., 104ff., 108, 110ff., 121ff., 192, 195, 325, 328f., 376f., 379, 387, 389, 392, 395
Boule 282
Brahmanen 286
Bund 113, 116, 191
Bundesschluss 116f.
Cassius Dio 286, 315ff., 319f., 322ff., 328f.
Charon 230, 281, 283, 289, 293
Chrysippos 282
damnatio memoriae 313, 323, 328

Dämon 98, 125, 337, 386, 388f., 393
Daseinsminderungen 5, 8ff., 15ff.
Davidpsalm 180
Davidpsalter 180, 196
Demonax 283, 291
Di Manes 305, 334
Diaspora 79, 99, 117
Diogenes 131f., 282
Dionysos 276, 285, 336, 352
Divinisierung 276, 287, 291f., 324, 330
Dualismus 119
dualistisch 98, 105, 110f., 116, 119, 124, 194
Effeminierung 326
Egeria 339, 342ff., 348ff.
Einwohnung 114f., 120
Ekklesía 282
Empedokles 282f., 285, 292
Engelgemeinschaft 188
Entmenschlichung 317, 326
epikureisch 289f.
Erbsünde 14, 16
Erkenntnisfähigkeit 9
erlösen 123
erwählen 117, 191
Erwählung 97, 114, 116f., 124
eschatologisch 100, 106, 121, 123, 190, 255
Eschatologisierung 101, 121
Eva 3, 6, 8f., 11ff., 102
ewiges Leben 10, 100, 122, 124, 190, 193
Ewigkeit 100, 107f., 122, 303, 391
Fährmann 288
Feuertod 284, 286f., 292
Finsternis 24, 35, 38, 187, 190, 192ff., 288, 379
Fluchspruch 8
Frevel 185f., 190ff., 334, 344, 384
Frevler 115f.
Frömmigkeit 327, 342, 344ff., 350, 394
Gebot 5f., 8f., 11f., 15f., 109
Geist 4, 111, 114, 123f., 182, 184, 186ff., 196, 327, 382, 398
Geist der Wahrheit 190ff.
Geist des Frevels 184, 190ff.

Geist, göttlicher 113
Geist, heiliger 114
gerecht 193, 327
Gerechter 100, 112, 115ff., 192, 194, 390
Gerechtigkeit 99, 109, 111f., 115, 120, 123, 125, 181, 186, 190, 192, 195, 317, 347, 380, 383, 386, 405ff., 409
Gericht 106, 186
Geschöpf 9, 101, 103, 119, 390
geschöpflich 100, 102f., 105, 121f.
Geschöpflichkeit 103ff., 108, 111
Gesellschaft 18, 28, 39, 118, 278, 280, 310f., 316, 330, 397, 405, 409
Gilgamesch 4, 7f., 18
Glaube 94, 100, 118, 121, 303
Gnade 8, 33, 181, 183, 190, 192, 387f.
Gottebenbildlichkeit 100, 122
Gottesbeziehung 33, 39, 106, 108, 116
Gotteserkenntnis 113, 117, 120
Gottesfurcht 120, 327, 341f., 345, 348, 350
Gottesleugner 99, 115f., 118
Gottloser, gottlos 112f., 115ff., 334, 354, 392
Grabhügel 290
Grabinschrift 296ff., 303, 305, 308, 311
Grabmal 295, 298, 302, 306ff., 325
Greif 390
Gut und Böse 4, 6f., 9, 104f., 111, 194, 376
Gymnosophisten 286
Hades 109f., 115f., 124, 149, 279ff., 285, 288f.
Halakha 16
Heil 33, 98, 109, 114, 125, 187ff., 193f., 196, 246, 252, 390
Hekate 279f., 302, 305
Herakles 262, 264, 276, 281, 284f., 292f., 299, 304, 311
Hermes 230, 283, 289
Herodes Atticus 291
Herodian 91, 315ff., 320, 322, 329, 331
Heros 284f., 293
Herrschertod 317
Herrscherwechsel 313
Hesiod 157, 280, 287
Historia Augusta 315, 318, 320ff., 327, 329f.
Homer 280, 287, 293, 364
Huld 33
impietas, impius 239, 334, 344
Individualisierung 97, 114ff., 120, 298

Israel 14, 29, 36f., 39, 48, 51ff., 69, 80, 83ff., 90f., 97ff., 114ff., 119f., 125, 136, 140, 172, 174, 192, 204, 210, 232ff., 247, 253ff., 271
Jenseitsgericht 394, 399, 406
Jenseitshoffnung 115
Judasevangelium 215
Justizvollzug 382
Kalanos 286
Kreatürlichkeit 185ff.
Kulturkontakt 11
Kyniker 276f., 283ff.
kynisch 279, 284
Leben 4f., 7ff., 12ff., 18, 21f., 32, 34, 36, 40f., 97, 99f., 102, 104, 106ff., 110ff., 114f., 117ff., 126, 180f., 187, 275, 282f., 285, 288f., 291ff., 298, 304, 310f., 315f., 319, 326, 333, 341f., 346, 350, 378f., 385, 392, 394f., 398, 401, 403
Leib 114, 191, 281ff., 321, 397
Leichenmahl 290
Leiden 100, 185, 352, 385, 390, 401
Leviathan 97
Libation 288
Licht 13, 190, 192ff., 253, 390
Lukian 275ff., 281ff., 287, 289ff.
Marc Aurel 276, 291, 313
Märtyrer 185, 284
Meer 24f., 27, 31, 34f., 97, 180, 194ff., 307, 333
memoria 298, 308, 313ff., 324
Menelaos 284
Menippos 277, 279, 282, 285, 289
Mensch 3ff., 17, 21, 24ff., 37, 39ff., 97ff., 102ff., 110ff., 120ff., 185ff., 281, 287, 289ff., 303ff., 308, 315, 318, 325ff., 333ff., 338f., 344ff., 350f., 378ff., 383ff., 389ff., 394, 398, 404
Menschenopfer 290, 339, 346, 350
Moiren 281
Monotheismus 32, 98, 110, 322
Natur 6ff., 11, 28, 39, 314, 317, 326ff., 346
necyomanteia 279, 282
Norden 24, 34
Numa 333, 335, 338ff., 352
Obolus 288
Odysseus 151, 157f., 160, 230, 269, 279

Oknos 403f.
Olymp 281, 284, 287
Olympia 276, 285
Olympische Spiele 284f.
Onesikritos 286
Opferpraxis 290
Orpheus 262, 283
Ovid 333, 335, 338ff., 363
Paideia 290f.
Paradies 3, 8ff., 12ff., 16f., 102ff., 111, 122, 125, 244, 253f., 304
Paradieserzählung 3, 5, 8, 12, 14, 16, 18f., 102f., 124f.
paradiesisch 102
Parion 287
Pentheus 283
Peregrinos 275ff., 284, 287, 292f.
Perilaos 283
Perser 290
Personifizierung 97f.
Petronius 287, 295
Phalaris 283
Philosophie 113, 280, 282, 285
Philostrat 277f.
Phönix 287
pietas 345, 349f.
Platon 59, 280, 282
Platoniker 279
Pluto 275, 281, 288
Polytheismus 117
prädestinatianisch 120f., 124
Prädestination 111, 125, 196
Prodigien 333, 342f.
Proteus 284, 286f., 292f., 344
protologisch 100, 122
Psalmen Salomos 82
Psephisma 282
Psychopompos 281, 289
Ptah 379
Pyramide 290
Pythagoräer 280
Randvölker 286
Raumvorstellungen, -metaphern 35f.
Reinigung 184, 320, 340, 343
Religionsbegriff 336f., 350
Religiosität 327, 335f., 347, 351f.

Rettung 22, 26f., 32ff., 41f., 120, 185, 187, 190, 193, 195
Rettungshandeln 38
Rhetorica ad Herennium 143
Ritual 345
Rituelle Vorschriften 334
Romanisierung 298
Sapientia Salomonis 11, 98f., 102, 106f., 109ff., 118f., 121ff., 125f.
Satan, satanisch 11, 13, 16f., 44f., 97, 110, 119, 121, 123f., 134, 179, 182, 184, 235
Scheol 11, 34, 179, 182ff., 187
Schlange 3, 5ff., 11ff., 16f., 97, 103, 105, 108, 276, 390
Schöpfer 9, 103ff., 110, 124, 303, 305
Schöpfung 16, 22, 41f., 98, 105, 108, 111, 116, 119, 121, 194, 379
Schöpfungsbericht 108, 122, 380
Schöpfungserzählung 100f., 107
Schöpfungstheologie 119
Seele 16, 114, 182f., 291f., 303, 404f.
Sinai 116, 170ff., 174, 267
Si-Osiris 226f., 396ff., 400, 403
Sisyphos 281
Skeptizismus 115
Skythen 290
Söhne Gottes 116
Sokrates 280, 282
Sonnengott 378f., 386, 395
Sophistik 278
Speiseopfer 288f.
Sterblichkeit 7ff., 14, 17, 105, 118, 122
Strafe, göttliche 5, 7, 380, 382, 384, 386, 401
Sünde 6, 11ff., 17f., 24, 27, 105, 114, 179, 181ff., 192, 194f., 394, 401, 403
Sündenfall 3, 6, 9, 11, 13, 16f., 99, 101, 105f., 125
Susanna 143
Tantalos 230, 281, 402ff.
Tartarus 280
Teufel 12, 100, 106ff., 113, 115, 118ff., 194
Tierfabel 378
Tityos 281
Todesart 283, 331
Todesdarstellung 315
Todesverhängnis 183
Todverfallenheit 100, 106, 122, 183f., 187

Totenbrauchtum 289ff.
Totengericht 281f., 315, 393, 399f., 405, 407f.
Totengott 109, 275
Totenkult 275, 287, 300, 306, 334, 352
Totenreich 187, 275, 287
Totenwelt 109f.
Trankopfer 289
Trauer 275, 277, 287, 295f., 301, 303, 307, 309, 317, 325
Trauerritus 275, 289
Tun-Ergehen-Zusammenhang 381
Übertretung 9, 179, 182ff., 186f.
Unglaube 100
Unheil 11, 22, 25, 28, 32f., 37, 40, 190, 193f.
Unreinheit 184ff., 190ff.
Unvergänglichkeit 100, 107, 119, 122
Vergehen 15, 24, 377, 379, 385, 391, 394, 401, 407
Wahrheit 100, 102, 118, 182, 186, 190ff., 278, 291, 305, 346, 379

Weg 22, 120
Weiser 14, 112, 288
Weisheit 4, 10, 17, 19, 21ff., 25, 28, 32f., 37, 40, 73, 98ff., 108, 111ff., 117ff., 123ff., 190ff., 196, 385, 405
Welt 3, 7, 11, 13ff., 22, 41, 100, 108ff., 113f., 116f., 123f., 195, 246, 289, 291ff., 303, 305, 311, 333, 340, 348, 377, 379, 395, 407
Wille Gottes 105, 113f., 117, 123, 385
Willensfreiheit 15, 108
Wunder 21, 24ff., 31, 38ff., 398
Zeus 109f., 281, 286, 290, 292, 305
Zion 35, 115
Zionstradition 114
Zuwendung 21, 23ff., 27, 29, 33f.
4. Esra 83, 85, 90, 129, 135, 241, 244

Index of Names and Subjects (English)

Abraham 15, 19, 54, 86, 90, 93f., 141ff., 145, 208, 223f., 226, 229, 232, 234, 237ff., 242, 245, 253f., 256f., 263
Animal 62ff., 71, 81, 137
Apocalypticism 63
Bacchylides 356, 358ff., 364f., 375
Book of Jannes and Jambres 231
Child 46ff., 53, 80f., 83, 88, 131, 133, 135, 143, 145, 199ff., 204ff., 210ff., 237, 240, 263, 363, 368f.
Comfort 67ff., 84
Creation 57, 62f., 65, 68f., 77f., 84, 86, 92, 128f., 131, 134, 136, 140, 144f., 147, 168, 236, 262
Cultus 259, 261, 263, 265ff., 269ff., 330
Curse 43, 45, 47ff., 237, 358
Deliverance 68, 71, 143f., 179f.
Desire 130, 132, 146, 370
Disciple, Discipleship 199ff., 207, 210f., 213f., 235f., 238, 243, 247, 249
Enoch's journey 149, 159, 164f.
Eschatology 94, 246
Ethic 75ff., 91ff., 148, 159, 233, 237, 247, 252, 254
Ethical 77ff., 81f., 84f., 89, 91ff., 128, 146f., 159, 171f., 232, 260, 268, 270
Expiation 264, 358f., 367
Faith 46, 50ff., 75, 87, 135, 137, 140, 143, 211f., 214, 216, 224, 238
Fate 58ff., 68, 72, 84, 87, 90, 138, 158, 223f., 227, 229, 231, 234, 236f., 240, 245f., 249, 356, 358, 364f., 367, 371, 373f.
Flood story 62, 65
Gehenna 229, 243, 245, 255
Grief 152, 239, 362ff., 371, 374f.
Guilt 360, 365, 373
Hades 149, 151f., 156ff., 160f., 223, 226, 230f., 238, 241ff., 245, 247, 283, 303
Heart 45, 49, 57, 61, 64ff., 68f., 71f., 83ff., 90, 128f., 132f., 141, 214, 235, 248, 265

Homer 150f., 157f., 160, 230, 253, 256, 356ff., 360f., 364f., 372, 376
Image 44f., 63, 65, 78, 92, 128, 131, 139, 150f., 153ff., 158, 160, 164, 226, 232, 267, 367, 369, 372
Immortality 53, 63, 94, 124ff., 141, 145, 161, 196, 218, 241
Isles of the Blessed 149, 156, 230
Job's wife 43ff., 51ff.
Judgment 57f., 64f., 67, 69ff., 77, 84, 89, 232, 236, 241f., 246, 267
Justice system 66f., 71
Lazarus 221ff., 228ff., 232, 234, 237f., 247ff., 252ff., 399, 405f.
Martyr 83, 128, 131, 135, 138, 140f., 144f., 238
Martyrdom 49, 77f., 92, 139, 142
Meleager 355ff., 361ff.
Misery 60, 69
Moral code 163, 172, 175
Mortality 58ff., 63ff., 199, 202, 207, 212, 265
Moses and the Prophets 91, 223, 247f.
Myth 157, 164, 269, 355ff., 364f., 367, 369, 371ff., 375
Nature 48f., 51f., 79, 86ff., 131, 172, 204, 232
Nekyia 149, 156, 176
Oppression 67ff., 83, 202, 236
Orphic 160, 163
Orphic teaching 160
Ovid 348, 356, 358, 360ff., 372, 375f.
Paradise 46, 125f., 151, 162, 165, 172, 239, 242ff.
Passion 47, 85, 127ff., 134ff., 138f., 141f., 144, 146
Piety 50, 87, 132, 139ff., 145, 226, 237f.
Post-mortem condition 149, 160f., 163
Poverty 226, 230, 233ff., 237
Punishment 52, 57, 65, 67, 72, 82, 84, 133f., 137f., 142, 144, 149, 152, 157ff., 162, 174, 228, 230f., 241, 245, 357
Pyriphlegethon 149ff., 154

Pythagorean tradition 156, 161f.
Resurrection 89, 94, 188, 196, 208, 218, 221, 223ff., 232, 239ff., 245ff., 252, 256
Revelation 47, 76, 89, 93f., 224, 229, 231, 235, 242, 246ff.
Rhetoric 71, 129, 143, 231, 254, 259f., 265f., 270, 272
Sanctuary 265ff., 269
Sarcophagus relief 371f.
Sin 83f., 162, 179, 230, 234, 241, 244, 248, 262, 264f.
Spirit 62f., 71, 86, 134, 144, 166ff., 211, 216, 227, 234, 236, 266, 358
Suffering 46ff., 50, 58, 67ff., 72, 82, 87, 92, 135, 138, 143, 152, 157, 168, 199, 211, 224, 233, 235f., 261ff., 266, 268ff.
Tale of Setme Khamuas 226
Torah 70, 76, 78f., 81f., 84, 88, 91, 93, 129ff., 137f., 142, 144f., 214, 228, 231
Vice 86f., 130, 138, 241
Virtue 45, 77, 79, 86f., 130ff., 137ff., 166, 241, 263, 361, 372
Wickedness 57ff., 64ff., 71f., 84
Wisdom 45, 47, 51ff., 55, 57ff., 73, 76f., 87ff., 92ff., 99, 125f., 133, 143, 146, 162, 262, 405f., 409
Zion 35, 266, 271

Bible Citation Index

Altes Testament

Genesis
1,26–27 100
1,26–29 65
1,27 122
1,30 62
1–2 99
1–3 97, 100f., 106, 110, 121f., 124
2,16–17 4, 102
2,17 6f.
2,18–2,25 5
2,7 7, 62f., 128
2,9 4, 10
3 3, 5ff., 18, 99, 101ff., 105ff., 110f., 113, 121, 123, 125
3,14–19 5
3,19 7f., 100
3,20–24 6
3,5 6, 107
3,6 5
3,7 5, 103, 125
3,8 104
4,7 6
6,17 62
6,5 64f., 69

Exodus
19 267
23,1–2 173
23,5–16 171
23,7 171, 174f.
33,22 170
7,13 117

Deuteronomium
1,39 4, 105
34,1 266
7,6–8 117
9,3 267

2. Samuel
7,14 266

1. Könige
3,9 4

Psalmen
107 21ff., 26f., 29ff., 42
107,1 29
107,2 29
107,33–42 23, 28, 31f.
107,43 21
107,6 34
146,7–8 188
16,10 242f.
21,23 263
23,4 68
37,32–33 169
37,33 174
8 259, 261
95 264, 266
95,11 264
95,7–8 265

Kohelet
12,7 71
12,9–14 70
2,13–17 59
3,16 64, 66
3,16–22 65f., 71
3,17 64, 71f., 168
3,18 64f., 69, 71
3,19–22 62ff.
3,21 63, 70f.
4,1 68, 168
4,1–3 67
5,7 67
7,13–14 68
7,29 66, 68
8,10–14 168
8,11–12 66
8,14–15 60
8,6b–7 69

9,1–3 60
9,3 57, 59, 66, 72
9,4 60, 67

Jesaja
14,11 242
2,10 167
2,21 170
24,17–18 167
24,22 167
28,15 116
51,3 244
53 233, 248
57,1–13 116
58,6 233
61,1–2 233f.
7,15–16 4, 105
8,17 263
8,18 263

Jeremia
31,31–34 266
31,33 266

Haggai
2,6 267

Apokryphen und Pseudepigraphen des Alten Testaments

2. Makkabäer
14,46 189
7,6 189

4. Makkabäer
13,17 238
7,18–19 238

Sapientia Salomonis
1–2 107, 109, 111, 120, 121
1,1 112, 115
1,1–15 99
1,1–6,21 99
1,4 113
1,12 112
1,13–15 108
1,14 109f.
1,16 112, 115f., 118f.
1,16–2,22 99
1,16–2,9 100
2 11, 115, 117
2,1–5 115
2,6–9 115
2,10 111
2,10–20 100, 117f.
2,17.18 117
2,21–24 99
2,22 120
2,23 107, 119, 122
2,23–24 100, 107ff., 124
2,24 11, 108f., 111, 118
3,4 107
7,26 262
9,5–6 120

Sirach
24,8 114
25,24 11

1. Henoch
1,3–9 166
14,18–22 153
17,4–5 153
17,4–8 150, 154
17,5–6 175
17,5–8 149
17,6–8 151
18,6–8 162
22 149, 162, 175, 241f., 254
22,1–13 149
22,12 170, 174
22,1–4 166f.
22,8–13 167
22,9 164, 172
24,4–5 162
94,8–10 236

Apokalypse des Mose
14 12
15–30 12
16–19 12
21 12
33,2–37,6 12

41,2 13
7 12
8 12
9 12

Testament Abrahams
20,10.12 239
20,14 239

Qumranisches Schrifttum

1QH
IX,23–29 185
XI,19–22 187

1QS
I,18 195
III,13–IV,26 189, 191, 194
III,4–12 184
IV,12–14 193
IV,15–26 193
IV,16–17 193
IV,20–21 184
IV,20–23 191
IV,23 193f.
IV,24–25 194
IV,2–6 192
IV,2–8 190
IV,6–8 193
IV,9–11 192f.
IV,9–14 190
XI,2–22 187

1QSa
1,10–11 4

4Q171
II,7,18 169

11QPs[a]
XIX,1–18 179f.
XVIII,16–17 181

Jüdisch-hellenistische Literatur

Josephus
– De bello Judaico
2,165 189

Neues Testament

Markus
10,13-16 206, 213
10,13–16 206
10,13–16 206
10,13–16 206
10,13–16 212
10,13–16 213
10,13–16 213
10,13–16 213
10,13–16 215
10,13–16 217
12,18–27 189
5 206
6 207f.
7 210
9 211, 215
9,33-37 213
9,33–37 204, 206, 212f.
9,33–37 213
9,33–37 213

Lukas
1,46–55 232
3 232
4 233, 235, 240, 247f.
4,18–19 233f.
6,20–26 236
7,22 234
9,28–36 247
10,15 242f., 245
12,4–5 243
13,28–29 238
14,13–14 240, 245
16,1–9 247
16,14–18 247
16,19-31 224
16,19–31 221f., 224, 232, 237, 239, 242, 247, 253f.

20,35–38 240
23,43 242ff., 246
24,25 248
24,27 248
24,44–47 248

Apostelgeschichte
2,27 243, 245
2,31 243
8,26–40 248
23,6–8 240
23,8 189
24,15 240f., 245

Römerbrief
5,12–21 13
7,14 184, 195
7,15 195
7,23 195
7,24 195
7,25a 195

Hebräerbrief
1,1 269
1,1–4 262
1,3 262
1,5 266
2 270
2,5–9 262
2,6 259
2,6–7 259
2,9 262, 269
2,10 265
2,10–13 262
2,10–18 262
2,12 263
2,13 263, 268
2,14–18 263
2,18 265
3 266
3,11 264
3,15 265
3,17 265
4,14 260
4,14–16 260
6,1 265
8,10 266

8,8–12 266
9–10 270
10,32–34 268
11 268
11,2 268
12 267
12,1 260, 268
12,18–19 267
12,22–24 266
12,25–26 267
12,26 267
13,1–3 268
13,12 269
13,13 269
13,22 260

Johannes-Apokalypse
12,9 13

Rabbinische Literatur

Babylonischer Talmud
– Baba Bathra
75a 15

– Sabbath
55b 14

Midraschim
– Bereshit Rabbah
12,6 15
17,8 16
19,7 15
19,8 15
20,6 16

– Pirqe de Rabbi Eliezer
13–14 16

– Tanchuma Bereshit (ed. Buber)
29 14

Antike pagane Literatur

Cicero
– Briefe an Atticus
12,38 307

Corpus Inscriptionum Latinorum
VI 15696 300
VI 7581 299
XIII 8706 300
XIV 2793 297

Homer
– Odyssee
11,1–640 230
11,36–43 158
11,568–571 158
6,561–569 158

Phaedrus
111d 152
111e 152
113a–114b 162
113a–b 152
114a 152

Pindar
2,72–74 162

www.ingramcontent.com/pod-product-compliance
Lightning Source LLC
Chambersburg PA
CBHW071809230426
43670CB00013B/2400